The REPO Handbook

Children do not converse. They say things. They ask, they tell, and they talk, but they know nothing of one of the great joys in life, conversation. Then, along about twelve, give or take a year on either side, two young people sitting on their bicycles near a front porch on a summer evening begin to talk about others that they know, and conversation is discovered. Some confuse conversation with talking, of course, and go on for the rest of their lives, never stopping, boring others with meaningless chatter and complaints. But real conversation includes asking questions, and asking the right questions before it is too late.

Charles M Schulz
You Don't Look 40, Charlie Brown!
Ravette Books 1990

The REPO Handbook

Moorad Choudhry

OXFORD AMSTERDAM BOSTON LONDON NEW YORK PARIS
SAN DIEGO SAN FRANCISCO SINGAPORE SYDNEY TOKYO

Butterworth-Heinemann
An imprint of Elsevier Science
Linacre House, Jordan Hill, Oxford OX2 8DP
225 Wildwood Avenue, Woburn MA 01801-2041

First published 2002

/H

Visit the author's web site at www.YieldCurve.com

British Library Cataloguing in Publication Data
A catalogue record for this book is available from the British Library

Library of Congress Cataloguing in Publication Data
A catalogue record for this book is available from the Library of Congress

ISBN 0 7506 5162 8

For information on all Butterworth-Heinemann publications
visit our website at www.bh.com

The views, thoughts and opinions expressed in this book are those of the author in his individual capacity
and should not in any way be attributed to JPMorgan Chase Bank, or to Moorad Choudhry as a
representative, officer, or employee of JPMorgan Chase Bank.

While every effort has been made to ensure accuracy, no responsibility for loss occasioned to any person
acting or refraining from action as a result of any material in this book can be accepted by the author,
publisher or any named person or entity.

Printed and Bound in Great Britain by Biddles Ltd, *www.biddles.co.uk*

To my Dad, Mr Saeed Choudhry, *RAF Halton apprentice, ex-British United Airlines, BOAC, and Kuwait Airways Corporation,* who can fix anything from an F-86 Sabre to an A340 Airbus, but who always wanted me to be an investment banker…

Butterworth-Heinemann – The Securities Institute
A publishing partnership

About The Securities Institute

Formed in 1992 with the support of the Bank of England, the London Stock Exchange, the Financial Services Authority, LIFFE and other leading financial organizations, the Securities Institute is the professional body for practitioners working in securities, investment management, corporate finance, derivatives and related businesses. Their purpose is to set and maintain professional standards through membership, qualifications, training and continuing learning and publications. The Institute promotes excellence in matters of integrity, ethics and competence.

About the series

Butterworth-Heinemann is pleased to be the official **Publishing Partner** of the Securities Institute with the development of professional level books for: Brokers/Traders; Actuaries; Consultants; Asset Managers; Regulators; Central Bankers; Treasury Officials; Compliance Officers; Legal Departments; Corporate Treasurers; Operations Managers; Portfolio Managers; Investment Bankers; Hedge Fund Managers; Investment Managers; Analysts and Internal Auditors, in the areas of: Portfolio Management; Advanced Investment Management; Investment Management Models; Financial Analysis; Risk Analysis and Management; Capital Markets; Bonds; Gilts; Swaps; Repos; Futures; Options; Foreign Exchange; Treasury Operations.

Series titles

- **Professional Reference Series**

  The Bond and Money Markets: *Strategy, Trading, Analysis*

- **Global Capital Markets Series**

  The REPO Handbook
  The Gilt-Edged Market
  Foreign Exchange and Money Markets: *theory, practice and risk management*
  IPO and Equity Offerings

For more information

For more information on **The Securities Institute** please visit their web site:

www.securities-institute.org.uk

and for details of all **Butterworth-Heinemann Finance** titles please visit Butterworth-Heinemann:

www.bh.com/finance

বিশ্ববিদ্যালয়ের হুমায়ুনের রুহিম

It's been a long, long, long time
How could I ever have lost you
When I loved you

It took a long, long, long time
Now I'm so happy I found you
How I love you

So many tears I was searching
So many tears I was wasting, oh, oh…

Now I can see you, be you
How can I ever misplace you
How I want you
Oh I love you
You know that I need you
Ooh I love you

Long Long Long, *The Beatles*
(Apple Records 1968)

Contents

Foreword

Anyone taking a stroll through the City's bookshops will be confronted by a vast array of books on the money and capital markets, their history, how they work and the academic theory which underpins market behaviour and pricing. But as someone who has spent many an hour in these bookshops I've often felt that the range of books on these fields which are comprehensive, readable and yet still informative to money and capital market practitioners is extremely limited. There is a surfeit of books which are very specialised, highly complex and at first glance impenetrable to most people. The cynic would say they are written to impress. At the other extreme, are very simple guides which do little to advance the knowledge of the practitioner. Moorad's triumph is in filling this gap with a comprehensive and lucid guide on a vital aspect of the global debt markets.

Part of the value of this book is that Moorad himself is a practitioner. He understands as well as anyone the academic and occasionally complex mathematical foundation of modern markets. But, and just as important, Moorad has also been a trader, and as such has a feel for how markets operate in the real world and how traders in this world think. As a result the academic will find a lot in this book to admire. The trader, however, will come to treat this book as his bible.

Moorad is a master of his subject. A true master in that he understands the complexities of his subject but is able to reach out and educate a wide audience. This is a rare skill. How many students are proficient at both the arts and sciences? The greatest example is probably John Maynard Keynes, who was a notable mathematician, and whose main works were based on highly complex and path-breaking theories, but whose writings were highly readable, indeed entertaining, and as a result had enormous influence.

This is a book about repo markets, the fulcrum of modern money markets and the bridge with the capital markets. Repo, or *sale and repurchase* agreement, is essentially a secured loan. Repo has an ever increasing role in the money markets due to it being the preferred instrument of most developed central banks for their open market operations. The United Kingdom was a laggard in this process, not introducing a repo market until the beginning of 1996; and, the Bank of England did not begin open market operations in repo for over a year after that. Prior to that, liquidity for the bond markets was provided solely by stock borrowing/lending and this is still the preferred method for many institutions, such as insurance companies and pension funds, despite being less flexible and somewhat cumbersome in comparison to repo.

Although stock borrowing/lending seeps through to the repo market anyway, through specialist money market institutions, it is one of the reasons why the growth of the repo market in the UK has been relatively slow. Other reasons include a contraction in the size of the gilt market and associated turnover, the lack of specials (with the authorities for a while actively discouraging such situations) and the lack of a central counterparty. The London Clearing House is currently addressing the last point through its RepoClear system, and when introduced this could lead, as it has in the United States, to an explosion in turnover. Hence it is crucial that all money market practitioners, who up to now have restricted themselves essentially to straight deposits and CDs, understand repo and become familiar with how the repo market trades.

However, a repo trader cannot concentrate solely on the money markets, he or she has to understand and monitor the associated government bond market as well. This is because the two markets are intimately linked, with the strongest link through the bond futures market. The most actively traded stocks in a government bond market are usually those in the basket of futures deliverable stocks, in particular the key *cheapest-to-deliver* bond. Which stock is the cheapest to deliver is a function not just of the cash price of the bond but also of its repo rate. It is the repo rate which turns the bond market's *gross basis* into the all-important *net basis*, which is more of a money market concept. Hence it is important for the repo trader to closely watch the basis stocks; in fact, in Germany most repo trading concentrates on the deliverables. Likewise it is crucial for the bond trader to understand and monitor the repo market, without which he or she cannot price cash stocks, particularly those directly linked to the futures market.

Knowledge of repo rates, apart from basis stocks, is also crucial for a bond trader. Any serious analysis of which stocks are cheap or dear cannot be undertaken without knowing the repo rates on those stocks. A stock may be expensive in the cash market merely because it is tight, or special, in the repo market. Any bear trade or switch out of that stock could come unstuck once the repo rate is taken into account.

The repo markets are therefore central to both the money and bond markets and their importance is likely to grow. Practitioners in both markets need to fully understand and monitor the repo market closely, even if they are not directly involved that market. As a result of the commitment shown by Moorad Choudhry in producing this study we now have a complete reference guide which will become the benchmark book for the international money markets.

David Wileman, Chief Executive
Derek Taylor, Manager, Gilt Repo
King & Shaxson Bond Brokers Limited,
subsidiary of Old Mutual plc

Preface

This book is about the repo markets. That is, it is about the instruments used in the world's repo markets, the mechanics of the instruments themselves, and the markets in which they are used. Repo, from "*sale and repurchase* agreement", is closely linked to other segments of the debt and equity markets, so the book does not look at repo in isolation but rather its use in the context of the global capital markets. These are comprised of the debt and equity capital markets, and although equity repo is increasingly important, it is government bond repo that is absolutely vital to the smooth running of the global debt markets. From its use as a financing instrument for market makers to its use in the open market operations of central banks, and its place between the bond markets and the money markets, repo integrates the various disparate elements of the marketplace and allows the raising of corporate finance across all sectors. Although used in bond and equity markets, this book concentrates on bond repo.

So, the repo market is a vital element of the global capital and money markets. The first repo transactions were initiated by the US Federal Reserve in 1918, since which time repo has become the main instrument of open market operations for many major central banks around the world. It is also a major component of the global money markets. The market experienced substantial growth during the 1990s and is now estimated to account for up to 50% of daily settlement activity in non-US government bonds worldwide; this is a phenomenal figure. Daily outstanding volume in international repo transactions has been estimated at anything between £420 to £450 billion, depending on your source.

The rapid growth in the use of repo worldwide has been attributed to several factors including the rise in non-bank funding and disintermediation, the expansion in public debt, the liquidity of the instrument itself and the high quality of collateral used – which is government debt in a majority of the transactions. Additional factors that have led to greater use of repo include the need for liquidity as market makers have sought to cover short positions; a greater awareness of counterparty risk, heightened in the wake of the collapse of Barings, and not least the more advantageous capital treatment that repo receives compared to unsecured transactions. Its flexibility has resulted in repo being used by a wide variety of market players, from securities houses and investment banks to fund managers, corporate treasurers and local authorities. All major markets in the world now have an established repo market, the facility is also increasingly being used in developing currency markets as well.

This book is aimed at those with little or no previous understanding of, or exposure to, the repo markets; however, it also investigates the markets in sufficient depth to be of use to the more experienced practitioner. It is primarily aimed at front office, middle office and back office banking and fund management staff who are involved to some extent in the repo markets. Others, including corporate and local authority treasurers and risk management and legal department staff may, also, find the contents useful. Comments on the text are welcome and should be sent to the author care of Butterworth-Heinemann.

Structure of the book

This book is organised into three parts. Part I deals with the repo instrument, but also seeks to place repo in the context of the wider debt capital markets. Repo market practitioners may go straight to Chapter 5, which begins our discussion of the market and instruments. Chapters 2, 3 and 4 describe the bond and money markets, which may be useful for newcomers to the industry. The more technically-minded may also be interested in Chapter 4, which deals with the term structure in some detail. However these chapters are not necessary for an understanding of repo. In addition to covering the basic repo instrument, its uses and economic function, we also cover repo-like transactions such as Total Return Swaps. There is also a chapter each on elementary trading strategy, and asset & liability management. Brief coverage is presented of a number of selected country markets, whilst Chapter 10 looks at the United Kingdom gilt repo market in some detail.

Part II of the book considers the institutional treatment of repo. So there are chapters on risk, accounting, tax and legal issues connected with repo. There is also a chapter on equity repo, which may more logically sit in Part I, but the author thought that this spoiled somewhat the aesthetic of Part I, which concentrates on bond repo.

Part III is a detailed treatment of one of the most exciting areas of the market: the government bond basis, implied repo rate and basis trading. This includes a detailed look at the United Kingdom gilt bond basis. Basis trading is a form of arbitrage trading, and it is a form of trading that doesn't reap dividends unless carried out exactly right, but there is considerable confusion about it in the market. The chapters in Part III are designed to demystify the subject to some extent.

A glossary concludes the book.

Study materials

Where possible, the main concepts and techniques we discuss have been illustrated with worked examples and case studies. Some of the content of this book was originally written as course notes, and used to form part of repo market courses taught at a number of professional bodies and teaching institutions, including the Securities Institute, International Faculty of Finance, and City University Business School. From these courses, a number of Microsoft Powerpoint slides have been made available for use as teaching aids, and may be downloaded from the author's web site at

www.YieldCurve.com

There is also a selection of the author's and his associates' fixed income research . The web site contains details of repo and other training courses that are available on repo and advanced bond market topics.

Acknowledgements – the book

This book has been a long time in the making. It would not have been completed without the help and influence, directly or indirectly, of a number of people.

A very, very big thank you to Mr Derek Taylor, who is not only a money markets expert but also a top chap, now with King & Shaxson Bond Brokers Limited, for his continued assistance, which includes the foreword to this book, and all his help in the past, starting when I was at Hoare Govett Securities Limited. Thanks for everything Del-Boy, and all the best. By the way, you share your name with the best bass player ever, Derek Taylor of Roachford. Thanks also to David Wileman at King's, a true gent. I appreciate the excellent foreword, really, you're too kind.

I am especially grateful for the endorsements provided for this book, all by people who are real experts in their field. First up, a big thank you to David Franklin, now at HBOS plc, but previously at LM Money Brokers and then Gerrand plc when I was a dealing counterparty of his – those were the days! Sorry I couldn't use your original comment about me ("A dubious character but with impeccable dress sense"), it might have harmed sales of the book! My very best wishes to you. A big, big thank you to Professor Elias Dinenis, and I look forward to working with you at the Centre for Mathematical Trading and Finance.

Thanks to Sean Baguley for recruiting me into the market, and John Lenton for introducing me to the subject of repo; my very best wishes gentlemen. Thanks to Tracy Shand, formerly at International Faculty of Finance, for inviting me to teach part of the IFF repo course. Thanks to Alison Brooks at FinTuition Limited and Zena Deane at the Securities Institute for asking me to teach their respective repo courses as well!

A big thank you to Nimish Thakker, formerly at LIFFE, for the long gilt future delivery data, I really appreciated the prompt responses to all my queries. Also, nice working with you on a possible CreditNOTE.

Thanks to Bill Curtin at the US Office of the Public Debt for all his assistance, and Karstein Bjastad and Chris Bessant at JPMorgan Chase for help with the equity repo chapter.

I'd like to thank the following individuals for their prompt attention in granting permission to reproduce various items in this book: Lindsey Gulley and Hayley Hewlett at Halifax plc, Peter Ratcliffe and Yvonne Schweizer at ISMA, Mike Sheard and Paul Cumbers at Garban ICAP, and the people at Bloomberg.

Thanks to Mike Cash at Butterworth-Heinemann for all his help with this book and his faith in my ability to deliver something half-way decent.

Thanks to Molga for the cartoons, and as the esteemed Orange Juice once said, *A Place In My Heart...*

Special thanks

Thanks to Alan Fulling, Rich Lynn, Neil Lewis and Richard McCarthy. 110%.

Thanks for the web site work Bogey, it's awesome, especially since I got you to change it to look more like Darren Gough's web site. A special thanks for all your help with the Associates. Sherif, the IT kit is still going strong, thanks… it's been 20 years since you bought *Crumbling the Antiseptic Beauty*, almost as long since that article in "International Musician and Recording World" alerted us to *This Charming Man* and right now I've got *Shock of Daylight* on (I haven't heard it in years)… nice one. You taught me a lot.

A big thank you to Mr Frank Fabozzi, it's a great pleasure to work with you on any subject in fixed income, and I appreciate your help with the section on dollar rolls for this book. Thanks also to my co-author (on *The Global Money Markets*) Professor Steven Mann, at the University of South Carolina, again, a real pleasure to work with you. I must mention Brian Eales (London Guildhall University), Philippe Priaulet (HSBC CCF), Professor Sheldon Ross (University of California at Berkeley), Kenneth Garbade (Federal Reserve Bank of New York), Dr Christine Oughton (Birkbeck, University of London), and Professor Steven Satchell (Trinity College, Cambridge), it's a real pleasure working with you all.

This book looks so good because it's been produced by Graham Douglas, a top chap and publishing expert. It was a lot of fun exchanging differences of editorial opinion at odd hours of the day. Thanks for all your input! I still think the design layout of pages 107–108 could be improved though…

Cheers to Rod Pienaar at Deutsche Bank and Richard Pereira at Dresdner Kleinwort Wasserstein who know capital market mathematics better than anyone, also Didier Joannas at

SunGard, another co-author and an old mate from Hoare Govett days, remember lads the team is everything!

Mike Hellmuth – when are we getting to an England game ?(cricket or football, you pick!). We need to discuss the team selections some more though. Ketul Tanna, Mark Jones, Hugh Stevens, Remi Bola, you guys know structured products better than half the mob over at you-know-where…! Thanks for your help.

A special thank you to Mr Tim Leonard, an artist and true master of his craft.

Hello to the four most gorgeous nieces anyone could have: Little Bitty Lee, Asia, and Jasmine , but most especially my friend Millie. Cheers Nik, and Clax, here's to the next 20 years…

Joanne Milbourn, you're an absolute darling, and Mark, surely you supplied the best endoresement a book could ever have ? ("I started reading it… but there was nothing to colour in"). The publishers weren't too keen on that though…

Thanks to Gary Raggett and Diane Spranger at the Personal Banking Office, NatWest Bank, for sorting out my banking needs and thereby reducing my stress levels .

Thanks to Margaret Lee at the Forest Road post office, Effingham Junction, for looking after my mail.

Thanks to Yasmin Imani for help at those PhD research seminars!

For inspiration I'd like to thank Simon Barnes, *No Escape Zone* by Lieutenant Nick Richardson RN; *Only Fools and Horses*; *What Difference Does It Make?* by The Smiths; Stuart Morrow, Martin Stephenson, Edwyn Collins, Lawrence, Maurice Deebank, Mick Lloyd, Gary Ainge, Nick King, Chris Dean, Martin Hewes, Lloyd Cole and The Commotions, and the late Adrian Borland of *The Sound* (R.I.P., 1999).

No thanks to those who doubted, and managers who couldn't lead themselves out of a wet paper bag, let alone lead a team of professionals. I'd like to give each of them a copy of Mike Brearley's book *The Art of Captaincy*, but of course they already know it all.

A passer-by saw three men building a wall, and stopped to ask them what they were doing.

"I'm laying bricks," said the first man.

"I'm earning 10 pound an hour," said the second man.

"I'm building a cathedral," said the third man, "and one day after its finished, I'm going to bring my kids and show them what a fabulous building it is, and tell them how their Dad helped to build it."

They'll be surprised and embarrassed to hear it, but my time playing football with the lads at JPMorgan Chase Institutional Trust Services has taught me to think more like the third man. They know who they are: thanks a lot chaps, it's been a real privilege, as well as a pleasure.

The same day I'm writing this, I'd just watched Mark Ramprakash score a century in the Fifth Test at the Oval, his first in England… 10 years after his Test debut. And against the Australians too. It was worth waiting for, as fabulous as it was inspirational. Brilliant. Keep on keeping on…

Moorad Choudhry
Surrey, England
25 August 2001

The JPMorgan Chase ITS "Dream Team" 1st XI

Chris Green
(*Brisbane Lions*)

Moorad Choudhry   **Alan Fulling (c)**   **Ben Burrell**   **Lucan Chavez-Munoz**
(*Wimbledon*)   (*Arsenal*)   (*Sheffield Wednesday*)   (*Manchester United*)

Rich Lynn   **Steve Fearon**   **Neil Lewis**   **Jonathan Rossington**
(*Tottenham*)   (*Liverpool*)   (*Manchester United*)   (*West Ham*)

                       Richard McCarthy   **Michael Nicoll**
                       (*Liverpool*)   (*Arsenal*)

Subs:
Bill Bolger (*Manchester City*), **Huw Williams** (*Manchester United*)
Remi Bola (*Tottenham*), **Clive Kentish** (*Luton Town*)
Nick Procter (*Leeds United*), **Matthew Neville** (*West Ham*)

Programme Notes

Chris Green	Safe hands
Alan Fulling	Key coach and motivator, first choice for Sven Goran Eriksson's No 2
Moorad	Between him and footballing success lies talent
Ben Burrell	A great stopper
Lucan	Mr Reliable
Rich Lynn	A Rolls Royce of a player, the team's Glenn Hoddle
Steve Fearon	The consummate team player in any position
Neil Lewis	The Boss. 'Nuff said…
Jon Ross	Supreme optimism and self-confidence from the Boy Wonder, quickest player on the pitch
Will Manns	Solid in midfield
Adam Miller	Cheers for keeping me on the Thursday game reserve list
Nick Procter	Archtypal tenacious Aussie
Stuart Medlen	Surely a professional footballer in a past life? A privilege to watch…
Dickie	Finishes like Fowler. First name on the team sheet
Nicoll	Sublime play from the man with the golden touch
Remi Bola	Motivated to the final whistle
Mat Neville	Always does his best
Kevin Francis	Key team player up front
Huw Williams	The natural team leader
Clive Kentish	Always raises his game for the big night
Bill Bolger	Solid at the back
George Okunega	Already a result simply when he turns up

Alternative Programme Notes by Michael Nicoll

Chris Green	Aussie! Says it all!!
Moorad	Good ball old chap!
Fulling	Left foot for standing only!
Burrell	Plays football like he's playing Rugby…
Lucan	Would kick his own Mother if she played!
Rich Lynn	Not the same player since Sol left…
Steve Fearon	Tall
Neil Lewis	Always the morning after the night before!
Rossington	Couldn't control a bag of cement! Poor man's Steve McManaman
Dickie	Couldn't hit a barn door from 5 yeards on a good day
Nicoll	LEGEND! Any team's Zidane
Remi Bola	If it moves he kicks it
Mat Neville	Occasional lapses is an understatement
Kevin Francis	Can't dribble, control a ball, shoot, pass or take people on. Otherwise a fine player…
Stuart Medlen	Not surprised he supports Charlton!
Huw Williams	A skuffed volley legend
Clive Kentish	Stick to them Moroccan Bongs!
Bill Bolger	A defender who thinks he's Ruud Van Nistelrooy
Nick Procter	Quick
George Okunega	Another Super Eagles enigma! Surprisingly enough…

Bibliography and references

All reference to previous research and published material is detailed in a bibliography at the end of each relevant chapter. We also list recommended texts and articles, which the author thinks readers will find interesting and/or benefit from looking at. A more comprehensive list of references and recommended readings on the subject of the global debt capital markets can be found at the end of each chapter in Choudhry (2001). The Blake (1990) and Fabozzi (1989) references listed below were the first ones ever purchased by the author shortly after he started work as a graduate trainee in the City of London in 1989; he is happy to say that (in their updated editions) they remain excellent reading for newcomers to the world of financial markets, and heartily recommends them. If any budding authors out there go on to recommend any of his works to future graduate trainees, the author will have achieved his primary goal in writing this book.

Blake, D., *Financial Market Analysis*, McGraw Hill, 1990.
Choudhry, M., *Bond Market Securities*, FT Prentice Hall, 2001.
Fabozzi, F., *Bond Markets: Analysis and Strategies*, 2nd edition, Prentice Hall, 1993.

About the Author

Moorad Choudhry is a vice-president in structured finance services with JPMorgan Chase in London. From joining the London Stock Exchange in 1989 he went on to Hoare Govett Securities Limited (later ABN Amro Hoare Govett Sterling Bonds Limited) where he worked as a sterling Treasury trader and gilt-edged market maker. He later set up and ran the Treasury division's sterling proprietary trading desk at Hambros Bank Limited. He worked in strategy and risk consulting for a number of commercial and investment banks before joining JPMorgan Chase Bank in February 2000.

Moorad has lectured on the bond and money markets at London Guildhall University, International Faculty of Finance and the Securities Institute. He is a senior Fellow at the Centre for Mathematical Trading and Finance, City University Business School.

Moorad was born in Bangladesh but moved at an early age to Surrey in England, where he lives today.

Part I
Repo Instruments and the Debt Capital Markets

In Part I of the book we introduce repo as a financial market instrument, and also spend three chapters placing repo in the context of the debt capital markets. Repo is an interesting product because although it is a money market product, by dint of the term to maturity of repo trades, the nature of the underlying collateral means that the repo desk must be keenly aware of the bonds that they "trade" as well. This multi-faceted nature of repo is apparent in the way that banks organise their repo trading. In some banks it is part of the money market or Treasury division, while in other banks it will be within the bond trading area. Equity repo is sometimes a back office activity, as is the longer-established stock borrowing desk. However, it is not only commercial and investment banks that engage in repo transactions. In the US dollar market repo is a well-established investment product, utilised by corporate treasuries and local authorities. Fund managers will also engage in repo. The practicality and simplicity of repo means that it can be taken up even in capital markets that are still at an "emerging" stage, and by a wide range of participants. If it is not traded in just about every country with a debt capital market in the world, then before long it most probably will be.

Part I introduces the repo instrument and places it in the context of the wider market. To this end we spend three chapters discussing bonds and money markets. We then move on to the nitty-gritty, Chapters 5 and 6, which look at the repo instrument and its principal uses and economic functions. There are two main types of repo: the classic repo and the sell/buy-back. As markets have developed in their own way and at different paces, they also have slightly different terminology. Wherever possible this is described and explained. This is followed by a review of the more structured repo-type products, such as total return swaps, and how they form part of the newer market in credit derivatives.

The importance of the financing function undertaken using repo needs to be placed in context, and for this reason we consider bank asset & liability management and basics of trading strategy. These are important areas if one wishes to understand the part repo plays in the capital markets. Once we have considered the instrument generically, we are ready to look at some specific markets. A detailed review is given of the UK gilt repo market, and there are briefer notes on selected "other country" markets.

"Yeah, there was this guy after one of the gigs and he was saying, 'Well, I don't know if I should stay around here for the show or go back and get this album moving!' Get this album moving!? Who did he think he was? John Wayne or something? What's he going to do at nine o'clock at night?"

– Paul Weller, quoted in Nicholls, M., *About the Young Idea: The Story of The Jam 1972–1982*. Proteus Books, 1984, p. 59.

1 Introduction to Repo

The global market in repurchase agreements or *repo* is both large and vitally important to the smooth running of the capital markets. The size of the market is always presented as an estimate, but it is safe to say that markets around the world experienced significant growth during the 1990s and continue to expand. Asset classes that can be subject to repo now include corporate and Eurobonds in both developed and emerging markets, as well as equities and equity baskets. The growth in repo has been attributed to several factors, which we will review in this and subsequent chapters. However in essence the simplicity of repo and the ability to adapt it to any market circumstance is key to its attraction to market participants, whether they are central banks, investment banks, borrowers, investors, or fund managers. The use of repo enhances the liquidity of bond and equity markets, which reduces costs for issuers of capital, and allows market makers to hedge positions with greater efficiency. Estimates of the size of the repo market vary. The turnover in euro-zone countries and the United Kingdom was in excess of $25 trillion in 1998.[1] The US Treasury repo market is estimated very roughly at $2 trillion. Repo generally carries a lower profile than other sectors of the market, but its size is substantial in comparison to them. For example the turnover through the Euroclear and Clearstream clearing systems alone was put at $13 trillion in 1998.[2] The introduction of a repo market has impact on areas other than the straightforward provision of secured lending and borrowing facilities. In the United Kingdom an open market in repo was introduced only in January 1996,[3] and it has been interesting to observe the impact of gilt repo on the unsecured money market and on the liquidity and turnover of the gilt market. For instance, data on the sterling average interbank overnight rate, known as SONIA, indicated a substantial reduction in the volume of unsecured overnight borrowing and lending from around $7 billion at the start of 1996 to under $4 billion at the start of 2000, as participants started to use repo more heavily. Evidence from the Bank of England also suggested that the volatility of overnight interest rates was reduced.[4] These and other issues in the sterling market are investigated in detail in a separate chapter.

Given its size and importance, it is surprising that repo has such a low profile; for example, there is little discussion of it in the financial press. This reflects the simple and straightforward nature of the instrument. Indeed, the fundamental essence of repo is its simplicity; the sale of securities coupled with an agreement to repurchase them at a future date. It is this simplicity and flexibility that has allowed repo to be used for a variety of purposes, or to meet a range of requirements. The determinants of the growth of repo in Europe are considered in more detail later, although one of the main factors was the need for investment banks and bond market makers to secure a lower funding rate for their long positions, and the ability to cover short positions more efficiently. The introduction of the Bund futures contract on London's LIFFE

---

[1] Source: ISMA.

[2] *Ibid.*

[3] This is the open market in gilt repo. A market in equity repo, for instance, had been in operation in the London market from around 1992.

[4] Volume figures from ISMA. Several Bank of England reports have studied the impact of gilt repo, but note particularly the *Quarterly Bulletin* for February 1998, August 1998 and February 1999.

exchange in 1988 also contributed to the growth of Bund repo, as market participants entered into cash-and-carry or *basis* trading, arbitraging between the cash and futures market. Such trading is not possible without an open repo market. From around the same time the increasing use of derivative instruments such as swaps and bond options also contributed to greater use of repo, as banks often used the repo market to manage their hedge positions.

There is a wide range of uses to which repo might be put. Structured transactions that are very similar to repo include total return swaps, and other structured repo trades include floating-rate repo which contains an option to switch to a fixed rate at a later date. In the equity market repo is often conducted in a basket of stocks, which might be constituent stocks in an index such as the FTSE100 or CAC40 or user-specified baskets. Market makers borrow and lend equities with differing terms to maturity, and generally the credit rating of the institution involved in the repo transaction is of more importance than the quality of the colla t-eral. Central banks' use of repo also reflects its importance; it is a key instrument in the implementation of monetary policy in many countries. Essentially then, repo markets have vital links and relationships with global money markets, bond markets, futures markets, swap markets and over-the-counter (OTC) interest rate derivatives.

In the remainder of this chapter we set the scene by discussing key features of the repo instrument, as well as the history of repo. Practitioners may wish to skip this part and move straight to the mechanics of repo in Chapter 5, while newcomers to the market may wish to proceed to the market background in the next chapter.

1.1   Key features

Repo is essentially a secured loan. The term comes from *sale and repurchase agreement*; however, this is not necessarily the best way to look at it. Although in a *classic repo* transaction legal title of an asset is transferred from the "seller" to the "buyer" during the term of the repo, in the author's opinion this detracts from the essence of the instrument: a secured loan of cash. It is therefore a money market instrument. In Chapter 3 we formally define repo and illustrate its use; for the moment we need only to think of it as a secured loan. The interest on this loan is the payment made in the repo.

There are a number of benefits in using repo, which concurrently have been behind its rapid growth. These include the following:

■ market makers generally are able to finance their long bond and equity positions at a lower interest cost if they repo out the assets; equally they are able to cover short positions;

■ there is greater liquidity in specific individual bond issues;

■ greater market liquidity lowers the cost of raising funds for capital market borrowers;

■ central banks are able to use repo in their open market operations;

■ repo reduces *counterparty risk* in money market borrowing and lending, because of the security offered by the collateral given in the loan;

■ investors have an added investment option when placing funds;

■ institutional investors and other long-term holders of securities are able to enhance their returns by making their inventories available for repo trading.

The maturity of the majority of repo transactions are between overnight and three months, although trades of six months and one year are not uncommon. It is possible to transact in longer term repo as well. Because of this, repo is best seen as a money market product.[5] However, because of the nature of the collateral, repo market participants must keep a close eye on the market of the asset collateral, whether this is the government bond market, Eurobonds, equity or other asset.[6] The counterparties to a repo transaction will have different requirements, for instance to "borrow" a particular asset against an interest in lending cash. For this reason it is common to hear participants talk of trades being *stock-driven* or *cash-driven*. A corporate treasurer who invests cash while receiving some form of security is driving a cash-driven repo, whereas a market maker that wishes to cover a short position in a particular stock, against which she lends cash, is entering into a stock-driven trade.

There is a close relationship between repo and both the bond and money markets. The use of repo has contributed greatly to the liquidity of government, Eurobond and emerging market bond markets. Although it is a separate and individual market itself, operationally repo is straightforward to handle, in that it generally settles through clearing mechanisms used for bonds. As a money market product, repo reduces the stress placed on the unsecured interbank market, and empirical evidence indicates a reduction in overnight interest-rate volatility.[7]

1.2   Market participants

The development and use of repo in each country to an extent dictates the nature and range of market participants. In a mature market repo counterparties include investors and cash-rich institutions, those seeking to finance asset positions and their intermediaries. Some firms will cross over these broad boundaries and engage in all aspects of repo trading. The main market parties are:

- *Financial institutions:* retail and commercial banks, building societies, securities houses and investment banks;

- *Investors:* fund managers, insurance companies and pension funds, investment funds, hedge funds, local authorities and corporate treasuries;

- *Intermediaries:* Inter-dealer brokers and money brokers. The main brokers are Cantor Fitzgerald, Prebon Yamane, Garban ICAP, Tullet & Tokyo and Tradition. Indiviual markets also have other brokers.

Financial institutions will engage in both repo and reverse repo trades. Investors also, despite their generic name, will be involved in both repo and reverse repo. Their money market funds will be cash-rich and engage in investment trades; at the same time they will run large fixed interest portfolios, the returns for which can be enhanced through trading in repo. Central banks are major players in repo markets and use repo as part of daily liquidity or *open market* operations and as a tool of monetary policy.

---

5   The textbook definition of a "money market" instrument is of a debt product issued with between one day and one year to maturity, while debt instruments of greater than one year maturity are known as capital market instruments. In practice the money market desks of most banks will trade the yield curve to up to two years maturity, so it makes sense to view a money market instrument as being of up to two years maturity.

6   This carries on to bank organisation structure. In most banks, the repo desk for bonds is situated in the money markets area, while in others it will be part of the bond division (the author has experience of banks employing each system). Equity repo is often situated as part of the back office settlement or Treasury function.

7   Bank of England (*ibid*).

Repo itself is an over-the-counter market conducted over the telephone, with rates displayed on screens. These screens are supplied by both brokers and market makers themselves. Increasingly, electronic dealing systems are being used, with live dealing rates displayed on screen and trades being conducted at the click of a mouse button.

1.3   Development of repo

1.3.1   *History*

A repo market was introduced by the US Federal Reserve in 1918, as the main tool of the Fed's open market operations. Repo was used both to drain liquidity, in the form of surplus cash, from the banking system, and to add liquidity as required. Initially, repo was transacted in bank bills known as Bankers Acceptances and the trades were known as *resale agreements*. Subsequently repo was undertaken in Treasury securities. The US government bond market and the repo market in US Treasuries are the largest in the world; daily volume in US repo is estimated at over $1,000 billion.

Repo has spread to other markets around the world, and exists in both developed and emerging economy capital markets. The instrument now covers corporate bonds, asset-backed bonds, agency securities and Eurobonds as well as equity and money market instruments. It began in the London market from around the time of "Big Bang" (1986), when investment banks began using repo to finance their bond positions. The driver behind the increasing use of repo was a need to obtain lower financing rates. Certain banks began what was essentially a market-making service in repo, making two-way prices in repo and in large size; this is known as *matched book* trading.[8] In the Eurobond market, the high cost of borrowing securities from the two main clearing mechanisms, Euroclear and Clearstream (or Cedel as it was known previously), was another driver in the growth of repo. As we noted earlier, repo also became more important when the Bund futures contract was introduced on LIFFE and when the Notionel contract was introduced on Matif in Paris. These events occurred in the late 1980s.

Other factors that led to the growth in repo across markets globally include:

- the ease of the transaction itself;
- expansion in public sector debt levels, leading to larger volume government bond markets;
- increased volatility in interest rates;
- arbitrage opportunities against other money market instruments and in derivatives markets;
- the use of repo in hedging, illustrating the link between the repo market and derivatives markets;

---

[8]   The term "matched book" is something of a misnomer, as banks rarely actually match the term of bid and offer transactions. It is essentially repo market-making, with the trader taking a view on the short-term yield curve and positioning her book accordingly. Some writers have stated that matched book trading is where a bank generates a profit by trading the bid–offer spread. However, this is an academic definition; it is the active trading of the book, deliberately mis-matching positions and taking a view on the future direction of interest rates, that generates the trader's profit. Another definition, which the author will accept, is trading activity to cover one's own positions only.

- as an alternative to bank deposits for corporate treasurers and others, as well as an alternative to unsecured instruments such as *certificates of deposit* and *commercial paper*. The existence of security however, results in a lower yield being available on repo, except at the very short end of the yield curve, where there is higher demand from market participants who do not have access to the interbank market. Repo that pays a rate of Libor will be for lower quality asset collateral.

In addition repo is used by large-scale holders of bonds such as institutional investors, who can gain additional income by making their assets available for repo. They can switch into a cash investment whilst maintaining their portfolios intact. The economic benefits of the assets of course remain with the original bondholder. The stock-lending market is attractive to such institutions for the same reason, and is preferred when institutions desire straight fee income in return for repoing out their portfolios.

The instrument is attractive to market participants due to its flexibility when compared to other money market instruments. Bondholders can pick up extra yield on their portfolios; there is also potential for reduction of borrowing costs allied to reduced credit risk due to collateralisation, and a facility to borrow bonds to cover short positions. Some of these uses will be explored later in the book.

As repo has developed in popularity it has been adopted by a greater range of participants, and for a wider range of assets. In the USA it is common for non-bank institutions such as corporate treasurers and local authorities to invest in repo, although this is not widespread in Europe. However this is only a matter of time. A recent development that will further encourage use of repo is the development of multilateral clearing and netting systems such as Repo-Clear. These act in a similar fashion to the clearing house systems used in futures exchanges, and will provide several key advantages for banks – including the ability to reduce counterparty risk exposure and free up lending lines. Netting is also discussed in a later chapter.

1.3.2   *Types of repo*

There are three main basic types of repo: the *classic* repo, the *sell/buy-back* and *tri-party repo*. A sell/buy-back, referred to in some markets as a *buy-sell*, is a spot sale and repurchase of assets transacted simultaneously. It does not require a settlement system that can handle the concept of a classic repo and is often found in emerging markets. A classic repo is economically identical but the repo rate is explicit and the transaction is conducted under a legal agreement that defines the legal transfer of ownership of the asset during the term of the trade. Classic repo, the type of transaction that originated in the USA, is a sale and repurchase of an asset where the repurchase price is unchanged from the "sale" price. Hence the transaction is better viewed as a loan and borrow of cash. In a tri-party repo a third party acts as an agent on behalf of both seller and buyer of the asset, but otherwise the instrument is identical to classic repo.

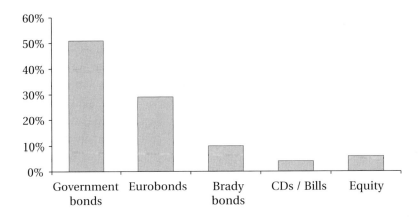

Figure 1.1: Assets used in repo transactions during 1999. Source: ISMA.

The rest of this book looks in detail at the use and application of repo, and its interplay with other markets.

Selected bibliography and references

Choudhry, M., *An Introduction to Repo Markets*, SI (Services) Publishing 1998
Corrigan, D., Georgiou, C., Gollow, J., *Repo: the ultimate guide*, Pearls of Wisdom Publishing 1999
Scott-Quinn, B., Walmsley, J., *The Repo Market in Euro: Making It Work*, ISMA 1997
Roth, P., *Mastering Foreign Exchange & Money Markets*, FT Prentice-Hall 1996
Steiner, B., *Mastering Repo Markets*, FT Prentice-Hall 1998

2 Market Background: *The Bond Markets I*

Repo is a money market instrument that demands that its users be keenly aware of the overall debt capital markets. For this reason in this chapter we present a review of financial arithmetic and bond mathematics. A separate chapter presents a brief description of money market instruments. We do not present an analysis of equities, on the basis that it is not necessarily required learning for repo market participants to be aware of issues such as equity valuation techniques. Readers should know that there are a number of readable texts that deal with this subject, including Blake (2000) and Van Horne (1995).

The analysis of bonds is frequently presented in what might be termed "traditional" terms, with description limited to gross redemption yield or *yield to maturity*. However these days basic bond maths analysis is presented in slightly different terms, as described in a range of books and articles such as those by Ingersoll (1987), Shiller (1990), Neftci (1996), Jarrow (1996), Van Deventer (1997) and Sundaresan (1997), among others.[1] For this reason we review the basic elements, strictly in overview fashion only, in this chapter. The academic approach and description of bond pricing, and a review of the term structure of interest rates, is considered in the next chapter. Interested readers may wish to consult the texts in the bibliography for further information.

Be prepared, this chapter is a long one as it attempts to summarise concepts generally covered in an entire book. However, readers unfamiliar with bonds are encouraged to work through it.

2.1 Time value of money

The principles of pricing in the bond market are exactly the same as those in other financial markets, which states that the price of any financial instrument is equal to the present value today of all the future cash flows from the instrument. Bond prices are expressed as per 100 nominal of the bond, or "per cent". So, for example, if the price of a US dollar denominated bond is quoted as "98.00", this means that for every $100 nominal of the bond a buyer would pay $98.[2] The interest rate or discount rate used as part of the present value (price) calculation is key, as it reflects where the bond is trading in the market and how it is perceived by the market. All the determining factors that identify the bond, including the nature of the issuer, the maturity, the coupon and the currency, influence the interest rate at which a bond's cash flows are discounted, which will be similar to the rate used for comparable bonds. First we consider the traditional approach to bond pricing for a plain vanilla instrument, making certain assumptions to keep the analysis simple, and then we present the more formal analysis commonly encountered in academic texts.

---

[1] This area of fixed income analytics has been extensively researched. The references given are, in the opinion of the author, some of the very best. In fact a reader could make do with reading and understanding the Jarrow, Shiller and Ingersoll references only, which are excellent.

[2] The convention in certain markets is to quote a price per 1000 nominal, but this is rare.

2.1.1 *Introduction*

Bonds or *fixed income*[3] instruments are debt capital market securities and therefore have maturities longer than one year. This differentiates them from money market securities. Bonds have more intricate cash flow patterns than money market securities, which usually have just one cash flow at maturity. This makes bonds more involved to price than money market instruments, and their prices more responsive to changes in the general level of interest rates. There is a large variety of bonds. The most common type is the *plain vanilla* (or *straight, conventional* or *bullet)* bond. This is a bond paying a regular (annual or semi-annual) fixed interest payment, or *coupon,* over a fixed period to maturity or redemption, with the return of principal (the par or nominal value of the bond) on the maturity date. All other bonds are variations on this.

The key identifying feature of a bond is its issuer, the entity that is borrowing funds by issuing the bond into the market. Issuers are generally categorised as one of four types: governments (and their agencies), local governments (or municipal authorities), supranational bodies such as the World Bank, and corporates. Within the municipal and corporate markets there are a wide range of issuers, each assessed as having differing abilities to maintain the interest payments on their debt and repay the full loan on maturity. This ability is identified by a *credit rating* for each issuer. The *term to maturity* of a bond is the number of years over which the issuer has promised to meet the conditions of the debt obligation. The *maturity* of a bond refers to the date that the debt will cease to exist, at which time the issuer will redeem the bond by paying back the principal. The practice in the bond market is to refer to the "term to maturity" of a bond as simply its "maturity" or "term". Some bonds contain provisions that allow either the issuer or the bondholder to alter a bond's term. The term to maturity of a bond is its other key feature. Firstly, it indicates the time period over which the bondholder can expect to receive coupon payments and the number of years before the principal is paid back. Secondly, it influences the yield of a bond. Finally, the price of a bond will fluctuate over its life as yields in the market change. The volatility of a bond's price is dependent on its maturity. All else being equal, the longer the maturity of a bond, the greater its price volatility resulting from a change in market yields.

The *principal* of a bond is the amount that the issuer agrees to repay the bondholder on maturity. This amount is also referred to as the *redemption value, maturity value, par value* or *face value.* The coupon rate, or *nominal rate,* is the interest rate that the issuer agrees to pay each year during the life of the bond. The annual amount of interest payment made to bondholders is the *coupon.* The cash amount of the coupon is the coupon rate multiplied by the principal of the bond. For example, a bond with a coupon rate of 8% and a principal of £1000 will pay annual interest of £80. In the United Kingdom the usual practice is for the issuer to pay the coupon in two semi-annual instalments. All bonds make periodic coupon payments, except for one type that makes none. These bonds are known as *zero-coupon bonds.* Such bonds are issued at a discount and redeemed at par. The holder of a zero-coupon bond real-

---

[3] The term *fixed income* originated at a time when bonds were essentially plain vanilla instruments paying a fixed coupon per year. In the United Kingdom the term *fixed interest* was used. These days many bonds do not necessarily pay a fixed coupon each year; for instance, asset-backed bond issues are invariably issued in a number of tranches, with each tranche paying a different fixed or floating coupon. The market is still commonly referred to as the fixed income market however (and certain sterling market diehards, like the author, will even call it the fixed interest market).

ises interest by buying the bond at this discounted value, below its principal value. Interest is therefore paid on maturity, with the exact amount being the difference between the principal value and the discounted value paid on purchase.

There are also *floating rate bonds* (FRNs). With these bonds coupon rates are reset periodically according to a predetermined benchmark, such as 3-month or 6-month LIBOR. For this reason FRNs typically trade more as money market instruments than conventional bonds.

A bond issue may include a provision that gives either the bondholder and/or the issuer an option to take some action against the other party. The most common type of option embedded in a bond is a *call feature*. This grants the issuer the right to call the debt, fully or partially, before the maturity date. A *put provision* gives bondholders the right to sell the issue back to the issuer at par on designated dates. A *convertible bond* is an issue giving the bondholder the right to exchange the bond for a specified number of shares (equity) in the issuing company. The presence of embedded options makes the valuation of such bonds more complex when compared with plain vanilla bonds.

2.1.2 *Present value and discounting*

As fixed income instruments are essentially a collection of cash flows, we begin by reviewing the key concept in cash flow analysis, that of discounting and *present value*. It is essential to have a firm understanding of the main principles given here before moving on to other areas. When reviewing the concept of the time value of money, assume that the interest rates used are the market determined rates of interest.

Financial arithmetic has long been used to illustrate that £1 received today is not the same as £1 received at a point in the future. Faced with a choice between receiving £1 today or £1 in one year's time we would be indifferent given a rate of interest of, say, 10% that was equal to our required nominal rate of interest. Our choice would be between £1 today or £1 plus 10p in one year's time – the interest on £1 for one year at 10% per annum. The notion that money has a time value is a basic concept in the analysis of financial instruments. Money has time value because of the opportunity to invest it at a rate of interest. A loan that has one interest payment on maturity is accruing *simple interest*. On short-term instruments there is usually only the one interest payment on maturity; hence simple interest is received when the instrument expires. The terminal value of an investment with simple interest is given by (2.1):

$$F = P(1 + r)$$ (2.1)

where

F is the terminal value or *future value*;
P is the initial investment or *present value*;
r is the interest rate.

The market convention is to quote interest rates as *annualised* interest rates, which is the interest that is earned if the investment term is one year. Consider a three-month deposit of £100 in a bank, placed at a rate of interest of 6%. In such a case the bank deposit will earn 6% interest for a period of 90 days. As the annual interest gain would be £6, the investor will expect to receive a proportion of this, which is calculated as

$$£6.00 \times \frac{90}{365} = £1.479.$$

So the investor will receive £1.479 interest at the end of the term. The total proceeds after the three months is therefore £100 plus £1.479. If we wish to calculate the terminal value of a short-term investment that is accruing simple interest we use the following expression:

$$F = P(1 + r \times (\text{days}/\text{year})).\tag{2.2}$$

The fraction (days/year) refers to the numerator, which is the number of days the investment runs, divided by the denominator which is the number of days in the year. In the sterling markets the number of days in the year is taken to be 365; however, most other markets (including the dollar and euro markets) have a 360-day year convention. For this reason we simply quote the expression as "days" divided by "year" to allow for either convention.

Let us now consider an investment of £100 made for three years, again at a rate of 6%, but this time fixed for three years. At the end of the first year the investor will be credited with interest of £6. Therefore for the second year the interest rate of 6% will be accruing on a principal sum of £106, which means that at the end of year 2 the interest credited will be £6.36. This illustrates how *compounding* works, which is the principle of earning interest on interest. The outcome of the process of compounding is the *future value* of the initial amount. The expression is given in (2.3).

$$FV = PV(1 + r)^n\tag{2.3}$$

where

FV	is the future value;
PV	is initial outlay or *present value*;
r	is the periodic rate of interest (expressed as a decimal);
n	is the number of periods for which the sum is invested.

When we compound interest we have to assume that the reinvestment of interest payments during the investment term is at the same rate as the first year's interest. That is why we stated that the 6% rate in our example was *fixed* for three years. We can see however that compounding increases our returns compared to investments that accrue only on a simple interest basis.

Now let us consider a deposit of £100 for one year, at a rate of 6% but with quarterly interest payments. Such a deposit would accrue interest of £6 in the normal way but £1.50 would be credited to the account every quarter, and this would then benefit from compounding. Again assuming that we can reinvest at the same rate of 6%, the total return at the end of the year will be:

$$100 \times ((1 + 0.015) \times (1 + 0.015) \times (1 + 0.015) \times (1 + 0.015)) = 100 \times (1 + 0.015)^4$$

which gives us 100×1.06136, a terminal value of £106.136. This is some 13 pence more than the terminal value using annual compounded interest.

In general, if compounding takes place m times per year, then at the end of n years mn interest payments will have been made and the future value of the principal is given by (2.4):

$$FV = PV\left(1 + \frac{r}{m}\right)^{mn}.\tag{2.4}$$

As we showed in our example the effect of more frequent compounding is to increase the value of the total return when compared to annual compounding. The effect of more frequent compounding is shown below, where we consider the annualised interest rate factors, for an annualised rate of 6%.

$$\text{Interest rate factor} = \left(1 + \frac{r}{m}\right)^m.$$

Compounding frequency	Interest rate factor	
Annual	$(1 + r)$	= 1.060000
Semi-annual	$\left(1 + \frac{r}{2}\right)^2$	= 1.060900
Quarterly	$\left(1 + \frac{r}{4}\right)^4$	= 1.061364
Monthly	$\left(1 + \frac{r}{12}\right)^{12}$	= 1.061678
Daily	$\left(1 + \frac{r}{365}\right)^{365}$	= 1.061831

This shows us that the more frequent the compounding the higher the interest rate factor. The last case also illustrates how a limit occurs when interest is compounded continuously. Equation (2.4) can be rewritten as follows:

$$\begin{aligned} FV &= PV\left(\left[1 + \frac{r}{m}\right]^{m/r}\right)^{rn} \\ &= PV\left(\left[1 + \frac{1}{m/r}\right]^{m/r}\right)^{rn} \\ &= PV\left(\left[1 + \frac{1}{n}\right]^{n}\right)^{rn} \end{aligned} \tag{2.5}$$

where $n = m/r$. As compounding becomes continuous and m and hence n approach infinity, the expression in the square brackets in (2.5) approaches a value known as e, which is shown below.

$$e = \lim_{n \to \infty}\left(1 + \frac{1}{n}\right)^n = 2.718281\ldots$$

If we substitute this into (2.5) this gives us:

$$FV = PVe^{rn} \tag{2.6}$$

where we have continuous compounding. In (2.6) e^{rn} is known as the *exponential function* of rn and it tells us the continuously compounded interest rate factor. If $r = 6\%$ and $n = 1$ year then:

$$e^r = 2.718281^{0.06} = 1.061837$$

This is the limit reached with continuous compounding.

The convention in both wholesale and personal (retail) markets is to quote an annual interest rate. A lender who wishes to earn the interest at the rate quoted has to place their funds on deposit for one year. Annual rates are quoted irrespective of the maturity of a deposit, from overnight to ten years or longer. For example, if one opens a bank account that pays interest at a rate of 3.5% but then closes it after six months, the actual interest earned will be equal to 1.75% of the sum deposited. The actual return on a three-year building society bond (fixed deposit) that pays 6.75% fixed for three years is 21.65% after three years. The quoted rate is the annual one-year equivalent. An overnight deposit in the wholesale or *interbank* market is still quoted as an annual rate, even though interest is earned for only one day.

The convention of quoting annualised rates is to allow deposits and loans of different maturities and different instruments to be compared on the basis of the interest rate applicable. We must be careful when comparing interest rates for products that have different payment frequencies. As we have seen from the previous paragraphs the actual interest earned will be greater for a deposit earning 6% on a semi-annual basis compared to 6% on an annual basis. The convention in the money markets is to quote the equivalent interest rate applicable when taking into account an instrument's payment frequency.

We saw how a *future value* could be calculated given a known *present value* and rate of interest. For example £100 invested today for one year at an interest rate of 6% will generate $100 \times (1 + 0.06) = £106$ at the end of the year. The future value of £100 in this case is £106. We can also say that £100 is the *present value* of £106 in this case.

In equation (2.3) we established the following future value relationship:

$$FV = PV(1+r)^n.$$

By reversing this expression we arrive at the present value calculation given at (2.7),

$$PV = \frac{FV}{(1+r)^n} \qquad (2.7)$$

where the symbols represent the same terms as before. Equation (2.7) applies in the case of annual interest payments and enables us to calculate the present value of a known future sum.

Example 2.1

◆ Nasser is saving for a trip around the world after university and needs to have £1000 in three years time. He can invest in a building society bond at 7% guaranteed fixed for three years. How much does he need to invest now?

To solve this we require the *PV* of £1000 received in three years' time.

$$PV = \frac{1000}{(1+.07)^3}$$

$$= \frac{1000}{1.225043} = 816.29787$$

Nasser therefore needs to invest £816.30 today.

To calculate the present value for a short-term investment of less than one year we will need to adjust what would have been the interest earned for a whole year by the proportion of days of the investment period. Rearranging the basic equation, we can say that the present value of a known future value is:

$$PV = \frac{FV}{\left(1+r \times \frac{days}{year}\right)}. \qquad (2.8)$$

Given a present value and a future value at the end of an investment period, what then is the interest rate earned? We can rearrange the basic equation again to solve for the *yield*.

When interest is compounded more than once a year, the formula for calculating present value is modified, as shown at (2.9),

$$PV = \frac{FV}{\left(1 + \dfrac{r}{m}\right)^{mn}} \tag{2.9}$$

where as before *FV* is the cash flow at the end of year *n*, *m* is the number of times a year interest is compounded, and *r* is the rate of interest or discount rate. Illustrating this, the present value of £100 received at the end of five years at a rate of interest rate of 5%, with quarterly compounding is:

$$PV = \frac{100}{\left(1 + \dfrac{0.05}{4}\right)^{(4)(5)}}$$
$$= £78.00.$$

Interest rates in the money markets are always quoted for standard maturities; for example, overnight, "tom next" (the overnight interest rate starting tomorrow, or "tomorrow to the next"), spot next (the overnight rate starting two days forward), 1 week, 1 month, 2 months and so on up to 1 year. If a bank or corporate customer wishes to deal for non-standard periods, an interbank desk will calculate the rate chargeable for such an "odd date" by *interpolating* between two standard period interest rates. If we assume that the rate for all dates in between two periods increases at the same steady state, we can calculate the required rate using the formula for *straight line* interpolation, shown at (2.10).

$$r = r_1 + (r_2 - r_1) \times \frac{n - n_1}{n_2 - n_1} \tag{2.10}$$

where

r	is the required odd-date rate for n days;
r_1	is the quoted rate for n_1 days;
r_2	is the quoted rate for n_2 days.

Let us imagine that the 1-month (30-day) offered interest rate is 5.25% and that the 2-month (60-day) offered rate is 5.75%. If a customer wishes to borrow money for a 40-day period, what rate should the bank charge? We can calculate the required 40-day rate using the straight line interpolation process. The increase in interest rates from 30 to 40 days is assumed to be 10/30 of the total increase in rates from 30 to 60 days. The 40-day offered rate would therefore be: 5.25% + (5.75% − 5.25%) × 10/30 = 5.4167%.

What about the case of an interest rate for a period that lies just before or just after two known rates and not roughly in between them? When this happens we *extrapolate* between the two known rates, again assuming a straight line relationship between the two rates and for a period after (or before) the two rates.

So if the 1-month offered rate is 5.25% while the 2-month rate is 5.75%, the 64-day rate is

5.25 + (5.75 − 5.25) × 34/30 = 5.8167%.

Straight-line interpolation and extrapolation is commonly used in the money markets.

2.2   Bond pricing and yield: the traditional approach

2.2.1   *Bond pricing*

The interest rate that is used to discount a bond's cash flows (hence called the *discount* rate) is the rate required by the bondholder. It is therefore known as the bond's *yield*. The yield on the bond will be determined by the market and is the price demanded by investors for buying it, which is why it is sometimes called the bond's *return*. The required yield for any bond will depend on a number of political and economic factors, including what yield is being earned by other bonds of the same class. Yield is always quoted as an annualised interest rate, so that for a semi-annually paying bond exactly half of the annual rate is used to discount the cash flows.

The *fair price* of a bond is the present value of all its cash flows. So, when pricing a bond we need to calculate the present value of all the coupon interest payments and the present value of the redemption payment, and sum these. The price of a conventional bond that pays annual coupons can therefore be given by (2.11).

$$P = \frac{C}{(1+r)} + \frac{C}{(1+r)^2} + \frac{C}{(1+r)^3} + \cdots + \frac{C}{(1+r)^N} + \frac{M}{(1+r)^N}$$

$$= \sum_{n=1}^{N} \frac{C}{(1+r)^n} + \frac{M}{(1+r)^N}$$

(2.11)

where

P	is the price;
C	is the annual coupon payment;
r	is the discount rate (therefore, the required yield);
N	is the number of years to maturity (therefore, the number of interest periods; in an annually-paying bond; for a semi-annual bond the number of interest periods is $N \times 2$);
M	is the maturity payment or par value (usually 100 per cent of currency).

For long-hand calculation purposes the first half of (2.11) is usually simplified and is sometimes encountered in one of the two ways shown in (2.12).

$$P = C\left(\frac{1 - \left(1/(1+r)^N\right)}{r}\right) \quad \text{or} \quad P = \frac{C}{r}\left(1 - \frac{1}{(1+r)^N}\right).$$

(2.12)

The price of a bond that pays semi-annual coupons is given by the expression at (2.13), which is our earlier expression modified to allow for the twice-yearly discounting:

$$P = \frac{C/2}{\left(1+\frac{1}{2}r\right)} + \frac{C/2}{\left(1+\frac{1}{2}r\right)^2} + \frac{C/2}{\left(1+\frac{1}{2}r\right)^3} + \cdots + \frac{C/2}{\left(1+\frac{1}{2}r\right)^{2N}} + \frac{M}{\left(1+\frac{1}{2}r\right)^{2N}}$$

$$= \sum_{t=1}^{2T} \frac{C/2}{\left(1+\frac{1}{2}r\right)^n} + \frac{M}{\left(1+\frac{1}{2}r\right)^{2N}}$$

(2.13)

$$= \frac{C}{r}\left(1 - \frac{1}{\left(1+\frac{1}{2}r\right)^{2N}}\right) + \frac{M}{\left(1+\frac{1}{2}r\right)^{2N}}.$$

Note how we set $2N$ as the power by which to raise the discount factor, as there are two interest payments every year for a bond that pays semi-annually. We also adjust the discount rate, r, by $\frac{1}{2}$. A more convenient exponential function to use might be the number of interest periods in the life of the bond, as opposed to the number of years to maturity, which we could set as n, allowing us to alter the equation for a semi-annually paying bond to:

$$P = \frac{C}{r}\left(1 - \frac{1}{\left(1 + \frac{1}{2}r\right)^n}\right) + \frac{M}{\left(1 + \frac{1}{2}r\right)^n}. \qquad (2.14)$$

The formula at (2.14) calculates the fair price on a coupon payment date, so that there is no *accrued interest* incorporated into the price. It also assumes that there is an even number of coupon payment dates remaining before maturity. The concept of accrued interest is an accounting convention, and treats coupon interest as accruing every day that the bond is held; this amount is added to the discounted present value of the bond (the *clean price*) to obtain the market value of the bond, known as the *dirty price*.

The date used as the point for calculation is the *settlement date* for the bond, the date on which a bond will change hands after it is traded. For a new issue of bonds the settlement date is the day when the stock is delivered to investors and payment is received by the bond issuer. The settlement date for a bond traded in the *secondary market* is the day that the buyer transfers payment to the seller of the bond and when the seller transfers the bond to the buyer. Different markets have different settlement conventions; for example, UK gilts normally settle one business day after the trade date (the notation used in bond markets is "T + 1") whereas Eurobonds settle on T + 3. The term *value date* is sometimes used in place of settlement date, however, the two terms are not strictly synonymous. A settlement date can only fall on a business date, so that a gilt traded on a Friday will settle on a Monday. However a value date can sometimes fall on a non-business day; for example, when accrued interest is being calculated.

If there is an odd number of coupon payment dates before maturity the formula at (2.14) is modified as shown in (2.15).

$$P = \frac{C}{r}\left(1 - \frac{1}{\left(1 + \frac{1}{2}r\right)^{2N+1}}\right) + \frac{M}{\left(1 + \frac{1}{2}r\right)^{2N+1}}. \qquad (2.15)$$

The standard formula also assumes that the bond is traded for a settlement on a day that is precisely one interest period before the next coupon payment. The price formula is adjusted if dealing takes place between coupon dates. If we take the *value date* for any transaction, we then need to calculate the number of calendar days from this day to the next coupon date. We then use the following ratio, i, when adjusting the exponent for the discount factor:

$$i = \frac{\text{Days from value date to next coupon date}}{\text{Days in the interest period}}.$$

The number of days in the interest period is the number of calendar days between the last coupon date and the next one, and it will depend on the day count basis used for that specific bond. The price formula is then modified as shown at (2.16),

$$P = \frac{C}{(1+r)^i} + \frac{C}{(1+r)^{1+i}} + \frac{C}{(1+r)^{2+i}} + \cdots + \frac{C}{(1+r)^{n-1+i}} + \frac{M}{(1+r)^{n-1+i}} \qquad (2.16)$$

where the variables C, M, n and r are as before. Note that (2.16) assumes r for an annually-paying bond and is adjusted to $r/2$ for a semi-annually paying bond.

Example 2.2

In these examples we illustrate the long-hand price calculation, using both expressions for the calculation of the present value of the annuity stream of a bond's cash flows.

2.2 (a)

Calculate the fair pricing of a UK Gilt, the 9% Treasury 2008, which pays semi-annual coupons, with the following terms:

C = £9.00 per £100 nominal
M = £100
N = 10 years (that is, the calculation is for value the 13th October 1998)
r = 4.98%

$$P = \frac{£9.00}{0.0498}\left(1 - \frac{1}{\left(1 + \frac{1}{2}(0.0498)\right)^{20}}\right) + \frac{£100}{\left(1 + \frac{1}{2}(0.0498)\right)^{20}}$$

$$= £70.2175 + £61.1463$$

$$= £131.3638.$$

The fair price of the gilt is £131.3638, which is composed of the present value of the stream of coupon payments (£70.2175) and the present value of the return of the principal (£61.1463).

2.2(b)

What is the price of a 5% coupon sterling bond with precisely 5 years to maturity, with semi-annual coupon payments, if the yield required is 5.40%?

As the cash flows for this bond are 10 semi-annual coupons of £2.50, and a redemption payment of £100 in 10 six-month periods from now, the price of the bond can be obtained by calculating the expression below, where we substitute C = 2.5, n = 10 and r = 0.027 into the price equation (the values for C and r reflect the adjustments necessary for a semi-annual paying bond).

$$P = 2.5\left(\frac{1 - \left(1/(1.027)^{10}\right)}{0.027}\right) + \frac{100}{(1.027)^{10}}$$

$$= £21.65574 + £76.61178$$

$$= £98.26752$$

The price of the bond is £98.2675 per £100 nominal.

2.2(c)

What is the price of a 5% coupon euro-denominated bond with five years to maturity paying annual coupons, again with a required yield of 5.4%?

In this case there are five periods of interest, so we may set C = 5, n = 5, with r = 0.05.

$$P = 5\left(\frac{1 - \left(1/(1.054)^{5}\right)}{0.054}\right) + \frac{100}{(1.054)^{5}}$$

$$= £21.410121 + £76.877092 = £98.287213$$

Note how the annual-paying bond has a slightly higher price for the same required annualised yield. This is because the semi-annual paying sterling bond has a higher *effective* yield than the euro-denominated bond, resulting in a lower price.

2.2(d)

Consider our 5% sterling bond again, but this time the required yield has risen and is now 6%. This makes $C = 2.5$, $n = 10$ and $r = 0.03$.

$$P = 2.5\left(\frac{1 - \left(1/(1.03)^{10}\right)}{0.03}\right) + \frac{100}{(1.03)^{10}}$$

$$= £21.325507 + £74.409391$$

$$= £95.7349$$

As the required yield has risen, the discount rate used in the price calculation is now higher, and the result of the higher discount is a lower present value (price).

2.2(e)

Calculate the price of our sterling bond, still with five years to maturity but offering a yield of 5.1%.

$$P = 2.5\left(\frac{1 - \left(1/(1.0255)^{10}\right)}{0.0255}\right) + \frac{100}{(1.0255)}$$

$$= £21.823737 + £77.739788$$

$$= £99.563525$$

To satisfy the lower required yield of 5.1% the price of the bond has fallen to £99.56 per £100.

2.2(f)

Calculate the price of the 5% sterling bond one year later, with precisely four years left to maturity and with the required yield still at the original 5.40%. This sets the terms in 2.2(a) unchanged, except now $n = 8$.

$$P = 2.5\left(\frac{1 - \left(1/((1.027)^{8})\right)}{0.027}\right) + \frac{100}{(1.027)^{8}}$$

$$= £17.773458 + £80.804668$$

$$= £98.578126$$

The price of the bond is £98.58. Compared to 2.2(b) this illustrates how, other things being equal, the price of a bond will approach par (£100 per cent) as it approaches maturity.

There also exist *perpetual* or *irredeemable* bonds which have no redemption date, so that interest on them is paid indefinitely. They are also known as *undated* bonds. An example of an undated bond is the 3½% War Loan, a UK gilt originally issued in 1916 to help pay for the 1914–1918 war effort. Most undated bonds date from a long time in the past and it is unusual to see them issued today. In structure the cash flow from an undated bond can be viewed as a continuous annuity. The fair price of such a bond is given from (2.11) by setting $N = \infty$, such that:

$$P = \frac{C}{r}. \tag{2.17}$$

In most markets bond prices are quoted in decimals, in minimum increments of 1/100ths. This is the case with Eurobonds, euro-denominated bonds and gilts, for example. Certain markets, including the US Treasury market, and South African and Indian government bond markets, for example, quote prices in *ticks*, where the minimum increment is 1/32nd. One tick is therefore equal to 0.03125. A US Treasury might be priced at "98-05" which means "98 and 5 ticks". This is equal to 98 and 5/32nds, which is 98.15625.

Example 2.3

◆ What is the total consideration for £5 million nominal of a gilt, where the price is 114.50?

The price of the gilt is £114.50 per £100, so the consideration is:

$$1.145 \times 5,000,000 = £5,725,000.$$

◆ What consideration is payable for $5 million nominal of a US Treasury, quoted at an all-in price of 99-16?

The US Treasury price is 99-16, which is equal to 99 and 16/32, or 99.50 per $100. The consideration is therefore:

$$0.9950 \times 5,000,000 = \$4,975,000.$$

If the price of a bond is below par the total consideration is below the nominal amount; whereas if it is priced above par the consideration will be above the nominal amount.

Bonds that do not pay a coupon during their life are known as *zero-coupon* bonds or *strips*, and the price for these bonds is determined by modifying (2.11) to allow for the fact that $C = 0$. We know that the only cash flow is the maturity payment, so we may set the price as:

$$P = \frac{M}{(1+r)^N} \qquad (2.18)$$

where M and r are as before and N is the number of years to maturity. The important factor is to allow for the same number of interest periods as coupon bonds of the same currency. That is, even though there are no actual coupons, we calculate prices and yields on the basis of a *quasi-coupon* period. For a US dollar or a sterling zero-coupon bond, a five-year zero-coupon bond would be assumed to cover ten quasi-coupon periods, which would set the price equation as:

$$P = \frac{M}{\left(1 + \frac{1}{2}r\right)^n}. \qquad (2.19)$$

We have to note carefully the quasi-coupon periods in order to maintain consistency with conventional bond pricing in the same market.

Example 2.4
2.4(a) Calculate the price of a gilt *strip* with a maturity of precisely 5 years, where the required yield is 5.40%.

These terms allow us to set $N = 5$ so that $n = 10$, $r = 0.054$ (so that $r/2 = 0.027$), with $M = 100$ as usual.

$$P = \frac{100}{(1.027)^{10}} = \text{£}76.611782$$

2.4(b) **Calculate the price of a French government zero-coupon bond with precisely five years to maturity, with the same required yield of 5.40%.**

$$P = \frac{100}{(1.054)^{5}} = \text{€}76.877092$$

Note the difference in prices.

An examination of the bond price formula tells us that the yield and price for a bond are closely related. A key aspect of this relationship is that the price changes in the opposite direction to the yield. This is because the price of the bond is the net present value of its cash flows; if the discount rate used in the present value calculation increases, the present values of the cash flows will decrease. This occurs whenever the yield level required by bondholders increases. In the same way, if the required yield decreases, the price of the bond will rise. This property was observed in Example 2.2. As the required yield decreased the price of the bond increased, and we observed the same relationship when the required yield was raised.

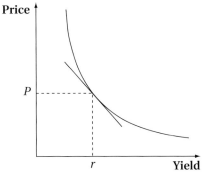

Figure 2.1: The price/yield relationship.

The relationship between any bond's price and yield at any required yield level is illustrated in Figure 2.1, which is obtained if we plot the yield against the corresponding price; this shows a *convex* curve. The graph shown at Figure 2.1 is exaggerated for illustrative purposes; in practice, the curve, while still convex, slopes at a more gentle angle.

Example 2.5: **Illustration of price/yield changes for two selected gilts**
Prices of selected gilts on 14 July 1999 for next-day settlement

UK Treasury stock 5% 2004

Price	Yield %
98.61750	5.324
98.64875	5.317
98.68000	5.309 (actual quoted price at the time of asking)
98.71100	5.302
98.74200	5.295

UK Treasury stock 5¾% 2009

Price	Yield %
104.73750	5.155
104.76875	5.151
104.80000	5.147 (actual quoted price at the time of asking)
104.83125	5.143
104.86250	5.140

Summary of the price/yield relationship

◆ At issue if a bond is priced at par, its coupon will equal the yield that the market requires from the bond.

◆ If the required yield rises above the coupon rate, the bond price will decrease.

◆ If the required yield goes below the coupon rate, the bond price will increase.

2.2.2 *Bond yield*

We have observed how to calculate the price of a bond using an appropriate discount rate known as the bond's *yield*. We can reverse this procedure to find the yield of a bond where the price is known, which would be equivalent to calculating the bond's *internal rate of return* (IRR). The IRR calculation is taken to be a bond's *yield to maturity* or *redemption yield* and is one of a number of yield measures used in the markets to estimate the return generated from holding a bond. In most markets bonds are generally traded on the basis of their prices but because of the complicated patterns of cash flows that different bonds can have, they are generally compared in terms of their yields. This means that a market-maker will usually quote a two-way price at which they will buy or sell a particular bond, but it is the *yield* at which the bond is trading that is important to the market-maker's customer. This is because a bond's price does not actually tell us anything useful about what we are getting. Remember that in any market there will be a number of bonds with different issuers, coupons and terms to maturity. Even in a homogenous market such as the gilt market, different gilts will trade according to their own specific characteristics. To compare bonds in the market therefore we need the yield on any bond and it is yields that we compare, not prices.

The yield on any investment is the interest rate that will make the present value of the cash flows from the investment equal to the initial cost (price) of the investment. Mathematically the yield on any investment, represented by r, is the interest rate that satisfies equation (2.20), which is simply the bond price equation we've already reviewed.

$$P = \sum_{n=1}^{N} \frac{C_n}{(1+r)^n} \qquad (2.20)$$

But as we have noted there are other types of yield measure used in the market for different purposes. The simplest measure of the yield on a bond is the *current yield*, also known as the *flat yield, interest yield* or *running yield*. The running yield is given by (2.21),

$$rc = \frac{C}{P} \times 100 \tag{2.21}$$

where rc is the current yield.

In (2.21) C is not expressed as a decimal. Current yield ignores any capital gain or loss that might arise from holding and trading a bond and does not consider the time value of money. It essentially calculates the bond coupon income as a proportion of the price paid for the bond, and to be accurate would have to assume that the bond was more like an annuity rather than a fixed-term instrument.

The current yield is useful as a "rough-and-ready" interest rate calculation; it is often used to estimate the cost of, or profit from, a short-term holding of a bond. For example, if other short-term interest rates such as the one-week or three-month rates are higher than the current yield, holding the bond is said to involve a *running cost*. This is also known as *negative carry* or *negative funding*. The term is used by bond traders and market makers and *leveraged* investors. The *carry* on a bond is a useful measure for all market practitioners as it illustrates the cost of holding or *funding* a bond. The funding rate is the bondholder's short-term cost of funds. A private investor could also apply this to a short-term holding of bonds.

The *simple yield to maturity* makes up for some of the shortcomings of the current yield measure by taking into account capital gains or losses. The assumption made is that the capital gain or loss occurs evenly over the remaining life of the bond. The resulting formula is:

$$rsm = \frac{C}{P} + \frac{100 - P}{N \cdot P} \tag{2.22}$$

where rsm is the simple yield to maturity.

The simple yield measure is useful for rough-and-ready calculations. However, its main drawback is that it does not take into account compound interest or the time value of money. Any capital gain or loss resulting is amortised equally over the remaining years to maturity. In reality as bond coupons are paid they can be reinvested, and hence interest can be earned. This increases the overall return from holding the bond. As such the simple yield measure is not overly useful and it is not commonly encountered in, say, the gilt market. However it is often the main measure used in the Japanese government bond market.

The y*ield to maturity* (YTM) or *gross redemption yield* is the most frequently used measure of return from holding a bond.[4] Yield to maturity takes into account the pattern of coupon payments, the bond's term to maturity and the capital gain (or loss) arising over the remaining life of the bond. We saw from our bond price formula in the previous section that these elements were all related and were important components in determining a bond's price. If we set the IRR for a set of cash flows to be the rate that applies from a start-date to an end-date we can assume the IRR to be the YTM for those cash flows. The YTM therefore is equivalent to the *internal rate of return* on the bond – the rate that equates the value of the discounted cash flows on the bond to its current price. The calculation assumes that the bond is held until maturity and therefore it is the cash flows to maturity that are discounted in the calculation. It also employs the concept of the time value of money.

As we would expect the formula for YTM is essentially that for calculating the price of a bond. For a bond paying annual coupons the YTM is calculated by solving equation (2.11). Of course, the expression at (2.11) has two variable parameters: the price P and yield r. It cannot

---

4   In this book the terms *yield to maturity* and *gross redemption yield* are used synonymously. The latter term is encountered in sterling markets.

be rearranged to solve for yield r explicitly and in fact the only way to solve for the yield is to use the process of numerical iteration. This involves estimating a value for r and calculating the price associated with the estimated yield. If the calculated price is higher than the price of the bond at the time, the yield estimate is lower than the actual yield, and so it must be adjusted until it converges to the level that corresponds with the bond price.[5] For the YTM of a semi-annual coupon bond we have to adjust the formula to allow for the semi-annual payments, shown at (2.13).

To differentiate redemption yield from other yield and interest rate measures described in this book, we henceforth refer to it as rm.

Example 2.6:   Yield to maturity for semi-annual coupon bond

A semi-annual paying bond has a dirty price of £98.50, an annual coupon of 6% and there is exactly one year before maturity. The bond therefore has three remaining cash flows, comprising two coupon payments of £3 each and a redemption payment of £100. Equation (2.11) can be used with the following inputs:

$$98.50 = \frac{3.00}{\left(1+\frac{1}{2}rm\right)} + \frac{103.00}{\left(1+\frac{1}{2}rm\right)^2}$$

Note that we use half of the YTM value rm because this is a semi-annual paying bond. The expression above is a quadratic equation, which is solved using the standard solution for quadratic equations, which is noted below.

$$ax^2 + bx + c = 0 \Rightarrow x = \frac{-b \pm \sqrt{b^2 - 4ac}}{2a}$$

In our expression if we let $x = (1 + rm/2)$, we can rearrange the expression as follows:

$$98.50x^2 - 3.0x - 103.00 = 0$$

We then solve for a standard quadratic equation, and as such there will be two solutions (when $b^2 - 4ac \geq 0$), only one of which gives a positive redemption yield. The positive solution is $rm/2 = 0.037929$ so that $rm = 7.5859\%$.

As an example of the iterative solution method, suppose that we start with a trial value for rm of $r_1 = 7\%$ and plug this into the right-hand side of equation (2.11). This gives a value for the right-hand side (which we shall call RHS_1) of $RHS_1 = 99.050$ which is higher than the left-hand side (LHS = 98.50); the trial value for rm was therefore too low. Suppose then that we next try $r_2 = 8\%$ and use this as the right-hand side of the equation. This gives $RHS_2 = 98.114$ which is lower than the LHS. Because RHS_1 and RHS_2 lie on either side of the LHS value we know that the correct value for rm lies between 7% and 8%. Using the formula for linear interpolation,

$$rm = r_1 + (r_2 - r_1)\frac{RHS_1 - LHS}{RHS_1 - RHS_2}$$

---

[5]   Bloomberg also uses the term *yield-to-workout* where "workout" refers to the maturity date for the bond.

our linear approximation for the redemption yield is $rm = 7.587\%$, which is near the exact solution.

Note that the redemption yield calculated as discussed in this section is the *gross redemption yield*, the yield that results from payment of coupons without deduction of any withholding tax. The *net redemption yield* is obtained by multiplying the coupon rate C by (1 – marginal tax rate). The net yield is what will be received if the bond is traded in a market where bonds pay coupon *net*, which means net of a withholding tax. The net redemption yield is always lower than the gross redemption yield.

We have already alluded to the key assumption behind the YTM calculation, namely that the rate rm remains stable for the entire period of the life of the bond. By assuming the same yield we can say that all coupons are reinvested at the same yield rm. For the bond in Example 2.6 this means that if all the cash flows are discounted at 7.59% they will have a total net present value of 98.50. This is patently unrealistic since we can predict with virtual certainty that interest rates for instruments of similar maturity to the bond at each coupon date will not remain at this rate for the life of the bond. In practice however investors require a rate of return that is equivalent to the price that they are paying for a bond and the redemption yield is, to put it simply, as good a measurement as any. A more accurate measurement might be to calculate present values of future cash flows using the discount rate that is equal to the market's view on where interest rates will be at that point, known as the *forward* interest rate. However forward rates are *implied* interest rates, and a YTM measurement calculated using forward rates can be as speculative as one calculated using the conventional formula. This is because the *actual* market interest rate at any time is invariably different from the rate implied earlier in the forward markets. So a YTM calculation made using forward rates would not be realised in practice either.[6] We shall see later in this chapter how the *zero-coupon* interest rate is the true interest rate for any term to maturity; however, the YTM is, despite the limitations presented by its assumptions, the main measure of return used in the markets.

Example 2.7:   Comparing the different yield measures

◆ The examples given in this section illustrate a five-year bond with a coupon of 6% trading at a price of £97.89. Using the three common measures of return we have:

Running yield = 6.129%
Simple yield = 6.560%
Redemption yield = 6.50%

We have noted the difference between calculating redemption yield on the basis of both annual and semi-annual coupon bonds. Analysis of bonds that pay semi-annual coupons incorporates semi-annual discounting of semi-annual coupon payments. This is appropriate for most UK and US bonds. However, government bonds in most of continental Europe and most Eurobonds pay annual coupon payments, and the appropriate method of calculating the redemption yield is to use annual discounting. The two yield measures are not therefore directly comparable. We could make a Eurobond directly comparable with a UK gilt by using semi-annual discounting of the Eurobond's annual coupon payments. Alternatively we could

---

6   Such an approach is used to price interest-rate swaps, however.

make the gilt comparable with the eurobond by using annual discounting of its semi-annual coupon payments. The price/yield formulae for different discounting possibilities we encounter in the markets are listed below (as usual we assume that the calculation takes place on a coupon payment date so that accrued interest is zero).

- **Semi-annual discounting of annual payments:**

$$P_d = \frac{C}{\left(1 + \frac{1}{2}rm\right)^2} + \frac{C}{\left(1 + \frac{1}{2}rm\right)^4} + \frac{C}{\left(1 + \frac{1}{2}rm\right)^6} + \cdots + \frac{C}{\left(1 + \frac{1}{2}rm\right)^{2N}} + \frac{M}{\left(1 + \frac{1}{2}rm\right)^{2N}} \tag{2.23}$$

- **Annual discounting of semi-annual payments:**

$$P_d = \frac{C/2}{\left(1 + rm\right)^{\frac{1}{2}}} + \frac{C/2}{\left(1 + rm\right)} + \frac{C/2}{\left(1 + rm\right)^{\frac{3}{2}}} + \cdots + \frac{C/2}{\left(1 + rm\right)^{N}} + \frac{M}{\left(1 + rm\right)^{N}} \tag{2.24}$$

Consider a bond with a dirty price of 97.89, a coupon of 6% and a five years to maturity. This bond would have the following gross redemption yields under the different yield calculation conventions:

Discounting	Payments	Yield to maturity (%)
Semi-annual	Semi-annual	6.500
Annual	Annual	6.508
Semi-annual	Annual	6.428
Annual	Semi-annual	6.605

This proves what we have already observed, namely that the coupon and discounting frequency will impact the redemption yield calculation for a bond. We can see that increasing the frequency of discounting will the lower the yield, while increasing the frequency of payments will raise the yield. When comparing yields for bonds that trade in markets with different conventions it is important to convert all the yields to the same calculation basis.

Intuitively we might think that simply doubling a semi-annual yield figure will give us the annualised equivalent; in fact this will result in an inaccurate figure due to the multiplicative effects of discounting and one that is an underestimate of the true annualised yield. The correct procedure for producing an annualised yield from semi-annual and quarterly yields is given by the expressions below.

The general conversion expression is given by (2.25),

$$rm_a = (1 + \text{interest rate})^m - 1 \tag{2.25}$$

where m is the number of coupon payments per year.

We can convert between yields using the expressions given at (2.26) and (2.27).

$$rm_a = \left(\left(1 + \tfrac{1}{2}rm_s\right)^2 - 1\right)$$
$$rm_s = \left(\left(1 + rm_a\right)^{1/2} - 1\right) \times 2 \tag{2.26}$$

$$rm_a = \left(\left(1 + \tfrac{1}{4}rm_q\right)^4 - 1\right)$$
$$rm_q = \left(\left(1 + rm_a\right)^{1/4} - 1\right) \times 4 \tag{2.27}$$

where rm_q, rm_s and rm_a are respectively the quarterly, semi-annually and annually compounded yields to maturity.

Example 2.8

◆ A UK gilt paying semi-annual coupons and a maturity of 10 years has a quoted yield of 4.89%. A European government bond of similar maturity is quoted at a yield of 4.96%. Which bond has the higher effective yield?

The effective annual yield of the gilt is:

$$rm = \left(1 + \tfrac{1}{2} \times 0.0489\right)^2 - 1 = 4.9498\%$$

Therefore the gilt does indeed have the lower yield.

The market convention sometimes is simply to double the semi-annual yield to obtain the annualised yields, despite the fact that this produces an inaccurate result. It is only acceptable to do this for rough calculations. An annualised yield obtained by multiplying the semi-annual yield by two is known as a *bond equivalent yield*.

While YTM is the most commonly used measure of yield, it has one disadvantage; implicit in the calculation of the YTM is the assumption that each coupon payment, as it becomes due, is re-invested at the rate rm. This is clearly unlikely, due to the fluctuations in interest rates over time, and as the bond approaches maturity. In practice the measure itself will not equal the actual return from holding the bond, even if it is held to maturity. That said, the market standard is to quote bond returns as yields to maturity, bearing the key assumptions behind the calculation in mind. We can demonstrate the inaccuracy of the assumptions by multiplying both sides of equation (2.13), the price/yield formula for a semi-annual coupon bond, by $(1 + (rm/2))^{2N}$, which gives us (2.28),

$$P_d\left(1 + \tfrac{1}{2}rm\right)^{2N} = (C/2)\left(1 + \tfrac{1}{2}rm\right)^{2N-1} + (C/2)\left(1 + \tfrac{1}{2}rm\right)^{2N-2} + \cdots + (C/2) + M. \qquad (2.28)$$

The left-hand side of (2.28) gives the value of the investment in the bond on the maturity date, with compounding at the redemption yield. The right-hand side gives the terminal value of the returns from holding the bond. The first coupon payment is reinvested for $(2N-1)$ half-years at the yield to maturity, the second coupon payment is reinvested for $(2N-2)$ half-years at the yield to maturity, and so on. This is valid only if the rate of interest is constant for all future time periods, that is, if we had the same interest rate for all loans or deposits, irrespective of the loan maturity. This would only apply under a flat *yield curve* environment. However, a flat yield curve implies that the yields to maturity of all bonds should be identical, and is very rarely encountered in practice. So we can discount the existence of flat yield curves in most cases.

Another disadvantage of the yield to maturity measure of return is where investors do not hold bonds to maturity. The redemption yield will not be of great use where the bond is not being held to redemption. Investors might then be interested in other measures of return, which we can look at later.

To reiterate then, the redemption yield measure assumes that:

■ the bond is held to maturity;

■ all coupons during the bond's life are reinvested at the same (redemption yield) rate.

Therefore the YTM can be viewed as an *expected* or *anticipated* yield and is closest to reality perhaps where an investor buys a bond on first issue and holds it to maturity. Even then the actual realised yield on maturity would be different from the YTM figure because of the inapplicability of the second condition above.

In addition, as coupons are discounted at the yield specific for each bond, it actually becomes inaccurate to compare bonds using this yield measure. For instance, the coupon cash flows that occur in two years' time from both a two-year and five-year bond will be discounted at different rates (assuming we do not have a flat yield curve). This would occur because the YTM for a five-year bond is invariably different to the YTM for a two-year bond. It would clearly not be correct to discount the two-year cash flows at different rates, because we can see that the present value calculated today of a cash flow in two years' time should be the same whether it is sourced from a short- or long-dated bond. Even if the first condition noted above for the YTM calculation is satisfied, it is clearly unlikely for any but the shortest maturity bond that all coupons will be reinvested at the same rate. Market interest rates are in a state of constant flux and hence this would affect money reinvestment rates. Therefore although yield to maturity is the main market measure of bond levels, it is not a true interest rate. This is an important result and we shall explore the concept of a true interest rate in Chapter 3.

2.3   Accrued interest, clean and dirty bond prices, and day counts

Our discussion of bond pricing up to now has ignored coupon interest. All bonds (except zero-coupon bonds) accrue interest on a daily basis, and this is then paid out on the coupon date. The calculation of bond prices using present value analysis does not account for coupon interest or *accrued interest*. In all major bond markets the convention is to quote price as a *clean price*. This is the price of the bond as given by the net present value of its cash flows, but excluding coupon interest that has accrued on the bond since the last dividend payment. As all bonds accrue interest on a daily basis, even if a bond is held for only one day, interest will have been earned by the bondholder. However, we have referred already to a bond's *all-in* price, which is the price that is actually paid for the bond in the market. This is also known as the *dirty price* (or *gross price*), which is the clean price of a bond plus accrued interest. In other words, the accrued interest must be added to the quoted price to get the total consideration for the bond.

Accruing interest compensates the seller of the bond for giving up all of the next coupon payment even though they will have held the bond for part of the period since the last coupon payment. The clean price for a bond will move with changes in market interest rates; assuming that this is constant in a coupon period, the clean price will be constant for this period. However, the dirty price for the same bond will increase steadily from one interest payment date until the next one. On the coupon date the clean and dirty prices are the same and the accrued interest is zero. Between the coupon payment date and the next *ex-dividend* date the bond is traded *cum dividend*, so that the buyer gets the next coupon payment. The seller is compensated for not receiving the next coupon payment by receiving accrued interest instead. This is positive and increases up to the next ex-dividend date, at which point the dirty price falls by the present value of the amount of the coupon payment. The dirty price at this point is below the clean price, reflecting the fact that accrued interest is now negative. This is because after the ex-dividend date the bond is traded "ex-dividend"; the seller not the buyer receives the next coupon and the buyer has to be compensated for not receiving the next coupon by means of a lower price for holding the bond.

The net interest accrued since the last ex-dividend date is determined as follows:

$$AI = C \times \left(\frac{N_{xt} - N_{xc}}{Day\ Base} \right) \tag{2.29}$$

where

AI is the next accrued interest;

C is the bond coupon;

N_{xc} is the number of days between the *ex-dividend* date and the coupon; payment date (7 business days for UK gilts);

N_{xt} is the number of days between the *ex-dividend* date and the date for the calculation;

Day Base   is the day count base (365 or 360).

Interest accrues on a bond from, and including, the last coupon date up to and excluding what is called the *value date*. The value date is almost always the *settlement* date for the bond, or the date when a bond is passed to the buyer and the seller receives payment. Interest does not accrue on bonds whose issuer has subsequently gone into default. Bonds that trade without accrued interest are said to be trading *flat* or *clean*. By definition therefore,

> clean price of a bond = dirty price – accrued interest.

For bonds that are trading ex-dividend, the accrued coupon is negative and would be subtracted from the clean price. The calculation is given by (2.30).

$$AI = -C \times \frac{\text{days to } next \text{ coupon}}{Day\ Base} \tag{2.30}$$

Certain classes of bonds, for example US Treasuries and Eurobonds, do not have an *ex-dividend* period and therefore trade *cum dividend* right up to the coupon date.

The accrued interest calculation for a bond is dependent on the day-count basis specified for the bond in question. When bonds are traded in the market the actual consideration that changes hands is made up of the clean price of the bond together with the accrued interest that has accumulated on the bond since the last coupon payment; these two components make up the dirty price of the bond. When calculating the accrued interest, the market will use the appropriate day-count convention for that bond. A particular market will apply one of five different methods to calculate accrued interest; these are:

actual/365   Accrued = Coupon × days/365

actual/360   Accrued = Coupon × days/360

actual/actual   Accrued = Coupon × days/actual number of days in the interest period

30/360   See below

30E/360   See below

When determining the number of days in between two dates, include the first date but not the second; thus, under the actual/365 convention, there are 37 days between 4 August and 10 September. The last two conventions assume 30 days in each month; so, for example, there are "30 days" between 10 February and 10 March. Under the 30/360 convention, if the first date falls on the 31st, it is changed to the 30th of the month, and if the second date falls on the 31st *and* the first date is on the 30th or 31st, the second date is changed to the 30th. The difference under the 30E/360 method is that if the second date falls on the 31st of the month it is automatically changed to the 30th.

Table 2.1 shows the bond accrued conventions for certain selected government bond markets.

Market	Coupon Frequency	Day Count Basis	Ex-dividend period
Australia	Semi-annual	actual/actual	Yes
Austria	Annual	actual/actual	No
Belgium	Annual	actual/actual	No
Canada	Semi-annual	actual/actual	No
Denmark	Annual	30E/360	Yes
Eurobonds	Annual	30/360	No
France	Annual	actual/actual	No
Germany	Annual	actual/actual	No
Eire	Annual	actual/actual	No
Italy	Annual	actual/actual	No
New Zealand	Semi-annual	actual/actual	Yes
Norway	Annual	actual/365	Yes
Spain	Annual	actual/actual	No
Sweden	Annual	30E/360	Yes
Switzerland	Annual	30E/360	No
United Kingdom	Semi-annual	actual/actual	Yes
United States	Semi-annual	actual/actual	No

Table 2.1: Selected government bond market conventions. Source: Author.

Van Deventer (1997) presents an effective critique of the accrued interest concept, stating essentially that is has little basis in economic reality. Nevertheless it is the convention that is followed in the market.

Example 2.9:   Accrual calculation for 7% Treasury 2002

◆   This gilt has coupon dates of 7 June and 7 December each year. £100 nominal of the bond is traded for value 27 August 1998. What is accrued interest on the value date?

On the value date 81 days have passed since the last coupon date. Under the old system for gilts, act/365, the calculation was:

$$7 \times \frac{81}{365} = 1.55342.$$

Under the current system of act/act, which came into effect for gilts in November 1998, the accrued calculation uses the actual number of days between the two coupon dates, giving us:

$$7 \times \frac{81}{183} \times 0.5 = 1.54918.$$

Example 2.10

◆ Mansur buys £25,000 nominal of the 7% 2002 gilt for value on 27 August 1998, at a price of 102.4375. How much does he actually pay for the bond?

The clean price of the bond is102.4375. The dirty price of the bond is:

102.4375 + 1.55342 = 103.99092

The total consideration is therefore $1.0399092 \times 25,000 = £25,997.73$.

Example 2.11

◆ A Norwegian government bond with a coupon of 8% is purchased for settlement on 30 July 1999 at a price of 99.50. Assume that this is 7 days before the coupon date and therefore the bond trades ex-dividend. What is the all-in price?

The accrued interest $= -8 \times \dfrac{7}{365} = -0.153424$. The all-in price is therefore $99.50 - 0.1534 = 99.3466$.

Example 2.12

◆ A bond has coupon payments on 1 June and 1 December each year. What is the day-base count if the bond is traded for value date on 30 October, 31 October and 1 November 1999 respectively? There are 183 days in the interest period.

	30 October	31 October	1 November
Act/365	151	152	153
Act/360	151	152	153
Act/Act	151	152	153
30/360	149	150	151
30E/360	149	150	150

Page "DCX" on the Bloomberg system enables users to check day-counts under the 30/360 system. The screen also gives the actual number of days for comparison. Figure 2.2 shows the day-count for the period 1 June 2001 to 30 October 2001, while Figures 2.3 and 2.4 show the same screen with the end-date shifted to 31 October and 1 November respectively. Note how under the 30/360 basis the number of days is unchanged in the last two examples.

Figure 2.2:
Bloomberg screen
DCX for period 1
June – 30 October
©Bloomberg L.P.
Used with
permission.

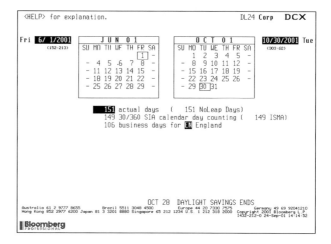

Figure 2.3:
Bloomberg screen
DCX for period 1
June – 31 October.
©Bloomberg L.P.
Used with
permission.

Figure 2.4:
Bloomberg screen
DCX for period
1 June –
1 November.
©Bloomberg L.P.
Used with
permission.

2.4   Duration, modified duration and convexity

Bonds pay part of their total return during their lifetime in the form of coupon interest, so that the term to maturity does not reflect the true period over which the bond's return is earned. If we wish to gain an idea of the trading characteristics of a bond, and compare this to other bonds of say, similar maturity, then term to maturity is insufficient and so we need a more accurate measure. In fact, if we were to analyse the properties of a bond, we should conclude quite quickly that its maturity gives us little indication of how much of its return is paid out during its life, nor any idea of the timing or size of its cash flows, and hence its sensitivity to moves in market interest rates. For example, if comparing two bonds with the same maturity date but different coupons, the higher-coupon bond provides a larger proportion of its return in the form of coupon income than does the lower-coupon bond. The higher-coupon bond provides its return at a faster rate; its value is theoretically therefore less subject to subsequent fluctuations in interest rates.

We may wish to calculate an average of the time to receipt of a bond's cash flows and use this measure as a more realistic indication of maturity. However, cash flows during the life of a bond are not all equal in value, so a more accurate measure would be to take the average time to receipt of a bond's cash flows, but weighted in the form of the cash-flows' present value. This is, in effect, *duration*. We can measure the speed of payment of a bond, and hence its price risk relative to other bonds of the same maturity by measuring the average maturity of the bond's cash flow stream. Bond analysts use duration to measure this property (it is sometimes known as *Macaulay's duration*, after its inventor, who first introduced it in 1938).[7] Duration is the weighted average time until the receipt of cash flows from a bond, where the weights are the present values of the cash flows, measured in years. At the time that he introduced the concept, Macaulay used the duration measure as an alternative for the length of time that a bond investment had remaining to maturity.

2.4.1   *Duration*

Recall that the price/yield formula for a plain vanilla bond is as given by (2.31) below, assuming complete years to maturity paying annual coupons, and with no accrued interest at the calculation date. The yield to maturity symbol reverts to r in this section.

$$P = \frac{C}{(1+r)} + \frac{C}{(1+r)^2} + \frac{C}{(1+r)^3} + \cdots + \frac{C}{(1+r)^n} + \frac{M}{(1+r)^n} \qquad (2.31)$$

If we take the first derivative of this expression we obtain (2.32).

$$\frac{dP}{dr} = \frac{(-1)C}{(1+r)^2} + \frac{(-2)C}{(1+r)^3} + \cdots + \frac{(-n)C}{(1+r)^{n+1}} + \frac{(-n)M}{(1+r)^{n+1}} \qquad (2.32)$$

If we rearrange (2.32) we will obtain the expression at (2.33), which is our equation to calculate the approximate change in price for a small change in yield.

$$\frac{dP}{dr} = -\frac{1}{(1+r)}\left(\frac{1C}{(1+r)} + \frac{2C}{(1+r)^2} + \cdots + \frac{nC}{(1+r)^n} + \frac{nM}{(1+r)^n} \right) \qquad (2.33)$$

---

7   Macaulay, F., *Some theoretical problems suggested by the movements of interest rates, bond yields and stock prices in the United States since 1865*, National Bureau of Economic Research, NY 1938. This book is now available as part of the *RISK* Classics Library.

Readers may feel a sense of familiarity regarding the expression in brackets in equation (2.33) as this is the weighted average time to maturity of the cash flows from a bond, where the weights are, as in our example above, the present values of each cash flow. The expression at (2.33) gives us the approximate measure of the change in price for a small change in yield. If we divide both sides of (2.33) by P we obtain the expression for the approximate percentage price change, given by (2.34).

$$\frac{dP}{dr}\frac{1}{P} = -\frac{1}{(1+r)}\left(\frac{1C}{(1+r)} + \frac{2C}{(1+r)^2} + \cdots + \frac{nC}{(1+r)^n} + \frac{nM}{(1+r)^n}\right)\frac{1}{P} \qquad (2.34)$$

If we divide the bracketed expression in (2.34) by the current price of the bond P, we obtain the definition of Macaulay duration, given by (2.35).

$$D = \frac{\dfrac{1C}{(1+r)} + \dfrac{2C}{(1+r)^2} + \cdots + \dfrac{nC}{(1+r)^n} + \dfrac{nM}{(1+r)^n}}{P}. \qquad (2.35)$$

Equation (2.35) is simplified using Σ notation as shown by (2.36).

$$D = \frac{1}{P}\sum_{n=1}^{N}\frac{nC_n}{(1+r)^n} \qquad (2.36)$$

where C represents all bond cash flows at time n. Example 2.13 calculates the Macaulay duration for a hypothetical bond, an 8% 2009 annual coupon bond.

Example 2.13:   Calculating the Macaulay duration for the hypothetical 8% 2009 annual coupon bond

Issued	30 September 1999
Maturity	30 September 2009
Price	102.497
Yield	7.634%

Period (n)	Cash flow	PV at current yield *	$n \times PV$
1	8	7.43260	7.4326
2	8	6.90543	13.81086
3	8	6.41566	19.24698
4	8	5.96063	23.84252
5	8	5.53787	27.68935
6	8	5.14509	30.87054
7	8	4.78017	33.46119
8	8	4.44114	35.529096
9	8	4.12615	37.13535
10	108	51.75222	517.5222
Total		102.49696	746.540686

* Calculated as $C/(1+r)^n$

Macaulay duration	=	746.540686/102.497
	=	7.283539998 years
Modified duration	=	7.28354/1.07634
	=	6.76695

Table 2.2: Duration calculation for the hypothetical 8% 2009 bond.

The Macaulay duration value given by (2.36) is measured in years. An interesting observation by Galen Burghardt in *The Treasury Bond Basis* is that, "measured in years, Macaulay's duration is of no particular use to anyone." (Burghardt (1994), page 90). The author has to agree! However, as a risk measure and hedge calculation measure, duration transformed into *modified duration* was the primary measure of interest rate risk used in the markets, and is still widely used despite the advent of the *value-at-risk* measure for market risk.

If we substitute the expression for Macaulay duration (2.35) into equation (2.34) for the approximate percentage change in price we obtain (2.37) below.

$$\frac{dP}{dr}\frac{1}{P} = -\frac{1}{(1+r)}D \tag{2.37}$$

This is the definition of modified duration, given by (2.38).

$$MD = \frac{D}{(1+r)} \tag{2.38}$$

Modified duration is clearly related to duration then, in fact we can use it to indicate that, for small changes in yield, a given change in yield results in an inverse change in bond price. We can illustrate this by substituting (2.38) into (2.37), giving us (2.39).

$$\frac{dP}{dr}\frac{1}{P} = -MD \tag{2.39}$$

If we are determining duration long-hand, there is another arrangement we can use to shorten the procedure. Instead of equation (2.31) we use (2.40) as the bond price formula, which calculates price based on a bond being comprised of an annuity stream and a redemption payment, and summing the present values of these two elements. Again we assume an annual coupon bond priced on a date that leaves a complete number of years to maturity and with no interest accrued.

$$P = C\left(\frac{1}{r}\left(1 - \frac{1}{(1+r)^n}\right)\right) + \frac{M}{(1+r)^n}. \tag{2.40}$$

This expression calculates the price of a bond as the present value of the stream of coupon payments and the present value of the redemption payment. If we take the first derivative of (2.40) and then divide this by the current price of the bond P, the result is another expression for the modified duration formula, given by (2.41).

$$MD = \frac{\frac{C}{r^2}\left(1 - \left(1/(1+r)^n\right)\right) + \frac{n(M - (C/r))}{(1+r)^{n+1}}}{P} \tag{2.41}$$

We have already shown that modified duration and duration are related; to obtain the expression for Macaulay duration from (2.41) we multiply it by $(1 + r)$. This short-hand formula is demonstrated in Example 2.14 for our hypothetical bond, the annual coupon 8% 2009.

Example 2.14:   8% 2009 bond: using equation (2.41) for the modified duration calculation

Coupon	8%, annual basis
Yield	7.634%
n	10
Price	102.497

Substituting the above terms into the equation we obtain:

$$MD = \frac{\frac{8}{(0.07634^2)}\left(1 - \frac{1}{(1.07634)^{10}}\right) + \frac{10(100 - (8/0.07634))}{(1.07634)^{11}}}{102.497}$$

$$= 6.76695.$$

To obtain the Macaulay duration we multiply the modified duration by $(1 + r)$, in this case 1.07634, which gives us a value of 7.28354 years.

For an irredeemable bond duration is given by:

$$D = \frac{1}{rc} \qquad\qquad (2.42)$$

where $rc = C/P_d$ is the *running yield* (or *current yield*) of the bond. This follows from equation (2.36) as $N \to \infty$, recognising that for an irredeemable bond $r = rc$. Equation (2.42) provides the limiting value to duration. For bonds trading at or above par, duration increases with maturity and approaches this limit from below. For bonds trading at a discount to par, duration increases to a maximum at around 20 years and then declines towards the limit given by (2.42). So in general, duration increases with maturity, with an upper bound given by (2.42).

2.4.2 *Properties of Macaulay duration*

A bond's duration is always less than its maturity. This is because some weight is given to the cash flows in the early years of the bond's life, which brings forward the average time at which cash flows are received. In the case of a zero-coupon bond, there is no present value weighting of the cash flows, for the simple reason that there are no cash flows, and so duration for a zero-coupon bond is equal to its term to maturity. Duration varies with coupon, yield and maturity. The following three factors imply higher duration for a bond:

■   the lower the coupon;

■   the lower the yield;

■   broadly, the longer the maturity.

Duration increases as coupon and yield decrease. As the coupon falls, more of the relative weight of the cash flows is transferred to the maturity date and this causes duration to rise. Because the coupon on index-linked bonds is generally much lower than on vanilla bonds, this means that the duration of index-linked bonds will be much higher than for vanilla bonds of the same maturity. As yield increases, the present values of all future cash flows fall, but the present values of the more distant cash flows fall relatively more than those of the nearer cash flows. This has the effect of increasing the relative weight given to nearer cash flows and hence of reducing duration.

■   *The effect of the coupon frequency.* As we have already stated, certain bonds, such as most Eurobonds, pay coupon annually compared to, say, gilts which pay semi-annual coupons. Thinking of duration as a balancing fulcrum, if we imagine that every coupon is divided into two parts, with one part paid a half-period earlier than the other, this will represent a shift in weight to the left of the fulcrum, as part of the coupon is paid earlier. Thus increasing the coupon frequency shortens duration, and of course decreasing coupon frequency has the effect of lengthening duration.

- **Duration as maturity approaches.** Using our definition of duration we can see that initially it will decline slowly, and then at a more rapid pace as a bond approaches maturity.

- **Duration of a portfolio.** Portfolio duration is a weighted average of the duration of the individual bonds. The weights are the present values of the bonds divided by the full price of the entire portfolio, and the resulting duration calculation is often referred to as a "market-weighted" duration. This approach is in effect the duration calculation for a single bond. Portfolio duration has the same application as duration for an individual bond, and can be used to structure an *immunised* portfolio.

2.4.3 *Modified duration*

Although it is common for newcomers to the market to think intuitively of duration much as Macaulay originally did, as a proxy measure for the time to maturity of a bond, such an interpretation is to miss the main point of duration, which is a measure of price volatility or interest rate risk.

Using the first term of a Taylor's expansion of the bond price function[8] we can prove the following relationship between price volatility and the duration measure, which is expressed as (2.43) below,

$$\Delta P = -\left(\frac{1}{(1+r)}\right) \times \text{Macaulay duration} \times \text{change in yield} \tag{2.43}$$

where r is the yield to maturity for an annual-paying bond (for a semi-annual coupon bond, we use $r/2$). If we combine the first two components of the right-hand side, we obtain the definition of modified duration. Equation (2.43) expresses the approximate percentage change in price as being equal to the modified duration multiplied by the change in yield. We saw in the previous section how the formula for Macaulay duration could be modified to obtain the *modified duration* for a bond. There is a clear relationship between the two measures. From the Macaulay duration of a bond can be derived its modified duration, which gives a measure of the sensitivity of a bond's price to small changes in yield. As we have seen, the relationship between modified duration and duration is given by (2.44),

$$MD = \frac{D}{1+r} \tag{2.44}$$

where MD is the modified duration in years. It also measures the approximate change in bond price for a 1% change in bond yield. For a bond that pays semi-annual coupons, the equation becomes:

$$MD = \frac{D}{\left(1 + \frac{1}{2}r\right)}. \tag{2.45}$$

This means that the following relationship holds between modified duration and bond prices:

$$\Delta P = MD \times \Delta r \times P. \tag{2.46}$$

---

[8]   For an accessible explanation of the Taylor expansion, see Butler, C., *Mastering Value-at-Risk*, FT Prentice Hall 1998, pp. 112–114.

In the UK markets the term *volatility* is sometimes used to refer to modified duration but this is becoming increasingly uncommon in order to avoid confusion with option markets' use of the same term, which often refers to *implied volatility* and is something different.

Example 2.15:   Using modified duration

◆ An 8% annual coupon bond is trading at par with a duration of 2.74 years. If yields rise from 8% to 8.50%, then the price of the bond will fall by:

$$\Delta P = -D \times \frac{\Delta(r)}{1+r} \times P$$

$$= -(2.74) \times \left(\frac{0.005}{1.080}\right) \times 100 = -£1.2685.$$

That is, the price of the bond will now be £98.7315.

The modified duration of a bond with a duration of 2.74 years and yield of 8% is obviously, $MD = 2.74/1.08$ which gives us MD equal to 2.537 years. This tells us that for a 1 per cent move in the yield to maturity, the price of the bond will move (in the opposite direction) by 2.54%.

We can use modified duration to approximate bond prices for a given yield change. This is illustrated with the following expression:

$$\Delta P = -MD \times (\Delta r) \times P. \tag{2.47}$$

For a bond with a modified duration of 3.99, priced at par, an increase in yield of 1 basis point (100 basis = 1 per cent) leads to a fall in the bond's price of:

$$\Delta P = (-3.24/100) \times (+0.01) \times 100.00$$
$$\Delta P = £0.0399, \text{ or } 3.99 \text{ pence.}$$

In this case 3.99 pence is the *basis point value* (BPV) of the bond, which is the change in the bond price given a 1 basis point change in the bond's yield. The basis point value of a bond can be calculated using (2.48).

$$BPV = \frac{MD}{100} \times \frac{P}{100}. \tag{2.48}$$

Basis point values are used in hedging bond positions. To hedge a bond position requires an opposite position to be taken in the hedging instrument. So if we are long a 10-year bond, we may wish to sell short a similar 10-year bond as a hedge against it. Similarly, a short position in a bond will be hedged through a purchase of an equivalent amount of the hedging instrument. In fact there are a variety of hedging instruments available, both on- and off-balance sheet. Once the hedge is put on, any loss in the primary position should in theory be offset by a gain in the hedge position, and vice-versa. The objective of a hedge is to ensure that the price change in the primary instrument is equal to the price change in the hedging instrument. If we are hedging a position with another bond, we use the BPVs of each bond to calculate the amount of the hedging instrument required. This is important because each bond will have different BPVs, so that to hedge a long position in say, £1 million nominal of a 30-year bond does not mean we simply sell £1 million of another similar-maturity bond. This is because the BPVs of the two bonds will almost certainly be different. Also there may not be another 30-year bond in that market. What if we have to hedge with a 10-year bond? How much nominal of this bond would be required?

We need to know the ratio given at (2.49) to calculate the nominal hedge position.

$$\frac{BPV_p}{BPV_h} \qquad\qquad (2.49)$$

where

BPV_p is the basis point value of the primary bond (the position to be hedged);
BPV_h is the basis point value of the hedging instrument.

The *hedge ratio* is used to calculate the size of the hedge position and is given at (2.50),

$$\frac{BPV_p}{BPV_h} \times \frac{\text{change in yield for primary bond position}}{\text{change in yield for hedge instrument}}. \qquad\qquad (2.50)$$

The second ratio in (2.50) is known as the *yield beta*. Example 2.16 illustrates use of the hedge ratio.

Example 2.16:   Calculating hedge size using basis point value

◆   A trader holds a long position of £1 million of the 8% 2019 bond. The modified duration of the bond is 11.14692 and its price is 129.87596. The basis point value of this bond is therefore 0.14477. The trader decides, to protect against a rise in interest rates, to hedge the position using the 0% 2009 bond, which has a BPV of 0.05549. If we assume that the yield beta is 1, what nominal value of the zero-coupon bond must be sold in order to hedge the position?

The hedge ratio is:

$$\frac{0.14477}{0.05549} \times 1 = 2.60894.$$

Therefore, to hedge £1 million of the 20-year bond the trader shorts £2,608,940 of the zero-coupon bond. If we use the respective BPVs to see the net effect of a 1 basis point rise in yield, the loss on the long position is approximately equal to the gain in the hedge position.

Example 2.17:   The nature of the modified duration approximation

				Yield					
6.00%	6.50%	7.00%	7.50%	7.99%	**8.00%**	8.01%	8.50%	9.00%	10.00%
114.72017	110.78325	107.02358	103.43204	100.0671311	**100.00000**	99.932929	96.71933	93.58234	87.71087

Bond	8% 2009	Yield change	Price change	Estimate using price duration
Maturity (years)	10			
Modified Duration	6.76695	down 1 bp	0.06713	0.06936
		up 1 bp	0.06707	0.06936
Price duration		down 200 bp	14.72017	13.872
of basis point	0.06936	up 200 bp	12.28913	13.872

Table 2.3: Nature of the modified duration approximation.

Table 2.3 shows the change in price for one of our hypothetical bonds, the 8% 2009, for a selection of yields. We see that for a 1 basis point change in yield, the change in price given by the dollar duration figure, while not completely accurate, is a reasonable estimation of the actual change in price. For a large move however, say 200 basis points, the approximation is significantly in error and analysts would not use it. Notice also for our hypothetical bond how the dollar duration value, calculated from the modified duration measurement, underestimates the change in price resulting from a fall in yields but overestimates the price change for a rise in yields. This is a reflection of the price/yield relationship for this bond. Some bonds will have a more pronounced convex relationship between price and yield and the modified duration calculation will underestimate the price change resulting from both a fall or a rise in yields.

2.4.4 *Convexity*

Duration can be regarded as a first-order measure of interest rate risk: it measures the *slope* of the present value/yield profile. It is however only an approximation of the actual change in bond price given a small change in yield to maturity. Similarly for modified duration, which describes the price sensitivity of a bond to small changes in yield. However, as Figure 2.5 illustrates, the approximation is an underestimate of the actual price at the new yield. This is the weakness of the duration measure.

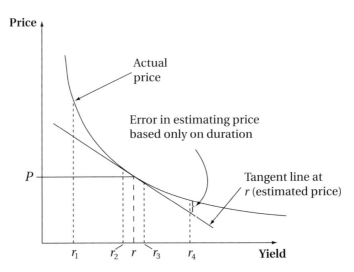

Figure 2.5: Approximation of the bond price change using modified duration.

Convexity is a second-order measure of interest rate risk; it measures the *curvature* of the present value/yield profile. Convexity can be regarded as an indication of the error we make when using duration and modified duration, as it measures the degree to which the curvature of a bond's price/yield relationship diverges from the straight-line estimation. The convexity of a bond is positively related to the dispersion of its cash flows; thus, other things being equal, if one bond's cash flows are more spread out in time than another's, then it will have a higher *dispersion* and hence a higher convexity. Convexity is also positively related to duration.

The second-order differential of the bond price equation with respect to the redemption yield r is:

$$\frac{\Delta P}{P} = \frac{1}{P}\frac{\Delta P}{\Delta r}(\Delta r) + \frac{1}{2P}\frac{\Delta^2 P}{\Delta r^2}(\Delta r)^2$$
$$= -MD(\Delta r) + \frac{CV}{2}(\Delta r)^2$$

(2.51)

where CV is the convexity.

From equation (2.51), convexity is the rate at which price variation to yield changes with respect to yield. That is, it describes a bond's modified duration changes with respect to changes in yield. It can be approximated by expression (2.52).

$$CV = 10^8\left(\frac{\Delta P'}{P} + \frac{\Delta P''}{P}\right)$$

(2.52)

where

$\Delta P'$ is the change in bond price if yield increases by 1 basis point (0.01);
$\Delta P''$ is the change in bond price if yield decreases by 1 basis point (0.01).

Appendix 2.1 provides the mathematical derivation of the formula.

Example 2.18

◆ A 5 per cent annual coupon bond is trading at par with three years to maturity. If the yield increases from 5.00 to 5.01 per cent, the price of the bond will fall (using the bond price equation) to:

$$P_d' = \frac{5}{(0.0501)}\left(1 - \frac{1}{(1.0501)^3}\right) + \frac{100}{(1.0501)^3}$$
$$= 99.97277262,$$

or by $\Delta P_d' = -0.02722738$. If the yield falls to 4.99 per cent, the price of the bond will rise to:

$$P_d'' = \frac{5}{(0.0499)}\left(1 - \frac{1}{(1.0499)^3}\right) + \frac{100}{(1.0499)^3}$$
$$= 100.02723695.$$

or by $\Delta P_d'' = 0.02723695$. Therefore

$$CV = 10^8\left(\frac{-0.02722738}{100} + \frac{0.02723695}{100}\right)$$
$$= 9.57$$

that is, a convexity value of approximately 9.57.

The unit of measurement for convexity using (2.52) is the number of interest periods. For annual coupon bonds this is equal to the number of years; for bonds paying coupon on a different frequency we use (2.53) to convert the convexity measure to years.

$$CV_{years} = \frac{CV}{C^2}.$$

(2.53)

The convexity measure for a zero-coupon bond is given by (2.54).

$$CV = \frac{n(n+1)}{(1+r)^2}.$$
(2.54)

Convexity is a second-order approximation of the change in price resulting from a change in yield. This is given by:

$$\Delta P = \frac{1}{2} \times CV \times (\Delta r)^2.$$
(2.55)

The reason we multiply the convexity by ½ to obtain the convexity adjustment is because the second term in the Taylor expansion contains the coefficient ½. The convexity approximation is obtained from a Talyor expansion of the bond price formula. An accessible illustration of the Taylor expansion of the bond price/yield equation is given in Appendix 9.3 of Choudhry (2001) and the Butler (1998) reference cited earlier.

The formula is the same for a semi-annual coupon bond.

Note that the value for convexity given by the expressions above will always be positive, since the approximate price change due to convexity is positive for both yield increases and decreases.

Example 2.19:   Second-order interest rate risk

◆ A 5 per cent annual coupon bond is trading at par with a modified duration of 2.54 and convexity of 7.45. If we assume a significant market correction and yields rise from 5 to 7 per cent, the price of the bond will fall by:

$$\Delta P_d = -MD \times (\Delta r) \times P_d + \frac{CV}{2} \times (\Delta r)^2 \times P_d$$

$$= -(2.54) \times (0.02) \times 100 + \frac{7.45}{2} \times (0.02)^2 \times 100$$

$$= -5.08 + 0.149$$

$$= -£4.93.$$

Thus the bond price will fall to to £95.07. The first-order approximation, using the modified duration value of 2.54, is –£5.08, which is an overestimation of the fall in price by £0.149.

Example 2.20

◆ The 5% 2009 bond is trading at a price of £96.23119 (a yield of 5.50%) and has precisely 10 years to maturity. If the yield rises to 7.50%, a change of 200 basis points, the percentage price change due to the convexity effect is given by:

$$(0.5) \times 96.23119 \times (0.02)^2 \times 100 = 1.92462\%$$

If we use an HP or other financial calculator to find the price of the bond at the new yield of 7.50% we see that it is £82.83980, a change in price of 13.92%. The convexity measure of 1.92462% is an approximation of the error we would make when using the modified duration value to estimate the price of the bond following the 200 basis point rise in yield.

If the yield of the bond were to fall by 200 basis points, the convexity effect would be the same, as given by the expression at (2.55).

In Example 2.20 we saw that the price change estimated using modified duration will be quite inaccurate, and that the convexity measure is the approximation of the size of the inaccuracy. The magnitude of the price change as estimated by both duration and convexity is obtained by summing the two values. However, it only makes any significant difference if the change in yield is very large. If we take our hypothetical bond again, the 5% 2009 bond, its modified duration is 7.64498. If the yield rises by 200 basis points, the approximation of the price change given by modified duration and convexity is:

Modified duration $= 7.64498 \times 2 = -15.28996$;

Convexity $= 1.92462$.

Note that the modified duration is given as a negative value, because a rise in yield results in a fall in price. This gives us a net percentage price change of 13.36534. As we saw in Example 2.20 the actual percentage price change is 13.92%. So in fact using the convexity adjustment has given us a noticeably more accurate estimation. Let us examine the percentage price change resulting from a fall in yield of 1.50% from the same starting yield of 5.50%. This is a decrease in yield of 150 basis points, so our convexity measurement needs to be recalculated. The convexity value is $(0.5) \times 96.23119 \times (0.0150)^2 \times 100 = 1.0826\%$. So the price change is based on:

Modified duration $= 7.64498 \times 1.5 = 11.46747$;

Convexity $= 1.0826$.

This gives us a percentage price change of 12.55007. The actual price change was 10.98843%, so here the modified duration estimate is actually closer! This illustrates that the convexity measure is effective for larger yield changes only. Example 2.21 shows us that for very large changes, a closer approximation for bond price volatility is given by combining the modified duration and convexity measures.

Example 2.21

◆ The hypothetical bond is the 5% 2009, again trading at a yield of 5.50% and priced at 96.23119. If the yield rises to 8.50%, a change of 300 basis points, the percentage price change due to the convexity effect is given by:

$(0.5) \times 96.23119 \times (0.03)^2 \times 100 = 4.3304\%$.

Meanwhile as before, the modified duration of the bond at the initial yield is 7.64498. At the new yield of 8.50% the price of the bond is 77.03528 (check using any financial calculator); comparative prices are also given in Table 2.3.

The price change can be approximated using:

Modified duration $= 7.64498 \times 3.0 = -22.93494$;

Convexity $= 4.3304$.

This gives a percentage price change of 18.60454%. The actual percentage price change was 19.9477%, but our estimate is still closer than that obtained using only the modified duration measure. The continuing error reflects the fact that convexity is also a dynamic measure and changes with yield changes; the effect of a large yield movement compounds the inaccuracy given by convexity.

Convexity is an attractive property for a bond to have. What level of premium will be attached to a bond's higher convexity? This is a function of the current yield levels in the market as well as market volatility. Remember that modified duration and convexity are functions of yield level, and that the effect of both is magnified at lower yield levels. As well as the relative level, investors will value convexity higher if the current market conditions are volatile. Remember that the cash effect of convexity is noticeable only for large moves in yield. If an investor expects market yields to move only by relatively small amounts, they will attach a lower value to convexity; and vice-versa for large movements in yield. Therefore the yield premium attached to a bond with higher convexity will vary according to market expectations of the future size of interest rate changes.

The convexity measure increases with the square of maturity, and it decreases with both coupon and yield. As the measure is a function of modified duration, index-linked bonds have greater convexity than conventional bonds. The price/yield profile will be more convex for a bond of higher convexity, and such a bond will outperform a bond of lower convexity whatever happens to market interest rates. High convexity is therefore a desirable property for bonds to have. In principle, a more convex bond should fall in price less than a less convex one when yields rise, and rise in price more when yields fall. That is, convexity can be equated with the potential to outperform. Thus, other things being equal, the higher the convexity of a bond the more desirable it should, in principle, be to investors. In some cases investors may be prepared to accept a bond with a lower yield in order to gain convexity. We noted also that convexity is, in principle, of more value if uncertainty, and hence expected market volatility, is high, because the convexity effect of a bond is amplified for large changes in yield. The value of convexity is therefore greater in volatile market conditions

For a conventional vanilla bond convexity is almost always positive. Negative convexity resulting from a bond with a concave price/yield profile would not be an attractive property for a bondholder; the most common occurrence of negative convexity in the cash markets is with callable bonds.

We illustrated that, for most bonds, and certainly when the convexity measure is high, the modified duration measurement for interest rate risk becomes more inaccurate for large changes in yield. In such situations it becomes necessary to use the approximation given by the convexity equation (2.52) to measure the error we have made in estimating the price change based on modified duration only. The expression was given earlier in this chapter.

The following points highlight the main convexity properties for conventional vanilla bonds.

- **A fall in yields leads to an increase in convexity.** A decrease in bond yield leads to an increase in the bond's convexity; this is a property of positive convexity. Equally, a rise in yields leads to a fall in convexity.

- **For a given term to maturity, higher coupon results in lower convexity.** For any given redemption yield and term to maturity, the higher a bond's coupon, the lower its convexity. Therefore, among bonds of the same maturity, zero-coupon bonds have the highest convexity.

- **For a given modified duration, higher coupon results in higher convexity**. For any given redemption yield and modified duration, a higher coupon results in a higher convexity. Contrast this with the earlier property; in this case, for bonds of the same modified duration, zero-coupon bonds have the lowest convexity.

Appendices

Appendix 2.1:   Measuring convexity

The modified duration of a plain vanilla bond is:

$$MD = \frac{D}{(1+r)}.$$ (2.56)

We know that:

$$\frac{dP}{dr}\frac{1}{P} = -MD.$$ (2.57)

This shows that for a percentage change in the yield we have an inverse change in the price by the amount of the modified duration value.

If we multiply both sides of (2.57) by any particular change in the bond yield, given by dr, we obtain expression (2.58).

$$\frac{dP}{P} = -MD \times dr$$ (2.58)

Using the first two terms of a Taylor expansion, we obtain an approximation of the bond price change, given by (2.59).

$$dP = \frac{dP}{dr}dr + \frac{1}{2}\frac{d^2P}{dr^2}(dr)^2 + \text{approximation error}$$ (2.59)

If we divide both sides of (2.59) by P to obtain the percentage price change the result is the expression at (2.60).

$$\frac{dP}{P} = \frac{dP}{dr}\frac{1}{P}dr + \frac{1}{2}\frac{d^2P}{dr^2}\frac{1}{P}(dr)^2 + \frac{\text{approximation error}}{P}$$ (2.60)

The first component of the right-hand side of (2.59) is the expression at (2.58), which is the cash price change given by the duration value. Therefore equation (2.59) is the approximation of the price change. Equation (2.60) is the approximation of the price change as given by the modified duration value. The second component in both expressions is the second derivative of the bond price equation. This second derivative captures the convexity value of the price/yield relationship and is the cash value given by convexity. As such it is referred to as *dollar convexity* in the US markets. The dollar convexity is stated as (2.61).

$$CV_{dollar} = \frac{d^2P}{dr^2}$$ (2.61)

If we multiply the dollar convexity value by the square of a bond's yield change we obtain the approximate cash value change in price resulting from the convexity effect. This is shown by (2.62).

$$dP = (CV_{dollar})(dr)^2$$ (2.62)

If we then divide the second derivative of the price equation by the bond price, we obtain a measure of the percentage change in bond price as a result of the convexity effect. This is the measure known as *convexity* and is the convention used in virtually all bond markets. This is given by the expression at (2.63).

$$CV = \frac{d^2 P}{dr^2} \frac{1}{P} \qquad (2.63)$$

To measure the amount of the percentage change in bond price as a result of the convex nature of the price/yield relationship we can use (2.64).

$$\frac{dP}{P} = \frac{1}{2} CV (dr)^2 \qquad (2.64)$$

For long-hand calculations note that the second derivative of the bond price equation is (2.65). The usual assumptions apply to the expressions, that the bond pays annual coupons and has a precise number of interest periods to maturity. If the bond is a semi-annual paying one, the yield value r is replaced by $r/2$.

$$\frac{d^2 P}{dr^2} = \sum_{n=1}^{N} \frac{n(n+1)C}{(1+r)^{n+2}} + \frac{n(n+1)M}{(1+r)^{n+2}} \qquad (2.65)$$

Alternatively, we differentiate to the second order the bond price equation as given by (2.66), giving us the alternative expression (2.67).

$$P = \frac{C}{r}\left(1 - \frac{1}{(1+r)^n}\right) + \frac{100}{(1+r)^n} \qquad (2.66)$$

$$\frac{d^2 P}{dr^2} = \frac{2C}{r^3}\left(1 - \frac{1}{(1+r)^n}\right) - \frac{2C}{r^2(1+r)^{n+1}} + \frac{n(n+1)(100 - (C/r))}{(1+r)^{n+2}} \qquad (2.67)$$

Selected bibliography and references

Allen, S.L., Kleinstein, A.D., *Valuing Fixed Income Investments and Derivative Securities*, New York Institute of Finance 1991

Bierwag, G.O., "Immunization, Duration and the term structure of interest rates," *Journal of Financial and Quantitative Analysis*, December 1977 pp.725–741

Bierwag, G.O., "Measures of duration," *Economic Inquiry 16*, October 1978, pp. 497–507

Blake, D., *Financial Market Analysis*, 2nd edition, Prentice Hall 2000

Burghardt, G., *The Treasury Bond Basis*, McGraw-Hill 1994

Choudhry, M., *Bond Market Securities*, FT Prentice Hall 2001

Fabozzi, F., *Bond Markets, Analysis and Strategies*, Prentice Hall 1989, Chapter 2

Fabozzi, F., *Bond Markets, Analysis and Strategies*, 2nd edition, Prentice Hall 1993

Fabozzi, F., *Fixed Income Mathematics*, 3rd edition, McGraw-Hill 1997, pp. 190–192

Higson, C., *Business Finance*, Butterworth 1995

Ingersoll, J., Jr., *Theory of Financial Decision Making*, Rowe & Littlefield 1987, Chapter 18

Jarrow, R., *Modelling Fixed Income Securities and Interest Rate Options*, McGraw-Hill 1996, Chapters 2, 3

Neftci, S., *An Introduction to the Mathematics of Financial Derivatives*, Academic Press 1996

Shiller, R., "The Term Structure of Interest Rates", in Friedman, B. Hahn, F, (editors), *Handbook of Monetary Economics*, volume 1, Elsevier Science Publishers, 1990

Van Deventer, D., Imai, K., *Financial Risk Analytics*, Irwin 1997, pp. 9–11

Weston, J.F., Copeland, T.E., *Managerial Finance*, Dryden, 1986

Van Horne, J., *Financial Management and Policy*, 10th edition, Prentice Hall International, 1995

3 Market Background: *The Bond Markets II*

In this chapter we present a brief overview of the main tenets of fixed income analysis as it appears in the current literature. Repo market practitioners may skip this chapter, and go straight to Chapter 5; however it is presented here on the grounds of completeness for any book that discusses the debt capital markets. First we illustrate basic concepts, which is followed by a discussion of yield curve analysis and the term structure of interest rates.

3.1 Basic concepts

We are already familiar with two types of fixed income security: *zero-coupon bonds*, also known as *discount bonds* or *strips*, and *coupon bonds*. A zero-coupon bond makes a single payment on its maturity date, whereas a coupon bond makes regular interest payments at regular dates up to and including its maturity date. A coupon bond may be regarded as a set of strips, with each coupon payment and the redemption payment on maturity being equivalent to a zero-coupon bond maturing on that date. This is not a purely academic concept; witness events before the advent of the formal market in US Treasury strips, when a number of investment banks had traded the cash flows of Treasury securities as separate zero-coupon securities.[1] The literature we review in this section is set in a market of default-free bonds, whether they are zero-coupon bonds or coupon bonds. The market is assumed to be liquid so that bonds may be freely bought and sold. Prices of bonds are determined by the economy-wide supply and demand for the bonds at any time, so they are *macroeconomic* and not set by individual bond issuers or traders.

3.1.1 *Zero-coupon bonds*

A zero-coupon bond is the simplest fixed income security. It is an issue of debt, the issuer promising to pay the face value of the debt to the bondholder on the date the bond matures. There are no coupon payments during the life of the bond, so it is a discount instrument, issued at a price that is below the face or *principal* amount. We denote as $P(t, T)$ the price of a discount bond at time t that matures at time T, with $T \geq t$. The term to maturity of the bond is denoted by n, where $n = T - t$. The price increases over time until the maturity date, when it reaches the maturity or *par* value. If the par value of the bond is £1, then the *yield to matur-*

---

[1] These banks included Merrill Lynch, Lehman Brothers and Salomon Brothers, among others (Fabozzi 1993). The term "strips" comes from Separate Trading of Registered Interest and Principal of Securities, the name given when the official market was introduced by the Treasury. The banks would purchase Treasuries which would then be deposited in a safe custody account. Receipts were issued against each cash flow from each Treasury, and these receipts traded as individual zero-coupon securities. The market-making banks earned profit due to the arbitrage difference in the price of the original coupon bond and the price at which the individual strips were sold. The US Treasury formalised trading in strips after 1985, after legislation had been introduced that altered the tax treatment of such instruments. The market in UK gilt strips trading began in December 1997.

ity of the bond at time t is denoted by $r(t,T)$, where r is actually "one plus the percentage yield" that is earned by holding the bond from t to T. We have:

$$P(t,T) = \frac{1}{[r(t,T)]^n}. \tag{3.1}$$

The yield may be obtained from the bond price and is given by

$$r(t,T) = \left[\frac{1}{P(t,T)} \right]^{1/n}, \tag{3.2}$$

which is sometimes written as

$$r(t,T) = P(t,T)^{-(1/n)}. \tag{3.3}$$

Analysts and researchers frequently work in terms of logarithms of yields and prices, or continuously compounded rates. One advantage of this is that it converts the non-linear relationship in (3.2) into a linear relationship.[2]

The bond price at time t_2 where $t \le t_2 \le T$ is given by

$$P(t_2,T) = P(t,T)e^{(t_2-t)r(t,T)} \tag{3.4}$$

which is natural given that the bond price equation in continuous time is

$$P(t,T) = e^{-r(t,T)(T-t)} \tag{3.5}$$

so that the yield is given by

$$r(t,T) = -\log\left(\frac{P(t,T)}{n} \right) \tag{3.6}$$

which is sometimes written as

$$\log r(t,T) = -\left(\frac{1}{n} \right)\log P(t,T). \tag{3.7}$$

The expression in (3.4) includes the exponential function, hence the use of the term "continuously compounded".

The *term structure of interest rates* is the set of zero-coupon yields at time t for all bonds ranging in maturity from $(t, t+1)$ to $(t, t+m)$ where the bonds have maturities of $\{0,1,2,...,m\}$. A good definition of the term structure of interest rates is given in Sundaresan (1997), who states that it:

---

2   A linear relationship in X would be a function $Y = f(X)$ in which the X values change via a power or index of 1 only, and are not multiplied or divided by another variable or variables. So, for example, terms such as $X^2, \sqrt{X}$ and other similar functions are not linear in X, nor are terms such as XZ or X/Z where Z is another variable. In econometric analysis, if the value of Y is solely dependent on the value of X, then its rate of change with respect to X, or the derivative of Y with respect to X, denoted dY/dX, is independent of X. Therefore, if $Y = 5X$, then $dY/dX = 5$, which is independent of the value of X. However, if $Y = 5X^2$, then $dY/dX = 10X$, which is not independent of the value of X. Hence this function is not linear in X. The classic regression function $E(Y \mid X_i) = \alpha + \beta X_i$ is a linear function with slope β and intercept α where $|\alpha| \ge 0$ and $|\beta| > 0$. The regression "curve" is represented geometrically by a straight line.

> "... refers to the relationship between the yield to maturity of default-free zero coupon securities and their maturities."

> (Sundaresan 1997, page 176)

The *yield curve* is a plot of the set of yields for $r(t, t+1)$ to $r(t, t+m)$ against m at time t. For example, Figures 3.1–3.3 show the log zero-coupon yield curve for US Treasury strips, UK gilt strips and French OAT strips on 27 September 2000. Each of the curves exhibit peculiarities in their shape, although the most common type of curve is gently upward-sloping, as is the French curve. The UK curve is *inverted*. We explore further the shape of the yield curve later in this chapter.

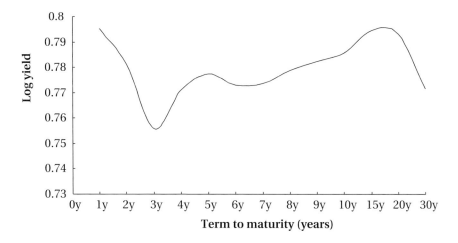

Figure 3.1: US Treasury zero-coupon yield curve in September 2000.
Yield source: Bloomberg.

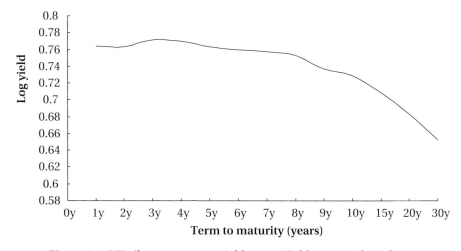

Figure 3.2: UK gilt zero-coupon yield curve. Yield source: Bloomberg.

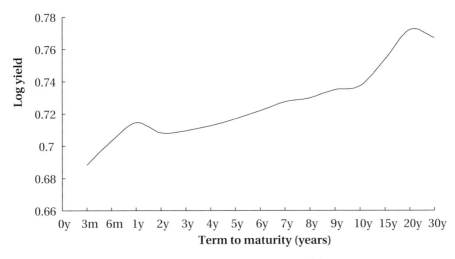

Figure 3.3: French OAT zero-coupon yield curve.
Yield source: Bloomberg.

3.1.2 *Coupon bonds*

The majority of bonds in the market make periodic interest or *coupon* payments during their life, and are known as coupon bonds. We have already noted that such bonds may be viewed as a package of individual zero-coupon bonds. The coupons have a nominal value that is a percentage of the nominal value of the bond itself, with steadily longer maturity dates, while the final redemption payment has the nominal value of the bond itself and is redeemed on the maturity date. We denote a bond issued at time i and maturing at time T as having a w-element vector of payment dates $(t_1, t_2, \dots, t_{w-1}, T)$ and matching date payments $C_1, C_2, \dots, C_{w-1}, C_w$. In the academic literature these coupon payments are assumed to be made in continuous time, so that the stream of coupon payments is given by a positive function of time $C(t)$, $i < t \leq T$. An investor who purchases a bond at time t that matures at time T pays $P(t, T)$ and will receive the coupon payments as long as they continue to hold the bond.[3]

The yield to maturity at time t of a bond that matures at T is the interest rate that relates the price of the bond to the future returns on the bond, that is, the rate that *discounts* the bond's cash flow stream C_w to its price $P(t, T)$. This is given by

$$P(t,T) = \sum_{t_i > t} C_i e^{-(t_i - t)r(t,T)} \tag{3.8}$$

which says that the bond price is given by the present value of the cash flow stream of the bond, discounted at the rate $r(t, T)$. For a zero-coupon bond (3.8) reduces to (3.6). In the academic literature, where coupon payments are assumed to be made in continuous time, the Σ summation in (3.8) is replaced by $\int$ (the integral). We will look at this in a moment.

---

3   In theoretical treatments this is the discounted clean price of the bond. For coupon bonds in practice, unless the bond is purchased for value on a coupon date, it will be traded with interest accrued. The interest that has accrued on a pro-rata basis from the last coupon date is added to the clean price of the bond to give the market "dirty" price that is actually paid by the purchaser.

In some texts the plot of the yield to maturity at time t for the term of the bonds m is described as the term structure of interest rates, but it is generally accepted that the term structure is the plot of zero-coupon rates only. Plotting yields to maturity is generally described as graphically depicting the yield curve, rather than the term structure. Of course, given no-arbitrage pricing, also known as the law of one price, there is a relationship between the yield to maturity yield curve and the zero-coupon term structure, and given the first value one can derive the second. See a standard text such as Hull (2000) for background on no-arbitrage pricing.

The expression at (3.8) obtains the continuously compounded yield to maturity $r(t,T)$. It is the use of the exponential function that enables us to describe the yield as continuously compounded.

The market frequently uses the measure known as *current yield* which is

$$rc = \frac{C}{P_d} \times 100,$$ (3.9)

where P_d is the dirty price of the bond. The measure is also known as the *running yield* or *flat yield*. Current yield is not used to indicate the interest rate or discount rate and therefore should not be mistaken for the yield to maturity.

3.2 Forward rates

An investor can combine positions in bonds of differing maturities to guarantee a rate of return that begins at a point in the future. That is, the trade ticket would be written at time t but would cover the period T to $T+1$ where $t < T$ (sometimes written as beginning at T_1 and ending at T_2, with $t < T_1 < T_2$). The interest rate earned during this period is known as the *forward rate*.[4] The mechanism by which this forward rate can be guaranteed is described in Example 3.1, following approaches described in texts such as Jarrow (1996) and Campbell *et al* (1997).

3.2.1 *The forward rate*

Example 3.1

◆ An investor buys, at time t, 1 unit of a zero-coupon bond maturing at time T, priced at $P(t,T)$ and simultaneously sells $P(t,T)/P(t,T+1)$ bonds that mature at $T+1$. From Table 3.1, below, we see that the net result of these transactions is a zero cash flow. At time T there is a cash inflow of 1, and then at time $T+1$ there is a cash outflow of $P(t,T)/P(t,T+1)$. These cash flows are identical to a loan of funds made during the period T to $T+1$, contracted at time t. The interest rate on this loan is given by

   $$P(t,T)/P(t,T+1),$$

   which is therefore the forward rate. That is,

   $$f(t,T) = \frac{P(t,T)}{P(t,T+1)}.$$ (3.10)

---

4   See the footnote on page 639 of Shiller (1990) for a fascinating insight on the origin of the term "forward rate", which Mr Shiller ascribes to John Hicks in his book *Value and Capital* (2nd edition, Oxford University Press 1946).

Together with our earlier relationships on bond price and yield, from (3.10) we can define the forward rate in terms of yield, with the return earned during the period $(T, T+1)$ shown as (3.11).

$$f(t,T,T+1) = \frac{1}{(P(t,T+1)/P(t,T))} = \frac{(r(t,T+1))^{(T+1)}}{r(t,T)^T}. \tag{3.11}$$

Transaction time	t	T	$T+1$
Cash flows			
Buy 1 T-period bond	$-P(t,T)$	1	
Sell $P(t,T)/P(t,T+1)$			
$T+1$ period bonds	$+(P(t,T)/P(t,T+1))P(t,T+1)$		$-P(t,T)/P(t,T+1)$
Net	0	1	$-P(t,T)/P(t,T+1)$

Table 3.1

From (3.10) we can obtain a bond price equation in terms of the forward rates that hold from t to T,

$$P(t,T) = \frac{1}{\prod_{k=t}^{T-1} f(t,k)}. \tag{3.12}$$

A derivation of this expression can be found in Jarrow (1996), Chapter 3. Expression (3.12) states that the price of a zero-coupon bond is equal to the nominal value, here assumed to be 1, receivable at time T after it has been discounted at the set of forward rates that apply from t to T.[5]

When calculating a forward rate, it is as if we are writing an interest rate contract today that is applicable at the forward start date; in other words, we trade a forward contract. The law of one price, or no-arbitrage, is used to calculate the rate. For a loan that begins at T and matures at $T+1$, similar to the way we described in the box above, consider a purchase of a $(T+1)$-period bond and a sale of p amount of the T-period bond. The net cash position at t must be zero, so p is given by

$$p = \frac{P(t,T+1)}{P(t,T)} \tag{3.13}$$

and to avoid arbitrage the value of p must be the price of the $(T+1)$-period bond at time T. Therefore the forward yield is given by

$$f(t,T+1) = -\frac{\log P(t,T+1) - \log P(t,T)}{(T+1) - T} \tag{3.14}$$

If the period between T and the maturity of the later-dated bond is reduced, so we now have bonds that mature at T and T_2, and $T_2 = T + \Delta t$, then the incremental change in time Δt

---

5   The symbol Π means "take the product of", and is defined as $\prod_{i=1}^{n} x_i = x_1 \cdot x_2 \cdot \cdots \cdot x_n$, so that

$$\prod_{k=t}^{T-1} f(t,k) = f(t,t) \cdot f(t,t+1) \cdot \cdots \cdot f(t,T-1)$$

which is the result of multiplying the rates that are obtained when the index k runs from t to $T-1$.

becomes progressively smaller until we obtain an instantaneous forward rate, which is given by

$$f(t,T) = -\frac{\partial}{\partial T}\log P(t,T).$$ (3.15)

This rate is defined as the forward rate and is the price today of forward borrowing at time T. The forward rate for borrowing today where $T = t$ is equal to the instantaneous short rate $r(t)$. At time t the spot and forward rates for the period (t, t) will be identical, at other maturity terms they will differ.

For all points other that at (t, t) the forward rate yield curve will lie above the spot rate curve if the spot curve is positively sloping. The opposite applies if the spot rate curve is downward sloping. Campbell *et al* (1997, pages 400–401) observe that this property is a standard one for marginal and average cost curves. That is, when the cost of a marginal unit (say, of production) is above that of an average unit, then the average cost will increase with the addition of a marginal unit. This results in the average cost rising when the marginal cost is above the average cost. Equally, the average cost per unit will decrease when the marginal cost lies below the average cost.

Example 3.2: The spot and forward yield curves

◆ From the discussion in this section we see that it is possible to calculate bond prices, spot rates and forward rates provided that one has a set of only one of these parameters. Therefore given the following set of zero-coupon rates, observed in the market, shown in Table 3.2, we calculate the corresponding forward rates and zero-coupon bond prices as shown.[6] The initial term structure is upward sloping. The two curves are illustrated in Figure 3.4.

Term to maturity $(0,T)$	Spot rate $r(0,T)^*$	Forward rate $f(0,T)$	Bond price $P(0,T)$
0			1
1	1.054	1.054	0.94877
2	1.055	1.056	0.89845
3	1.0563	1.059	0.8484
4	1.0582	1.064	0.79737
5	1.0602	1.068	0.7466
6	1.0628	1.076	0.69386
7	1.06553	1.082	0.64128
8	1.06856	1.0901	0.58833
9	1.07168	1.0972	0.53631
10	1.07526	1.1001	0.48403
11	1.07929	1.1205	0.43198

* Interest rates are given as $(1 + r)$.

Table 3.2: Hypothetical zero-coupon yield and forward rates.

6 This is explained in top fashion by Olivier de la Grandville in his book *Bond Pricing and Portfolio Analysis*, MIT Press, 2001; Chapter 9 and pages 240–244.

There are technical reasons why the theoretical forward rate has a severe kink at the later maturity, but we shall not go into an explanation of this as it is outside the scope of this book.

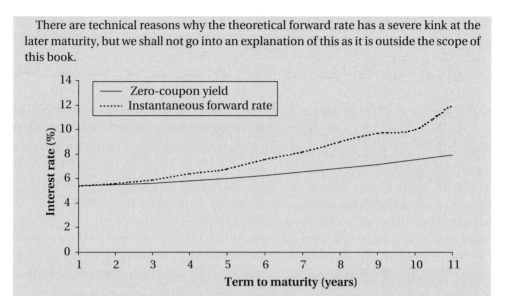

Figure 3.4: Hypothetical zero-coupon and forward yield curves.

3.3   Bond price in continuous time[7]

3.3.1 *Fundamental concepts*

In this section we present an introduction to the bond price equation in continuous time.[8] Consider a trading environment where bond prices evolve in a w-dimensional process

$$X(t) = [X_1(t), X_2(t), X_3(t), \ldots, X_w(t)], \qquad t > 0$$

where the random variables are termed *state variables* that reflect the state of the economy at any point in time. The markets assume that the state variables evolve through a process described as *geometric Brownian motion* or a *Weiner process*. It is therefore possible to model the evolution of these variables in the form of a stochastic differential equation.

The market assumes that the cash flow stream of assets such as bonds and (for equities) dividends is a function of the state variables. A bond is characterised by its coupon process

$$C(t) = \tilde{C}[X_1(t), X_2(t), X_3(t), \ldots, X_w(t), t]. \tag{3.16}$$

---

7   This section follows the approach used in Avellaneda (2000), Baxter and Rennie (1996), Neftci (2000), Campbell *et al* (1997), Ross (1999), and Shiller (1990). These are all excellent texts of very high quality, and strongly recommended. For an accessible and highly readable introduction, Ross's book is worth buying for Chapter 4 alone, as is Avellaneda's for his Chapter 12. For a general introduction to the main pricing concepts see Campbell *et al* (1997), Chapter 10. In addition Chapter 3 in Jarrow (1996) is an accessible introduction for discrete-time bond pricing. Sundaresan (1997) is an excellent overview text on the fixed income market as a whole, and is highly recommended.

8   The necessary background on price processes is not introduced, but interested readers will find this covered in Chapter 43 and pages 865–871 of the author's book *The Bond and Money Markets*, (Butterworth-Heinemann 2001).

The coupon process represents the cash flow that the investor receives during the time that they hold the bond. Over a small incremental increase in time of dt from the time t the investor can purchase $1 + C(t)\mathrm{d}t$ units of the bond at the end of the period $t + \mathrm{d}t$. Assume that there is a very short-term discount security such as a Treasury bill that matures at $t + \mathrm{d}t$, and during this period the investor receives a return of $r(t)$. This rate is the annualised short-term interest rate, or *short rate*, which in the mathematical analysis is defined as the rate of interest charged on a loan that is taken out at time t and which matures almost immediately. For this reason the rate is also known as the *instantaneous rate*. The short rate is given by

$$r(t) = r(t,t) \tag{3.17}$$

and

$$r(t) = -\frac{\partial}{\partial T} \log P(t,t). \tag{3.18}$$

If we continuously reinvest the short-term security such as the T-bill at this short rate, we obtain a cumulative amount that is the original investment multiplied by (3.19).[9]

$$M(t) = \exp\left[\int_t^T r(s)\,ds \right] \tag{3.19}$$

where M is a money market account that offers a return of the short rate $r(t)$, to the time T.

If we say that the short rate is constant, making $r(t) = r$, then the price of a risk-free bond that pays £1 on maturity at time T is given by

$$P(t,T) = e^{-r(T-t)}. \tag{3.20}$$

What (3.20) states is that the bond price is simply a function of the continuously-compounded interest rate, with the right-hand side of (3.20) being the discount factor at time t. At $t = T$ the discount factor will be 1, which is the redemption value of the bond and hence the price of the bond at this time.

Consider the following scenario: a market participant may undertake the following:

- it can invest $e^{-r(T-t)}$ units of cash in a money market account today, which will have grown to a sum of £1 at time T;

- it can purchase the risk-free zero-coupon bond today, which has a maturity value of £1 at time T.

The market participant can invest in either instrument, both of which we know beforehand to be risk-free, and both of which have identical payouts at time T and have no cash flow between now and time T. As interest rates are constant, a bond that paid out £1 at T must have the same value as the initial investment in the money market account, which is $e_t^{-r(T-t)}$. Therefore, equation (3.20) must apply. This is a restriction placed on the zero-coupon bond price by the requirement for markets to be arbitrage-free.

If the bond was not priced at this level, arbitrage opportunities would present themselves. Consider if the bond was priced higher than $e_t^{-r(T-t)}$. In this case, an investor could sell short the bond and invest the sale proceeds in the money market account. On maturity at time T, the short position will have a value of –£1 (negative, because the investor is short the bond)

---

[9]   This expression uses the integral operator. The integral is the tool used in mathematics to calculate sums of an infinite number of objects, that is, where the objects are uncountable. This is different to the Σ operator which is used for a countable number of objects. For a readable and accessible review of the integral and its use in quantitative finance, see Neftci (2000), pp. 59–66.

while the money market will have accumulated £1, which the investor can use to pay the proceeds on the zero-coupon bond. However, the investor will have surplus funds because at time t

$$P(t,T) - e^{-r(T-t)} > 0,$$

and so will have profited from the transaction at no risk to himself.

The same applies if the bond is priced below $e_t^{-r(T-t)}$. In this case the investor borrows $e_t^{-r(T-t)}$ and buys the bond at its price $P(t, T)$. On maturity the bond pays £1 which is used to repay the loan amount; however, the investor will gain because

$$e^{-r(T-t)} - P(t,T) > 0.$$

Therefore, the only price at which no arbitrage profit can be made is if

$$P(t,T) = e^{-r(T-t)}. \tag{3.21}$$

In the academic literature the price of a zero-coupon bond is given in terms of the evolution of the short-term interest rate, in what is termed the *risk-neutral measure*.[10] The short rate $r(t)$ is the interest rate earned on a money market account or short-dated risk-free security such as the T-Bill suggested above, and it is assumed to be continuously compounded. This makes the mathematical treatment simpler. With a zero-coupon bond we assume a payment on maturity of 1 (say $1 or £1), a one-off cash flow payable on maturity at time T. The value of the zero-coupon bond at time t is therefore given by

$$P(t,T) = \exp\left(-\int_t^T r(s)\mathrm{d}s\right) \tag{3.22}$$

which is the redemption value of 1 divided by the value of the money market account, given by (3.19). The bond price for a coupon bond is given in terms of its yield as

$$P(t,T) = \exp(-(T-t)r(T-t)). \tag{3.23}$$

Expression (3.22) is very commonly encountered in the academic literature. Its derivation is not so frequently occurring however; we present it in Appendix 3.1, which is a summary of the description given in Ross (1999). This reference is highly recommended reading. It is also worth referring to Neftci (2000), Chapter 18.

The expression (3.22) represents the zero-coupon bond pricing formula when the spot rate is continuous or *stochastic*, rather than constant. The rate $r(s)$ is the risk-free return earned during the very short, or *infinitesimal*, time interval $(t, t + \mathrm{d}t)$. The rate is used in the expressions for the value of a money market account (3.19) and the price of a risk-free zero-coupon bond (3.23). For coupon bonds the price equation in continuous time is given as

$$P_c = 100e^{-rN} + \int_n^N Ce^{-rn}\mathrm{d}t \tag{3.24}$$

which in discrete time and substituting Df to denote the discount factor part of the expression and assuming an annual coupon, is

$$P = 100 \cdot Df_N + \sum_{n:t_n \geq t}^N C \cdot Df_n , \tag{3.25}$$

which states that the market value of a risk-free bond on any date is determined by the

---

10   This is part of the *arbitrage pricing theory*. For detail on this see Cox *et al* (1985), while Duffie (1996) is a fuller treatment for those with a strong grounding in mathematics.

discount function on that date.

We know from Chapter 2 that the actual price paid in the market for a bond includes accrued interest from the last coupon date, so that price given by (3.25) is known as the clean price and the traded price, which includes accrued interest, is known as the *dirty price*.

3.4 The term structure

We have already referred to the yield curve or *term structure of interest rates*. Strictly speaking, only a spot rate yield curve is a term structure, but one sometimes encounters the two expressions being used synonymously. At any time *t* there will be a set of coupon and/or zero-coupon bonds with different terms to maturity and cash flow streams. There will be certain fixed maturities that are not represented by actual bonds in the market, as there will be more than one bond maturing at or around the same redemption date. The debt capital markets and the pricing of debt instruments revolves around the term structure, and for this reason this area has been extensively researched in the academic literature. There are a number of ways to estimate and interpret the term structure, and in this section we review the research highlights.

3.4.1 *Deriving the spot rate curve from coupon bond prices and yields, using a simple approach*[11]

In this section we describe how to obtain zero-coupon and forward rates from the yields available from coupon bonds, using the *boot-strapping* technique. In a government bond market such as that for US Treasuries or gilts, the bonds are considered to be *default-free*. The rates from a government bond yield curve describe the risk-free rates of return available in the market *today*; however, they also *imply* (risk-free) rates of return for *future time periods*. These implied future rates, known as *implied forward rates*, or simply *forward rates*, can be derived from a given spot yield curve using boot-strapping. This term reflects the fact that each calculated spot rate is used to determine the next period spot rate, in successive steps.

Table 3.3 shows an hypothetical benchmark yield curve for value as at 2 January 2000. The observed yields of the benchmark bonds that compose the curve are displayed in the last column. All rates are annualised and assume semi-annual compounding. The bonds all pay on the same coupon dates of 2 January and 2 July, and as the value date is a coupon date, there is no accrued interest. Note also that all the bonds are priced at par.

Hypothetical government benchmark bond yields as at 2 January 2000					
Bond	Term to maturity (years)	Coupon	Maturity date	Price	Gross redemption yield
6-month	0.5	4%	02-Jul-00	100	4%
1-year	1	5%	02-Jan-01	100	5%
1.5-year	1.5	6%	02-Jul-01	100	6%
2-year	2	7%	02-Jan-02	100	7%
2.5-year	2.5	8%	02-Jul-02	100	8%
3-year	3	9%	02-Jan-03	100	9%

Table 3.3: Hypothetical coupon bond yields.

---

[11] This section follows the approach used in Windas (1994). The technique described here is usually referred to as "bootstrapping" the zero-coupon curve.

The gross redemption yield or *yield-to-maturity* of a coupon bond describes the single rate that present-values the sum each of its future cash flows to a given price. This yield measure suffers from a fundamental weakness in that each cash flow is present-valued at the same rate; an unrealistic assumption in anything other than a flat yield curve environment. The bonds in Table 3.3 pay semi-annual coupons on 2 January and 2 July and have the same time period – six months – between 2 January 2000, their valuation date, and 2 July 2000, their next coupon date. However, since each issue carries a different yield, the next six-month coupon payment for each bond is present-valued at a different rate. In other words, the six-month bond present-values its six-month coupon payment at its 4% yield to maturity, the one-year at 5%, and so on.

Because each of these issues uses a different rate to present-value a cash flow occurring at the same future point in time, it is unclear which of the rates should be regarded as the true interest rate or benchmark rate for the six-month period from 2 January 2000 to 2 July 2000. This problem is repeated for all other maturities. We require a set of true interest rates, however, and so these must be derived from the redemption yields that we can observe from the benchmark bonds trading in the market. These rates we designate as rs_i, where rs_i is the *implied spot rate* or *zero-coupon rate* for the term beginning on 2 January 2000 and ending at the end of period i.

We begin calculating implied spot rates by noting that the six-month bond contains only one future cash flow – the final coupon payment and the redemption payment on maturity. This means that it is, in effect, trading as a zero-coupon bond. Since this cash-flow's present value, future value and maturity term are known, the unique interest rate that relates these quantities can be solved using the compound interest equation (3.26) below.

$$FV = P \times \left(1 + \frac{rs_i}{m}\right)^{nm}$$

$$rs_i = m \times \left(\sqrt[nm]{\frac{FV}{P}} - 1\right)$$

(3.26)

where

FV	is the future value;
P	is the present value (or price);
rs_i	is the implied i-period spot rate;
m	is the number of interest periods per year;
n	is the number of years in the term.

The first rate to be solved is referred to as the implied six-month spot rate and is the true interest rate for the six-month term beginning on 2 January 2000 and ending on 2 July 2000.

Equation (3.26) relates a cash-flow's present value and future value in terms of an associated interest rate, compounding convention and time period. Of course if we rearrange it we may use it to solve for an implied spot rate. For the six-month bond the final cash flow on maturity is £102, comprised of the £2 coupon payment and the par redemption amount. So we have, for the first term, $i = 1$, $FV = £102$, $P = £100$, $n = 0.5$ years and $m = 2$. This allows us to calculate the spot rate as follows:

$$rs_i = m \times \left(\sqrt[nm]{FV/P} - 1 \right)$$
$$rs_1 = 2 \times \left(\sqrt[0.5\times2]{£102/£100} - 1 \right)$$
$$rs_1 = 0.04000$$
$$rs_1 = 4.000\%.$$

(3.27)

Thus the implied six-month spot rate or zero-coupon rate is equal to 4%.[12] We now need to determine the implied one-year spot rate for the term from 2 January 2000 to 2 January 2001. We note that the one-year issue has a 5% coupon and contains two future cash flows: a £2.50 six-month coupon payment on 2 July 2000 and a £102.50 one-year coupon and principal payment on 2 January 2001. Since the first cash flow occurs on 2 July – six months from now – it must be present-valued at the 4% six-month spot rate established above. Once this present value is determined, it may be subtracted from the £100 total present value of the one-year issue to obtain the present value of the one-year coupon and cash flow. Again we then have a single cash flow with a known present value, future value and term. The rate that equates these quantities is the implied one-year spot rate. From equation (3.26) the present value of the six-month £2.50 coupon payment of the one-year benchmark bond, discounted at the implied six-month spot rate, is:

$$P_{\text{6-mo cash flow, 1-yr bond}} = £2.50/\left(1 + 0.04/2\right)^{(0.5\times2)}$$
$$= £2.45098.$$

The present value of the one-year £102.50 coupon and principal payment is found by subtracting the present value of the six-month cash flow, determined above, from the total present value (current price) of the issue:

$$P_{\text{1-yr cash flow, 1-yr bond}} = £100 - £2.45098$$
$$= £97.54902.$$

The implied one-year spot rate is then determined by using the £97.54902 present value of the one-year cash flow determined above:

$$rs_2 = 2 \times \left(\sqrt[(1\times2)]{£102.50/£97.54902} - 1 \right)$$
$$= 0.0501256$$
$$= 5.01256\%.$$

The implied 1.5-year spot rate is solved in the same way:

$$P_{\text{6-mo cash flow, 1.5-yr bond}} = £3.00/\left(1 + 0.04/2\right)^{(0.5\times2)}$$
$$= £2.94118$$
$$P_{\text{1-yr cash flow, 1.5-yr bond}} = £3.00/\left(1 + 0.0501256/2\right)^{(1\times2)}$$
$$= £2.85509$$
$$P_{\text{1.5-yr cash flow, 1.5-yr bond}} = £100 - £2.94118 - £2.85509$$
$$= £94.20373.$$

---

[12] Of course, intuitively we would have concluded that the six-month spot rate was 4 per cent, without the need to apply the arithmetic, as we had already assumed that the six-month bond was a quasi-zero-coupon bond.

$$rs_3 = 2 \times \left(\sqrt[(1.5 \times 2)]{£103 \ / \ £94.20373} - 1 \right)$$
$$= 0.0604071$$
$$= 6.04071\%.$$

Extending the same process for the remaining bonds, we calculate the implied two-year spot rate rs_4 to be 7.0906%, and rates rs_5 and rs_6 to be 8.1614% and 9.25403% respectively.

The interest rates rs_1, rs_2, rs_3, rs_4, rs_5 and rs_6 describe the true zero-coupon or spot rates for the 6-month, 1-year, 1.5-year, 2-year, 2.5-year and 3-year terms that begin on 2 January 2000 and end on 2 July 2000, 2 January 2001, 2 July 2001, 2 January 2002, 2 July 2002 and 2 January 2003 respectively. They are also called implied spot rates because they have been calculated from redemption yields observed in the market from the benchmark government bonds that were listed in Table 3.3.

Note that the 1-, 1.5-, 2-, 2.5- and 3-year implied spot rates are progressively greater than the corresponding redemption yields for these terms. This is an important result, mentioned briefly in the previous section,[13] and occurs whenever the yield curve is positively sloped. The reason for this is that the present values of a bond's shorter-dated cash flows are discounted at rates that are lower than the redemption yield; this generates higher present values that, when subtracted from the current price of the bond, produce a lower present value for the final cash flow. This lower present value implies a spot rate that is greater than the issue's yield. In an inverted yield curve environment we observe the opposite result, that is, implied rates that lie below the corresponding redemption yields. If the redemption yield curve is flat, the implied spot rates will be equal to the corresponding redemption yields.

Once we have calculated the spot or zero-coupon rates for the 6-month, 1-year, 1.5-year, 2-year, 2.5-year and 3-year terms, we can determine the rate of return that is implied by the yield curve for the sequence of six-month periods beginning on 2 January 2000, 2 July 2000, 2 January 2001, 2 July 2001 and 2 January 2002. These period rates are referred to as *implied forward rates* or *forward-forward rates* and we denote these as rf_i, where rf_i is the implied six-month forward interest rate today for the ith period.

Since the implied six-month zero-coupon rate (spot rate) describes the return for a term that coincides precisely with the first of the series of six-month periods, this rate describes the risk-free rate of return for the first six-month period. It is therefore equal to the first period spot rate. Thus we have $rf_1 = rs_1 = 4.0\%$, where rf_1 is the risk-free forward rate for the first six-month period beginning at period 1. The risk-free rates for the second, third, fourth, fifth and sixth six-month periods, designated rf_2, rf_3, rf_4, rf_5 and rf_6 respectively, may be solved from the implied spot rates.

The benchmark rate for the second semi-annual period, rf_2, is referred to as the one-period forward six-month rate, because it goes into effect one six-month period from now ("one-period forward") and remains in effect for six months ("six-month rate"). It is therefore the six-month rate in six months' time, and is also referred to as the 6-month forward-forward rate. This rate, in conjunction with the rate from the first period, rf_1, must provide returns that match those generated by the implied one-year spot rate for the entire one-year term. In other words, one pound invested for six months from 2 January 2000 to 2 July 2000 at the first period's benchmark rate of 4% and then reinvested for another six months from 2 July 2000 to 2 January 2001 at the second period's (as yet unknown) implied *forward* rate must enjoy

---

[13] See Campbell *et al* (1997).

the same returns as one pound invested for one year from 2 January 2000 to 2 January 2001 at the implied one-year *spot* rate. This reflects the law of no-arbitrage.

A moment's thought will convince us that this must be so. If it were not the case, there might exist an interest rate environment in which the return over any given term would depend on whether an investment is made at the start period for the entire maturity term, or over a succession of periods within the whole term and re-invested at points in between. If there were any discrepancies between the returns received from each approach, there would exist an unrealistic arbitrage opportunity, in which investments for a given term carrying a lower return might be sold short against the simultaneous purchase of investments for the same period carrying a higher return, thereby locking in a risk-free, cost-free profit. Therefore, forward interest rates must be calculated so that they are *arbitrage-free*. Excellent mathematical explanations of the no-arbitrage property of interest-rate markets are contained in Ingersoll (1987), Jarrow (1996), and Shiller (1990) among others.

The existence of a no-arbitrage market of course makes it straightforward to calculate forward rates; we know that the return from an investment made over a period must equal the return made from investing in a shorter period and successively reinvesting to a matching term. If we know the return over the shorter period, we are left with only one unknown – the full-period forward rate, which is then easily calculated. In our example, having established the rate for the first six-month period, the rate for the second six-month period – the one-period forward six-month rate – is determined below.

The future value of £1 invested at rf_1, the period 1 forward rate, at the end of the first six-month period is calculated as follows:

$$FV_1 = £1 \times \left(1 + \frac{rf_1}{2}\right)^{(0.5\times2)}$$

$$= £1 \times \left(1 + \frac{0.04}{2}\right)^1$$

$$= £1.02000.$$

The future value of £1 at the end of the one-year term, invested at the implied benchmark one-year spot rate, is determined as follows:

$$FV_2 = £1 \times \left(1 + \frac{rs_2}{2}\right)^{(1\times2)}$$

$$= £1 \times \left(1 + \frac{0.0501256}{2}\right)^2$$

$$= £1.050754.$$

The implied benchmark one-period forward rate, rf_2, is the rate that equates the value of FV_1 (£1.02) on 2 July 2000 to FV_2 (£1.050754) on 2 January 2001. From equation (3.26) we have:

$$rf_2 = 2 \times {}^{(0.5\times2)}\sqrt{\frac{FV_2}{FV_1}} - 1$$

$$= 2 \times \left(\frac{£1.050754}{£1.02} - 1\right)$$

$$= 0.060302$$

$$= 6.0302\%.$$

In other words, £1 invested from 2 January to 2 July at 4.0% (the implied forward rate for the first period) and then reinvested from 2 July to 2 January 2001 at 6.0302% (the implied forward rate for the second period) would accumulate the same returns as £1 invested from 2 January 2000 to 2 January 2001 at 5.01256% (the implied one-year spot rate).

The rate for the third six-month period – the two-period forward six-month interest rate – may be calculated in the same way:

$$FV_2 = £1.050754$$
$$FV_3 = £1 \times (1 + rs_3/2)^{(1.5 \times 2)}$$
$$= £1 \times (1 + 0.0604071/2)^3$$
$$= £1.093375$$
$$rf_3 = 2 \times \left(\sqrt[(0.5 \times 2)]{\frac{FV_3}{FV_4}} - 1 \right)$$
$$= 2 \times \left(\sqrt[3]{£1.093375/£1.050754} - 1 \right)$$
$$= 0.081125$$
$$= 8.1125\%.$$

In the same way the three-period forward six-month rate, rf_4, is calculated to be 10.27247%, and rates rf_5 and rf_6 are shown to be 12.59% and 15.23% respectively.

The results of the implied spot (zero-coupon) and forward rate calculations along with the given yield curve are displayed in Table 3.4, and illustrated graphically in Figure 3.5.

Term to maturity (years)	Cash market yield	Implied spot rate	Implied one-period forward rate
0.5	4.00000%	4.00000%	4.00000%
1	5.00000%	5.01256%	6.03023%
1.5	6.00000%	6.04071%	8.11251%
2	7.00000%	7.09062%	10.27247%
2.5	8.00000%	8.16140%	12.59782%
3	9.00000%	9.25403%	15.23100%

Table 3.4: Implied spot and forward rates.

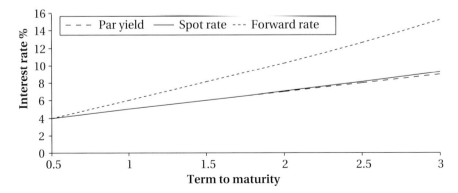

Figure 3.5: Implied spot and forward rates.

This methodology can be applied using a spreadsheet for actual market redemption yields, although in practice we will not have a set of bonds with exact and/or equal periods to maturity and coupons falling on the same date; thus it is necessary to use another technique such as *cubic spline* interpolation. In designing a spreadsheet spot rate calculator therefore, the coupon rate and maturity date is entered as standing data and usually interpolation is used when calculating the spot rates for bonds with uneven maturity dates.

The theoretical approach described above is neat and appealing, but in practice there are a number of issues that will complicate the attempt to extract zero-coupon rates from bond yields. The main problem is that it is highly unlikely that we will have a set of bonds that are both precisely six months (or one interest period) apart in maturity and priced precisely at par. We also require our procedure to fit as smooth a curve as possible. Setting our coupon bonds at a price of par simplified the analysis in our illustration of bootstrapping, so in reality we need to apply more advanced techniques . A basic approach for extracting zero-coupon bond prices is described in the next section.

3.4.2 *Calculating spot rates in practice*

Researchers have applied econometric techniques to the problem of extracting a zero-coupon term structure from coupon bond prices. The most well-known approaches are described in McCulloch (1971, 1975), Schaefer (1981), Nelson and Siegel (1987), Deacon and Derry (1994), Adams and Van Deventer (1994) and Waggoner (1997), to name but a few. The most accessible article is probably the one by Deacon and Derry.[14] In addition, a good overview of all the main approaches is contained in James and Webber (2000); Chapters 15–18 of their book provide an excellent summary of the research highlights to date.

We have noted that a coupon bond may be regarded as a portfolio of zero-coupon bonds. By treating a set of coupon bonds as a larger set of zero-coupon bonds, we can extract an (implied) zero-coupon interest rate structure from the yields on the coupon bonds.

If the actual term structure is observable, so that we know the prices of zero-coupon bonds of £1 nominal value $P_1, P_2, \ldots, P_N$, then the price, P_C, of a coupon bond of nominal value £1 and coupon C is given by

$$P_C = P_1 C + P_2 C + \cdots + P_N (1 + C). \qquad (3.28)$$

Conversely, if we can observe the coupon bond yield curve, so that we know the prices P_{C1}, $P_{C2}, \ldots, P_{CN}$, then we may use (3.28) to extract the implied zero-coupon term structure. We begin with the one-period coupon bond, for which the price is

$$P_{C1} = P_1 (1 + C),$$

so that

$$P_1 = \frac{P_{C1}}{(1 + C)}. \qquad (3.29)$$

This process is repeated. Once we have the set of zero-coupon bond prices $P_1, P_2, \ldots, P_{N-1}$ we obtain P_N using

$$P_N = \frac{P_{CN} - P_{N-1} C - \cdots - P_1 C}{1 + C}. \qquad (3.30)$$

---

[14] This is in the author's opinion. Those with a good grounding in econometrics will find all these references both readable and accessible. Further recommended references are given in the bibliography.

At this point we apply a regression technique known as *ordinary least squares* (OLS) to fit the term structure. Discussing this is outside the scope of this book; interested readers should consult Chapters 2–8 of Gujarati (1995). This is an introduction to econometrics and is highly readable.

Expression (3.28) restricts the prices of coupon bonds to be precise functions of the other coupon bond prices. In fact this is unlikely in practice because specific bonds will be treated differently according to liquidity, tax effects and so on. For this reason we add an *error term* to (3.28) and estimate the value using cross-sectional regression against all the other bonds in the market. If we say that these bonds are numbered $i = 1, 2, \dots, I$ then the regression is given by

$$P_{C_i N_i} = P_1 C_i + P_2 C_i + \cdots + P_{N_i}(1 + C_i) + u_i \tag{3.31}$$

for $i = 1, 2, \dots, I$ and where C_i is the coupon on the ith bond and N_i is the maturity of the ith bond. In (3.31) the regressor parameters are the coupon payments at each interest period date, and the coefficients are the prices of the zero-coupon bonds P_1 to P_N where $i = 1, 2, \dots, N$. The values are obtained using OLS as long as we have a complete term structure and that $I \geq N$.

In practice we will not have a complete term structure of coupon bonds and so we are not able to identify the coefficients in (3.20). McCulloch (1971, 1975) describes a *spline estimation* method, which assumes that zero-coupon bond prices vary smoothly with term to maturity. In this approach we define P_N, a function of maturity $P(N)$, as a *discount function* given by

$$P(N) = 1 + \sum_{j=1}^{J} a_j f_j(N) \tag{3.32}$$

The function $f_j(N)$ is a known function of maturity, N, and the coefficients a_j must be estimated. We arrive at a regression equation by substituting (3.32) into (3.31) to give us (3.33), which can be estimated using OLS.

$$\prod_i = \sum_{j=1}^{J} a_j X_{ij} + u_i \qquad i = 1, 2, \dots, I \tag{3.33}$$

where

$$\prod_i \equiv P_{C_i N_i} - 1 - C_i N_i$$

$$X_{ij} \equiv f_j(N_i) + C_i \sum_{l=1}^{N_i} f_j(l)$$

The function $f_j(N_i)$ is usually specified by setting the discount function as a polynomial. In certain texts, including McCulloch, this is carried out by applying what is known as a *spline* function. Considerable academic research has gone into the use of spline functions as a yield-curve fitting technique; however, we are not able to go into the required level of detail here, so readers should refer to the bibliography for further information. For a specific discussion on using regression techniques for spline-curve fitting methods see Suits *et al* (1978).

3.5   Term structure hypotheses

As befits a subject that has been the target of extensive research, a number of hypotheses have been put forward that seek to explain the term structure of interest rates. These hypotheses describe why yield curves assume certain shapes, and relate maturity terms with spot and forward rates. In this section we briefly review these hypotheses.

3.5.1 *The expectations hypothesis*

Simply put the *expectations hypothesis* states that the slope of the yield curve reflects the market's expectations about future interest rates. There are in fact four main versions of the hypothesis, each distinct from the other and each not compatible with the others. The expectations hypothesis has a long history, first being described in 1896 by Fisher and later developed by Hicks (1946) among others.[15] As Shiller (1990) describes, the thinking behind it probably stems from the way market participants discuss their view on future interest rates when assessing whether to purchase long-dated or short-dated bonds. For instance, if interest rates are expected to fall, investors will purchase long-dated bonds in order to "lock in" the current high long-dated yield. If all investors act in the same way, the yield on long-dated bonds will of course decline as prices rise in response to demand. This yield will remain low as long as short-dated rates are expected to fall, and will revert to a higher level only once the demand for long-term rates is reduced. Therefore, downward-sloping yield curves are an indication that interest rates are expected to fall, whilst an upward-sloping curve reflects market expectations of a rise in short-term interest rates.

Let us briefly consider the main elements of the discussion. The *unbiased expectations hypothesis* states that current forward rates are unbiased predictors of future spot rates. Let $f_t(T, T+1)$ be the forward rate at time t for the period from T to $T+1$. If the one-period spot rate at time T is r_T then according to the unbiased expectations hypothesis

$$f_t(T, T+1) = E_t[r_T];$$ (3.34)

which states that the forward rate $f_t(T, T+1)$ is the expected value of the future one-period spot rate given by r_T at time T.

The *return-to-maturity expectations hypothesis* states that the return generated from an investment of term t to T by holding a $(T-t)$-period bond will be equal to the expected return generated by a holding a series of one-period bonds and continually rolling them over on maturity. More formally we write

$$\frac{1}{P(t,T)} = E_t[(1+r_t)(1+r_{t+1})\cdots(1+r_{T-1})].$$ (3.35)

The left-hand side of (3.35) represents the return received by an investor holding a zero-coupon bond to maturity, which is equal to the expected return associated with rolling over £1 from time t to time T by continually re-investing one-period maturity bonds, each of which has a yield of the future spot rate r_t. A good argument for this hypothesis is contained in Jarrow (1996, page 52), which states that essentially in an environment of *economic equilibrium* the returns on zero-coupon bonds of similar maturity cannot be significantly different, otherwise investors would not hold the bonds with the lower return. A similar argument can be put forward with relation to coupon bonds of differing maturities. Any difference in yield would not, therefore, disappear as equilibrium was re-established. However there are a number of reasons why investors will hold shorter-dated bonds, irrespective of the yield available on them, so it is possible for the return-to-maturity version of the hypothesis not to apply.[16] In essence this version of the hypothesis represents an equilibrium condition in

---

[15] See the footnote on page 644 of Shiller (1990) for a fascinating historical note on the origins of the expectations hypothesis. An excellent overview of the hypothesis itself is contained in Ingersoll (1987, pages 389–392).

[16] See Rubenstein (1999, pp. 82–85) for an accessible explanation of why this can happen.

which expected *holding period returns* are equal, although it does not state that this return will be the same from different bond-holding strategies.

From (3.34) and (3.35) we see that the unbiased expectations hypothesis and the return-to-maturity hypothesis are not compatible with each other, unless there is no correlation between future interest rates. As Ingersoll (1987) notes, although it would be both possible and interesting to model such an economic environment, it is not related to economic reality, as interest rates are highly correlated. Given positive correlation between rates over a period of time, bonds with maturity terms longer than two periods will have a higher price under the unbiased expectations hypothesis than under the return-to-maturity version. Bonds of exactly two-period maturity will have the same price.

The *yield-to-maturity expectations hypothesis* is described in terms of yields. It is given by

$$\left[\frac{1}{P(t,T)}\right]^{\frac{1}{T-t}} = E_t\left[\left((1+r_t)(1+r_{t+1})\cdots(1+r_{T-1})\right)^{\frac{1}{T-t}}\right],\qquad(3.36)$$

where the left-hand side specifies the yield-to-maturity of the zero-coupon bond at time t. In this version the expected holding period *yield* on continually rolling over a series of one-period bonds will be equal to the yield that is guaranteed by holding a long-dated bond until maturity.

The *local expectations hypothesis* states that all bonds will generate the same expected rate of return if held over a small term. It is given by

$$\frac{E_t[P(t+1,T)]}{P(t,T)} = 1+r_t.\qquad(3.37)$$

This version of the hypothesis is the only one that is consistent with no-arbitrage, because the expected rates of return on all bonds are equal to the risk-free interest rate. For this reason the local expectations hypothesis is sometimes referred to as *the risk-neutral* expectations hypothesis.

3.5.2 *Liquidity premium hypothesis*

The liquidity premium hypothesis arises from the natural desire for borrowers to borrow long while lenders prefer to lend short. It states that current forward rates differ from future spot rates by an amount that is known as the *liquidity premium*. It is expressed as

$$f_t(T,T+1) = E_t[r_T] + \pi_t(T,T+1)\qquad(3.38)$$

where π_t is the liquidity premium.

Expression (3.38) states that the forward rate $f_t(T,T+1)$ is the expected value of the future one-period spot rate given by r_T at time T plus the liquidity premium, which is a function of the maturity of the bond (or term of loan). This premium reflects the conflicting requirements of borrowing and lenders, while traders and speculators will borrow short and lend long, in an effort to earn the premium. The liquidity premium hypothesis has been described in Hicks (1946).

3.5.3 *Segmented markets hypothesis*

The *segmented markets hypothesis* seeks to explain the shape of the yield curve by stating that different types of market participants invest in different sectors of the term structure, according to their requirements. So for instance, the banking sector has a requirement for short-dated bonds, while pension funds will invest in the long end of the market. This was first described in Culbertson (1957). There may also be regulatory reasons why different investors have preferences for particular maturity investments. A *preferred habitat* theory was described in Modigliani and Sutch (1967), which states not only that investors have a preferred maturity but also that they may move outside this sector if they receive a premium for so doing. This would explain "humped" shapes in yield curves. The preferred habitat theory may be viewed as a version of the liquidity preference hypothesis, where the preferred habitat is the short-end of the yield curve, so that longer-dated bonds must offer a premium in order to entice investors to hold them. This is described in Cox, Ingersoll and Ross (1981).

Appendices

Appendix 3.1:   The derivation of the bond price equation in continuous time

This section summarises the description given in Ross (1999), on pages 54–56, and describes the derivation of the standard bond price equation. This reference is excellent, very readable and accessible, and is highly recommended. We replace Ross's terminology of investment at time 0 for maturity at time *t* with the terms *t* and *T* respectively, which is consistent with the price equations given in the main text in this chapter. We also use the symbol *M* for the maturity value of the money market account, again to maintain consistency with the expressions used in this book.

Assume a continuously compounded interest rate $r(s)$ that is payable on a money market account at time s. This is the instantaneous interest rate at time s. Assume further that an investor places x in this account at time s; after a very short time period of time, h, the account would contain

$$x_h \approx x(1 + r(s)h). \tag{3.39}$$

Suppose that $M(T)$ is the amount that will be in the account at time T if an investor deposits £1 at time t. To calculate $M(T)$ in terms of the spot rate, $r(s)$, where $t \le s \le T$, for an incremental change in time of h, we have

$$M(s + h) \approx M(s)(1 + r(s)h) \tag{3.40}$$

which leads us to

$$M(s + h) - M(s) \approx M(s)r(s)h \tag{3.41}$$

and

$$\frac{M(s + h) - M(s)}{h} \approx M(s)r(s). \tag{3.42}$$

The approximation given by (3.42) turns into an equality as the time represented by h becomes progressively smaller. At the limit given as h approaches zero, we say

$$M'(s) = M(s)r(s) \tag{3.43}$$

which can be rearranged to give

$$\frac{M'(s)}{M(s)} = r(s). \tag{3.44}$$

From expression (3.44) we imply that in a continuous time process

$$\int_t^T \frac{M'(s)}{M(s)} ds = \int_t^T r(s) ds,$$

(3.45)

and that

$$\log(M(T)) - \log(M(t)) = \int_t^T r(s) ds.$$

(3.46)

However we deposited £1 at time t, that is $M(t) = 1$, so from (3.46) we obtain the value of the money market account at T to be

$$M(T) = \exp\left(\int_t^T r(s) ds\right),$$

(3.47)

which was our basic equation shown as (3.19).

Let us now introduce a risk-free zero-coupon bond that has a maturity value of £1 when it is redeemed at time T. If the spot rate is constant, then the price at time t of this bond is given by

$$P(t,T) = e^{-r(T-t)}$$

(3.48)

where r is the continuously compounded instantaneous interest rate. The right-hand side of (3.48) is the expression for the present value of £1, payable at time T, discounted at time t at the continuously compounded, constant interest rate r.

So we say that $P(t,T)$ is the present value at time t of £1 to be received at time T. Since a deposit of $1/M(T)$ at time t will have a value of 1 at time T, we are able to say that

$$P(t,T) = \frac{1}{M(T)} = \exp\left(-\int_t^T r(s) ds\right),$$

which is our bond price equation in continuous time.

If we say that the *average* of the spot interest rates from t to T is denoted by $rf(T)$, so we have $rf(T) = (1/T)\int_t^T r(s) ds$, then the function $rf(T)$ is the term structure of interest rates.

Selected bibliography and references

Adams, K., Van Deventer, D., "Fitting Yield Curves and Forward Rate Curves with Maximum Smoothness", *Journal of Fixed Income* 4, 1994, pp. 52–62
Avellaneda, M., *Quantitative Modelling of Derivative Securities*, Chapman & Hall 2000
Baxter, M., Rennie, A., *Financial Calculus*, Cambridge University Press 1996, Chapter 5
Cambell, J., Lo, A., MacKinlay, A., *The Econometrics of Financial Markets*, Princeton University Press 1997, Chapters 10–11
Cox, J., Ingersoll, J., Ross, S., "An Inter-Temporal General Equilibrium Model of Asset Prices", *Econometrica* 53, 1985
Culbertson, J., "The Term Structure of Interest Rates", *Quarterly Journal of Economics*, LXII, 1957, pp. 489–504
Deacon, M., Derry, A., "Estimating the Term Structure of Interest Rates", *Bank of England Working Paper Series* No 24, July 1994
Duffie, D., *Dynamic Asset Pricing Theory*, Princeton University Press, 1996
Fabozzi, F., *Bond Markets, Analysis and Strategies*, 2nd edition, Prentice Hall 1993, Chapter 5
Fabozzi, F., *Fixed Income Mathematics*, McGraw-Hill 1997
Gujarati, D., *Basic Econometrics*, 3rd edition, McGraw-Hill 1995

Hicks, J., *Value and Capital*, 2nd edition, Oxford University Press 1946

Ingersoll, J. Jr., *Theory of Financial Decision Making*, Rowman & Littlefield 1987, Chapter 18

Jarrow, R., *Modelling Fixed Income Securities and Interest Rate Options*, McGraw-Hill 1996, Chapter 3

James, J., Webbe, N., *Interest Rate Modelling*, Wiley 2000

McCulloch, J., "Measuring the Term Structure of Interest Rates", *Journal of Business* 44, 1971, pp. 19–31

McCulloch, J., "The Tax-Adjusted Yield Curve", *Journal of Finance* 30, 1975, pp. 811–830

Modigliani, F., Sutch, R., "Innovations in Interest Rate Policy", *American Economic Review* 56, 1967, pp. 178–197

Neftci, S., *An Introduction to the Mathematics of Financial Derivatives*, 2nd edition, Academic Press 2000, Chapter 18

Nelson, C., Siegel, A., "Parsimonious Modelling of Yield Curves, *Journal of Business* 60(4), 1987, pp. 473–489

Ross, Sheldon M., *An Introduction to Mathematical Finance*, Cambridge University Press 1999

Rubinstein, M., *Rubinstein on Derivatives*, RISK Books, 1999, pp. 82–85

Schaefer, S., "Measuring a Tax-Specific Term Structure of Interest Rates in the Market for British Government Securities", *Economic Journal* 91, 1981, pp. 415–438

Shiller, R., "The Term Structure of Interest Rates", in Friedman, B., Hanh, F., (eds), *Handbook of Monetary Economics*, Volume 1, North Holland 1990, Chapter 13

Suits, D., Mason, A., Chan, L., "Spline Functions Fitted by Standard Regression Methods", *Review of Economics and Statistics*, 60, 1978, pp. 132–139

Sundaresan, S., *Fixed Income Markets and Their Derivatives*, South-Western 1997

Van Deventer, D., Imai, K., *Financial Risk Analytics*, Irwin 1997

Van Horne, J., *Financial Management and Policy*, 10th edition, Prentice Hall 1995

Waggoner, D., "Spline Methods for Extracting Interest Rate Curves from Coupon Bond Prices", *Working Paper, Federal Reserve Bank of Atlanta*, 97-10, 1997

Windas, T., *An Introduction to Option-Adjusted Spread Analysis*, Bloomberg Publishing 1993

4 Market Background: *The Money Markets*

Repo is essentially a money market instrument. In terms of trading volumes, the *money markets* are the largest and most active market in the world. Money market securities are securities with maturities of up to twelve months, so they are short-term debt obligations. Money market debt is an important segment of the global financial markets, and facilitates the smooth running of the banking industry as well as providing working capital for industrial and commercial corporate institutions. The market allows issuers, who are financial organisations as well as corporates, to raise funds for short-term periods at relatively low interest rates. These issuers include sovereign governments, who issue Treasury bills, corporates issuing commercial paper and banks issuing bills and certificates of deposit. At the same time, investors are attracted to the market because the instruments are highly liquid and carry relatively low credit risk. Investors in the money market include banks, local authorities, corporations, money market investment funds and individuals; however, the money market essentially is a wholesale market and the denominations of individual instruments are relatively large.

Although the money market is traditionally defined as the market for instruments maturing in one year or less, frequently the money market desks of banks trade instruments with maturities of up to two years, both cash and off balance-sheet.[1] In addition to the cash instruments that go to make up the market, the money markets also consist of a wide range of over-the-counter off-balance sheet derivative instruments. These instruments are used mainly to establish future borrowing and lending rates, and to hedge or change existing interest rate exposure. This activity is carried out by banks, central banks and corporates. The main derivatives are short-term interest rate futures, forward rate agreements, and short-dated interest rate swaps.

In this chapter we review the cash instruments traded in the money market as well as the two main money market derivatives: interest-rate futures and forward-rate agreements.

4.1 Overview

The cash instruments traded in the money market include the following:

- Treasury bill;
- Time deposit;
- Certificate of Deposit;
- Commercial Paper (CP);
- Bankers acceptance;
- Bill of exchange.

---

[1] The author has personal experience in market-making on a desk that combined cash and derivative instruments of up to two years maturity as well as government bonds of up to three years maturity.

70

A Treasury bill is used by sovereign governments to raise short-term funds, while certificates of deposit (CDs) are used by banks to raise finance. The other instruments are used by corporates and occasionally banks. Each instrument represents an obligation on the borrower to repay the amount borrowed on the maturity date together with interest if this applies. The instruments above fall into one of two main classes of money market securities: those quoted on a *yield* basis and those quoted on a *discount* basis. These two terms are discussed below.

The calculation of interest in the money markets often differs from the calculation of accrued interest in the corresponding bond market. Generally, the day-count convention in the money market is the exact number of days that the instrument is held divided by the number of days in the year. In the sterling market the year base is 365 days, so the interest calculation for sterling money market instruments is given by (4.1).

$$i = \frac{n}{365} \tag{4.1}$$

Money markets that calculate interest based on a 365-day year are listed at Appendix 4.1. The majority of currencies including the US dollar and the euro calculate interest based on a 360-day base. The process by which an interest rate quoted on one basis is converted to one quoted on the other basis is shown in Appendix 4.1.

Settlement of money market instruments can be for value today (generally only when traded before midday), tomorrow or two days forward, known as *spot*.

4.2 Securities quoted on a yield basis

Two of the instruments in the list above are yield-based instruments.[2]

4.2.1 *Money market deposits*

These are fixed-interest term deposits of up to one year with banks and securities houses. They are also known as *time deposits* or *clean deposits*. They are not negotiable so cannot be liquidated before maturity. The interest rate on the deposit is fixed for the term and related to the London Interbank Offer Rate (LIBOR or Libor) of the same term. Interest and capital are paid on maturity.

LIBOR

The term LIBOR or "Libor" comes from London Interbank Offer Rate and is the interest rate at which one London bank offers funds to another London bank of acceptable credit quality in the form of a cash deposit. The rate is "fixed" by the British Bankers Association at 1100 hours every business day morning (in practice the fix is usually about 20 minutes later) by taking the average of the rates supplied by member banks. The term LIBID is the banks' "bid" rate, that is, the rate at which they pay for funds in the London market. The quote spread for a selected maturity is therefore the difference between LIBOR and LIBID. The convention in London is to quote the two rates as LIBOR-LIBID, thus matching the yield convention for other instruments. In some other markets the quote convention is reversed. EURIBOR is the interbank rate offered for euros as reported by the European Central Bank. Other money centres also have their rates fixed, so for example STIBOR is the Stockholm banking rate, while pre-euro the Portuguese escudo rate fixing out of Lisbon was LISBOR.

---

[2]   And to these two products we may also add the classic repo instrument.

The effective rate on a money market deposit is the annual equivalent interest rate for an instrument with a maturity of less than one year.

4.2.2   *Certificates of Deposit*

Certificates of Deposit (CDs) are receipts from banks for deposits that have been placed with them. They were first introduced in the sterling market in 1958. The deposits themselves carry a fixed rate of interest related to LIBOR and have a fixed term to maturity, so cannot be withdrawn before maturity. However, the certificates themselves can be traded in a secondary market, that is, they are negotiable.[3] CDs are therefore very similar to negotiable money market deposits, although the yields are about 0.15% below the equivalent deposit rates because of the added benefit of liquidity. Most CDs issued are of between one and three months maturity, although they do trade in maturities of one to five years. Interest is paid on maturity except for CDs lasting longer than one year, where interest is paid annually or, occasionally, semi-annually.

Banks, merchant banks and building societies issue CDs to raise funds to finance their business activities. A CD will have a stated interest rate and fixed maturity date and can be issued in any denomination. On issue a CD is sold for face value, so the settlement proceeds of a CD on issue always equal its nominal value. The interest is paid, together with the face amount, on maturity. The interest rate is sometimes called the *coupon*, but unless the CD is held to maturity this will not equal the yield, which is of course, the current rate available in the market and varies over time. In the United States CDs are available in smaller denomination amounts to retail investors.[4] The largest group of CD investors are banks themselves, money market funds, corporates and local authority treasurers.

Unlike coupons on bonds, which are paid in rounded amounts, CD coupon is calculated to the exact day.

CD yields. The coupon quoted on a CD is a function of the credit quality of the issuing bank, its expected liquidity level in the market, and of course the maturity of the CD, as this will be considered relative to the money market yield curve. As CDs are issued by banks as part of their short-term funding and liquidity requirement, issue volumes are driven by the demand for bank loans and the availability of alternative sources of funds for bank customers. The credit quality of the issuing bank is the primary consideration; in the sterling market the lowest yield is paid by "clearer" CDs, which are CDs issued by the clearing banks such as RBS NatWest, HSBC and Barclays plc. In the US market "prime" CDs, issued by highly-rated domestic banks, trade at a lower yield than non-prime CDs. In both markets CDs issued by foreign banks, such as French or Japanese banks, will trade at higher yields.

Euro-CDs, which are CDs issued in a different currency to the home currency, also trade at higher yields, in the US because of reserve and deposit insurance restrictions.

If the current market price of the CD, including accrued interest, is P and the current quoted yield is r, the yield can be calculated (given the price) using (4.2).

$$r = \left(\frac{M}{P} \times \left(1 + C\left(\frac{N_{im}}{B} \right) \right) - 1 \right) \times \left(\frac{B}{N_{sm}} \right). \tag{4.2}$$

Given the yield, the price can be calculated using (4.3).

---

3   A small number of CDs are non-negotiable.
4   This was first introduced by Merrill Lynch in 1982.

$$P = M \times \frac{(1 + C(N_{im}/B))}{(1 + r(N_{sm}/B))}$$

$$= F/(1 + r(N_{sm}/B)) \tag{4.3}$$

where

C	is the quoted coupon on the CD;
M	is the face value of the CD;
B	is the year day-basis (365 or 360);
F	is the maturity value of the CD;
N_{im}	is the number of days between issue and maturity;
N_{sm}	is the number of days between settlement and maturity;
N_{is}	is the number of days between issue and settlement.

After issue a CD can be traded in the secondary market. The secondary market in CDs in the UK is very liquid, and CDs will trade at the rate prevalent at the time, which will invariably be different from the coupon rate on the CD at issue. When a CD is traded in the secondary market, the settlement proceeds will need to take into account interest that has accrued on the paper and the different rate at which the CD has now been dealt. The formula for calculating the settlement figure is given by (4.4), which applies to the sterling market and its 365-day count basis.

$$\text{Proceeds} = \frac{M \times \text{tenor} \times C \times 100 + 36500}{\text{days remaining} \times r \times 100 + 36500} \tag{4.4}$$

The *tenor* of a CD is the life of the CD in days, while *days remaining* is the number of days left to maturity from the time of trade.

The return on holding a CD is given by (4.5).

$$\text{Return} = \left(\frac{(1 + \text{purchase yield} \times (\text{days from purchase to maturity}/B))}{1 + \text{sale yield} \times (\text{days from sale to maturity}/B)} - 1 \right) \times \frac{B}{\text{days held}} \tag{4.5}$$

Example 4.1

◆ A three-month CD is issued on 6 September 1999 and matures on 6 December 1999 (maturity of 91 days). It has a face value of £20,000,000 and a coupon of 5.45%. What are the total maturity proceeds?

$$\text{Proceeds} = 20 \text{ million} \times \left(1 + 0.0545 \times \frac{91}{365} \right) = £20,271,753.42.$$

◆ What is the secondary market price on 11 October if the yield for short 60-day paper is 5.60%?

$$P = \frac{20.271\text{m}}{\left(1 + 0.056 \times \frac{56}{365} \right)} = £20,099,066.64.$$

◆ On 18 November the yield on short three-week paper is 5.215%. What rate of return is earned from holding the CD for the 38 days from 11 October to 18 November?

$$R = \left(\frac{1 + 0.0560 \times (56/365)}{1 + 0.05215 \times (38/365)} - 1 \right) \times \frac{365}{38} = 9.6355\%.$$

4.3   Securities quoted on a discount basis

The remaining money market instruments are all quoted on a *discount* basis, and so are known as "discount" instruments. This means that they are issued on a discount to face value, and are redeemed on maturity at face value. Treasury bills, bills of exchange, bankers acceptances and commercial paper are examples of money market securities that are quoted on a discount basis, that is, they are sold on the basis of a discount to par. The difference between the price paid at the time of purchase and the redemption value (par) is the interest earned by the holder of the paper. Explicit interest is not paid on discount instruments; rather, interest is reflected implicitly in the difference between the discounted issue price and the par value received at maturity. Note that in some markets Commercial Paper is quoted on a yield basis, but not in the UK or in the US where they are discount instruments.

4.3.1   *Treasury bills*

Treasury bills, or T-bills, are short-term government "IOUs" of short duration, often three-month maturity. For example, if a bill is issued on 10 January it will mature on 10 April. Bills of one-month and six-month maturity are also issued, but only rarely in the UK market.[5] On maturity the holder of a T-bill receives the par value of the bill by presenting it to the Central Bank. In the UK most such bills are denominated in sterling but issues are also made in euros. In a capital market, T-bill yields are regarded as the *risk-free* yield, as they represent the yield from short-term government debt. In emerging markets they are often the most liquid instruments available for investors.

A sterling T-bill with £10 million face value issued for 91 days will be redeemed on maturity at £10 million. If the three-month yield at the time of issue is 5.25%, the price of the bill at issue, under the old formula, was

$$P = \frac{10,000,000}{\left(1 + 0.0525 \times \frac{91}{365}\right)} = £9,870,800.69.$$

In the UK and US markets the interest rate on discount instruments is quoted as a *discount rate* rather than a yield. This is the amount of discount expressed as an annualised percentage of the face value, and not as a percentage of the original amount paid. By definition the discount rate is always lower than the corresponding yield. If the discount rate on a bill is *d*, then the amount of discount is given by (4.6) below.

$$d_{value} = M \times d \times \frac{n}{B} \tag{4.6}$$

The price *P* paid for the bill is the face value minus the discount amount, given by (4.7).

$$P = 100 \times \left(1 - \frac{d \times (N_{sm}/365)}{100}\right) \tag{4.7}$$

If we know the yield on the bill then we can calculate its price at issue by using the simple present value formula, as shown at (4.8).

---

[5]   The BoE issued six-month bills very rarely. The DMO reserves the right to issue six-month or 364-day bills.

$$P = \frac{M}{1 + r \times (N_{sm}/365)} \tag{4.8}$$

The discount rate d for T-bills is calculated using (4.9).

$$d = (1 - P) \times \frac{B}{n} \tag{4.9}$$

The relationship between discount rate and true yield is given by (4.10).

$$d = \frac{r}{(1 + r \times (n/B))}$$
$$r = \frac{d}{1 - d \times (n/B)} \tag{4.10}$$

During 2001, the UK Debt Management Office changed the basis under which UK T-bill yields were calculated. They are now issued at tenders on a money market yield basis, with the yield calculated to three decimal places. The price formula is now

$$P = \frac{N}{\left(1 + \dfrac{r \times n}{36500}\right)} \tag{4.10a}$$

where n is the number of calendar days from the settlement date to the maturity date. The settlement proceeds P are rounded up to the nearest penny. The rate r is the yield, quoted to three decimal places.

Example 4.2

◆ A 91-day £100 Treasury bill is issued with a yield of 4.75%. What is its issue price?

$$P = \frac{£100}{1 + 0.0475(91/365)}$$
$$= £98.82.$$

◆ A UK T-bill with a remaining maturity of 39 days is quoted at a discount of 4.95% What is the equivalent yield?

$$r = \frac{0.0495}{1 - 0.0495 \times (39/365)}$$
$$= 4.976\%.$$

If a T-bill is traded in the secondary market, the settlement proceeds from the trade are calculated using (4.11).

$$\text{Proceeds} = M - \left(\frac{M \times \text{ days remaining} \times d}{B \times 100}\right). \tag{4.11}$$

Bond equivalent yield. In certain markets including the UK and US markets, the yields on government bonds that have a maturity of less than one year are compared to the yields of treasury bills; however, before the comparison can be made the yield on a bill must be converted to a "bond equivalent" yield. The bond equivalent yield of a US Treasury bill is the coupon of a theoretical Treasury bond trading at par that has an identical maturity date. If the bill has 182 days or less until maturity, the calculation required is the conventional conversion from discount rate to yield, with the exception that it is quoted on a 365-day basis (in the UK market, the quote basis is essentially the same unless it is a leap year. So the conversion element in (4.12) is not necessary). The calculation for the US market is given by (4.12),

$$rm = \frac{d}{(1 - d \times (days/360))} \times \frac{365}{360} \qquad (4.12)$$

where rm is the bond-equivalent yield that is being calculated.

Note that if there is a bill and a bond that mature on the same day in a period under 182 days, the bond-equivalent yield will not be precisely the same as the yield quoted for the bond in its final coupon period, although it is a very close approximation. This is because the bond is quoted on an actual/actual basis, so its yield is actually made up of twice the actual number of days in the interest period.

4.3.2   Bankers acceptances

A bankers acceptance is a written promise issued by a borrower to a bank to repay borrowed funds. The lending bank lends funds and in return accepts the bankers acceptance. The acceptance is negotiable and can be sold in the secondary market. The investor who buys the acceptance can collect the loan on the day that repayment is due. If the borrower defaults, the investor has legal recourse to the bank that made the first acceptance. Bankers acceptances are also known as *bills of exchange*, *bank bills*, *trade bills* or *commercial bills*.

Essentially bankers acceptances are instruments created to facilitate commercial trade transactions. The instrument is called a *bankers acceptance* because a bank accepts the ultimate responsibility to repay the loan to its holder. The use of bankers acceptances to finance commercial transactions is known as *acceptance financing*. The transactions for which acceptances are created include import and export of goods, the storage and shipping of goods between two overseas countries, where neither the importer nor the exporter is based in the home country,[6] and the storage and shipping of goods between two entities based at home. Acceptances are discount instruments and are purchased by banks, local authorities and money market investment funds. The rate that a bank charges a customer for issuing a bankers acceptance is a function of the rate at which the bank thinks it will be able to sell it in the secondary market. A commission is added to this rate. For ineligible bankers acceptances (see below) the issuing bank will add an amount to offset the cost of the additional reserve requirements.

Eligible bankers acceptance. An accepting bank that chooses to retain a bankers acceptance in its portfolio may be able to use it as collateral for a loan obtained from the central bank during open market operations, for example the Bank of England in the UK and the Federal Reserve in the US. Not all acceptances are eligible to be used as collateral in this way, as they must meet certain criteria set by the central bank. The main requirement for eligibility is that the acceptance must be within a certain maturity band (a maximum of six months in the US and three months in the UK), and that it must have been created to finance a self-liquidating commercial transaction. In the US eligibility is also important because the Federal Reserve imposes a reserve requirement on funds raised via bankers acceptances that are ineligible. Bankers acceptances sold by an accepting bank are potential liabilities of the bank, but reserve requirements impose a limit on the amount of eligible bankers acceptances that a

---

6   A bankers acceptance created to finance such a transaction is known as a *third-party acceptance*.

bank may issue. Bills eligible for deposit at a central bank enjoy a finer rate than ineligible bills, and also act as a benchmark for prices in the secondary market.

4.3.3   *Commercial paper*

Commercial paper (CP) is a short-term money market funding instrument issued by corporates. In the UK and US it is a discount instrument. They trade essentially as T-bills but with higher yields as they are unsecured corporate obligations.

Companies fund part of their medium- and long-term capital requirements in the debt capital markets, through the issue of bonds. Short-term capital and *working* capital is usually sourced directly from banks, in the form of bank loans. An alternative short-term funding instrument is commercial paper (CP), which is available to corporates that have a sufficiently strong credit rating. Commercial paper is a short-term unsecured promissory note. The issuer of the note promises to pay its holder a specified amount on a specified maturity date. CP normally has a zero coupon and trades at a *discount* to its face value. The discount represents interest to the investor in the period to maturity. CP is typically issued in bearer form, although some issues are in registered form.

Outside of the United States, CP markets were not introduced until the mid-1980s, and in 1986 the US market accounted for over 90% of outstanding commercial paper globally.[7] In the US however, the market was developed in the late nineteenth century, and as early as 1922 there were 2200 issuers of CP with $700 million outstanding. In 1998 there was just under $1 trillion outstanding. CP was first issued in the United Kingdom in 1986, and subsequently in other European countries.

Originally the CP market was restricted to borrowers with high credit rating, and although lower-rated borrowers do now issue CP, sometimes by obtaining credit enhancements or setting up collateral arrangements, issuance in the market is still dominated by highly-rated companies. The majority of issues are very short-term, from 30 to 90 days in maturity; it is extremely rare to observe paper with a maturity of more than 270 days or nine months. This is because of regulatory requirements in the US,[8] which states that debt instruments with a maturity of less than 270 days need not be registered. Companies therefore issue CP with a maturity lower than nine months and so avoid the administration costs associated with registering issues with the SEC.

There are two major markets, the US dollar market, and the Eurocommercial paper market with outstanding value of $290 billion at the end of 1998.[9] Commercial paper markets are wholesale markets, and transactions are typically very large size. In the US over a third of all CP is purchased by money market unit trusts, known as mutual funds; other investors include pension fund managers, retail or commercial banks, local authorities and corporate treasurers.

Although there is a secondary market in CP, very little trading activity takes place since investors generally hold CP until maturity. This is to be expected because investors purchase CP that match their specific maturity requirement. When an investor does wish to sell paper, it can be sold back to the dealer or, where the issuer has placed the paper directly in the market (and not via an investment bank), it can be sold back to the issuer.

---

[7]   OECD (1989).
[8]   This is the Securities Act of 1933. Registration is with the Securities and Exchange Commission.
[9]   Source: BIS.

	US CP	Eurocommercial CP
Currency	US dollar	Any Euro currency
Maturity	1–270 days	2–365 days
Common maturity	30–50 days	30–90 days
Interest	Zero coupon, issued at discount	Usually zero-coupon, issued at discount
Quotation	On a discount rate basis	On a discount rate basis or yield basis
Settlement	T + 0	T + 2
Registration	Bearer form	Bearer form
Negotiable	Yes	Yes

Table 4.1: Comparison of US CP and Eurocommercial CP.

4.3.4 *Commercial paper programmes*

The issuers of CP are often divided into two categories of company: banking and financial institutions and non-financial companies. The majority of CP issues are by financial companies. These include not only banks but the financing arms of corporates such as General Motors, Ford Motor Credit and Chrysler Financial. Most of the issuers have strong credit ratings, but lower-rated borrowers have tapped the market, often after arranging credit support from a higher-rated company, such a *letter of credit* from a bank, or by arranging collateral for the issue in the form of high-quality assets such as Treasury bonds. CP issued with credit support is known as *credit-supported commercial paper*, while paper backed with assets is known, naturally enough, as *asset-backed commercial paper*. Paper that is backed by a bank letter of credit is termed *LOC paper*. Although banks charge a fee for issuing letters of credit, borrowers are often happy to arrange for this, since by so doing they are able to tap the CP market. The yield paid on an issue of CP will be lower than a commercial bank loan.

Although CP is a short-dated security, typically of three- to six-month maturity, it is issued within a longer term programme, usually for three to five years for euro paper; US CP programmes are often open-ended. For example, a company might arrange a five-year CP programme with a limit of $500 million. Once the programme is established the company can issue CP up to this amount, say for maturities of 30 or 60 days. The programme is continuous and new CP can be issued at any time, daily if required. The total amount in issue cannot exceed the limit set for the programme. A CP programme can be used by a company to manage its short-term liquidity, that is, its working capital requirements. New paper can be issued whenever a need for cash arises, and for an appropriate maturity.

Issuers often roll over their funding and use funds from a new issue of CP to redeem a maturing issue. There is a risk that an issuer might be unable to roll over the paper where there is a lack of investor interest in the new issue. To provide protection against this risk issuers often arrange a stand-by line of credit from a bank, normally for all of the CP programme, to draw against in the event that it cannot place a new issue.

There are two methods by which CP is issued, known as *direct-issued* or *direct paper* and *dealer-issued* or *dealer paper*. Direct paper is sold by the issuing firm directly to investors, and no agent bank or securities house is involved. It is common for financial companies to issue CP directly to their customers, often because they have continuous programmes and constantly roll-over their paper. It is therefore cost-effective for them to have their own sales arm and sell their CP direct. The treasury arms of certain non-financial companies also issue direct paper; this includes, for example, British Airways plc corporate treasury, which runs a continuous direct CP programme. This is used to provide short-term working capital for the company. Dealer paper is paper that is sold using a banking or securities house intermediary. In the US, dealer CP is effectively dominated by investment banks, as retail (commercial) banks were until recently forbidden from underwriting commercial paper. This restriction has since been removed and now both investment banks and commercial banks underwrite dealer paper.

Although CP is issued within a programme, like medium-term notes (MTNs), there are of course key differences between the two types of paper, reflecting CP's status as essentially a money market instrument. The CP market is issuer-driven, with daily offerings to the market. MTNs in contrast are more investor-driven; issuers will offer them when demand appears. In this respect MTN issues are often "opportunistic", taking advantage of favourable interest rate conditions in the market.

4.4   Commercial paper yields

Commercial paper is a discount instrument. There have been issues of coupon CP, but this is very unusual. Thus CP is sold at a discount to its maturity value, and the difference between this maturity value and the purchase price is the interest earned by the investor. The CP day-count base is 360 days in the US and euro markets, and 365 days in the UK. The paper is quoted on a discount yield basis, in the same manner as Treasury bills. The yield on CP follows that of other money market instruments and is a function of the short-dated yield curve. The yield on CP is higher than the T-bill rate; this is due to the credit risk that the investor is exposed to when holding CP; for tax reasons (in certain jurisdictions interest earned on T-bills is exempt from income tax) and because of the lower level of liquidity available in the CP market. CP also pays a higher yield than Certificates of Deposit (CD), due to the lower liquidity of the CP market.

Although CP is a discount instrument and trades as such in the US and UK, euro currency Eurocommercial paper trades on a yield basis, similar to a CD. The discount rate for an instrument was discussed in Chapter 2. The expressions below are a reminder of the relationship between true yield and discount rate.

$$P = \frac{M}{1 + r \times (\text{days}/\text{year})} \tag{4.13}$$

$$rd = \frac{r}{1 + r \times (\text{days}/\text{year})} \tag{4.14}$$

$$r = \frac{rd}{1 - rd \times (\text{days}/\text{year})} \tag{4.15}$$

where M is the face value of the instrument, rd is the discount rate and r is the true yield.

Example 4.3

4.3(a)
A 60-day CP note has a nominal value of $100,000. It is issued at a discount of 7½ per cent per annum. The discount is calculated as:

$$\text{discount} = \frac{\$100,000(0.075 \times 60)}{360} = \$1,250.$$

The issue price for the CP is therefore $100,000 – $1,250, or $98,750.
The money market yield on this note at the time of issue is:

$$\left(\frac{360 \times 0.075}{360 - (0.075 \times 60)} \right) \times 100\% = 7.59\%.$$

Another way to calculate this yield is to measure the capital gain (the discount) as a percentage of the CP's cost, and convert this from a 60-day yield to a one-year (360-day) yield, as shown below.

$$r = \frac{1,250}{98,750} \times \frac{360}{60} \times 100\%$$

$$= 7.59\%.$$

Note that these are US dollar CP and therefore have a 360-day base.

4.3(b)
ABC plc wishes to issue CP with 90 days to maturity. The investment bank managing the issue advises that the discount rate should be 9.5 per cent. What should the issue price be, and what is the money market yield for investors?

$$\text{discount} = \frac{100(0.095 \times 90)}{360}$$

$$= 2.375.$$

The issue price will be 97.625.

The yield to investors will be $\frac{2.375}{97.625} \times \frac{360}{90} \times 100\% = 9.73\%.$

US Treasury bills
The Treasury bill market in the United States is one of the most liquid and transparent debt markets in the world. Consequently the bid-offer spread on them is very narrow. The Treasury issues bills at a weekly auction each Monday, made up of 91-day and 182-day bills. Every fourth week the Treasury also issues 52-week bills as well. As a result there are large numbers of Treasury bills outstanding at any one time. The interest earned on Treasury bills is not liable to state and local income taxes.

Federal funds
Commercial banks in the US are required to keep reserves on deposit at the Federal Reserve. Banks with reserves in excess of required reserves can lend these funds to other banks, and these interbank loans are called *federal funds* or *fed funds* and are usually overnight loans. Through the fed funds market, commercial banks with excess funds are able to lend to banks that are short of reserves, thus facilitating liquidity. The transactions are very large denominations, and are lent at the *fed funds rate*, which is a very volatile interest rate because it fluctuates with market shortages.

Prime rate
The *prime interest rate* in the US is often said to represent the rate at which commercial banks lend to their most creditworthy customers. In practice many loans are made at rates below the prime rate, so the prime rate is not the best rate at which highly-rated

firms may borrow. Nevertheless the prime rate is a benchmark indicator of the level of US money market rates, and is often used as a reference rate for floating-rate instruments. As the market for bank loans is highly competitive, all commercial banks quote a single prime rate, and the rate for all banks changes simultaneously.

4.5   Money market derivatives

The market in short-term interest-rate derivatives is a large and liquid one, and the instruments involved are used for a variety of purposes. Here we review the two main contracts used in money markets trading, the short-term *interest rate future* and the *forward rate agreement* (FRA). In Chapter 3 we introduced the concept of the forward rate. Money market derivatives are priced on the basis of the forward rate, and are flexible instruments for hedging against or speculating on forward interest rates. The FRA and the exchange-traded interest-rate future both date from around the same time, and although initially developed to hedge forward interest-rate exposure, they now have a range of uses. Here, the instruments are introduced and analysed, and there is a review of the main uses that they are put to. Readers interested in the concept of *convexity* bias in swap and futures pricing may wish to refer to Choudhry (2001) listed in the bibliography, which is an accessible introduction.

4.5.1   *Forward rate agreements*

A *forward rate agreement* (FRA) is an over-the-counter (OTC) derivative instrument that trades as part of the money markets. It is essentially a forward-starting loan, but with no exchange of principal, so that only the difference in interest rates is traded. Trading in FRAs began in the early 1980s and the market now is large and liquid; turnover in London exceeds $5 billion each day. So an FRA is a forward-dated loan, dealt at a fixed rate, but with no exchange of principal – only the interest applicable on the notional amount between the rate dealt at and the actual rate prevailing at the time of settlement changes hands. That is, FRAs are *off-balance-sheet* (OBS) instruments. By trading today at an interest rate that is effective at some point in the future, FRAs enable banks and corporates to hedge interest rate exposure. They are also used to speculate on the level of future interest rates.

An FRA is an agreement to borrow or lend a *notional* cash sum for a period of time lasting up to twelve months, starting at any point over the next twelve months, at an agreed rate of interest (the FRA rate). The "buyer" of a FRA is borrowing a notional sum of money while the "seller" is lending this cash sum. Note how this differs from all other money market instruments. In the cash market, the party buying a CD or Bill, or bidding for stock in the repo market, is the lender of funds. In the FRA market, to "buy" is to "borrow". We use the term "notional" because in an FRA no borrowing or lending of cash actually takes place, as it is an OBS product. The notional sum is simply the amount on which interest payment is calculated.

So when an FRA is traded, the buyer is borrowing (and the seller is lending) a specified notional sum at a fixed rate of interest for a specified period, the "loan" to commence at an agreed date in the future. The *buyer* is the notional borrower, and so if there is a rise in interest rates between the date that the FRA is traded and the date that the FRA comes into effect, they will be protected. If there is a fall in interest rates, the buyer must pay the difference between the rate at which the FRA was traded and the actual rate, as a percentage of the notional sum. The buyer may be using the FRA to hedge an actual exposure, that is an actual borrowing of money, or simply speculating on a rise in interest rates. The counterparty to the transaction, the *seller* of the FRA, is the notional lender of funds, and has fixed the rate for lending funds. If there is a fall in interest rates the seller will gain, and if there is a rise in rates the seller will pay. Again, the seller may have an actual loan of cash to hedge, or be a speculator or market-maker.

In FRA trading only the payment that arises as a result of the difference in interest rates changes hands. There is no exchange of cash at the time of the trade. The cash payment that does arise is the difference in interest rates between that at which the FRA was traded and the actual rate prevailing when the FRA matures, as a percentage of the notional amount. FRAs are traded by both banks and corporates and between banks. The FRA market is very liquid in all major currencies and rates are readily quoted on screens by both banks and brokers. Dealing is over the telephone or over a dealing system such as Reuters.

The terminology quoting FRAs refers to the borrowing time period and the time at which the FRA comes into effect (or matures). Hence if a buyer of an FRA wished to hedge against a rise in rates to cover a three-month loan starting in three months' time, they would transact a "three-against-six month" FRA, or more usually a 3x6 or 3-vs-6 FRA. This is referred to in the market as a "threes-sixes" FRA, and means a three-month loan in three months time. So a "ones-fours" FRA (1v4) is a three-month loan in one month's time, and a "three-nines" FRA (3v9) is six-month money in three months' time.

Example 4.4

A company knows that it will need to borrow £1 million in three months time for a twelve-month period. It can borrow funds today at Libor + 50 basis points. Libor rates today are at 5% but the company's treasurer expects rates to go up to about 6% over the next few weeks. So the company will be forced to borrow at higher rates unless some sort of hedge is transacted to protect the borrowing requirement. The treasurer decides to buy a 3x15 ("threes-fifteens") FRA to cover the twelve-month period beginning three months from now. A bank quotes 5½% for the FRA which the company buys for a notional £1 million. Three months from now rates have indeed gone up to 6%, so the treasurer must borrow funds at 6½% (the Libor rate plus spread); however, they will receive a settlement amount which will be the difference between the rate at which the FRA was bought and today's twelve-month Libor rate (6%) as a percentage of £1 million, which will compensate for some of the increased borrowing costs.

In virtually every market FRAs trade under a set of terms and conventions that are identical. The British Bankers Association (BBA) has compiled standard legal documentation to cover FRA trading. The following standard terms are used in the market.

- **Notional sum:** The amount for which the FRA is traded.
- **Trade date:** The date on which the FRA is dealt.
- **Spot date:** the date from which the FRA becomes effective.
- **Settlement date:** The date on which the notional loan or deposit of funds becomes effective, that is, is said to begin. This date is used, in conjunction with the notional sum, for calculation purposes only as no actual loan or deposit takes place.
- **Fixing date:** This is the date on which the *reference rate* is determined, that is, the rate to which the FRA dealing rate is compared.
- **Maturity date:** The date on which the notional loan or deposit expires.
- **Contract period:** The time between the settlement date and maturity date.

- **FRA rate:** The interest rate at which the FRA is traded.
- **Reference rate:** This is the rate used as part of the calculation of the settlement amount, usually the Libor rate on the fixing date for the contract period in question.
- **Settlement sum:** The amount calculated as the difference between the FRA rate and the reference rate as a percentage of the notional sum, paid by one party to the other on the settlement date.

These terms are illustrated in Figure 4.1.

Figure 4.1: Key dates in an FRA trade.

The spot date is usually two business days after the trade date; however, it can by agreement be sooner or later than this. The settlement date will be the time period after the spot date referred to by the FRA terms; for example, a 1x4 FRA will have a settlement date one calendar month after the spot date. The fixing date is usually two business days before the settlement date. The settlement sum is paid on the settlement date, and as it refers to an amount calculated over a period of time but which is paid up-front (at the start of the contract period) the sum is discounted. This is because a normal payment of interest on a loan/deposit is paid at the end of the time period to which it relates; because an FRA makes this payment at the *start* of the relevant period, the settlement amount is a discounted figure.

With most FRA trades the reference rate is the LIBOR fixing on the fixing date.

The settlement sum is calculated after the fixing date, for payment on the settlement date. We may illustrate this with an hypothetical example. Consider a case where a corporate has bought £1 million notional of a 1v4 FRA, and dealt at 5.75%, and that the market rate is 6.50% on the fixing date. The contract period is 90 days. In the cash market the extra interest charge that the corporate would pay is a simple interest calculation, and is:

$$\frac{6.50 - 5.75}{100} \times 1,000,000 \times \frac{91}{365} = £1869.86.$$

This extra interest that the corporate is facing would be payable with the interest payment for the loan, which (as it is a money market loan) is when the loan matures. Under a FRA then, the settlement sum payable should, if it was paid on the same day as the cash market interest charge, be exactly equal to this. This would make it a perfect hedge. As we noted above though, FRA settlement value is paid at the start of the contract period, that is, the beginning of the underlying loan and not the end. Therefore the settlement sum has to be adjusted to account for this, and the amount of the adjustment is the value of the interest that would be earned if the unadjusted cash value was invested for the contract period in the money market. The amount of the settlement value is given by (4.16).

$$Settlement = \frac{\left(r_{ref} - r_{FRA}\right) \times M \times (n/B)}{1 + \left(r_{ref} \times (n/B)\right)} \tag{4.16}$$

where

r_{ref} is the reference interest fixing rate;

r_{FRA} is the FRA rate or *contract rate*;
M is the notional value;
n is the number of days in the contract period;
B is the day-count base (360 or 365).

The expression at (4.16) simply calculates the extra interest payable in the cash market, resulting from the difference between the two interest rates, and then discounts the amount because it is payable at the start of the period and not, as would happen in the cash market, at the end of the period.

In our hypothetical illustration, as the fixing rate is higher than the dealt rate, the corporate buyer of the FRA receives the settlement sum from the seller. This then compensates the corporate for the higher borrowing costs that they would have to pay in the cash market. If the fixing rate had been lower than 5.75%, the buyer would pay the difference to the seller, because the cash market rates will mean that they are subject to a lower interest rate in the cash market. By using the FRA, the corporate is hedged so that whatever happens in the market, it will pay 5.75% on its borrowing.

A market maker in FRAs is trading short-term interest rates. The settlement sum is the value of the FRA. The concept is identical to that of trading short-term interest-rate futures; a trader who buys an FRA is running a long position, so that if on the fixing date $r_{ref} > r_{FRA}$, the settlement sum is positive and the trader realises a profit. What has happened is that the trader, by buying the FRA, "borrowed" money at an interest rate which subsequently rose. This is a gain, exactly like a *short* position in an interest-rate future, where if the price goes down (that is, interest rates go up), the trader realises a gain. Equally, a "short" position in an FRA, put on by selling an FRA, realises a gain if on the fixing date $r_{ref} < r_{FRA}$.

FRA pricing

As their name implies, FRAs are forward rate instruments and are priced using the forward rate principles we established in Chapter 3. Consider an investor who has two alternatives, either a six-month investment at 5% or a one-year investment at 6%. If the investor wishes to invest for six months and then roll-over the investment for a further six months, what rate is required for the roll-over period such that the final return equals the 6% available from the one-year investment? If we view an FRA rate as the breakeven forward rate between the two periods, we simply solve for this forward rate and that is our approximate FRA rate. This rate is sometimes referred to as the interest rate "gap" in the money markets (not to be confused with an interbank desk's *gap risk*, the interest rate exposure arising from the net maturity position of its assets and liabilities).

We can use the standard forward-rate breakeven formula to solve for the required FRA rate; we established this relationship earlier when discussing the calculation of forward rates that are arbitrage-free. The relationship given at (4.17) connects simple (bullet) interest rates for periods of time up to one year, where no compounding of interest is required. As FRAs are money market instruments we are not required to calculate rates for periods in excess of one year,[10] where compounding would need to be built into the equation. The expression is given by (4.17),

$$(1 + r_2 t_2) = (1 + r_1 t_1)(1 + r_f t_f) \tag{4.17}$$

---

[10] It is of course possible to trade FRAs with contract periods greater than one year, for which a different pricing formula must be used.

where

r_2 is the cash market interest rate for the long period;
r_1 is the cash market interest rate for the short period;
r_f is the forward rate for the gap period;
t_2 is the time period from today to the end of the long period;
t_1 is the time period from today to the end of the short period;
t_f is the forward gap time period, or the contract period for the FRA.

This is illustrated diagrammatically in Figure 4.2.

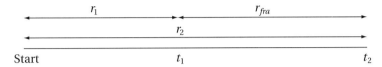

Figure 4.2: Rates used in FRA pricing.

The time period t_1 is the time from the dealing date to the FRA settlement date, while t_2 is the time from the dealing date to the FRA maturity date. The time period for the FRA (contract period) is $t_2 - t_1$. We can replace the symbol "t" for time period with "n" for the actual number of days in the time periods themselves. If we do this and then rearrange the equation to solve for r_{fra}, the FRA rate, we obtain (4.18).

$$r_{fra} = \frac{r_2 n_2 - r_1 n_1}{n_{fra}\left(1 + r_1 \dfrac{n_1}{365}\right)} \tag{4.18}$$

where

n_1 is the number of days from the dealing date or spot date to the settlement date;
n_2 is the number of days from the dealing date or spot date to the maturity date;
r_1 is the spot rate to the settlement date;
r_2 is the spot rate from the spot date to the maturity date;
n_{fra} is the number of days in the FRA contract period;
r_{fra} is the FRA rate.

If the formula is applied to the US or euro money markets, the 365 in the equation is replaced by 360, the day-count base for these markets.

In practice FRAs are priced off the exchange-traded short-term interest rate future for that currency, so that sterling FRAs are priced off LIFFE short sterling futures. Traders normally use a spreadsheet pricing model that has futures prices fed directly into it. FRA positions are also usually hedged with other FRAs or short-term interest rate futures.

FRA prices in practice

The dealing rates for FRAs are possibly the most liquid and transparent of any non-exchange traded derivative instrument. This is because they are calculated directly from exchange-traded interest-rate contracts. The key consideration for FRA market-makers however is how the rates behave in relation to other market interest rates. The forward rate calculated from two period spot-rates must, as we have seen, be set such that it is arbitrage-free. If for example, the six-month spot rate was 8.00% and the nine-month spot rate was 9.00%, the 6v9 FRA would have an approximate rate of 11%. What would be the effect of a change in one or both of the spot rates? The same arbitrage-free principle must apply. If there is an increase in the short-rate period, the FRA rate must decrease to make the total return unchanged. The extent of the change in the FRA rate is a function of the ratio of the contract period to the long period. If the rate for the long period increases, the FRA rate will increase by an amount related to the ratio between the total period to the contract period. The FRA rate for any term is generally a function of the three-month LIBOR rate generally, the rate traded under an interest-rate future. A general rise in this rate will see a rise in FRA rates.

Example 4.5:   Valuation of an existing FRA

◆   In order to value an FRA, it must be decomposed into its constituent parts, which are equivalent to a loan and deposit. Both these parts are then present valued, and the value of the FRA is simply the net present value of both legs. For example, a 6v9 FRA is equivalent to a six-month asset and a nine-month liability. If we assume that the six-month rate is 9% and the nine-month rate is 10%, on a notional principal of £1 million, the value of the FRA is given by:

Value	Term (yr)	Rate (%)	PV
£1 million	0.49	9.00	£957,503
–£1 million	0.745	10.00	–£955,373

The value of the FRA is therefore £2,129.

4.6   Short-term interest rate futures

4.6.1   *Description*

A *futures* contract is a transaction that fixes the price today for a commodity that will be delivered at some point in the future. Financial futures fix the price for interest rates, bonds, equities and so on, but trade in the same manner as commodity futures. Contracts for futures are standardised and traded on exchanges. In London the main futures exchange is LIFFE, although commodity futures are also traded on, for example, the International Petroleum Exchange and the London Metal Exchange. The money markets trade short-term interest rate futures, which fix the rate of interest on a notional fixed term deposit of money (usually for 90 days or three months) for a specified period in the future. The sum is notional because no actual sum of money is deposited when buying or selling futures; the instrument is off-balance sheet. Buying such a contract is equivalent to making a notional deposit, while selling a contract is equivalent to borrowing a notional sum.

The three-month interest-rate future is the most widely used instrument used for hedging interest-rate risk.

The LIFFE exchange in London trades short-term interest rate futures for major currencies including sterling, euro, yen and Swiss franc. Table 4.2 summarises the terms for the short sterling contract as traded on LIFFE.

Name	90-day sterling Libor future
Contract size	£500,000
Delivery months	March, June, September
Delivery date	First business day after last trading day
Last trading day	Third Wednesday of delivery month
Price quotation	100 minus yield
Tick size	0.005
Tick value	£6.25
Trading hours	0805 – 1800
	LIFFE CONNECT™ electronic screen trading

Table 4.2: Description of LIFFE short sterling future contract.

The original futures contracts related to physical commodities, which is why we speak of *delivery* when referring to the expiry of financial futures contracts. Exchange-traded futures such as those on LIFFE are set to expire every quarter during the year. The short sterling contract is a deposit of cash, so as its price refers to the rate of interest on this deposit, the price of the contract is set as

$$P = 100 - r$$

where P is the price of the contract and r is the rate of interest at the time of expiry implied by the futures contract. This means that if the price of the contract rises, the rate of interest implied goes down, and vice versa. For example, the price of the June 1999 short sterling future (written as Jun99 or M99, from the futures identity letters of H, M, U and Z denoting contracts expiring in March, June, September and December respectively) at the start of trading on 13 March 1999 was 94.880, which implied a three-month Libor rate of 5.12% on expiry of the contract in June. If a trader bought 20 contracts at this price and then sold them just before the close of trading that day, when the price had risen to 94.96, an implied rate of 5.04%, they would have made 16 ticks profit or £2000. That is, a 16 tick upward price movement in a long position of 20 contracts is equal to £2000. This is calculated as follows:

Profit = ticks gained × tick value × number of contracts
Loss = ticks lost × tick value × number of contracts

The tick value for the short sterling contract is straightforward to calculate, since we know that the contract size is £500,000, there is a minimum price movement (tick movement) of 0.005% and the contract has a three-month "maturity".

$$\text{Tick value} = 0.005\% \times £500,000 \times \frac{3}{12}$$

$$= £6.25$$

The profit made by the trader in our example is logical because if we buy short sterling futures we are depositing (notional) funds; if the price of the futures rises, it means the interest rate has fallen. We profit because we have "deposited" funds at a higher rate beforehand. If we expected sterling interest rates to rise, we would sell short sterling futures, which is equivalent to borrowing funds and locking in the loan rate at a lower level.

Note how the concept of buying and selling interest rate futures differs from FRAs: if we buy an FRA we are borrowing notional funds, whereas if we buy a futures contract we are depositing notional funds. If a position in an interest rate futures contract is held to expiry, cash settlement will take place on the delivery day for that contract.

Short-term interest rate contracts in other currencies are similar to the short sterling contract and trade on exchanges such as Eurex in Frankfurt and MATIF in Paris.

4.6.2 *Pricing interest rate futures*

The price of a three-month interest rate futures contract is the implied interest rate for that currency's three-month rate at the time of expiry of the contract. Therefore there is always a close relationship and correlation between futures prices, FRA rates (which are derived from futures prices) and cash market rates. On the day of expiry the price of the future will be equal to the Libor rate as fixed that day. This is known as the Exchange Delivery Settlement Price (EDSP) and is used in the calculation of the delivery amount. During the life of the contract its price will be less closely related to the actual three-month Libor rate *today*, but closely related to the *forward rate* for the time of expiry.

Equation (4.17) was our basic forward rate formula for money market maturity forward rates, which we adapted to use as our FRA price equation. If we incorporate some extra terminology to cover the dealing dates involved it can also be used as our futures price formula. Let us say that:

T_0 is the trade date;
T_M is the contract expiry date;
T_{CASH} is the value date for cash market deposits traded on T_0;
T_1 is the value date for cash market deposits traded on T_M;
T_2 is the maturity date for a three-month cash market deposit traded on T_M.

We can then use equation (4.18) as our futures price formula to obtain P_{fut}, the futures price for a contract up to the expiry date.

$$P_{fut} = 100 - \left(\frac{r_2 n_2 - r_1 n_1}{n_f \left(1 + r_1 \left(n_1/365\right)\right)} \right) \tag{4.19}$$

where

P_{fut} is the futures price;
r_1 is the cash market interest rate to T_1;
r_2 is the cash market interest rate to T_2;
n_1 is the number of days from T_{CASH} to T_1;
n_2 is the number of days from T_{CASH} to T_2;
n_f is the number of days from T_1 to T_2.

The formula uses a 365 day count convention which applies in the sterling money markets; where a market uses a 360-day base this must be used in the equation instead.

In practice the price of a contract at any one time will be close to the theoretical price that would be established by (4.19) above. Discrepancies will arise for supply and demand reasons in the market, as well as because Libor rates are often quoted only to the nearest sixteenth or 0.0625. The prices of FRAs and futures are very closely correlated, in fact banks will often price FRAs using futures, and use futures to hedge their FRA books. When hedging an FRA book with futures, the hedge is quite close to being exact, because the two prices track each other almost tick-for-tick. However, the tick value of a futures contract is fixed, and uses (as we saw above) a 3/12 basis, while FRA settlement values use a 360- or 365-day base. The FRA trader will be aware of this when putting on their hedge.

In our discussion of forward rates in Chapter 3 we emphasised that they were the market's view on future rates using all information available today. Of course a futures price today is very unlikely to be in line with the actual three-month interest rate that is prevailing at the time of the contract's expiry. This explains why prices for futures and actual cash rates will differ on any particular day. Up until expiry the futures price is the implied forward rate; of course there is always a discrepancy between this forward rate and the cash market rate *today*. The gap between the cash price and the futures price is known as the *basis*. This is defined as

> basis = cash price – futures price.

At any point during the life of a futures contract prior to final settlement – at which point futures and cash rates converge – there is usually a difference between current cash market rates and the rates implied by the futures price. This is the difference we've just explained; in fact the difference between the price implied by the current three-month interbank deposit and the futures price is known as *simple basis*, but it is what most market participants refer to as the basis. Simple basis consists of two separate components, *theoretical basis* and *value basis*. Theoretical basis is the difference between the price implied by the current three-month interbank deposit rate and that implied by the theoretical fair futures price based on cash market forward rates, given by (4.18). This basis may be either positive or negative depending on the shape of the yield curve.

Futures contracts do not in practice provide a precise tool for locking into cash market rates today for a transaction that takes place in the future, although this is what they are in theory designed to do. Futures do allow a bank to lock in a rate for a transaction to take place in the future, and this rate is the *forward rate*. The basis is the difference between today's cash market rate and the forward rate on a particular date in the future. As a futures contract approaches expiry, its price and the rate in the cash market will converge (the process is given the name *convergence*). As we noted earlier this is given by the EDSP and the two prices (rates) will be exactly in line at the exact moment of expiry.

4.6.3   *Hedging using interest rate futures*

Banks use interest rate futures to hedge interest rate risk exposure in cash and OBS instruments. Bond trading desks also often use futures to hedge positions in bonds of up to two or three years maturity, as contracts are traded up to three years maturity. The liquidity of such "far month" contracts is considerably lower than for near month contracts and the "front month" contract (the current contract, for the next maturity month). When hedging a bond with a maturity of say, two years maturity, the trader will put on a *strip* of futures contracts that matches as near as possible, the expiry date of the bond. The purpose of a hedge is to protect the value of a current or anticipated cash market or OBS position from adverse changes in interest rates. The hedger will try to offset the effect of the change in interest rate on the value of his cash position with the change in value of their hedging instrument. If the hedge is an exact one the loss on the main position should be compensated by a profit on the hedge position. If the trader is expecting a fall in interest rates and wishes to protect against such a fall they will buy futures, known as a long hedge, and will sell futures (a short hedge) if wishing to protect against a rise in rates.

Bond traders also use three-month interest-rate contracts to hedge positions in short-dated bonds; for instance, a market maker running a short-dated bond book would find it more appropriate to hedge his book using short-dated futures rather than the longer-dated bond futures contract. When this happens it is important to accurately calculate the correct number of contracts to use for the hedge. To construct a bond hedge it will be necessary to use a *strip* of contracts, thus ensuring that the maturity date of the bond is covered by the longest-dated futures contract. The hedge is calculated by finding the sensitivity of each cash flow to changes in each of the relevant forward rates. Each cash flow is considered individually and the hedge values are then aggregated and rounded to the nearest whole number of contracts.

Example 4.6:   Forward rate calculation for money market term

Consider two positions:

- a repo of £250 million gilts GC from 2 January 2000 for 30 days at 6.500%;
- a reverse repo of £250 million gilts GC from 2 January 2000 for 60 days at 6.625%.

The two positions generate a 30-day forward 30-day interest rate exposure (a 30- versus 60-day forward rate). This exposure can be hedged by buying an FRA that matches the gap, or by selling a strip of futures. What forward rate must be used if the trader wished to hedge this exposure, assuming no bid-offer spreads and a 365-day count base?

The 30-day by 60-day forward rate can be calculated using the forward-rate formula at (4.20).

$$rf = \left(\left(\frac{1+(rs_2 \times (L/M))}{1+(rs_1 \times (S/M))}\right) - 1\right) \times \frac{M}{L-S} \tag{4.20}$$

where

rf	is the forward rate;
rs_2	is the long period rate;
rs_1	is the short period rate;
L	is the long period days;
S	is the short period days;
M	is the day-count base.

Using this formula we obtain a 30v60 day forward rate of 6.713560%. This assumes no bid-offer spread.

This interest rate exposure can be hedged using interest rate futures or forward rate agreements (FRAs). Either method is an effective hedging mechanism, although the trader must be aware of:

- *basis* risk that exists between repo rates and the forward rates implied by futures and FRAs;
- date mismatched between expiry of futures contracts and the maturity dates of the repo transactions; therefore, an FRA will probably be preferred.

Appendices

Appendix 4.1:   Currencies using money market year base of 365 days

Sterling	Hong Kong dollar
Malaysian ringgit	Singapore dollar
South African rand	Taiwan dollar
Thai baht	

In addition the domestic markets, but not the international markets, of the following currencies also use a 365-day base:

Australian dollar	Canadian dollar
Japanese yen	New Zealand dollar

To convert an interest rate i quoted on a 365-day basis to one quoted on a 360-day basis (i^*) use the expressions given at (4.21).

$$i = i^* \times \frac{365}{360}$$
$$i^* = i \times \frac{360}{365}. \tag{4.21}$$

Appendix 4.2:   Selected country money market conventions

Repo interest is calculated using the money market convention for the market in question. The accrued interest for bond collateral is calculated using the appropriate day-count basis for the relevant bond market.

Country	Money market	Bond day count basis
Australia	act/365	act/act
Austria	act/360	act/act
Belgium	act/361	act/act
Canada	act/365	act/act
Finland	act/360	act/act
France	act/360	act/act
Germany	act/360	act/act
Italy	act/360	act/act
Japan	act/365	act/365
New Zealand	act/365	act/365
Norway	various	act/366
South Africa	act/365	act/365
Spain	act/360	act/act
United Kingdom	act/365	act/act
United States	act/360	act/act

Table 4.3

Selected bibliography and references

Blake, D., *Financial Market Analysis*, Wiley 2000

Chicago Board of Trade, *Interest rate Futures for Institutional Investors*, CBOT, 1987

Choudhry, M., *The Bond and Money Markets: Strategy, Trading, Analysis*, Butterworth-Heinemann 2001, Chapter 34

Figlewski, F., *Hedging with Financial Futures for Institutional Investors*, Probus Publishing 1986

French, K., "A Comparison of Futures and Forwards Prices", *Journal of Financial Economics* 12, November 1983, pp. 311–342

Hull, J., *Options, Futures and Other Derivatives*, 4th edition, Prentice-Hall Inc.1999

Jarrow, R., Oldfield, G., "Forward Contracts and Futures Contracts", *Journal of Financial Economics* 9, December 1981, pp. 373–382

OECD, *Competition in Banking*, OECD 1989

Stigum, M., Robinson, F., *Money Market and Bond Calculations*, Irwin 1996

Stigum, M., *The Money Market*, Dow-Jones Irwin 1990

5 The Repo Instrument

In this chapter we define repo and illustrate its use. We will see that the term *repo* is used to cover one of two different transactions: the *classic repo* and the *sell/buy-back*, and sometimes is spoken of in the same context as another instrument, the *stock loan*. A fourth instrument, known as the *total return swap*, is economically similar in some respects to a repo so we will also look in some detail at this product. It is now commonly encountered as part of the market in credit derivatives. However, although these transactions differ in terms of their mechanics, legal documentation and accounting treatment, the economic effect of each of them is often very similar. The structure of any particular market and the motivations of particular counter-parties will determine which transaction is entered into; there is also some crossover between markets and participants.

Market participants enter into classic repo because they wish to invest cash, for which the transaction is deemed to be *cash-driven*, or because they wish to borrow a certain stock, for which purpose the trade is *stock-driven*. A sell/buy-back, which is sometimes referred to as a *buy-sell*, is entered into for similar reasons but the trade itself operates under different mechanics and documentation.[1] A stock loan is just that, a borrowing of stock against a fee. Long-term holders of stock will therefore enter into stock loans simply to enhance their portfolio returns. We will look at the motivations behind the total return swap in a later chapter.

In this chapter we look in detail at the main repo structures, their mechanics and the different reasons for entering into them. It's a long chapter, but well worth studying closely.

5.1 Repo instruments

5.1.1 *Definition*

A repo agreement is a transaction in which one party sells securities to another, and at the same time and as part of the same transaction commits to repurchase identical securities on a specified date at a specified price. The seller delivers securities and receives cash from the buyer. The cash is supplied at a predetermined rate of interest – *the repo rate* – that remains constant during the term of the trade. On maturity the original seller receives back collateral of equivalent type and quality, and returns the cash plus repo interest. One party to the repo requires either the cash or the securities and provides *collateral* to the other party, as well as some form of compensation for the temporary use of the desired asset. Although legal title to the securities is transferred, the seller retains both the economic benefits and the market risk of owning them. This means that the "seller" will suffer loss if the market value of the collateral drops during the term of the repo, as they still retain beneficial ownership of the collateral. The "buyer" in a repo is not affected in profit/loss account terms if the value of the collateral drops, although as we shall see later, there will be other concerns for the buyer if this happens.

---

[1]   We shall use the term "sell/buy-back" throughout this book. A repo is still a repo whether it is cash-driven or stock-driven, and one person's stock-driven trade may well be another's cash-driven one.

We have given here the legal definition of repo. However, the purpose of the transaction as we have described above is to borrow or lend cash, which is why we have used inverted commas when referring to sellers and buyers. The "seller" of stock is really interested in borrowing cash, on which they will pay interest at a specified interest rate. The "buyer" requires security or *collateral* against the loan they have advanced, and/or the specific security to borrow for a period of time. The first and most important thing to state is that repo is a secured loan of cash, and would be categorised as a money market yield instrument.[2]

5.2   The classic repo

The *classic repo* is the instrument encountered in the US, UK and other markets. In a classic repo one party will enter into a contract to sell securities, simultaneously agreeing to purchase them back at a specified future date and price. The securities can be bonds or equities but also money market instruments such as T-bills. The buyer of the securities is handing over cash, which on the termination of the trade will be returned to them, and on which they will receive interest.

The seller in a classic repo is selling or *offering* stock, and therefore receiving cash, whereas the buyer is buying or *bidding* for stock, and consequently paying cash. So if the one-week repo interest rate is quoted by a market-making bank as "5½ - 5¼", this means that the market maker will bid for stock, that is, lend the cash, at 5.50% and offers stock or pays interest on borrowed cash at 5.25%. In some markets the quote is reversed.

5.2.1   *Illustration of classic repo*

There will be two parties to a repo trade, let us say Bank A (the seller of securities) and Bank B (the buyer of securities). On the trade date the two banks enter into an agreement whereby on a set date, the *value* or *settlement* date Bank A will sell to Bank B a nominal amount of securities in exchange for cash.[3] The price received for the securities is the market price of the stock on the value date. The agreement also demands that on the termination date Bank B will sell identical stock back to Bank A at the previously agreed price; consequently, Bank B will have its cash returned with interest at the agreed repo rate.

In essence a repo agreement is a secured loan (or *collateralised* loan) in which the repo rate reflects the interest charged on the cash being lent.

On the value date, stock and cash change hands. This is known as the start date, *on-side* date, *first leg* or *opening leg*, while the termination date is known as the *second leg*, *off-side leg* or *closing leg*. When the cash is returned to Bank B, it is accompanied by the interest charged on the cash during the term of the trade. This interest is calculated at a specified rate known as the *repo rate*. It is important to remember that although in legal terms the stock is initially "sold" to Bank B, the economic effects of ownership are retained with Bank A. This means that if the stock falls in price it is Bank A that will suffer a capital loss. Similarly, if the stock

---

[2]   That is, a money market product quoted as a yield instrument, similar to a bank deposit or a Certificate of Deposit. The other class of money market products are *discount* instruments such as a Treasury Bill or Commercial Paper.

[3]   The two terms are not necessarily synonymous. The value date in a trade is the date on which the transaction acquires value; for example, the date from which accrued interest is calculated. As such it may fall on a non-business day such as a weekend or public holiday. The settlement date is the day on which the transaction settles or *clears*, and so can only fall on a business day.

involved is a bond and there is a coupon payment during the term of the trade, this coupon is to the benefit of Bank A, and although Bank B will have received it on the coupon date, it must be handed over on the same day or immediately after to Bank A. This reflects the fact that although legal title to the collateral passes to the repo buyer, economic costs and benefits of the collateral remain with the seller.

A classic repo transaction is subject to a legal contract signed in advance by both parties. A standard document will suffice; it is not necessary to sign a legal agreement prior to each transaction.

Note that although we have called the two parties in this case "Bank A" and "Bank B", it is not only banks that get involved in repo transactions, and we have used these terms for the purposes of illustration only.

The basic mechanism is illustrated in Figure 5.1.

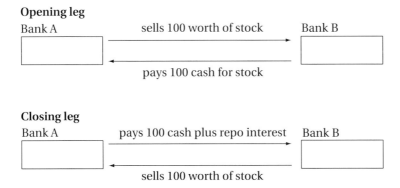

Figure 5.1: Classic repo transaction for 100-worth of collateral stock.

A seller in a repo transaction is entering into a repo, whereas a buyer is entering into a *reverse repo*. In Figure 5.1 the repo counterparty is Bank A, while Bank B is entering into a reverse repo. That is, a reverse repo is a purchase of securities that are sold back on termination. As is evident from Figure 5.1 every repo is a reverse repo, and the name given is dependent on from whose viewpoint one is looking at the transaction.[4]

5.2.2   *Examples of classic repo*

The basic principle is illustrated with the following example. This considers a *specific* repo, that is, one in which the collateral supplied is specified as a particular stock, as opposed to a *general collateral* (GC) trade in which a basket of collateral can be supplied, of any particular issue, as long as it is of the required type and credit quality.

---

4   Note that the guidelines to the syllabus for the Chartered Financial Analyst examination, which is set by the Association for Investment Management and Research, defines repo and reverse repo slightly differently. This states, essentially, that a "repo" is conducted by a bank counterparty and a "reverse repo" is conducted by an investment counterparty or non-financial counterparty. Another definition states that a "repo" is any trade where the bank counterparty is offering stock (borrowing cash) and a "reverse repo" is any trade where the non-bank counterparty is borrowing cash.

We consider first a classic repo in the United Kingdom gilt market between two market counterparties, in the 5.75% Treasury 2009 gilt stock. The terms of the trade are given in Table 5.1 and illustrated in Figure 5.2.

Trade date	5 July 2000
Value date	6 July 2000
Repo term	1 week
Termination date	13 July 2000
Collateral (stock)	UKT 5.75% 2009
Nominal amount	£10,000,000
Price	104.60
Accrued interest (29 days)	0.4556011
Dirty price	105.055601
Settlement proceeds (*wired amount*)	£10,505,560.11
Repo rate	5.75%
Repo interest	£11,584.90
Termination proceeds	£10,517,145.01

Table 5.1: Terms of classic repo trade.

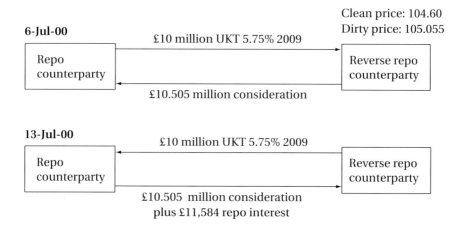

Figure 5.2: Classic repo trade.

The repo counterparty delivers to the reverse repo counterparty £10 million nominal of the stock, and in return receives the purchase proceeds. The clean market price of the stock is £104.60. In this example no *margin* has been taken so the start proceeds are equal to the market value of the stock which is £10,505,560.11. It is common for a rounded sum to be transferred on the opening leg. The repo interest is 5.75%, so the repo interest charged for the trade is

$$10,505,560 \times 5.75\% \times \frac{7}{365}$$

or £11,584.01. The sterling market day-count basis is actual/365, and the repo interest is based on a seven-day repo rate of 5.75%. Repo rates are agreed at the time of the trade and are quoted, like all interest rates, on an annualised basis. The settlement price (dirty price) is used because it is the market value of the bonds on the particular trade date and therefore indicates the cash value of the gilts. By doing this the cash investor minimises credit exposure by equating the value of the cash and the collateral.

On termination the repo counterparty receives back its stock, for which it hands over the original proceeds plus the repo interest calculated above.

Market participants who are familiar with the Bloomberg trading system will use screen RRRA for a classic repo transaction. For this example the relevant screen entries are shown in Figure 5.3. This screen is used in conjunction with a specific stock, so in this case it would be called up by entering

UKT 5.75 09 <GOVT> RRRA <GO>

where "UKT" is the ticker for UK gilts. Note that the date format for Bloomberg screens is the US style, which is mm/dd/yy. The screen inputs are relatively self-explanatory, with the user entering the terms of the trade that are detailed in Table 5.1. There is also a field for calculating margin, labelled "collateral" on the screen. As no margin is involved in this example, it is left at its default value of 100.00%. The bottom of the screen shows the opening leg cash proceeds or "wired amount", the repo interest and the termination proceeds.

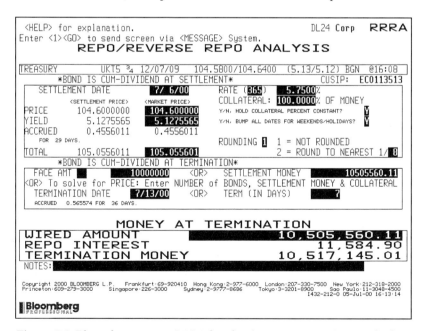

Figure 5.3: Bloomberg screen RRRA for classic repo transaction, trade date 5 July 2000. ©Bloomberg L.P. Reproduced with permission.

What if a counterparty is interested in investing £10 million against gilt collateral? Let us assume that a corporate treasury function with surplus cash wishes to invest this amount in repo for a one-week term. It invests this cash with a bank that deals in gilt repo. We can use Bloomberg screen RRRA to calculate the nominal amount of collateral required. Figure 5.4 shows the screen for this trade, again against the 5.75% Treasury 2009 stock as collateral. We see from Figure 5.4 that the terms of the trade are identical to that in Table 5.1, including the bond price and the repo rate; however, the opening leg wired amount is entered as £10 million, which is the cash being invested. Therefore the nominal value of the gilt collateral required will be different, as we now require a market value of this stock of £10 million. From the screen we see that this is £9,518,769. The cash amount is different from the example in Figure 5.3 so of course the repo interest charged is different, and is £11,027 for the seven-day term. The diagram at Figure 5.5 illustrates the transaction details.

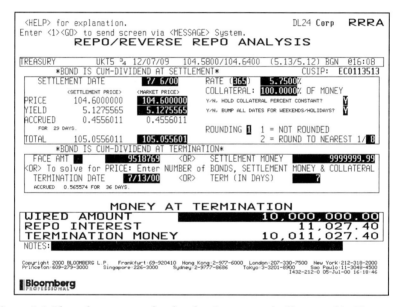

Figure 5.4: Bloomberg screen for the classic repo trade illustrated in Figure 5.5.
©Bloomberg L.P. Reproduced with permission.

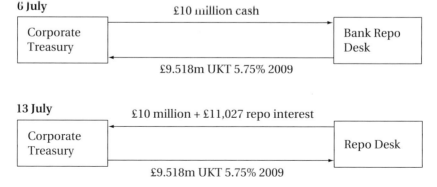

Figure 5.5: Corporate treasury classic repo.

> **Example 5.1:   Classic repo**
>
> ◆ On 21 June 1998, a corporate wishes to invest DEM 50 million against German gov-
> ernment bonds for 7 days. The collateral is the 5½% bunds due in April 2003. The
> repo rate is agreed at 5.60%. The bund price is 101.2305 clean, which together with
> 1.0542 accrued interest (69 days) gives a dirty price of 102.2847.
>
> The borrower of cash will need to determine the face value of bunds required at the
> current market price which will equate to DEM 50 million. This is shown below.
>
> $$\frac{102.2847}{100.0000} = \frac{50,000,000}{X}$$
>
> The nominal value of bunds required (X) is 48,883,000. This is rounded to the nearest
> 1,000 because bunds traded in denominations of 1,000 prior to the introduction of the
> euro. (Euroland bonds trade down to nominal value EUR 0.01).
>   The trade details are summarised below.
>
> | | |
> |---|---|
> | Nominal | DEM 48,883,000 of Bund 5½% 2003 |
> | Clean start price | 101.2305 |
> | Accrued | 1.0542 |
> | Dirty start price | 102.2847 |
> | Settlement money | DEM 50,000,000 |
> | Dirty end price | 102.2847 |
> | Repo interest | DEM 54,444 (50,000,000 × 5.60% × 7/360) |
> | Termination money | DEM 50,054,444 |
>
> Note that the sale and repurchase prices are the same.

5.3   The sell/buy-back

5.3.1 *Definition*

In addition to classic repo there exists *sell/buy-back*. A sell/buy-back is defined as an outright
sale of a bond on the value date, and an outright repurchase of that bond for value on a *forward* date. The cash flows therefore become a sale of the bond at a *spot* price, followed by
repurchase of the bond at the *forward* price. The forward price calculated includes the interest
on the repo, and is therefore a different price to the spot price.[5] That is, repo interest is realised as the difference between the spot price and forward price of the collateral at the start and
termination of the trade. The sell/buy-back is entered into for the same reasons as a classic
repo, but was developed initially in markets where no legal agreement existed to cover repo
transactions, and where the settlement and IT systems of individual counterparties were not
equipped to deal with repo. Over time, sell/buy-backs have become the convention in certain
markets, most notably Italy, and so the mechanism is still used. In many markets therefore,

---

5   The "forward price" is calculated only for the purpose of incorporating repo interest; it should not be
    confused with a forward interest rate, which is the interest rate for a term starting in the future and
    which is calculated from a spot interest rate. Nor should it be taken to be an indication of what the
    market price of the bond might be at the time of trade termination, the price of which could differ
    greatly from the sell/buy-back forward price.

sell/buy-backs are not covered by a legal agreement, although the standard legal agreement used in classic repo now includes a section that describes them.[6]

A sell/buy-back is a spot sale and forward repurchase of bonds transacted simultaneously, and the repo rate is not explicit, but is implied in the forward price. Any coupon payments during the term are paid to the seller; however, this is done through incorporation into the forward price, so the seller will not receive it immediately, but on termination. This is a disadvantage when compared to classic repo. However there will be compensation payable if a coupon is not handed over straight away, usually at the repo rate used in the sell/buy-back. As sell/buy-backs are not subject to a legal agreement in most cases, in effect the seller has no legal right to any coupon, and there is no provision for marking-to-market and *variation margin*. This makes the sell/buy-back a higher-risk transaction when compared to classic repo, even more so in volatile markets.

A general diagram for the sell/buy-back is given in Figure 5.6.

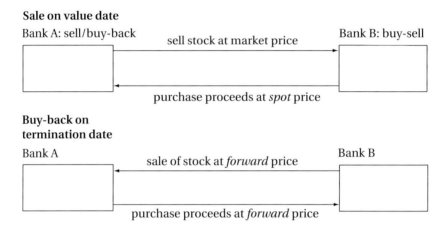

Figure 5.6: Sell/buy-back transaction.

5.3.2   *Examples of sell/buy-back*

We use the same terms of trade given in Table 5.1 in section 5.2.2 but this time the trade is a sell/buy-back.[7] In a sell/buy-back we require the forward price on termination, and the difference between the spot and forward price incorporates the effects of repo interest. It is important to note that this forward price has nothing to with the actual market price of the collateral at the time of forward trade. It is simply a way of allowing for the repo interest that is the key factor in the trade. Thus in sell/buy-back the repo rate is not explicit (although it is the key consideration in the trade) rather, it is implicit in the forward price.

In this example, one counterparty sells £10 million nominal of the UKT 5.75% 2009 at the spot price of 104.60, this being the market price of the bond at the time. The consideration for this trade is the market value of the stock, which is £10,505,560 as before. Repo interest is calculated on this amount at the rate of 5.75% for one week, and from this the termination

---

6   This is the PSA/ISMA Global Master Repurchase Agreement, which is reviewed in Chapter 14.
7   The Bank of England discourages sell/buy-backs in gilt repo and it is unusual, if not unheard of, to observe them in this market. However, we use these terms of trade for comparison purposes with the classic repo example given in the previous section.

proceeds are calculated. The termination proceeds are divided by the nominal amount of stock to obtain the forward dirty price of the bond on the termination date. For various reasons, the main one being that settlement systems deal in clean prices, we require the forward clean price, which is obtained by subtracting from the forward dirty price the accrued interest on the bond on the termination date. At the start of the trade the 5.75% 2009 had 29 days' accrued interest, therefore on termination this figure will be 29 + 7 or 36 days.

Bloomberg users access a different screen for sell/buy-backs, which is BSR. This is shown in Figure 5.7. Entering in the terms of the trade, we see from Figure 5.7 that the forward price is 104.605876. However the fundamental nature of this transaction is evident from the bottom part of the screen: the settlement amount ("wired amount"), repo interest and termination amount are identical for the classic repo trade described earlier. This is not surprising; the sell/buy-back is a loan of £10.505 million for one week at an interest rate of 5.75%. The mechanics of the trade do not differ on this key point.

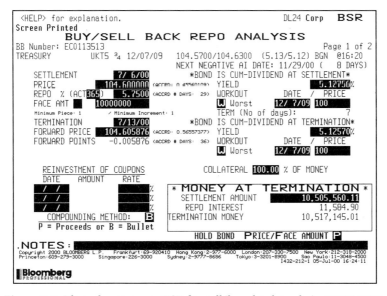

Figure 5.7: Bloomberg screen BSR for sell/buy-back trade in 5.75% 2009, trade date 5 July 2000. ©Bloomberg L.P. Used with permission.

Screen BSR on Bloomberg has a second page, which is shown at Figure 5.8. This screen summarises the cash proceeds of the trade at start and termination. Note how the repo interest is termed "funding cost". This is because the trade is deemed to have been entered into by a bond trader who is funding his book. This will be considered later, but we can see from the screen details that during the one week of the trade the bond position has accrued interest of £10,997. This compares unfavourably with the repo funding cost of £11,584.

If there is a coupon payment during a sell/buy-back trade and it is not paid over to the seller until termination, a compensating amount is also payable on the coupon amount, usually at the trade's repo rate. When calculating the forward price on a sell/buy-back where a coupon will be paid during the trade, we must subtract the coupon amount from the forward price. Note also that sell/buy-backs are not possible on an open basis, as no forward price can be calculated unless a termination date is known.

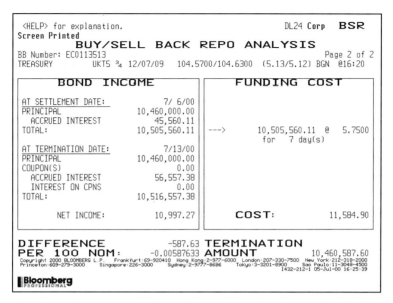

Figure 5.8: Bloomberg screen BSR page 2 for sell/buy-back trade in 5.75% 2009 gilt.
©Bloomberg L.P. Reproduced with permission.

Example 5.2:   Sell/buy-back transaction

Consider the same terms as Example 5.1 above, but in this case as a sell/buy-back transaction. We require the forward bond price, and this is calculated by converting the termination money.

$$\frac{\text{DEM } 50,054,444}{\text{DEM } 48,883,000} \times 100 = 102.39642$$

The accrued interest *at the time of termination* is subtracted from this price to obtain a forward clean price, as shown below.

$$102.39642 - 1.1611 \text{ [76 days]} = 101.23532.$$

The trade details are summarised below.

Nominal	DEM 48,833,000 of Bund 5½% 2003
Clean start price	101.2305
Accrued	1.0542
Dirty start price	102.2847
Settlement money	DEM 50,000,000
Termination money	DEM 50,064,290 (includes repo interest of DEM 64,167)
Dirty end price	102.39642
Accrued	1.1611
Clean end price	101.23532

Note that the sale and repurchase prices are now different.

5.4   Comparing classic repo and sell/buy-back

Fundamentally both classic repo and sell/buy-backs are money market instruments that are a means by which one party may lend cash to another party, secured against collateral in the form of stocks and bonds. Both transactions are a contract for one party to sell securities, with a simultaneous agreement to repurchase them at a specified future. They also involve:

- in economic terms, an exchange of assets, usually bonds but also money market paper or equities as collateral against cash;

- the supplier of cash being compensated through the payment of interest, at an explicit (repo) or implicit (sell/buy-back) rate of interest;

- short-covering of positions by market makers or speculative sellers, when they are stock-driven trades.

In certain respects however, there are significant differences between the two instruments. A classic repo trade is carried out under formal legal documentation, which sets out the formal position of each counterparty in the event of default. Sell/buy-backs have traditionally not been covered by this type of documentation, although this is no longer the case as standard documentation now exists to cater for them. There is no provision for *marking-to-market* and variation margining in sell/buy-backs, issues we shall look at shortly.

A summary of the main features of both types of trade is given in Table 5.2.

Classic repo	Sell/buy-back
"Sale" and repurchase	Outright sale; forward buy-back
Bid at repo rate: bid for stock, lend the cash (Offer at repo rate: offer the stock, take the cash)	Repo rate implicit in forward buy-back price
Sale and repurchase prices identical	Forward buy-back price different
Return to cash lender is repo interest on cash	Return to cash lender is difference between sale price and forward buy-back price (the "repo" interest!)
Bond coupon received during trade is returned to seller	Coupon need not be returned to bond seller until termination (albeit with compensation)
Standard legal agreement (BMA/ISMA GMRA)	No standard legal agreement (but may be traded under the GMRA)
Initial margin may be taken	Initial margin may be taken
Variation margin may be called	No variation margin unless transacted under a legal agreement
Specific repo dealing systems required	May be transacted using existing bond and equity dealing systems

Table 5.2: Summary of highlights of classic repo and sell/buy-back.

5.5   Stock lending

5.5.1   *Definition*

Stock lending or *securities lending* is defined as a temporary transfer of securities in exchange for collateral. It is not a repo in the normal sense; there is no sale or repurchase of the securities. The temporary use of the desired asset (the stock that is being borrowed) is reflected in a fixed fee payable by the party temporarily taking the desired asset. In stock loan, the lender does not monitor interest rates during the term of the trade, but instead realises value by receiving this fixed fee during the term of the loan. This makes administration of stock lending transactions less onerous compared to repo. The formal definition of a stock loan is a contract between two parties in which one party lends securities to another for a fixed or *open* term. The party that borrows must supply collateral to the stock lender, which can be other high-quality securities, cash or a letter of credit. This protects against credit risk. Fabozzi (2001) states that in the US the most common type of collateral is cash; however, in the UK market it is quite common for other securities to be given as collateral, typically gilts. In addition the lender charges a fixed fee, usually quoted as a basis point charge on the market value of the stock being lent, payable by the borrower on termination. The origins and history of the stock-lending market are different from that of the repo market. The range of counterparties is also different, although of course a large number of counterparties are involved in both markets. Most stock loans are on an "open" basis, meaning that they are confirmed (or terminated) each morning, although term loans also occur.

Institutional investors such as pension funds and insurance companies often prefer to enhance the income from their fixed interest portfolios by lending their bonds, for a fee, rather than entering into repo transactions. This obviates the need to set up complex settlement and administration systems, as well as the need to monitor what is, in effect, an interest rate position. Initial *margin* is given to institutional lenders of stock, usually in the form of a greater value of collateral stock than the market value of the stock being lent.

5.5.2   *Basic concepts*

Stock lending transactions are the transfer of a security or basket of securities from a lending counterparty, for a temporary period, in return for a fee payable by the borrowing counterparty. During the term of the loan the stock is lent out in exchange for collateral, which may be in the form of other securities or cash. If other securities are handed over as collateral, they must be high-quality assets such as Treasuries, gilts or other highly-rated paper. Lenders are institutional investors such as pension funds, life assurance companies, local authority treasury offices and other fund managers, and loans of their portfolio holdings are often facilitated via the use of a broking agent, known as a *prime broker* or a clearing agent custodian such as Euroclear or Clearstream. In addition, banks and securities houses that require stock to cover short positions sometimes have access to their own source of stock lenders; for example, clients of their custody services.

Stock lending is not a sale and repurchase in the conventional sense but is used by banks and securities houses to cover short positions in securities put on as part of market-making or proprietary trading activity. In some markets (for example, the Japanese equity market) regulations require a counterparty to have arranged stock lending before putting on the short trade.

Other reasons why banks may wish to enter into stock loan (or stock borrowing, from their viewpoint) transactions include:

- where they have effected a purchase, and then sold this security on, and their original purchase has not settled, putting them at risk of failing on their sale;
- as part of *disintermediation* between the stock loan market and the repo and unsecured money market.

An institution that wishes to borrow stock must pay a fee for the term of the loan. This is usually a basis point charge on the market value of the loan, and is payable in arrears on a monthly basis. In the Eurobond market the fee is calculated at the start of the loan, and unless there is a significant change in the market value of the stock, it will be paid at the end of the loan period. In the UK gilt market the basis point fee is calculated on a daily basis on the market value of the stock that has been lent, and so the total charge payable is not known until the loan maturity. This arrangement requires that the stock be *marked-to-market* at the end of each business day. The fee itself is agreed between the stock borrower and the stock lender at the time of each loan, but this may be a general fee payable for all loans. There may be a different fee payable for specific stocks, so in this case the fee is agreed on a trade-by-trade basis, depending on the stock being lent out. Any fee is usually for the term of the loan, although it is possible in most markets to adjust the rate through negotiation at any time during the loan. The fee charged by the stock lender is a function of supply and demand for the stock in the market. A specific security that is in high demand in the market will be lent out at a higher fee than one that is in lower demand. For this reason it is important for the bank's Treasury desk[8] to be aware of which stocks are in demand, and more importantly to have a reasonable idea of which stocks will be in demand in the near future. Some banks will be in possession of better *market intelligence* than others. If excessive demand is anticipated, a prospective short seller may borrow stock in advance of entering into the short sale.

The term of a stock loan can be fixed, in which case it is known as a *term loan*, or it can be open. A term loan is economically similar to a classic repo transactions. An open loan is just that: there is no fixed maturity term, and the borrower will confirm on the telephone at the start of each day whether it wishes to continue with the loan or will be returning the security.

As in a classic repo transaction, coupon or dividend payments that become payable on a security or bond during the term of the loan will be to the benefit of the stock lender. In the standard stock loan legal agreement, known as the OSLA agreement,[9] there is no change of beneficial ownership when a security is lent out. The usual arrangement when a coupon is payable is that the payment is automatically returned to the stock lender via its settlement system. Such a coupon payment is known as a *manufactured dividend*.

Clients of prime brokers and custodians will inform their agent if they wish their asset holdings to be used for stock-lending purposes. At this point a stock-lending agreement is set up between the holder of the securities and the prime broker or custodian. Borrowers of stock are also required to set up an agreement with brokers and custodians. The return to the broker or custodian is the difference between the fee paid by the stock borrower and that paid to the stock lender. Banks that have their own internal lending lines can access this stock at a lower

---

8   Or whichever desk is responsible for covering short positions by borrowing or reverse-repoing stock.
9   After the trade association overseeing the stock loan market.

borrowing rate. If they wish to pursue this source they will set up a stock-lending agreement with institutional investors directly.

5.5.3   *Example of stock loan*

We illustrate a stock loan where the transaction is "stock-driven". Let us assume that a securities house has a requirement to borrow a UK gilt, the 5.75% 2009, for a one-week period. This is the stock from our earlier classic repo and sell/buy-back examples. We presume the requirement is to cover a short position in the stock, although there are other reasons why the securities house may wish to borrow the stock. The bond that it is offering as collateral is another gilt, the 6.50% Treasury 2003. The stock lender, who we may assume is an institutional investor such as a pension fund, but may as likely be another securities house or a bank, requires a margin of 5% as well as a fee of 20 basis points. The transaction is summarised in Table 5.3.

Value date	6 July 2000
Termination date	13 July 2000
Stock borrowed	5.75% 2009
Nominal borrowed	£10 million
Term	1 week
Loan value	£10,505.560.11
Collateral	6.50%
Clean price	102.1
Accrued interest (29 days)	0.5150273
Dirty price	102.615027
Margin required	5%
Market value of collateral required =10,505,560 × 1.05	£11,030,837.35
Nominal value of collateral	£10,749,729
Stock loan fee (20 bps)	£402.95

Table 5.3: Stock loan transaction.

Note that in reality, in the gilt market the stock loan fee (here 20 bps) is calculated on the daily mark-to-market stock price, automatically within the gilt settlement mechanism known as CREST–CGO, so the final charge is not known until termination. Within the Eurobond market, for example in Clearstream, the fee on the initial loan value is taken, and adjustments are made only in the case of large movements in stock price.

There is no specialist screen for stock loan transactions on Bloomberg, but it is sometimes useful to use the RRRA screen for calculations and analysis; for example Figure 5.9 shows this screen being used to calculate the nominal amount of collateral required for the loan of £10 million nominal of the 5.75% 2009 gilt shown in Table 5.3. The margin-adjusted market value of the collateral is £11,030,838, and if this is entered into the "wired amount" field on the screen, with the current price of the stock, we see that it shows a required nominal of £10,749,729 of the 6.50% 2003 gilt.

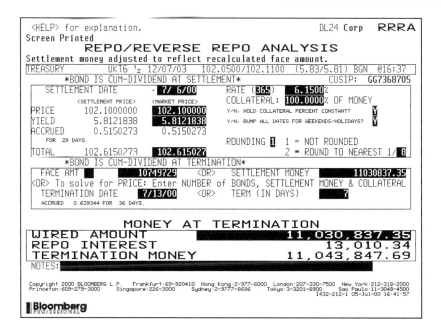

Figure 5.9: Bloomberg screen used to calculate nominal value of collateral required in a stock loan transaction. ©Bloomberg L.P. Used with permission.

5.6 Comparing classic repo and stock lending

A stock loan transaction in which the collateral is in the form of cash is similar in some ways to a classic repo trade. Here we compare the two transactions. Consider the following situation: ABC is an entity, perhaps a bank or fund manager, that owns government bond G. Bank XYZ is a bank that requires bond G in order to deliver into a short sale that it has transacted in G. To temporarily acquire bond G to cover the short sale Bank XYZ may enter into either a stock loan or a classic repo. Table 5.4 looks at the similarities between the two, and the differences.

Similarities	
ABC transfers bond G to XYZ.	
XYZ passes cash to the market value of G to ABC.	
At the termination of the transaction, XYZ returns bond G to ABC.	
At termination, ABC returns the cash it received at the start of the transaction to XYZ.	
Classic repo transaction	**Stock loan transaction**
ABC is the stock seller. It may be viewed as the borrower of funds, but not in the context of this trade.	ABC is the stock lender.

Continued overleaf ▶

XYZ is the stock buyer.	XYZ is the stock borrower.
ABC places cash received from XYZ on deposit, or otherwise invests it.	ABC receives cash from XYZ, which is collateral for the loan, and which is placed on deposit. The interest earned is payable to XYZ.
On termination, ABC returns the cash received at the start, together with interest charged at the repo rate.	On termination, ABC returns the cash to XYZ, together with the interest earned on it. XYZ pays over the fee charged by ABC for making the loan.
The net gain to ABC is based on the difference between the repo rate paid to XYZ and the rate earned on the cash placed on deposit.	The gain to ABC is considered as the stock loan fee.
If there is a coupon payment on bond G, this is paid by XYZ to ABC.	If there is a coupon payment on bond G, this is paid by XYZ to ABC.
On termination, ABC "buys back" bond G from XYZ at the repurchase price agreed at the trade start. As this is classic repo, the repurchase price is identical to the sale price, but the cash flow includes repo interest.	On termination, XYZ returns bond G to ABC, who returns the cash collateral it received at the start.

Table 5.4: Comparison of stock loan transaction with repo.

5.7   Repo variations

In the earlier section we described the standard classic repo trade, which has a fixed term to maturity and a fixed repo rate. Generally, classic repo trades will range in maturity from overnight to one year, however it is possible to transact longer maturities than this if required. The overwhelming majority of repo trades are between overnight and three months in maturity, although longer-term trades are not uncommon. A fixed-maturity repo is sometimes called a *term repo*. One could call this the "plain vanilla" repo. It is usually possible to terminate a vanilla repo before its stated maturity date if this is required by one or both of the counterparties.[10]

A repo that does not have a specified fixed maturity date is known as an *open repo*. In an open repo the borrower of cash will confirm each morning that the repo is required for a further overnight term. The interest rate is also fixed at this point. If the borrower no longer requires the cash, or requires the return of his collateral, the trade will be terminated at one day's notice.

In the remainder of this section we present an overview of the most common variations on the vanilla repo transaction that are traded in the markets.

---

[10] The term *delivery repo* is sometimes used to refer to a vanilla classic repo transaction where the supplier of cash takes delivery of the collateral, whether in physical form or as a book-entry transfer to his account in the clearing system (or his agent's account).

5.7.1 *Tri-party repo*

The tri-party repo mechanism is a relatively recent development and is designed to make the repo arrangement accessible to a wider range of market counterparties. Essentially it introduces a third-party agent in between the two repo counterparties, who can fulfil a number of roles from security custodian to cash account manager. The tri-party mechanism allows bond and equity dealers full control over their inventory, and incurs minimal settlement cost to the cash investor, but gives the investor independent confirmation that their cash is fully collateralised. Under a tri-party agreement, the securities dealer delivers collateral to an independent third-party custodian, such as Euroclear or Clearstream,[11] who will place it into a segregated tri-party account. The securities dealer maintains control over which precise securities are in this account (multiple substitutions are permitted) but the custodian undertakes to confirm each day to the investor that their cash remains fully collateralised by securities of suitable quality. A tri-party agreement needs to be in place with all three parties before trading can commence. This arrangement reduces the administrative burden for the cash-investor, but is not, in theory, as secure as a conventional delivery-versus-payment structure. Consequently the yield on the investor's cash (assuming collateral of identical credit quality) should be slightly higher. The structure is shown in Figure 5.10.

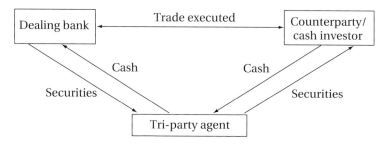

Figure 5.10: Tri-party repo structure.

The first tri-party repo deal took place in 1993 between the European Bank for Reconstruction and Development (EBRD) and Swiss Bank Corporation.[12]

A tri-party arrangement is, in theory, more attractive to smaller market participants as it removes the expense of setting up in-house administration facilities that would be required for conventional repo. This is mainly because the delivery and collection of collateral is handled by the tri-party agent. Additional benefits to cash-rich investors include:

- no requirement to install repo settlement and monitoring systems;
- no requirement to take delivery of collateral, or to maintain an account at the clearing agency;
- independent monitoring of market movements and margin requirements;
- in the event of default, a third-party agent that can implement default measures.

---

[11] Clearstream was previously known as Cedel Bank. Other tri-party providers include JPMorgan Chase and Bank of New York.

[12] Stated in Corrigan *et al* (1999), page 27.

Set against the benefits is of course the cost of tri-party repo, essentially the fee payable to the third-party agent. This fee will include a charge for setting up accounts and arrangements at the tri-party agent, and a custodian charge for holding securities in the clearing system.

As well as being attractive to smaller banks and cash-rich investors, the larger banks will also use tri-party repo, in order to be able to offer it as a service to their smaller-size clients. The usual arrangement is that both dealer and cash investor will pay a fee to the tri-party agent based on the range of services that are required, and this will be detailed in the legal agreement in place between the market counterparty and the agent. This agreement will also specify, among other detail, the specific types of security that are acceptable as collateral to the cash lender; the repo rate that is earned by the lender will reflect the nature of collateral that is supplied. In every other respect however, the tri-party mechanism offers the same flexibility of conventional repo, and may be transacted from maturities ranging from overnight to one year.

The tri-party agent is an agent to both parties in the repo transaction. It provides a collateral management service overseeing the exchange of securities and cash, and managing collateral during the life of the repo. It also carries out daily marking-to-market, and substitution of collateral as required. The responsibilities of the agent can include:

- the preparation of documentation;
- the setting up of the repo account;
- monitoring of cash against purchased securities, both at inception and at maturity;
- initial and ongoing testing of *concentration* limits;
- the safekeeping of securities handed over as collateral;
- managing the substitution of securities, where this is required;
- monitoring the market value of the securities against the cash lent out in the repo;
- issuing margin calls to the borrower of cash.

The tri-party agent will issue close-of-business reports to both parties. The contents of the report can include some or all of the following:

- tri-party repo cash and securities valuation;
- corporate actions;
- pre-advice of expected income;
- exchange rates;
- collateral substitution.

The extent of the duties performed by the tri-party agent is dependent of the sophistication of an individual party's operation. Smaller market participants who do not wish to invest in extensive infrastructure may outsource all repo-related functions to the tri-party agent.

Tri-party repo was originally conceived as a mechanism through which repo would become accessible to smaller banks and non-bank counterparties. It is primarily targeted at cash-rich investors. However users of the instrument range across the spectrum of market participants, and include, on the investing side, cash-rich financial institutions such as banks, fund managers including life companies and pension funds, and savings institutions such as UK building societies. On the borrowing side users include bond and equity market makers, and banks with inventories of high-quality assets such as government bonds and highly-rated corporate bonds.[13]

Tri-party repo: further discussion

The process of cash and collateral flow in a tri-party repo trade is illustrated in Figure 5.11.

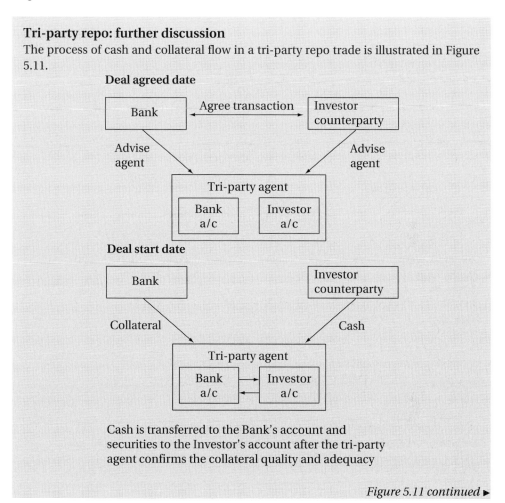

Cash is transferred to the Bank's account and securities to the Investor's account after the tri-party agent confirms the collateral quality and adequacy

Figure 5.11 continued ▶

---

[13] Fabozzi (2001) also refers to *four-party repos*. The difference between tri-party and four-party repo is given as follows: "in a four-party repo there is a sub-custodian that is the custodian for the lender." This might occur because of legal considerations; for instance, local regulations stating that the custodian in a repo transaction must be a financial institution or must be based in a particular location.

Termination date

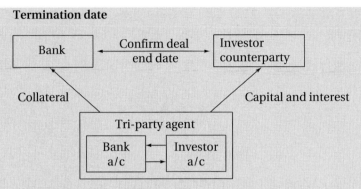

The tri-party agent effects a simultaneous transfer of
cash (original capital plus repo interest) versus
securities

Figure 5.11: Tri-party repo flow.

Table 5.5 shows the acceptable collateral types as advised by the institutional trust arm
of a US investment bank. Table 5.6 shows typical yields available on the different collateral types as at September 2000, and the amount of margin required. Not surprisingly,
bonds such as Treasuries and gilts are marked at 100% of their market value, with the
highest margin required for collateral such as listed equities that are outside of a recognised index.

Government bonds	Cash
Government guaranteed/	Certificate of Deposits
local authority bonds	Delivery by Value (DBV)
Supranational bonds	Letters of credit
Eurobonds	Equities
Corporate bonds	American Depositary Receipts
ABS/MBS	Warrants
Convertible bonds	

Table 5.5: Tri-party acceptable collateral: US Investment bank.

Collateral type	Valuation for mark-to-market purposes	Indicative yield spread to Libor (basis points)
OECD Sovereign bonds (e.g., UK gilts, US Treasuries, Bunds, 0–20 year maturity)	100%	–7 to –11
Bank CDs, LOCs (A1/P1 rated), Supranational securities	97.56%	–2 to –5
OECD Sovereign bonds (e.g., UK gilts, US Treasuries, Bunds, >20-year maturity), and other OECD government debt rated AA– or better	97.56%	+0 to –2
G7 OECD domiciled corporate bonds rated AA– or better	97.56%	–2 to –7
G10 prime index equities (e.g., FTSE100, S&P500, Nikkei225, CAC40, DAX30, IBEX35, MIB30)	97.56%	+5
Other prime index equities (e.g., OMX, BEL, HEX, TSE, OBX, KFX, NZSE, also FTSE and S&P convertibles rated AA– or better	95.24%	+8 to +15
Equities in Singapore SST30, Hong Kong HSI33	93.03%	+8 to +15
Equities in Johannesburg ASI40, Lisbon BVL30	90.91%	+8 to +15
G7 OECD domiciled corporate bonds and convertibles rated between AA– and BBB–	90.91%	+10 to +15
All other collateral, provided it is exchange-traded and with individual SEDOL numbers of less than $5 million value, and no more than $25 million total category value	71.43%	+ 8 to +15

Table 5.6: Tri-party yields, September 2000.
Source: JPMorgan Chase Bank.

5.7.2 Hold-in-custody repo

This is part of the general collateral (GC) market, and is more common in the United States than elsewhere. Consider the case of a cash-rich institution investing in GC as an alternative to deposits or commercial paper. The better the quality of collateral, the lower the yield the institution can expect, while the mechanics of settlement may also affect the repo rate. The most secure procedure is to take physical possession of the collateral. However if the dealer needs one or more substitutions during the term of the trade, the settlement costs involved may make the trade unworkable for one or both parties. Therefore, the dealer may offer to hold the securities in his own custody against the investor's cash. This is known as a *hold-in-custody* (HIC) repo. The advantage of this trade is that since securities do not physically move, no settlement charges are incurred. However, this carries some risk for the investor because they only have the dealer's word that their cash is indeed fully collateralised in the event of default. Thus this type of trade is sometime referred to as a "Trust Me" repo; it is also referred to as a *due-bill repo* or a *letter repo*.

In the US market there have been cases in which securities houses that went into bank-ruptcy and defaulted on loans were found to have pledged the same collateral for multiple HIC repo trades. Investors dealing in HIC repo must ensure:

■ they only invest with dealers of good credit quality, since an HIC repo may be perceived as an unsecured transaction;

■ they receive a higher yield on their cash in order to compensate them for the higher credit risk involved.

A *safekeeping repo* is identical to an HIC repo whereby the collateral from the repo seller is not delivered to the cash lender but held in "safe keeping" by the seller. This has advantages in that there is no administration and cost associated with the movement of stock. The risk is that the cash lender must entrust the safekeeping of collateral to the counterparty, and has no means of confirming that the security is indeed segregated, and only being used for one transaction.

Due to the counterparty risk inherent in an HIC repo, it is rare to see it transacted either in the US market or elsewhere. Certain securities are not suitable for delivery; for example, the class of mortgage securities known as *whole loans* in the US, and these are often funded using HIC repo (termed *whole-loan repo*).

5.7.3   Borrow/loan vs cash

This is similar in almost all respects to a classic repo/reverse repo. A legal agreement between the two parties is necessary, and trades generally settle *delivery-versus-payment*. The key difference is that under a repo agreement legal title over the collateral changes hands. Under a securities lending agreement this is not necessarily the case. The UK standard securities lending agreement does involve transfer of title, but it is possible to construct a securities lending agreement where legal title does not move. This can be an advantage for customers who may have accounting or tax problems in doing a repo trade. Such institutions will opt to transact a *loan versus cash*. The UK standard lending agreement also covers items such as dividends and voting rights, and is therefore the preferred transaction structure in the equity repo market.

5.7.4   Bonds borrowed/collateral pledged

In the case of a bonds borrowed/collateral pledged trade the institution lending the bonds does not want or need to receive cash against them, as it is already cash-rich and would only have to re-invest any further cash generated. As such this transaction only occurs with *special collateral*. The dealer borrows the special bonds and pledges securities of similar quality and value (general collateral). The dealer builds in a fee payable to the lending institution as an incentive to do the trade.

Example 5.3:   Bonds borrowed/collateral pledged

◆ ABC Bank plc wishes to borrow DKK 300 million of the Danish government bond 8% 2001. ABC owns the Danish government bond 7% 2007. ABC is prepared to pay a customer a 40 basis point fee in order to borrow the 8% 2001 for one month.

The market price of the 8% 2001 (including accrued interest) is 112.70. The total value of DKK 300 million nominal is therefore DKK 338,100,000.

The market price of the 7% 2007 (including accrued interest) is 102.55.

In order to fully collateralise the customer ABC needs to pledge 338,100,000/1.0255 which is 329,692,832.76; when rounded to the nearest DKK 1 million this becomes DKK 330 million nominal of the 7% 2007.

In a bonds borrowed/collateral pledged trade, both securities are delivered free of payment and ABC Bank plc would pay the customer a 40bp borrowing fee upon termination. In our example the fee payable would be:

$$338,100,000 \times 31/360 \times 0.4/100 = \text{DKK } 112,700.$$

5.7.5   *Borrow versus letter of credit*

This instrument is used when an institution lending securities does not require cash, but takes a third-party bank letter of credit as collateral. However, since banks typically charge 25–50 basis points for this facility, transactions of this kind are relatively rare.

5.7.6   *Cross-currency repo*

All of the examples of repo trades discussed so far have used cash and securities denominated in the same currency, for example gilts trading versus sterling cash, and so on. In fact there is no requirement to limit oneself to single-currency transactions. It is possible to trade say, gilts versus US dollar cash (or any other currency), or pledge Spanish government bonds against borrowing Japanese government bonds. A cross-currency repo is essentially a plain vanilla transaction, but where collateral that is handed over is denominated in a different currency to that of the cash lent against it. Other features of cross-currency repo include:

- possible significant daylight credit exposure on the transaction if securities cannot settle versus payment;
- a requirement for the transaction to be covered by appropriate legal documentation;
- fluctuating foreign exchange rates, which mean that it is likely that the transaction will need to be marked-to-market frequently in order to ensure that cash or securities remain fully collateralised.

It is also necessary to take into account the fluctuations in the relevant exchange rate when marking securities used as collateral, which are obviously handed over against cash that is denominated in a different currency.

Example 5.4:   Cross-currency repo

◆ On 4 January 2000 a hedge fund manager funds a long position in US Treasury securities against sterling, for value the following day. It is offered a bid of 4.90% in the one-week, and the market maker also requires a 2% margin. The one-week Libor rate is 4.95% and the exchange rate at the time of trade is £1/$1.63. The terms of the trade are given below.

Trade date	4 January 2000
Settlement date	5 January 2000
Stock (collateral)	US Treasury 6.125% 2001
Nominal amount	$100 million
Repo rate	4.90% (sterling)

Term	7 days
Maturity date	12 January 2001
Clean price	99-19
Accrued interest	5 days (0.0841346)
Dirty price	99.6778846
Gross settlement amount	$99,677,884.62
Net settlement amount (after 2% haircut)	$97,723,416.29
Net wired settlement amount in sterling	£59,953,016.13
Repo interest	£56,339.41
Sterling termination money	£60,009,355.54

The repo market has allowed the hedge fund to borrow in sterling at a rate below the cost of unsecured borrowing in the money market (4.95%). The repo market maker is "overcollateralised" by the difference between the value of the bonds (in £) and the loan proceeds (2%). A rise in USD yields or a fall in the USD exchange rate value will adversely affect the value of the bonds, causing the market maker to be undercollateralised.

5.7.7   *Dollar rolls*[14]

Dollar rolls are repo-type trades specific to the US mortgage-backed bond market.[15] A dollar roll is so-called because the buyer "rolls in" the security and then may well return, or "roll out", a different security, but one from the same issuer and with the same coupon rate. The procedure developed due to the special characteristics of mortgage-backed securities, as a means by which market makers could borrow stock to deliver into short positions. In essence dollar rolls are very similar to classic repo, as they are secured loans that involve the sale and simultaneous forward repurchase of a security. The main difference is that the party buying in the securities is not required to return the exact identical securities on termination, but only "substantially identical securities". To be deemed identical, the returned security must have the same coupon rate, issuer and type of mortgage collateral. This is required because (amongst other reasons) with a mortgage pass-through issue, for a given coupon and programme there are a number of pass-through securities representing different underlying pools of mortgage loans. Therefore the dealer bank may not return a security with the identical underlying pool of mortgages. The dealer bank thus has some flexibility with regard to the collateral, and in return does not receive any margin. That is, the cash proceeds are those of the market value of the securities transferred. This in turn results in some cases in the repo rate being lower than the GC repo rate. The other significant difference is that coupon payments made during the term of the trade are retained by the buying party, thus making dollar rolls more akin to a true sale.

The mechanics of the forward market have an influence on dollar roll activity. The difference between the spot or cash price of an MBS issue and its forward price is known as the *drop*, and in a positive-sloping yield curve environment, the drop is always positive (in other

---

14 My thanks and appreciation to Mr Frank Fabozzi for his assistance with this section.
15 For a good introduction to mortgage-backed bonds see Hu (2001). The MBS chapters in Mr Fabozzi's *Handbook* also provide an excellent description and review of the main analytical techniques.

words, the cash price of an MBS tranche is always higher than the forward price in this situation). Fund managers may exploit this difference by selling their holding of an MBS issue and buying it back forward, and making use of the sale proceeds in the intervening period. It is this feature of the mortgage bonds market that led to the development of dollar rolls, and from our description of it we can already observe its similarities to repo, although it is conceptually closer to a sell/buy-back. The cash proceeds in a dollar roll can be used by the seller during the term of the trade, as in a repo trade. However the key difference between dollar rolls and repo, sell/buy-back and securities lending is of course that in a dollar roll, the seller forfeits the coupon interest and the principal repayment on the security during the term of the trade.

The term of a dollar roll can vary from one week to six months, although most trades are around one month in duration. In market terminology, selling the bond and buying it back forward is known as "selling the roll", while buying the bond and selling it forward is "buying the roll". The Bond Market Association (BMA) publishes a calendar of dollar roll settlement dates at the start of each year. The accounting authorities have stated that for a dollar roll to be deemed a "financing" trade rather than an actual sale of assets, the bonds must have been owned by the seller for a period of 35 days prior to their sale. Savings and loans institutions (*thrifts*) must take delivery of dollar rolls within 12 months, although other financial institutions need not take delivery.

Unlike in a classic repo, the funding rate on a dollar roll is a function of a number of special factors, assuming that the dealing bank is buying securities and lending cash. These include:

■ the security sale and repurchase price;

■ the size of any expected coupon payment;

■ the level of expected principal repayments during the term of the trade;

■ the level of prepayments during the term of the trade;

■ the features of the similar security that is returned on maturity of the trade;

■ the level of under- or over-delivery of securities allowed.

Since the repurchase price in a dollar roll must take into account any coupon payment, the repurchase price is frequently lower than the opening leg purchase price (bear in mind that mortgage-backed securities usually pay a monthly coupon). This contrasts with a classic repo, where, depending on one's interpretation, the repurchase price is either greater than the sale price (the difference representing repo interest) or the same as the sale price, with repo interest an additional amount on the final cash flow. The amount of principal payments and prepayments also affects the financing rate, because all principal payments during the term of the trade are retained by the buyer. The buyer realises a gain if the security was originally purchased below par, as principal is paid off at par; if the security was purchased at a price above par, the buyer will realise a loss when principal is paid off. The total level of principal payments cannot be determined with certainty at the start of the trade, and this represents a risk to the buyer. Another material factor is what features the returned security possesses. This represents a risk for the seller.

There are additional esoteric factors that make dollar rolls differ from repo. The seller of securities may "under-deliver" the amount of securities by up to 0.1% of the agreed nominal value, and will do so if the price of the bonds has risen between the trade date and delivery date.[16] An over-delivery will occur if the price of the bonds has fallen in this time. The funding cost associated with dollar rolls can only be estimated, based on assumptions of prepayment, and is not known with certainty until the termination of the trade. If no prepayments of the underlying security actually take place during the term, the funding cost for the bond seller will rise, as there will be a lower amount to offset against the foregone coupon. This is illustrated in Example 5.5.

A good account of dollar rolls is given in Fabozzi and Yuen (1998). Example 5.5 of a dollar roll in the US agency market follows their approach.

Example 5.5:   Dollar roll and calculation of financing rate

A fund manager holds $1 million nominal of the GNMA 7.5% 30-year bond. It enters into a one-month dollar roll with a repo dealer bank in which it sells the bond holding at a price of 100-05 and buys it back at a forward price of par. This gives a *drop* of 5/32nds, and although the trade assumes that $1 million nominal of the bonds will be bought back, there may be an under-delivery if part of the bond principal has repaid during the term of the trade.

The bonds are sold at 100-05, therefore the cash consideration is $1,001,562.50. On the buy-back date the fund manager will receive back the same or identical bonds for a price of par, or consideration of $1,000,000. Hence the value of the drop is $1,562 and is the difference between the sale and repurchase prices.

In return for this feature the fund manager must forgo the coupon interest that is receivable during the roll period, which is 7.50% on $1 million nominal for a period of 30/360 of a year. This is calculated as

$$(7.50\% \times 1,000,000) \times (30/360)$$

or $6,250.

In a dollar roll the dealing back is also entitled to scheduled and unscheduled prepayments of the bond's principal balance. In our example the repayment of principal would result in a loss of 5 ticks per cent of par value, as the dealer has purchased the bonds by this much above par. This is a negative feature for the dealing bank but a positive feature for the fund manager. In common with all mortgage-backed securities analysis, in order to assess what level of prepayment can be expected, interested parties must assume a level of prepayment.[17] For the purposes of illustration we assume that this particular bond has a scheduled payment of principal of $5,000 per month and an assumed prepayment of $15,000 per month. As the dealing bank will lose 5/32nds per $100 nominal repaid, from these levels we can calculate that it will lose

$$0.15625 \times (5,000/100)$$

or $7.81 as a result of the scheduled principal repayment and

---

16   The facility to under- or over-deliver securities is known as the *tolerance* and has fallen from a 1% level when dollar rolls were first introduced.

17   See either of the previously mentioned references for an introduction to the prepayment "speeds" used in the analysis of MBS issues. These are known as "PSA100", "PSA200", and so on, after the Public Securities Association (since renamed The Bond Market Association) that initially introduced them, and refer to an assumed level of prepayment of the underlying mortgages that are used as asset backing in an MBS transaction.

$$0.15625 \times (15,000/100)$$

or \$23.44 as a result of prepayments.
We can now calculate the overall funding cost for the one-month period, as follows:

Coupon interest foregone	6,250.00
Drop	1,562.00
Principal repayment	31.25
Total offset	1,593.25
Total funding cost	4,656.75

Therefore the funding cost for the one-month term of the trade is

4,656.75/1,001,52.50

or 0.46495%.
The simple annualised financing rate is therefore 5.579%.
If during the term of the trade no repayments or prepayments had actually taken place, the offset against the foregone coupon would be lower, and consequently the funding cost for the fund manager would have risen.

In Example 5.5 the dollar roll funding rate will be compared to the repo rate available to the fund manager in a classic repo trade, using the same Ginnie Mae 7.5s as repo collateral. However the two trades are not strictly comparable due to the higher risks associated with the dollar roll for the dealing bank.

The size of the drop can be a key motivation for entering into a dollar roll. As Hu states:

> "Given the size of the drop, the implied financing rate is mathematically determined by the coupon rate of the mortgage pass-through [a type of MBS] and the monthly prepayment during the roll period."
>
> (Hu 2001, page 141).

Sometimes dealing banks will sell the roll because there is an arbitrage opportunity and short-term financing can be obtained at a favourable rate. Under certain circumstances, given the coupon of an MBS issue, its prepayment rate, current price and the market reinvestment rate, the current drop value will imply a certain funding rate. As the drop rises, the funding rate will decline, and vice versa. The point at which the value of the drop implies a funding rate that is equal to the market short-term repo rate is known as the *break-even drop*. At the break-even drop value, the mortgage bond holder will observe no difference from entering into a dollar roll or from continuing to hold the bond.

5.7.8   *Repo-to-maturity*

A *repo-to-maturity* is a classic repo where the termination date on the repo matches the maturity date of the bond in the repo. We can discuss this trade by considering the Bloomberg screen used to analyse repo-to-maturity, which is REM. The screen used to analyse a reverse repo-to-maturity is RRM.

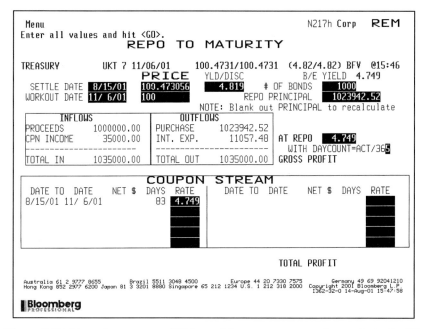

Figure 5.12: Bloomberg screen REM; used for repo-to-maturity analysis, for UK Treasury 7% 2001 on 14 August 2001. ©Bloomberg L.P. Reproduced with permission.

Screen REM is used to analyse the effect of borrowing funds in repo to purchase a bond, where the bond is the collateral security. This is conventional and we considered this earlier. In essence, the screen will compare the financing costs on the borrowed funds to the coupons received on the bond up to and including maturity. The key determining factor is the repo rate used to finance the borrowing. From Figure 5.12 we see that the screen calculates the break-even rate, which is the rate at which the financing cost equals the bond return. The screen also works out cash flows at start and termination, and the borrowed amount is labelled as the "repo principal". This is the bond total consideration. Under "outflows" we see the repo interest at the selected repo rate, labelled as "Int. Exp". Gross profit is the total inflow minus total outflow, which in our example is zero because the repo rate entered is the break-even rate. The user will enter the actual repo rate payable to calculate the total profit.

A reverse repo-to-maturity is a reverse repo with matching repo termination and bond expiry dates. This shown at Figure 5.13.

Repo-to-maturity is a low-risk trade as the financing profit on the bond position is known with certainty to the bond's maturity. For financial institutions that operate on an accruals basis rather mark-to-market basis, the trade can guarantee a profit and not suffer any losses in the interim while they hold the bond.

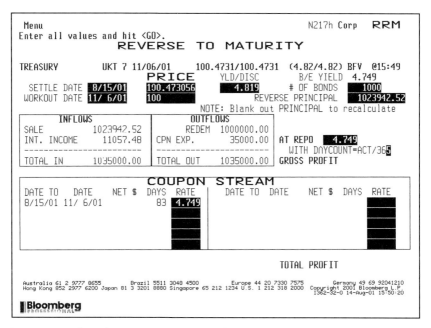

Figure 5.13: Bloomberg screen RRM, used for reverse repo-to-maturity analysis, for UK Treasury 7% 2001 on 14 August 2001. ©Bloomberg L.P. Used with permission.

5.7.9 *Whole loan repo*

Whole loans are a fixed income instrument in the domestic US market; the term is typically used to refer to mortgage securitisation products such as pass-throughs but also covers other underlying assets such as retail asset receivables; for example, credit card loans. Whole loan repo is a repo using a whole loan as the collateral. The market developed in the US because of the demand for higher yields in a falling interest rate environment. The whole loan repo rate trades above the Treasury GC repo rate because of the lower quality of the collateral. In addition, the collateral itself suffers from prepayment risk – the risk that all or part of the outstanding amount is paid off ahead of the stated maturity date. This will have the effect of cancelling a repo trade that has been entered into using the whole loan as collateral. For these reasons, in general the whole loan repo trades at an average of 25–30 basis points above the Treasury repo rate

5.8   Repo mechanics

5.8.1 *Repo collateral*

The collateral in a repo trade is the security passed to the lender of cash by the borrower of cash. It is not always secondary to the transaction; in stock-driven transactions the requirement for specific collateral is the motivation behind the trade. However, in a classic repo or sell/buy-back, the collateral is always the security handed over against cash.[18] In a stock loan

---

18   So that even in a stock-driven reverse repo the collateral is the security handed over against the borrowing of cash by the repo seller.

transaction, the collateral against stock lent can be other securities or cash. Collateral is used in repo to provide security against default by the cash borrower. Therefore it is protection against counterparty risk or *credit risk*; the risk that the cash borrowing counterparty defaults on the loan. A secured or *collateralised* loan is theoretically a lower credit risk exposure for a cash lender compared to an unsecured loan.

The most commonly encountered collateral is government bonds, and the repo market in government bonds is the largest in the world. Other forms of collateral include Eurobonds, other forms of corporate and supranational debt, asset-backed bonds, mortgage-backed bonds, money market securities such as T-bills, and equities.

In any market where there is a defined class of collateral of identical credit quality, this is known as *general collateral* or "GC". So for example, in the UK gilt market a GC repo is one where any gilt will be acceptable as repo collateral. Another form of GC might be "AA-rated sterling Eurobonds". In the US market the term *stock collateral* is sometimes used to refer to GC securities. In equity repo it is more problematic to define GC and by definition almost all trades are specifics; however, it is becoming more common for counterparties to specify any equity being acceptable if it is in an established index; for example, a FTSE100 or a CAC40 stock, and this is the nearest equity market equivalent of general collateral. If a specific security is required in a reverse repo or as the other side of a sell/buy-back, this is known as a *specific* or *specific collateral*. A specific stock that is in high demand in the market, such that the repo rate against it is significantly different from the GC rate, is known as a *special*. We will look at specials again in Chapter 8.[19] In the US market another term for special is *hot*.

Where a coupon payment is received on collateral during the term of a repo, it is to the benefit of the repo seller. Under the standard repo legal agreement, legal title to collateral is transferred to the buyer during the term of the repo, but it is accepted that the economic benefits remain with the seller. For this reason, coupon is returned to the seller. In classic repo (and in stock lending) the coupon is returned to the seller on the dividend date, or in some cases on the following date. In a sell/buy-back the effect of the coupon is incorporated into the repurchase price. This includes interest on the coupon amount that is payable by the buyer during the period from the coupon date to the buy-back date.

5.8.2 *Repo return*

The return on a repo is the interest paid on the cash that is lent out as part of the transaction. It is therefore received by the supplier of cash, the repo buyer. This return is the repo rate, the money market rate for the relevant maturity term which is a function of the central bank base rate as well as supply and demand in the money market and repo market. As we noted earlier, this repo rate is explicit in classic repo and implicit in sell/buy-back. In a stock loan transaction, return is quoted as a fixed fee in basis points. This fee is also a function of supply and demand in the stock loan market. There will be some interaction between the stock loan and repo markets. Where cash is received as collateral in a stock loan, the stock lender must pay interest on this cash during the term of the loan, and the stock loan fee will reflect this interest liability.

Where a specific stock is in high demand, the repo rate payable on cash lent against must reflect this demand in a way that benefits the owner of this stock (the repo seller). Therefore

---

[19] Note that it is not technically correct to refer to a specific as a special unless its repo rate is materially different to the GC rate. A repo in a specific stock that trades at or near the GC rate is just that, a specific repo, and not a special.

the specific repo rate will be lower than the GC rate, and becomes known as a *special* rate. The benefit to the owner of a special stock is that they pay a lower rate of interest on cash that they have borrowed, compared to if they had borrowed the cash in a GC trade or in the unsecured market.

5.8.3   *Repo risks*

We look at risks in dealing in repo later on in this book, but here we provide a basic overview. The primary risk in a money market transaction is *credit risk*, the risk that the borrower of cash will default during the term of the loan. Repo reduces this risk to the supplier of cash as it is secured. However the risk is not eliminated, and even where AAA-rated collateral is supplied, there is still a legal process to be entered into that is time-consuming and administratively costly. There is also a risk in the nature of the collateral itself, which is sometimes known as *issuer risk* – the risk that the issuer of bonds defaults or is declared bankrupt. The supplier of cash will wish to ensure that the market value of collateral is at least equal to the value of cash lent; there is a greater risk that this will not be the case for long-term trades, or where the collateral is highly price-volatile. To counter this repo buyers often specify *margin* to guarantee a minimum value for collateral; they will also prefer that bonds supplied as collateral are of low modified duration and so have lower *market risk*.

Market risk is the risk that the value of a financial instrument falls due to the fluctuations in market price levels. For a bond this is the risk that its price falls due to changes in market interest rates.[20] This is a risk for the repo buyer, the lender of cash, and is addressed through incorporating margins. The repo seller is of course also exposed to this market risk, as they are still the owner of the stock and will mark the loss on their balance sheet throughout the term of the repo trade.

5.8.4   *Legal treatment*

Classic repo is carried out under a legal agreement that defines the transaction as a full transfer of the title to the stock. The standard legal agreement is the BMA/ISMA GMRA, which we review in Chapter 14. It is now possible to trade sell/buy-backs under this agreement as well. This agreement was based on the standard BMA legal agreement used in the US domestic market, and was compiled because certain financial institutions were not allowed to legally borrow or lend securities. By transacting repo under the BMA agreement, these institutions were defined as legally buying and selling securities rather than borrowing or lending them.[21]

5.9   Margin

To reduce the level of risk exposure in a repo transaction it is common for the lender of cash to ask for a margin, which is where the market value of collateral is higher than the cash value of cash lent out in the repo. This is a form of protection should the cash-borrowing counterparty default on the loan. Another term for margin is *overcollateralisation* or *haircut*. There are two types of margin: an *initial margin* taken at the start of the trade, and *variation margin* which is called if required during the term of the trade.

---

[20]   The risk that its price falls due to a downgrade in its credit quality is of course credit risk.
[21]   The Bond Market Association (BMA) was previously known as the Public Securities Association (PSA), so the GMRA is, in some quarters, still referred to as the PSA/ISMA agreement.

5.9.1   *Initial margin*

The cash proceeds in a repo are typically no more than the market value of the collateral. This minimises credit exposure by equating the value of the cash to that of the collateral. The market value of the collateral is calculated at its *dirty* price, not clean price – that is, including accrued interest. This is referred to as *accrual pricing*. To calculate the accrued interest on the (bond) collateral we require the day-count basis for the particular bond.

The start proceeds of a repo can be less than the market value of the collateral by an agreed amount or percentage. This is known as the *initial margin* or *haircut*. The initial margin protects the buyer against:

■ a sudden fall in the market value of the collateral;

■ illiquidity of collateral;

■ other sources of volatility of value (for example, approaching maturity);

■ counterparty risk.

The margin level of repo varies from 0–2% for collateral such as UK gilts to 5% for cross-currency and equity repo, to 10–35% for emerging market debt repo.

In both classic repo and sell/buy-back, any initial margin is given to the supplier of cash in the transaction. This remains true in the case of specific repo. For initial margin the market value of the bond collateral is reduced (or given a "*haircut*") by the percentage of the initial margin and the nominal value determined from this reduced amount. In a stock loan transaction the lender of stock will ask for margin.

There are two methods for calculating the margin; for a 2% margin this could be one of the following:

■ (dirty price of the bonds) $\times 0.98$

■ (dirty price of the bonds)$/1.02$

The two methods do not give the same value! The RRRA repo page on Bloomberg uses the second method for its calculations and this method is turning into something of a convention.

For a 2% margin level the BMA/ISMA GMRA defines a "margin ratio" as:

$$\frac{\text{collateral value}}{\text{cash}} = 102\%.$$

The size of margin required in any particular transaction is a function of the following:

■ the credit quality of the counterparty supplying the collateral; for example, a central bank counterparty, interbank counterparty and corporate will all suggest different margin levels;

■ the term of the repo; an overnight repo is inherently lower risk than a one-year risk;

■ the duration (price volatility) of the collateral; for example, a T-bill compared to the long bond;

■ the existence or absence of a legal agreement; repo traded under a standard agreement is considered lower risk.

Certain market practitioners, particularly those that work on bond research desks, believe that the level of margin is a function of the volatility of the collateral stock. This may be either, say, one-year historical volatility or the implied volatility given by option prices. Given a volatility level of say, 10%, suggesting a maximum expected price movement of –10% to +10%, the margin level may be set at, say, 5% to cover expected movement in the market value of the collateral. This approach to setting initial margin is regarded as onerous by most repo traders, given the differing volatility levels of stocks within GC bands. The counterparty credit risk and terms of trade remain the most influential elements in setting margin, followed by quality of collateral.

In the final analysis margin is required to guard against market risk – the risk that the value of collateral will drop during the course of the repo. Therefore the margin call must reflect the risks prevalent in the market at the time; extremely volatile market conditions may call for large increases in initial margin.

5.9.2   *Variation margin*

The market value of the collateral is maintained through the use of *variation margin*. So if the market value of the collateral falls, the buyer calls for extra cash or collateral. If the market value of the collateral rises, the seller calls for extra cash or collateral. In order to reduce the administrative burden, margin calls can be limited to changes in the market value of the collateral in excess of an agreed amount or percentage, which is called a *margin maintenance limit*.

The standard market documentation that exists for the three structures covered so far includes clauses that allow parties to a transaction to call for variation margin during the term of a repo. This can be in the form of extra collateral (if the value of the collateral has dropped in relation to the asset exchanged) or a return of collateral, if the value has risen. If the cash-borrowing counterparty is unable to supply more collateral where required, they will have to return a portion of the cash loan. Both parties have an interest in making and meeting margin calls, although there is no obligation. The level at which variation margin is triggered is often agreed beforehand in the legal agreement put in place between individual counterparties. Although primarily viewed as an instrument used by the supplier of cash against a fall in the value of the collateral, variation margin can of course also be called by the repo seller if the value of the collateral has risen in value.

An illustration of variation margin being applied during the term of a trade is given in Example 5.6.

Example 5.6:   Variation margin

◆ Figure 5.14 shows a 60-day repo in the 5% Treasury 2004, a UK gilt, where a margin of 2% is taken. The repo rate is 5½%. The start of the trade is 5 January 2000. The clean price of the gilt is 95.25.

Nominal amount	1,000,000
Principal	£952,500.00
Accrued interest (29 days)	£3961.75
Total consideration	**£956,461.75**

The consideration is divided by 1.02, the amount of margin, to give £937,707.60. Assume that this is rounded up to the nearest pound.

Loan amount	£937,708.00
Repo interest at 5½%	£8477.91
Termination proceeds	**£946,185.91**

Assume that one month later there has been a catastrophic fall in the bond market and the 5% 2004 gilt is trading down at 92.75. Following this drop, the market value of the collateral is now:

Principal	£927,500
Accrued interest (59 days)	£8082.19
Market value	**£935,582.19**

However, the repo desk has lent £937,708 against this security, which exceeds its market value. Under a variation margin arrangement it can call margin from the counterparty in the form of general collateral securities or cash.

The formula used to calculate the amount required to restore the original margin of 2% is given by:

Margin adjustment =

((original consideration + repo interest charged to date) × (1 + initial margin))

−(new all-in price × nominal amount)

This therefore becomes:

$$((937,708 + 4238.96) \times (1 + 0.02)) - (0.93558219 \times 1,000,000) = £25,203.71.$$

The margin requirement can be taken as additional stock or cash. In practice, margin calls are made on what is known as a portfolio basis, based on the net position resulting from all repos and reverse repos in place between the two counterparties, so that a margin delivery may be made in a general collateral stock rather than more of the original repo stock. The diagrams below show the relevant cash flows at the various dates.

5 January

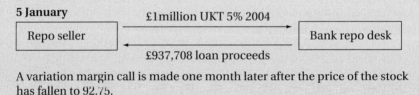

A variation margin call is made one month later after the price of the stock has fallen to 92.75.

7 February

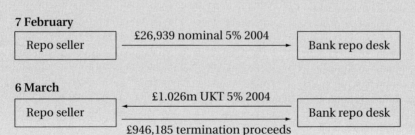

6 March

Figure 5.14

Selected bibliography and references

Bollenbacher, G., *The Professional's Guide to the United States Government Securities Markets; Treasuries, Agencies, Mortgage-Backed Instruments*, New York Institute of Finance 1988, Chapters 7–11

Choudhry, M., *An Introduction to Repo Markets*, 2nd edition, SI (Services) Publishing 2001

Choudhry, M., *The Bond and Money Markets*, Butterworth-Heinemann 2001, Chapter 34

Cooke, S., "Too many crooks spoilt the froth", *Euromoney* July 1994, pp. 21–24

Corrigan, D., Georgiou, C., Gollow, J., *Repo: the Ultimate Guide*, Pearls of Wisdom Publishing 1999

Fabozzi, F., (ed.), *Securities Lending and Repurchase Agreements*, FJF Associates 1997

Fabozzi, F., *Bond Portfolio Management*, 2nd edition, FJF Associates 2001, pp. 192, 196, 198.

Fabozzi, F., Yuen, D., *Managing MBS Portfolios*, FJF Associates 1998, Chapter 9

Hogg, S., "Ready, steady, repo", Emerging Markets Investor 2, 1995, pp. 10–12

Hu, J., *Basics of Mortgage-Backed Securities*, 2nd edition, FJF Associates 2001

Lumpkin, S., "Repurchase and reverse repurchase agreements" in Cook, T., and Rowe, T., *Instruments of the Money Market*, 6th edition, Federal Reserve Bank of Richmond, 1986

Mahn, J., "Lending in the Repo Market: Taking Advantage of Special Issues", *Bloomberg Magazine*, May 1998

Rugg, D., "Repurchase agreements", in Fabozzi, F. (ed.), *Handbook of Fixed Income Securities*, Irwin 1991

Steiner, R., *Mastering Repo Markets*, FT Pitman 1998

Sollinger, A., "The tri-party is just beginning", *Institutional Investor*, January 1996, pp. 133–135

Stigum, M., *The Repo and Reverse Markets*, Irwin, 1989.

6 The Uses and Economic Functions of Repo

Like most things that are simple and straightforward, repo is a flexible instrument that offers users a number of benefits. It is a means by which market participants ranging from banks to corporates can borrow and lend cash and securities. In Chapter 1 we stated that repo should be treated as a money market transaction, irrespective of the motivation behind the trade. Certain texts state that repo should also be regarded as a capital market instrument when it is a stock-driven transaction, although this is essentially an academic fine point.[1] The sale-and-repurchase element of the trade, and the transfer of legal title, also should not confuse users of the fundamental economics of the transaction.

In this chapter we review some of the uses of repo and its benefits to particular users.

6.1   Economic effects

Irrespective of the legal implications of a classic repo or a sell/buy-back conducted under a legal agreement, the transfer of collateral and cash is recognised as temporary in a repo. This contrasts with an outright sale or an outright purchase of a stock. Therefore the economic benefits of ownership remain with the original seller of stock or lender of cash. Hence, the repo seller will continue to mark-to-market the price of the stock on his book each day, and is also entitled to any coupon or dividend payable on the stock during the term of the trade. A drop in value of the stock is an unrealised loss on its daily profit-and-loss, while a rise in value is an unrealised profit.

The repo rate in a transaction is not a function of the current price of the collateral, its expected price on maturity, or its modified duration. Nor is the decision to enter into the repo a function of any of these values. This reflects the economics of repo. For a corporate, investing cash in the repo market is an alternative to a bank money market deposit.

6.2   Uses of repo

In this section we review some of the main uses of repo amongst market participants. Using repo enables market participants to realise value from holding assets in demand. The repo mechanism allows for compensation for use of a desired asset. If cash is the desired asset, the

---

[1]   In a stock-driven trade, a bank entering into reverse repo may well be motivated by the need to cover a short position; however, it is long of cash precisely because it is short of stock, and therefore needs to place this cash in the money market. By placing cash in the repo market though, which presupposes a demand by an external party to borrow short-term cash, the bank will deal with both its cash and stock requirements in one trade. Whichever way one looks at it, repo is a secured loan. The issue of legal transfer of title is part of the mechanics of the trade, but only because it allows parties to the transaction to proceed without worrying about issues such as translation risk in the event of default. Repo is a secured loan. Period. As for repo being a capital market instrument, most textbooks define "capital markets" to be debt with a maturity longer than one year, or equity. Very few repo trades are over one year in maturity, and all are priced relative to the money market yield curve. So again, an academic fine point.

compensation for its use is simply the repo rate of interest paid on it. If bonds are the desired asset, the buyer (lender of cash) compensates the seller (borrower of cash) by accepting a below-market repo rate of interest on the cash he has lent.

6.2.1 *Funding positions*

Often the primary purpose associated with repo is its use as a funding instrument for bond traders. In the normal course of business a bond trader or market-maker will need to finance their book positions. Figure 6.1 illustrates the basic principle for a bond trader who has purchased or shorted bonds.

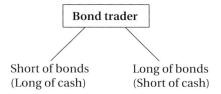

Figure 6.1

To finance the long position the bond trader can borrow money unsecured in the interbank market, assuming that they have a credit line in this market. This may not always be the case. However a collateralised loan will invariably be offered to them at a lower rate, and counterparties are more likely to have a credit line for the bond trader if the loan is secured. Therefore by financing the long position in the repo market rather than in the interbank market, the funding cost associated with running the position itself will be reduced. To "finance" the short position there is no alternative to an open repo market, where the market maker can enter into a reverse repo to cover the short.[2] Figure 6.2 is a generic illustration.

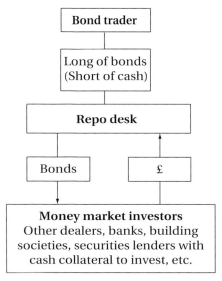

Figure 6.2

---

[2]   With regard to terminology, generally market participants use the term "finance" for a long bond position and "cover" for a short bond position. Sometimes the terms are interchanged.

Cash-rich money market investors finance bond traders by lending out cash in a repo. They receive *general collateral* (GC) in return for their cash, which is any bond of the required credit quality. Legally this is a sale and repurchase of bonds; economically it is a secured loan of cash. The cash investor receives the repo rate of interest for making the loan.

The advantages of a repo transaction for the cash investor are:

■ it is a secured investment;

■ the returns are competitive with bank deposits and occasionally higher;

■ this is a diversification from the usual practice of placing cash deposits with a bank.

A bond trader will enter into a *reverse repo* when they require a specific issue to deliver into a short sale. In this case the trader is effectively borrowing bonds and putting up cash as collateral. The market maker will receive interest on the cash they have lent out in the reverse repo; if this is below the coupon on the bond, the position will be funded at a loss.

The position is shown in Figure 6.3.

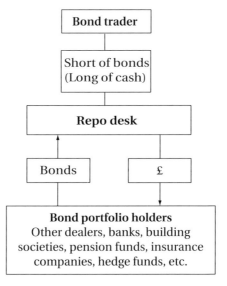

Figure 6.3

In this transaction the bond lender's compensation is the difference between the repo rate paid on the dealer's cash and the market rate at which they can reinvest the cash. If the bond is particularly sought after, that is it is *special*, the repo rate may be significantly below the GC rate. Special status in a bond will push the repo rate downwards. Zero rates and even negative rates are possible when dealing in specials.

The repo rate will reflect supply and demand in the market. In a financing transaction, the dealer is paying the repo rate on the investor's cash. The GC rate tends to trade below the LIBOR rate, and also below the LIBID rate, reflecting its status as a secured loan. In a positioning transaction, the dealer receives the repo rate on their cash. If the bond being borrowed (for this is, in effect, what is happening) is special, the repo rate receivable will be lower to reflect the demand for the bond.

6.2.2   Yield enhancement

Active players in repo and interbank markets can enhance yield by lending bonds at the GC rate and then reinvesting the cash at a higher rate. This would of course introduce an element of credit risk. A market counterparty could also borrow bonds in the stock-lending market, on-lend these bonds via repo and invest the cash proceeds in say, CDs, using the CDs as collateral for the stock loan. Where the collateral is government bonds, the institution will usually be receiving a higher rate on the CD than the repo rate it is paying in the repo. The use of repo for arbitrage and basis trading will be considered in Chapters 17–19.

6.2.3   Borrowers and lenders of cash

As a money market secured loan, repo has a number of uses as a cash borrowing or lending instrument. We have noted how bond traders can finance their books at a lower rate in the repo market; however for some market participants the interbank market will not be accessible to them and repo is the only means by which they can borrow cash. As a cash-lending instrument, repo is used where security is required. There are a number of advantages in secured lending, in addition to the reduction in credit risk, the main one being the lower capital charges that result compared to unsecured lending. There is also greater liquidity in government bond repo, as this is the main method by which central banks provide liquidity to the money market.

The other main use of repo is as a stock borrowing-and-lending instrument. Specific securities can be borrowed in repo to cover short positions. A short in a bond will be put on by a bank or bond trader in the following instances:

- in the normal course of market-making business;
- as a speculative trade in anticipation of a rise in market interest rates;
- as a hedge against a long position in another bond or an off-balance-sheet instrument;[3]
- as part of an arbitrage-type trade, such as a cash-and-carry or *basis* trade.

Institutional investors with large holdings of bonds and blue-chip equities can use repo to enhance income, for example investing the cash in high-quality investments such T-bills or clearing bank CDs. Such institutions have long used the stock loan market, where they can receive a fixed fee for lending stock, but the repo market often enables them to realise greater value from special stock.

6.2.4   Market participants

The simplicity of the repo instrument means that virtually any participant in the financial markets can use it. The main market players include:

- **investment banks:** including the global integrated banks that combine commercial banking and investment banking activity; examples include JPMorgan Chase, ABN Amro, Morgan Stanley, Barclays Capital, RBS NatWest, and so on. Some of these banks will provide a market-making service in some markets, but simply fund their books in other markets. They are active as both cash lenders and borrowers and stock lenders and borrowers;

---

[3]   For example, a possible hedge against a short position in an interest-rate swap, where the bank receives fixed-rate interest, is a short position in a similar-duration bond (in which the bank pays fixed-rate interest).

■ **cash-rich institutions:** these include commercial banks, building societies (known as Savings and Loan or *thrifts* in the US market), corporate treasurers, and money market funds. These will usually lend cash against security collateral;

■ **fund managers:** these include institutional investors, pension funds, local authority investment funds and other entities that are large-scale, long-term holders of securities including bonds and equities. They may repo-out their stock directly to market counterparties such as investment banks, or via brokers and clearing agents such as Euroclear and Clearstream. They are also active in the stock loan market;

■ in the UK market, **former discount houses** such as Gerrard & National and King & Shaxson, now known as Gerrard & King (and part of the Old Mutual group) and Cater Allen (part of Abbey National plc);

■ **brokers:** repo brokers will act as agents between the parties to a repo;

■ **Euroclear and Clearstream:** the clearing and custodian banks that provide tri-party repo services.

This is a diverse range of market participants, and this range is most widely developed in the US market, where repo is regarded as simply another money market instrument. In less mature markets the diversity of market players is less evident.

6.3   Benefits of using repo

The advantages of using repo for the various counterparties are summarised below. For the holders of securities they include:

■ a means by which cash may be borrowed to fund long positions in securities, irrespective of whether the securities are held for investment, speculative or arbitrage reasons;

■ the ability to finance at lower rates of interest, as the collateral is often government securities, particularly for institutions that lack direct access to the interbank markets;

■ in a positive yield curve environment, a funding gain available as the return on the holding of longer-term instruments is higher than the cost of short-term repo finance;

■ access to cash without having to liquidate the securities they are holding, which may be undesirable and which might crystallise market losses.

The benefits of reverse repo for the suppliers of cash include:

■ a secure, collateralised use of surplus cash or a long cash position. This reduces credit risk and frees up unsecured credit lines for use in other business;

■ capital charges under the Basel rules and the European Union capital adequacy directive (CAD) are reduced;

■ the freedom to go short of securities if they believe that the price of a repoable security is likely to fall.

6.4   Market practice

6.4.1   *The repo trade*

Repo trades themselves are effected by front-office dealers who may sit either on the Treasury desk, money market desk or government bonds desk.[4] The front office manages the book and will take a view on the short-term yield curve. Trades are settled by the operations area of the bank or financial institution, sometimes referred to as the "back office". In classic repo a legal agreement is in place between a bank and each of its counterparties, as well as any brokers that it deals through. The following details are agreed at the time of trade:

- the type of collateral, whether general collateral (GC) or a specific issue. If it is a GC trade, the actual collateral that is used is not usually known at the time of trade, and will be arranged by the back office; in this case the trader will simply write "GC" on the trade ticket. For government bond repo there is a standard list of acceptable collateral, documented by ISMA;

- start date or *value date*, and the maturity of the trade; if the termination date falls on a holiday or non-business day, it will be moved forward to the next business day. The most common convention is *modified following business day*, which means that the maturity date will be moved forward to the next business day unless this would result in the trade terminating in a different month, in which case it will be moved back to the nearest business day.[5] Trades taking place across borders cannot have start or termination dates that fall on a public holiday in either money centre;

- the repo rate for the transaction;[6]

- the amount of the repo trade. In the UK the convention is to *bid* and *offer* stock, which means lending or borrowing cash respectively. This is identical to CDs for example, so the bid rate on CDs is the rate at which one would buy paper, that is, lend cash. Therefore the amount quoted usually means nominal amount of stock; however, it is possible to effect a trade quoting an amount of actual cash;

- the price of the stock. It is common for front-office dealers to use a reference price; for example, the previous day's stock exchange or other official list closing price, which saves both parties from having to agree a current market price. Such a reference price will be a

---

4   The author has experienced each of these setups! It is more usual for the repo desk to be situated within the money markets division of a bank. Equity repo is frequently carried out by the Treasury arm of the operations area, often considered a "back office" department.

5   So for example, in the London market a one-month repo with value date 30 March 2000 would have a calendar maturity date of 30 April 2000; however, this day was a Sunday; ordinarily the termination date would be moved forward to the next working day, which was 2 May 2000 (1 May was a public holiday, known as a *bank holiday*, in the UK); however, under the MFBD convention the termination date would be brought back to 28 April 2000, which is in the same month as the calendar maturity date of April. Under the *following business day* convention the maturity date would be 2 May 2000.

6   This is the rate for short-term secured money, with short-term defined as any term from overnight to one-year. The complete set of rates for this period may be considered the repo term structure of interest rates, and is a function of the supply and demand for short-date money, the demand for specific stocks, and the behaviour and volatility of other money market rates. The money market yield curve often acts independently of the bond yield curve, at least over the short term, so a liquid and positively sloped bond curve may not necessarily imply the same in the money market, and vice-versa.

clean price, and the back-office will then calculate actual market values using the dirty price. In the gilt repo market counterparties usually use the Debt Management Office (DMO) reference price, previously known as the CGO reference price, which is the average of the previous day's market-makers closing prices. For Eurobonds the price is usually obtained from a third party such as Bloomberg or Reuters;

■ the level of any initial margin, if required. The standard margin level in the US Treasury market is 2.5%, while in gilt repo it is common for no margin to be taken amongst whole-sale market counterparties. Banks often have different margin level requirements depending on the credit quality of specific counterparties.

United Kingdom gilt repo general collateral

Term rates are regularly quoted in GC for all maturities from overnight to one-year. In the UK market a GC transaction will be quoted in terms of nominal of stock, so the actual cash lent in the transaction is not known until the actual collateral is identified. This must be done within five minutes of the trade taking place. If the repo buyer is unwilling to accept some types of stock, for example index-linked gilts, this must be specified at the outset. A deal in £50 million GC refers to £50 million nominal of stock, although if a counterparty requires, it can specify the actual amount of cash it wishes to deal in, which requires the repo seller to calculate the nominal amount of stock that must be passed over.

Rates are also quoted for "DBV" which refers to delivery-by-value, this differs from GC in that the actual stock that will be received is not necessarily identified until later in the day, around 3.50 pm; so the cash lender does not know what stock it will be receiving. Bonds to the value of the cash are handed over in the repo, hence the term used to identify this type of trade. Again, any CREST–CGO stock can be delivered in a DBV repo.

Certain details pertaining to a trade will have been agreed for each counterparty in advance, and are usually standing data applicable to all transactions. These include:

■ arrangements and procedures on the settlement or clearing of the trades; for instance, whether this is over a clearance system such as Euroclear or Clearstream Banking, or over a domestic clearance system such as CREST–CGO in the London market;

■ details on any rights or instructions on the substitution of one type or issue of collateral for another;

■ the treatment of coupons and dividends paid during a trade; in classic repo the manu-factured dividend is paid on the coupon date while in sell/buy-back it may be held until termination, in which case interest is payable at either the same repo rate or another rate, or paid on the coupon date;

■ margin arrangements; the GMRA master repo agreement states that the margin receiver may elect to receive it in the form of stock or cash. If stock is provided it is usually a form of general collateral; while if cash is provided, interest is payable to the cash provider at an agreed rate.

6.4.2   Credit risk and margin

Transactions in the money market expose the cash-lending party to credit risk and repo is no exception to this. The presence of security may be viewed as reducing the inherent credit risk exposure; however, it does not remove the need for credit assessment and "know your counterparty".[7] A bank will assess each counterparty for its creditworthiness, as well as the quality of the collateral, and assign a net repo trading limit (net of repo and reverse repo). A margin rate will be agreed on the basis of this assessment. In classic repo, as traded under the GMRA master agreement, this includes initial margin and ongoing variation margin. A variation margin arrangement will include:

- daily marking-to-market of each stock that has been accepted as repo collateral. If there is a standard reference price this will be taken as the mark, otherwise a third-party price source will be used;

- the level at which variation margin will be called, that is the threshold level below the initial margin point.

Margin is recommended for lower credit-quality counterparties but it is common to observe banks not incorporating it in their trades. This may be because counterparties have a certain dealing relationship, or view the market as low-risk on the whole. In some cases there is no standard margin level for counterparties, rather, specific trades are assessed on margin requirement depending on their particular risk profile. Another common occurrence in repo trades is a zero initial margin, but a provision for variation margin if market prices drop by a significant amount. Trades conducted via a broker in developed markets are rarely subject to initial margin, including longer-term transactions.

If variation margin is required during a trade, there are a number of ways in which this may be met. These are at the option of the supplier of collateral and are summarised below.

- **Provision of cash amount of margin.** If cash equal to the margin amount is supplied, the trade can be closed out for the day following the original start date and re-priced as a new trade for a start date on the same day. The maturity date in the new trade is of course identical to that in the original trade. The collateral remains with the repo buyer[8] and the cash amount is passed over to them. When cash is passed over as margin, interest is payable either at the original repo rate or at another interest rate, or may not be paid at all. This is for agreement amongst the counterparties.

- **Provision of security collateral to value of margin.** This can be done in two ways. The original trade can be closed out as before, on the day following the start date, and a new trade written for this day to the original termination date. The original cash investment amount remains unchanged and securities to the value of the margin call is passed to the repo buyer. The alternative method is to leave the original trade unchanged, running it to maturity, and pass securities to margin value as a *free delivery*. This additional amount is

---

7 Certain practitioners and academics suggest that repo should only be undertaken with counterparties for whom there exists an unsecured credit line. This appears to be excessively cautious, and renders the provision of security irrelevant. Although it is sensible to maintain credit analysis and regularly review lending limits, the availability of security does put a new slant on the credit risk element, but prudence would suggest a less risk-averse attitude to repo. This does not always happen; in the wake of the deterioration in credit quality of independent UK merchant banks (admittedly, a rare breed at the start of the 21st century!) following the collapse of Barings in 1995, a number of building societies would not enter into gilt repo with firms such as Hambros Bank Limited, despite the AAA-rated security collateral element attached to this business.

8 That is, the cash investor.

in effect a new repo, at a zero repo rate and with bonds *also* priced at zero, running to the same termination date as the original repo trade. It is more common to observe the re-pricing method being observed, and a corresponding netting of cash flows, so that it is not necessary to have stock movements in both directions.

6.5   Case study exercise

On Monday 4 January 2000 the gilt repo desk at ABC Bank plc receives or makes the following telephone calls from counterparties regarding different repo transactions, all with value dates of Tuesday 5 January 2000. Table 6.1 shows a composite screen of money market prices and rates, together with bond prices, for the day in question. Attached after the rates table are four sample trade tickets for each of the trades. Readers are invited to complete the trade tickets for each of the transactions, and then consider the discussion points at the end of each ticket.

Money market rates	Rate
GBP interbank – 1 week	4.95%
GBP interbank – 1 month	5.65%
UK T-bill – 1 month	5.20%
UK T-bill – 3 month	5.40%
AA+ name CD (3 month)	6.00%
Repo 1 week GC	4.90%
Repo 1 month GC	5.50%
Repo – 86 days GC	5.75%

Cable rate
GBP/USD = 1.63

Bonds	Price	Days accrued
5% Treasury 2004	95.25	29 days
5.75% Treasury 2009	100.79	29 days
United States Treasury 6.125% 2001	99.59375	5 days
7.25% Treasury 2007	107.84	29 days
6.5% Treasury 2003	100.42	29 days

Table 6.1: Case study rates.

Trade 1

A classic repo conducted with Commercial Bank plc; after ABC Bank plc quotes a bid-offer price in one-month GC repo of 5 9/16% – 5½%, the offer is lifted and ABC Bank plc deals £50 million GC at 5.50% for one month. The collateral stock supplied is 5% Treasury 2004. Commercial Bank plc have requested that the deal amount is actual cash value, rather than the market convention of quoting nominal amount of stock.

Trade 2

A sell/buy-back with Henry Marshall Securities, with ABC Bank plc offering £30 million nominal of 5¾% 2009 for 86 days at 5.00%.

Trade 3

A cross-currency repo with Quanto Asset Management, with ABC Bank plc bidding for $100 million of a US Treasury at 4.90% for a one-week term against sterling cash; a 2% margin is also required by ABC Bank plc.

Trade 4

A stock-loan deal, with ABC Bank plc borrowing £100 million of 7¼ Treasury 2007 for 14 days, with collateral supplied of 6½ Treasury 2003, paying a fee of 40 basis points, from Rasheed Pension Fund. Rasheed Pension Fund require a margin of 5% on the collateral supplied.

Trade tickets follow overleaf ▶

Trade 1

ABC Bank plc

ABC Repo Trading Ticket

Counterparty   <u>Commercial Bank plc</u>

Trade date   _____   Settlement date   _____

Collateral   _____   Nominal amount _____

Repo rate   _____

Term _____ days (From _____ To _____)   Check calendar!

Clean price   _____   (CREST Reference price – given)

Accrued   _____   Note: The UK gilt market uses act/act
for accrued interest

The coupon dates are 7 June
and 7 December

Dirty price   _____

Settlement amount (Wired Amount)   _____

Repo interest _____   (Repo interest day count: act/365)

Termination Money _____

---

1. What is the yield spread compared to Libor?
2. What is the repo rate compared to the rate on unsecured paper?
3. Suggest reasons why Commercial Bank's treasurer might make this investment rather than deposit the funds in a bank or purchase a T-bill.
4. What is the running yield on the 5% 2004? Should we use the bond clean or dirty price? If the trade is ABC plc in effect funding its long position in this stock, what is the funding gain (loss) during the 1-month period?

Trade 2

> ### *ABC Bank plc*
>
> **ABC Buy/Sell-back Trading Ticket**
>
> Counterparty   Henry Marshall Securities
>
> Trade date   _____ _____   Settlement date   _____
>
> Collateral   UKT 5¾% 2009 _____   Nominal amount _____
>
> Repo rate   _____
>
> Term _____ days (From _____ To _____)
>
> Clean price   _____
>
> Accrued   _____   (act/act; coupon dates
>   7 June and 7 December)
> Dirty price   _____
>
> Settlement amount (Wired Amount)   _____
>
> Repo interest _____
>
> Termination amount _____
>
> Forward dirty price   _____
>
> Forward accrued   _____
>
> Forward clean price   _____

1. What is the premium on the equivalent maturity GC rate?
2. By investing the proceeds in CDs, what gain in basis points will be earned over the three-week period (on an annualised basis)?
3. How can ABC Bank plc invest the proceeds for a risk-free gain?

Trade 3

```
┌─────────────────────────────────────────────────────────────────────────┐
│                                                                           │
│   ABC Bank plc                                                            │
│                                                                           │
│   ABC Reverse Repo Trading Ticket                                         │
│                                                                           │
│   Counterparty   Quanto Asset Management                                  │
│                                                                           │
│   Trade date  _____      Settlement date  _____     │
│                                                                           │
│   Collateral   US Treasury 6 1/8% 2001   Nominal amount _____    │
│                                                                           │
│   Repo rate    _____                                          │
│                                                                           │
│   Term _____ days (From _____ To _____ )                       │
│                                                                           │
│   Clean price   _____    US day-count method is  act/act –    │
│                                      coupon dates 30 June, 31 Dec          │
│   Accrued       _____                                         │
│                                                                           │
│   Dirty price   _____                                           │
│                                                                           │
│   Gross settlement amount in USD       _____                    │
│                                                                           │
│   Net settlement amount after haircut in USD    _____           │
│                                                                           │
│   Net settlement amount (Wired Amount) in GBP _____             │
│                                                                           │
│   GBP repo interest    _____                                  │
│                                                                           │
│   GBP termination money  _____                                  │
│                                                                           │
└─────────────────────────────────────────────────────────────────────────┘
```

1. What is Quanto Asset Management's cost of funds compared to what they can achieve with an unsecured borrowing?
2. Who is overcollateralised?

Trade 4

ABC Bank plc

ABC Stock Loan Ticket

Counterparty   Rasheed Pension Fund

Trade date _____ _   Settlement date _____

Bonds borrowed _____   Nominal amount _____

Fee _____

Term _____ days (From _____ To _____)

Clean price   _____

Accrued   _____   (Gilt is act/act; coupon dates
                                            7 June and 7 December)
Dirty price   _____

Loan value   _____

- -

Clean price of collateral (UKT 6½% 2003)   _____

Accrued of collateral   _____

Dirty price of collateral   _____

Value of collateral required, given 5% margin   _____

Nominal of collateral required   _____

---

1. Calculate the cash charge made by Rasheed Pension Fund for lending the bonds. What
   assumptions are required when making this calculation?

Selected bibliography and references

Fabozzi, F., (ed.), *The Handbook of Fixed Income Securities*, 5th edition, McGraw-Hill 1997, Chapter 10

7 Repo and Structured Financial Products

7.1   Introduction

A natural progression within fixed interest markets is the development of ever more sophisticated structures. This occurs for a number of reasons. As liquidity increases and yield spreads decline, banks need to look at newer structures for the same relative value. Investors may also wish to increase exposure to more risky markets in the search for yield; this may take the form of high quality credit counterparties issuing paper in "exotic" currencies or linked to emerging market indices. The imagination of bank financial engineers is the only constraint to the continued development of sophisticated structures. Customers can have instruments customised to meet their exact investment parameters and risk appetite. When engineering structured notes it is important to identify clients who may wish to invest in more sophisticated structures, and also to identify their specific requirements.

Repo has not been immune to the application of financial engineering techniques, notwithstanding the fact that it is probably the most plain vanilla sector of the global financial markets. Structured repo instruments were initially developed mainly in the US market where repo is widely accepted as a retail investment and money placement instrument. Following the introduction of new repo types it is also possible now to transact them in other markets. In this chapter we very briefly review some of the more common examples of structured repo. We then look at the *total return swap* (TRS), an instrument that is formally defined as part of the growing market in *credit derivatives*, but which has many similarities to repo and is sometimes used by repo traders to manage their books. Finally we consider repo and its use in a synthetic *collateralised loan obligation* (CLO) transaction.

7.2   Simple repo structures

7.2.1   *Cross-currency repo*

A cross-currency repo is not actually a structured repo, but simply a repo of a security used as collateral for a loan made in a different currency to the one in which the collateral is denominated. Banks and fund managers engage in cross-currency repo if they perceive funding gains in a currency other than that of the security currency. There is an element of foreign-exchange risk if the exchange rate between the security currency and the loan currency alters significantly during the trade. For this reason margin is always taken in cross-currency repo.

7.2.2   *Callable repo*

In this arrangement the lender of cash in a term fixed-rate repo has the right to terminate the repo early, or call back a portion of the cash. In effect the lender of cash benefits from an interest rate option, which becomes valuable if interest rates rise during the life of the repo. Should rates rise the lender will call back the cash and reinvest it at the higher rates now available. For this reason a callable repo will trade at lower fixed rates than a conventional repo, the difference being the value of the implicit interest-rate option.

7.2.3   *Whole loan repo*

In the US there is a large and liquid market in bonds formed from the securitisation of residential and commercial mortgages. In the issue of a *whole loan* mortgage security,[1] no pass-through security is created from the original pool of mortgages; rather, cash flows from all the mortgages form directly the cash flows of the notes. The whole loan repo structure originated in the US market as a response to investor demand for higher yields in a falling interest rate environment. Whole loan repo trades at higher rate than conventional repo because a lower quality collateral is used in the transaction. There are generally two types: mortgage whole loans and consumer whole loans. Both are unsecuritised loans or interest receivables. The loans can also be credit card payments and other types of consumer loans. The repo uses the BMA repo agreement. Owners of whole loan repos are exposed to credit risk but also, due to the nature of the collateral, prepayment risk. This is the risk that the loan package is paid off earlier than the maturity date, which is often the case with consumer loans. For these reasons the yield on whole loan repo is higher than government bond repo, trading at around 20–30 basis points over Libor.

Example 7.1:   Financing an investment position with a cross-currency repo

A fund manager holding a US government bond wishes to fund the position in sterling. A repo trader offers a 4.90% rate in sterling for a seven day-term with a "haircut" (margin) of 2%. The sterling/dollar exchange rate at the time of the trade is 1.63.

Collateral	US Treasury 6.125% 2001
GBP Repo rate	7.375%
Term	7 days (5 January 2000 – 12 January 2000)

The collateral has a clean price of 99-19 and a haircut of 2% is applied to the loan proceeds. Note that US Treasury securities are priced in "ticks", which are 1/32nd of a point. Hence 19 ticks is 0.59375.

Accrued	0.0841346 [(6.125 × 5/182 × 0.5)]
Dirty price	99.6778846
Gross settlement amount	USD 99,677,884.62
Net wired settlement amount	USD 97,723,416.29
Net settlement amount (GBP)	£59,953,016.13
Repo interest	£56,339.41

On 12 January 2000 the repo trader returns the collateral to the fund manager in exchange for a payment of £60,009,355.54 which is the original principal plus repo interest. Note that it is likely that actual transferred amounts will be rounded, so that cash flows are not made down to pennies!

The repo market has allowed the fund manager to borrow in sterling, which we can safely assume (as it is backed with high quality collateral) will be at a lower rate than the

---

[1]   Known as a *collateralised mortgage obligation* or CMO.

unsecured rate. The fund manager could have borrowed in dollars or another currency for the same loan-cost benefits. The repo trader is "overcollateralised" by the difference between the value of the bonds and the loan proceeds, that is 2%. A rise in dollar yields or a fall in the value of the dollar will leave the trader undercollateralised, in which case further collateral ("margin call") will be sought from the fund manager.

Example 7.2:   Using repo to finance the hedging of an interest rate swap

A trader transacts a $100 million five-year interest rate swap with a corporate customer. The trader pays fixed at 6.63% (five-year US treasury yield plus 28 basis points) and receives three-month dollar Libor, initially set at 5.875%. As it stands the trader is exposed to the risk of a fall in interest rates, so decides to hedge the position by buying the five-year treasury bond. The trader plans to offset the original swap with a pay floating swap of the same maturity. The bid-offer spread will be the profit. The sell-side five-year swap spread at the time of the original swap is 31 basis points. The trader finances the bond purchase with overnight repo at a rate of 5.50%. This rate is 8 basis points below the overnight repo rate for general collateral (GC) because of market makers' demand for the current five-year issue. After 14 days the trader is able to place an offsetting pay floating swap. The five-year US treasury yield has increased by 6 basis points to 6.41% and sell-side swap spreads have widened by one basis point to 32 basis points. The average overnight repo rate during the holding period is 5.60%.

Trade date 5 January 2000
Collateral   US Treasury 6.125% 2000
Repo rate   5.60% (average over holding period)
Term   14 days (5–19 January 2000)

The collateral has a dirty price of 99.678 for a current yield of 6.145%.

Collateral gross proceeds $99,677,884
Sale price of five-year bond   97.742 (6.41% yield; 19 January 2000)
Receive fixed swap rate   6.73% (19 January 2000)

The trader suffers a loss of $250,240 on the sale of the five-year treasury security. However, this is offset by the net gain in value of the present values of the five-year swaps, which is a gain of 10 basis points (the present value of the difference between 6.63% and 6.73% for five years). The trader was exposed to changes in the swap spread during the hedge period; in this case the widening swap spread was to the trader's benefit. Positive carry on the treasury slightly exceeded the negative carry on the swap during the hedge period.

7.3 The Total Return Swap

A total return swap (TRS), sometimes known as a *total rate of return swap* or *TR swap*, is an agreement between two parties that exchanges the total return from a financial asset between them. This is designed to transfer the credit risk from one party to the other. It is one of the principal instruments used by banks and other financial instruments to manage their credit risk exposure, and as such is a credit derivative. We discuss TR swaps here because of the economic similarities between repo and TR swaps; in this section we review the basic concepts behind TR swaps and the use that can be made of this instrument by repo traders.

7.3.1   *Basic concepts*

Credit derivatives are instruments that enable an institution to transfer its credit exposure onto another party, in return for the payment of some payment or premium, so removing the need to dispose of the asset that is the source of the credit risk. As such they are a form of insurance against losses arising from credit events. An introduction to credit derivatives is given in Appendix 7.1.

One definition of a TRS is given in Francis *et al* (1999), which states:

> "A total return swap is a swap agreement in which the *total return* [my italics] of a bank loan(s) or credit-sensitive security(s) is exchanged for some other cash flow, usually tied to LIBOR or some other loan(s) or credit-sensitive security(s)."
>
> (Francis *et al*, 1999, page 29)

In some versions of a TRS the actual underlying asset is actually sold to the counterparty, with a corresponding swap transaction agreed alongside; in other versions there is no physical change of ownership of the underlying asset. The TRS trade itself can be to any term to maturity, that is, it need not match the maturity of the underlying security. In a TRS the total return from the underlying asset is paid over to the counterparty in return for a fixed or floating cash flow. This makes it slightly different from other credit derivatives, as the payments between counterparties to a TRS are connected to changes in the market value of the underlying asset, as well as changes resulting from the occurrence of a *credit event* (see Appendix 7.1).

Figure 7.1 illustrates a generic TR swap. The two counterparties are labelled as banks, but the party termed "Bank A" may be another financial institution, including cash-rich institutions such as insurance companies and hedge funds. In Figure 7.1, Bank A has contracted to pay the "total return" on a specified reference asset, while simultaneously receiving a Libor-based return from Bank B. The reference or underlying asset can be a bank loan such as a corporate loan or a sovereign or corporate bond. The total return payments from Bank A include the interest payments on the underlying loan as well as any appreciation in the market value of the asset. Bank B will pay the Libor-based return; it will also pay any difference if there is a depreciation in the price of the asset. The economic effect is as if Bank B owned the underlying asset, so TR swaps are synthetic loans or securities. A significant feature is that Bank A will usually hold the underlying asset on its balance sheet, so that if this asset was originally on Bank B's balance sheet, this is a means by which the latter can have the asset removed from its balance sheet for the term of the TR swap.[2] If we assume Bank A has access to Libor funding, it will receive a spread on this from Bank B. Under the terms of the swap, Bank B will pay the difference between the initial market value and any depreciation, so it is sometimes termed the "guarantor" while Bank A is the "beneficiary".

---

2   Although it is common for the receiver of the Libor-based payments to have the reference asset on its balance sheet, this is not always the case.

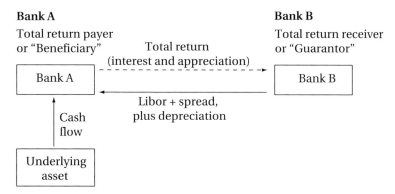

Figure 7.1: Total return swap.

The total return on the underlying asset is the interest payments and any change in the market value if it is an appreciation. The value of an appreciation may be cash settled, or alternatively there may be physical delivery of the reference asset on maturity of the swap, in return for a payment of the initial asset value by the total return "receiver". The maturity of the TR swap need not be identical to that of the reference asset, and in fact it is rare for it to be so.

The swap element of the trade will usually pay on a quarterly or semi-annual basis, with the underlying asset being re-valued or *marked-to-market* on the re-fixing dates. The asset price is usually obtained from an independent third party source such as Bloomberg or Reuters, or as the average of a range of market quotes. If the *obligor* of the reference asset defaults, the swap may be terminated immediately, with a net present value payment changing hands according to what this value is, or it may be continued with each party making appreciation or depreciation payments as appropriate. This second option is only available if there is a market for the asset, which is unlikely in the case of a bank loan. If the swap is terminated, each counterparty is liable to the other for accrued interest plus any appreciation or depreciation of the asset. Commonly, under the terms of the trade, the guarantor bank has the option to purchase the underlying asset from the beneficiary bank, and then dealing directly with loan defaulter.

7.3.2   *Uses and pricing of TR swaps*

There are a number of reasons why banks and financial institutions may wish to enter into TR swap arrangements. One of these is to reduce or remove credit risk. Using TR swaps as a credit derivative instrument, a party can remove exposure to an asset without having to sell it. In a vanilla TR swap the total return payer retains rights to the reference asset, although in some cases servicing and voting rights may be transferred. The total return receiver gains an exposure to the reference asset without having to pay out the cash proceeds that would be required to purchase it. As the maturity of the swap rarely matches that of the asset, the swap receiver may gain from the positive funding, or *carry*, that derives from being able to roll over short-term funding of a longer-term asset.[3] The total return payer, on the other hand, benefits from protection against market and credit risk for a specified period of time, without having to

---

3   This assumes a positively-sloping yield curve.

liquidate the asset itself.[4] On maturity of the swap the total return payer may reinvest the asset if it continues to own it, or it may sell the asset in the open market. Thus the instrument may be considered a synthetic repo. A TR swap agreement entered into as a credit derivative is a means by which banks can take on unfunded off-balance-sheet credit exposure. Higher-rated banks that have access to Libid funding can benefit by funding on-balance-sheet assets that are credit protected through a credit derivative such as a TR swap, assuming the net spread of asset income over credit protection premium is positive.

A TR swap conducted as a synthetic repo is usually undertaken to effect the temporary removal of assets from the balance sheet. This may be desirable for a number of reasons; for example, if the institution is due to be analysed by credit rating agencies or if the annual external audit is to fall due shortly. Another reason a bank may wish to temporarily remove lower credit-quality assets from its balance sheet is if it is in danger of breaching capital limits in between the quarterly return periods. In this case, as the return period approaches, lower quality assets may be removed from the balance sheet by means of a TR swap, which is set to mature after the return period has passed.

Banks have employed a number of methods to price credit derivatives and TR swaps. A review of these techniques is outside the scope of this book, although interested readers may wish to refer to some of the publications listed in the bibliography. Essentially the pricing of credit derivatives is linked to that of other instruments; however, the main difference between credit derivatives and other off-balance-sheet products such as equity, currency or bond derivatives, is that the latter can be priced and hedged with reference to the underlying asset, which can be problematic when applied to credit derivatives. Credit products pricing uses statistical data on likelihood of default, probability of payout, level of risk tolerance and a pricing model. The basic ingredients of a TR swap are that one party "funds" an underlying asset and transfers the total return of the asset to another party, in return for a (usually) floating return that is a spread to Libor. This spread is a function of:

- the credit rating of the swap counterparty;
- the amount and value of the reference asset;
- the credit quality of the reference asset;
- the funding costs of the beneficiary bank;
- any required profit margin;
- the capital charge associated with the TR swap.

The TR swap counterparties must consider a number of risk factors associated with the transaction, which include:

- the probability that the TR beneficiary may default while the reference asset has declined in value;
- the reference asset obligor defaults, followed by default of the TR swap receiver before payment of the depreciation has been made to the payer or "provider".

---

[4]   This may be desired for relationship reasons; for example, a bank wanting to be seen to be maintaining the bank loan of a corporate client (but transfering away the associated credit risk for a temporary period).

The first risk measure is a function of the probability of default by the TR swap receiver and the market volatility of the reference asset, while the second risk is related to the joint probability of default of both factors as well as the recovery probability of the asset.

7.3.3 Asset swap pricing

Credit derivatives are commonly valued using the asset swap pricing technique. In addition to its use by dealers, risk management departments who wish to independently price such swaps also adopt this technique. The asset swap market is a reasonably reliable indicator of the returns required for individual credit exposures, and provides a mark-to-market framework for reference assets as well as a hedging mechanism.[5]

A par asset swap typically combines the sale of an asset such as a fixed-rate corporate bond to a counterparty, at par and with no interest accrued, with an interest-rate swap. The coupon on the bond is paid in return for Libor, plus a spread if necessary. This spread is the asset swap spread and is the price of the asset swap. In effect the asset swap allows market participants that pay Libor-based funding to receive the asset swap spread. This spread is a function of the credit risk of the underlying bond asset, which is why it, in effect, becomes the cornerstone of the price payable on a credit default swap written on that reference asset.

The generic pricing is given by (7.1):

$$Y_a = Y_b - ir \tag{7.1}$$

where

Y_a is the asset swap spread;
Y_b is the asset spread over the benchmark;
ir is the interest-rate swap spread.

The asset spread over the benchmark is simply the bond (asset) redemption yield over that of the government benchmark. The interest-rate swap spread reflects the cost involved in converting fixed-coupon benchmark bonds into a floating-rate coupon during the life of the asset (or default swap), and is based on the swap rate for that maturity.

7.3.4 Asset swap pricing example

XYZ plc is a Baa2-rated corporate. The seven-year asset swap for this entity is currently trading at 93 basis points; the underlying seven-year bond is hedged by an interest-rate swap with an Aa2-rated bank. The risk-free rate for floating-rate bonds is Libid minus 12.5 basis points (assume the bid-offer spread is 6 basis points). This suggests that the credit spread for XYZ plc is 111.5 basis points. The credit spread is the return required by an investor for holding the credit of XYZ plc. The protection seller is conceptually long the asset, and so would short the asset as a hedge of its position. This is illustrated in Figure 7.2. The price charged for the default swap is the price of the shorting the asset, which works out as 111.5 basis points each year.

Therefore we can price a credit default written on XYZ plc as the present value of 111.5 basis points for seven years, discounted at the interest-rate swap rate of 5.875%. This computes to a credit swap price of 6.25%.

---

5   However, for an introductory discussion on the shortcomings of the asset-swap pricing technique for credit default swaps, see the article "Issues in the asset-swap pricing of credit default swaps" available (as an Acrobat PDF file) on the author's web site www.YieldCurve.com.

Reference	XYZ plc
Term	Seven years
Interest-rate swap rate	5.875%
Asset swap	Libor plus 93 bps

Default swap pricing:

Benchmark rate	Libid minus 12.5 bps
Margin	6 bps
Credit default swap	111.5 bps
Default swap price	6.252%

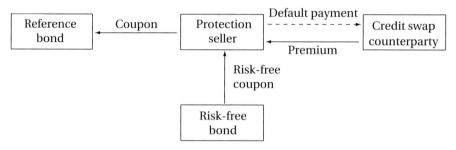

Figure 7.2: Credit default swap and asset swap hedge.

Example 7.3:   Classic repo and total return swap

A trader wishes to finance a bond position for one month (30 days). A cash investor agrees collateral of £1m nominal UK Treasury 7% 2001 gilt, which is trading at 104.46, plus four days' accrued interest which is 0.076087. The agreed repo rate is one month Libor flat, which is 6.00%. There is no haircut.

The following diagrams illustrate how the classic repo trade is structured and priced compared to the TR swap.

◆ **Classic repo**

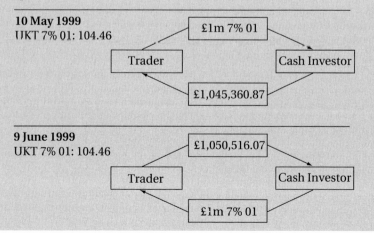

In this transaction the interest at 6% for 30 days is £5,155.20, so termination money is £1,050,516.07. In the example there is no change in price on termination. In any case, if, say, on 9 June the 7% 2001 was trading at the higher price of 105.10, as this is a classic repo there would still be no change in the cash flows.

◆ **Total return swap ("short swap")**

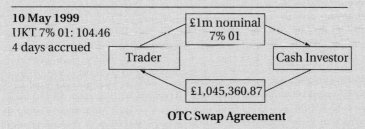

10 May 1999
UKT 7% 01: 104.46
4 days accrued

£1m nominal
7% 01

Trader

Cash Investor

£1,045,360.87

OTC Swap Agreement

Trader enters into a one-month swap in which they will **receive** the total return on a notional £1m nominal 7% 2001 and **pay** one-month Libor flat, that is 6%.

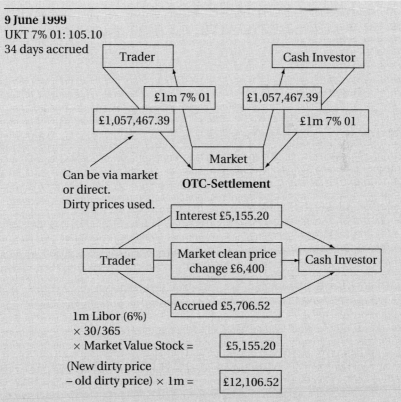

9 June 1999
UKT 7% 01: 105.10
34 days accrued

Trader

Cash Investor

£1m 7% 01

£1,057,467.39

£1,057,467.39

£1m 7% 01

Market

Can be via market
or direct.
Dirty prices used.

OTC-Settlement

Interest £5,155.20

Trader

Market clean price
change £6,400

Cash Investor

Accrued £5,706.52

1m Libor (6%)
× 30/365
× Market Value Stock =   £5,155.20

(New dirty price
– old dirty price) × 1m =   £12,106.52

As there has been a rise in price the trader pays over the difference to the cash investor. If there had been a drop in price the difference would have been paid by the cash investor to the trader.

7.3.5 *Total return swap and repo*

Readers may have perceived that there are economic similarities between a TR swap and a classic repo transaction. A repo seller does not remove the collateral bond from its balance sheet, and there is no transfer of economic effects, including market and credit risk. In a TR swap the total return payer or beneficiary lays off these risks to the swap counterparty. The counterparty desires this economic exposure, but the TR swap enables it to achieve this without taking on the associated financing cost. However both trades are funding transactions, in effect financed purchases of an asset, and in that respect are similar.

Consider a situation where the potential total return receiver owns an asset such as a bond, and requires financing for it (or is about to purchase the asset and requires financing). It could sell the bond to a counterparty that is prepared to be a TR payer and simultaneously enter into a TR swap with this counterparty. This is illustrated in Figure 7.3. In Figure 7.3, if Bank A had entered into a classic repo with Bank B, with the repo rate set at Libor plus a spread, the repo trade would be economically identical to the bond sale and TR swap.[6]

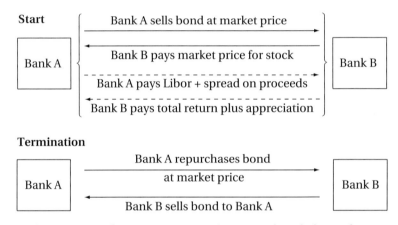

Figure 7.3: Total return swap removing assets from balance sheet.

The main difference is that the transaction is governed by the International Swap Dealers Association (ISDA) Swap agreement as opposed to a repo agreement. This changes the way the trade is reflected on the bank's balance sheet, and takes it off-balance-sheet. This is one of the main motivations for entering into this type of trade. So the transaction works as follows: (a) the institution sells the security at its market price; (b) the institution then executes a swap transaction for a fixed term, exchanging the total return on the security for an agreed rate on the relevant cash amount; (c) on maturity of the swap the institution repurchases the security at the market price.

In theory each leg of the transaction can be executed separately with different counterparties; in practice, the trade is bundled together and so is economically identical to a repo.

The similarities between repo and TR swaps has resulted in repo traders employing the latter to help manage their books. The swaps are used if they offer a cheaper funding rate and if there is a need to remove assets from the balance sheet for the term of the swap. Often TR swaps are used as financing instruments by equity market makers. It is unlikely that a repo

---

6   This trade is also common with equity underlying assets.

trader would employ TR swaps for short-term funding, or longer-term funding in high-quality assets such as gilts. However, long-term funding and funding of high-yield or exotic assets may need to be funded via a TR swap. In addition, repo desks are exposed to credit risk in the same way that other lending desks are so exposed; a TR swap or other credit derivative may be used to reduce this credit exposure where the bank does not wish to physically sell the asset.

In another application, assume that a bond trader believes that a particular bond that is not currently on his book is about to decline in price. To reflect this view the trader may:

- sell the bond in the market and cover the resulting short position in repo. The cash flow out is the coupon on the bond, with capital gain if the bond falls in price. Assume that the repo rate is floating, say Libor plus a spread. The trader must be aware of the funding costs of the trade, so that unless the bond can be covered in repo at GC,[7] the funding will be at a loss. The yield on the bond must also be lower than the Libor plus spread received in the repo;

- as an alternative, enter into a TR swap in which they pay the total return on the bond and receives Libor plus a spread. If the bond yield exceeds the Libor spread, the funding will be negative; however, the trade will gain if the trader's view is proved correct and the bond falls in price by a sufficient amount. If the breakeven funding cost (which the bond must exceed as it falls in value) is lower in the TR swap, this method will be used rather than the repo approach. This is more likely if the bond is special.

Total return swaps are increasingly used as synthetic repo instruments, most commonly by investors that wish to purchase the credit exposure of an asset without purchasing the asset itself. This is conceptually similar to what happened when interest-rate swaps were introduced, which enabled banks and other financial institutions to trade interest-rate risk without borrowing or lending cash funds.

7.3.6 *Balance sheet impact*

Under a TR swap an asset such as a bond position may be removed from the balance sheet. As we noted earlier, in order to avoid adverse impact on regular internal and external capital and credit exposure reporting a bank may use TR swaps to reduce the amount of lower-quality assets on the balance sheet. This can be done by entering into a short-term TR swap with, say, a two-week term that straddles the reporting date.

Bonds are removed from the balance sheet if they are part of a sale plus TR swap transaction. This is because legally, the bank selling the asset is not required to repurchase bonds from the swap counterparty, nor is the total return payer obliged to sell the bonds back to the counterparty (or indeed sell the bonds at all on maturity of the TR swap). This does not occur under a classic repo or sell/buy-back, which remain balance sheet transactions.

7.4 Repo and its use in collateralised debt obligation structures

Collateralised debt obligations, or CDOs, are a more recent innovation in the debt markets, and are a development of securitisation structures such as asset-backed and repackaged securities. In both the US market and Europe repo is used as part of a particular type of CDO

---

[7]   That is, the bond cannot be special.

structure known as a *synthetic CDO* transaction. This is a relatively recent feature in CDO transactions, and has not been observed in a majority of deals. It is relevant in the context of this book, because if the investment bank underwriters of the deal design a transaction incorporating repo, the repo desk of the same bank, or another counterparty, will need to get involved from the start of the deal. In this section we discuss how repo forms part of these deals. For beginners an introduction to CDOs and synthetic CDOs is given in Appendix 7.2.

Figure 7.4 illustrates a generic synthetic collateralised loan obligation or synthetic *CLO* structure, featuring a combination of credit default swaps and note issuance. It shows how the special purpose vehicle (SPV) receives the proceeds of the note issue; it then enters into a repo with a banking counterparty, lending cash and taking in securities as collateral. In effect the transaction has been collateralised by the repo securities. In most cases the repo counterparty is the repo desk of the originating bank. The repo securities are usually AAA-rated government debt, and margin of around 2–3% is supplied. The repo term can in theory, be matched to the term of the transaction, at the agreement of the repo desk. However, as the maturity term can be up to 10 years or longer, it is more likely for the repo to be rolled over at much shorter maturities. Figures 7.5 and 7.6 illustrate the repo mechanics.

Examples of CDO transactions that incorporated a repo arrangement in their structure include the Iceberg and Ice Cube deals from UBS Warburg in 1999.

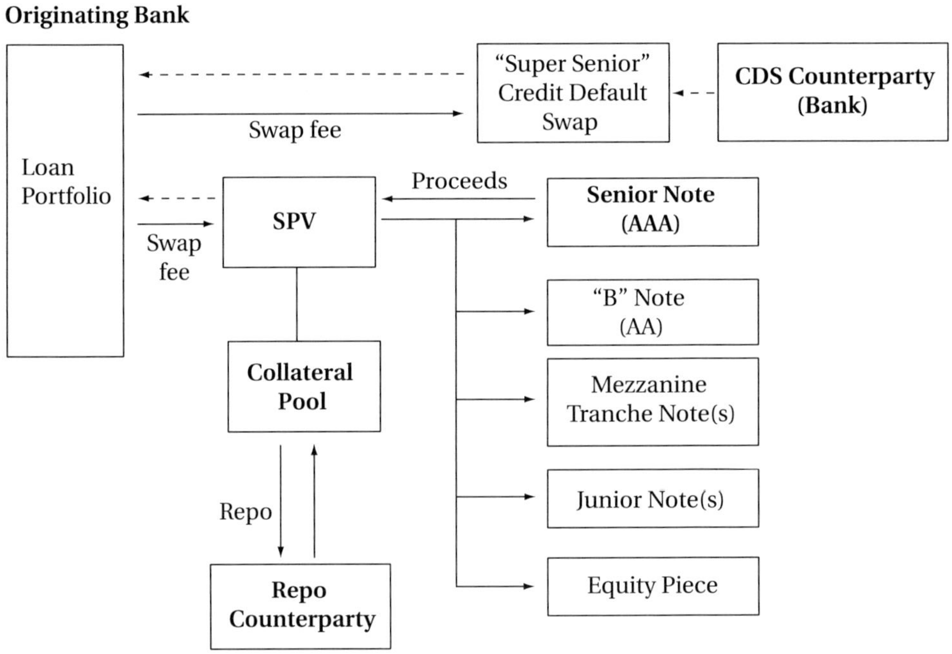

Originating Bank

Figure 7.4: Generic synthetic CLO structure.

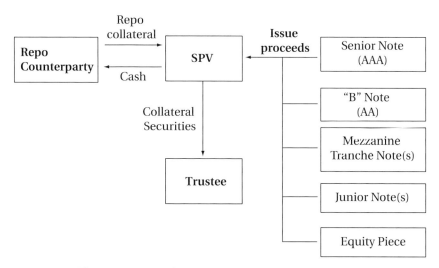

Figure 7.5: Repo element in CLO structure, at start leg.

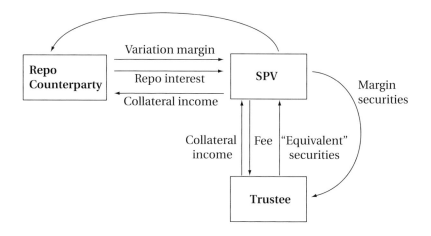

Figure 7.6: Repo mechanics including margin.

Figure 7.7 illustrates the repo arrangement forming part of a synthetic CBO structure, again where the majority element comprises the super senior credit default swap. The proceeds from the issued notes are lent out in repo and secured with AAA-rated collateral. In this example the repo earns interest at the overnight rate, and is rolled-over daily for the life of the transaction.

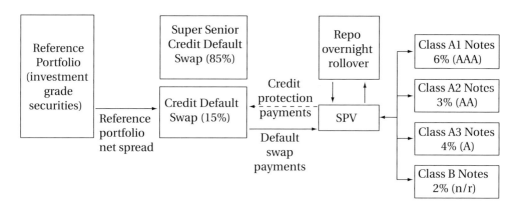

Figure 7.7: Synthetic CBO, with credit default swaps and repo arrangement.

Case study: Brooklands Euro CDO 2001-1 Limited

In this example we illustrate the use of a repo arrangement in a synthetic CDO structure. The terms of the deal state that the repo is set to match the expected life of the transaction. The issue is a synthetic CDO structured and underwritten by UBS Warburg, with Salomon Smith Barney as co-arranger. The purpose of the transaction is to transfer the credit risk of the reference portfolio off the balance sheet of UBS AG (London). The Issuer is the SPV, Brooklands CDO, and which sells credit protection to UBS AG by means of a credit default swap. The credit swap is written on a reference pool of EUR 1 billion of bond assets. As part of the structure the Issuer pledges collateral to UBS AG to support the credit swap, which forms the first loss piece of the issue, and is financed through the issue of EUR 172 million of Floating Rate Notes. These are listed in Figure 7.8. The collateral is invested in AAA-rated securities by means of a repo agreement between the Issuer and UBS AG (London).

Therefore in this arrangement the repo element secures the collateral that is provided as part of the credit protection for the structure. The repo is entered into under the BMA/ISMA GMRA agreement, and its mechanics are in every way similar to the classic repo trades we considered in Chapter 5. The terms of the repo are as follows:

Start date	Transaction closing date
Opening leg "price"	The market value of the Notes on issue, with the required margin taken on the purchased collateral securities. The securities are re-priced (and margin is reset) at the start of each interest period every quarter
Collateral	AAA-rated euro-denominated securities of maximum 13-year (fixed coupon) or 30-year (floating coupon) maturity
Margin	The purchased securities will be of value ranging from 102% (floating-rate government securities) to 113% (fixed coupon corporate securities) of the *required amount*, this being the principal amount of the issued Notes plus accrued interest
Day-count	Act/360

Final repo maturity	The legal maturity date of the issued Notes (December 2013)
Closing leg price	The purchased securities will be repurchased at a price that returns the original start proceeds to the repo counterparty
Variation margining	The purchased securities are marked-to-market by the repo counterparty each day; margin will be applied at the relevant specified level. If required, additional securities will be delivered if there is a shortfall, or returned if there is a surplus
Early termination	The repo is set to match the term of the Notes; however, early termination will result in the event of bankruptcy, failure to pay margin or interest, and a number of other specified events
Custodian	The purchased collateral securities are held in custody by JPMorgan Chase, the third-party repo verification agent.

The credit default swap is set up between the Issuer and the swap counterparty which is UBS AG (London) under the terms of the 1992 ISDA master agreement. Under the swap, credit protection on the reference portfolio is bought by the swap counterparty from the issuer. Under the swap the swap counterparty pays premium to the issuer, and the issuer will pay out to the swap counterparty following occurrence of a credit event. The nature of a credit event is set out in the transaction documentation.

The terms of the credit default swap are as follows:

Start date	Transaction closing date
Termination date	December 2013
Early termination	The credit default swap may be terminated ahead of the scheduled date in the event of bankruptcy, failure to pay, and so forth, as specified in the transaction documentation
Notional amount	EUR 1 billion
Premium	The premium will be an amount sufficient to cover interest payment on the issued Notes, Senior Income Notes and Junior Income Notes, together with interest on the repo, payable quarterly, semi-annually and annually respectively
Payout	This is referred to as the *credit protection payment* (CPP) or *floating amount* and is payable on occurrence of a credit event or partial credit event in regard to one or more of the assets in the reference portfolio. A credit event is specified in the transaction documentation and includes failure to pay interest or principal, reduction in principal amount, downgrade of credit rating to C or lower, restructuring, etc
CPP	This is calculated as: [(1 − Highest reference price) × Notional amount] minus Net partial CPP

Partial CPP	As above
Net partial CPP	Aggregate of Partial CPP minus aggregate of Partial CPP reimbursement
Partial CPP reimbursement	Reimbursement of excess of recalculated value, obtained from new reference price, over previous total of Partial CPP

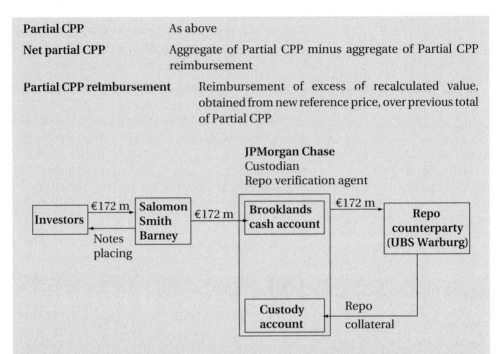

Figure 7.8: Brooklands CDO 2001-1 structure arrangement.

The repo is entered into under the BMA/ISMA GMRA legal agreement. The Brooklands transaction documentation carries an annex that details which parts of the GMRA do not apply; so for example, the paragraphs relating to buy/sell-back transactions and net-paying securities are stated as not being applicable. There are other paragraphs in the annex stating terms and conditions relating to margin, set-off in the event of default and the types of securities that are eligible as collateral.

Tranche	Nominal size (€ million)	Reference pool (%)	Rating	Coupon	Coupon frequency	Call date	Scheduled maturity date	Legal maturity date
Senior credit swap	828.0	82.80%	AAA				20-Dec-2011	20-Dec-2013
Class A Notes	50.0	5.00%	Aaa/AAA	3m Euribor + 30 bp	Quarterly	20-Dec-2006	20-Dec-2011	20-Dec-2013
Class B Notes	50.0	5.00%	Aa3/AA-	3m Euribor + 43 bp	Quarterly	20-Dec-2006	20-Dec-2011	20-Dec-2013
Class C Notes	32.0	3.20%	Baa2/BBB	3m Euribor + 68 bp	Quarterly	20-Dec-2006	20-Dec-2011	20-Dec-2013
Class D Notes	12.5	1.25%	Ba2/BB+	3m Euribor + 135 bp	Quarterly	20-Dec-2006	20-Dec-2011	20-Dec-2013
Senior Income Notes	22.0	2.20%	BB	17.5%	Semi-annually	20-Dec-2006	20-Dec-2011	20-Dec-2013
Junior Income Notes	5.5	0.55%	N/R	35%	Annually	20-Dec-2006	20-Dec-2011	20-Dec-2013

Transaction Closing Date 25 July 2001
First coupon date 12 December 2001
Final maturity date 20 December 2013

Figure 7.9: Brooklands CDO 2001–1 tranche structure.

Appendices

Appendix 7.1:   An introduction to credit derivatives

Credit derivatives are a relatively recent innovation, having been introduced in significant volumes in the mid-1990s. They are financial instruments originally designed to protect banks and other institutions against losses arising from *credit events*. A succinct definition would be that they are instruments designed to lay off or take on credit risk. Since their inception, they have also been used to trade credit for speculative purposes, and as hedging instruments.

A payout under a credit derivative is triggered by a credit event. As banks define default in different terms, the terms under which a credit derivative is executed usually include a specification of what constitutes a credit event. Typically this can be:

- bankruptcy or insolvency of the reference asset obligor;
- a financial restructuring; for example, occasioned under administration or as required under US bankruptcy protection;
- technical default; for example, the non-payment of interest or coupon when it falls due;
- a change in credit spread payable by the obligor above a specified maximum level;
- a downgrade in credit rating below a specified minimum level.

A user of credit derivatives may be any institution that has an exposure to or desires an exposure to credit risk. This includes investment banks and commercial banks, insurance companies, corporates, fund managers, and hedge funds.

The most common credit derivative, and possibly the simplest, is the *credit default swap*, *credit swap*. This is a contract in which a periodic fixed fee or a one-off premium is paid to a *protection seller*, in return for which the seller will make a payment on the occurrence of a specified credit event. The fee is usually quoted as a basis point fee of the nominal value. The swap can refer to a single asset, known as the reference asset or underlying asset, or a basket of assets. The default payment can be paid in whatever way suits the protection buyer or both counterparties. For example, it may be linked to the change in price of the reference asset or another specified asset, it may be fixed at a predetermined recovery rate, or it may be in the form of actual delivery of the reference asset at a specified price. However it is structured, the credit default swap enables one party to transfer its credit exposure to another party. Banks may use default swaps to trade sovereign and corporate credit spreads without trading the actual assets themselves; for example, someone who has gone long a default swap (the protection buyer) will gain if the reference asset obligor suffers a rating downgrade or a technical default, and can sell the default swap at a profit if they can find a buyer counterparty. This is because the cost of protection on the reference asset will have increased as a result of the credit event. The original buyer of the default swap need never have owned a bond issued by the reference asset obligor.

The maturity of the swap does not have to match the maturity of the reference asset and in most cases does not. On default the swap is terminated and default payment by the protection seller or guarantor is calculated and handed over. The guarantor may have the asset delivered to them and pay the nominal value, or may *cash settle* the swap contract.

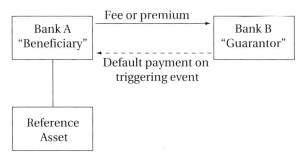

Figure 7.10: Credit default swap.

Another type of credit derivative is the *credit-linked note*. These exist in a number of forms, but all of them contain a link between the return payable on them and the credit-related performance of the underlying reference asset. A standard credit-linked note is a loan or security, usually issued by an investment-graded entity, that has an interest payment and fixed maturity structure similar to a vanilla bond. The performance of the note however, including the maturity value, is linked to the performance of specified underlying assets as well as that of the issuing entity. An accessible introduction to credit-linked notes is given in Kasapi (1999).

Credit options are another form of credit derivative. Like other options a credit option is a contract designed to meet specific hedging or speculative requirements of an entity, which may purchase or sell the option to meet its objectives. A credit call option gives the buyer the right, without the obligation, to purchase the underlying credit-sensitive asset, or a credit spread, at a specified price and specified time (or period of time). A credit put option gives the buyer the right without the obligation to sell the underlying credit-sensitive asset or credit spread. By purchasing credit options banks and other institutions can take a view on credit spread movements for the cost of the option premium only, without recourse to actual loans issued by an obligor. The writer of credit options seeks to earn fee income.

Banks use credit derivatives for a number of reasons. Some of these are summarised below.

Diversifying the credit portfolio
A bank may wish to take on credit exposure by providing credit protection on assets that it already owns, in return for a fee. This enhances income on their portfolio. They may sell credit derivatives to enable non-banking clients to gain credit exposures, if these clients do not wish to purchase the assets directly. In this respect the bank performs a credit intermediation role.

Reducing credit exposure
Another use of credit derivatives is to reduce credit exposure, either for an individual asset or a sectoral concentration, by buying a credit default swap. This may be desirable for assets in their portfolio that cannot be sold for relationship or tax reasons.

Acting as a credit derivatives market maker
A bank may wish to set itself up as a market maker in credit derivatives, hence becoming a credit trader. In this case the trader may or may not hold the reference assets directly, depending on their appetite for risk and the liquidity of the market enabling them to offset derivative contracts as and when required.

Appendix 7.2:   An introduction to Collateralised Debt Obligations (CDOs)

A CDO is essentially a securitisation in which a special purpose vehicle (SPV) issues bonds or notes against an investment in a diversified pool of assets. These assets can be bonds, loans such as commercial bank loans or a mixture of both bonds and loans. Where assets are bonds, these are usually high-yield bonds that provide a spread of interest over the interest liability of the issued notes; where the assets are loans, the CDO acts as a mechanism by which illiquid loans can be pooled into a marketable security or securities. The third type of CDO is known as a synthetic CDO and refers to a structure in which credit derivatives are used to construct the underlying pool of assets.

The investments are funded through the issue of the notes, and interest and principal payments on these notes are linked to the performance of the underlying assets. These underlying assets act as the *collateral* for the issues notes, hence the name. The key difference between CDOs, ABS and multi-asset repackaged securities is that in a CDO the collateral pool is more actively managed by a portfolio or collateral manager. Generally, CDOs feature a multi-tranche structure, with a number of issued securities, most or all of which are rated by a ratings agency. The priority of payment of the issued securities reflects the credit rating for each note, with the most senior note being the highest-rated. The term *waterfall* is used to refer to the order of payments; sufficient underlying cash flows must be generated by the issuing vehicle in order to meet the fees of third-party servicers and all the note issue liabilities. In Europe, issued securities may pay a fixed or floating coupon, usually on a semi-annual, quarterly or monthly basis,[8] with senior notes issues rated from AAA to A and junior and mezzanine notes rated BBB to B. There may be unrated subordinated and equity pieces issued. Investors in the subordinated notes receive coupon after payment of servicing fees and the coupon on senior notes. The equity and subordinated note are the first loss pieces and, as they carry the highest risk, have a higher expected return compared to that of the underlying collateral.

There are two types of CDO: *collateralised bond obligations* (CBOs) and *collateralised loan obligations* (CLOs). As the names suggest, the primary difference between each type is the nature of the underlying assets; a CBO will be collateralised by a portfolio of bonds while a CLO will represent an underlying pool of bank loans. CDOs have also been collateralised by credit derivatives and credit-linked notes. Following this distinction, CDOs can be broken into two main types: *balance sheet* CDOs and *arbitrage* CDOs. Balance sheet CDOs are most akin to a traditional securitisation; they are created to remove assets from the balance sheet of the originating bank or financial institution, usually for reduce capital requirements, increase return on capital or free-up lending lines. An arbitrage CDO is created when the originator, who may be a bank or fund manager for instance, wishes to exploit the yield differential between the underlying assets and the overlying notes. This may be achieved by active management of the underlying portfolio, which might consist of high-yielding or emerging market bonds. Arbitrage CDOs are categorized further into *cash flow* and *market value* CDOs. Almost invariably balance sheet CDOs are cash flow transactions. Put simply, a cash flow CDO is one in which the underlying collateral generates sufficient cash flow to pay the

---

8   Hence proving once and for all that Eurobonds, defined as international securities issued by a syndicate of banks and clearing in Euroclear and Clearstream, may pay coupon on frequencies other than an annual basis!

principal and interest on the issued notes, as well as the servicing fees of third party agents. In a *market value* CDO, the collateral manager actively runs the portfolio and, by means of this trading activity, generates sufficient returns to pay the CDO obligations.

Banks and financial institutions use CDOs to diversify their sources of funding, to manage portfolio risk and to obtain regulatory capital relief. Investors are attracted to the senior notes in a transaction because these allow them to earn relatively high yields compared to other asset-backed bonds of a similar credit rating. Other advantages for investors include:

- exposure to a diversified range of credits;
- access to the fund management and credit analysis skills of the portfolio manager;
- generally, a lower level of uncertainty and risk exposure compared to a single bond of similar rating.

A good overview introduction to CDOs is given in Fabozzi (2000). We show a "family tree" of CDOs in Figure 7.11. The most common CDOs are balance sheet deals; however, a later development, the *synthetic* CDO, now accounts for a large number of transactions.

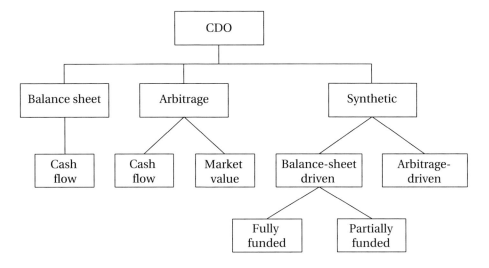

Figure 7.11: The CDO family.

Cash flow CDO

These are intuitively the easiest to understand and are similar to other asset-backed securitisation involving an SPV. In essence assets such as bonds or loans are pooled together and the cash flows from these assets used to back the obligations of the issued notes. As the underlying assets are sold to the SPV, they are removed from the originator's balance sheet; hence the credit risk associated with these assets is transferred to the holders of the issued notes. The originator also obtains funding by issuing the notes. The structure is illustrated, admittedly in simple fashion, in Figure 7.12.

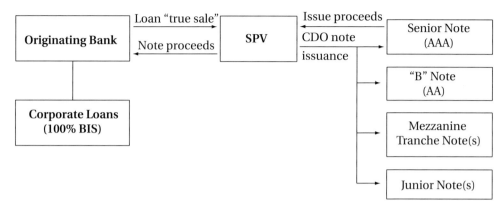

Figure 7.12: Cash flow CDO.

Synthetic CDO

A synthetic CDO is so-called because the transfer of credit risk is achieved "synthetically" via the sale of a credit derivative, rather than a "true sale" to the SPV. Thus in a synthetic CDO the credit risk of the underlying loans or bonds is transferred to the SPV using credit default swaps and/or total return swaps (TRS). The assets themselves may not be legally transferred to the SPV, and may sometimes remain on the originator's balance sheet. Using a synthetic CDO, the originator can obtain regulatory capital relief and manage the credit risk on its balance sheet, but will not be receiving any funding. A typical structure is shown in Figure 7.13.[9]

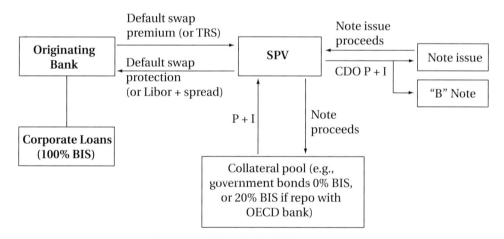

Figure 7.13: Synthetic CDO structure.

Synthetic CDOs are popular in the European market because they are simpler and can be brought to the market quickly; in practice, in certain countries the legal infrastructure has not been sufficiently developed to enable to true sale securitisation to be undertaken. In addition, when the underlying asset pool is composed of bonds from different countries, a cash funded CDO may present too many administrative difficulties. A synthetic CDO removes such issues

---

[9]   "P + I" is a common abbreviation for note (or loan) principal and interest.

by using credit derivatives, and, in theory, can be brought to market more quickly than a cash flow arrangement (although in practice this is not always the case). Synthetic CDOs have been issued as arbitrage CDOs or balance sheet CDOs. We briefly describe each type.

A synthetic arbitrage CDO is generally originated by collateral managers who wish to exploit the difference in yield between that obtained on the underlying assets and that payable on the CDO, both in note interest and servicing fees. The generic structure is as follows: the specially-created SPV enters into a TRS with the originating bank or financial institution, referencing the bank's underlying portfolio (the *reference portfolio*). The portfolio is actively managed and is funded on the balance sheet by the originating bank. The SPV receives the "total return" from the reference portfolio, and in return it pays Libor plus a spread to the originating bank. The SPV also issues notes that are sold into the market to CDO investors, and these notes can be rated as high as AAA because they are backed by high-quality collateral, which is purchased using the note proceeds. A typical structure is shown in Figure 7.14.

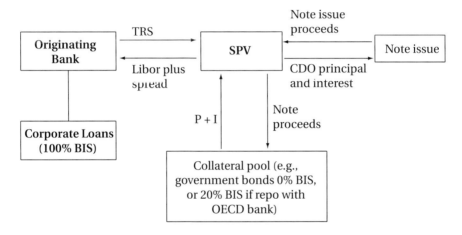

Figure 7.14: Synthetic arbitrage CDO structure.

Balance sheet synthetic CDOs are employed by banks that wish to manage regulatory capital. As before, the underlying assets are bonds, loans and credit facilities originated by the issuing bank. In a balance sheet CDO the SPV enters into a credit default swap agreement with the originator, again with the specific collateral pool designated as the reference portfolio. The SPV receives the premium payable on the default swap, and thereby provides credit protection on the reference portfolio. There are two types of CDO within this structure. In a *partially funded* CDO, only the highest credit risk segment of the portfolio is transferred. The cash flow that would be needed to service the synthetic CDO overlying liability is received from the AAA-rated collateral that is purchased by the SPV with the proceeds of the note issue. An originating bank obtains maximum regulatory capital relief by means of a partially funded structure, through a combination of the synthetic CDO and what is known as a *super senior swap* arrangement with an OECD banking counterparty. A super senior swap provides additional protection to that part of the portfolio, the senior segment, that is already protected by the funded portion of the transaction.

A generic partially funded transaction is shown in Figure 7.15. It shows an arrangement whereby the issuer enters into two credit default swaps; the first with an SPV that provides protection for losses up to a specified amount of the reference pool,[10] while the second swap is set up with the OECD bank or, occasionally, an insurance company.[11]

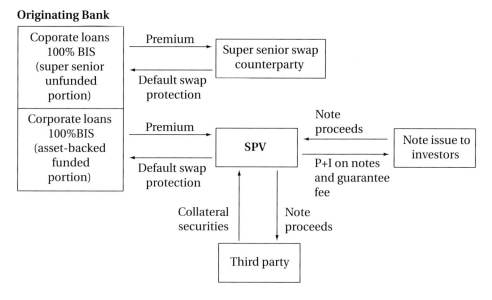

Figure 7.15: Partially funded synthetic CDO structure.

A *fully funded* CDO is a structure where the credit risk of the entire portfolio is transferred to the SPV via a credit default swap. In a fully funded (or just "funded") synthetic CDO the issuer enters into the credit default swap with the SPV, which itself issues notes to the value of the assets on which the risk has been transferred. The proceeds from the notes are invested in risk-free government or agency debt such as gilts, bunds or Pfandbriefe, or in senior unsecured bank debt. Should there be a default on one or more of the underlying assets, the required amount of the collateral is sold and the proceeds from the sale paid to the issuer as recompense for the losses. The premium paid on the credit default swap must be sufficiently high to ensure that it covers the difference in yield between that on the collateral and that on the notes issued by the SPV. The generic structure is illustrated in Figure 7.16.

Fully funded CDOs are relatively uncommon. One of the advantages of the partially funded arrangement is that the issuer will pay a lower premium compared to a fully funded synthetic CDO, because it is not required to pay the difference between the yield on the collateral and the coupon on the note issue (the unfunded part of the transaction). The downside is that the issuer will receive a reduction in risk weighting for capital purposes to 20% for the risk transferred via the super senior default swap.

---

[10] In practice, to date this portion has been between 5% and 15% of the reference pool.
[11] An "OECD" bank, thus guaranteeing a 20% risk weighting for capital ratio purposes, under Basel I rules.

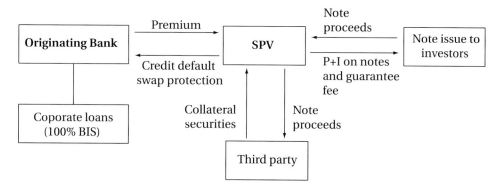

Figure 7.16: Fully funded synthetic balance sheet CDO structure.

Within the European market synthetic balance sheet CDOs are the most common structure. The reasons that banks originate them are two-fold:

- **capital relief:** banks can obtain regulatory capital relief by transferring lower-yield corporate credit risk, such as corporate bank loans, off their balance sheet. Under Basel I rules all corporate debt carries an identical 100% risk-weighting; therefore with banks having to assign 8% of capital for such loans, higher-rated (and hence lower-yielding) corporate assets will require the same amount of capital but will generate a lower return on that capital. A bank may wish to transfer such higher-rated, lower-yield assets from its balance sheet, and this can be achieved via a CDO transaction. The capital requirements for a synthetic CDO are lower than for corporate assets; for example the funded segment of the deal will be supported by high-quality collateral such as government bonds, and via a repo arrangement with an OECD bank would carry a 20% risk weighting, as does the super senior element;

- **transfer of credit risk:** the cost of servicing a fully funded CDO, and the premium payable on the associated credit default swap, can be prohibitive. With a partially funded structure, the issue amount is typically a relatively small share of the asset portfolio. This lowers substantially the default swap premium. Also, as the CDO investors suffer the first loss element of the portfolio, the super senior default swap can be entered into at a considerably lower cost than that on a fully funded CDO.

In essence, structuring synthetic CDOs presents a relatively straightforward transaction process and legal documentation requirements, and this has been behind their popularity in the European market.

Selected bibliography and references

Bessis, J., *Risk Management in Banking*, John Wiley & Sons 1998, pp. 17–18

Crosbie. P., "Modelling Default Risk", in *Credit Derivatives: Key Issues*, British Bankers Association 1997

Das, Sanjiv, "Credit Risk Derivatives", *Journal of Derivatives*, Spring 1995, pp. 7–23

Fabozzi, F., (ed.), *Investing in Asset-Backed Securities*, FJF Associates 2000, Chapters 13–14, 17

Francis, J., Frost, J., Whittaker, J.G., *Handbook of Credit Derivatives*, McGraw-Hill 1999

Jarrow, R., Turnbull, S., "Credit Risk", in Alexander, C., (ed.), *Handbook of Risk Management and Analysis*, Wiley 1996

JPMorgan Chase, *CDO Handbook*, 29 May 2001

Kasapi, A., *Mastering Credit Derivatives*, FT Prentice Hall 1999, Chapter 4

Longstaff, F., Schwartz, E., "Valuing Credit Derivatives", *Journal of Fixed Income*, June 1995, pp. 6–14

Lucas, D., "Default Correlation and Credit Analysis", *Journal of Fixed Income*, June 1995 pp. 32–41

Pierides, Y., "The Pricing of Credit Risk Derivatives", *Journal of Economic Dynamics and Control*, Vol. 5, 1997 pp. 1579–1611

Whittaker, G., Frost, J., "An Introduction to Credit Derivatives", *Journal of Lending and Credit Risk Management*, May 1997, pp. 15–25

Whittaker, G., Kumar, S., "Credit Derivatives: A Primer", in Dattatreya, R., (ed.), *Handbook of Fixed Income Derivatives*, Probus 1996

8 Trading and Hedging I: *Introduction*

In this chapter we introduce the basics of trading and hedging as employed by a repo desk. The instruments and techniques used form the fundamental building blocks of asset & liability management (ALM), so the reader can imagine that a full and comprehensive treatment of this subject would require a book in its own right.[1] Our purpose here is to acquaint the newcomer to the market with the essentials, with further recommended reading suggested in the bibliography.

The repo desk has a vital function on the trading floor, supporting the fixed-interest sales desk, hedging new issues, and working with the swaps and over-the-counter (OTC) options desks. In some banks and securities houses it will be placed within the Treasury or money markets areas, whereas other firms will organise the repo desk as part of the bond operation. It is also not unusual to see equity repo carried out in a different area from bond repo. Wherever it is organised, the need for clear and constant communication between the repo desk and other operating areas of the bank is paramount. For the repo desk itself, as it is dealing with a short-term interest-rate product, its remit falls under the general asset & liability management policy of the bank or financial institution of which it is a part. We present an overview of ALM, liquidity and interest-rate strategy in the next chapter; here we look at specific uses of repo in the context of yield enhancement and market-making.

8.1 Trading approach

8.1.1 *The yield curve and interest rate expectations*

When the yield curve is positively sloped, the conventional approach is to fund the book at the short end of the curve and lend at the long end. In essence therefore if the yield curve resembled that shown in Figure 8.1 a bank would borrow say, one-week funds while simultaneously lending out at say, the three-month maturity. This is known as *funding short*. A bank can effect the economic equivalent of borrowing at the short end of the yield curve and lending at the longer end through repo transactions – in our example, a one-week repo and a three-month reverse repo. The bank then continuously rolls over its funding at one-week intervals for the three-month period. This is also known as *creating a tail*; here the "tail" is the gap between one week and three months – the interest rate "gap" that the bank is exposed to. During the course of the trade, as the reverse repo has locked in a loan for six months, the bank is exposed to interest rate risk should the slope or shape of the yield curve change. In this case if short-dated interest rates rise, the bank may see its profit margin shrink or turn into a funding loss.

As we noted in Chapter 3, there are a number of hypotheses advanced to explain the shape of the yield curve at any particular time. A steeply positively-shaped curve may indicate that the market expects interest rates to rise over the longer term, although this is also sometimes given as the reason for an inverted curve with regard to shorter-term rates. Generally

---

1   And a very large and interesting book it would be too!

speaking, trading volumes are higher in a positively-sloping yield curve environment, compared to a flat or negative-shaped curve.

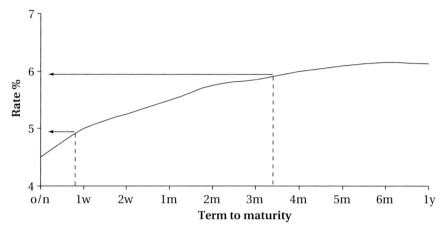

Figure 8.1: Positive yield curve funding.

In the case of an inverted yield curve, a bank will (all else being equal) lend at the short end of the curve and borrow at the longer end. This is known as *funding long* and is shown in Figure 8.2.

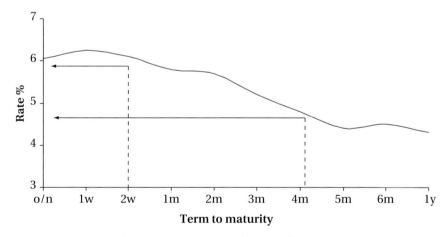

Figure 8.2: Negative yield curve funding.

The example in Figure 8.2 shows a short cash position of two-week maturity against a long cash position of four-month maturity. The interest rate *gap* of 10 weeks is the book's interest rate exposure. The inverted shape of the yield curve may indicate market expectations of a rise in short-term interest rates. Further along the yield curve the market may expect a benign inflationary environment, which is why the premium on longer-term returns is lower than normal.

8.1.2   *Credit intermediation*

The government bond repo market will trade at a lower rate than other money market instruments, reflecting its status as a secured instrument and the best credit. This allows the spreads between markets of different credits to be exploited. The following are examples of credit intermediation trades:

- a repo dealer lends general collateral currently trading at a spread below Libor, and uses the cash to buy CDs trading at a smaller spread below Libor;

- a repo dealer borrows specific collateral in the stock-lending market, paying a fee, and sells the stock in the repo market at the GC rate; the cash is then lent in the interbank market at a higher rate, for instance through the purchase of a clearing bank Certificate of Deposit. The CD is used as collateral in the stock loan transaction. A bank must have dealing relationships with both the stock loan and repo markets to effect this trade. An example of the trade that could be put on using this type of intermediation is shown in Figure 8.3 for the UK gilt market; the details are given below, and show that the bank would stand to gain 17 basis points over the course of the three-month trade;

- a repo dealer trades repo in the GC market, and using this cash reverses in emerging market collateral at a spread say, 400 basis points higher.

These are only three examples of the way that repo can be used to exploit the interest-rate differentials that exist between markets of varying credit qualities, and between the secured and unsecured markets.

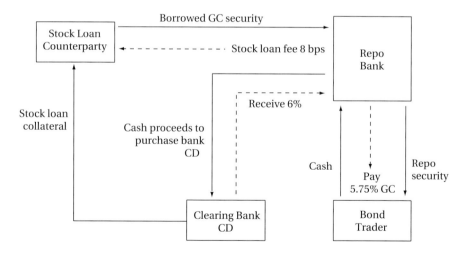

Figure 8.3: Intermediation between stock loan and repo markets; an example using UK gilts.

Figure 8.3 shows the potential gains that can be made by a repo dealing bank (market maker) that has access to both the stock loan and general collateral repo market. It illustrates the rates available in the gilt market on 31 October 2000 for three-month maturities, which were:

| 3-month GC repo | $5.83 - 5.75\%$ |
| 3-month clearing bank CD | $6\frac{1}{32} - 6.00\%$. |

The stock loan fee for this term was quoted at 5–10 basis points, with the actual fee paid being 8 basis points. Therefore the repo trader borrows GC stock for three months, and offers this in repo at 5.75%;[2] the cash proceeds are then used to purchase a clearing bank CD at 6.00%. This CD is used as collateral in the stock loan. The profit is market risk-free as the terms are locked, although there is an element of credit risk in holding the CD. On these terms in £100 million stock the profit for the three-month period is approximately £170,000.

The main consideration for the dealing bank is the capital requirements of the trade. Gilt repo is zero-weighted for capital purposes, and indeed clearing bank CDs are accepted by the Bank of England for liquidity purposes, so the capital cost is not onerous. The bank will need to ensure that it has sufficient credit lines for the repo and CD counterparties.

8.1.3 *Yield curve trading*

We describe here a first-principles type of *relative value* trading common on fixed-interest desks, and the role played by the repo desk in funding the trade. If a trader believes that the shape of the yield curve is going to change, thus altering the yield *spread* between two bonds of differing maturities, they can position the book to benefit from such a move. A yield spread arbitrage trade is not market directional, that is, it is not necessarily dependent on the direction that market moves in, but rather the move in the shape of the yield curve. As long as the trade is *duration weighted* there is no first-order interest-rate risk involved, although there is second-order risk in that if the shape of the yield curve changes in the opposite direction to that expected, the trader will suffer a loss.

Consider the yield spread between two hypothetical bonds, one of two-year and the other five-year maturity; the trader believes that this spread will widen in the near future. The trade therefore looks like this:

- buy £*x* million of the two-year bond and fund in repo;
- sell £*y* million of the five-year bond and cover in reverse repo.

The nominal amount of the five-year bond will be a ratio of the respective *basis point values* multiplied by the amount of the two-year bond.

The trader will arrange the repo transaction simultaneously (or instruct the repo desk to do so). The funding for both bonds forms an important part of the rationale for the trade. As repo rates can be fixed for the anticipated term of the trade, the trader will know the net funding cost – irrespective of any change in market levels or yield spreads – and this cost is the breakeven cost for the trade. A disciplined trader will have a time horizon for the trade, and the trade will be reviewed if the desired spread increase has not occurred by the expected time. In the case of the repo, however, the repo trader may wish to fix this at a shorter interval than the initial time horizon, and roll over as necessary. This will depend on the trader's (or repo desk's) view of repo rates.

Figure 8.4 illustrates the yield curve considerations involved.

---

[2] The repo dealer is the market maker, and so offers stock in repo at the offered side, which is 5.75%. However, this trade still turns in a profit if the bank dealt at another market maker's bid side of 5.83%, with a profit of 9 basis points on the cash sum. Rates are quoted from King & Shaxson Bond Brokers Limited.

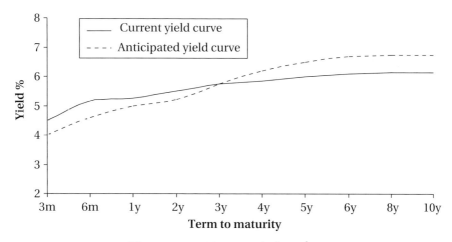

Figure 8.4: Yield curve relative value.

The solid curve in Figure 8.4 represents the yield curve at the time the trade is put on, while the dotted curve shows the curve that is *anticipated* by the trader at the end of their time horizon for the trade. If this proves correct, at this point profit is taken and the trade is unwound. The increase in the two-year versus five-year spread is the profit made from the trade, minus the net funding.

This yield curve spread trade is an example of relative value trading. There are many variations on this, including trades spanning different currencies and markets.

For example, around the sping of 1999 the spread between 10-year UK gilts and 10-year German bunds had narrowed from a high of 160 basis points six months previously to a level of 91 basis points. A trader looking at this may believe that this spread will widen out again in the near future. To reflect this view, a trade can be put on in which the trader sells the gilt and buys the bund in anticipation of the change in spread. Both trades are funded/covered in the respective repo markets. The net funding cost is a vital consideration of whether the trade should be put on or not; any anticipation of the widening of bond yield spread must take the funding into account. A trade such as this also requires that the trader have a view on the currency exchange rate, as any profit from the trade could be reduced or eliminated by adverse movements in the exchange rate.

Note that disciplined trading will require a "stop-loss" point at which the trade wil be unwound if the trader's view is proved incorrect. This is usually half the anticipated gain; for example, if the trader has an objective to take profit if spreads change in their favour by say, 10 basis points, the stop-loss will be put on at five basis points, or even less, should the trade not prove successful.[3]

Figure 8.5 illustrates the starting point for the trade.

---

[3]   It is easier to say this than it is to do it!

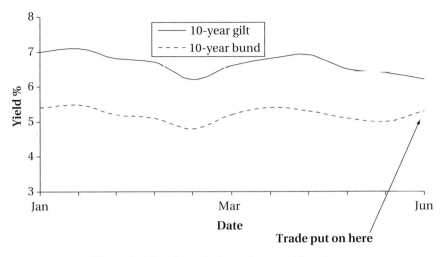

Figure 8.5: Further relative value considerations.

Example 8.1:   Spread trade repo funding calculator
The spreadsheet shown in Figure 8.6 calculates the net funding cost associated with running a spread position of two bonds, and was written by Dr Didier Joannas when he was at ABN Amro Hoare Govett Sterling Bonds Limited. It comprises an Excel front-end and Visual Basic program. The bonds shown in the spreadsheet are gilts. The user selects which bonds to enter into the spreadsheet; the first half shows benchmark bonds, which represent the short position of a trade, and the bond that is taken on as the long position is entered into a cell in the lower half. The specific repo rate that applies to each bond is also entered, as is the term of the trade. The calculator then works out the net funding, which if it is a loss is the traders breakeven cost for the trade. Any combination of bonds can be selected. The spreadsheet also calculates each bond's basis point value (bpv) and bpv ratio, because of course this is used to determine the nominal value of the bond positions. A spread trade is first-order risk neutral because both the long and short positions are duration-weighted. Note that a trade made up of a long position in the 8.50% 2005, against a short position in the 8% 2021, makes a 1.29 basis point gain in funding over a 30-day period, so that if the yield curve stays unchanged during that time, which admittedly is unlikely, the trade would still make a net gain for the book, composed of the funding profit. The funding of bond trades is a vital ingredient in devising trade strategy.

Yield Spread

UK gilt | Settlement: 18Feb00 | 21Feb00

SHORT		Cpn	Maturity	Yield	bpv	3	5	10	20	funding in pence	Repo Rate	TERM 23Feb00	Basis points gain 2	Days
2	103.24	103.75	7.00	07-Jun-02	5.234	2.08	2 40	1	-1	-50	0.09	5	103.740	0.04	98
3	107.50	107	8.00	10-Jun-03	5.638	2.86	3	-39	-42	-91	-0.18	5.9	106.991	-0.06	101
5	114.66	116.0625	8.50	07-Dec-05	5.244	4.59	3	5	-2	-51	-0.17	5.5	116.051	-0.04	98
10	104.30	104	5.75	07-Dec-09	5.221	7.39			10	-49	-0.18	5.5	104.000	-0.02	98
20	141.82	143.5625	8.00	07-Jun-21	4.730	11.86					-0.72	6	143.566	-0.06	98
30	120.60	120.03125	6.00	07-Dec-28	4.720	17.92					0.11	4.5	120.028	0.01	98

LONG		Cpn	Maturity	Yield	bpv	Benchmark	Spread	bpv ratio	funding gain	forward spread	funding in pence	Repo Rate	TERM 23Feb00	gain 2	Days
UK	114.66	116.0625	8.5	07-Dec-05	5.24389915	5.41	20	51.39	0.45631285	0.14	51.54	0.44	4.5	116.045	0.08	98
UK	141.82	143.5625	8	07-Jun-21	4.72997011	17.23	30	1.04	0.96180726	-0.04	0.99	-0.6490288	5.5	143.562	-0.04	98
UK	103.24	103.75	7	07-Jun-02	5.2336894	2.19	10	1.28	0.2958155	-0.06	1.22	-0.1901567	5.5	103.743	-0.09	98

Figure 8.6: Spread trade funding calculator. ©Didier Joannas and M. Choudhry.

8.2   Bond spread relative value trade and funding: example from the gilt market

The UK gilt yield curve for 1 November 2000 is shown in Figure 8.7. This is the Bloomberg screen "IYC". The trader believes that the spread between the two-year benchmark bond, the UK Treasury 7% 2002 and the five-year bond, the UK Treasury 8.5% 2005, will widen, and puts on a spread position, sometimes referred to as a *swap* or *switch*[4] that is long the two-year and short the five-year. The respective bond yields also suit this trade because the inverted yield curve produces a higher return for the two-year stock. If we assume the trader goes long of £10 million of the 7% 2002 bond, Bloomberg screen "SW" can be used to calculate the equivalent nominal amount of five-year bond to short. From Figure 8.8 we see that this is £3.23 million nominal. This ratio is calculated using the respective basis point values for each stock, which Bloomberg terms the *risk* values. This calculation basis is user-selected, as shown by the number "4" being entered in the box marked "Swap Type" in Figure 8.8. The two-year bond has a redemption yield of 5.732%, against the yield on the five-year of 5.565%; a yield pick-up of 16.7 basis points. The trader has one-month and three-month horizon periods, that is, the trade will be reviewed at these points in time. The funding element is crucial. The trader obtains the following specific repo rates from a repo market maker:

One-month	8.5% 2005	5.82–5.77%
	7% 2002	5.78–5.70%
Three-month	8.5% 2005	5.83–5.75%
	7% 2002	5.77–5.72%

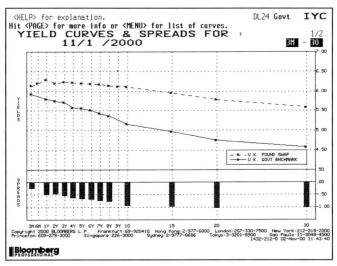

Figure 8.7: Bloomberg screen IYC showing yield curve.
©Bloomberg. Used with permission.

The trader uses Bloomberg screen "CCS" to check the funding, inserting the rates given above. This shows the net funding cost and breakeven amount for the trade; any widening of

---

4   Not to be confused with a swap, the derivative instrument.

spread must be by at least the breakeven amount to account for the funding cost. The calculations are shown in Figure 8.9. If the yield spread has widened by the trader's target after one month or three months, the trade is unwound and profit taken. If the spread has not widened by that amount after one month, the trade is reviewed and may be continued, but if it has narrowed by the stop-loss amount at any time it is immediately unwound.

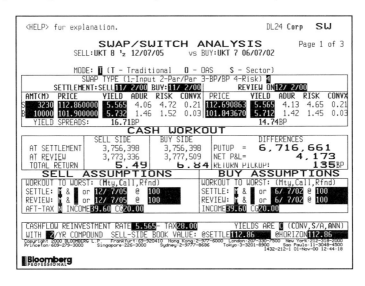

Figure 8.8: Bloomberg screen SW showing bond spread trade calculation.
©Bloomberg. Used with permission.

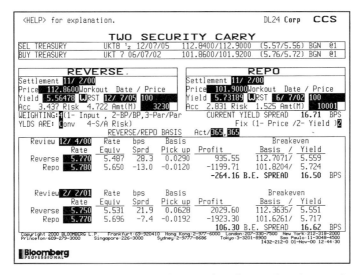

Figure 8.9: Bloomberg screen CCS showing bond spread trade repo funding.
©Bloomberg. Used with permission.

8.3   Specials trading

The existence of an open repo market allows the demand for borrowing and lending stocks to be cleared by the price mechanism, in this case the repo rate. This facility also measures supply and demand for stocks more efficiently than traditional stock lending. It is to be expected that when specific stocks are in demand, for a number of reasons, the premium on obtaining them rises. This is reflected in the repo rate associated with the specific stock in demand, which falls below the same-maturity GC repo rate. The repo rate falls because the entity repoing out stock (that is, borrowing cash) is in possession of the desired asset: the specific bond. So the interest rate payable by this counterparty falls, as compensation for lending out the desired bond.

Factors contributing to individual securities becoming *special* include:

■   government bond auctions; the bond to be issued is shorted by market makers in antici-
    pation of new supply of stock and due to client demand;

■   outright short selling, whether deliberate position-taking on the trader's view, or market
    makers selling stock on client demand;

■   hedging, including bond underwriters who will short the benchmark government bond
    that the corporate bond is priced against;

■   derivatives trading such as basis ("cash-and-carry") trading creating demand for a specific
    stock.

Natural holders of government bonds can benefit from issues *going special*, which is when the demand for specific stocks is such that the rate for borrowing them is reduced. The lower repo rate reflects the premium for borrowing the stock. Note that the party borrowing the special stock is lending cash; it is the rate payable on the cash that they have lent which is depressed.

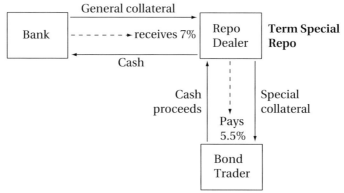

Figure 8.10: Funding gain from repo of a special stock.

The holder of a stock that has gone special can obtain cheap funding for the issue itself, by lending it out. Alternatively, the holder can lend the stock and obtain cash in exchange in a repo, for which the rate payable is lower than the interbank rate. These funds can then be lent out as either secured funding (in a repo), or as unsecured funding, enabling the specials holder to lock in a funding profit. For example, consider a situation where a repo dealer holds an issue that is trading at 5.5% in one-week repo. The equivalent GC rate is 7%, making the specific issue very special. By lending the stock out the dealer can lock in the profit by lending one-week cash at 7%, or at a higher rate in the interbank market. This is illustrated in Figure 8.10.

There is a positive correlation between changes in a stock trading expensive to the yield curve and changes in the degree to which it trades special. Theory would predict this, since traders will maintain short positions for bonds with high funding (repo) costs only if the anticipated fall in the price of the bond is large enough to cover this funding premium. When stock is perceived as being expensive, for example after an auction announcement, this creates a demand for short positions and hence greater demand for the paper in repo. At other times the stock may go tight in the repo market, following which it will tend to be bid higher in the *cash* market as traders closed out existing shorts (which had become expensive to finance). At the same time traders and investors may attempt to buy the stock outright since it will now be cheap to finance in repo. The link between dearness in the cash market and special status in the repo market flows both ways.

8.4   An analysis of special repo rates

Elsewhere in this chapter we have looked at why certain bonds may go special in the repo market. The subject is not extensively researched in the academic literature, and empirical results are scarce. In this section we consider some further issues associated with special repo rates, concentrating on the Treasury and Gilt markets for observations and anecdotal illustrations.

8.4.1   *Introduction*

In government markets there are specific rates for every security, and the highest of these rates is essentially the GC rate. The repo rate on a specific named bond issue becomes *special* when it is trading at over, say, 10–15 basis points below the GC rate for stock of equivalent credit quality and from the same issuer. A special rate is a manifestation of the demand for the specific stock from dealers in the market, most commonly because they are covering a short position in that stock. The measure of a security's *specialness* is the spread in basis points below the equivalent-maturity GC rate. In government markets, which are characterised by an easily-defined GC rate, there is invariably a number of stocks that are special. In the US Treasury market the most liquid benchmark securities, known as *on-the-run* issues, are usually special to a certain extent. This contrasts with the UK gilt market where the current benchmark is only rarely special. Since a bond can be marked as "special" when trading anywhere from a (relatively) small premium away from the GC rate as well as down to a negative rate, special status does not necessarily signify great shortages; a stock can go in and out of being special from one day to the next.

Figure 8.11 is an illustration of the fluctuation of the extent of specialness for the 10-year gilt benchmark during 2000–2001. Specialness is measured in basis points below the overnight GC rate. The benchmark bond, a status assigned by the market in this instance as the bond also being the cheapest-to-deliver bond for the gilt future, changed from the 5¾% 2009 stock to the 6¼% 2010 stock during this time.

As we noted in the previous section, special status for a bond can arise for a number of reasons. Whatever the background factors are, a bond will go special because of a shortage of supply in the market, and the extent of specialness will reflect the amount of shortage as well as the inability of owners of stock to make it available for lending in repo.

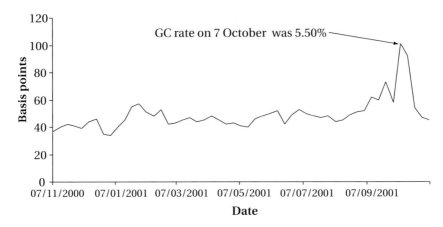

Figure 8.11: Extent of specialness for 10-year benchmark gilt, overnight repo rates.

The specific repo rate on a particular stock also reflects in part, the price volatility of that stock in the market, and this volatility may influence the margin level for that stock in repo. Although in theory government stocks all have the same credit risk, the differing market risk may result in variations in margin levels. The general rule, as we noted in Chapter 5, is that stocks of high modified duration are generally traded with higher margin.[5] A high demand to cover short stock positions using reverse repo can depress repo rates to special levels, and has been observed for some time; for example, see Cornell and Shapiro (1989) for an illustration using the Treasury long bond in 1986. This is not surprising when viewed in terms of orthodox economic theory, as the supply and demand equilibrium for individual stocks is reached via the interest rate in reverse repo. Amihud and Mendelson (1991) state that in the US Treasury market most on-the-run securities, as the most liquid stocks, are used for both hedging and speculative purposes and therefore dealers frequently maintain large short position in these bonds. The current benchmarks are almost always to some extent special for this reason. Due to the constant issue in the Treasury market, the market shifts its active trading into each successive on-the-run security, as it is issued. Reduced cash market trading as a stock ceases to become the benchmark can also lead to specialness.

8.4.2   *The market-determined repo rate*

Viewed purely as a loan of cash and using the theory of forward prices, the overnight repo rate would be identical to the overnight interest rate. This is summarised in Appendix 8.1. This, of course, ignores the existence of collateral and the impact this has on the repo rate. Duffie (1996) shows how the upper level on repo rates is the GC rate. Market observation indicates that the overnight GC rate is at, or very close to, the interbank market overnight rate, which is

---

[5]   To re-emphasise though, this depends on the counterparty. Professional wholesale market counter-parties in the gilt market frequently enter into short-term repo with no margin, irrespective of the stock being given up as collateral. Where the counterparty is not as "trusted", margin will be taken or dealers may offer to trade via tri-party arrangements. Further references are listed in the Chapter 5 bibliography. Obscure observation: the case that tarnished the reputation for hold-in-custody repo in the US domestic market was that concerning Drysdale Government Securities.

for unsecured funds.[6] This is illustrated in Figure 8.12, which compares sterling Libor and GC rates in the overnight during 2001. The GC rate tracks the interbank rate very closely, and on occasion is seen to lie above it. This reflects the supply and demand for short-date repo compared to interbank borrowing and lending. Where specific repo rates start to diverge from the GC rate and become special, market participants who are long of the stock can make risk-free gain from repoing out the stock at the reduced interest rate, and investing the cash proceeds into GC or the interbank market. The interest amount paid out in the reverse repo trade will be below that received in the repo or interbank trade. As Duffie states (*ibid,* page 503) this is not an arbitrage trade because the profit potential of the trade is a function of the amount of stock that is held and which is repoed out. Duffie also confirms market practice that trading repo, whether one is long of the special bond or not, is a speculative rather than arbitrage activity, since the market does not know whether individual stocks will go special, the extent of their specialness and when they will cease being special.

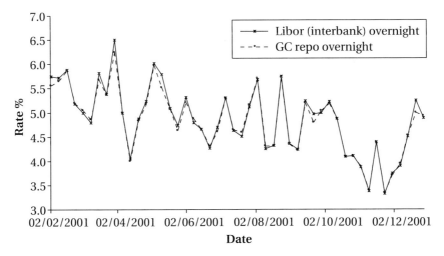

Figure 8.12: Sterling overnight Libor and GC repo rates compared, February–December 2001. Source: British Bankers Association.

Repo rates therefore reflect the individual supply and demand of specific stocks *whenever a specific stock is requested or offered as collateral* (as opposed to a trade stated at the outset as a GC trade), with the upper level being the GC rate. A large demand for a specific stock in reverse repo will result in the stock going special unless the stock is made available either in the stock-lending market or very shortly afterwards in the repo market. If no stock is available in either market, perhaps because the overall issue size is small or institutional holders are unable or unwilling to release supply to the market, the repo rate will become special. Hence the specific repo rate is the market clearing price for supply and demand for that stock.

8.4.3   *Duffie's model of special repo rates*

Here we present an overview of a model on equilibrium in cash and repo markets, presented by Darrell Duffie in the *Journal of Finance* in 1996. The model assumes that all repo is over-

---

6   See Chapter 10, section 10.1, for observations and reasoning on why overnight GC repo is very close to interbank overnight in the gilt market.

night and not term, implying that traders continually roll over and cover their short positions in overnight repo. A further assumption is that the "quantity of specific collateral that must be reversed in… is therefore inelastic to the specialness of the issue." (*ibid*, page 506).[7]

To formulate the model, Duffie describes the following market environment:

- a specific bond with a current price P' and a value of X in the next period;
- general collateral with a current price of P that also has a value in the next period of X;
- a risk-free one-period bond that pays one unit in the next period. The interest rate for borrowing or lending funds in connection with buying or selling this bond is r;
- a general collateral repo rate of R;
- a reverse repo trade in the specific bond, carried out by buying the bond at a price of P' and simultaneously agreeing to re-sell the bond in the next period for $P'(1+R)$;
- a repo trade in the specific bond, where the repurchase price is also $P'(1+R)$.

A market participant holding q units of the specific bond can set up a portfolio made up of a combination of the four investments described above, given by

$$aP' + bP + \frac{c}{1+r} + \frac{d}{1+R} = 0, \tag{8.1}$$

representing a costless portfolio. Further, we have two constraints: first, that only a market participant holding the specific bond may enter into collateralised borrowing; second, that the participant can only short the specific bond by entering into reverse repo, which means that funds must be lent at the specific repo rate. These constraints are described as

$$d < 0 \Rightarrow (a+q)P' \geq -\frac{d}{1+R} \tag{8.2}$$

$$a+q < 0 \Rightarrow (a+q)P' = -\frac{d}{1+R} \tag{8.3}$$

respectively.

By adapting (8.1) for general collateral the interest rate r can also be viewed as the GC repo rate, the funding rate for the general collateral bond.

Duffie goes on to show that to have market equilibrium where we have the set of prices and interest rates (P, P', r, R), we have

$$P' = P(1+r)/(1+R). \tag{8.4}$$

This is his Proposition 1 and can be proved by no-arbitrage arguments, and states that the price of the specific bond is given by the price of the general collateral bond and the relative funding rates. Further, in any equilibrium

$$R \leq r, \tag{8.5}$$

---

[7]   However anecdotal evidence from the UK gilt market suggests that increasing specialness does often lead to traders closing out short positions, as the funding cost becomes prohibitive. Therefore, although Duffie's assertion that increasing specialness does not make it attractive to close out a short position in the cash market is demonstrated by him in Proposition 1 of his paper, from anecdotal evidence we know that there are circumstances when excessive specialness does lead to cash market buying of stock, despite the cash market price rising with increasing specialness.

again proved by the no-arbitrage argument. The extent of the specialness s of the specific bond is therefore given by

$$s = r - R. \tag{8.6}$$

A further conclusion from the paper is that other things being equal, given two Treasury securities the more liquid of the two bonds will be more special in repo. This is somewhat counterintuitive but verified by Duffie on pages 517–518, who also cites empirical evidence from Beim (1992) and Cornell (1993). However, from observation in the gilt market the extent of specialness of liquid benchmark bonds would appear to be very slight, and only material with the CTD bond for the LIFFE long gilt future. Illiquid gilts are frequently more special than benchmark gilts.[8] Additionally, one measure of liquidity is the extent of its specialness in repo, given the argument that a high level of specialness restricts cash market trading in the stock.

8.4.4 Implications of the Duffie model

Duffie's model sets out the relationship between repo rate specialness, the overnight interest rate and cash market bond prices. The extent of specialness, measured by s, can be viewed as an additional dividend yield on the specific bond. One implication of the finding that liquid Treasuries are more special than less liquid issues is that market participants may wish to use off-the-run securities prices when constructing their zero-coupon yield curve, because on-the-run bond prices are biased by the built-in special status. Alternatively, the prices used for on-the-run bonds may be adjusted to remove the effect of the specialness. The process is, given a specific issue, to adjust the observed market price by

$$\frac{(1+R)}{(1+r)},$$

where R and r are the specific repo rate and GC repo rate as before, for whatever the term required.

Whatever the reasons for a stock going special, it will remain special until supply of the issue is made available in the repo market. There may be institutional restrictions amongst certain market participants that prevents them from entering into repo trades, and this leads to, or increases, specialness. The extent of specialness is also a function of demand for stock due to short covering requirements, and this as a function of overall issue size. The price of specific stock observed in the market increases "dollar-for-dollar" with the extent of specialness, and the measure of this given by s is the additional dividend yield on the stock. The amount s is the adjustment in price and is given by the difference between the GC repo rate and the specific repo rate. Duffie concludes that the expected return on holding the stock is the specific repo rate.

Finally, we conclude from a reading of the Duffie model that, other things being equal, one should expect the more liquid of two securities to be more special in repo.[9] However, repo rates generally, and specific repo rates in particular, reflect a number of factors, ranging from class of counterparty to issue size and trading patterns, and this needs to be borne in mind by market participants.

---

[8]   The author hopes to undertake empirical study of gilt repo and special repo rates in due course.
[9]   This could, however, conversely lead to a reduction in liquidity, as market participants reduced trading in the bond, and/or as market makers widened bid-offer spreads as a result.

8.5   Matched book trading

The growth and development of repo markets has led to repo match book trading desks. Essentially this is market-making in repo; dealers make two-way trading prices in various securities, irrespective of their underlying positions. In fact the term "matched book" is a misnomer; most matched books are deliberately mismatched as part of a view on the short-term yield curve. Another commonly encountered definition of the term "matched book" is of a bank that trades repo solely to cover its long and short bond positions, and does not enter into trades for other reasons.[10] It is *not* matching cash lent and borrowed however, or trading to profit from the bid–offer spread, and not any sundry other definitions that have been given in previous texts.

Traders running a matched book put on positions to take advantage of (i) short-term interest rate movements and (ii) anticipated supply and demand in the underlying stock. Many of the trading ideas and strategies described in this book are examples of matched book trading. Matched book trading can involve the following types of trade:

- taking a view on interest rates; for example, the dealer bids for one-month GC and offers three-month GC, expecting the yield curve to invert;

- taking a view on specials; for example, the trader borrows stock in the stock-lending market for use in repo once (as they expect) it goes *special*;

- credit intermediation; for example, a dealer reverses in Brady bonds from a Latin American bank, at a rate of Libor +200 and offers this stock to a US money market investor at a rate of Libor +20.

Principals and principal intermediaries with large volumes of repos and reverse repos, such as the market makers mentioned above, are said to be running matched books. An undertaking to provide two-way prices is made to provide customers with a continuous financing service for long and short positions and also as part of proprietary trading. Traders will mismatch positions in order to take advantage of a combination of two factors, which are short-term interest rate movements and anticipated supply/demand in the underlying bond.

8.6   Hedging tools

For dealers who are not looking to trade around term mismatch or other spreads, there is more than one way to hedge the repo trade. The best hedge for any trade is an exact offsetting trade. This is not always possible, nor indeed always desirable as it may reduce profit, or may use up valuable capital and credit lines. However, the advantage of a similar offsetting trade is that it reduces *basis risk* exposure. The residual risk will be that between say, GC and special or interest-rate gap risk.

It is the interest-rate risk exposure that the repo trader may need to hedge. This is part of managing the book and will be considered in more detail in the next chapter, as the considerations are similar to other money market desks. Here we introduce the main hedging tools.

---

[10]   Thanks to Del-boy at King & Shaxson Bond Brokers Limited for pointing this out, although I still reckon that my definition is the right one!

8.6.1 *Interest-rate futures*

A forward term interest-rate gap exposure can be hedged using interest rate futures. These instruments were introduced in Chapter 4. In the sterling market typically the instrument will be the 90-day short sterling future traded on LIFFE. A strip of futures can be used to hedge the term gap. The trader buys futures contracts to the value of the exposure and for the term of the gap. Any change in cash rates should be hedged by offsetting moves in futures prices.

8.6.2 *Forward rate agreements*

Forward rate agreements (FRAs) are similar in concept to interest rate futures and are also off-balance-sheet instruments. Under an FRA a buyer agrees notionally to borrow and a seller to lend a specified notional amount at a fixed rate for a specified period; the contract to commence on an agreed date in the future. On this date (the "fixing date") the actual rate is taken and, according to its position versus the original trade rate, the borrower or lender will receive an interest payment on the notional sum equal to the difference between the trade rate and the actual rate. The sum paid over is present-valued as it is transferred at the start of the notional loan period, whereas in a cash market trade interest would be handed over at the end of the loan period. As FRAs are off-balance-sheet contracts no actual borrowing or lending of cash takes place, hence the use of the term "notional". In hedging an interest rate gap in the cash period, the trader will buy an FRA contract that equates to the term gap for a nominal amount equal to their exposure in the cash market. Should rates moves against them in the cash market, the gain on the FRA should (in theory) compensate for the loss in the cash trade.

Further detail on FRAs was introduced in Chapter 4 of this book.

8.6.3 *Interest-rate swaps*

An interest rate swap is an off-balance-sheet agreement between two parties to make periodic interest payments to each other. Payments are on a predetermined set of dates in the future, based on a notional principal amount; one party is the *fixed-rate payer*, the rate agreed at the start of the swap, and the other party is the *floating-rate payer*, the floating rate being determined during the life of the swap by reference to a specific market rate or index. There is no exchange of principal, only of the interest payments on this principal amount. Note that our description is for a plain vanilla swap contract; it is common to have variations on this theme, for instance *floating–floating* swaps where both payments are floating rate, as well as *cross-currency* swaps where there is an exchange of an equal amount of different currencies at the start- and end-dates for the swap.

An interest rate swap can be used to hedge the fixed-rate risk arising from the purchase of a bond during a repo arbitrage or spread trade. The terms of the swap should match the payment dates and maturity date of the bond. The idea is to match the cash flows from the bond with equal and opposite payments in the swap contract, which will hedge the bond position. For example, if a trader has purchased a bond, they will be receiving fixed-rate coupon payments on the nominal value of the bond. To hedge this position the trader buys a swap contract for the same nominal value in which they will be paying the same fixed-rate payment; the net cash flow is a receipt of floating interest rate payments. A bond issuer, on the other hand, may issue bonds of a particular type because of the investor demand for such paper, but prefer to have the interest exposure on their debt in some other form. So for example, a UK company issues fixed-rate bonds denominated in say, Australian dollars, swaps the proceeds into sterling and pays floating-rate interest on the sterling amount. As part of the swap they will be receiving fixed-rate Australian dollars which neutralises the exposure arising from the bond issue. At the termination of the swap (which must coincide with the maturity of the bond) the original currency amounts are exchanged back, enabling the issuer to redeem the holders of the bond in Australian dollars.

For a readable and accessible introduction to interest-rate swaps and their applications see Galitz (1995) or Decovny (1998). Another quality article is the one by Ramamurthy (1998), whilst a more technical approach is given in Jarrow and Turnbull (2000). The mother of all swaps books is Das (1994), which is worth purchasing just to make the bookshelf look impressive. The author also suggests (but will leave a recommendation to someone else!) Fabozzi, Mann and Choudhry (2002), which includes a very accessible and comprehensive chapter on swaps.

Appendices

Appendix 8.1:   Confirming the forward interest rate

The forward price that drives the repo rate suggests that the latter should be equal to the overnight rate. This of course ignores the impact of the existence of collateral. The argument is the standard no-arbitrage one, which we summarise here. As usual we assume no bid-offer spreads.

A bond is trading at a price of P and the overnight interest rate for cash borrowing or lending is r. Assuming we are able to short the bond at P, the funding cost for the overnight forward price is

$$P_{fwd} = P(1+r).$$ (8.7)

This price is based on the principle of no-arbitrage, because if we had

$$P_{fwd} > P(1+r)$$ (8.8)

it would be possible to undertake the following:

- purchase the bond at price P;
- agree forward delivery;
- borrow funds at rate r to fund the trade.

The repayment of borrowed funds is at $(1+r)$. The bond is delivered at the forward date and given (8.8) above we know that this would yield a profit of

$$P_{fwd} - P(1+r) > 0.$$

This would be a risk-free profit and so cannot be allowed under market no-arbitrage principles. A similar argument is used to demonstrate that we cannot have

$$P_{fwd} < P(1+r)$$

because traders would then short the bond today and simultaneously buy the bond for forward delivery, investing sale proceeds at the interest rate of r. This would yield a risk-free profit of $P(1+r) - P_{fwd} > 0$.

Applying the same reasoning to the repo market, the forward price P_{fwd} would be given from the repo rate r_{repo} and is $P_{fwd} = P(1 + r_{repo})$. This implies that $r_{repo} = r$.

Selected bibliography and references

Amihud, Y., Mendelson, H., "Liquidity, maturity and the yields on U.S. government securities, *Journal of Finance*, Vol. 4, 1991, pp. 1411–1425

Beim, D., "Estimating bond liquidity", 1992, cited in Duffie (1996)

Cornell, B., "Adverse selection, squeezes, and the bid-ask spread on Treasury securities", *Journal of Fixed Income* June 1993, pp. 39–47

Cornell, B., Shapiro, A., "The mispricing of US Treasury bonds: A case study", *Review of Financial Studies 3*, Vol. 3, 1989, pp. 297–310

Das, S., *Swaps and Financial Derivatives*, 2nd edition, IFR Books 1994

Decovny, S., *Swaps*, 2nd edition, FT Prentice Hall 1998

Duffie, D., "Special Repo Rates", *Journal of Finance*, Vol. LI, No 2, June 1996, pp. 492–526

Fabozzi, F., Mann, S., Choudhry, M., *The Global Money Markets*, Wiley 2002

Galitz, L., *Financial Engineering*, FT Pitman 1995, Chapters 9, 14

Jarrow, R., Turnbull, S., *Derivative Securities*, 2nd edition, South-Western College Publishing 2000, Chapter 14

Ramamurthy, S., "Hedging Fixed-Income Securities with Interest-Rate Swaps", in Fabozzi, F., (ed.), *Perspectives on Interest Rate Risk Management for Money Managers and Traders*, FJF Associates 1998

9 Trading and Hedging II: *Asset & Liability Management* (ALM)

Repo is frequently the key funding tool used by a wide variety of banks and financial institutions. As such its use falls into the strategy employed by an institution to manage its banking or funding book, which is part of the asset & liability management of the entity. Asset & liability management (ALM) is the term covering tools and techniques used by a bank to minimise exposure to market risk and *liquidity* risk whilst achieving its profit objectives, through holding the optimum combination of assets and liabilities. In the context of a banking book, pure ALM would attempt to match precisely the timing and value of cash outflows of assets with the inflows of liabilities. Given the nature of a bank's activities however, this would be difficult if not impossible to structure, and would be expensive in terms of capital and opportunities foregone. For this reason a number of other approaches are followed to manage the risks of the banking book in a way that maximises potential revenue. Asset & liability management also covers banking procedures dealing with balance sheet structure, funding policy, regulatory and capital issues and profit targets; this side of ALM is not discussed here. The aspect of ALM we are interested in is that dealing with policy on liquidity and interest-rate risk, and how these are hedged. In essence the ALM policy of a commercial bank will be keep this risk at an acceptable level, given the institution's appetite for risk and expectations of future interest rate levels. Liquidity and interest-rate risk are interdependent issues, although the risks they represent are distinct.

In this chapter we present an introduction to asset & liability management. This is, of course, a multidimensional and complex subject, not to mention a fascinating one, and it is not possible to consider all the possible strategies and issues in the space of one brief chapter. The reader might consider this a "primer" on the topic, with further recommended reading detailed in the bibliography. Marshall and Bansal (1992) is an excellent introduction to the financial markets as a whole, with a particularly interesting chapter on ALM, while a more rigorous and technical approach is given in the RISK publication (1998).

9.1 Basic concepts

In the era of stable interest rates that preceded the breakdown of the Bretton–Woods agreement, ALM was a more straightforward process, constrained by regulatory restrictions and the saving and borrowing pattern of bank customers.[1] The introduction of the negotiable

---

[1] For instance, in the US banking sector the terms on deposit accounts were fixed by regulation, and there were restrictions on the geographic base of customers and the interest rates that could be offered. Interest-rate volatility was also low. In this environment ALM consisted primarily of asset management, in which the bank would use depositors' funds to arrange the asset portfolio that was most appropriate for the liability portfolio. This involved little more than setting aside some of the assets in non-interest reserves at the central bank authority and investing the balance in short-term securities, while any surplus outside of this would be lent out at very short-term maturities.

Certificate of Deposit by Citibank in the 1960s enabled banks to diversify both their investment and funding sources. With this there developed the concept of the *interest margin*, which is the spread between the interest earned on assets and that paid on liabilities. This led to the concept of the *interest gap* and the management of the gap, which is the cornerstone of modern-day ALM. The increasing volatility of interest rates, and the rise in absolute levels of rates themselves, made gap management a vital part of running the banking book. This development meant that banks could no longer rely permanently on the traditional approach of borrowing short (funding short) to lend long, as a rise in the level of short-term rates would result in funding losses. The introduction of derivative instruments such as FRAs and swaps in the early 1980s removed the previous uncertainty and allowed banks to continue the traditional approach while hedging against medium-term uncertainty.

9.1.1 *Foundations of ALM*

The general term *asset and liability management* entered common usage from the mid-1970s onwards. In the changing interest rate environment, it became imperative for banks to manage both assets and liabilities simultaneously, in order to minimise interest rate and liquidity risk and maximise interest income. ALM is a key component of any financial institution's overall operating strategy. As described in previous texts (for example, see Marshall and Bansal 1992, pp. 498–501) ALM is defined in terms of four key concepts, which are described below.

The first is *liquidity*, which in an ALM context does not refer to the ease with which an asset can be bought or sold in the secondary market, but the ease with which assets can be converted into cash.[2] A banking book is required by the regulatory authorities to hold a specified minimum share of its assets in the form of very liquid instruments. Liquidity is very important to any institution that accepts deposits because of the need to meet customer demand for instant-access funds. In terms of a banking book the most liquid assets are overnight funds, while the least liquid are medium-term bonds. Short-term assets such as T-bills and CDs are also considered to be very liquid.

The second key concept is the money market *term structure* of interest rates. The shape of the yield curve at any one time, and expectations as to its shape in the short- and medium-term, impact to a significant extent on the ALM strategy employed by a bank. Market risk in the form of *interest-rate sensitivity* is significant, in the form of present-value sensitivity of specific instruments to changes in the level of interest rates, as well as the sensitivity of floating-rate assets and liabilities to changes in rates. Another key factor is the *maturity profile* of the book. The maturities of assets and liabilities can be matched or unmatched; although the latter is more common the former is not uncommon depending on the specific strategies that are being employed. Matched assets and liabilities lock-in return in the form of the spread between the funding rate and the return on assets. The maturity profile, the absence of a locked-in spread and the yield curve combine to determine the total interest-rate risk of the banking book.

The fourth key concept is *default risk*: the risk exposure that borrowers will default on interest or principal payments that are due to the banking institution.

These issues are placed in context in the simple hypothetical situation described in the following box "ALM considerations".

---

2   The marketability definition of liquidity is also important in ALM. Less liquid financial instruments must offer a yield premium compared to liquid instruments.

ALM considerations

Assume that a bank may access the markets for three-month and six-month funds, whether for funding or investment purposes. The rates for these terms are shown in Table 9.1. Assume no bid-offer spreads. The ALM manager also expects the three-month Libor rate in three-months time to be 5.10%. The bank can usually fund its book at Libor, while it is able to lend at Libor plus 1%.

Term	Libor	Bank rate
90-day	5.50%	6.50%
180-day	5.75%	6.75%
Expected 90-day rate in 90 days' time	5.10%	6.10%
3v6 FRA	6.60%	

Table 9.1: Hypothetical money market rates.

The bank could adopt any of the following strategies, or a combination of them.

- Borrow three-month funds at 5.50% and lend this out in the three-month at 6.50%. This locks-in a return of 1% for a three-month period.

- Borrow six-month funds at 5.75% and lend in the six-month at 6.75%; again this earns a locked-in spread of 1%.

- Borrow three-month funds at 5.50% and lend this in the six-month at 6.75%. This approach would require the bank to re-fund the loan in three months' time, which it expects to be able to do at 5.10%. This approach locks-in a return of 1.25% in the first three-month period, and an expected return of 1.65% in the second three-month period. The risk of this tactic is that the three-month rate in three months time does not fall as expected to, by the ALM manager, reducing profits and possibly leading to loss.

- Borrow in the six-month at 5.75% and lend these for a three-month period at 6.50%. After this period, lend the funds in the three-month or six-month. This strategy does not tally with the ALM manager's view however, who expects a fall in rates and so should not wish to be long of funds in three months' time.

- Borrow three-month funds at 5.50% and again lend this in the six-month at 6.75%. To hedge the gap risk, the ALM manager simultaneously buys a 3v6 FRA to lock-in the three-month rate in three months time. The first period spread of 1.25% is guaranteed, but the FRA guarantees only a spread of 15 basis points in the second period. This is the cost of the hedge (and also suggests that the market does not agree with the ALM manager's assessment of where rates will be three months from now!), the price the bank must pay for reducing uncertainty, the lower spread return. Alternatively, the bank could lend in the six-month period, funding initially in the three-month, and buy an interest-rate cap with a ceiling rate of 6.60% and pegged to Libor, the rate at which the bank can actually fund its book.

Although simplistic, these scenarios serve to illustrate what is possible, and indeed there are many other strategies that could be adopted. The approaches described in the last option show how derivative instruments can be used actively to manage the banking book, and the cost that is associated with employing them.

9.1.2 *Liquidity and gap management*

We have noted that the simplest approach to ALM is to match assets with liabilities. For a number of reasons, which include the need to meet client demand and to maximise return on capital, this is not practical and banks must adopt more active ALM strategies. One of the most important of these is the role of the gap and gap management. This term describes the practice of varying the asset and liability *gap* in response to expectations about the future course of interest rates and the shape of the yield curve. Simply put this means increasing the gap when interest rates are expected to rise, and decreasing it when rates are expected to decline. The gap here is the difference between floating-rate assets and liabilities, but gap management must also be pursued when one of these elements is fixed rate.

Such an approach is of course an art and not a science. Gap management assumes that the ALM manager is proved to be correct in his/her prediction of the future direction of rates and the yield curve.[3] Views that turn out to be incorrect can lead to unexpected widening or narrowing of the gap spread, and losses. The ALM manager must choose the level of trade-off between risk and return.

Gap management also assumes that the profile of the banking book can be altered with relative ease. This was not always the case, and even today may still present problems, although the evaluation of a liquid market in off-balance-sheet interest-rate derivatives has eased this problem somewhat. Historically it has always been difficult to change the structure of the book, as many loans cannot be liquidated instantly and fixed-rate assets and liabilities cannot be changed to floating-rate ones. Client relationships must also be observed and maintained, a key banking issue. For this reason it is much more common for ALM managers to use off-balance-sheet products when dynamically managing the book. For example, FRAs can be used to hedge gap exposure, while interest-rate swaps are used to alter an interest basis from fixed to floating, or vice-versa. The last strategy presented in the box above presented, albeit simplistically, the use that could be made of derivatives. The widespread use of derivatives has enhanced the opportunities available to ALM managers, as well as the flexibility with which the banking book can be managed, but it has also contributed to the increase in competition and the reduction in margins and bid-offer spreads.

9.2 Interest rate risk and source

9.2.1 *Interest rate risk*

Put simply, interest rate risk is defined as the potential impact, adverse or otherwise, on the net asset value of a financial institution's balance sheet and earnings resulting from a change in interest rates. Risk exposure exists whenever there is a maturity date mismatch between assets and liabilities, or between principal and interest cash flows. Interest rate risk is not necessarily a negative thing; for instance, changes in interest rates that increase the net asset value of a banking institution would be regarded as positive. For this reason, active ALM seeks

---

3   Or, is proved to be correct at least 3 times out of 5...!

to position a banking book to gain from changes in rates. The Bank for International Settlements splits interest rate risk into two elements: *investment risk* and *income risk*. The first risk
type is the term for potential risk exposure arising from changes in the market value of fixed
interest-rate cash instruments and off-balance-sheet instruments, and is also known as *price
risk*. Investment risk is perhaps best exemplified by the change in value of a plain vanilla
bond following a change in interest rates, and from Chapter 2 we know that there is an
inverse relationship between changes in rates and the value of such bonds (see Example 2.2).
Income risk is the risk of loss of income when there is a non-synchronous change in deposit
and funding rates, and it this risk that is known as gap risk.

ALM covering the formulation of interest-rate risk policy is usually the responsibility of
what is known as the asset-liability committee or ALCO, which is made up of senior management personnel including the Finance Director and the heads of Treasury and Risk Management. ALCO sets bank policy for balance sheet management and the likely impact on revenue
of various scenarios that it considers may occur. The size of ALCO will depend on the com-
plexity of the balance sheet and products traded, and the amount of management information available on individual products and desks.

The process employed by ALCO for ALM will vary according to the particular internal
arrangement of the institution. A common procedure involves a monthly presentation to
ALCO of the impact of different interest-rate scenarios on the balance sheet. This presentation
may include:

- an analysis of the difference between the actual net interest income (NII) for the previous
  month and the amount that was forecast at the previous ALCO meeting. This is usually
  presented as a gap report, broken by maturity buckets and individual products;

- the result of discussion with business unit heads on the basis of the assumptions used   in
  calculating forecasts and impact of interest-rate changes; scenario analysis usually   assumes an unchanging book position between now and one month later, which is essentially unrealistic;

- a number of interest-rate scenarios, based on assumptions of (a) what is expected to
  happen to the shape and level of the yield curve, and (b) what may happen to the yield
  curve; for example, extreme scenarios. Essentially, this exercise produces a value for the
  forecasted NII due to changes in interest rates;

- an update of the latest actual revenue numbers.

Specific new or one-off topics may be introduced at ALCO as circumstances dictate; for
example, the presentation of the approval process for the introduction of a new product.

9.2.2 *Sources of interest rate risk*

Assets on the balance sheet are affected by absolute changes in interest rates as well as
increases in the volatility of interest rates. For instance, fixed-rate assets will fall in value in
the event of a rise in rates, while funding costs will rise. This decreases the margins available.
We noted that the way to remove this risk was to lock-in assets with matching liabilities;
however, this is not only not always possible, but also sometimes undesirable, as it prevents
the ALM manager from taking a view on the yield curve. In a falling interest-rate environment,
deposit-taking institutions may experience a decline in available funds, requiring new

funding sources that may be accessed at less favourable terms. Liabilities are also impacted by a changing interest-rate environment.

There are five primary sources of interest-rate risk inherent in an ALM book, which are described below.

- **Gap risk** is the risk that revenue and earnings decline as a result of changes in interest rates, due to the difference in the maturity profile of assets, liabilities and off-balance-sheet instruments. Another term for gap risk is *mismatch risk*. An institution with gap risk is exposed to changes in the level of the yield curve, a so-called *parallel shift*, or a change in the shape of the yield curve or *pivotal shift*. Gap risk is measured in terms of short- or long-term risk, which is a function of the impact of rate changes on earnings for a short or long period. Therefore the maturity profile of the book, and the time to maturity of instruments held on the book, will influence whether the bank is exposed to short-term or long-term gap risk.

- **Yield curve risk** is the risk that non-parallel or pivotal shifts in the yield curve cause a reduction in NII. The ALM manager will change the structure of the book to take into account their views on the yield curve. For example, a book with a combination of short-term and long-term asset- or liability-maturity structures[4] is at risk from a yield curve inversion, sometimes known as a *twist* in the curve.

- **Basis risk** arises from the fact that assets are often priced off one interest rate, while funding is priced off another interest rate. Taken one step further, hedge instruments are often linked to a different interest rate to that of the product they are hedging. In the US market the best example of basis risk is the difference between the Prime rate and Libor. Term loans in the US are often set at Prime, or a relationship to Prime, while bank funding is usually based on the Eurodollar market and linked to Libor. However, the Prime rate is what is known as an "administered" rate and does not change on a daily basis, unlike Libor. While changes in the two rates are positively correlated, they do not change by the same amount, which means that the spread between them changes regularly. This results in the spread earning on a loan product changing over time. Figure 9.1 illustrates the change in spread during 1998–9.

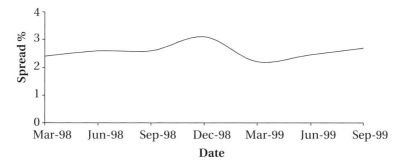

Figure 9.1: Change in spread between three-month Prime rate and three-month Libor 1998–9. Source: Bloomberg.

---

4   This describes a *barbell* structure, but this is really a bond market term.

■ Another risk for deposit-taking institutions such as clearing banks is **run-off risk**, associated with the non-interest bearing liabilities (NIBLs) of such banks. The level of interest rates at any one time represents an opportunity cost to depositors who have funds in such facilities. However, in a rising interest-rate environment, this opportunity cost rises and depositors will withdraw these funds, available at immediate notice, resulting in an outflow of funds for the bank. The funds may be taken out of the banking system completely; for example, for investment in the stock market. This risk is significant and therefore sufficient funds must be maintained at short notice, which is an opportunity cost for the bank itself.

■ Many banking products entitle the customer to terminate contractual arrangement ahead of the stated maturity term; this is sometimes referred to as **option risk**. This is another significant risk as products such as CDs, cheque account balances and demand deposits can be withdrawn or liquidated at no notice, which is a risk to the level of NII should the option inherent in the products be exercised.

9.2.3 *Gap and net interest income*

We noted earlier that gap is a measure of the difference in interest-rate sensitivity of assets and liabilities that revalue at a particular date, expressed as a cash value. Put simply it is

$$Gap = A_{ir} - L_{ir} \tag{9.1}$$

where A_{ir} and L_{ir} are the interest-rate sensitive assets and interest-rate sensitive liabilities. Where $A_{ir} > L_{ir}$ the banking book is described as being *positively gapped*, and when $A_{ir} < L_{ir}$ the book is said to be *negatively gapped*. The change in NII is given by

$$\Delta NII = Gap \times \Delta r \tag{9.2}$$

where r is the relevant interest rate used for valuation. The NII of a bank that is positively gapped will increase as interest rates rise, and will decrease as rates decline. This describes a banking book that is asset sensitive; the opposite, when a book is negatively gapped, is known as liability sensitive. The NII of a negatively-gapped book will increase when interest rates decline. The value of a book with zero gap is immune to changes in the level of interest rates. The shape of the banking book at any one time is a function of customer demand, the treasury manager's operating strategy, and view of future interest rates.

Gap analysis is used to measure the difference between interest-rate sensitive assets and liabilities, over specified time periods. Another term for this analysis is *periodic gap*, and the common expression for each time period is maturity *bucket*. For a commercial bank the typical maturity buckets are:

0 – 3 months;
3 – 12 months;
1 – 5 years;
> 5 years.

although another common approach is to group assets and liabilities by the buckets or grid points of the *Riskmetrics* value-at-risk methodology. Any combination of time periods may be used, however. For instance, certain US commercial banks place assets, liabilities and off-balance-sheet items in terms of *known maturities*, *judgemental maturities* and *market-driven maturities*. These are defined as:

- **known maturities:** fixed-rate loans and CDs;
- **judgemental maturities:** passbook savings accounts, demand deposits, credit cards, non-performing loans;
- **market-driven maturities:** option-based instruments such as mortgages, and other interest-rate sensitive assets.

The other key measure is *cumulative gap*, defined as the sum of the individual gaps up to one year maturity. Banks traditionally use the cumulative gap to estimate the impact of a change in interest rates on NII.

9.2.4 *Assumptions of gap analysis*

A number of assumptions are made when using gap analysis, assumptions that may not reflect reality in practice. These include:

- the key assumption that interest rate changes manifest themselves as a parallel shift in the yield curve; in practice changes do not occur as a parallel shift, giving rise to basis risk between short-term and long-term assets;
- the expectation that contractual repayment schedules are met; if there is a fall in interest rates, prepayments of loans by borrowers who wish to refinance their loans at lower rates will have an impact on NII. Certain assets and liabilities have option features that are exercised as interest rates change, such as letters of credit and variable rate deposits; early repayment will impact a bank's cash flow;
- that repricing of assets and liabilities takes place in the mid-point of the time bucket;
- the expectation that all loan payments will occur on schedule; in practice certain borrowers will repay the loan earlier.

Recognised weaknesses of the gap approach include:

- no incorporation of future growth, or changes in the asset/liability mix;
- no consideration of the time value of money;
- arbitrary setting of time periods.

Limitations notwithstanding, gap analysis is used extensively. Gup and Brooks (1993, page 59) state the following reasons for the continued popularity of gap analysis:

- it was the first approach introduced to handle interest-rate risk, and provides reasonable accuracy;
- the data required to perform the analysis is already compiled for the purposes of regulatory reporting;
- the gaps can be calculated using simple spreadsheet software;
- it is easier (and cheaper) to implement than more sophisticated techniques;
- it is straightforward to demonstrate and explain to senior management and shareholders.

Although there are more sophisticated methods available, gap analysis remains in widespread use.

9.3   Liquidity and the interest rate gap

9.3.1   *The liquidity gap*

A bank funding book will contain assets and liabilities of differing size and maturities; these differences generate liquidity risk. If assets exceed liabilities a funding gap exists that must be met in the market; if the opposite is the case there are excess funds that must be invested. The difference between assets and liabilities at all future dates is known as the liquidity gap. This gap needs to be managed in a way that ensures that expected funding deficits can be met under normal circumstances. Gaps are the source of liquidity risk. The existence of surplus liabilities over assets does not generate liquidity risk per se; however, it is a source of interest-rate risk since the income from invested surplus is not known with certainty. If a bank does not match terms or lock-in liquidity, it will pay the cost of longer-term term funding. This cost is a function of the slope of the yield curve. By definition the liquidity gap for a bank is a snapshot in time, and is measured as the net balance between assets and liabilities. As the bank carries out its duties each day, new assets and liabilities are added so that the gap profile alters.

The *gap profile* is usually tabulated, as shown by the hypothetical example in Table 9.2. Alternatively, it is given in graphical form as shown in Figure 9.2, which is shown along the maturity structure. The deficits shown in the hypothetical gap profile in Figure 9.2 represent the cumulative funding requirement for all the periods projected. The *marginal gap* is the difference between changes in assets and liabilities over a given period. Of course the cumulative funding is not the same as the new funding requirement at each maturity period, since debt issued in the past does not necessarily amortise at subsequent periods.

Maturity bucket	overnight	1 week	2 weeks	1 month	2 months	3 months
Assets	1900	1860	890	740	1300	900
Liabilities	2000	2230	670	550	1500	660
Gap	100	370	−220	−190	200	−240
Asset amortisation		−40	−970	−150	560	−400
Liability amortisation		230	−1560	−120	950	−840
Marginal gap		−270	590	−30	−390	440

- The gap is calculated as the difference between assets and liabilities. A negative gap is an excess of funds that must be invested, while a positive gap is a difference that requires funding in the market.

- The marginal gap is the variation of assets minus liabilities between one maturity point and the previous time period. A positive gap is a funds outflow, while a negative gap is a funds inflow.

Table 9.2: Hypothetical assets and liabilities by maturity bucket, and liquidity gap.

The simplest approach to liquidity management is *cash matching*, which is when the time profile of assets and liabilities are identical. This can be carried further, to match interest-rate profiles, so that different item fixed rates are identical and floating rates are re-fixed on the same day, for instance. Under cash matching the liquidity gap is zero. In practice, cash matching does not mean that loans precisely match deposits; as both of these reflect customer demand, this would be difficult to accomplish in any case. Instead the debt position is adjusted to mirror the time profile of the assets, since the amortisation schedule of the loan portfolio is known. Cash matching is suitable only for the smallest banking institutions, and therefore banks that do not implement this procedure must manage liquidity gaps, which will require funding or placement in the market at future dates.

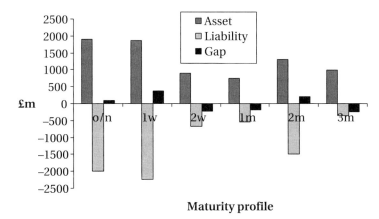

Figure 9.2: The gap profile.

The interest rates at which future gaps will be managed are not known, as they occur in the future. This is the key source of interest-rate risk for the liquidity manager, the uncertainty of future revenue and cost levels. Uncertainty on rates is reduced through hedging, often using off-balance-sheet instruments.

9.3.2   *Gap risk and limits*

Liquidity gaps are measured by taking the difference between outstanding balances of assets and liabilities over time. At any point a positive gap between assets and liabilities is equivalent to a deficit, and this is measured as a cash amount. The *marginal gap* is the difference between the changes of assets and liabilities over a given period. A positive marginal gap means that the variation in value of assets exceeds the variation in value of liabilities. As new assets and liabilities are added over time, as part of the ordinary course of business, the gap profile changes.

The gap profile is tabulated or charted (or both) during and at the end of each day as a primary measure of risk. For illustration, a tabulated gap report is shown in Table 9.3 and is an actual example from a UK banking institution. It shows the assets and liabilities grouped into maturity *buckets* and the net position for each bucket. It is a snapshot today of the exposure, and hence funding requirement of the bank for future maturity periods.

Table 9.3 is very much a summary figure, because the maturity gaps are very wide. For risk-management purposes the buckets would be much narrower, for instance the period between zero and 12 months might be split into 12 different maturity buckets. An example of a more detailed gap report is shown at Figure 9.7, which is from another UK banking institution. Note that the overall net position is zero, because this is a balance sheet and therefore, not surprisingly, it balances. However, along the maturity buckets or grid points there are net positions which are the gaps that need to be managed.

	Total		Time periods								
			0–6 months		6–12 months		1–3 years		3–7 years		7+ years
Assets	40,533	6.17%	28,636	6.08%	3,801	6.12%	4,563	6.75%	2,879	6.58%	654	4.47%
Liabilities	40,533	4.31%	30,733	4.04%	3,234	4.61%	3,005	6.29%	2,048	6.54%	1,513	2.21%
Net Cumulative												
Positions	0		1.86%	(2,097)		567		1,558		831		(859)
Margin on total assets:			2.58%									
Average margin on total assets:			2.53%									

Table 9.3: Example gap profile, UK banking institution.

Limits on a banking book can be set in terms of gap limits. For example a bank may set a six-month gap limit of £10 million. The net position of assets and maturities expiring in six months' time could then not exceed £10 million. An example of a gap limit report is shown at Figure 9.3, with the actual net gap positions shown against the gap limits for each maturity. Again, this is an actual limit report from a UK banking institution.

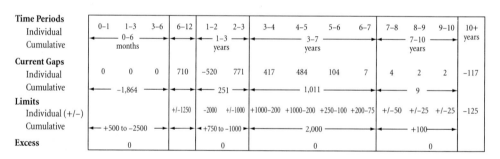

Figure 9.3: Gap limit report.

The maturity gap can be charted to provide an illustration of net exposure, and an example is shown in Figure 9.4, from another UK banking institution. In some firms' reports both the assets and the liabilities are shown for each maturity point, but in our example only the net position is shown. This net position is the gap exposure for that maturity point. A second example, used by the overseas subsidiary of a Middle Eastern commercial bank, which has no funding lines in the interbank market and so does not run short positions, is shown in Figure 9.5, while the gap report for a UK high-street bank is shown in Figure 9.6. In Figure 9.6, note the large short gap under the maturity labelled "Non-int"; this stands for *non-interest bearing liabilities* and represents the balance of current accounts (cheque or "checking" accounts) which are funds that attract no interest and are, in theory very, short-dated (because they are demand deposits, so may be called at instant notice).

Gaps represent cumulative funding required at all dates. The cumulative funding is not necessarily identical to the new funding required at each period, because the debt issued in previous periods is not necessarily amortised at subsequent periods. The new funding between, for example, months 3 and 4 is not the accumulated deficit between months 2 and 4 because the debt contracted at month 3 is not necessarily amortised at month 4. Marginal gaps may be identified as the new funding required, or the new excess funds of the period that should be invested in the market. Note that all the reports are snapshots at a fixed point in time and the picture is of course a continuously moving one. In practice the liquidity position of a bank cannot be characterised by one gap at any given date, and the entire gap profile must be used to gauge the extent of the book's profile.

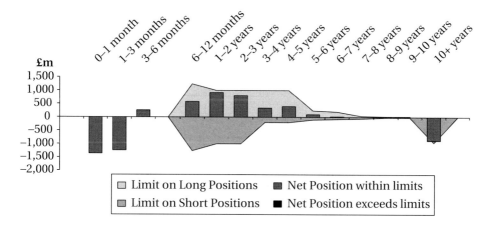

Figure 9.4: Gap maturity profile in graphical form.

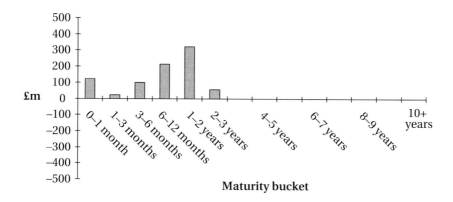

Figure 9.5: Gap maturity profile for a Middle Eastern bank with no short funding allowed.

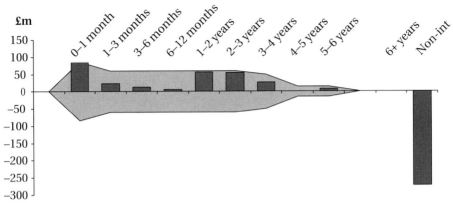

Figure 9.6: Gap maturity profile, UK high-street bank.

The liquidity book may decide to match its assets with its liabilities. This is known as *cash matching* and occurs when the time profiles of both assets and liabilities are identical. By following such a course the bank can lock-in the spread between its funding rate and the rate at which it lends cash, and run a guaranteed profit. Under cash matching the liquidity gaps will be zero. Matching the profile of both legs of the book is done at the overall level; that is, cash matching does not mean that deposits should always match loans. This would be difficult as both result from customer demand, although an individual purchase of, say, a CD can be matched with an identical loan. Nevertheless, the bank can elect to match assets and liabilities once the net position is known, and keep the book matched at all times. Still, it is highly unusual for a bank to adopt a cash matching strategy.

9.3.3 *Liquidity management*

The continuous process of raising new funds or investing surplus funds is known as liquidity management. If we consider that a gap today is funded, thus balancing assets and liabilities and squaring-off the book, the next day a new deficit or surplus is generated which also has to be funded. The liquidity management decision must cover the amount required to bridge the gap that exists the following day as well as position the book across future dates in line with the bank's view on interest rates. Usually in order to define the maturity structure of debt a target profile of resources is defined. This may be done in several ways. If the objective of ALM is to replicate the asset profile with resources, the new funding should contribute to bringing the resources profile closer to that of the assets, that is, more of a matched book looking forward. This is the lowest-risk option. Another target profile may be imposed on the bank by liquidity constraints. This may arise if for example, the bank has a limit on borrowing lines in the market so that it could not raise a certain amount each week or month. For instance, if the maximum that could be raised in one week by a bank is £10 million, the maximum period liquidity gap is constrained by that limit. The ALM desk will manage the book in line with the target profile that has been adopted, which requires it to try to reach the required profile over a given time horizon.

Managing the banking book's liquidity is a dynamic process, as loans and deposits are known at any given point, but new business will be taking place continuously and the profile of the book looking forward must be continuously re-balanced to keep it within the target profile. There are several factors that influence this dynamic process, the most important of which are reviewed below.

	Total (£m)	Up to 1 month	1–3 months	3–6 months	6 months to 1 year	1–2 years	2–3 years	3–4 years	4–5 years	5–6 years	6–7 years	7–8 years	8–9 years	9–10 years	10+ years
ASSETS															
Cash & Interbank Loans	2,156.82	1,484.73	219.36	448.90	3.84	0.00	0.00	0.00	0.00	0.00	0.00	0.00	0.00	0.00	0.00
Certificates of Deposit purchased	1,271.49	58.77	132.99	210.26	776.50	92.96	0.00	0.00	0.00	0.00	0.00	0.00	0.00	0.00	0.00
Floating Rate Notes purchased	936.03	245.62	586.60	12.68	26.13	45.48	0.00	0.00	19.52	0.00	0.00	0.00	0.00	0.00	0.00
Bank Bills	314.35	104.09	178.36	31.90	0.00	0.00	0.00	0.00	0.00	0.00	0.00	0.00	0.00	0.00	0.00
Other Loans	13.00	0.00	1.00	0.00	0.00	7.00	1.00	0.00	0.00	0.00	2.00	2.00	0.00	0.00	0.00
Debt Securities/Gilts	859.45	0.00	25.98	7.58	60.05	439.06	199.48	26.81	100.50	0.00	0.00	0.00	0.00	0.00	0.00
Fixed rate Mortgages	4,180.89	97.72	177.37	143.13	964.98	1,452.91	181.86	661.36	450.42	22.78	4.30	3.65	3.10	2.63	14.67
Variable & Capped Rate Mortgages	14,850.49	14,850.49	0.00	0.00	0.00	0.00	0.00	0.00	0.00	0.00	0.00	0.00	0.00	0.00	0.00
Commercial Loans	271.77	96.62	96.22	56.52	0.86	2.16	1.12	3.64	8.85	1.06	0.16	0.17	0.16	0.00	4.23
Unsecured Lending and Leasing	3,720.13	272.13	1,105.20	360.03	507.69	694.86	400.84	195.19	79.98	25.45	14.06	10.03	10.44	10.82	33.42
Other Assets	665.53	357.72	0.00	18.77	5.00	0.00	0.00	0.00	0.00	0.00	0.00	0.00	0.00	0.00	284.03
TOTAL CASH ASSETS	29,239.95	17,567.91	2,523.06	1,289.77	2,345.05	2,734.43	783.31	888.00	659.26	49.28	20.53	15.85	13.71	17.68	332.12
Swaps	9,993.28	3,707.34	1,462.32	1,735.59	1,060.61	344.00	146.50	537.60	649.00	70.00	5.32	200.00	75.00	0.00	0.00
Forward Rate Agreements	425.00	0.00	50.00	0.00	220.00	5.00	150.00	0.00	0.00	0.00	0.00	0.00	0.00	0.00	0.00
Futures	875.00	0.00	300.00	0.00	175.00	400.00	0.00	0.00	0.00	0.00	0.00	0.00	0.00	0.00	0.00
TOTAL	40,533.24	21,275.24	4,335.38	3,025.36	3,800.66	3,483.43	1,079.81	1,425.60	1,308.26	119.28	25.84	215.85	88.71	17.68	332.12
LIABILITIES (£m)															
Bank Deposits	3,993.45	2,553.85	850.45	233.03	329.06	21.07	1.00	5.00	0.00	0.00	0.00	0.00	0.00	0.00	0.00
Certificates of Deposit issued	1,431.42	375.96	506.76	154.70	309.50	60.00	20.00	3.50	1.00	0.00	0.00	0.00	0.00	0.00	0.00
Commercial Paper – CP & Euro	508.46	271.82	128.42	108.21	0.00	0.00	0.00	0.00	0.00	0.00	0.00	0.00	0.00	0.00	0.00
Subordinated Debt	275.00	0.00	0.00	0.00	0.00	0.00	0.00	0.00	0.00	0.00	0.00	200.00	75.00	0.00	0.00
Eurobonds + Other	2,582.24	768.75	1,231.29	121.94	53.86	9.77	13.16	150.43	150.53	0.00	7.51	0.00	0.00	0.00	75.00
Customer Deposits	17,267.55	15,493.65	953.60	311.70	340.50	129.10	6.60	24.90	7.50	0.00	0.00	0.00	0.00	0.00	0.00
Other Liabilities (incl capital/reserves)	3,181.83	1,336.83	0.00	0.00	741.72	0.00	0.00	0.00	0.00	0.00	0.00	0.00	0.00	0.00	1,103.28
TOTAL CASH LIABILITIES	29,239.96	20,800.86	3,670.52	929.58	1,774.64	219.93	40.76	178.83	156.53	7.50	7.51	200.00	75.00	0.00	1,178.28
Swaps	9,993.28	1,754.70	1,657.59	1,399.75	1,254.24	1,887.97	905.06	770.52	281.44	15.76	6.48	7.27	8.13	13.06	31.30
FRAs	425.00	0.00	150.00	70.00	55.00	150.00	0.00	0.00	0.00	0.00	0.00	0.00	0.00	0.00	0.00
Futures	875.00	0.00	0.00	300.00	150.00	425.00	0.00	0.00	0.00	0.00	0.00	0.00	0.00	0.00	0.00
TOTAL	40,533.24	22,555.56	5,478.11	2,699.33	3,233.89	2,682.90	1,083.90	927.05	404.88	104.28	13.99	207.27	83.13	13.06	1,209.58
Net Positions	0.00	-1,351.09	-1,234.54	265.58	583.48	803.46	341.70	404.88	104.28	11.85	8.58	5.57	4.62	13.06	-877.45

Figure 9.7: Detailed gap profile.

Demand deposits

Deposits placed on demand at the bank, such as current accounts (known in the US as "checking accounts"), have no stated maturity and are available on demand at the bank. Technically they are referred to as "non-interest bearing liabilities" because the bank pays no, or very low, rates of interest on them, so they are effectively free funds. The balance of these funds can increase or decrease throughout the day without any warning, although in practice the balance is quite stable. There are a number of ways that a bank can choose to deal with these balances, which are:

- to group all outstanding balances into one maturity bucket at a future date that is the preferred time horizon of the bank, or a date beyond this. This would then exclude them from the gap profile. Although this is considered unrealistic because it excludes the current account balances from the gap profile, it is nevertheless a fairly common approach;
- to rely on an assumed rate of amortisation for the balances, say 5% or 10% each year;
- to divide deposits into stable and unstable balances, of which the core deposits are set as a permanent balance. The amount of the core balance is set by the bank based on a study of the total balance volatility pattern over time. The excess over the core balance is then viewed as very short-term debt. This method is reasonably close to reality as it is based on historical observations;
- to make projections based on observable variables that are correlated with the outstanding balances of deposits. For instance, such variables could be based on the level of economic growth plus an error factor based on the short-term fluctuations in the growth pattern.

Pre-set contingencies

A bank will have committed lines of credit, the utilisation of which depends on customer demand. Contingencies generate outflows of funds that are by definition uncertain, as they are contingent upon some event; for example, the willingness of the borrower to use a committed line of credit. The usual way for a bank to deal with these unforeseen fluctuations is to use statistical data based on past observation to project a future level of activity.

Prepayment options of existing assets

Where the maturity schedule is stated in the terms of a loan, it may still be subject to uncertainty because of prepayment options. This is similar to the prepayment risk associated with a mortgage-backed bond. An element of prepayment risk renders the actual maturity profile of a loan book to be uncertain; banks often calculate an "effective maturity schedule" based on prepayment statistics instead of the theoretical schedule. There are also a range of prepayment models that may be used, the simplest of which use constant prepayment ratios to assess the average life of the portfolio. The more sophisticated models incorporate more parameters, such as one that bases the prepayment rate on the interest rate differential between the loan rate and the current market rate, or the time elapsed since the loan was taken out.

Interest cash flows

Assets and liabilities generate interest cash inflows and outflows, as well as the amortisation of principal. The interest payments must be included in the gap profile as well.

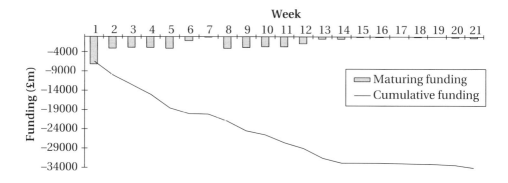

Figure 9.8: Liquidity analysis – example of UK bank profile of maturity of funding.

9.3.4 *The interest-rate gap*

The interest-rate gap is the standard measure of banking book interest-rate risk exposure. This gap is defined as the difference between fixed-rate assets and fixed-rate liabilities, as well as the difference between interest-rate sensitive assets and liabilities. It applies to fixed maturity periods in the future, although the term *marginal gap* is used to refer to variations in asset and liability balances over time. Readers may detect that the interest-rate gap is similar to the liquidity gap, and this is correct; the main difference is that while the entire asset and liability base comprises the liquidity risk, only assets and liabilities with a fixed interest rate are used for the interest-rate gap. A specified period must also be used for the interest-rate gap. The gap itself is the sensitivity of the interest margin to changes in the level of interest rates. In an *immunised* book the interest-rate gap would be zero.

The ALM manager is responsible for controlling the level of interest-rate risk exposure by dynamically adjusting the gap after funding is complete. If this gap is zero after the funding has been arranged, the net margin is in theory not at risk from any change in interest rates.

The convention for calculating gaps is important for interpretation. The "fixed-rate" gap is the opposite of the "variable-rate" gap when assets and liabilities are equal. They differ when assets and liabilities do not match and there are many reference rates. When there is a deficit, the "fixed-rate gap" is consistent with the assumption that the gap will be funded through liabilities for which the rate is unknown. This funding is then a variable-rate liability and is the bank's risk, unless the rate has been locked-in beforehand. The same assumption applies when the banks runs a cash surplus position, and the interest rate for any period in the future is unknown. The gap position at a given time bucket is sensitive to the interest rate that applies to that period.

The gap is calculated for each discrete time bucket, so there is a net exposure for say, 0–1 month, 1–3 months and so on. Loans and deposits do not, except at the time of being undertaken, have precise maturities like that, so they are "mapped" to a time bucket in terms of their relative weighting. For example, a £100 million deposit that matures in 20 days' time will have most of its balance mapped to the three-week time bucket, but a smaller amount will also be allocated to the two-week bucket. Interest-rate risk is measured as the change in present value of the deposit, at each grid point, given a 1 basis point change in the interest rate. So a £10 million one-month CD that was bought at 6.50% will have its present value move upwards if on the next day the one-month rate moves down by a basis point.

The net change in present value for a 1 basis point move is the key measure of interest-rate risk for a banking book and this is what is usually referred to as a "gap report", although strictly speaking it is not. The correct term for such a report is a "PVBP" or "DV01" report, which are acronyms for "present value of a basis point" and "dollar value of an 01 [1 basis point]" respectively. The calculation of interest-rate sensitivity assumes a *parallel shift* in the yield curve, that is, that every maturity point along the term structure moves by the same amount (here one basis point) and in the same direction. An example of a PVBP report is given in Table 9.4, split by different currency books, but with all values converted to sterling.

	1 day	1 week	1 month	2 months	3 months	6 months	12 months	2 years
GBP	8,395	6,431	9,927	8,856	(20,897)	(115,303)	(11,500)	(237,658)
USD	1,796	(903)	10,502	12,941	16,784	17,308	(13,998)	(18,768)
Euro	1,026	1,450	5,105	2,877	(24,433)	(24,864)	(17,980)	(9,675)
Total	11,217	6,978	25,534	24,674	(28,546)	(122,859)	(43,478)	(266,101)

	3 years	4 years	5 years	7 years	10 years	15 years	20 years	30 years
GBP	(349,876)	(349,654)	5,398	(5,015)	(25,334)	(1,765)	(31,243)	(50,980)
USD	(66,543)	(9,876)	(1,966)	237	2,320	(5,676)	(1,121)	0
Euro	(11,208)	(3,076)	1,365	1,122	3,354	(545)	(440)	(52)
Total	(427,627)	(362,606)	4,797	(3,656)	(19,660)	(7,986)	(32,804)	(51,032)

GBP total: (1,160,218); USD total: (56,963); Euro total: (75,974); Grand total: (1,293,155)
All figures in £

Table 9.4: Banking book PVBP grid report.

The basic concept in the gap report is the net present value (NPV) of the banking book, which was introduced in Chapter 2. The PVBP report measures the difference between the market values of assets and liabilities in the banking book. To calculate NPV we require a discount rate, and it represents a *mark-to-market* of the book. The rates used are always the zero-coupon rates derived from the government bond yield curve, although some adjustment should be made to this to allow for individual instruments.

Gaps may be calculated as differences between outstanding balances at one given date, or as differences of variations of those balances over a time period. A gap number calculated from variations is known as a *margin gap*. The cumulative margin gaps over a period of time, plus the initial difference in assets and liabilities at the beginning of the period, are identical to the gaps between assets and liabilities at the end of the period.

The interest-rate gap differs from the liquidity gap in a number of detailed ways, which include:

■ whereas for liquidity gap all assets and liabilities must be accounted for, only those that have a fixed rate are used for the interest-rate gap;

■ the interest-rate gap cannot be calculated unless a period has been defined because of the fixed-rate/variable-rate distinction. The interest-rate gap is dependent on a maturity period and an original date.

The primary purpose in compiling the gap report is in order to determine the sensitivity of the interest margin to changes in interest rates. As we noted earlier the measurement of the gap is always "behind the curve" as it is an historical snapshot; the actual gap is a dynamic value as the banking book continually undertakes day-to-day business.

Case study:[5]   Position management

Starting the day with a flat position, a money market interbank desk transacts the following deals:

1. £100 million borrowing from 16/9/99 to 7/10/99 (3 weeks) at 6.375%.
2. £60 million borrowing from 16/9/99 to 16/10/99 (1 month) at 6.25%.
3. £110 million loan from 16/9/99 to 18/10/99 (32 days) at 6.45%.

The desk reviews its cash position and the implications for refunding and interest-rate risk, bearing in mind the following:

- there is an internal overnight roll-over limit of £40 million (net);
- the bank's economist feels more pessimistic about a rise in interest rates than most others in the market, and has recently given an internal seminar on the dangers of inflation in the UK as a result of recent increases in the level of average earnings;
- today there are some important figures being released including inflation (RPI) data. If today's RPI figures exceed market expectations, the dealer expects a tightening of monetary policy by *at least* 0.50% almost immediately;
- a broker's estimate of daily market liquidity for the next few weeks is one of low shortage, with little central bank intervention required, and hence low volatilities and rates in the overnight rate;
- brokers' screens indicate the following term repo rates:

O/N	6.350%–6.300%
1 week	6.390%–6.340%
2 week	6.400%–6.350%
1 month	6.410%–6.375%
2 month	6.500%–6.450%
3 month	6.670%–6.620%

- the indication for a 1v2 FRA is:

  | 1v2 FRA | 6.680%–6.630% |

- the quote for an 11-day forward borrowing in 3 weeks' time (the "21v32 rate") is 6.50% bid.

The book's exposure looks like this:

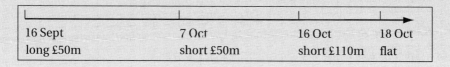

16 Sept	7 Oct	16 Oct	18 Oct
long £50m	short £50m	short £110m	flat

---

5   This example follows the approach used on FinTuition Limited's repo course, which the author taught during 1998/1999. The original example was introduced to the course by Alison Brooks.

What courses of action are open to the desk, bearing in mind that the book needs to be squared off such that the position is flat each night?

Possible solutions

Investing early surplus

From a cash management point of view, the desk has a £50 million surplus from 16 September up to 7 October. This needs to be placed in the market. It may be able to negotiate a 6.31% loan with the market for overnight, or 6.35% term deposit for 1 week to 6.38% for 1 month.

The overnight roll is the most flexible but offers a worse rate, and if the desk expects the overnight rate to remain both low and stable (due to forecasts of low market shortages), it may not opt for this course of action.

However, it may make sense from an interest-rate risk point of view. If the desk agrees with the bank's economist, it should be able to benefit from rolling at higher rates soon – possibly in the next three weeks. Therefore it may not want to lock-in a term rate now, and the overnight roll would match this view. However, it exposes them to lower rates, if their view is wrong, which will limit the extent of the positive funding spread. The market itself appears neutral about rate changes in the next month, but appears to factor in a rise thereafter.

The forward "gap"

Looking forward, the book is currently on course to exceed the £40 million overnight position limit on 7 October, when the refunding requirement is £50 million. The situation gets worse on 16 October (for two days) when the refunding requirement is £110 million. The desk needs to fix a term deal before those dates to carry it over until 18 October when the funding position reverts to zero. A borrowing from 7 October to 18 October of £50 million will reduce the rollover requirement to within limit.

However, given that interest rates will rise, should the desk wait until the 7th to deal in the cash? Not if it has a firm view. They may end up paying as much as 6.91% or higher for the funding (after the 0.50% rate rise). So it would be better to transact now a forward starting repo to cover the period, thus locking in the benefits obtainable from today's yield curve. The market rate for a 21x32 day repo is quoted at 6.50%. This reflects the market's consensus that rates may rise in about a month's time. However, the desk's own expectation is of a larger rise, hence its own logic suggests trading in the forward loan. This strategy will pay dividends if their view is right, as it limits the extent of funding loss.

An alternative means of protecting the interest-rate risk alone is to BUY a 1v2 Forward Rate Agreement (FRA) for 6.68%. This does not exactly match the gap, but should act as an effective hedge. If there is a rate rise, the book gains from the FRA profit. Note that the cash position still needs to be squared-off. Should the desk deal before or after the inflation announcement? That is, of course, down to its judgement but most dealers like, if at all possible, to sit tight immediately ahead of releases of key economic data.

9.4   Introduction to generic ALM policy

The management of interest-rate risk is a fundamental ingredient of commercial banking. Bank shareholders require comfort that interest-rate risk is measured and managed in a satisfactory manner. A common approach to risk management involves the following:

- the preparation and adoption of a high-level interest-rate risk policy at managing board level; this sets general guidelines on the type and extent of risk exposure that can be taken on by the bank;
- setting limits on the risk exposure levels of the banking book; this can be by product type, desk, geographic area and so on, and will be along the maturity spectrum;
- actively measuring the level of interest-rate risk exposure at regular, specified intervals;
- reporting to senior management on general aspects of risk management, risk exposure levels, limit breaches and so on;
- the monitoring of risk management policies and procedures by an independent "middle office" risk function.

The risk management approach adopted by banks will vary according to their specific markets and appetite for risk. Certain institutions will have their activities set out or proscribed for them under regulatory rules. For instance, building societies in the UK are prohibited from trading in certain instruments under the regulator's guidelines.[6] In this section we present, purely for the purposes of illustration, the ALM policies of three hypothetical banks, called Bank S, Bank M and Bank L. These are respectively, a small banking entity with assets of £500 million, a medium-sized bank with assets of £2.5 billion and a large bank with assets of £10 billion. The following serves to demonstrate the differing approaches that can be taken according to the environment that a financial institution operates in.

9.4.1　ALM policy for Bank S (assets = £500 million)

The aim of the ALM policy for Bank S is to provide guidelines on risk appetite, revenue targets and rates of return, as well as risk management policy. Areas that may be covered include capital ratios, liquidity, asset mix, rate-setting policy for loans and deposits, and investment guidelines for the banking portfolio. The key objectives should include:

- to maintain capital ratios at the planned minimum, and to ensure safety of the deposit base;
- to generate a satisfactory revenue stream, both for income purposes and to further protect the deposit base.

The responsibility for overseeing the operations of the bank to ensure that these objectives are achieved is lodged with the ALM Committee. This body monitors the volume and mix of the bank's assets and funding (liabilities), and ensures that this asset mix follows internal guidelines with regard to banking liquidity, capital adequacy, asset base growth targets, risk exposure and return on capital. The norm is for the committee to meet on a monthly basis; at a minimum the membership of the committee will include the finance director, head of Treasury and risk manager. For a bank the size of Bank S the ALM committee membership will possibly be extended to the chief executive, the head of the loans business and the chief operating officer.

As a matter of course the committee will wish to discuss and review the following on a regular basis:

---

[6]　This is the UK Financial Services Authority, which was established as a "super regulator" for all financial market activities.

- overall macroeconomic conditions;
- financial results, and key management ratios such as share price analysis and rates of return on capital and equity;
- the house view on the likely direction of short-term interest rates;
- the current lending strategy, and suggestions for changes to this, as well as the current funding strategy;
- any anticipated changes to the volume and mix of the loan book, and that of the main sources of funding; in addition, the appropriateness or otherwise of alternative sources of funding;
- suggestions for any alteration to the bank's ALM policy;
- the maturity gap profile and anticipated and suggested changes to it.

The committee will also wish to consider the interest rates offered currently on loans and deposits, and whether these are still appropriate.

Interest-rate sensitivity is monitored and confirmed as lying within specified parameters; these parameters are regularly reviewed and adjusted if deemed necessary according to changes in the business cycle and economic conditions. Measured using the following ratio:

$$A_{ir} / L_{ir} \, ,$$

typical risk levels would be expected to lie between 90–120% for the maturity period 0–90 days, and between 80–110% for the maturity period over 90 days and less than 365 days.

Put simply, the objective of Bank S would be to remain within specified risk parameters at all times, and to maintain as consistent level of earnings as possible (and one that is immune to changes in the stage of the business cycle).

9.4.2 *ALM policy for Bank M (assets = £2.5 billion)*

Bank M is our hypothetical "medium sized" banking institution. Its ALM policy would be overseen by an Asset–Liability Management Committee or ALCO. Typically, the following members of senior management would be expected to be members of ALCO:

- deputy chief executive
- finance director
- head of retail banking
- head of corporate banking
- head of Treasury
- head of risk management
- head of internal audit

together with others such as product specialists who are called to attend as and when required. The finance director will often chair the meeting.

The primary responsibilities of ALCO are detailed below.

Objectives

ALCO is tasked with reviewing the bank's overall funding strategy. Minutes are taken at each meeting, and decisions taken are recorded on the minutes and circulated to attendees and designated key staff. ALCO members are responsible for undertaking regular review of the following:

- minutes of the previous meeting;

- the ratio of the interest-rate sensitive assets to liabilities, gap reports, risk reports and the funding position;

- the bank's view on expected level of interest rates, and how the book should be positioned with respect to this view; and related to this, the ALCO view on anticipated funding costs in the short- and medium-term;

- stress testing in the form of "what if?" scenarios, to check the effect on the banking book of specified changes in market conditions; and the change in parameters that may be required if there is a change in market conditions or risk tolerance;

- the current interest rates for loans and deposits, to ensure that these are in accordance with the overall lending and funding strategy;

- the maturity distribution of the liquidity book (expected to be comprised of T-bills, CDs and very short-dated government bonds); the current liquidity position and the expected position in the short- and medium-term.

As ALCO meets on a regular monthly basis, it may not be the case that every aspect of their responsibility is discussed at every meeting; the agenda is set by the chair of the meeting in consultation with committee members. The policies adopted by ALCO should be dynamic and flexible, and capable of adaptation to changes in operating conditions. Any changes will be made on agreement of committee members. Generally, any exceptions to agreed policy can only be with the agreement of the CEO and ALCO itself.

Interest-rate risk policy

The objective will be to keep earnings volatility resulting from an upward or downward move in interest rates to a minimum. To this end, at each ALCO meeting members will review risk and position reports and discuss these in the light of the risk policy. Generally, the six-month and 12-month A_{ir}/L_{ir} cumulative ratio will lie in the range 90–110%. A significant move outside this range will most likely be subject to corrective action. The committee will also consider the results of various scenario analyses on the book, and if these tests indicate a potential earnings impact of greater than, say, 10%, instructions may be given to alter the shape and maturity profile of the book.

Liquidity policy

A primary responsibility of ALCO is to ensure that an adequate level of liquidity is maintained at all times. We define liquidity as:

> "… the ability to meet anticipated and unanticipated operating cash needs, loan demand, and deposit withdrawals, without incurring a sustained negative impact on profitability."

> (Gup and Brooks, 1993, page 238)

Generally, a Bank-M type operation would expect to have a target level for loans to deposits of around 75–85%, and a loans to core deposits ratio of 85–95%. The loan/deposit ratio is reported to ALCO and reviewed on a monthly basis, and a reported figure significantly outside these ranges (say, by 5% or more) will be reviewed and asked to be adjusted to bring it back into line with ALCO policy.

9.4.3   ALM policy for Bank L (assets = £10 billion)

The management policy for ALM at a larger entity will build on that described for a medium-sized financial institution. If Bank L is a group company, the policy will cover the consolidated balance sheet as well as individual subsidiary balance sheets; the committee will provide direction on the management of assets and liabilities, and the off-balance-sheet instruments used to manage interest-rate and credit risk. A well-functioning management process will be proactive and concentrate on direction in response to anticipated changes in operating conditions, rather than reactive responses to changes that have already taken place. The primary objectives will be to maximise shareholder value, with target returns on capital of 15–22%.

The responsibility for implementing and overseeing the ALM management policy will reside with ALCO. The ALCO will establish the operating guidelines for ALM, and review these guidelines on a periodic basis. The committee will meet on a more frequent basis that would be the case for Bank M, usually on a fortnightly basis. As well as this, it will set policies governing liquidity and funding objectives, investment activities and interest-rate risk. It will also oversee the activities of the investment banking division. The head of the ALM desk will prepare the interest-rate risk sensitivity report and present it to ALCO.

Interest-rate risk management

ALCO will establish an interest-rate risk policy that sets direction on acceptable levels of interest-rate risk. This risk policy is designed to guide management in the evaluation of the impact of interest-rate risk on the bank's earnings. The extent of risk exposure is a function of the maturity profile of the balance sheet, as well as the frequency of repricing, the level of loan prepayments and funding costs. Managing interest-rate risk is, in effect, the adjustment of risk exposure upwards or downwards, which will be in response to ALCO's views on the future direction of interest rates. As part of the risk management process the committee will monitor the current risk exposure and duration gap, using rate sensitivity analysis and simulation modelling to assess whether the current level of risk is satisfactory.

Measuring interest-rate risk

Notwithstanding the widespread adoption of value-at-risk as the key market risk measurement tool, funding books such as repo books continue to use the gap report as a key measure of interest-rate risk exposure. This enables ALCO to view the risk sensitivity along the maturity structure. Cumulative gap positions, and the ratio of assets revaluation to liabilities revaluation, are calculated and compared to earnings levels on current the asset/liability position. Generally the 90-day, six-month and one-year gap positions are the most significant points along the term structure at which interest-rate risk exposure is calculated. The ratio of gap to earnings assets will be set at the ±15% to ±20% level.

As it is a traditional duration-based approach, gap reporting is a static measure that measures risk sensitivity at one specific point in time. It for this reason that banks combine a value-at-risk measure as well, or only use VaR. It is outside the scope of this book to consider VaR, we cite a useful introductory reference at the end of this chapter.

9.4.4   Simulation modelling

Simulation modelling is a procedure that measures the potential impact on the banking book, and hence earnings levels, of a user-specified change in interest rates and/or a change in the shape of the book itself. This process enables senior management to gauge the risk associated with particular strategies. Put simply the process is:

- construct a "base" balance sheet and income statement as the starting point (this is derived from the current shape of the banking book, and any changes expected from current growth trends that have been projected forward);

- assess the impact on the balance sheet of changes under selected scenarios; these might be no change in rates; a 100 basis point and 250 basis point upward parallel shift in the yield curve; a 100 basis point and 250 basis point downward parallel shift; a 25 basis point steepening and flattening of the yield curve, between the three-month to the three-year maturity points; a combination of a parallel shift with a pivotal shift at a selected point; an increase or decrease in three-month T-bill yield volatility levels; and a 20 basis point change in swap spreads;

- compare the difference in earnings resulting from any of the scenarios to the anticipated earnings stream under the current environment.

Generally the committee will have set guidelines about the significance of simulation results; for example, there may be a rule that for a 100 basis point change in interest rates should not impact NII by more than 10%. If results indicate such an impact, ALCO will determine if the current risk strategy is satisfactory or whether adjustments are necessary.

Selected bibliography and references

Asset & Liability Management, RISK books (1998)

Butler, C., *Mastering Value-at-Risk*, FT Prentice Hall, 1998

Cornyn, A., Mays, E., (eds.), *Interest Rate Risk Models: Theory and Practice*, Glenlake Publishing/Fitzroy Dearborn Publishers 1997, Chapters 6, 15

Fabozzi, F., Konishi, A., *The Handbook of Asset/Liability Management*, revised edition, Irwin McGraw-Hill 1996, Chapters 3, 6, 7, 8, 12

Gup, B., Brooks, R., *Interest Rate Risk Management*, Irwin Professional Publishing 1993

Kamakura Corporation, *Asset & Liability Management: A Synthesis of New Methodologies*, Risk Publications 1998

Marshall, J., Bansal, V.K., *Financial Engineering*, New York Institute of Finance 1992, Chapter 20

Schaffer, S., "Interest Rate Risk", *Business Review,* Federal Reserve Bank of Philadelphia, May–June 1991, pp. 17–27

Stigum, M., *The Money Market*, 3rd edition, Dow Jones Irwin 1990

Toevs, A., Haney, W., *Measuring and Managing Interest Rate Risk*, Morgan Stanley publication 1984

10 The United Kingdom Gilt Repo Market

In this chapter we describe and examine the market in United Kingdom gilt repo, a recent development but an example of an efficient and liquid market. The introduction of repo was part of a range of structural changes and reform undertaken in the gilt market by the Bank of England during the 1990s to bring market practice up to date. These changes included changes in quotation convention to decimals in place of tick pricing, and the introduction of a market in zero-coupon gilts or strips. The repo market has been arguably the most successful element of these market reforms.

10.1 Introduction

The repo market in the United Kingdom is relatively new, dealing in gilt repo having begun only on 2 January 1996. It was introduced as a "big bang" with all institutions and structures in place before the start of trading, and implementation was smooth and trouble-free. Before the advent of an open market in repo, stock borrowing and lending in the gilt market was available only to *gilt-edged market makers* (GEMMs), dealing through approved intermediaries known as *Stock Exchange Money Brokers* (SEMBs). The introduction of an open gilt repo market allowed all market participants to borrow and lend gilts. Additional market reforms also liberalised gilt stock lending by removing the restrictions on who could borrow and lend stock, thus ensuring a "level playing field" between the two types of transaction. The *gilt-edged stock lending agreement* (GESLA) was also updated to ensure that it dovetailed with the new gilt repo legal agreement; the revised GESLA was issued in December 1995 and repo and stock lending are interlinked aspects of the new market.

In the run-up to the start of repo trading, market practitioners and regulators compiled a set of recommended market practices, set out in the Gilt Repo Code of Best Practice. The associated legal agreement is the PSA/ISMA Global Master Repurchase Agreement,[1] with an annexe describing special features of gilts such as the use of delivery-by-value (DBV) within the CREST settlement mechanism.

The market participants in gilt repo and include commercial and investment banks, fund managers and local authority and corporate treasurers.

The repo market grew to about £50 billion of repos and stock lending outstanding in the first two months of operation, and further growth took it to nearly £95 billion by February 1997, of which £70 billion was in repos. This figure fell to about £75 billion by November 1998, compared with £100 billion for sterling certificates of deposit (CDs). During 1999 the size of the market stabilised and grew by only a relatively small amount; the amount outstanding stood at £100 billion in November 1999. Following rapid initial growth, a Bank of England report suggested that further significant growth in the market would require "structural

---

[1]   Now known as the BMA/ISMA global repo agreement.

innovation".[2] These would include the introduction of repo *netting* and more widespread electronic trading mechanisms.

Table 10.1 shows the composition of the sterling money market during 2000 and 2001; gilt repo, interbank deposits and CDs make up by far the largest share of the market by amount outstanding. This is noteworthy given the relatively recent introduction of repo, while its introduction coincided with an increase in the size of the stock loan market. Table 10.2 shows that the average daily turnover in gilt repo approached £16 billion during 1999.

Sterling Money Markets: Amounts outstanding in £ bln
(1990 and 1995 data are end-March; otherwise end-year)

	Interbank	CDs	T-bills	Bank bills	CP	Gilt repo	Sell/ buy-backs	Stock lending	Local Authority bills	Other[b]	Total
1990	89	53	9	23	5	–	–	–	2	6	187
1995	93	66	8	20	6	–	–	–	2	7	202
1998	150	122	1	17	10	95[a]	2	35[a]	1	6	309
1999	155	135	4	14	13	99[a]	3	49[a]	0	6	330
Feb 2000	155	127	2	14	13	100	2	51	0	7	471
May 2000	165	138	2	14	17	123	3	54	0	6	522
Q4 2000	151	130	3	11	18	127	6	57	0	9	512
Q1 2001	171	141	–	13	19	126	–	67	–	7	544

[a] End-November data.
[b] "Other" comprises T-bills, sell/buy-backs and local authority bills.

Table 10.1: Sterling money markets. Source: BoE, *QB* 8/00, Spring 2001, Summer 2001. Used with permission.

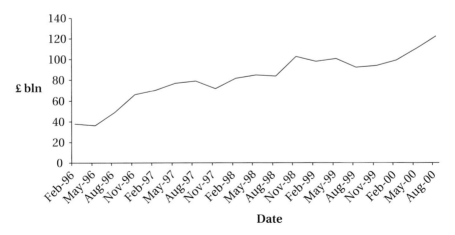

Figure 10.1: Gilt repo outstanding. Source: BoE. Used with permission.

---

2   *Quaterly Bulletin*, February 2000.

£ billion	1998	1999				2000				2001	
		Q1	Q2	Q3	Q4	Q1	Q2	Q3	Q4	Q1	Q2
Gilts											
Conventional	7.0	7.0	6.0	6.0	5.0	6.0	6.0	4.0	4.5	4.8	5.2
Index-linked	0.2	0.1	0.2	0.1	0.1	0.1	0.1	0.0	0.1	0.1	0.2
Money markets											
Gilt repo	14.8	11.4	16.8	14.7	15.5	12.6	13.5	15.8	12.4	15.7	17.9
Overnight interbank	6.1	7.7	7.8	7.1	7.4	8.2	8.3	7.8	7.6	11.1	9.3

Table 10.2: Average daily market turnover, nominal amounts.
Source: BoE, London Stock Exchange.

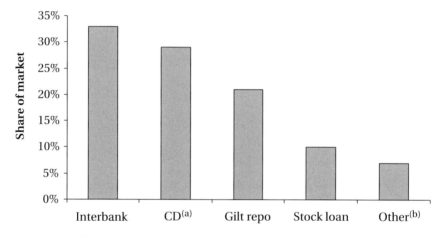

(a) Bank and building society CDs
(b) Includes Treasury bills, eligible and local authority bills,
commercial paper, and sell/buy-backs.

Figure 10.2: Sterling money markets: outstanding amounts,
November 1999. Source: BoE.

Table 10.1 and Figure 10.2 illustrate some interesting developments in sterling money markets since the advent of gilt repo. The Certificate of Deposit (CD) market has grown substantially, partly because the growth of the gilt repo and stock-lending market has contributed to demand for CDs for use as collateral in stock loans, and also because banks will use the CD market to enhance yields, as part of credit intermediation between the money market and gilt repo. The BoE suggested this growth occurred partly as a result of two factors:[3]

■ the liquidity regime for sterling money markets, introduced by the Bank in 1996, increased the attractions of CD funding for banks, as their required liquidity holdings were allowed to be offset by holding of other banks' CDs;

---

[3]   See *Quarterly Bulletin*, February 2000 pp. 40–41.

■ as we noted above, the use of CD as collateral in the stock loan market (making possible the stock loan/repo market intermediation trade we described in Chapter 8) increases the demand to hold these instruments.

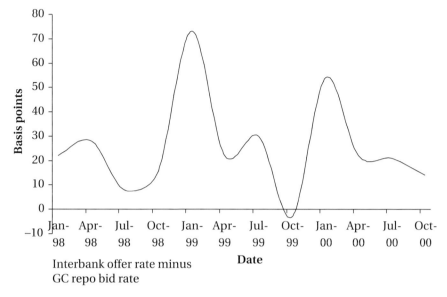

Interbank offer rate minus
GC repo bid rate

Figure 10.3: Spread between one-month repo and interbank rates.
Source: Bank of England.

Similarly, the stock loan market grew from £35 billion to £49 billion in the year to November 1999. This growth resulted from the "complementary relationship" (BoE, *ibid*) between the stock loan and repo markets, and intermediation between them by participants who had access to both markets. The continuing popularity of stock lending reflects its popularity with institutional investors – many of the smaller institutions prefer to lend their portfolio holdings for a fee, rather than sell in repo. This obviates the need for them to monitor an interest-rate position or reinvest cash collateral.

So gilt repo has developed alongside growth in the existing unsecured money markets. There has been a visible shift in short-term money market trading patterns from unsecured to secured money. According to the Bank, market participants estimate that gilt repo now accounts for about half of all overnight transactions in the sterling money markets. The repo general collateral (GC) rate tends to trade below the interbank rate, on average about 10–15 basis points below, reflecting its status as government credit. The gap is less obvious at very short maturities, due to the lower value of such credit over the short term and also reflecting the higher demand for short-term funding through repo by securities houses that may not have access to unsecured money. Hence, it is common to observe very little spread between overnight interbank and GC repo rates. Even at longer maturities, supply and demand factors can reduce the spread, as shown by Figure 10.3. Figures 10.4 and 10.5 show the spread through interbank for three-month GC repo early on during the market, and for the two-week and one-month GC repo during 1999. Another effect of gilt repo on the money market is a possible association with a reduction in the volatility of overnight unsecured rates. Fluctuations in the overnight unsecured market have been reduced since the start of an open repo market, although the evidence is not conclusive. This may be due to repo providing an alternative funding method for market participants, which may have reduced pressure on the unsecured market in overnight funds. It may also have enhanced the ability of financial intermediaries to distribute liquidity.

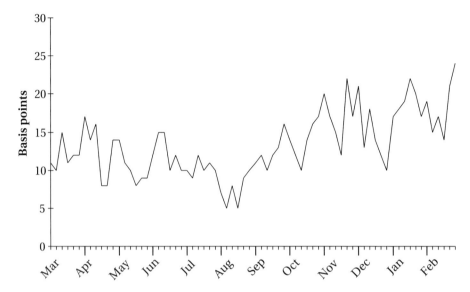

Figure 10.4: Three-month interbank rate minus three-month gilt repo GC rate during 1997/1998. Source: Bank of England, Bloomberg.

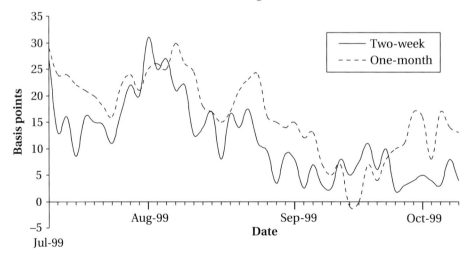

Figure 10.5: Two-week and one-month GC repo and interbank spreads during 1999. Source: BoE.

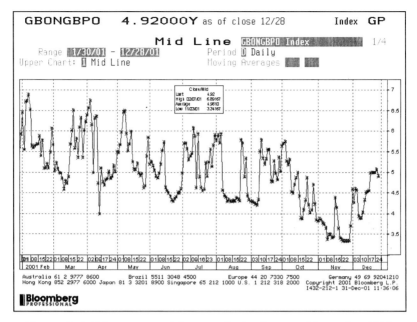

Figure 10.6: Gilt repo overnight rates during January–December 2001, as shown on Bloomberg screen GP. LIBOR rates during the same period are shown in Figure 10.7. © Bloomberg L.P.

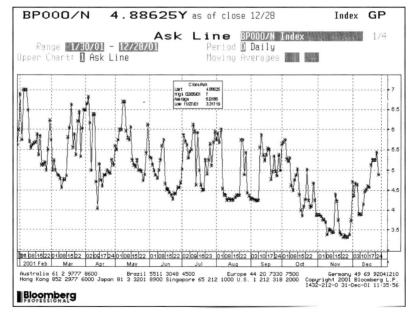

Figure 10.7: Overnight sterling LIBOR rates during January–December 2001, on Bloomberg screen GP (ticker BP00O/N). © Bloomberg L.P.

10.2 Market structure

10.2.1 *Introduction*

One of the stated objectives behind introducing gilt repo was to enhance the liquidity of the gilt market and the attraction of gilts as an investment, particularly to overseas investors. The positive impact on this with regard to dealing sizes and bid–offer spreads is difficult to measure however as the excess of demand for gilts over supply, particularly at the long end of the yield curve, has resulted in some illiquidity in the market since repo was introduced. Gilt repo has, however, contributed to improvements in the gilt-edged market-making function, *viz*, because the ability to undertake gilt repo with any counterparty enhances the ability of market makers (GEMMs) to make markets in gilts by improving their access to stock to cover short positions. There is therefore a reduced cost of running shorts (in theory); overall there has been a reduction in the cost of financing long positions, from above Libor to below Libid. The average cost of borrowing stock has also fallen, according to the BoE. These lower financing and borrowing costs are also available to other market participants. On anecdotal evidence it would appear that gilts are now less likely to trade at anomalous prices, and data from the Bank of England indicates that the divergence of GEMM quoted yields from its own fitted yield curve has decreased. However, it is difficult to strip out other factors contributing to developments such as these; for instance, the extremely competitive world of gilts market-making would also appear to have contributed to gilt prices and quote spreads becoming very keen. At the longer end of the term structure, the lack of supply of long-dated gilts has contributed to illiquidity at times.

The ability of all market participants to short gilts and to take and finance or cover their desired positions might be expected to improve the efficiency and liquidity of the gilt market. There is scope for empirical study in this regard. The development of a liquid market in secured money has widened the range of funding and money placement options open to financial and non-financial firms. It may also be associated with a reduction in volatility of overnight interest rates.[4]

Figure 10.8 shows the breakdown of gilt repo market activity between banking institutions and non-banking institutions, which include securities houses, fund managers and broking firms. Although banks' share of the market is higher, recent growth in activity is sourced more from non-banking entities. The latter are more likely to use gilt repo when positioning their book to reflect views on interest rates, whereas banks can also use unsecured money market instruments to do this. The Financial Services Authority's regulatory requirements on liquidity is favourable to banks who hold short-dated gilt portfolios, which leads to corresponding activity in repo.

---

[4]   On anecdotal evidence, based on a sample limited to the author and his acquaintances in the market (!), the volatility of overnight rates would certainly appear to be much lower in the second half of the 1990s compared to the first half.

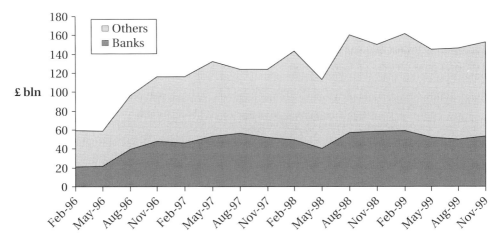

Figure 10.8: Breakdown of repo activity by banks and non-banking institutions.
Source: Bank of England.

10.2.2 *Market participation*

The UK market structure comprises both gilt repo and gilt stock lending. Although there are institutions which undertake only one type of activity, there are many institutions trading actively in both areas. For example, an institution that is short of a particular gilt may cover its short position (which could result from an either an outright sale or a repo) in either the gilt repo or the stock-lending market. Certain institutions prefer to use repo because they feel that the value of a *special* stock is more rapidly and more accurately reflected in the repo rather than the stock-lending market. Some firms have preferred to remain in stock lending because their existing systems and control procedures can accommodate stock lending more readily than repo. For example, a firm may have no cash reinvestment facility or experience of managing interest-rate risk. Such a firm will prefer to receive collateral against a stock loan for a fee, rather than interest-bearing cash in a repo. They may also feel that their business does not need, or cannot justify, the costs of setting up a repo trading facility. In addition the stock-lending market has benefited from securities houses and banks who trade in both it and repo; for example, borrowing a stock in the lending market, repoing this and then investing the cash in, say, the CD market.

Other firms have entered into trading in repo due, for instance, to the perception that value from tight stock is more readily obtained in the repo market than in the stock lending market.

Prior to the introduction of repo, no facility was made for the registration of dedicated market makers in gilt repo, in the belief that the market mechanism would result in this occuring as a matter of course. This turned out to be the case; virtually from the start of the market some firms have provided what is, in effect, a market-making function in gilt repo. These firms include the former stock exchange money brokers (SEMBs), and banks that run large matched books. There are approximately 20 firms, mostly banks and securities houses, which quote two-way repo rates on request for GC, specifics and specials, up to three months' maturity; longer-dated trades may also be transacted with relative ease. Examples of such firms are former SEMBs such as Gerrard & King (part of the Old Mutual group), Lazards, Rowe & Pitman (part of the UBS group), and banks such as RBS Financial Markets, Barclays Capital and HSBC. Some firms will quote only to established customers, such as ABN AMRO Securities Ltd. Some firms will quote indicative repo rates on screen services such as Reuters and Bloomberg; for example, the sterling markets screen from Halifax plc, "HFX2", which appears on Bloomberg is shown in Figure 10.9.

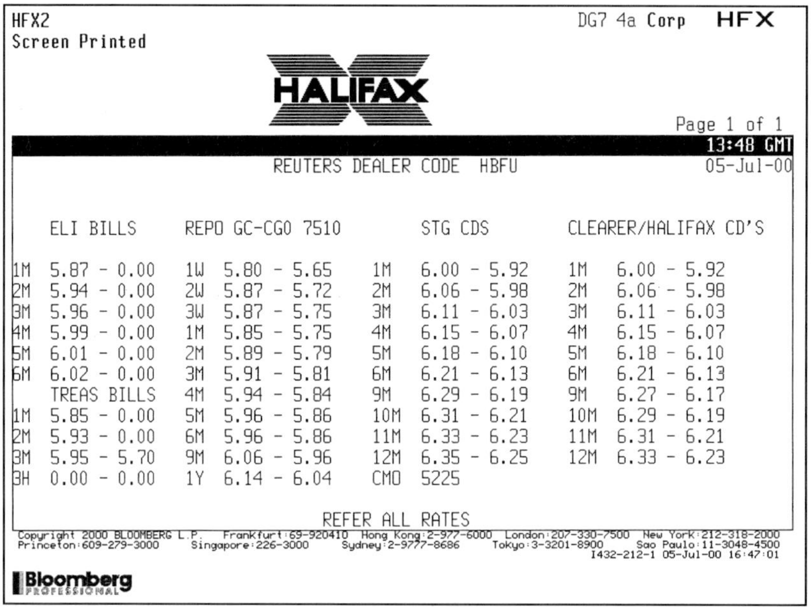

```
HFX2                                            DG7 4a Corp   HFX
Screen Printed
                          HALIFAX
                                                      Page 1 of 1
                                                          13:48 GMT
                    REUTERS DEALER CODE   HBFU             05-Jul-00


    ELI BILLS     REPO GC-CG0 7510       STG CDS        CLEARER/HALIFAX CD'S

1M  5.87 - 0.00   1W  5.80 - 5.65    1M  6.00 - 5.92   1M  6.00 - 5.92
2M  5.94 - 0.00   2W  5.87 - 5.72    2M  6.06 - 5.98   2M  6.06 - 5.98
3M  5.96 - 0.00   3W  5.87 - 5.75    3M  6.11 - 6.03   3M  6.11 - 6.03
4M  5.99 - 0.00   1M  5.85 - 5.75    4M  6.15 - 6.07   4M  6.15 - 6.07
5M  6.01 - 0.00   2M  5.89 - 5.79    5M  6.18 - 6.10   5M  6.18 - 6.10
6M  6.02 - 0.00   3M  5.91 - 5.81    6M  6.21 - 6.13   6M  6.21 - 6.13
    TREAS BILLS   4M  5.94 - 5.84    9M  6.29 - 6.19   9M  6.27 - 6.17
1M  5.85 - 0.00   5M  5.96 - 5.86   10M  6.31 - 6.21  10M  6.29 - 6.19
2M  5.93 - 0.00   6M  5.96 - 5.86   11M  6.33 - 6.23  11M  6.31 - 6.21
3M  5.95 - 5.70   9M  6.06 - 5.96   12M  6.35 - 6.25  12M  6.33 - 6.23
3H  0.00 - 0.00   1Y  6.14 - 6.04   CMO  5225

                       REFER ALL RATES
Copyright 2000 BLOOMBERG L.P.   Frankfurt:69-920410  Hong Kong:2-977-6000  London:207-330-7500  New York:212-318-2000
Princeton:609-279-3000          Singapore:226-3000   Sydney:2-9777-8686    Tokyo:3-3201-8900    Sao Paulo:11-3048-4500
                                                                           I432-212-1 05-Jul-00 16:47:01
Bloomberg
PROFESSIONAL
```

Figure 10.9: Halifax plc screen on Bloomberg for 5 July 2000.
©Halifax plc ©Bloomberg L.P. Used with permission.

A number of sterling broking houses are active in gilt repo. Counterparties still require signed legal documentation to be in place with each other, along with credit lines, before trading can take place. This is not the case in the interbank broking market. A gilt repo agreement is not required with the broker, although of course firms will have counterparty agreements in place with them. Typical of the firms providing broking services are Tullet & Tokyo, Tradition Bond Brokers, Prebon Yamane and King & Shaxson Bond Brokers Limited. Brokers tend to specialise in different segments of the gilt market. For example, some concentrate on GC repo, and others on specials and specifics; some on very short maturity transactions and others on longer-term trades. Brokerage is usually 1 basis point of the total nominal amount of the bond transferred for GC, and 2 basis points for specific and special repo.[5] Brokerage is paid by both sides to a gilt repo.

The range of participants and end-users has grown as the market has expanded. The overall client base now includes banks, building societies, overseas banks and securities houses, hedge funds, fund managers (such as Standard Life, Scottish Amicable, and so on), insurance companies and overseas central banks. Certain corporates have also begun to undertake gilt repo transactions. The slow start in the use of tri-party repo in the UK market has probably

---

5   Volume discounts are available to customers who transact a large amount of business via brokers. If you see your broker driving down the road in a Rolls-Royce, you may also wish to negotiate such a discount. Thanks Del-boy, for the original observation…! (Deemed worthy of a cartoon…)

constrained certain corporates and smaller financial institutions from entering the market. Tri-party repo would be attractive to such institutions because of the lower administrative burden that comes from having an external custodian. The largest users of gilt repo will remain banks and building societies, who are required to hold gilts as part of their BoE liquidity requirements.

10.2.3 *Repo market activity*

Generally repo trading has been found to be more active when the yield curve is positively sloped, with overnight GC trading at lower rates than 1–2 weeks up to 1 month. This allows the repo trader to enjoy positive funding by borrowing cash overnight on repo while lending funds in the 1 week or 1 month. The trader is of course exposed to unexpected upward movements in overnight rates while covering their positions.

It should be remembered that the short-term money market curve acts independently of the cash gilt curve, especially with regard to long gilt yields, and sometimes is uncorrelated with its movements (an observation in regard to this is given in Example 10.1).

Example 10.1

A good illustration of the lower correlation between the short-term money market yield curve and the gilt yield curve took place in summer 1997. Following the granting of interest rate setting responsibility to the Bank of England, the gilt yield curve changed from a positive to a negative (inverted) curve; the Treasury 8% 2021 was yielding 6.54% in September 1997 and by December was yielding 6.37%. (The yield as at September 1998 was 5.15%). Some firms' view was that the short-term curve would behave in the same manner. One market participant bid for 1 year GC at 7.18% at that time (September 1997), but by December 1997 this rate was 7.58%! An expensive trade…

In this case the gilt yield curve had behaved as the trader had expected but the short-term money market curve had not. Note the the market convention is to *bid* for stock, which is to *lend* cash.

Hedging positions in other markets is one of the main motives for some participants' involvement in gilt repo. This is evident in the sterling bond market, where underwriters have benefited from the ability to hedge the interest rate risk on their (long) underwriting positions, by taking an offsetting short position in the gilt they are using to price their bond. This improves the quality of their interest rate hedge. The underwriter uses (reverse) repo to cover the resulting short position in the gilt. Previously underwriters that weren't GEMMs would have used less exact hedges such as the long gilt future. The introduction of open repo has therefore benefited the sterling bond market, in that those securities houses issuing sterling bonds can now put on a more effective hedge against their bond position.

Gilt repo activity is concentrated at the very short end of the yield curve, with a majority of deals trading at overnight to one week maturity. This is longer-term than stock lending, which is generally undertaken overnight or on call. As liquidity has improved the volume, if not the proportion, of longer-maturity trades has increased. Trades of up to three months maturity are common, and three month repo rates are routinely quoted with a spread of around 5 basis points. Trades of up to 6 months are also not unusual. Figure 10.10 shows the maturity of trades in gilt repo in the three years to November 1999, data reproduced with the permission of the Bank of England.

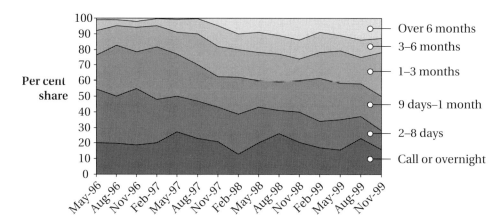

Figure 10.10: Maturity of gilt repo transactions. Source: BoE, *Quarterly Bulletin*, February 2000. Used with permission.

10.2.4 *Specials trading*

The emergence of *specials* trading is a natural part of a repo market. At the start of the market the BoE stated that one purpose in introducing a repo market was to allow the demand to borrow and lend stocks to be cleared by the price mechanism. Hence it is natural that when stocks are in demand, for example because firms wish to cover short positions arising from underwriting or other reasons, the premium on obtaining them rises. This manifests itself in a reduction in the repo rate for such stocks, as the interest rate payable on cash lent against them decreases compared to the GC rate.

The Bank of England has conducted a study into the relationship between cash prices and repo rates for stocks that have traded special. This showed a positive correlation between changes in a stock trading expensive to the yield curve and changes in the degree to which it trades special. This is to be expected: traders maintain short positions for paper which has high associated funding costs only if the anticipated fall in the price of the paper is large enough to give a profit. One implication of this is that longer-duration stocks should be less expensive for a given specials premium, because their prices are more sensitive to changes in yields and therefore a given rise in yields will give a trader running a short position a higher profit to offset any increase in the cost of the repo.

Both types of cause and effect may be due to the following:

■ stock may be perceived as expensive; for example, after an *auction* announcement. This creates a greater demand for short positions, and hence greater demand for the paper in repo (to cover short positions);

■ at other times stock might go tight in the repo market. It would then tend to be bid higher in the *cash* market as traders closed out existing shorts, which were now too expensive to run; another reason would be that traders and *investors* would try to buy the stock outright since it would now be cheap to finance by repoing out.

There are a number of reasons why a particular bond may go special. Some of these include:

- government bond auctions: when the authorities announce an auction of an existing stock, market makers will run a short position in this stock going into the auction, reflecting institutional investor demand for the issue. This demand may lead to the stock going special;

- outright short selling by proprietary trading desks of banks. In connection with the last point noted below, this can lead to stocks going special;

- hedging/bond underwriting: for example, a bank that is the underwriter for a Eurobond issue will, unless the issue is 100% successful, have a long position in some of the stock (it will be left *wearing* the stock). This will be hedged with the government benchmark security against which the Eurobond is priced; if this is done in sufficient size, the benchmark may go special;

- derivatives trading, such as basis trading, resulting in excessive demand for *the cheapest-to-deliver* stock;

- buy-back or cancellation of debt: if an issue is bought-back, for example as happened when a sovereign government announced cancellation of some of the nominal outstanding of one of its Brady bonds, there will be a sudden shortage of stock that can lead to special rates and even negative repo rates when this occurs;

- small size issues leading to low liquidity: if a particular issue exists only in very small size, it may go special either due to periodic shortages of tradeable stock or as a result of market manipulation creating this shortage. For example, in the gilt market there were a number of esoteric high-coupon bonds, such as the 15% 1997 and others, that existed in sizes of under £1 billion. These stocks periodically experienced special status due to their illiquidity in the secondary market.

Sometimes a combination of these factors can result in a stock going special. In the Japanese government bond markets it is quite common for stock to be special or trade at negative repo rates, as the base interest rates are close to 1%, and have been so for some time now.

The Bank of England has suggested that the link between dearness in the cash market and specialness in the repo market flows both ways: in some cases changes in dearness have preceded changes in specialness and in other cases the sequence has been the other way round. In both cases the stock remains expensive until existing holders take profits by selling their stock or making it available for repo or lending.

An analysis by Garban Europe's gilt repo broking team (Garban ICAP Europe, 1998) of the relationship between the specialness of issues and their turnover in the specials market (therefore excluding any GC turnover in the stock) suggested that the level of specialness peaked at around 125 basis points. In other words, special status increased up to a point until cumulative turnover reached around £10 billion, at which point the special spread was 125 basis points, and then declined from this point.

In the gilt strips market,[6] stock is special on an almost permanent basis. This reflects the low volume and liquidity in the cash market in strips, which has struggled to rise above 3% of

---

6   Gilt strips are zero-coupon gilts created by "stripping" coupons from conventional gilts, creating a package of single cash flow bonds, in effect zero-coupon bonds, that comprise the individual coupons and the principal repayment of the original ("source") gilt. The market is relatively new, trading having commenced in December 1997. For further information on gilt strips, consult the references in the bibliography.

nominal amount of the conventional market. Only benchmark stocks that are designated as strippable may be stripped. As an example of the special status of these securities, in May 1999 in the stock loan market the 8% Treasury 2021 gilt itself could be borrowed on an open basis (that is, no fixed term) at approximately 10 basis points; the equivalent stock loan fee for the 8% 2021 principal strip was in the range of 50–100 basis points.[7] It is also rare to see repo in coupon strips, reflecting the low volumes of these instruments traded in the cash market.

Example 10.2:   Market intervention

On rare occasions the Bank will intervene to relieve excess demand: in November 1996 there was an increase in demand for 7.75% Treasury 2006, mainly because investors switched out of a similar maturity stock as it approached its ex-dividend period. Market makers sold the stock to meet this demand and then simultaneously covered their shorts in the repo market. This sudden demand, coupled with the fact that a large amount of this issue was held by investors that did not lend it out, led to the special rate trading at close to 0%. The Bank issued £100 million of the stock as a *tap* to help relieve demand.

For delivery into the March 1998 LIFFE long gilt futures contract, the BoE made supplies of the cheapest-to-deliver stock (Treasury 9% 2008) available if required, albeit at a rate of 0%! The author is not aware that any market participant made use of this facility.

Example 10.3:   Specials trading during 1999

During 1999 three stocks experienced significant special status. The 6% 1999, a stock that matured in August that year, approached a 0% rate and briefly was reported as trading at a negative repo rate. From the start of the repo market it had periodically traded special, which was explained as being a lack of tradeable stock, as it was actually a large size issue with nearly £7 billion nominal outstanding.

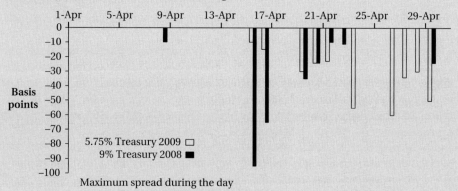

Figure 10.11: Selected specials spreads during April 1999.
Source: Garban ICAP Europe's *Gilt Repo Monitor*.

The 6% 2028 was consistently special due to heavy demand for this stock from institutional investors in the cash market. This heavy demand was put forward as part explanation for the inverted shape of the gilt yield curve from July 1997.

---

[7]   Thanks to Simon Adams, a former dealing counterparty of mine, and now at RBS Trust Bank, for pointing this out to me.

The 9% 2008 was in heavy demand in the cash market due to it being the cheapest-to-deliver bond for the long gilt future traded on LIFFE. It was also cheapest by a significant margin compared to other bonds in the delivery basket, so that in repo it traded anything from 20 basis points to several hundred basis points through GC. From the March 2000 contract the cheapest-to-deliver bond was the 5.75% 2009 gilt, which resulted in the 9% 2008 losing its special status.

For further details on these stocks see the February 2000 issue of the *Quarterly Bulletin*.

10.3 Open market operations

10.3.1 *Introduction*

The Bank introduced gilt repo into its open market operations in March 1997. The Bank aims to meet the banking system's liquidity needs each day via its open market operations. Almost invariably the market's position is one of a shortage of liquidity, which the Bank generally relieves via open market operations conducted at a fixed official interest rate.[8] The Bank's repo operation in this case is actually a reverse repo, as it will reverse in gilts and eligible bills. On the rare occasion that there is a surplus in the market, the Bank will sell bills in the market to "mop up" this excess. The reason central banks choose repo as the money market instrument to relieve shortages is because it provides a combination of security (government debt as collateral) and liquidity to trade in large size.

The average daily shortage in February 2000 was £1.3 billion, compared with £1.7 billion for six months previously. Figure 10.12 shows how the Bank's daily refinancing was provided during the first quarter of 2000; about 63% was by repo of gilts and eligible bills.

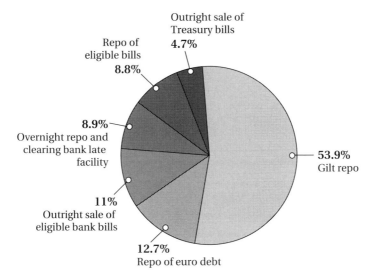

Figure 10.12: Breakdown of instruments used in daily open market operations, Q1 2000. Source: BoE.

---

8   During five years in the sterling money market, the author observed a surplus on just a handful of occasions. As with the peculiar circumstances arising during trading between Christmas and New Year, such occurrences were an exciting anomaly.

The average size of the daily money market shortage is given at Table 10.3. The stock of eligible bank bills (bills that may be sold to the BoE as part of its daily operations) was roughly unchanged during 2000, at £21 billion. Therefore the introduction of gilt repo to the daily operation could be seen to be a significant element in the market being able to deal with the larger volume of daily shortages.

	£ million		£ million
1996	900	2001:	
1997	1,200	Quarter 1	2,500
1998	1,400	Quarter 2	2,300
1999	1,200	July	2,200
2000	2,100	August	2,600

Table 10.3: Average daily money market shortages.
Source: BoE, *Quarterly Bulletin*, Winter 2001.
Used with permission.

Date of facility	Amount (£ million)
13 October	3,000
20 October	3,000
27 October	1,315
3 November	600
1 December	50

Table 10.4: Refinancing provided by three-month repos during 1999.
Source: BoE, *Quarterly Bulletin*, February 2000. Used with permission.

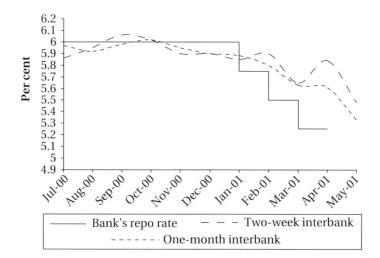

Figure 10.13: BoE repo rate, two-week and one-month interbank mid-rates. Source:
BoE, *Quarterly Bulletin*, Spring 2001. Used with permission.

The Bank's standard repo facility is a two-week reverse repo; during the last quarter of 1999 a three-month repo was made available on a one-off basis to preserve liquidity and market confidence running into the new millennium.[9] In addition, during 1999 the Bank widened the range of eligible collateral that could be used in open market operations conducted with it, such that from September that year the list of such eligible securities was extended to cover government securities issued by countries of the European Economic Area, denominated in euros. This increased the stock of eligible collateral by £2 trillion. During the final quarter of 2000 gilt repo made up just over 70% of the collateral accepted by the Bank in its open market operations, while euro-denominated securities made up about 11% of the total, or £1.7 billion worth. The full set of eligible securities is listed on the Bank's web site at

```
http://www.bankofengland.co.uk/markets/money/eligiblesecurities.htm
```

10.3.2 *Counterparties*

The BoE deals with a wide range of financial institutions active in the gilt repo and/or bill markets, all of whom must satisfy a number of financial criteria, designed to ensure that operations function efficiently and that the liquidity supplied is available to all market participants. Counterparty banks, building societies and securities houses must satisfy the BoE requirements that they:

- have the technical capability to respond quickly and efficiently to the Bank's operations;
- maintain an active presence in the gilt repo and/or bill markets, thus contributing to the distribution of liquidity;
- participate regularly in the Bank's operations; and
- provide the Bank with useful information on market conditions and movements.

There is no formal underwriting commitment, but the BoE monitors compliance with its functional requirements and reserves the right to cease dealing with any counterparty at its own discretion.

The Bank of England and the sterling money markets

By dint of its money market open market operations, the BoE maintains a regular dealing relationship with participants in the sterling money markets. By means of this relationship the Bank is able to discuss and be aware of market expectations and conditions, as well as keep an eye on market liquidity. Two committees exist that act as a conduit for the Bank to maintain regular contact, the Sterling Money Markets Liaison Group (MMLG) and the Stock Lending and Repo Committee (SLRC), both of which are chaired by the BoE's head of Gilt-Edged and Money Markets Division.

The SLRC was established in 1990, originally as the Stock Borrowing and Lending Committee. It is essentially a forum in which all market participants and interested parties can meet to discuss developments in the sterling repo and stock-lending markets. As well as banks, securities houses and other stock lending and repo practitioners, those represented include the Debt Management Office, the Financial Services Authority (FSA), CRESTCo, the British Bankers Association, the London Stock Exchange and the

---

[9]   See the *Quarterly Bulletin* for November 1999, pp. 325–326.

London Clearing House (LCH). There is also representation from the European Repo Council and the US Bond Market Association; this enables discussion of topics of common interest, such as developments in legal and structural treatment of repo.

The SLRC is involved in providing guidelines and direction on market good practice for repo and stock lending. It produced the Gilt Repo Code in 1995, as well as the Stock Borrowing and Lending Code. This type of work is ongoing, and the Committee keeps under review progress in repo documentation issues; for example, in 2000 it produced the revised Gilts Annexe to accompany the revised BMA/ISMA GMRA (see Appendix A at the back of this book). During 2000 and 2001 the SLRC debated a number of new developments in the market, including:

- potential impact on stock lending and repo of the Basel II capital adequacy rules;
- the new regulatory environment that took effect in the UK in December 2001, under the overview of the FSA;
- the impact of delivery-versus-payment and how this involves CRESTCo;
- the progress of the new RepoClear electronic trading and netting system at LCH, and the proposed introduction of gilt repo within this system.

Minutes of the SLRC meetings are available on the BoE's web site at

`http://www.bankofengland.co.uk/markets/index.htm`

10.4 Gilt settlement and CREST/CGO

10.4.1 *Overview*

The CREST service is operated by CRESTCo, the body set up to run the London equity market dematerialised settlement system. The Central Gilts Office (CGO), part of the Bank of England, was merged with CREST in July 2000, so that equity, gilt and money market clearing is now conducted through one system.[10] The CGO service was originally established in 1986 by the BoE and the London Stock Exchange to facilitate the settlement of specified securities, essentially gilts and certain sterling bonds such as Bulldogs for which the BoE acts as registrar, and was upgraded by the BoE in 1997. In particular, the service was upgraded to enhance gilt repo trading activity and to cater for the introduction of the gilt strips facility in December 1997. It also provides a vehicle for the development of real-time Delivery-versus-Payment (DVP) through links to the Real Time Gross Settlement System (RTGS) for wholesale payments, which was introduced in mid-1996.

The basic concept of CREST/CGO remains the same as when it was introduced, that is the provision of secure settlement for gilt-edged securities through an efficient and reliable system of electronic book entry transfers in real time against an assured payment. CREST is a real-time, communication-based system. Settlement on the specified business day (T+1 for normal gilt trades) is dependent on the matching by CREST of correctly input and authenticated instructions by both of the trading parties, and the successful completion of pre-settlement checks on the parties' stock account balances and credit "headroom".

---

[10] A small number of non-British government securities or "Bulldogs" did not migrate to the CREST system.

The upgraded CGO provided additional features including:

- greater control by settlement banks over the credit risks run on their customers (by means of a debit-capped payment mechanism);
- the movement of stock free of payment;
- matching of instructions between counterparties;
- a flexible membership structure (allowing the names of "sponsored" as well as "direct" members to appear on the register);
- multiple account designations.

Note that firms must have an account at CREST in order to settle via the system; due to the charges payable for this service many banks opt for an agent settlement bank to handle their transactions. It is now possible to settle gilts through Euroclear and Clearstream Banking. both of which have accounts at CREST.

10.4.2 *Gilt reference prices*[11]

After a repo trade has been agreed, the back offices of both parties will often use the gilt reference price as the basis for settlement proceeds and other calculations. CREST/CGO uses data supplied by GEMMs for the calculation of these reference prices, which are bid-offer closing prices for each gilt reported to the Debt Management Office (DMO) at the close of business each day. The reference prices for conventional CREST/CGO stocks are based on the clean mid-market closing (normally 4.15pm) prices supplied by members of the GEMM Association. These mid-prices are then adjusted to include accrued interest and quoted to five decimal places, expressed in £100 nominal of stock. Reference prices are updated daily.

Gilt strips trade on a yield basis. The reference price for strips is calculated from gross redemption yields using an "actual/actual" formula, that is, compound interest for all strips divided by the actual number of days in the coupon period.

10.4.3 *Delivery-by-value*

Delivery-by-value (DBV)[12] is a mechanism whereby a CREST member may borrow money from or lend money to another CREST member against overnight gilt collateral. The CREST system automatically selects and delivers securities to a specified aggregate value on the basis of the previous night's DMO reference prices; equivalent securities are returned the following business day. The DBV functionality allows the giver and taker of collateral to specify the classes of security to be included within the DBV. The options available for DBV stock are:

- all classes of security held within CREST, including strips, index-linked stock and Bulldogs;
- coupon-bearing gilts and Bulldogs;
- coupon-bearing gilts and strips;
- only coupon-bearing gilts.

---

[11] In the author's time these were known as CGO reference prices; I have since heard them referred to variously as "DMO reference prices", "gilt reference prices" and "CREST reference prices". Take your pick.

[12] Yes, not delivery-by-van (thanks, Del!).

DBV repo is a repo transaction in which the delivery of the securities is by the DBV mechanism in CREST; a series of DBV repos may be constructed to form an "open" or "term" DBV repo. The DBV functionality allows repo interest to be automatically calculated and paid.

Note that repo rates can be quoted for "GC" as well as for "DBV"; for instance, see the GiltKING dealing screen in Figure 10.14. If we remember that the market convention for both is to bid and offer for nominal amount of stock, which translates into a sum of cash that is the market value of the stock if we ignore any margin, there is a key difference between the two types of repo: if one deals in GC, the seller of stock must inform the counterparty what specific stock is being passed over within around five minutes of the trade being agreed. In a DBV repo, the seller may deliver any eligible gilt, and this may not be specified up until 3pm the day of the trade. In this scenario, the repo buyer may not know what stock they are getting until considerably later than the time of trade, only that it will be a CREST/CGO stock. Given that this might conceivably be an index-linked gilt that is trading at considerably over par, this will impact the amount of cash that will be passed over against the gilt. A party trading DBV repo will accept this situation; however, when trading GC, certain buying parties will specify what stock they are prepared or not prepared to receive. For instance, they may state that index-linked gilts or strips are not acceptable.

A final word on market convention: as repo rates refer to bids and offer for stock, a corporate counterparty that wished to invest a specific amount of cash must clearly state that it has a cash amount to invest. So for example, if we assume that a corporate has £50 million cash to lend, simply lifting a market-maker's screen offer in "£50 million GC" may see it receive more (or less) than £50 million-worth of stock, depending on the price of the collateral. Therefore it must clearly state beforehand that it has an exact amount of cash to lend, to avoid confusion.

10.5 Code of best practice

The *Gilt Repo Code of Best Practice* sets out standards of best practice for gilt repo. It was introduced by the BoE in November 1995 ahead of the commencement of gilt repo trading in January 1996. The Code is set out in various sections, which we summarise below.

Preliminary Issues

Market participants should ensure that they have adequate systems and controls for the business they intend to undertake. This includes internal controls, credit-risk control systems, written procedures and systems for accounting and taxation.

Market Professionals

Before dealing with a client for the first time, market professionals should either confirm that the client is already aware of the Code or draw it to the client's attention.

Legal Agreement

Gilt repo transactions should be subject to a legal agreement between the two parties concerned. A market standard is the *Gilt Repo Legal Agreement*, and participants to gilt repo are strongly recommended to adopt this. This agreement is based on the BMA/ISMA Global Master Repurchase Agreement (see Appendix A, at the back of this book).

Margin

Participants in gilt repo should negotiate suitable initial margin levels, reflecting both their assessment of their counterparty's creditworthiness and the market risks (for example, duration of collateral) involved in the transaction. Participants should also monitor their net exposure to all counterparties on a daily basis.

Custody

Clients need to ensure that stock loan and repo transactions are identified accordingly to their custodian.

Default and Close-Out

Once the decision to default has been taken it is important that the process be carried out carefully. This includes the non-defaulting party doing everything in its power to ensure that default market values used in the close-out calculations are fair.

10.6 Electronic gilt repo trading

Various forms of electronic trading exist in repo markets, ranging from screen-based repo rates to fully automated systems. In this section we describe two systems in operation in the gilt repo market.

10.6.1 *Automated electronic trading: GiltKING*

King & Shaxson Bond Brokers Limited (KSBB) is part of Gerrard and King, part of the Old Mutual group. Gerrard & King was formed from the merger of two discount houses, Gerrard & National and King & Shaxson. The firm is active in sterling and other markets as cash bond brokers as well as repo brokers. In September 1998 KSBB introduced "GiltKING", an automated electronic trading system for gilt repo. GiltKING offers the speed and freedom of dealer input whilst retaining the benefits of voice broking, the traditional method employed by brokers in the bond and money markets. Dealers connected to the system can view real-time GC and specific rates. If they wish to trade on a price they activate a "hit" or "lift" on the screen at the touch of a mouse button. The system will prompt the dealer to confirm the trade, after which the trade goes through.

The markets available on GiltKING are currently limited to gilt repo, cash gilts and sterling swaps. The trading screen displays real-time live prices from the market, input by repo dealers. Prices are displayed anonymously and may be dealt on directly through the screen. A single command button enables the dealer to *refer* all his prices in an instant. This is when a dealer wishes to change his prices from being live to being under reference, which would require a counterparty to confirm the price before dealing. The right-hand side of the rates screen is a dialogue box where dealers input and maintain prices, with additional sections showing trade confirmations and trade history. There is also an "on call" help facility that puts the dealer in touch with the KSBB broking team.

Figure 10.14 shows an extract from the trading screen on GiltKING, which has been reproduced with permission. The screen displays the overnight rates for gilt GC and specials and the sizes at which the dealer inputting the price is prepared to deal. The bottom half shows term rates for a specific stock, the 8½% Treasury 2005, abbreviated to "8H 05". Other pages will show the rates for term rates up to one year. The page is in colour so that on the trader's screen the firm's own prices are in green. Prices are firm (unless indicated as referred) and can be dealt on immediately on-screen. The small figure prefix is the "big figure", while the small figure suffix is the dealing size in millions nominal up to which the trader is prepared to deal.

Figure 10.15 shows a sample trade history box taken from the right-hand side of the screen. This shows time of trade, stock dealt, term of trade, whether buy or sell, size of bargain and rate dealt.

			Overnight			
^{7}62$_{17}$	^{7}61$_{12}$	^{7}60$_{50}$	GC	^{7}60$_{121}$	^{7}55$_{50}$	^{7}52$_{20}$
^{7}60$_{50}$	^{7}59$_{50}$	^{7}57$_{50}$	DBV	^{7}56$_{15}$	^{7}50$_{97}$	^{7}48$_{75}$
		^{7}52$_{45}$	6 99	^{7}50$_{50}$		
			8 00	^{7}45$_{76}$		
	^{7}51$_{25}$	^{7}49$_{30A}$	7 01	^{7}46$_{25}$	^{7}42$_{18}$	
			7 02	^{7}47$_{60}$		
	^{7}44$_{10}$	^{7}41$_{15}$	8 03			
		^{7}43$_{19}$	6H 03	^{7}38$_{76}$		
	^{7}45$_{25}$	^{7}41$_{23}$	6T 04			
		^{7}35$_{30}$	8H 05	^{7}29$_{160}$	^{7}27$_{80}$	^{7}25$_{25}$
	^{7}23$_{50}$	^{7}21$_{20}$	7H 06	^{7}11$_{30}$		
		^{7}10$_{75}$	7Q 07			

			8H 05			
		^{7}35$_{30}$	ON	^{7}29$_{160}$	^{7}27$_{80}$	^{7}25$_{25}$
		^{7}37$_{45}$	TN			
		^{7}55$_{20}$	1W	^{7}45$_{15}$		
		^{7}45$_{20}$	1M			
			2M			
	^{7}42$_{25}$	^{7}37$_{20}$	3M	^{7}35$_{20}$		
			6M			
			9M			
			1Y			

Figure 10.14: Extract from GiltKING dealing screen.
© K&S BB. Used with permission.

11:26:36	7H 06	ON	B	30	7.11
11:15:24	8 03	1W	B	15	7.27
10:49:14	8 00	ON	B	76	7.45
09:49:42	6 99	ON	S	56	7.18
09:12:00	DBV	ON	B	50	7.55

Figure 10.15: Trade history screen extract from GiltKING.
© K&S BB. Used with permission.

10.6.2 *Garban ICAP*

From June 1998 Garban Europe provided a full screen-broking service for its gilt repo clients. Prices on the screen are firm and offer a real view of the market, although dealing itself is not automated – the trader still needs to deal over the telephone. As is customary, a dealer will see his own prices highlighted while all other prices on-screen will be anonymous.

Where clients make prices available, the screen shows term rates for all stocks as well as for GC. An illustration of how the screen may look at any time is given at Figure 10.16.

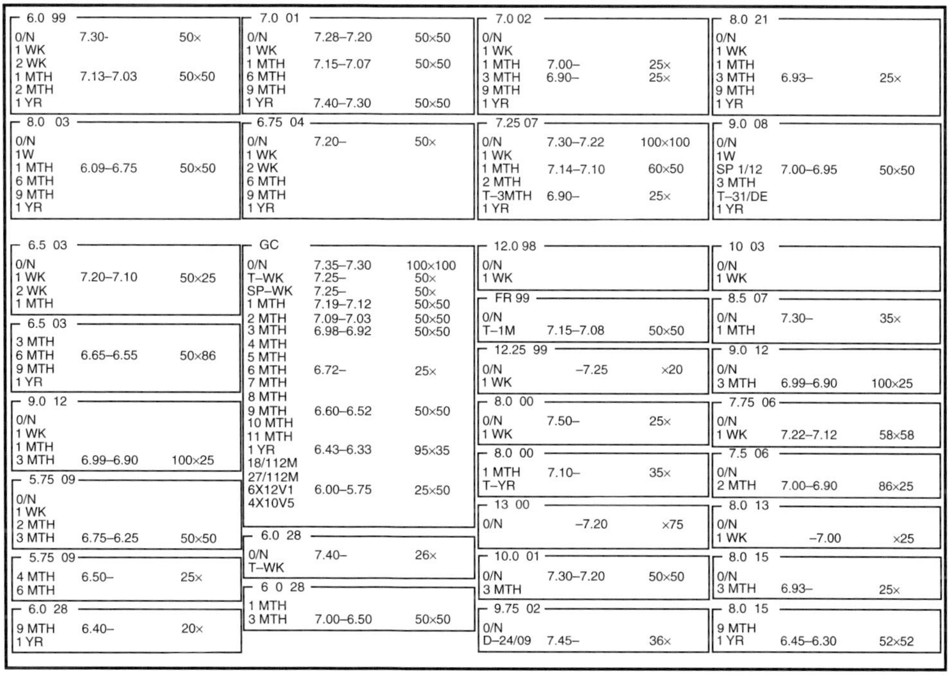

```
┌─ 6.0  99 ──────┐  ┌─ 7.0  01 ──────┐  ┌─ 7.0 02 ───────┐  ┌─ 8.0 21 ───────┐
│ 0/N    7.30-  50×│ 0/N   7.28-7.20 50×50│ 0/N            │ 0/N            │
│ 1 WK           │  │ 1 WK           │  │ 1 WK           │  │ 1 WK           │
│ 2 WK           │  │ 1 MTH 7.15-7.07 50×50│ 1 MTH  7.00-  25×│ 1 MTH          │
│ 1 MTH 7.13-7.03 50×50│ 6 MTH      │  │ 3 MTH  6.90-  25×│ 3 MTH 6.93-  25×│
│ 2 MTH          │  │ 9 MTH          │  │ 9 MTH          │  │ 9 MTH          │
│ 1 YR           │  │ 1 YR   7.40-7.30 50×50│ 1 YR        │  │ 1 YR           │
├─ 8.0  03 ──────┤  ├─ 6.75  04 ─────┤  ├─ 7.25 07 ──────┤  ├─ 9.0 08 ───────┤
│ 0/N            │  │ 0/N    7.20-  50×│ 0/N   7.30-7.22 100×100│ 0/N        │
│ 1W             │  │ 1 WK           │  │ 1 WK           │  │ 1W             │
│ 1 MTH 6.09-6.75 50×50│ 2 WK       │  │ 1 MTH 7.14-7.10 60×50│ SP 1/12 7.00-6.95 50×50│
│ 6 MTH          │  │ 6 MTH          │  │ 2 MTH          │  │ 3 MTH          │
│ 9 MTH          │  │ 9 MTH          │  │ T-3MTH 6.90-  25×│ T-31/DE        │
│ 1 YR           │  │ 1 YR           │  │ 1 YR           │  │ 1 YR           │
└────────────────┘  └────────────────┘  └────────────────┘  └────────────────┘

┌─ 6.5  03 ──────┐  ┌─ GC ───────────┐  ┌─ 12.0 98 ──────┐  ┌─ 10 03 ────────┐
│ 0/N            │  │ 0/N  7.35-7.30 100×100│ 0/N         │  │ 0/N            │
│ 1 WK  7.20-7.10 50×25│ T-WK  7.25-  50×│ 1 WK          │  │ 1 WK           │
│ 2 WK           │  │ SP-WK 7.25-   50×│                 │  └────────────────┘
│ 1 MTH          │  │ 1 MTH 7.19-7.12 50×50│             │  ┌─ FR 99 ────────┐
├─ 6.5  03 ──────┤  │ 2 MTH 7.09-7.03 50×50│             │  │                │
│ 3 MTH          │  │ 3 MTH 6.98-6.92 50×50│             │  ├─ 8.5 07 ───────┤
│ 6 MTH 6.65-6.55 50×86│ 4 MTH       │     │ 0/N         │  │ 0/N    7.30-  35×│
│ 9 MTH          │  │ 5 MTH          │  │ T-1M  7.15-7.08 50×50│ 1 MTH      │
│ 1 YR           │  │ 6 MTH  6.72-  25×│ ├─ 12.25 99 ────┤  ├─ 9.0 12 ───────┤
├─ 9.0  12 ──────┤  │ 7 MTH          │  │ 0/N           │  │ 0/N            │
│ 0/N            │  │ 8 MTH          │  │ 0/N     -7.25  ×20│ 0/N            │
│ 1 WK           │  │ 9 MTH 6.60-6.52 50×50│ 1 WK       │  │ 3 MTH 6.99-6.90 100×25│
│ 1 MTH          │  │ 10 MTH         │  ├─ 8.0 00 ───────┤  ├─ 7.75 06 ──────┤
│ 3 MTH 6.99-6.90 100×25│ 11 MTH     │  │ 0/N    7.50-  25×│ 0/N            │
├─ 5.75 09 ──────┤  │ 1 YR  6.43-6.33 95×35│ 1 WK        │  │ 1 WK  7.22-7.12 58×58│
│ 0/N            │  │ 18/112M        │  ├─ 8.0 00 ───────┤  ├─ 7.5 06 ───────┤
│ 1 WK           │  │ 27/112M        │  │ 1 MTH  7.10-  35×│ 0/N            │
│ 2 MTH          │  │ 6X12V1 6.00-5.75 25×50│ T-YR      │  │ 2 MTH 7.00-6.90 86×25│
│ 3 MTH 6.75-6.25 50×50│ 4X10V5      │  ├─ 13 00 ────────┤  ├─ 8.0 13 ───────┤
├─ 5.75 09 ──────┤  ├─ 6.0 28 ───────┤  │ 0/N     -7.20  ×75│ 0/N            │
│ 4 MTH  6.50-  25×│ 0/N    7.40-  26×│                    │ 1 WK    -7.00  ×25│
│ 6 MTH          │  │ T-WK           │  ├─ 10.0 01 ──────┤  ├─ 8.0 15 ───────┤
├─ 6.0 28 ───────┤  ├─ 6 0 28 ───────┤  │ 0/N   7.30-7.20 50×50│ 0/N        │
│ 9 MTH  6.40-  20×│ 1 MTH          │  │ 3 MTH           │  │ 3 MTH 6.93-  25×│
│ 1 YR           │  │ 3 MTH 7.00-6.50 50×50│ ├─ 9.75 02 ──┤  ├─ 8.0 15 ───────┤
└────────────────┘  └────────────────┘  │ 0/N           │  │ 9 MTH          │
                                          │ D-24/09 7.45- 36×│ 1 YR 6.45-6.30 52×52│
                                          └────────────────┘  └────────────────┘
```

Figure 10.16: Garban ICAP repo screen.
© Garban ICAP. Used with permission.

10.7 Examples of gilt repo trades

The following examples of gilt repo trades illustrate market conventions on pricing, settlement and margin. The examples relate to both stock-driven trades and cash-driven trades. The terms of trades for Examples 10.4–10.7 are as follows:

Amount	£10,000,000
Security	5% Treasury 2004
Term repo	One month
Start date	5 January 2000
End date	7 February 2000
Clean price	£95.25
Repo rate	5½%

Example 10.4

The standard case assumes no initial margin, and no significant price movements during the trade, so no variation margining.

Calculating the all-in or dirty market value

$$\text{Nominal} \times \text{clean price} = £10,000,000 \times 0.9525$$
$$= 9,525,000$$

Accrued interest (29 days) = £39,617.49

Consideration = £9,564,617.49

Therefore the dirty "price" for the purposes of entering into the settlement system is:

$$\frac{\text{consideration}}{\text{nominal}} \times 100 = \frac{9,564,617.49}{10,000,000} \times 100 = 95.65$$

In this example the dirty price is calculated to two decimal places but where the trade is cash-driven the dirty price may be taken to more significant figures. Counterparties may agree between themselves how exact the calculation of the nominal amount of stock should be.

Setting the "opening leg"
In the case of a stock-driven trade the seller of securities passes £10 million nominal of stock to the purchaser in return for consideration of £9,564,617.49.

Calculating the repurchase price
The repurchase "price" equals the initial consideration of £9,564,617.49 plus the repo interest payable.

The repo interest payable is given by:

consideration × repo rate × number of days (act/365 basis)

which is £9,564,617.49 × 5½% × 33/365 = £47,561.04.

Note that the term specified was one month, which would ordinarily make the termination date 5 February 2000; however, this day is a non-business day, so the maturity date is moved forward to the nearest business day, which makes the trade a 33-day term transaction.

Setting the closing leg
The original seller of securities receives back his £10 million nominal of stock and pays £9,612,178.53 cash to the original purchaser (this is £9,564,617.49 opening amount or "wired amount" plus £47,561.04 repo interest).

Example 10.5
With initial margin: here we assume that the person repoing out stock provides initial margin of 2.0.% (this is factored into the dirty price).

Calculating the terms of the transaction

Consideration = £9,564,617.49 (as before)

divide by 1.020 initial margin level = £9,377,075,97

Therefore the adjusted all-in or dirty price, rounded to 2 decimal places, is £93.77. The terms of the trade are therefore:

Nominal	£10,000,000
Issue	5% Treasury 2004
Repo rate	5½%
Accrued	£39,617.49

All-in price	£93.77
Purchase date (value date)	5 January
Repurchase date	7 February
Total purchase consideration	£9,377,000
Repo interest	£46,628.10
Total repurchase consideration	£9,423,628.10

Note that if the person repoing out the stock receives the initial margin, rather than pays it, the calculation would be £9,564,617.49 × 1.020 or £9,755,909.84 and the adjusted all-in price would be 97.55.

Example 10.6

Making margin calls: using Example 10.5, here we assume a fall in the market price of the stock from 95.25 to 92.25 occurring on 6 January.

Examples 10.6 and 10.7 show two methods to re-margin repo trades. The objective is to eliminate the exposure which has arisen from a movement in market prices. Counterparties must agree the approach they will adopt between themselves.

Following the drop in price of the bond, the collateral is now worth:

Principal	£9,225,000
Accrued interest (30 days)	£40,983.61
Total	£9,265,983.61

The repo buyer (provider of cash) has, however, lent £9,377,000 against this security, and so is now undercollateralised; in addition, one day's interest has accrued on the cash lent and an initial margin requirement of 2.0% must be restored.

Calculating the amount of the collateral shortfall

To restore the original margin of 2.0%, the cash provider in this example would need to call for the following amount:

(original consideration + repo interest accrued on consideration) ×
(1 + initial margin) *less* (New all-in price × nominal amount)

This is shown to be:

((£9,377,000 + £1,412.97) × 1.02) − (£0.926598 × 10,000,000)
= £300,001.23 margin shortfall.

Note that if the person repoing out stock receives initial margin, rather than pays it, the calculation would be:

$$\frac{\text{original consideration} + \text{interest on consideration}}{1 + \text{initial margin}}$$

less

(new all-in price × nominal amount)

This would be:

$$\frac{£9,755,909 + £1,470.07}{1.02} - £0.926598 \times 10,000,000$$
$$= £300,016.15 \text{ margin shortfall.}$$

Margin call: Provided the agreed variation margin has been triggered by the price movement, the purchaser has the right to make a margin call on the provider of securities to eliminate the credit exposure. The Gilt Repo Code regards it as essential protection that calls are made when a collateral shortfall exceeds the variation margin. The party being called for margin has the right to choose whether margin shall be delivered in securities or cash.

Free delivery of sufficient additional bonds is a frequent method of eliminating the shortfall. If any additional amount of the original bond (5% 2004) is delivered, then the nominal amount required would be £300,001.23/0.926598 = £323,766.33 of stock. The parties may agree on whether this exact amount or a rounded amount, say £323,000, is delivered.

Alternatively cash may be posted as collateral. For single repo transactions cash can earn interest at the repo rate of the underlying transaction. Margin is held on a pool basis covering a number of repo transactions, that cash earns interest at a rate agreed between the parties as being applicable to such funds.

Example 10.7

This illustrates margin calls with a term repo transaction through close-out and repricing, but is otherwise similar to Example 10.6.

A less frequently used approach is to close-out the original transaction and then re-open it or "re-price" it with new terms to reflect the movement in the value of the collateral. Counterparties again have the option of making the adjustment to either cash or securities.

(a) *adjusting cash*

The original trade agreed on 5 January, as in Example 10.6, is closed-out for value on 6 January and re-opened the same day. The consideration for the close-out is calculated by adding one day's repo interest to the original transaction:

$$£9,377,000 + £1,412.97 = £9,378,412.97$$

The new purchase price is calculated by re-pricing the collateral at the new all-in price. In this case the price would be:

$$\frac{£92.65983}{1.02} = 90.84 \text{ rounded to 2 decimal places.}$$

This would give a new total purchase price of £9,084,000 (rounded). In settlement the close-out trade matches the start leg of the new trade – bonds therefore do not move – and the cash difference of £294,412.97 (that is, £9,378,412.97 less £9,084,000) is paid to the provider of cash. In this process interest has been "cleaned up", that is, the cash transfer includes one day's repo interest.

The terms of the trade are now:

Nominal	£10,000,000
Issue	5% Treasury 2004
Repo rate	5½%
All-in price	90.84
Purchase date	6 January
Repurchase date	7 February
Total purchase consideration	£9,084,000

(b) *adjusting securities*

The consequence of closing-out and re-pricing via transfers of cash is to vary the amount of cash consideration on which the repo interest is payable. In a cash-driven trade, adjusting the amount of securities is more likely to be appropriate, as it is considered administratively simpler.

The original trade – at a dirty price of 93.77 – is closed-out for value on 6 January and a new trade booked from 6 January to 7 February, still at a dirty price of 90.84. The nominal amount of stock in the new transaction needs to be increased to reflect its fall in value. The new nominal amount is calculated so as to produce a total purchase price for the new transaction at the new price which matches that of the old.

Thus the new nominal value is

$$\frac{9,377,000}{0.9084} = £10,322,545.13.$$

A free delivery of £322,545.13 (or an agreed rounded amount) of stock is required, plus a payment of one day's repo interest (£1,412.97) from the old transaction.

The terms of trade for the new transaction (if repo interest is settled) are:

Nominal	£10,322,545
Issue	5% Treasury 2002
Repo rate	5½%
All-in price	90.84
Purchase date	6 January
Repurchase date	7 February
Total purchase consideration	£9,377,000

Where repo interest up to 6 January is not to be settled, a corresponding further amount of stock would need to be supplied.

Example 10.8: Repo of a gilt strip

In this example the principal strip maturing on 7 December 2009 is repoed over the same time period with the seller in this example providing margin of 3.0%.

Gilt strips trade on a yield basis which are then converted into a price. If the UK Treasury Principal strip December 2009 is yielding 4.521% on 2 March 1999, then its price will be 61.804. The repo is carried out in the normal way. Initial margin, if required, may reflect the greater price volatility of strips compared with coupon bonds. There will obviously be no accrued interest on the collateral involved in the calculation, as this is a strip. If £10,000,000 nominal of the strip is repoed with an initial margin of 3.0% then the overall purchase price will be:

$$\frac{10,000,000 \times 0.61804}{1.03} = £6,000,388.35.$$

The terms of the trade are:

Nominal	£10,000,000
Issue	Treasury Principal strip December 2009
Repo rate	5½%
All-in price	60.003884
Purchase date	2 March
Repurchase date	2 April
Total purchase consideration	£6,000,388.35
Repo interest	£27,125.04
Total repurchase consideration	£6,027,513.40

If the strip maintained a yield of 4.521% throughout the trade then its price on 2 April would be 62.108627 and no margin would have been called.

Selected bibliography and references

Bank of England, *Quarterly Bulletin*, November 1999, February 2000, August 2000
Choudhry, M., *Introduction to the Gilt Strips Market*, SI (Services) Publishing 1999
Garban ICAP Europe, *Gilt Repo Monitor*, May 1998

11 Selected Country Repo Markets

There are developed and liquid repo markets in existence around the world, in North America, Europe, Asia and Japan. There is a considerable amount of cross-border trading, as well as repo in so-called emerging markets. The size and liquidity of different markets varies but the aggregate whole is considerable, with a large volume of stock being repoed at any one time. There is a dearth of reference material on country market repo, outside those mentioned in earlier chapters; consequently we give a brief overview here in the hope that this will spur readers on to further research and perhaps more formal documentation of the structures and conventions in these markets.

The depth and liquidity of repo markets in Europe and the US varies by each country. Practitioners new to any particular market often contact relevant brokers for specific operating details. Figure 11.1 illustrates the depth of selected repo markets, showing the ratio of outstanding repo volume to nominal value of government debt outstanding. Not surprisingly, by this measure the US market is shown to have the greatest liquidity.

In this chapter we review briefly the structure and composition of five country repo markets. We also look at issues in emerging markets repo and central bank repo.

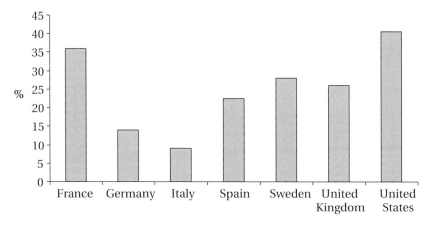

Figure 11.1: Depth of selected repo markets, measured as ratio of repo volume outstanding to government debt outstanding. ©RISK, November 2000. Used with permission.

	Daily turnover (EUR bln)	Nominal outstanding (EUR bln)
Belgium	26.2	86.5
France	42.3	292
Germany	60	137.7
Italy	53	113.3
Spain	21.3	54.4
United States	not available	1528.9

Table 11.1: Approximate daily turnover in selected country markets,
June 2000. Source: Euroclear, Clearstream, SICOVAM, Nomura.

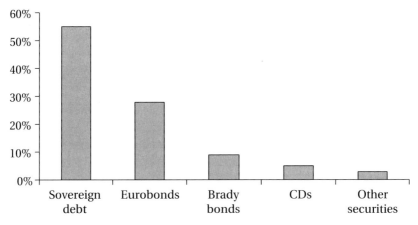

Figure 11.2: Breakdown of instruments used in repo, 2000.
Source: Garban ICAP.

Figure 11.3: Euro GC rates on Garban ICAP repo screen, showing "Euro GC",
German government, Jumbo Pfandbriefe, French government, Italian government
and Greek government repo rates, 9 January 2001.
© Garban ICAP. Used with permission.

11.1 France

11.1.1 *Overview*

Development of the repo market in government securities has been actively encouraged by the authorities in France, indeed the Banque de France views the instrument as one method by which bank systemic risk, inherent in unsecured interbank lending, can be reduced. From December 1993 repo has been formally described in legislation that also describes provisions for *netting*, repo and derivatives, among other areas.[1] Under this legislation repo is defined as a transaction that involves transfer of securities, with both counterparties committed to sell and buy-back (or buy and sell, as appropriate) the securities transferred at an agreed price and date. Under this definition the transaction cannot be described as a secured loan. The repo legal agreement in France is the *Pension Livree* although generally referred to simply as the *Pension*. Repo can be undertaken in the following instruments:

■ securities listed on a French or foreign stock exchange;

■ securities listed on the *seconde marché*;

■ negotiable debt instruments traded on a French or foreign regulated market, including government paper such as BTANs, OATs, and Treasury bills, as well as CDs and certain other securities.

Other features of the French repo market legal agreement include:

■ the ability for any corporate, local authority or financial entity to engage in repo;

■ a description of margin, without making its use compulsory;

■ a description of the process followed by the stock buyer in the event of default, including a capability to hold stock sold as collateral;

■ an allowance for *set-off* and netting in the event of default and insolvency.

Repo in France is straightforward classic repo and an on-balance-sheet instrument. The market is large and liquid, with daily average turnover of around EUR40 billion and volume outstanding of approximately EUR200 billion as at June 2000.[2] The average term of trade is 14 days. Along with countries such as Germany and the Netherlands in the euro area, French government repo rates invariably trade at a slight premium to the euro GC curve, although as we note later, there is no uniform GC rate due to the perceived credit differences between euro-denominated debt of different sovereign issuers. A BIS study reported that during the first quarter of 1998 French government repo traded approximately 4–5 basis points below the interbank rate in the short dates (that is, overnight to one week) and 8–10 basis points below for one- to three-month maturities.[3]

There are a number of unusual features in the French repo market, in addition to the definition of repo in domestic law. These include a registered market-making system, as one observes in the cash government market, and a significant volume of floating-rate repo.

---

[1] See ISMA (1997).
[2] Source is SICOVAM.
[3] Bank for International Settlements, *Implications of repo markets for central banks*, March 1999.

11.1.2 *Registered market-making structure*

As of June 2000 there were 11 firms registered as market makers or primary dealers in French government debt repo. These were originally known as *Spécialistes de la Pension sur Valeurs du Trésor* or SPVTs but are now termed SVTs; they are registered at the French Treasury and are required to make two-way prices in government security repo out to a three-month maturity. The ready dealing size that must be quoted is a maximum of EUR100 million for overnight trades, decreasing to EUR 20 million for three-month trades. This formal market-making system dates from 1994 and firms that are registered as both cash and repo market-makers include Societe Generale, BNP Paribas and Credit Commercial de France. These firms post prices on standard vendor services such as Reuters and Bloomberg.

11.1.3 *Floating-rate repo*

An unusual and possibly unique feature of French government repo is the floating-rate repo, which makes up more than half of repo transactions. Before the introduction of the euro, this transaction was based on the French franc interbank unsecured overnight rate known as the *Taux Moyen Pondéré* or TMP. It is now based on the euro overnight rate or EONIA. This rate is the general overnight rate and so practically immune to market manipulation, given the size of the euro interbank market. In a floating-rate repo trade the final rate paid by the stock seller is calculated as the mean of the overnight offer rate applicable each day during the term of the loan. Depending on the credit quality of the stock seller, the actual repo rate may be a spread over or under EONIA.

11.1.4 *Settlement*

The main securities settlement mechanisms in France is SICOVAM, the central securities depositary system. This body operates a system known as *Relit Grand Vitesse* or RGV, an integrated real-time settlement mechanism for bonds, money market instruments and equities. It provides real-time matching, settlement and reporting cycles, and operates for 22 hours out of 24. Put simply, the settlement process works as follows:

■ SICOVAM continuously calculates each market participant's purchasing power on the basis of cash positions, securities held that can be used as collateral, and collateral and other guarantees held outside the system;

■ if a participant has insufficient funds to settle a security transfer during the day, the Banque de France automatically enters into a repo trade with it to guarantee final payment; this eliminates intra-day cash shortfall, thus reducing intra-day settlement risk.

Repo trades initiated by the Banque de France are settled by close-of-business that day. Thus irrevocable settlement is guaranteed by the Banque de France, and the use of these intra-day repos provides liquidity in central bank money to the bank money transfer system, known as TBF.

	1999 Q1	1999 Q2
Repo trades		
• value (EUR bln)	2.046	1.893
• average size (EUR mln)	39	37
• outstanding value (EUR bln)	184.06	171.17
Collateral		
• OAT	54.50%	59%
• BTF	13%	9.50%
• BTAN	30.50%	29%
• Total French government	98%	97.50%
• Other securities	2%	2.50%
Repo rate		
• fixed rate	41.50%	39.91%
• floating rate	58.30%	59.91%
• zero	0.20%	0.18%

Table 11.2: Breakdown of French government bond repo, 1999.
Source: SICOVAM.

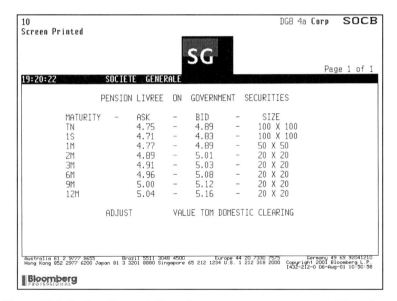

Figure 11.4: Societe Generale French government repo rates on Bloomberg,
6 August 2001. ©Societe Generale, ©Bloomberg L.P. Reproduced with permission.

11.2 Spain

The repo market in Spain has a number of distinctive features. One of the most significant of these is that the market trades sell/buy-backs rather than classic repo, and by local convention there are two types of transaction: *simultneas* for market professionals and *repos* traded by other entities such as investment funds and which are also sell/buy-backs. The Bank of Spain defines a sell/buy-back as a transfer of ownership of stock. The main difference between the two types is that in repos the bonds bought (borrowed) are frozen by the Central de Anotaciones, which is the Bank of Spain book-entry system, until the maturity of the transaction. This feature reduces the inherent credit risk, albeit with the restriction that the bonds are locked away for the term of the trade. In simultneas trades, the bonds are not frozen and so may be sold short. For this reason the majority of domestic professional trading, and virtually all non-resident trading, is conducted in the form of simultneas, with repos being undertaken by domestic investment funds, retail investors and third parties known as *terceros*. The professional market is dominated by commercial banks. The Spanish market is possibly unique in that domestic savings institutions, known as *Cajas*, market repo as a retail savings product to private customers, who are able to invest in this product at local branches.

The repo market in government securities comprises T-bills known as *Letras*, bonds of between three and five years maturity (*Bonos*) and bonds of 10–15 years maturity (*Obligaciones*). Repo in Letras was introduced first, in 1987. At the start of 2000 there was approximately EUR 251.3 billion nominal of government debt outstanding; repo volume was approximately EUR 141 billion per month.[4]

The money market in Spain, as in other euro-area markets, is quoted on a 360-day basis. From the start of the euro, as expected Spanish government collateral trades at a premium to the euro overnight rate (EONIA), although the margin is not great, usually around 5–10 basis points below. Repo in specific issues is on average around 7–9 basis points below Spanish government "GC" rates. There is no real "GC" as such in euro government repo, as certain collateral trades cheap and others expensive. For instance, German government collateral trades roughly around 5 basis points below others, but for various reasons connected with special status of certain stocks, Spanish collateral also traded through GC. Certain government collateral, for example Italian and Belgian bonds, trade above German, Dutch and Spanish collateral. Generic euro repo rates are posted on the British Bankers Association page on Bloomberg, shown in Figure 11.9.

Settlement of Spanish repo is via the Bank of Spain's book-entry system, which allows same-day settlement. For non-resident counterparties settlement is next-day.

Spanish government repo rates are posted on numerous vendors including Bloomberg and Reuters; rates can be viewed on Bloomberg page CIMD and Reuters page CIMF among others.

11.3 Germany

11.3.1 *German government repo*

The market in German government bonds or *Bund* market is large and liquid, possibly the most liquid in continental Europe. Sizes of individual issues are at least €10 billion, often larger, and this has allowed Bunds to achieve benchmark status, in a manner similar to US Treasury securities. The Bund repo market reflects the underlying liquidity of cash Bund securities; euro GC prices are those of Bund and French government securities, while remaining euro-area repo rates are quoted as a spread to these GC rates. The market informally ranks Bund repo as the lowest euro GC rates, which are rated as equal to French and Dutch government repo for credit quality but considered to be more liquid.

---

4   Source: ISMA (according to trades matched via TRAX).

Government bond repo is carried out in the instruments listed in Table 11.3, with ISMA-approved GC securities marked with a '*'.

Instrument	Maturity
Treasury bills	1–12 months
Bundesschatzanweisungen	1–2 years
Bundesrepublik (Bundes)*	1–30 years
German Unity Fund*	1–3 years
ERP Sondervermoegen	1–4 years
Bundesobligation (BOBL, OBL)*	1–5 years
Treuhandanstalt*	1–30 years
Treuhand–Obligation (TOBL)*	1–5 years

Table 11.3: German government securities used in repo.

Formally repo is described under German commercial law, and classic repo does not require a master agreement in order to be enforceable. The standard legal agreement in any case is the German Master Agreement, applicable to domestic deals. The legal framework is well established. Most market participants use the BMA/ISMA GMRA for international business, although a considerable volume of domestic business is carried out via undocumented sell/buy-backs. The GMRA, as applied to repo in Germany, contains an annexe to make it effective under local law, the domestic "Rahmenvertrag für echte Wertpapierpensionsgeschäfte".

Buy/sell-backs are also common in the German market; the legal arrangements for them are covered by a buy/sell-back annexe of the BMA/ISMA Global Master Repurchase Agreement. Traditionally, securities financing has been undertaken using buy/sell-backs; however, this is no longer the case and today classic repo is more prevalent. The main reason for the increasing popularity of classic repo was (and is) that unlike buy/sell-back, classic repo was described by the GMRA and allowed margining and re-pricing of securities.

The market is a traditional OTC one, with trades conducted on the telephone directly between banking counterparties or via brokers. There are a number of electronic trading platforms being developed primarily for the interbank market.

During 2000 Bund GC traded in a range around 2–10 basis points below Euribor in the short dates, while on occasion trading in specials went down to 90 basis points below the GC rate. As in other markets, there are a number of reasons why government stocks become special in the German market; however, the primary factor is the extent of its deliverability into the Bund futures contract. For illustration we show, in Figure 11.5, the spread below GC for repo in the DBR 3.75% January 2009 bond, the 10-year benchmark and also the cheapest-to-deliver (CTD) issue for the March 1999 Bund contract. However, it was not the CTD bond after expiry of June 1999 contract, and the extent of specialness declined after this point. Interestingly this bond remained in the delivery basket for subsequent contracts and its special status fluctuated. Arbitrage traders who wish to exploit the repo rate differential between benchmark and "off-the-run" issues and GC and special stocks are active participants in the Bund repo market.[5]

---

5   See Part III for a complete account of deliverable stocks, CTD bonds, the basis and a host of other fascinating detail concerning repo and exchange-traded government bond futures.

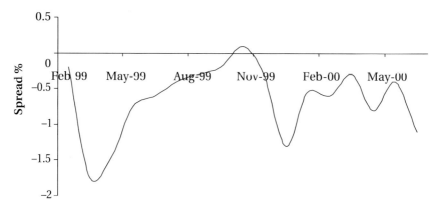

Figure 11.5: The specific repo rate spread to the GC rate for the DBR 3.75% January
2009 bond, 1999–2000. Source: Deutsche Bank. Used with permission.

11.3.2 *Pfandbriefe repo*

Pfandbriefe are domestic mortgage-backed securities, backed with the full faith and credit of
the federal government. As such they may be considered to be similar in status to government
agency securities in the US dollar market. Large-size issues are known as "Jumbo Pfandbriefe". There is an active market in Pfandbriefe repo, and from January 1999 a market maker
facility was introduced, which contributed substantially to liquidity. Essentially, the arrangement is that the underwriting bank (or lead manager) behind the issue of a cash market
security also undertakes to make a market in repo in that issue. The only conditions are that
the individual stock has a minimum issue size of €1.25 billion and has at least two years to
maturity. Market makers are required to quote two-way prices in up to €15 million, with a
maximum quote spread of 20 basis points.

Jumbo issues generally trade with the euro overnight rate (EONIA), although the smaller-
sized issues sometimes go special. The offered side in repo is dominated by investment funds
and the mortgage bank issuers themselves.

Figure 11.6:
German govern-
ment two- and
five-year collat-
eral, repo rates on
Garban ICAP
screen, 9 January
2001. Reproduced
with permission.

GC	GC	DMK - 10 Year	Germany	Italy	Italy CCT / CTZ	Belgium	UK - Gilts	French	Eurobonds

2 year		
DEC02TRH		
TREU 7.125 JAN03		
C-20/3	4.62 -	25.0x
OBL 126		
6,75AP03		
APR03TRH		
OBL 127		
JUN03TRH		

Others			
9,0JAN01			
FEB01UNT			
OBL 118			
MAR01SCH			
OBL 119			
8,37MY01			
JUN01SCH			
OBL 120			
AUG01UNT			
SEP01SCH			
8,25SP01			
OBL 121			
C-9/2	- 4.70	x100.0	
JUN02 SCHATZ			2<
T-12/1	4.75 -	5.0x	
C-7/2	- 4.68	x25.0S	
SEP02SCH			
BUND 7.125 DEC02			2<
C1M	4.72 - 4.65	25.0x25.0	
C-20/3	4.50 - 4.40	25.0x50.0S	
OBL 135			
S1M	- 4.68	x25.0S	
6,0JAN07			
BUND 5.25 JAN08			
T1W	4.74 -	20.0x	
BUND 6.25 JAN24			
S-15/1	4.75 -	14.0x	
BUND 6.25 JAN30			
S-17/1	- 4.75	x5.0S	

5 Year			
6,5OCT05			
6,0JAN06			
6,0FEB06			
BUND 6.25 APR06			2<
SN	4.67 -	50.0x	
C-20/3	4.62 - 4.57	25.0x50.0S	

Figure 11.7: German government 10-year collateral, repo rates on Garban ICAP screen, 9 January 2001. Reproduced with permission.

| GC | GC | DMK - 10 Year | Germany | Italy | Italy CCT / CTZ | Belgium | UK - Gilts | French | Eurobonds |

10 Year				10 Year		
NEW 7.08				BUND 5.375 JAN10		8<
BUND OLD JUL08				SN	- 4.65	x22.0
SN	- 4.50	x19.0		S1W	4.70 - 4.55	25.0x50.0
BUND 3.75 JAN09		2<		C1W	4.70 - 4.55	25.0x25.0S
T-12/1	4.74 -	5.0x		C2W	4.60 - 4.40	25.0Sx25.0S
S-31/1	4.75 - 4.68	25.0x25.0S		C-20/3	4.50 - 4.42	50.0x25.0
BUND NEW JUL09				C-20/6	4.33 - 4.23	25.0Sx25.0S
TN	4.77 -	70.0x		MARJUN	- 4.15	x25.0
BUND OLD JUL09		2<		C1Y	4.27 - 4.15	25.0x25.0
T1W	4.75 -	25.0x		BUND 5.25 JUL10		6<
S1W	- 4.67	x37.5		C-25/1	4.75 -	22.0x
				C1M	4.73 - 4.65	25.0x25.0S
				C-20/3	4.65 - 4.57	25.0x25.0
				C-20/6	4.55 - 4.35	25.0x25.0
				JUNSEP	4.10 - 3.80	25.0x25.0
				C1Y	4.25 - 4.20	50.0x50.0S
				BUND 5.25 JAN11		5<
				SN	- 4.60	x22.0
				C-14/3	4.65 -	25.0x
				C-20/6	4.50 - 4.35	25.0x25.0
				C-20/9	4.38 - 4.25	25.0x25.0S
				C1Y	4.30 - 4.15	25.0x25.0

11.4 Italy

The Italian repo market dates from 1970 and is the oldest repo market in Europe. It is also the largest European market. Due to historical tax and legal complications with classic repo, trades are actually sell/buy-backs, although confusingly they are called "repo".[6] Until recently Italian government bonds paid coupons net of tax, hence this created different opportunities for different users of the repo market. Non-resident institutions were able to reclaim withholding tax via a domestic custodian, while resident institutions accessed the repo market to generate tax credits which were then used as an offset against income from other sources. From January 1997 bonds paid coupon gross to non-residents. Repo rates are quoted on both a net and gross basis due to taxable coupon issue, depending on domicile of the investor. Due to the requirement for a domestic custodian all trades are settled onshore. As in the US the domestic market has a strong retail involvement with interest from savings institutions and fund managers.

The size of the repo market reflects the size of the cash market in government bonds, which is the largest in Europe. The instruments used in the market are listed in Table 11.4. Securities marked with a "~" are listed by ISMA as euro GC securities. Most transactions are one-week maturity, while, unusually for repo, overnight trades are rarer. This may be because stamp duty is chargeable at a flat rate on domestic deals, and so this is an incentive for market participants to undertake longer-duration repo trades.

Instrument	Maturity
Buoni Ordinari del Tesoro (BOT)~	1–12 months
Buoni Poliennali del Tesoro (BTP)~	2–30 years
Certificati di Credito del Tesoro (CCT)~	2–10 years
Certificati di Credito del Tesoro (ICTZ)~	1–2 years
Credito Tesoro (CTES)	1–2 years

Table 11.4: Italian government securities used in repo.

[6] Italian repo remains predominantly sell/buy-back because of taxation and other issues. These include the retail origination and emphasis of the transaction, and the fact that both legs of a repo may be treated as separate transactions and attract two lots of stamp duty.

Repo settlement is carried out via a domestic custodian bank or via Euroclear or Clearstream Banking. Generally BTPs, CCTs and BOTs settle domestically while CTEs settle though Euroclear and/or Clearstream. The stock-lending market is virtually non-existent, as there is no official facility and banks are not keen to enter into a stock loan, as they remain unfamiliar with the concept.

ISMA's Italian regional committee produced an annexe which adapts Annex III of the GMRA (which contains provision for sell/buy-backs) for transactions involving an Italian party or Italian securities.

Figure 11.8 shows bid-offer repo rates for specific Italian government collateral on a typical broker screen. The dealing size is also indicated, so for instance the December 2001 CCT issue is bid at 4.72% and offered at 4.65%, both up to EUR 25 million. Not all issues have a two-way price posted.

GC	GC	DMK - 10 Year	Germany	Italy	Italy CCT / CTZ

	CCT		< >
CCTAPR01			
CCTDEC01			
	C2W	4.72 - 4.65	25.0x25.0
CCTFEB02			
CCTNOV02			
	C2W	4.75 - 4.65	25.0x25.0
CCTDEC02			
CCTFEB03			
	C2W	4.74 - 4.69	25.0x25.0
CCTJUL03			
	C1W	4.70 -	25.0x
CCTNOV03			2<
	TN	4.65 -	10.0x
	SN	4.70 -	15.0x
CCTJAN04			2<
	SN	4.60 -	60.0x
	C1W	4.60 -	40.0x
CCTMAR04			
	SN	4.65 - 4.60	7.5x7.5
CCTSEP04			
	ON	4.65 -	2.5x
CCTMAY05			
	ON	4.65 -	2.5x
CCTOCT05			
CCTMAR06			
	C1W	4.72 -	25.0x
CCTDEC06			2<
	SN	- 4.70	x25.0
	C1W	4.74 -	25.0x

Figure 11.8: Repo rates for specific Italian government collateral, Garban ICAP screen on 9 January 2001. Reproduced with permission.

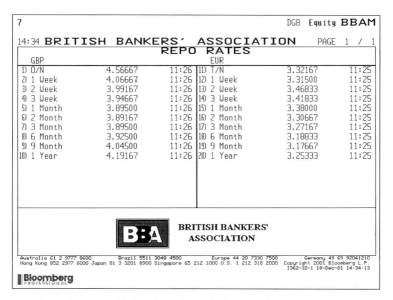

Figure 11.9: British Bankers Association sterling and euro repo rates for 17 December 2001, part of Bloomberg page BBAM. ©Bloomberg L.P. Used with permission.

11.5 United States

11.5.1 *Overview*

The US repo market is the oldest and largest such market in the world. The Federal Reserve initiated repo trading in 1918, when it began a buy and sell-back transaction in T-bills. The size of the domestic market was quoted as $1 trillion over ten years ago, the estimate today is perhaps two to three times this figure. The rapid growth of the US Treasury bond market during the 1980s was mirrored in the Treasury repo market, with overnight repo volumes exceeding $200 billion nominal and term repo volumes running at over $300 billion (Wong, 1993). The average daily volume outstanding in Treasury and agency repo, as dealt by primary dealers, is given in Appendix 11.2. The core of the market remains dealing in Treasury bills, notes and bonds as well as government agency paper. The US market is invariably the source of new developments in repo, including asset-backed bond repo, whole loan (for mortgage-backed securities) and high-yield debt. The key players are the primary dealers, money market mutual funds and local authorities (municipal authorities), although provincial banks and other money institutions also take part. Trades are often carried out through inter-dealer brokers. As the market has developed, market participants have been able to deal on a more automated basis, with real-time live prices displayed on vendor screens. Most business is conducted between 0800–1000 hours; the Federal Reserve conducts its repo operation at 1130 hours. The Fed "wire" mechanism allows same-day domestic settlement, similar to the settlement arrangement in the UK market. As might be expected, the majority of trades are in the overnight to three month area of the yield curve, although liquidity is maintained out to two-year term trades.

Generally, the overnight GC rate is slightly lower than the overnight Federal Funds rate, but of course rates will vary according to the tightness of money as well as the supply and demand of specific collateral securities.

A generic repo screen is page MMR on Bloomberg. The main screen on Reuters is REPO.

```
Press 98<GO> to make a copy, 99<GO> to clear news alerts.        Corp    MMR

16:22        REPO/REVERSE  RP  O/N  &  TERM           Page 1 / 3
94<GO> View News.
 SECURITY         ║ TIME  ║ LAST  ║ CHANGE ║ OPEN  ║ HIGH  ║ LOW   ║ CLOSE
GOVERNMENT
 Repo
Dealer pays int
  4)RPGT01D        16:15    6.38    -.13    6.37    6.38    6.37    6.51
  5)RPGT01W        16:15    6.35    +.05    6.35    6.35    6.35    6.30
  6)RPGT02W        16:15    6.45    +.10    6.45    6.45    6.45    6.35
  7)RPGT03W        16:15    6.38    +.03    6.38    6.38    6.38    6.35
  8)RPGT01M        16:15    6.34    --      6.34    6.34    6.34    6.34
  9)RPGT02M        16:15    6.39    +.04    6.39    6.39    6.39    6.35
 10)RPGT03M        16:15    6.45    +.02    6.45    6.45    6.45    6.43
 Reverse Repo
Dealer earns int
 13)RVGT01D        16:15    6.43    -.13    6.42    6.45    6.42    6.56
 14)RVGT01W        16:15    6.42    +.02    6.42    6.42    6.42    6.40
 15)RVGT02W        16:15    6.50    +.05    6.50    6.50    6.50    6.45
 16)RVGT03W        16:15    6.45    +.04    6.45    6.45    6.45    6.41
 17)RVGT01M        16:15    6.40    -.01    6.40    6.40    6.40    6.41
 18)RVGT02M        16:15    6.44    +.01    6.44    6.44    6.44    6.43
 19)RVGT03M        16:15    6.50    +.02    6.50    6.50    6.50    6.48
PAGE FOR MTGE REPO
Copyright 2000 BLOOMBERG L.P.  Frankfurt:69-920410  Hong Kong:2-977-6000  London:207-330-7500  New York:212-318-2000
Princeton:609-279-3000        Singapore:226-3000     Sydney:2-9777-8686   Tokyo:3-3201-8900    Sao Paulo:11-3048-4500
                                                                                    I432-212-0 07-Jul-00 16:17:19

Bloomberg
PROFESSIONAL
```

Figure 11.10: US Treasury repo Bloomberg page for 7 July 2000.
©Bloomberg L.P. Used with permission.

11.5.2 *Market structure*

The market in USD repo is comprised of several distinct sectors, although many participants will deal across sectors. The largest segment, mirroring its scale in the cash market, is the US Treasury repo market. There was over $3.3 trillion nominal of Treasury securities outstanding at the end of 1999, and repo volume outstanding at this time was over $1.4 trillion. Government repo rates are posted on "GovPX" which is a screen on vendor services.

The main market participants include bond market-makers, known as bond dealers in the US, investment entities such as hedge funds, central banks, and commercial banks.

In addition to the US Treasury repo market, there are substantial repo markets in securities such as agency mortgage-backed securities, domestic securities and high-yield bonds. Unlike in Europe, repo is also the principle method of short-term corporate investment. The minimum size for a US Treasury repo is $1 million, although the usual smallest size is $5 million. Interest is calculated on a 30/360 day basis and transactions are settled via the Federal Book Entry (FBE) system.

The FBE does not allow for matching of trades prior to settlement, so it is therefore common for banks' back offices to either check counterparty confirmations or call-back trades prior to settlement to avoid any unnecessary fails. The settlement process is initiated by the repo seller who electronically delivers securities to the purchaser in exchange for immediate credit to its account. Securities and cash settle on a real-time gross basis. Since securities are dematerialised, there is no depository, but the Federal Reserve Bank acts as a central registrar for all securities.

Treasury securities transactions are usually traded for next day value. A dealer can view the open position on any given value date and cover with a repo transaction. Participants in the cash Treasury market may also use either the repo market or the securities lending market to remedy any failed trades and since the market is very liquid, fails are infrequent.

The Federal Reserve Bank is a major participant in the Treasury repo market on a daily basis for its own purposes, known as *system repo*, both in order to stimulate liquidity and again when it needs to signal a change in its interest rate policy. These transactions are dealt with primary dealers in US Government securities. The Federal Reserve Bank also trades customer repos on behalf of customers such as foreign central banks and supranational bodies who have cash positions with it. The Federal Reserve uses Treasury repo as the primary instrument in its daily open market operations. A shortage in the market is alleviated by the Fed carrying out reverse repo with banks and primary dealers, which takes place at 11:30am EST each morning. Occasional surplus funds are drained using "matched sale/purchases" or MSPs. The repo rate at which the Fed deals is an indicator of its direction on monetary policy.

The domestic and interbank markets are screen-based and dominated by the large banks; there are also a number of active brokers. Screens are generally used by broker–dealers and telephone brokers. Clearing is carried out via the Government Securities Clearing Corporation (GSCC). Dealing through GSCC enables repo *netting* to be employed between member counterparties. There is a large and liquid market in mortgage-backed securities, in which thrifts are active in addition to securities houses and banks. Other markets exist in corporate bonds, high-yield bonds and emerging market sovereign collateral, principally Brady bonds.

The development of tri-party repo was pioneered in the United States, and has been instrumental in transforming repo from a product used primarily by bond market makers into a vanilla money market instrument and short-term investment product. Almost half of all repo transactions carried out in the US market are tri-party repo, and banks such as JPMorgan Chase and Citibank offer a full tri-party broking service. Smaller market participants may prefer to use tri-party as it reduces their administrative and operational burden, and is popular in equity repo and for financing a portfolio or basket of assets. An example is a repo of a portfolio of equities for an agreed fee, or a *portfolio swap*, in which an holding of Treasury securities is exchanged for lower-rated assets such as corporate bonds in return for a specified fee.

The legal documentation for domestic USD repo is the Master Repurchase Agreement compiled by the Bond Markets Association, whose previous identity as the Public Securities Association gave its name to the PSA/ISMA agreement. The MRA was used as the basis of the GMRA legal agreement. The PSA MRA was introduced in 1986.

Repo rates for US dollar GC securities are posted on a number of vendor systems. Figures 11.11 to 11.13 give repo and reverse repo rates for specified maturity terms as appearing on Bloomberg, for 19 December 2001. They also illustrate how the repo interest rate differs according to term and type of collateral. Figure 11.11 shows the rates for US Treasury collateral, while Figures 11.12 and 11.13 show the rates for mortgage and agency securities respectively.

Figure 11.14 shows the rates for Treasury, mortgage and agency securities as given on Garban International's page on Bloomberg, also for 19 December 2001.

```
Press 98<GO> to make a copy, 99<GO> to clear news alerts.      Corp   MMR

12:48        REPO/REVERSE  RP  O/N  &  TERM            Page 1 / 3
94<GO> View News.
 SECURITY        | TIME  || LAST  || CHANGE || OPEN  || HIGH  || LOW   || CLOSE
GOVERNMENT
 Repo
Dealer pays int
  4)RPGT01D       12/18    1.74     --       1.74     1.74     1.74     1.74
  5)RPGT01W       12/18    1.72     --       1.72     1.72     1.72     1.72
  6)RPGT02W       12/18    1.72     --       1.72     1.72     1.72     1.72
  7)RPGT03W       12/18    1.74     --       1.74     1.74     1.74     1.74
  8)RPGT01M       12/18    1.73     --       1.73     1.73     1.73     1.73
  9)RPGT02M       12/18    1.70     --       1.70     1.70     1.70     1.70
 10)RPGT03M       12/18    1.67     --       1.67     1.67     1.67     1.67
 Reverse Repo
Dealer earns int
 13)RVGT01D       12/18    1.79     --       1.79     1.79     1.79     1.79
 14)RVGT01W       12/18    1.77     --       1.77     1.77     1.77     1.77
 15)RVGT02W       12/18    1.77     --       1.77     1.77     1.77     1.77
 16)RVGT03W       12/18    1.79     --       1.79     1.79     1.79     1.79
 17)RVGT01M       12/18    1.77     --       1.77     1.77     1.77     1.77
 18)RVGT02M       12/18    1.74     --       1.74     1.74     1.74     1.74
 19)RVGT03M       12/18    1.72     --       1.72     1.72     1.72     1.72
PAGE FOR MTGE REPO
Australia 61 2 9777 8600      Brazil 5511 3048 4500      Europe 44 20 7330 7500      Germany 49 69 92041210
Hong Kong 852 2977 6000 Japan 81 3 3201 8900 Singapore 65 212 1000 U.S. 1 212 318 2000  Copyright 2001 Bloomberg L.P.
                                                                     I362-32-0 19-Dec-01 12:48:49
Bloomberg
PROFESSIONAL
```

Figure 11.11: Repo and reverse repo for US Treasury GC Securities, 19 December 2001. © Bloomberg L.P. Used with permission.

```
Press 98<GO> to make a copy, 99<GO> to clear news alerts.      Corp   MMR

12:48        REPO/REVERSE  RP  O/N  &  TERM            Page 2 / 3
94<GO> View News.
 SECURITY        | TIME  || LAST  || CHANGE || OPEN  || HIGH  || LOW   || CLOSE
MORTGAGE
 Repo
  3)RPMB01D       12/18    1.74     --       1.74     1.74     1.74     1.74
  4)RPMB01W       12/18    1.77     --       1.77     1.77     1.77     1.77
  5)RPMB02W       12/18    1.80     --       1.80     1.80     1.80     1.80
  6)RPMB03W       12/18    1.81     --       1.81     1.81     1.81     1.81
  7)RPMB01M       12/18    1.80     --       1.80     1.80     1.80     1.80
  8)RPMB02M       12/18    1.80     --       1.80     1.80     1.80     1.80
  9)RPMB03M       12/18    1.73     --       1.73     1.73     1.73     1.73

 Reverse Repo
 12)RVMB01D       12/18    1.80     --       1.80     1.80     1.80     1.80
 13)RVMB01W       12/18    1.80     --       1.80     1.80     1.80     1.80
 14)RVMB02W       12/18    1.83     --       1.83     1.83     1.83     1.83
 15)RVMB03W       12/18    1.85     --       1.85     1.85     1.85     1.85
 16)RVMB01M       12/18    1.84     --       1.84     1.84     1.84     1.84
 17)RVMB02M       12/18    1.85     --       1.85     1.85     1.85     1.85
 18)RVMB03M       12/18    1.78     --       1.78     1.78     1.78     1.78
PAGE FOR
AGENCY REPO
Australia 61 2 9777 8600      Brazil 5511 3048 4500      Europe 44 20 7330 7500      Germany 49 69 92041210
Hong Kong 852 2977 6000 Japan 81 3 3201 8900 Singapore 65 212 1000 U.S. 1 212 318 2000  Copyright 2001 Bloomberg L.P.
                                                                     I362-32-0 19-Dec-01 12:48:55
Bloomberg
PROFESSIONAL
```

Figure 11.12: Repo rates for US Mortgage Securities, 19 December 2001. © Bloomberg L.P. Used with permission.

```
Press 98<GO> to make a copy, 99<GO> to clear news alerts.      Corp   MMR

12:49      REPO/REVERSE  RP  O/N  &  TERM         Page 3 / 3
94<GO> View News.
  SECURITY      ║ TIME  ║ LAST  ║ CHANGE ║ OPEN  ║ HIGH  ║ LOW   ║ CLOSE
 AGENCY
  Repo                      .
   3)RPAG01D      12/18    1.77    --     1.77    1.77    1.77    1.77
   4)RPAG01W      12/18    1.79    --     1.79    1.79    1.79    1.79
   5)RPAG03W      12/18    1.83    --     1.83    1.83    1.83    1.83
   6)RPAG01M      12/18    1.83    --     1.83    1.83    1.83    1.83
   7)RPAG02M      12/18    1.76    --     1.76    1.76    1.76    1.76
   8)RPAG03M      12/18    1.74    --     1.74    1.74    1.74    1.74

  Reverse Repo
  11)RVAG01D      12/18    1.81    --     1.81    1.81    1.81    1.81
  12)RVAG01W      12/18    1.83    --     1.83    1.83    1.83    1.83
  13)RVAG02W      12/18    1.84    --     1.84    1.84    1.84    1.84
  14)RVAG03W      12/18    1.88    --     1.88    1.88    1.88    1.88
  15)RVAG01M      12/18    1.87    --     1.87    1.87    1.87    1.87
  16)RVAG02M      12/18    1.81    --     1.81    1.81    1.81    1.81
  17)RVAG03M      12/18    1.80    --     1.80    1.80    1.80    1.80


 Australia 61 2 9777 8600       Brazil 5511 3048 4500       Europe 44 20 7330 7500      Germany 49 69 92041210
 Hong Kong 852 2977 6000 Japan 81 3 3201 8900 Singapore 65 212 1000 U.S. 1 212 318 2000 Copyright 2001 Bloomberg L.P.
                                                                          1362-32-0 19-Dec-01 12:49:00
 ▌Bloomberg
```

Figure 11.13: Repo rates for US Agency Securities,
19 December 2001. © Bloomberg L.P. Used with permission.

```
 Page                                               DG8  Corp    GARB

 12:57 GARBAN  INTERNATIONAL                            PAGE  1  /  2

   Term          Bid          Time    Term           Ask          Time
   REPURCHASE AGREEMENT-AGENCY    │  REPURCHASE AGREEMENT-AGENCY
  1) O/N          1.810        .    12/18 18) O/N           1.770        12/18
  2) 1 Week       1.830             12/18 19) 1 Week        1.790        12/18
  3) 2 Week       1.840             12/18 20) 2 Week        1.800        12/18
  4) 3 Week       1.880             12/18 21) 3 Week        1.830        12/18
  5) 1 Month      1.870             12/18 22) 1 Month       1.830        12/18
  6) 2 Month      1.810             12/18 23) 2 Month       1.760        12/18
  7) 3 Month      1.800             12/18 24) 3 Month       1.740        12/18
   REPURCHASE AGREEMENT-GOVT      │  REPURCHASE AGREEMENT-GOVT
  8) O/N          1.790             12/18 25) O/N           1.740        12/18
  9) 1 Week       1.770             12/18 26) 1 Week        1.720        12/18
 10) 2 Week       1.770             12/18 27) 2 Week        1.720        12/18
 11) 3 Week       1.790             12/18 28) 3 Week        1.740        12/18
 12) 1 Month      1.770             12/18 29) 1 Month       1.730        12/18
 13) 2 Month      1.740             12/18 30) 2 Month       1.700        12/18
 14) 3 Month      1.720             12/18 31) 3 Month       1.670        12/18
   REPURCHASE AGREEMENT-MTG-BACKED │  REPURCHASE AGREEMENT-MTG-BACKED
 15) O/N          1.800             12/18 32) O/N           1.740        12/18
 16) 1 Week       1.800             12/18 33) 1 Week        1.770        12/18
 17) 2 Week       1.830             12/18 34) 2 Week        1.800        12/18
 Australia 61 2 9777 8600       Brazil 5511 3048 4500       Europe 44 20 7330 7500      Germany 49 69 92041210
 Hong Kong 852 2977 6000 Japan 81 3 3201 8900 Singapore 65 212 1000 U.S. 1 212 318 2000 Copyright 2001 Bloomberg L.P.
                                                                          1362-32-0 19-Dec-01 12:57:22
 ▌Bloomberg
```

Figure 11.14: Garban International repo screen for US Treasury, Mortgage and
Agency Securities, 19 December 2001. © Bloomberg L.P and Garban.
Used with permission.

The ISMA European Repo Market Survey

In June 2001 the International Securities Market Association (ISMA) conducted a survey amongst repo market participants, the first in what is intended to be a semi-annual event. For the benefit of readers we air some of the findings here. The full survey methodology and results are available at www.isma.org.

Those taking part in the survey were members of ISMA's European Repo Council and comprised 48 banks and securities houses. The survey was commissioned essentially due to the lack of published information being available on the size and composition of the repo market across Europe, although individual country central authorities do publish full and comprehensive statistics on their markets; for example, the Bank of England on the sterling repo market.

Survey highlights

- Total volume of repo business outstanding amongst all participants was €1.83 billion, comprised of 49.6% as repo and 50.4% as reverse repo (gross values). Only a small volume of trades, 6%, was made up of tri-party repo.
- Repo was conducted primarily in euros (73%), with remaining trades being conducted in sterling (11%), US dollars (10%) and other currencies (6%). The "other" currencies were Japanese yen, Swedish krona, Danish krone and other European currencies.
- A large part of collateral used in repo was issued in Europe or euro-zone countries, with 34% being issued in Germany, 18% in Italy and 12% in the UK. Over 91% of collateral was sovereign debt.
- An overwhelming majority of repo trades were conducted as fixed-rate repo, at over 91%. The remaining trades were made up of floating-rate repo (5%) and open repo (4%). However, the small number of floating-rate trades was put down to the small number of French banks taking part in the survey, France being the principal market where such trades are common.
- Geographical analysis – see Figure 11.15.
- Maturity analysis – see Figure 11.16.
- Somewhat surprisingly, classic repo made up a large part of repo trading, at 84% of outstanding contracts, with 16% being sell/buy backs. Of these trades, 92% were conducted under the BMA/ISMA GMRA, while 8% (and all of these being sell/buy-backs) were undocumented trades. The low volume of sell/buy-backs is explained by the survey's author, Mr Richard Comotto, as being due to the small number of banks taking part that were based in Italy and Spain, where the predominant trade type is sell/buy-back.

The ISMA survey has revealed that the European repo market, as represented by the 48 banks taking part (the full list of participants is given in the report itself), is somewhat larger than expected. This would appear to imply that the instrument is important to the smooth functioning of the money markets across the region.

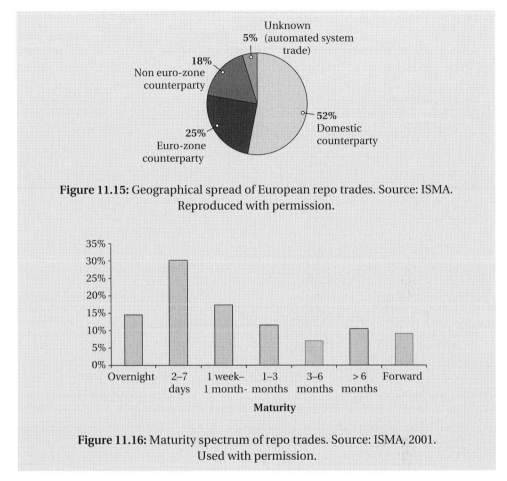

Figure 11.15: Geographical spread of European repo trades. Source: ISMA. Reproduced with permission.

Figure 11.16: Maturity spectrum of repo trades. Source: ISMA, 2001. Used with permission.

11.6 Emerging market repo

11.6.1 *Introduction*

One of the most exotic developments in repo in recent years has been an increasing interest in the so-called "emerging markets". Although this term would tend to imply that the countries that come under this label form a homogeneous entity, in fact they are a diverse group and some have very little in common with each other. The term has at various times grouped relatively developed markets such as Taiwan and Singapore along with true capital market minnows such as those in Jordan and Zambia, and the whole range of countries in between. The enthusiasm for emerging market assets cooled somewhat following the crisis with East Asian currencies in the second half of 1997, followed rapidly by the credit and currency problems in Russia and Brazil in 1998. However one of the main reasons behind the initial enthusiasm for emerging markets, namely the requirement by investment managers for higher yields, remains in place and this has seen renewed growth in investment in these markets.

Until recently, repo in emerging markets was restricted to international issues such as Brady bonds and sovereign Eurobonds issued by countries such as Argentina and Poland. Brady bonds remain the most liquid, reflecting their status as dollar-denominated US government-backed paper (and as such offering some degree of credit protection). International bonds can settle via Euroclear and Clearstream and are also fairly easy to trade. Domestic emerging market repo confers considerably more risk as settlement is in the local market and the local currency will be fairly illiquid. As yields continue to decline in developed markets and products, investors will justify the higher risk involved in emerging markets.

Repo in emerging markets invariably centres around the government debt market. Volumes have been dominated by Latin American markets. The size of the debt markets in certain countries is shown in Figure 11.17. Often, these markets have restrictions that will affect the nature of trading; this includes restrictions on amounts that local banks can borrow and thus will restrict activity in repo.

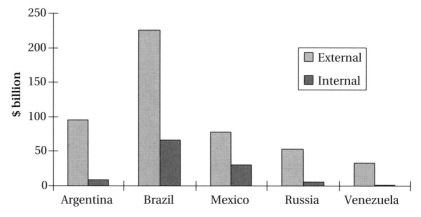

Figure 11.17: Selected emerging debt market volume, December 1999.
Source: ING Barings.

Trading volumes in emerging market repo ranged between $100 million and $850 million between December 1998 and December 1999 for Brazilian "C" bonds alone, a phenomenal figure. Emerging market debt is priced off US treasuries, and widening spreads through 1998 reflected the increasing investor concerns with the sector as economic problems grew during the year. For instance, the spread on Argentina 30-year bonds was around 480 basis points above the equivalent Treasury bond in June 1998, this had widened to 600 bps by December 1998; likewise, spreads had increased from 570 to 980 bps in Brazil, 420 to 600 bps in Mexico, 580 to 1156 bps in Venezuela and 725 to 4144 bps in Russia during this period.[7] Short-term debt spreads had also increased by a proportionate amount.

Repo in these markets is characterised by counterparty risk that is significantly greater than that met in developed markets. For this reason margins on repo trades need to be higher. Margins also need to reviewed constantly due to the higher price-volatility experienced by the underlying bond. The experience of Russia during the summer of 1998, when there was a widespread belief that the government would default on coupon payments for its long-dated USD "MinFin" bond, proved that margins had been too low and not monitored frequently enough (that is, daily). It is not uncommon for repo traders to ask for haircuts of up to 50% for term trades in emerging market repo.

---

7   Source: ING Barings.

As trading is domestic, settlement risk is also higher in emerging markets. Often there is a requirement to use local custodians, the reliability of whom is occasionally open to question.[8] For this reason settlement risk and the quality of the custodian must also be priced into the repo.

11.6.2 *Trading approach*

As the repo market is less transparent and liquid in developing economies there is greater potential to gain advantage by engaging in relative value trading. This might include the following approaches:

- **intra-country trades:** for example, positions in collateralised versus uncollateralised bonds. Certain Brady bonds for instance are collateralised by strips (zero-coupon bonds) while others are not; for example, the Mexico Par 6¼% 2019 versus Mexico 11½% 2026. Other trades have involved fixed- versus floating-rate notes, where there is a yield differential that may be earned, and curve spreads;

- **inter-country trades:** for example, a relative value position in Brazil EI 2006 versus Argentina FRB 2005;

- **cross-currency trades**.

It is indicative of the lessons learned since many banks and investors suffered large losses in markets such as Russia in 1998 and 1999 that, at the time of writing, attention is being focused on those more developed emerging markets. These include Eastern Europe and South Africa; for instance:

- **Poland:** an already developed T-bill repo market and a fledgling bond special market are reflective of a more mature market;

- **Czech Republic:** this market has a developing bond repo market in which term trades of up to one month maturity are common. Compared to Poland, the market nevertheless lacks liquidity as it is dominated by local institutions. Western European banks will access this market but more usually for specific needs only, such as meeting customer demand, and borrowing bonds; there is little matched book trading;

- **South Africa:** repo in this market is already developed; however, developing country interest is currently constrained by counterparty risk (which affects all domestic emerging market repo). This may lead to the development of a two-tier market, with a market in South Africa and an offshore market in London.

Although trading activity in emerging markets is constrained by the difficulties faced by investors in both trading and settling, the demand will remain due to the decline in spreads and absolute yields in developed asset markets. If any lesson is learned by recent high market volatility and depreciation of currencies during 1997–1999, it should be that investors enter such markets only with full awareness and understanding of the risks involved.

11.7 Central bank operations

Central banks are an important customer base for repo business. In addition, many central banks use repo as a tool of monetary policy to manage liquidity in the domestic money market. A central bank "repo" operation is actually a reverse repo, as the bank is buying in eligible

---

8   Not, he hastens to add, by the author however.

securities, typically domestic government debt, against lending out cash to a list of eligible counterparties. The net effect of this is a short-term injection of cash into the market, which alleviates shortages in the money market. This is referred to as central banks injecting liquidity. Central banks prefer to use repo as a money market instrument because of the security afforded by the high quality of collateral, and because of the size of the government bond market. There is usually no direct impact on the cash bond market. The duration of transactions will vary but is usually a two-week or four-week term. Trades can be at a fixed rate determined by the central bank or (less common) at a variable rate resulting from auction amongst eligible participants. A variable-rate auction approach is used in the French market. In addition to the objective of controlling market liquidity, central banks' operations are also undertaken in some countries to send a signal to the market on the intended direction of short-term interest rates.

The European Central Bank (ECB) sets the base rate for euro by announcing its lending rate to central banks of member countries. Pre-euro the German Bundesbank actively used repo in all aspects of its money market operations. This included long-term adjustments involving outright bond purchases, interim financing using repo and "fine tuning" using two-to ten-day repo. The Banque de France has a five- to ten-day lending facility at its ceiling rate, and uses repo on a once-weekly basis dealt at its floor (base) rate. Repo trades are usually overnight or two-day maturity. Only primary dealers in repo can take part. The domestic market in France is unusual in that primary dealers are registered not only in cash government bond trading (which is conventional) but also in the repo market. This is not the case, for example, in the UK where no formal repo market-making arrangement exists.

In the US, primary dealers in Treasury notes and bonds are the only counterparties in the US market. The Federal Reserve conducts a daily repo operation, dealing in overnight, term and open repo.

Appendices

Appendix 11.1:   General collateral as defined by the ISMA CRD repo sub-committee

On 22 February 1999 ISMA listed the following securities as being acceptable as general collateral, unless a counterparty specifically states that one or more of the security types is unacceptable prior to undertaking a trade. When finalising a trade, the stock buyer must specify if a trade goes over a record date for gross-paying GC securities. For net-paying securities the stock seller must specify if this occurs. For Spanish Bonos the seller will specify if the bonds pass over a record date up to 30 days before the trade.

Australia
Government bonds and bills
New South Wales bonds
Queensland Treasury Corp

Austria
Government bonds and bills

Belgium
Phillipe bonds
Government bonds and bills

Canada
Government bonds and bills

France
OATs, BTANs
BTF

Germany
Bund DBR
BOBL
TOBL
Treuhand THA
Schatz BKO
German Unity Fund DBRUF
BUBILL
World Bank global

Italy
BTP
BOT
CCT
CTO
CTZ

Japan
Clean JGBs

Netherlands
Dutch state loans DSL
Treasury bills

Spain
Bonos

Sweden, Denmark, Norway
Government bonds and bills

Appendix 11.2:   Financing by US government securities dealers, repo and reverse repo average daily amount outstanding

	Repo ($ bln)	Reverse repo ($ bln)	Total ($ bln)
1981	65.4	46.7	112.1
1982	95.2	75.1	170.3
1983	102.4	81.7	184.1
1984	132.6	112.4	245.0
1985	172.9	147.9	320.8
1986	244.5	207.7	452.2
1987	292.0	275.0	567.0
1988	309.7	313.6	623.3
1989	398.2	383.2	781.4
1990	413.5	377.1	790.6
1991	496.6	417.0	913.6
1992	628.2	511.1	1139.3
1993	765.6	594.1	1359.7
1994	825.9	651.2	1477.1
1995	821.5	618.8	1440.3
1996	973.7	718.1	1691.8
1997	1159.0	883.0	2042.0
1998	1414.0	1111.4	2525.4
1999	1361.0	1070.1	2431.1
2000	1439.6	1093.3	2532.9

Table 11.5: Volumes for transactions in US Treasury, Federal Agency, and Federal Agency MBS securities. Source: The Bond Market Association, www.bondmarkets.com, citing data from the Federal Reserve Bank of New York, www.newyorkfed.org.

Selected bibliography and references

International Securities Market Association, *European Repo Market Survey*, ISMA June 2001
Rhein, M., Riehm, K-H., *Reaping Repo Rewards*, RISK Product Report, November 2000
Scott-Quinn, B., Walmsley, J., *The Repo Market in Euro: Making It Work*, ISMA 1997
Wong, M. A., *Fixed Income Arbitrage*, Wiley 1993, pp. 25–6

Part II
Institutional Treatment of Repo

In Part II we look at institutional treatment of repo. To wit, the way repo is handled in terms of accounting, taxation and legal documentation. The nature of repo, and the distinctions between secured loans and true sale of an asset, means that these areas must be considered very carefully by market participants before they commence trading. As this is not a textbook on accounting or tax (or law), only a brief overview can be considered; however, we hope that this serves at least its main purpose, that of highlighting how repo is treated administratively.

We also introduce repo netting, a topical subject and the focus of much attention from banks and service providers. This is an area that is currently being developed, and there will almost certainly be something new to write about by the time this book is published. Finally, we consider equity repo, an established but still developing market in North America, Europe and Japan.

Ask me why, and I'll die
And if you must go to work tomorrow
well, if I were you I wouldn't bother
for there are brighter sides to life
and I should know because I've seen them
but not very often…

Still Ill
The Smiths
Rough Trade Records, 1984

12 Repo Dealing Risks

Repo is by nature a relatively low-risk instrument for counterparties to deal in, being a loan of cash against security. In the majority of transactions, this security is very high quality, usually AAA-rated. Classic repo is conducted under legal documentation that is in place on a bilateral basis between an institution and all its counterparties. Hence our belief that repo is a low-risk instrument, and one that lends itself to use by a wide range of corporate entities, rather than only financial institutions. As with all capital market transactions though there *are* risks attached to trading in repo, although these risks are not unique to repo; rather, they are almost invariably of the type that are extant in banking operations generally. These risks can be grouped into the following areas:

- credit risk, split into counterparty risk and collateral risk;
- legal risk;
- market risk;
- daylight exposure;
- systems and controls (operational risk).

There are a number of additional risks. In certain cases the risk exposure by a market counterparty will be a function of more than one of the above, and the market sometimes refer to these risks as being *interdependent* risks. Generally, credit risk, issuer risk, legal risk and market risk can be thought of as functions of counterparty risk, as opposed to operational risk which is usually an internal issue (unless a firm is affected by operational weakness in a counterparty).

In this chapter we review those elements of risk exposure inherent in repo trading and look at some methods of managing such risk.

12.1 Characterising risk

12.1.1 *Introduction*

In the financial markets risk is essentially a measure of the volatility of asset returns, although we prefer the broader definition as being any type of uncertainty as to future outcomes. The types of risk that a bank or securities house is exposed to as part of its *general* operations in the capital markets may be characterised as follows:

- **Market risk.** Risk arising from movements in prices in financial markets. As such, this risk reflects uncertainty as to an asset's price when it is sold. For bondholders it is the risk arising from movement in interest rates, and this is specifically referred to as *interest-rate risk*. Other examples of market-type risks include *volatility* risk, which affects option traders, and *basis* risk, which has a wider impact. Basis risk arises whenever one kind of risk exposure is hedged with an instrument that behaves in a similar, but not necessarily identical manner. One example would be a company using three-month interest rate futures to hedge its commercial paper programme. Although eurocurrency rates, to which futures prices respond, are well correlated with commercial paper rates, they do not invariably move in lock step. If short-term paper rates moved up by 20 basis points but futures prices dropped by only 17 basis points, the three basis point gap is the basis risk.

- **Credit risk.** This refers to the risk that an issuer of debt will default. *Counterparty risk* refers to the risk that a counterparty from whom one has dealt with will cease trading, making recovery of funds owed difficult.

- **Liquidity risk.** This term covers two quite different risks. One is the risk that a bank has insufficient funding to meet commitments as they arise. For a securities house, it is the risk that the market for its assets becomes too thin to enable fair and efficient trading to take place.

- **Operational risk.** Risk of loss associated with non-financial matters such as fraud, system failure, accidents and natural disaster.

- **Concentration risk.** Any organisation with too great a proportion of its assets invested in one type of instrument, or in one specific geographical or industrial sector, is exposed to concentration risk. Banks will seek to limit this type of risk exposure by diversifying across investment types and geographical and country boundaries.

- **Reinvestment risk.** If an asset makes any payments before the investor's horizon, whether it matures or not, the cash flows will have to be reinvested until the horizon date. Since the reinvestment rate is unknown when the asset is purchased, the final cash flow is uncertain.

- **Sovereign risk.** This is a type of credit risk specific to a government bond. There is minimal risk of default by an industrialised country. A developing country may default on its obligation (or declare a debt "moratorium") if debt payments relative to national domestic product reach unsustainable levels.

- **Model risk.** Some of the latest financial instruments such as exotic options are heavily dependent on complex mathematical models for pricing and hedging. If the model is incorrectly specified, is based on questionable assumptions or does not accurately reflect the true behaviour of the market, banks trading these instruments could suffer extensive losses.

- **Legal risk.** Also known as translation risk, the risk arising from failure to agree on a single interpretation of legal documentation. Legal risk also refers to the difficulty in enforcing legal agreements in the event of default.

All participants in the capital markets are exposed to these risks to one degree or another.

12.1.2 *Risk management*

Risk management in financial institutions has grown steadily in size and importance since the early 1990s. The development of the risk-management function and risk-management departments was not instituted from a desire to eliminate the possibility of all unexpected losses, should such an outcome indeed be feasible; rather, from a wish to control the frequency, extent and size of trading losses in such a way as to provide the minimum surprise to senior management and shareholders.

Risk exists in all competitive business although the balance between financial risks of the types described above and general and management risk varies with the type of business that is being engaged in. The key objective of the risk-management function within a financial institution is to allow for a clear understanding of the risks and exposures the firm is engaged in, such that any monetary loss is deemed acceptable by the firm's shareholders. The accept-ability of any loss should be on the basis that such (occasional) loss is to be expected as a result of the firm being engaged in a particular business activity. If the bank's-risk manage-ment function is effective, there will be no overreaction to any unexpected losses, which may increase eventual costs to many times the original loss amount.

While there is no one agreed organisation structure for the risk-management function, the following may be taken as being indicative of the typical banking institution arrangement:

- an independent, "middle office" department responsible for drawing up and explicitly stating the bank's approach to risk, and defining trading limits and the areas of the market that the firm can have exposure to;

- the head of the risk function reporting to an independent senior manager, who is a mem-ber of the Executive Board;

- monitoring the separation of duties between front, middle and back office, often in con-junction with an internal audit function;

- reporting to senior management, including the firm's overall exposure and adherence of the front office to the firm's overall risk strategy;

- communication of risks and risk strategy to shareholders;

- where leading-edge systems are in use, employment of the risk-management function to generate competitive advantage in the market as well as control.

The risk-management function is more likely to deliver effective results when there is clear lines of responsibility and accountability. "Dotted lines" of responsibility or a lack of clear accountability hamper effective decision-making in a crisis. Generally the risk-management department interacts closely with other areas of the front and back office. The following are often accepted as ingredients of a market best-practice risk-management framework in an institution that is engaged in investment banking and trading activity:

- daily overview of risk exposure profile and profit & loss reports (p&l);

- *Value-at-Risk* as a common measure of risk exposure, in addition to other measures including "jump risk" to allow for market corrections;[1]

- independent daily monitoring of risk utilisation by middle-office risk-management function;

- independent production of daily p&l, and independent review of front-office closing prices on a daily basis;

- independent validation of market pricing, and pricing and VaR models.

The risk manager will be concerned with the extent of market risk that the bank is exposed to, but also with communicating this to senior management and liasing with the front office to keep in touch with latest developments. Risk management therefore is an understanding

---

[1] There is a considerable literature on value-at-risk; the author strongly recommends Butler, C., *Mastering Value-at-Risk* (FT Prentice Hall, 1998) for its detail and accessibility. He hesitates to recommend his own *An Introduction to Value-at-Risk* (SI (Services) Publishing 1998) as it reads in slightly quirky fashion and may be out of print; it is, at least, priced relatively cheaply however...

of how the value of the banking and trading books changes in line with movements in under-lying risk factors (such as interest rates).

It is recognised that the traditional risk measures used in the past, for example duration-based measures, suffered from drawbacks as they capture linear risk only. The emphasis now is more on second-order risk measures, that is, the convexity exposure on a portfolio, or *gamma* in an option book. It is the area of options trading that has observed the most devel-opment in risk-management techniques, as options – which, unlike all other financial instru-ments, do not have a linear payout profile – were not well served by the traditional risk measures. The new approach to risk management, developed in response to high profile banking failures, focuses on measurement of *gamma* and *vega* risks[2] as well as greater emphasis on likely future impact on the banking portfolio of such risks.

The-risk management function is now recognised as an important function in commer-cial and investment banking. A set of formal processes and procedures is now recognised as being essential to minimise the possibility of loss due to movements in the market, counter-party credit issues and internal issues. The art of risk management encompasses more than a measurement tool such as value-at-risk; internal controls to ensure the separation of duties, and adequate provision for the provision of effective management information are also vital.

12.1.3 *Risks in repo*

We conclude this introductory section by looking at the potential risk exposures inherent in a repo transaction, shown in Table 12.1.

Credit risk	Market risk	Liquidity risk	Operational risk	Legal risk
Counterparty risk	Interest-rate risk	Market (interest rate) illiquidity	System failure	Lack of documentation
• default	Collateral price volatility	Collateral illiquidity	Settlement failure	Translation risk
• operational risk	Foreign exchange risk	Banking liquidity exposure	Fraud, procedural risk, etc	
• regulatory failure	Interest-rate gap exposure	Interest-rate gap exposure		
Collateral risk				
• Issuer default				
• Lack of liquidity				
• Collateral price volatility				

Table 12.1: Repo risk exposures.

12.2 Credit risk

The two forms of credit risk in a repo transaction are the key risks associated with the instru-ment. In a classic repo, a lender of cash is faced with risk exposure to the counterparty and the risk of downgrade of the quality of the collateral.

---

2   *Ibid.*

12.2.1 *Counterparty risk*

Counterparty risk is the risk that the counterparty defaults on the transaction, due to financial difficulty or going out of business entirely. Although this is a serious issue, it is more so for unsecured creditors of the company, including those who have dealt in (unsecured) inter-bank transactions with the company. A market participant that has entered into a classic repo transaction may feel that it is protected by the collateral in its possession. Under English law, the counterparty has the right to recover its loan losses by disposing of the collateral in the market. In addition, losses suffered in a repo that is covered by a legal agreement are theoretically recoverable, as long as the agreement is enforceable in the jurisdiction of the counterparty. Losses incurred on an undocumented repo or sell/buy-back transaction have a lower recovery possibility and are therefore higher risk.

Banks and other market participants guard against counterparty credit risk by internally rating all their counterparties, and assigning trading limits to each of them. The trading limit may be higher for repo compared to interbank trading, or set at the same level. In some cases counterparties deemed unsuitable for an interbank limit are not assigned secured lending limits either. An example of this occurred after the collapse of Barings merchant bank in 1995; many UK building societies withdrew or drastically reduced limits for other similar merchant banks in the unsecured market. This continued to be the case when the gilt repo market was introduced the following year, despite the fact that gilt repo involves the transfer of risk-free collateral.

Banks measure their counterparty default risk as a net exposure for each counterparty; this is then aggregated. There are two elements to net counterparty exposure: *current exposure* or replacement cost, and *potential exposure* or add-on risk. Current exposure is measured as the difference between the value of all assets held by the bank and the value of assets held by its counterparty. In practice, the existence of a master repo agreement such as GMRA results in current exposure being measured on a portfolio basis, comprised of market value of all assets and cash lent out against market value of all assets and received as collateral. The net counterparty exposure of a bank is the sum of the current exposure and the potential exposure.

Current exposure

- **Lender of cash in repo:** calculate current exposure as the excess of loan value, including repo interest accrued to date, over the current market value of collateral held by the lending institution. If there is an excess, this represents current exposure risk; generally therefore this excess should be zero or negative, representing *overcollateralisation* of the lender.

- **Borrower of cash in repo:** calculate current exposure as the excess of the current market value of collateral transferred to the counterparty over the value of the loan on the firm's books.

- **Stock loan counterparty, non-cash collateral:** calculate current exposure as excess of market value of securities borrowed over market value of collateral transferred.

Potential exposure is measured as any loss, in addition to current exposure, that a firm is exposed to as a result of collateral price volatility subsequent to counterparty default being announced. Where a variation margin arrangement is in place, in effect this is the extent of decline in value of collateral from the last margin call to the announcement of default. Banks measure potential exposure in a number of ways, most often by the value-at-risk (VaR) method. VaR is a quantitative measure of the potential losses that can be suffered over a user-specified time period, under certain statistical assumptions. Using VaR a bank will calculate potential exposure arising in the period from notice of default to eventual sale of the collateral in the market.

A key risk-management arrangement in repo is the variation margin or haircut requirement. The amount of margin demanded by a cash lender is usually calculated as a function of the potential exposure. This is logical because margin is a risk-reduction tool associated with movements in collateral value after initial margin has been taken. Therefore, banks generally set the margin at a level above the potential exposure measure, the additional amount being set depending on prevailing market conditions. Example 12.1 illustrates the basic principles.

Example 12.1:   Setting the margin level

For an hypothetical portfolio we suggest margin levels depending on the credit rating of the counterparty. The potential exposure is measured using individual asset volatility levels. For high-quality counterparties, with whom there is an unsecured credit limit in place, it is common for no margin to be taken, even if the collateral quality is not gilt-edged. This reflects the fact that the most important risk factor in repo is counterparty risk; if the counterparty is deemed low-risk, the quality of collateral is usually ignored. As the counterparty status is lowered, margin is required. An initial margin and margin *threshold* (the point at which variation margin is called) are set and added to the collateral volatility value to obtain the margin level required. Some banks do not engage in repo with counterparties with whom they do not have an unsecured line in place; this will depend on how risk-averse the cash-lending institution is.

Stock	Volatility	Min margin threshold	AA-counterparty (with unsecured line) Margin	A-counterparty (with unsecured line)	Margin	BB-counterparty (no unsecured line)	Margin
Gilt	1.90%	0%	0%	2.50%	2.50%	5.00%	5.00%
A-rated industrial Eurobond	3.70%	0%	0%	2.50%	2.50%	5.00%	9%
BBB-rated Eurobond	6.20%	0%	0%	2.50%	2.50%	5.00%	12%
Brady bond	7.10%	0%	0%	2.50%	10.00%	5.00%	13%
Emerging market sovereign	7.45%	0%	8.00%	2.50%	10.00%	5.00%	13%
High yield bond	8.29%	0%	8.50%	2.50%	11.00%	5.00%	14%

Essentially, margin levels are a function of the credit standing of the counterparty, followed by collateral quality, market volatility and settlement risk. The existence of an unsecured lending line does not always result in zero or low margin.

12.2.2 *Credit ratings*

Counterparty risk of an individual corporate entity is assessed in the first instance by recourse to the firm's credit rating. These are assigned by one or more of the international credit rating agencies.[3] Ultimately these are qualitative assessments, and an individual company's credit quality fluctuates over time and with the business cycle, such that credit ratings migrate across different grades. The different credit ratings of market participants are reflected in the rates paid by each of them in the debt market.

Appendix 12.1 lists the corporate bond ratings assigned by the main international credit rating agencies, which include Moody's and Standard & Poor's. Although the rating agencies specify all paper at the level of Baa3/BBB– and above as being of "investment grade", in practice often only banks and corporates rated at Baa1/BBB+ or higher are deemed suitable counterparties for unsecured transactions. To illustrate the different market behaviour of entities across each rating category, Table 12.2 in Appendix 12.1 lists the default rates for each category of rating, and the average one-year loss rates for each category, as published by Moody's in 2000.

12.2.3 *Collateral risk*

Collateral risk, or issuer risk, is the risk that the quality of collateral held during the term of the repo will suffer because the fortunes of the issuer decline. The worst-case scenario in this case is that the issuer is declared bankrupt and the collateral declines in value to just a few cents on the dollar.[4] For this reason many repo market participants will only accept AAA-rated paper such as government bonds as collateral. In the case of equity repo, usually only blue-chip shares are accepted; for example, the shares of FTSE100 or S&P 500 companies. The market for lower-quality collateral is less liquid, and the equivalent "GC" rate will be higher than that for government collateral, reflecting the higher risk involved.[5]

However, deterioration of collateral quality is by no means a sure sign that losses will follow. Assuming that the counterparty remains solvent and a going concern, the collateral should be replaced with one of acceptable quality. In other words, when there is a fall in collateral value, losses in a repo transaction will occur only if there is a simultaneous default on the repo by the counterparty. There is greater issuer risk if a loan of cash is made to a counterparty that transfers collateral that has been issued by itself. This is expressly prohibited by many banks' internal risk guidelines.

The quality of collateral is measured by its credit rating, followed by the extent of liquidity in that issue and current market volatility.

12.3 Market risk

Market risk covers a number of exposures. We referred to collateral risk above, the risk of fall in value of collateral. This is a form of market risk. Essentially market risk is any risk of loss arising as a result of moves in market rates during the term of the trade; the risk of a change in

---

[3]   For an assessment of the criteria employed by rating agencies when reviewing bond issues see Part 3 of Fabozzi (1997).

[4]   Bonds rarely fall to zero in price; there is almost always assumed to be some residual value left in a bond.

[5]   In the UK the blue-chip equity repo rate typically trades at around 35–50 basis points over the government rate, with a higher spread during times of market volatility.

the value of an asset due to moves in market levels/prices. For repo market participants this can cover, as well as collateral risk, interest-rate risk and foreign exchange risk. One reason for the continuing popularity of the stock-lending market is that lenders such as fund managers and insurance companies prefer to lend stock in return for a fixed fee rather than engage in repo, which requires a dealing desk and interest-rate management, and exposes the lender to market risk.

We have already discussed collateral price volatility, so here we consider interest-rate risk and foreign exchange risk.

12.3.1 *Position risk*

Repo trading is trading in loans and deposits, in other words it is interest-rate trading. A term repo, unless it is matched by a reverse repo of identical size and maturity date, opens up an interest rate position in a banking book as it has to be financed by a reverse repo. This "gap" is an interest rate position, and this can be marked at a loss if interest rate movements are unfavourable.

In some textbooks this *position risk* is viewed in terms of the bonds in the transaction; for example, a long position in a bond that is being financed in a repo is a long position that is exposed to a rise in interest rates. This type of position risk is more relevant to a bond trader than a repo trader, and we will not dwell on it.

12.3.2 *Foreign exchange risk*

Foreign exchange risk exposure exists in cross-currency repo transactions. It is the risk of loss arising from a fall in value of collateral as a result of adverse moves in the foreign exchange rate, rather than a rise in interest rates causing the bond price to fall. However loss will only occur if the counterparty subsequently defaults before having supplied additional margin or replaced the collateral.

12.4 Liquidity risk

Liquidity risks in repo are closely connected with market risk and collateral issuer risk. In the context of collateral, as with issuer risk, liquidity risk only becomes material in the event of counterparty default. Ideally there should be sufficient liquidity such that in the event of counterparty default, the collateral may be sold off in the market, at its fair value, and the loss made good. For all but the longest-dated repo trades then, this risk exposure is not great. The risk exists in instances where collateral exhibited low liquidity at the start of the trade, that is, the cash lender is aware of it. In such cases the liquidity must be monitored in case it reaches unacceptable levels.

When stock is illiquid, it may be difficult to obtain a reliable valuation for it. This makes marking-to-market, which is essential for variation margin purposes, difficult to undertake. Such stock should only be taken as collateral when the counterparty is rated as top quality in terms of credit risk, such as a AA-rated and highly-capitalised banking institution. When dealing with institutions that are not regarded as being of superior credit quality, the colla - teral taken ideally must be liquid AAA-rated securities. Of course in certain cases this may not be possible, such as dealing in emerging market government repo with local counterparties.

The initial margin required in a repo will take the liquidity of collateral into account. One approach is to base the amount of margin on the estimated fall in price of the collateral in the time from the margin-call date to the disposal of the stock following notice of default. This period of time is based, in part, on the liquidity of the collateral security; liquid securities are assumed to be liquidated in one business day. A bank's risk-management department will estimate the extra time required to dispose of illiquid stock.

Most markets have provision for a set-off mechanism in the event of default, known as *netting*. This means that:

- all outstanding loans/repos are recalled or repurchased;

- each party's obligations to the other are valued and converted into a monetary amount;

- the resulting cash sums are set-off and only the net balance is payable by the party owing the greater amount.

The response to exposure to market risk and liquidity risk is to engage in *margining*. In order for margin calls to take place, market participants have to engage in *marking-to-market* of all their positions. This means that a bond would be marked at its current market price at the close of business. Where the value has fallen by a predetermined amount, the lender of cash will ask for margin. This is not a watertight arrangement in the event of default. The cash lender may still find itself short of a sufficient amount of collateral, due to the following:

- there may have been adverse market movements between the last margin call and payment;

- there may be an element of *concentration risk*, associated with illiquid issues, where the lender of cash is holding a high proportion of bonds from the same issuer, which then become illiquid and difficult to realise.

Therefore banks also engage in daily margin calls.

12.5 Legal risk

Credit risk is still relevant in a secured transaction such as repo. There may be an inclination to attach a lower level of importance to credit risk, compared to that in an unsecured transaction. This is not market best practice, because the holding of collateral may still create problems in the event of default, as the lender of cash may not have legal title to the collateral, or a sufficient amount of collateral. When a counterparty is in default, the process of liquidation or administration can be a lengthy one; it also may not be possible to enforce ownership through legal title, as other creditors may be "ahead of the queue". This is an example of *insolvency risk*, as the liquidator may be able to "cherry pick" the assets of the company, which may include the assets held by the repo counterparty. Ultimately the most effective means of dealing with the various risks is to "know your counterparty". Some market participants go further, and only engage in repo with firms with whom they would also deal in the unsecured market. This is considered excessively risk-averse by some though.

Legal risk also exists where the legal documentation covering repo trades is insufficient or inadequate. This may result in the cash lender being unable to pursue its claim in the courts. Inadequate documentation would for example, not allow for variation margin or default netting. Measures adopted to reduce the legal risk exposure in repo trading have included:

- a formal binding legal agreement, of which the BMA/ISMA agreement is the best example. In the UK gilt repo market for example, parties are required to sign this document before being able to commence dealing. A participant has to have the signed agreement in place with each counterparty it deals with;

- the International Stock Lenders Association OSLA agreement;
- standard domestic agreements (such as the *pension livree* in France).

Essentially, legal risk is minimised by the adoption of standard agreements between counterparties.

12.6 Operational risk

12.6.1 *System risk*

Operational risk is not a repo-specific risk. All participants in the capital markets are exposed to operational risk to a greater or lesser extent. It refers to all the risks that are internal to a firm, such as system failure, procedural inadequacy, fraud, and so on. Banks rely on information technology to a great extent, and repo trading systems are generally highly sophisticated pieces of kit. Modern repo trading systems are used across the bank, from front-office trading to back-office settlement, together with middle-office risk management, accounting and product control. They are used by traders to book trades and monitor book position, and also provide daily data on margin call requirements, current exposure and profit & loss. As such a failure in any part of the system can have potentially serious consequences for a bank, especially if it prevents the bank from dealing normally.

To reduce system operational risk, operating procedures are formalised and communicated to all users. In addition, regular reconciliations are performed of data held by the front, middle and back offices, and of counterparty standing data. The other operational risks are minimised by strict adherence to formal procedures and monitoring by the risk management, internal audit and compliance departments.

12.6.2 *Settlement risk*

The other key operational risk is settlement risk, also known as *delivery risk*. It too is not unique to repo but exists in all capital market trading business. In repo it is the risk that a counterparty does not deliver on its commitment on the due date, either at the opening or closing leg. Thus, settlement risk may lead to loss if a bank delivers the stock (cash) before the counterparty delivers the corresponding cash (stock). In most markets a system of delivery-versus-payment (DVP) operates, which eliminates this risk. However, in certain markets DVP is not always possible, thus leading to an element of settlement risk. The extent of the risk is the maximum potential loss that may be suffered if the firm suffers failed delivery.

Settlement risk is low, indeed practically non-existent in developed markets, with participants dealing with well-established counterparties. However, a temporary delay in delivery is always possible even in such circumstances. This is because of the large number (and variety) of counterparties and the types of collateral traded; delivery failure by one firm, say because a specific stock has become temporarily illiquid,[6] can have knock-on effects that cause other firms to fail delivery in their trades.

To minimise settlement risk, repo should not be conducted, or conducted only very rarely, on anything other than on a DVP basis, with lower-rated counterparties.

---

[6]   Such that the stock is not available for borrowing in the securities-lending market, and/or is available at a negative repo rate.

Appendices

Appendix 12.1:   Rating agency credit ratings

FitchIBCA	Moody's	Standard & Poor's	Summary description
Investment Grade – High credit quality			
AAA	Aaa	AAA	Risk-free; gilt edged, prime, lowest risk
AA+	Aa1	AA+	
AA	Aa2	AA	High-grade, high credit quality
AA–	Aa3	AA–	
A+	A1	A+	
A	A2	A	Upper–medium grade
A–	A3	A–	
BBB+	Baa1	BBB+	
BBB	Baa2	BBB	Lower–medium grade
BBB–	Baa3	BBB–	
Speculative (sub-investment grade) – Lower credit quality			
BB+	Ba1	BB+	
BB	Ba2	BB	Low grade; speculative
BB–	Ba3	BB–	
B+	B1	B+	
B	B2	B	Highly speculative
B–	B3	B–	
Highly speculative, substantial risk or in default			
		CCC+	
CCC	Caa	CCC	Considerable risk, in poor standing
		CCC–	
CC	Ca	CC	May already be in default, very speculative
C	C	C	Extremely speculative
		CI	Income bonds – no interest being paid
DDD			
DD			Default
D		D	

Credit rating	Default rate	One-year loss rate
Aaa	0.00%	0.00%
Aa	0.02%	0.02%
A	0.03%	0.03%
Baa	0.15%	0.07%
Ba	1.46%	0.73%
B	6.92%	3.69%

Table 12.2: Moody's average default rates and average one-year loss rate, by credit rating. Source: *Moody's Default Rates of Corporate Issuers Report*, 2000.

Selected bibliography and references

Fabozzi, F. (ed.), *The Handbook of Fixed Income*, 5th edition, McGraw-Hill, 1997

13 Accounting, Tax and Capital Issues

In this chapter we discuss the accounting and taxation implications of repo for financial institutions. As each market jurisdiction follows its own accounting rules, we are only able to present an overview account, the basic principles adhered to in most markets. Readers requiring specific rules and regulations for a particular market will need to seek local specialist advice.[1] We also consider the capital adequacy rules and their relevance to repo, and discuss the proposed Basel II capital rules.

13.1 Accounting treatment

As we discovered in Part I, the legal definition of a repo trade is given as a "sale" of an asset, with an agreement at the time of sale to "repurchase" the same or an identical asset at a specified date in the future. However, ignoring repo in specific securities for the moment, the transaction is undertaken because one party wishes to lend cash on a secured basis, and the asset "sold" is merely transferred to the cash lender to act as collateral for the loan, to be returned on loan maturity. The key issue with regard to accounting treatment is whether the transaction should be treated as an actual sale by the selling counterparty, or treated as a financing instrument in which the asset is used as collateral for a loan of cash. In most jurisdictions the accounting treatment of repo reflects the business realities of the transaction, which is a *secured loan*, and ignores its legal definition.

In a repo transaction then, while legal title to collateral is transferred to the "buyer", the accounting treatment (in most jurisdictions) recognises that the economic impact of the collateral remains with the "seller". Therefore, for the seller, bonds given as collateral remain on its balance sheet. The corresponding double-entry liability is the repo cash. Coupon or dividend cash flow from the asset continues to accrue to the seller. The book-keeping entries are the opposite for the repo buyer. So in its accounting treatment a repo trade appears as a secured loan and not an actual sale transaction. As a collateralised financing transaction, repos are on-balance-sheet transactions. With regard to the profit & loss account, the repo interest (repo return) is treated as the payment of interest and is taken as a charge on an accruals basis, that is, it is entered in the books at the time of the transaction.

13.1.1 *Overview of accounting rules*

Accounting authorities stress that treatment of an entity's business transactions must reflect their *commercial substance*; this aspect of any transaction is assessed by considering the rewards and risks that are associated with an asset or liability. If an asset is recorded in a company balance sheet, for that asset to be removed from the balance sheet the substantial

---

[1]   The author also confesses that accounting and taxation are not areas of his immediate expertise, another reason for the brevity of this chapter! A more detailed treatment is given in the Euromoney publication *Repo Handbook* (Euromoney, 1995).

part of economic impact attached to it must be transferred to another entity. This is known as *de-recognition*.[2] For the seller in repo trade, de-recognition cannot take place because the risks and rewards associated with the asset are not transferred to another entity. Equally, the repo buyer entering into a reverse repo trade does not take on the risks and rewards associated with the collateral transferred, so that these assets are not recorded on its balance sheet. Thus since a repo trade (unlike say, a total return swap) cannot be defined in a way that would allow de-recognition, accounting authorities treat repo as a financing transaction. Note that repo trading under a matched book or market-making scenario can, under some jurisdictions, have their cash balance element marked-to-market on the bank's balance sheet, but not in the UK or US.

The treatment of variation margin also varies according to accounting jurisdiction. To recap, additional margin is transferred between counterparties if there is a triggering movement in the value of the collateral during the term of the trade. This margin may be sent in the form of cash or securities. In the UK cash may be offset against the amount of the original repo, or added to it, providing that this procedure is described in the relevant legal documentation and that settlement is on a net basis. If securities are transferred, the balance sheet treatment follows that employed for the original securities.

The general rules applicable in most accounting regimes are summarised in Table 13.1.

Repo seller (cash borrower)	Repo buyer (cash lender)
Securities transferred are retained on the balance sheet, and the usual valuation approach maintained during the term of the trade (mark-to-market or at cost). Securities used as collateral are identified in the accounts.	Securities transferred are not entered in the balance sheet; changes in the market value of the securities have no effect on the buyer's balance sheet.
The cash loan is entered as a liability on the balance sheet, and the seller is obliged to repay the cash borrowed from the buyer together with interest at the agreed repo rate. The liability is identified on the balance sheet as "assets (securities) sold under a repurchase agreeement".	The cash lent to the seller is recorded on the balance sheet as an asset. It is identified on the balance sheet as "assets (securities) purchased under a repurchase agreement, to be sold on maturity".
The interest charged on the loan is entered on an accruals basis, identified as a financing cost during the term of the repo agreement.	The interest earned on the loaned funds is entered on an accruals basis during the term of the repo agreement.
Treatment of repo to be explained in the Notes to the Financial Statements.	Treatment of repo to be explained in the Notes to the Financial Statements.

Table 13.1: Summary of general accounting approach.

---

[2]   In some jurisdictions de-recognition with regard to repo is assessed by determining which counterparty has actual control over the asset used as collateral.

13.1.2 *United Kingdom accounting*

The accounting authority in the UK is the Accounting Standards Board. It issues statements of required accounting practice in what are known as *Financial Reporting Standards* (FRS). The treatment of repo would appear to fall under FRS 5, entitled *Reporting the Substance of Transactions*. It states that generally repo transactions are not to be considered as a sale, and therefore securities transferred must remain on the seller's balance sheet, thus defining a repo in terms of its economic impact and not in legal terms. This continues to apply even where different securities, of identical credit quality, are returned. Under certain circumstances it may be possible to de-recognise assets in a repo, depending on whether the buyer has some recourse to "use" of the asset. In addition, a *repo to maturity* may be treated as a sale transaction if the repo matures on the expiry date of the collateral.

Prior to this formal statement, the British Bankers Association issued a *Statement of Recommended Practice* (SORP) in 1990 that contained direction on the accounting treatment and recording of repo transactions. This predated the introduction of repo in the sterling market by nearly six years.

FRS 5 also contains provisions in paragraphs 21–30 relating to *netting* of multiple trades with the same counterparty. This refers to the practice of offsetting repo and reverse repo trades against each other on the balance sheet, that is, offsetting the assets recorded as secured loans against the liabilities arising from borrowing of cash. This is also known as *balance sheet netting*. FRS 5 states that assets and liabilities may be netted against each other if certain conditions exist, including that the values involved are material and either of the same currency or of liquid currencies that can be converted into the reporting currency easily. In addition, there must be a provision for net settlement between the reporting entity and the counterparty, and this must be legally enforceable against the counterparty in the event of default.

Appendix 13.1 quotes relevant extracts from FRS 5 relevant to accounting treatment for repo transactions.

13.1.3 *United States accounting*

The equivalent regulatory pronouncements in the US jurisdiction are the Statements of Financial Accounting Standards (SFAS). SFAS 125 from January 1990, *Accounting for Transfers and Servicing of Financial Assets and Extinguishments of Liabilities*, covers the treatment of repo. Its states that in any repo trade in which the seller will repurchase from the buyer securities sold to it at the start of the trade, the treatment of the transaction should be as a secured loan. This assumes that the securities repurchased are identical to those sold, or at least identical in terms of issuing entity, coupon and maturity date, and not due to mature during the term of the trade. In addition, the trade must be honoured under any circumstance, including the default of the buyer. SFAS 125 assumes that the seller retains control of securities transferred during the term of the trade, and therefore must continue to record the value of the securities during this time. The buyer also does not record the securities on its balance sheet. However, if the repo does not allow the seller to terminate it at short notice, the buyer may record the item in its balance sheet as a buy, while the seller is still allowed to record the trade as a secured loan.

Under US Securities and Exchange Commission regulations, it is a requirement that repo trades be disclosed separately on the balance sheet.

Repos to maturity are treated as sales and purchases of the securities concerned, under the US SFAS 125, and not as financing transactions, assuming that the seller is not affected by the securities in the event of bankruptcy. This is because the securities will not be repurchased.

Netting provisions in the US market are described under general accounting principle rules known as Financial Accounting Standards Board statements. FASB 39 sets out a number of conditions under which cash payable under a repo agreement may be offset against cash receivable as part of a reverse repo transaction, so that a net cash value may be reported. Netting is permissible provided that:

- repo and reverse repo trades concerned have all been undertaken with the same counterparty, and have identical maturity dates;

- a provision for netting is contained in the legal documentation describing repo between the counterparties;

- the entity uses one bank account to handle cash flows arising from both repo and reverse repo trades;

- settlement of both repo and reverse repo is via a clearing system and securities are transferred across this clearing system in electronic book-entry form.

The FASB has also indicated that these provisions apply to transactions settling across any suitable electronic clearing system.

13.2 Taxation treatment

The tax treatment of repo differs in each jurisdiction. In the UK the return on the cash leg of a repo is treated as interest and is taxed as income. Coupon payments during the term of a repo are treated for tax purposes as being to the benefit of the counterparty, the taxable date of which is taken to be the dividend date. To allow for this treatment, which recognises the economic reality of repo rather than its legal form, the UK enacted specific legislation. However, as taxation treatment of repo does differ across tax regimes, when trading in overseas markets where the tax treatment is uncertain, institutions must investigate the principal tax issues, both from the point of view of repo seller and buyer.

13.2.1 *Basic principles*

For tax purposes the transfer of securities at the start of the trade does not count as a disposal, which tallies with the accounting treatment. However tax treatment is different for the income in a repo.

- **Repo seller:** For the seller, the principal issue is whether the "sale" of securities will trigger a taxable event and/or result in transfer taxes. The type of institution engaged in the trade may affect the resulting tax treatment, as it may be taxable or tax-exempt, as will the firm's country of residence, as there may be a form of double taxation treaty. For a cross-border trade the accounting treatment in both countries must be taken into consideration, and whether the repo is treated as a sale or not. The basic accounting treatment is that a repo is not a sale; however, this is not the case in all countries.

- **Repo buyer:** For the buyer, the principal issue to ascertain is whether the "purchase" of securities will result in transfer taxes.

A taxation issue may arise whenever a coupon payment is made during the term of a repo. If a repo runs over a record date (coupon date) a "manufactured dividend" will arise. In the UK this is treated as income accruing to the beneficial owner of the securities, and therefore not the income of the cash lender. For this reason the dividend is deductible for the cash lender. There is an additional issue if the coupon is actually paid net of any withholding taxes or gross. The coupon on government bonds is usually paid gross, the major exception being Japanese government bonds which pay coupon net. The UK introduced (in 1998) gross payment of coupon for government bonds (previously foreign-domiciled investors had to register to receive gross coupons). However, holders are still liable to tax which is paid in the normal course of tax assessment.

The tax authorities recognise that the substance of repo is as a financing transaction, and a collateralised loan. Any difference between the sale price and repurchase price is treated for tax purposes as interest, which is paid on maturity of the trade. This is, in effect, viewing repo as a sell/buy-back trade, where the repurchase price is different from the initial sale price, this differential being the way loan interest is priced into the deal. The tax treatment is described in Section 730 of the Income and Corporation Taxes Act 1988 (ICTA).

13.2.2 *Manufactured dividends*

Manufactured dividends is the term for coupon or dividend paid out on a security that has been transferred for collateral purposes to the buyer in a repo transaction. In legal terms, the right to the coupon or dividend payable on a security also transfers to the buyer. The seller, who retains economic benefits of the collateral, therefore must be compensated for the implied loss of income during the term of the repo, thus preserving the cash flows received had the seller not entered into a repo.

A manufactured dividend is effected so that the seller is compensated. This can be done using either of the following methods:

- in a classic repo, the buyer pays the value of the coupon or dividend over to the seller, on the dividend date or the following business day; this is, in effect, the definition of a manufactured dividend;

- in a sell/buy-back, the repurchase price is adjusted by the amount of the coupon or dividend (it is subtracted from the buy-back price); this is known as a *roll up*. This means that the value of the may not be received until some time after the dividend date, in which case the buy-back price will also be adjusted by a compensating amount, usually the repo rate payable on the dividend amount from the dividend date to the termination date.

The tax treatment of manufactured dividends reflects their economic substance, so that they are viewed as actual dividends received by the seller. Manufactured dividends in classic repo are described in Section 737 of the ICTA. This states that the buyer in a repo is assumed to have paid a manufactured dividend when it falls due, equal in value to the actual dividend. This assumes that the real dividend is not also received directly by the seller, and that the repurchase price takes into account that the seller did not receive the real dividend (irrelevant in classic repo where the repurchase price is identical to the sale price). Where a withholding tax obligation arises, the repo buyer is required to account for this to the Inland Revenue as an amount due.

In the UK, bonds pay coupon gross of interest; however, equities pay a net dividend. Rules pertaining to withholding taxes are in Schedule 23 of the ICTA. Note that in a sell/buy-back, the taxable date is deemed to be the dividend date, even though the value will not be recovered until the maturity date of the trade.

13.3 Capital treatment

The Bank for International Settlements (BIS) originally introduced a standard for capital adequacy in July 1988. This is known as the Basel Capital Accord and it specified a relatively uniform system for defining exactly how much capital a bank required. The rules came into effect at the end of 1992. They set a minimum ratio of capital to *weighted risk assets* of 8%, also known as the Cooke ratio after the chairman of the Basel Committee at the time. Each asset on the bank's balance sheet is assigned a weighting, which can be from 0% for assets considered riskless, to 100% for the most risky assets. For example, most interbank deposits are given a 20% weighting, while most bank lending receives the full 100% weighting. A £100 million corporate loan would therefore consume £8 million of the bank's capital (that is, the bank would have to set aside £8m against the loan), while a £100 million interbank deposit would require a £1.6 million allocation of bank capital. The risk weighting applied varies with the type of counterparty; broadly speaking, the weightings are:

0%	Cash, Zone A Central Governments/Banks
20%	EIB, Zone B Credit Institutions
50%	Fully secured loans
100%	Zone A or Zone B non-bank sectors (for example, corporates)

An institution's basic capital charge calculation is therefore:

Principal value × Risk weighting × Capital charge [8%].

The sum of the exposures is taken. Firms may use netting or portfolio modelling to reduce the total principal value.

The capital requirements for off-balance-sheet instruments are lower because for these instruments the *principal* is rarely at risk. Interest-rate derivatives such as Forward Rate Agreements (FRAs) of less than one year's maturity have no capital requirement at all, while a long-term currency swap requires capital of between 0.08% and 0.2% of the nominal principal. For example, a £100 million five-year currency swap between banks would require capital allocation of £80,000. This is considerably lower than the equivalent nominal value transactions considered above.

The reasoning behind bank capital

The market views the extent of a banking institution's credit costs as having a cumulative probability distribution, as illustrated in Figure 13.1. The concept behind this is that a significant proportion of credit costs are deemed to be expected, and that therefore accurate product pricing, together with loss provisions should be sufficient to cover predicted losses. However, due to market uncertainty regulators believe that perfect predictive ability is most unlikely and hence a further cushion is required, to cover unforeseen eventualities. This cushion is provided by bank's regulatory capital, defined in terms of the equity capital of the bank. Regulatory capital is only a cushion and may not prove to be sufficient; indeed, the only way to *completely* protect against all eventual outcomes would be for a bank to hold an identical amount of capital as assets. Clearly this would be excessive and unrealistic, as the return on capital would be very low and insufficient to attract equity investment. So there is a capital reserves level beyond which it becomes uneconomic to hold further capital, but before which financial regulators feel is sufficient to protect against most eventualities. A bank might still suffer a catastrophic loss, which would exceed the capital cover, and which would then result either in a rescue by the authorities and/or other banks, or failure and bankruptcy. The Barings crisis in 1995 is an example of such a catastrophic event. Where banking institutions are in a weak state, the authorities may engineer higher capital ratios in order to boost investor and consumer confidence; for example, the government may take over non-performing loans from commercial banks, as happened in Thailand and the Czech Republic, or regulators may apply a definition of bad debt that still presents a façade of adequate capital cover. For this reason, the Basel Committee proposed its original capital rules so that a consistent approach to banking capital treatment was adopted in all jurisdictions.

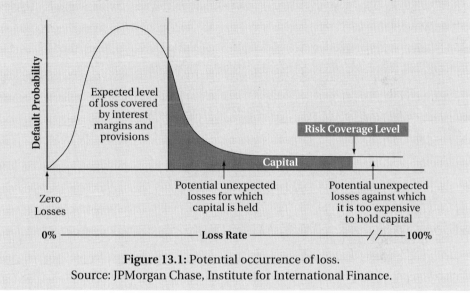

Figure 13.1: Potential occurrence of loss.
Source: JPMorgan Chase, Institute for International Finance.

The BIS makes a distinction between *banking book* transactions as carried out by retail and commercial banks (primarily deposits and lending) and *trading book* transactions as carried out by investment banks and securities houses. Capital treatment can differ between banking and trading books.

In this section we summarise the current regime and introduce the proposed Basel II arrangements, and illustrate capital calculations.

13.3.1 *Capital adequacy treatment*

In the UK capital adequacy treatment differs according to the type of entity concerned. Banking institutions follow the requirements set out in the Banking Act (1987), now supervised by the Financial Services Authority (FSA), while investment banks capital adequacy requirements are described in the Financial Services Act. The minimum acceptable capital requirements for securities houses are laid out in the European Union's Capital Adequacy Directive (CAD), which was implemented throughout the EU in January 1996. In the UK the CAD is followed by means of the FSA capital adequacy rules. Trading activity for both banks and securities houses is therefore regulated for capital adequacy by the CAD, and this also covers repo trading. However, the precise capital treatment for repo activity differs according to whether the transaction is classified as being on the banking book or the trading book.[3] As repo business results in both counterparty default risk exposure and (for the seller) continuing market risk exposure of the underlying asset, it gives rise to a counterparty risk charge and market risk. Thus in most cases repo business is considered trading book activity.

13.3.2 *UK repo capital treatment: counterparty risk*

In this section we introduce capital treatment for securities houses. The FSA *Guide to Banking Supervisory Policy* (1996) states that a bank's trading book includes all exposures arising from repo agreements and stock lending where the underlying securities are placed in the trading book, and all reverse repo and stock borrowing transactions. The FSA makes a distinction between "documented" and "undocumented" repo transactions, or business that comes under a specific legal agreement or not. Undocumented repo business results in a higher capital requirement.

- **Documented repo treatment:** a repo trade is considered to be documented if it is covered by a legal agreement that includes provision for variation margin adjustment on up to a daily basis during the term of the trade, and provision for netting in the event of counterparty default.

  The counterparty risk capital charge for a repo trade is given by

  $$CA = \max[((C_{mv} - S_{mv}) \times 8\% \times RW), 0] \tag{13.1}$$

  where

C_{mv}	is the value of cash proceeds;
S_{mv}	is the market value of securities;
RW	the counterparty risk weighting (as percentage).

  For reverse repo the capital allocation is given by

  $$CA = \max[((S_{mv} - C_{mv}) \times 8\% \times RW), 0] \tag{13.2}$$

  If one or both of the above legal requirements are not described in the legal agreement, the repo is treated as undocumented.

- **Undocumented repo treatment:** a repo trade is considered undocumented if it is not covered by a legal agreement as described above. The best example is an undocumented sell/buy-back transaction. Undocumented repo attracts higher capital charges.

  The counterparty risk calculation for a sell/buy-back or repo transaction is given by

  $$CA = (C_{rct} + CE) \times 8\% \times RW \tag{13.3}$$

  where

C_{rct}	is the contract replacement cost;
CE	is the potential future credit exposure;

---

[3] The banking book refers to more traditional banking operations, such as lending activity and deposit-taking, including longer-term lending. It would also cover repo business, but only where the primary motive for such business was not "trading". The trading book includes activities such as short-term trading and market-making, as well as most off-balance-sheet business. It also includes most repo business.

and C_{rct} is given by $\max\left[(C_{mv} - S_{mv}), 0\right]$. The potential future credit exposure CE is the trade's forward delivery value multiplied by the security *risk cushion factor* (RCF). The RCF applicable will range from 0.25% to 6% depending on the type of security and its term to maturity.

The counterparty risk exposure in a buy/sell-back or reverse repo is given by

$$CA = \left[(C_{rct} + CE) \times 8\% \times RW\right]$$

where C_{rct} is given by $\max\left[(S_{mv} - C_{mv}), 0\right]$ and CE is the trade's value for forward delivery, multiplied by the *risk cushion factor* (RCF) for the security concerned. If the collateral RCF is higher than the security RCF, this is used in the calculation instead.

■ **Repo netting:** a bank that has entered into a number of repo trades with one counterparty may calculate its counterparty risk measure on the basis of netting the trades, provided that this is described in legal documentation covering the transactions. This must contain a provision for close-out netting arrangements in the event of counterparty, or its own default or insolvency.

Recap: CAD treatment for repo

A repo transaction attracts a charge on the *trading book*. The formula for calculating the capital allocation is:

$$CA = \max\left[((C_{mv} - S_{mv}) \times 8\% \times RW), 0\right] \qquad (13.4)$$

where

C_{mv}	is the value of cash proceeds;
S_{mv}	is the market value of securities;
RW	the counterparty risk weighting (as percentage).

Example 13.1

The CAD charge for a repo transaction with the following terms:

Clean price of collateral	100
Accrued interest	0
Cash proceeds on £50m nominal	£50,000,000
Counterparty	OECD bank
Counterparty risk weighting	20%

is $CA = \max\left[((50,000,000 - 50,000,000) \times 8\% \times 20\%), 0\right] = 0.$

The CAD charge for a loan/deposit transaction of the same size would be as follows:

Unsecured loan	£50,000,000
Counterparty	OECD bank
Counterparty risk weighting	20%

$$CA = \max\left[((50,000,000) \times 8\% \times 20\%), 0\right] = £800,000.$$

Repo conducted under legal documentation, such as the BMA/ISMA agreement, are given favourable treatment for CAD purposes compared with undocumented repo.

Buy/sell-backs attract the full charge based on the counterparty risk weighting. Documented repos attract a capital charge at the counterparty risk weighting based on the mark-to-market value of all positions between the parties.

Example 13.2:   Repo and reverse repo treatment
Bank ABC repos £10 million nominal of a five-year government bond marked-to-market at a price of £101 and receives £10 million cash from Bank XYZ. Both banks carry a 20% counterparty risk weighting.
Bank ABC counterparty risk calculation is:

$$CA = \max[((10.1m - 10m) \times 8\% \times 20\%), 0] = \pounds1,600.$$

Bank XYZ calculation is:
$$CA = \max[((10m - 10.1m) \times 8\% \times 20\%), 0] = \pounds0.$$

Example 13.3:   Undocumented repo and reverse repo treatment
Bank ABC repos £10 million of a five-year government bond priced at £101 to Bank XYZ and receives £10 million cash from Bank XYZ. Both banks carry a 20% risk weighting. The risk cushion factors are 1.25% for the bond and 0% for the cash. The trade's contract value for forward delivery is £10 million.

Bank ABC counterparty risk requirement is:

Replacement cost:	max [(£10.1m – £10m), 0]
Potential future exposure:	£10m × 1.25%

Capital charge = (£100,000 + £125,000) × 8% × 20%
                = £3,600

Bank XYZ counterparty risk requirement is:

Replacement cost:	max [(£10m – £10.1m), 0]
Potential future exposure:	£10m × 1.25%

Capital charge = (£125,000) × 8% × 20%
                = £2,000

13.3.3 *UK repo treatment for banking book*

Generally repo that comes under the banking book is treated similarly to secured lending. On the banking book assets are assigned a risk weighting according to the categorisation given in Section 13.3. This risk weight is then multiplied by the 8% minimum charge and the value of the loan. A *credit conversion factor* is used to convert items such as repo and off-balance-sheet entries into a *credit equivalent amount*; for repo the conversion factor is 100%. The credit equivalent amount is multiplied by the 8% minimum capital charge and the appropriate risk weighting. Because repo is treated as a secured deposit on the banking book, no counterparty risk exposure need be calculated.

Reverse repo is treated as a secured loan, and the risk exposure is considered a counterparty risk exposure. However the amount of exposure (and corresponding capital charge) is lowered if the collateral is of high quality, such as certain government debt or supranational debt, as the risk weighting is lower for these securities.

13.3.4 *Securities houses capital treatment*

The trading operations of investment banks and securities houses are regulated by the Securities and Futures Authority (SFA), one of the regulatory bodies subsumed into the FSA in November 2001. The capital treatment for repo described in the SFA rules is broadly similar to those described above for banking institutions.

Documented repo attracts more favourable treatment compared to undocumented repo. A repo is considered to be documented if it is conducted under the following conditions:

- there is provision for daily variation margining, and (to facilitate this) the security or other collateral is marked-to-market on a daily basis;

- there is provision for set-off against the claims of the counterparty in the event of counterparty default;

- the legal agreement is used only to cover transactions conducted for the purpose described.

Undocumented transactions attract a capital charge that is twice that of an otherwise identical documented transaction.

13.4 Basel II rules

In June 1999 the Basel Committee on banking supervision circulated its proposals for an update to the existing capital rules, the so-called Basel II proposals. Originally it had been intended that a market consultation process would follow, up to June 2001, and the new proposals would be adopted in 2004. Due to the high level of market reaction to the original proposals the consultation period was extended by one year, and the Committee announced that implementation of the new capital rules in their final firm would now take place in 2005. Since the original rules were implemented in 1992, it had become commonplace thinking that they were no longer adequate for the more sophisticated markets and products that existed. There was also a belief that some very large and active banking institutions were insufficiently capitalised, and that certain firms were advantaged due to their more benign capital regimes.[4] The increasing use of off-balance-sheet derivative instruments and the differing regimes also sometimes allowed substantial capital opportunities, and a resulting misallocation of regulatory capital. The June 1999 Basel paper was devised as an attempt to update the risk calculation associated with banking assets. In this section we briefly introduce the main points behind Basel II and also discuss its impact on repo market participants.

13.4.1 *The Basel II proposals and critique*

The June 1999 consultative paper from the Basel Committee put forward three "pillars" of capital adequacy, these being minimum capital requirements, the supervisory review process, and market discipline. The first pillar, that of minimum capital requirements, has been the

---

[4]   Remember that the Basel Committee is not itself a regulatory body, and its role is confined to making recommendations to national regulators. Banking supervision rules and capital requirements are set by a particular regulator in any jurisdiction. However as the Committee is made up of regulators of the G10 countries, unsurprisingly the rules adopted in at least the G10 countries come very close to recommendations of the Basel Committee.

focus of most market reaction to the proposals to date. The main recommendation in the consultative paper is that risk weightings for assets be based on ratings assigned to borrowers by external credit rating agencies. The main change from the Basel I rules concerns risk weights for OECD sovereign borrowers and banks, which had previously been weighted at 0% and 20% respectively; these would now be weighted according to their credit ratings. The new proposals are listed in Table 13.2.

		AAA to AA–	A+ to A–	BBB+ to BBB–	BB+ to B–	Below B–	Unrated
Sovereign		0%	20%	50%	100%	150%	100%
Banks	Option 1 (1)	20%	50%	100%	100%	150%	100%
	Option 2 (2)	20%	50% (3)	50% (3)	100% (3)	150%	50% (3)
Corporates		20%	100%	100%	100%	150%	100%

Notes

(1) Risk weighting based on risk weighting of the sovereign in which the bank is incorporated.

(2) Risk weighting based on the assessment of the individual bank.

(3) Claims on banks of a short original maturity, for example less than six months, would receive a weighting that is one notch above the usual risk weight on the bank's claim.

(Source: BIS, Basel Committee on Banking Supervision)

Table 13.2: Basel II proposals, risk weightings.

A significant change in Basel II was the specification of a required charge to cover *operational risk*. This has been referred to as the McDonough ratio, again after the incumbent Committee chairman. The original Cooke ratio is given by

$$\text{Cooke} = \frac{\text{Tier 1} + \text{Tier 2}}{RW} = \frac{\text{Core Capital} + \text{Secondary Capital}}{\sum(\text{Assets} \times RW)} \tag{13.5}$$

while the McDonough ratio is given by

$$\text{McDonough} = \frac{\text{Tier 1} + \text{Tier 2}}{(\text{Credit} + \text{market} + \text{operational})\text{risk}} \tag{13.6}$$

Under Basel II terms a bank will need to calculate three parts to its risk exposure; for credit risk it will weight assets according to the nature of the counterparty and the chosen risk weighting, whether internal or external (see below). Market and operational risks would be calculated as the sum of all risk-weighted assets plus 12.5 times the sum of the capital charges. Operational risk is deemed to cover all risks inherent to a bank's business, such as IT failure, fraud, procedural error, and such like. As currently proposed the Basel Committee has suggested that operational risk would account for 20% of the calculation basis for the capital requirement, a figure which has attracted widespread negative comment.[5]

The proposals attracted a wide range of comment, with the most common one being that although they were an improvement on the current inflexible regime, there still remained considerable problems with their scope. A widely held criticism is that, as the incidence of external credit ratings outside the US is relatively low, the proposals as they stand represent a disadvantage to non-US banks and borrowers. Another fundamental issue is that the assignment of a specific credit rating implies a level of likelihood of full and timely payment of

---

[5] This issue was still being debated at the time of writing, with signs that the 20% level might be lowered to 15% or 10%.

interest and principal; however the current proposal carries different risk weights to sovereigns, banks and corporates of identical ratings. This inconsistency would create arbitrage-type dealing and would be a distortion of the Committee's intent, which is surely to align regulatory and economic capital requirements. In addition the credit rating agencies are not enthusiastic about the proposals, as they might lead to a change in emphasis of their role, and perhaps to some form of external regulation. Being private profit-making entities, there is also concern about the liability exposure should a credit rating prove to have been inappropriate.

Other critical comment received by the Basel Committee includes the following:

- bank risk weightings as described under option 1 have been generally deemed unacceptable, as a weighting on the basis of the sovereign's rating suggests that all of a bank's risk is related to its national government. As the intention is to implement a new standard that matches capital allocation with actual risk exposure, such practice would render a bank's individual economic strength irrelevant, which cannot be what the Committee is seeking;
- option 2 has been accepted as the basis of a new standard, although the 50% weighting for A-rated banks has attracted comment has excessive and harsh;
- it is common for banks to carry different ratings according to which ratings agency is quoted; which rating would then be used for capital allocation purposes?

Credit risk managers have also observed that the risk weighting matrix does not map to the historical default loss probabilities that is observed Moody's and Standard & Poor's data. That is, under the proposals there would be a relatively large amount of excess capital held against higher quality credits, but a relatively low amount held against much more risky assets. This is illustrated in Figure 13.2, which shows the amount of Tier 1 capital that the Basel II standard would require for corporate assets, compared to the default probabilities using Standard & Poor's rating categories and default probabilities, for a sample of 20 banks. It would appear to indicate that the Basel II proposals diverge significantly from economic capital requirements. This has led to the Basel Committee investigating the use of an internal ratings-based approach to capital adequacy.

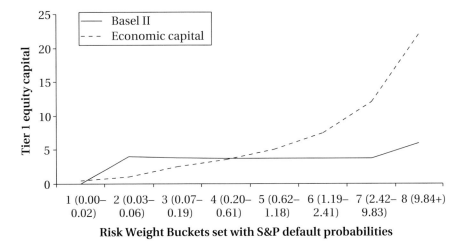

Figure 13.2: Basel II proposed capital requirements compared to S&P default probabilities. Source: JPMorgan Chase Bank; Institute of International Finance.

13.4.2 *The internal ratings-based approach*

The internal ratings-based approach to capital adequacy (IRB) is a method by which capital ratios reflect each bank and the precise composition of the asset base and the risk-reduction procedures that have been followed (that is, hedging). A bank will require a lower level of capital to support a given capital ratio if it holds high quality assets, and has advanced credit-risk management procedures and internal ratings. Equally a bank with low-quality assets and lower levels of hedging will require more capital to support the same ratio.

In order to adopt an IRB approach a bank will need to demonstrate an ability to internally assess the likelihood of default of the loans on its loan book. That is, the bank estimates the solvency and the credit risk of each borrower, with the aggregate results being the basis of an estimate of future loss levels. This calculation is used to derive the bank's capital requirements. The larger, more sophisticated banks will have a greater ability to carry this out, and hence a greater ability to implement an IRB approach. Banks that cannot demonstrate an adequate ability to carry out this "self-assessment" will continue to have their capital requirement calculated by their regulator. However as regulators are more cautious than the banks themselves, and thus calculate a greater capital requirement than the bank itself, this is a strong incentive for banks to improve their data collection and IRB methodologies so that they are assessed as being able to adopt the IRB approach. It is expected that generally a minimum of three years' historic data is required by regulators before they are prepared to sign-off on an internal ratings-based approach.

A key criticism from bank researchers[6] is that internal ratings should not be considered to be relevant until a minimum of five years' data (observations) has been compiled by a bank seeking to implement an IRB approach. In addition, regulatory authorities should seek to ensure that there is a certain homogeneity across the internal ratings procedures of different banks.

13.4.3 *Basel II and impact on repo*

The Basel Committee proposals include references to collateralisation as a means of reducing credit risk exposure. If collateralised trading follows a number of specified standards, under the new standard it is possible, in theory, for a bank's regulatory capital requirement to be reduced substantially. The response of repo market participants would appear to suggest that capital requirements may be substantially increased, and that the proposals require re-working.

The proposals specify "simple" and "comprehensive" approaches to the treatment of collateral. The comprehensive approach may be followed by institutions that possess the necessary infrastructure, such as in-house margin methodologies. In order to obtain maximum capital relief, an institution must adhere to the following five "standards":

- **Legal opinion.** Regular legal opinion must be sought on the legal documentation in place between a bank and its counterparties. This is to ensure that signed agreements in place to support collateralised trading can in fact be enforced in the event of counterparty default; in order to obtain capital relief, a bank must be able to demonstrate that it has legal title to collateral it holds, and that it may liquidate such collateral if the counterparty is declared insolvent. Note that the mere existence of say, a signed BMA/ISMA repo agreement would

---

[6]   For example, see February 2001 *Credit Research* from CDC IXIS Capital Markets, or June 2000 *Guide to Bank Bonds* from Chase Manhattan Bank (now JPMorgan Chase Bank).

not be sufficient to meet this requirement: it must be frequently reviewed by external counsel for opinion that the agreement can indeed be enforced in the event of default. This requirement may be considered a significant material cost to firms.

- **Collateral and exposure correlation.** Collateral held must have "low correlation" to the exposure that it is being used to secure. For example, a UK bank entering into repo with a bank based in Argentina accepts Argentinian government bonds as collateral. In the event of an economic crisis in Argentina, the credit quality of the counterparty will worsen, but one expects that so will the quality of the collateral. If there is an element of correlation, then no capital relief is available. This requirement has attracted much unfavourable comment from market participants. In addition there is a potential conflict with another element in the new proposals, which state that an 8% "foreign exchange risk" margin be levied on collateral that is denominated in a different currency to the exposure; however, there is the previously stated requirement that there be low correlation between collateral and exposure!

- **Risk-management processes.** Institutions must compile and implement robust risk-management procedures and processes covering legal, operational, liquidity and market risks. This includes collateral management risk procedures. The areas that must be covered include: a policy on use of collateral; acceptable collateral and margin levels; procedures for making margin calls; policies and procedures to identify and manage legal risk; and policies and procedures to deal with close-out and liquidation of collateralised positions in the event of counterparty default.

- **Eligible collateral.** Institutions should identify the range of acceptable collateral, and required margin levels. The requirements differ according to whether the simple or comprehensive approach is adopted. Although the range of eligible collateral has been greatly expanded compared to Basel I rules, the margin calculation requirements are also consequently more onerous. The range of collateral now covers: cash; securities rated BB– and above issued by sovereigns; securities rated BBB– and above issued by bank and corporates; index-listed equities; and gold.

- **The collateral "floor".** The collateral floor is a new concept, applicable only under the comprehensive approach, in which a floor factor w is applied to that part of the risk exposure secured by collateral. This is an additional capital cushion designed to cover legal and documentation risks associated with holding collateral.[7] Under the existing proposal the value of w will be uniform, regardless of the type of documentation in place and the domicile of counterparty banks. However this floor can be varied down to 0% in some circumstances where the counterparty is a specified type of "core" market professional counterparty.

As with the general Basel II proposals, the new proposals with regard to repo have attracted much adverse comment. A sample of market participants' responses include the following:[8]

- as they currently stand, the capital requirements for repo counterparties will increase significantly; this would appear to run counter to the Committee's intent, which is for

---

[7] Forgive an audible grin from the author here, wondering if it's better then, in this case, to avoid such "risk" and lend cash without accepting collateral!

[8] These responses have been gauged by the author in discussion with repo market participants.

capital allocation to reflect more accurately the actual risk of specific transactions, since repo is recognised as a low-risk business;

■ there is no reference to repo netting in the proposals, although netting arrangements reduce potential risk exposures by a considerable degree. The proposals should state guidelines for netting arrangements;

■ the *w*-factor floor requirement serves no purpose and should be removed, as it would not appear to be representing any specific risk. In addition, the stated "legal" and "documentation" risk that it is designed to cover should already be covered by the initial and variation margin taken.

The British Bankers Association (BBA), in its joint response with the London Investment Banking Association (LIBA) to the Committee proposals, has suggested that in terms of capital treatment repo should be viewed as a standalone transaction, of its own standing, rather than merely as a collateralised loans. It has suggested that as it currently stands, the Basel proposals may lead to an increase in capital requirements of up to 600% for active market participants. It remains to be seen how the outcome of the consultation process leads to a modification of the final recommendations ahead of implementation in 2005.

Appendices

Appendix 13.1: Financial Reporting Standard 5

Paragraph 14 of FRS 5 states:

> "… a reporting entity's financial statements should report the *substance* [author's italics] of transactions into which it has entered. In determining the substance of a transaction, all its aspects and implications should be identified and greater weight given to those more likely to have a commercial effect in practice."

> (FRS 5, Accounting Standards Board, May 1994)

Paragraph 21 states:

> "… where a transaction involving a previously recognised asset results in no significant change in (a) the entity's rights or other access to benefits relating to that asset, or (b) its exposure to the risks inherent in those benefits; [then] the entire asset should continue to be recognised. In particular, this will be the case for any transaction that is in substance a financing of a previously recognised asset…"

> (FRS 5, Accounting Standards Board, May 1994)

Paragraph 184 refers specifically to repo and states:

> "In a straightforward case, the substance of a sale and repurchase agreement will be that of a secured loan – i.e., the seller will retain all significant rights to benefits relating to the original asset and all significant exposure to the risks inherent in those benefits and will have a liability to the buyer for the *whole* [author's italics] of the proceeds received… The seller should account for this type of arrangement by showing the original asset on its balance sheet together with a liability for the amounts received from the buyer."

> (FRS 5, Accounting Standards Board, May 1994)

Selected bibliography and references

Financial Services Act (1986), Schedule I, Part III

Financial Services Authority, *Guide to Banking Supervisory Policy*, FSA, 1996

Financial Services Authority, *London Code of Conduct*, FSA, June 1999

Securities and Futures Authority, *Rulebook,* 1991

Stanschus, C., Clarke, M., "Credit, collateral, capital", *RISK*, August 2001

14 Legal and Documentation Issues

The legal treatment of repo differs across jurisdictions. Therefore it is not possible to offer anything other than an introductory account in this book. Readers who wish greater detail relevant to the particular area they are operating in will need to consult with local capital markets lawyers. The aim of this chapter is to describe the legal framework for repo, as applicable under English law, and the key points that arise. We also discuss the BMA/ISMA Global Master Repurchase Agreement, the standard documentation adopted for classic repo and, from September 2000, for sell/buy-backs.[1]

14.1 Legal treatment

14.1.1 *Introduction*

From our discussion in Chapter 1 we know that the legal definition of repo is the principal factor in its identity as a capital market instrument. We have been at pains to suggest that while repo is, and should be viewed as, a loan of cash against security, it is also important to remember the legal definition as a sale and simultaneous repurchase of an asset between two counterparties. Viewed in this way, the legal treatment of repo becomes very important, because it describes the procedures to be followed in the event of default.

Legal jurisdictions elect to treat repo in one of two ways, either passing legislation that is designed specifically to deal with repo or leaving the legal issues associated with repo to fall under general capital markets legislation. An example of the former treatment occurs in France, while the UK treatment is an example of the latter approach. The UK approach can lead to difficulties in interpretation compared to the more traditional activities of outright sales and purchases, and lending and borrowing; generally, however, the introduction of the open gilt repo market has been trouble-free with regard to legal treatment. This reflects partly on the use of the standard GMRA documentation from the outset. Sell/buy-back transactions are, by their definition, more straightforward instruments in terms of their legal treatment, being defined as actual sales and purchases, however they are rare in bond repo in the UK market.

14.1.2 *Definition*

In legal terms a repo is a sale of assets, whether bonds or equities, from one party to another, entered into in conjunction with a simultaneous agreement by the seller to purchase back the assets at a specified later date. A sell/buy-back is defined in much the same way. As a repo is a sale of securities from one party to another, the transaction is defined as a contractual agreement, and subject to the legal obligations stated under contract law. For a contract to be legally enforceable it must be accepted by both parties as a legally binding document, and the transaction must be executed under agreed terms such as the term of the contract and

---

1   The original PSA/GMRA was updated in September 2000, and following a name change is now known as the TBMA/ISMA GMRA.

the price of the goods sold. The terms must be unambiguous and, to the best of both parties' knowledge, complete. As with the vast majority of capital market transactions (especially in the OTC market), there is no requirement that the contract must be in writing: a verbal agreement to undertake the transaction constitutes a conclusion of the contract, which is legally binding on both parties. This allows deals to be conducted over the telephone, which are then confirmed in writing by documents such as contract notes, shortly after the trade is agreed.[2] This is the case in the money markets generally, and not only in repo and sell/buy-back trading.

The terms stipulated in the contract are variable and specific terms, applicable to a particular trade only and not any other, may be inserted into the contract on agreement of both parties. After the trade is concluded, confirmation in writing is sent out by one or both parties; the best example of this is the *contract note* sent out by stockbrokers confirming a retail investor bargain or share deal. In, for instance, gilt repo trading this confirmation is sent out electronically by both counterparties, and must be agreed before stock and cash can be transferred across.

14.1.3 *Differentiating repo from collateralised loans*

Early in this book we emphasised that repo should be viewed as a secured loan for the purposes of analysis, or when considering the motivations of parties for entering into them as trades. We now want to reverse this, and consider the legal definition.[3] An important distinction in repo, compared to secured loans, is that legal title of the securities transferred passes to the buyer. This confers a greater degree of protection to the cash lender because in the event of default or insolvency, the buyer is in possession of the security and can use this to make good the potential loss of principal. In a secured loan, there would be a period of time when it may have to join the queue of general creditors, and there would be some time before the security could be sold off to cover losses. In such circumstances there is also a chance that the assets may not be realisable. In defining repo therefore it is key that, in its legal treatment, the transaction is indeed viewed as an outright sale of assets in return for the cash proceeds, and not as a loan of cash against assets pledged as security for the loan. The risk that repo is treated as a secured loan and not an outright sale is known as *recharacterisation* risk.

In the event of recharactersiation, the repo buyer may be required to hand over the security collateral to the counterparty's administrator or liquidator, and then enter into a process of recovering the losses, or it may be prevented by the administrator or the courts from selling the securities in the market, on the basis that it does not possess the required level of ownership to sell them. The risk is increased because as a transaction the tax and accounting authorities (and not least the parties to the trade) consider its underlying economics, which is as a secured loan, and not its legal status. For market participants it is vital that this potential ambiguity does not exist with regard to its legal treatment. The legal documentation describing repo trades must therefore always refer only to the legal definition applied to them and not the underlying economics that are discussed in other contexts. In some jurisdictions there may be some risk of recharactersiation because of the language used by

---

2   The binding nature of a contract concluded over the telephone is the primary reason why bank dealing desks record all telephone conversations – to resolve queries in the event of dispute. This doesn't mean that there is someone listening in to your call (!), just that records are available that may be checked against in the event of a dispute.

3   I know: Make up your mind!

market participants themselves when describing repo, and which has been used consistently in this book; for example, we have referred to *security* or *collateral* being passed over, and the payment of repo *interest* on the maturity date of the trade. This implies a secured loan. The origin of the term "repo", from "sale and repurchase", also might be taken to mean that the stock must be held by the buyer and this same stock bought back by the seller, which implies that the buyer does not have full ownership and cannot sell them in the open market. This is why legal agreements such as the GMRA and the Gilt Repo Agreement refer to the repurchase of *equivalent* securities, and we will look at this later in the chapter.

Notwithstanding the importance of documenting the legal definition carefully, the courts may recharacterise a repo trade under special conditions; for example, if they decide that the real motivation behind the trade was not as documented, and the transaction was entered into to cover other activity, or if the economic impact of the trade is not in line with the description given to it by the parties themselves.

14.1.4 *Legal authority of counterparties*

In a famous case, the supreme legal authority in the UK, the House of Lords, ruled that a number of local authorities were not authorised to conduct interest-rate swap transactions, and that therefore they were not liable to the losses they had incurred on these trades. This ruling mean that the swap counterparties, the market-making banks, had to cover the losses themselves.[4] The legal term for this occurrence is *capacity*, the power of a party to enter into a particular transaction, and there is a risk for repo market-makers that a transaction may be deemed to be outside the authority of one of the parties, and hence ruled null-and-void.

There is slightly less risk in this regard for a repo counterparty, principally because of the collateral held by the buyer; however, if the trade is ruled void, the buyer may be required by the courts to return the collateral. To minimise this risk, a bank can scrutinise the legal and constitutional documents of the counterparty, which describe the activities it undertakes, although in general terms. The documentation of the counterparty's regulator may also be relevant; for example, the activities of UK building societies (known as *thrifts* or Savings & Loan institutions in the US) are proscribed by the Building Societies Commission.[5] Banks dealing with counterparties that fall under other company legislation, such as foreign corporates, will need to scrutinise the relevant legal documentation for those counterparties.

14.2 The Global Master Repurchase Agreement

The development of the repo market in the US and across Europe, and subsequently globally, has been accompanied by the development of legal documentation to describe the transaction. Initially a bank compiled its own form of legal agreement and this was put in place between itself and each counterparty. Hence each agreement would be tailored to the requirements of the originating bank, and they differed from agreements drawn up by other

---

[4]   The actual case brought to court involved the London Borough of Hammersmith and Fulham, in 1987, although the final ruling was not until 1991. There were a number of other local authorities involved, and a number of banks, including Chemical Bank. From his limited knowledge of Company Law, the author remembers that if a transaction is outside the power of an entity, it is *ultra vires* and may not therefore be enforceable.

[5]   The Building Societies Commission was merged into the new "super regulator", the Financial Services Authority, under parliamentary legislation that was finalised in 2001 (the Financial Services Act (2001) referred to in the market as "N2").

banks. This process was labour-intensive and expensive in terms of legal fees and staff time, and repo participants sought to develop market standard documentation that could be implemented with little delay and amendments. This led to the Global Master Repurchase Agreement or GMRA, which we discuss in this section.

The GMRA as updated in September 2000 is reproduced in Appendix A, at the back of this book, with the kind permission of the Bond Markets Association and the International Securities Market Association.

14.2.1 *Origins*

The Public Securities Association (PSA; subsequently renamed the Bond Market Association) is a US-based body that acts as a trade association and supervisory body for the US domestic bond market. It developed a market standard documentation for repo in the US domestic market, introduced in February 1986. In the early 1990s a committee acting jointly in the name of the PSA and the International Securities Market Association (ISMA), used the PSA's domestic repo agreement as the basis of the new international repo legal agreement, the GMRA. This is the market standard repo document used as the legal basis for repo in non-US dollar markets, and was introduced in November 1992. It was revised in November 1995 and updated again in September 2000. The updates have included various new treatments, include UK gilts, buy–sell transactions and equities.

The GMRA is written under English law but can be applied to international and domestic markets across jurisdictions. Following its introduction it has been adopted as the repo legal agreement across Europe, Asia and South America.

14.2.2 *Key features*

The GMRA covers transactions between parties and includes repo, buy/sell-back and agency trades, and has recently been adapted for securities paying net coupons, as well as for equities.

The key features of the agreement are that:

- repo trades are structured as outright sales and repurchases;
- full ownership is conferred of securities transferred;
- there is an obligation to return "equivalent" securities;
- there is provision for initial and variation margin;
- coupon is paid over to the repo seller at the time of payment;
- legal title to collateral is confirmed in the event of default.

As well as enabling market participants to enter into repo trading in quicker time and at lower expense, the main advantages of the GMRA are:

- its allowance for close-out and netting is capital efficient for CAD purposes;
- it specifies action in the event of default;
- its rules on margining;
- its market acceptance means that new entrants to repo trading can sign up to it in the knowledge that it represents the market's view on fairness and convenience;
- it reduces translation risk in the courts.

Another advantage of the GMRA is its structure, in the form of a standard legal agreement that can be instantly entered into between two counterparties. Its provisions can be applied to any type of classic repo, while the various annexes added to it in the years since it was introduced illustrate how it can be adapted for different markets with relative ease. After an entity has signed the agreement between itself and its prospective counterparty, there is no requirement for any other legal documentation. Confirmations are exchanged between the parties immediately after each transaction, but this is the norm in virtually all capital market transactions.

The GMRA also is written in very careful legal terms. For example, to reduce recharacter-tersiation risk it speaks of the obligation of the buyer in the closing leg to return *equivalent* securities, which backs up the legal definition of repo as a true sale of the securities.[6] As originally drafted the agreement described only gross-paying securities, thus omitting most obviously equity instruments, and was not designed for use with US Treasury securities. Since its original inception it has been amended to cover net-paying securities and equities, as well as sell/buy-back transactions, and has also been used by parties to US Treasury repo trading. A list of the annexes to the GMRA is given in Appendix B, at the back of the book.

14.2.3 *Margin provision*

The description of initial margin and variation margin[7] in repo trades is an important aspect of the GMRA. The treatment of margin is contained in paragraph 4 of the agreement. As we noted in Chapter 5, to protect the repo buyer against a fall in the value of the collateral supplied, the seller will provide securities over the value of the loan amount as initial margin, and falls in the value of the collateral will result in additional margin being transferred. Equally, a rise in collateral value will result in part of the collateral being returned to the seller. The GMRA makes provision for this adjustment feature to take place daily.

In the GMRA language the initial margin is known as the *margin ratio*. A repo trade has a *transaction exposure* which is the current value of the securities as a percentage of the purchase price at the opening leg; a negative difference compared to the margin ratio is an exposure for the buyer. The aggregate exposure for all of a counterparty's trades is then calculated, and if there is a shortfall for the buyer or a surplus for the seller, the relevant party may call for variation margin or, in the words of the GMRA, a *margin transfer*. Generally, only material amounts are called for. If a seller is required to pass margin to the buyer, this is in the form of additional collateral of acceptable credit quality, known as *equivalent margin securities*, or as cash. If the latter is taken, in effect the seller is reducing the amount of the loan. As in the opening leg, a margin transfer from the seller is an outright sale, so that complete ownership

---

6   The wording is that the buyer returns "securities of the same issuer, forming part of the same issue and of an identical type, a nominal value, description and amount as the purchased securities". It also explicitly refers to the fact that the use of the term "repurchase" should not be indicated to imply anything other than a legal transfer of title. The wording in paragraph 6 states "Notwithstanding the use of expressions such as Repurchase Date, Repurchase Price, margin, ..., which are used to reflect terminology used in the market for transactions... all rights, title and interest in and to securities and money transferred or paid under this Agreement shall pass to the transferee upon transfer or payment, the obligation of the party receiving purchased securities or margin securities being an obligation to transfer Equivalent Securities...".
7   Some writers use the term "margin" to refer to both types, while some participants use the term "daily margin" instead of variation margin. In the US market, and increasingly across global markets, the term "haircut" is used instead of margin.

of the securities is transferred to the buyer. If a buyer is required to return a portion of the collateral, it is required to transfer equivalent securities.

In some markets margin calls are handled by what is known as *close out and repricing* or simply *repricing*. Here the original transaction is terminated, and a new trade, at the initial margin level, entered into for maturity to the original expiry date. The cash flows for the two trades are netted out, and this net difference only transferred across. Repricing is detailed in paragraph 4(j) of the GMRA.

14.2.4 *Manufactured dividends*

Paragraph 5 of the GMRA refers to *income payments*, which arise when the term of a repo runs over the collateral security's coupon date. Securities transferred as collateral are held by the buyer, so that a coupon payment would be made to the buyer. In practice securities are held electronically as book-entries in clearing systems such as CREST/CGO or Clearstream International, so that the coupon payment will be made into the account of the buyer (or an appropriate nominee or *custody* account). However the seller retains the right to this coupon, and under the GMRA the buyer must pay the exact coupon amount to the seller on the same day. The market refers to such a payment as a *manufactured dividend*, as opposed to the actual dividend that would have been received by the seller if there had been no repo.

14.2.5 *Collateral substitution*

Paragraph 8 of the GMRA describes the right of sellers to ask for the return of securities transferred in a repo before the expiry date, with the agreement of the buyer, and their substitution by securities of identical credit quality and value. This right may be exercised for a number of reasons; for example, the seller may have really sold the stock in the market, and requires them in order to make good delivery; or, the stock may have gone special and the seller could repo them out at a more advantageous repo rate in another transaction.

The market refers to this as substitution, but to reduce recharactersiation risk the term itself is not used outside the heading of paragraph 8 . This is because a court may view the right of substitution as implying that the buyer must hang on to the securities during the term of the trade, suggesting that there has not been full transfer. Instead the GMRA states that substitution is effected by terminating the original trade on the day the securities are called, and instituting a new trade under the same original terms, with different collateral transferred.

14.2.6 *Tri-party repo*

Generally parties entering into tri-party repo will sign the GMRA between the two main parties and a separate legal service agreement between themselves and the third-party provider. Although the parties will therefore have legal obligations under the service agreement, the terms of the GMRA still apply.

14.2.7 *GMRA annexes*

Since its introduction in 1992 a number of annexes have been added to the standard GMRA. These have included further generic treatments as well as more market-specific ones. A full list of the annexes as at October 2000 is given in Appendix B, at the back of the book. We consider three of the annexes here.

Gilt Repo Legal Agreement

The Gilt Repo Legal Agreement is an amended version of the revised (November 1995) PSA/ISMA agreement for the UK gilt repo market. The PSA/ISMA agreement was extended by supplemental terms and conditions for gilt repo forming Part 2 to Annex I of the PSA/ISMA agreement and modified by a side letter in connection with the upgrade to the Central Gilts Office (now CREST) service in November 1997. The PSA/ISMA is now referred to as the BMA/ISMA reflecting the name change to the Bond Market Association.

Participants in the gilt repo market are recommended to adopt the Gilt Repo Legal Agreement for gilt repo transactions, as set out in the Gilt Repo Code of Best Practice. The Code was issued by the Bank of England. Use of the legal agreement is subject to legal confirmation of its effectiveness, if the specific circumstances in which it is to be used are not straightforward. The agreement is recommended as the umbrella documentation for all types of repo, including buy/sell-back.

The agreement provides for the following:

- the absolute transfer of title to securities;

- daily marking-to-market;

- appropriate initial margin and for maintenance of margin whenever the mark-to-market reveals a material change of value;

- clear events of default and the consequential rights and obligations of the counterparties;

- in the event of default, full setoff of claims between counterparties;

- clarification of rights of parties regarding substitution of collateral and the treatment of coupon payments;

These are essentially the provisions as contained in the BMA/ISMA agreement.

The agreement is governed by English law, as is the GMRA itself.

Buy/sell-back annexe

Notwithstanding that we have been referring to it throughout this book as *sell/buy-back*, the GMRA annexe is known as the buy/sell-back annexe. From Chapter 5 we know that previously the key distinctions between classic repo and buy/sell-back were that the latter was undocumented, and had no provision for margin. Another difference was that there was no arrangement for manufactured dividend; instead, the coupon was incorporated into the sell-back price. These factors increased the risk exposure for the cash lender compared to a classic repo, and also meant that buy/sell-backs carried a higher capital charge. However, for a number of reasons, including market tradition and familiarity, and the fact that they can be handled by fairly unsophisticated settlement systems, buy/sell-backs have been preferred to classic repo in certain markets, and for this reason an annexe covering them was added to the GMRA in 1995, as Annexe III. This removed one of the key weaknesses from buy/sell-backs, namely that they were not covered by a legal agreement.

Annexe III adapts a number of provisions from the standard GMRA to make them applicable to buy/sell-backs. These include the provisions for margin and close-out. The principle adaptation to the buy/sell-back itself is that an explicit repo rate is now quoted, unlike previously when the repo rate was implied and factored into the forward buy-back price.

Equity repo annexe

Annexe IV of the GMRA deals with the special conditions that arise in equity repo, reflecting the characteristics of the equity instrument. These include provisions relating to:

- treatment of corporate actions such as rights issues, capital restructuring, and exercise of voting rights in the event of a merger or acquisition situation;
- dividend payments of equities, which in the UK are paid net of basic rate tax;
- taxation treatment of equities.

The underlying logic for legal treatment of equity repo follows that of bond repo: there is a need to reflect that economic benefits of stock ownership remain with the seller, but recharactersiation risk must be minimised, if not removed altogether. With equities though the matter is complicated by the circumstances arising from corporate events. The annexe recognises that, full ownership having been transferred, the buyer is entitled to sell the equities during the term of the repo, and is obliged to return only equivalent securities. The annexe attempts to resolve the potential conflict by stating that the buyer must inform the seller whenever it receives notice of a corporate action or event. The seller then may, if it wishes, terminate the repo ahead of the maturity date and the specific corporate event. It can then exercise its view on the corporate action as it wishes. If the seller elects not to wind up the repo, where a vote is required (for instance, in an acquisition) the seller notifies the buyer of the form in which it wishes to receive the securities on trade termination, thereby adjusting the definition of "equivalent securities". Specific voting instructions may be passed by the seller to the buyer, and under the GMRA the buyer is in fact obliged to exercise its voting rights under the instructions supplied. In addition, in a rights issue the seller is required to supply sufficient funds to the buyer in order for it to purchase the extra shares. Where no vote is required, such as a bonus or scrip issue, the definition of equivalent securities is automatically adjusted such that the buyer delivers the correct number of shares in their new form.

If a dividend payment is received during the repo term, the seller must substitute the stock for one with no forthcoming dividend date. Alternatively it may close-out the repo ahead of the dividend date. If no action is taken and the buyer receives the dividend, it must pass over all sums received, in addition to any amount that is recoverable for tax by the seller.

Equity repo is considered briefly in Chapter 16.

15 Repo Netting and Electronic Trading

Repo netting is one of the most exciting developments in the repo markets in recent years, and is viewed as the way forward in both developed and emerging economies. In essence it has the potential to bring the liquidity and lack of counterparty risk associated with exchange-traded futures trading to repo. Taken together with the rise of electronic trading platforms, the market should benefit at all stages, from front-office trading, middle-office risk management and product control and back-office settlement and clearing. The benefits of a netting system that is taken up by a large part of the market were made apparent after the introduction by the Government Securities Clearance Corporation (GSCC) of a repo netting service in the US market; trading volumes were substantially increased and the product range was extended to a wider set of market participants. Liquidity in longer-dated repo trades also increased.

In this chapter we introduce the concept of repo netting and explain its benefits. We also consider the London Clearing House *RepoClear* system and consider the main issues in electronic trading.

15.1 Introduction to netting

15.1.1 *Definition*

Put simply *netting* is when a multiple set of obligations arising from outstanding loans and deposits between two counterparties are aggregated and offset against each other to produce one net figure owed by one counterparty to the other. As we've just described it, this is *bilateral* netting, and there is also *multilateral* netting of the type that we observe with a futures exchange clearing house, where a multiple number of parties are involved. Even bilateral netting brings with it a number of advantages to both parties, reducing administrative burden and improving efficiency. However significant economic benefits are derived from multilateral netting, including reduction of capital requirements and credit risk, and the freeing-up of bilateral lending limits. We will consider these again later.

Netting may be undertaken in different ways. The most common method is known as *close out* netting, which comes into effect on default or insolvency of one of the counterparties. When this occurs, all transactions between the two parties are closed out and netted, to be replaced by a single net payment obligation. Another method is netting by *novation*, which is when the sum of obligations involving gross amounts is replaced by an aggregate figure of a net amount. The third main method is *settlement* netting, which is settlement of all transactions on a net basis. When applied to repo trading via a central clearing counterparty, the clearing house becomes the counterparty to all market participants, and netting can then be applied to a banking entity's entire banking book (assuming everyone else it deals with is also a member of the clearing house), and the bank will have one net figure for all its repo trading exposures.

15.1.2 *Advantages of repo netting*

Repo markets across many markets are usually large and liquid, with a wide variety of market participants, and for this reason, although centralised netting presents obvious advantages to everyone in the market, it will be some time before it is the norm. The great majority of repo trades are bilateral contracts, and although capital requirements are not necessarily onerous, this may change in some cases under Basel II. The custom is for trades to be OTC between counterparties, either directly or via a broker. Hence a repo market-maker will have a large number of bilateral exposures with a large number of counterparties, requiring capital allocation and using up credit lines, and will also have high brokerage costs. The capital and credit line issues are increased with longer-maturity trades. The advantages of centralised clearing and netting include the following.

Balance sheet netting

As repo is an on-balance-sheet instrument, its use is sometimes restricted among large-scale users due to return on capital and capital adequacy considerations. Conducting repo via a centralised clearing and netting system means that banks can net their trading for balance sheet reporting purposes. Using balance-sheet netting, the aggregate assets and liabilities arising from repo and reverse repo trading can be offset on the balance sheet. This enables banks to enter into more transactions and also longer-term transactions. Even bilateral balance-sheet netting carries with it advantages, as aggregate assets and liabilities with a single counterparty are netted out.

Freeing-up bilateral credit lines and reducing credit risk

Following exactly the same principle with exchange-traded futures, repo trading via a centralised clearing system means that an existing bilateral relationship is removed, and instead there is a relationship between the repo bank and the clearing house. This removes the repo exposure to the counterparty bank, which means that the existing credit line can now be used for other trading, such as unsecured lending, additional repo, or other business such as structured financial products. The repo bank also has one repo exposure, to the clearing system,[1] and has reduced its credit risk exposure to market counterparties.

Centralised variation margin administration

Clearing repo trades through a centralised system means that the calculations are required for one counterparty only, which produces efficiency gains in margin transfers, settlement and administration. The clearing house will mark-to-market all repo positions each day, calculate the margin required and collect or pay the variation margin required. This also reduces the accounting workload for each member firm, including accounting for repo interest and margin interest. Another benefit is that member firms will now all be treated on a common basis for initial and variation margin calculations.

Settlement netting

In standard classic repo there is a movement of stock against cash between two counterparties at the start and end of the trade. In centralised netting the clearing house nets all settlements

---

[1] Again, we assume that all the bank's trading counterparties are also members of the centralised clearing system. This is not likely to be the case for some time, so bilateral repo exposures will remain. Also, there may be some intra-day exposure until both parties have settled with the clearing house, and if the trade is too late for reporting to the clearing system it will also remain a bilateral trade.

that are due to or from each member firm. This reduces dramatically the number of settlements taking place in national or international clearing systems such as CREST/CGO and
Clearstream, and reduces the operations workload at each member firm. As an example, a
normal trade between Banks A, B and C, where A has repoed bonds to B, which then lends or
repos them to C, will results in bilateral movements involving all three banks. Under centralised netting Bank B will not have to make any deliveries. This increases settlement efficiency
and also reduces the potential for failed trades in the market.

Member firms will have a single net long or net short position each day for each stock and
for each clearing system. This has been observed in the US with the GSCC system, where net
settlements has resulted in a big reduction in the number of trades actually settling. This has
produced efficiency gains for banks as the administrative burden has been reduced.

A further benefit is real-time reporting of settlement notification.

Same-day margin movement
Member firms are guaranteed that margin collateral will be moved on the same day.

Coupon pass-back
The central clearing system will pay out coupons on selling parties' securities, removing
manufactured dividend responsibilities of member firms.

Operational risk
This follows on from settlement efficiency gains. The reduced settlement activity resulting
from netting also reduces operational risk, because the activity level of bilateral negotiations
and operational issues is reduced. A clearing house will use standard legal documentation
and terminology for repo trading with all counterparties, and will undertake the marking-to-
market and variation margining. This also serves to reduce potential operational risk exposure as the level of bilateral price checking and margin movements is reduced.

Lower operational costs
All of the above, combined with standardised processes and procedures, a lower level of
settlements and failed trades, elimination of manual marking-to-market and automated
coupon payments will result in lower operational cost.

Anonymous trading
By definition, normal trading and brokered trading, which operates on a name give-up basis,
means that each party to a repo trade is identified.[2] Centralised netting systems allow the
potential of dealing anonymously. For example, the London-based RepoClear, while it is not
a trading system, allows third-party automated trading systems to offer anonymous interbank trading if both parties clear through it, as they send trade directly to RepoClear. In this
case, neither the automated trading system or RepoClear would reveal each counterparty's
identity to the other.

15.2 Benefits of cross-product trading

Centralised clearing systems such as RepoClear offer other products besides repo. The
London Clearing House (LCH), which runs RepoClear, also clears the futures and options

---

[2]   Obviously dealing direct means one knows who one is talking to! Trading via a broker, once you have
      agreed to the trade, names are passed so that each party can check credit limits. This still applies in
      electronic screen-based trading.

traded on LIFFE. The LCH also operates SwapClear, the interest-rate swaps netting system. This means that margin offsets with LIFFE futures and SwapClear products may be offered to member firms that deal across all three markets. This frees up collateral that can then be used elsewhere, or cash that can be used to fund other positions.

15.2.1 *Settlement netting and novation*

Centralised clearing systems accommodate the two main methods used in netting. Under settlement netting, the clearing house, which acts as the counterparty to all member firms, nets the aggregate trade exposures so that each member firm has one net long or short position for each security. That is, the net security and net cash position is calculated for each firm for the start and end legs of every repo transaction. This net position is settled in the member firm's clearing system or *depositary*, so in the UK this would be CREST/CGO, in the US it is the Fed Wire system, and in Clearnet it is SICOVAM.

Novation netting refers to the replacement of a set of exposures with another set. It describes the process that is operated when a derivatives exchange clearing house acts as the counterparty to all exchange traders. Under a centralised clearing system this means that repo and reverse trades are "novated" to the clearing house, which takes on the other side to every trade. In other words, the clearing house comes in between two counterparties in a bilateral contract and acts as the other side to each party. Another term for novation is *registration* (that is, every trade is "registered" with the clearing house). The same process allows multilateral netting to take place. In a multilateral context, all repo trades are still covered by standard documentation such as the GMRA, but they also fall under the clearing house standard legal documentation.

15.2.2 *Electronic trade capture*

All centralised clearing and netting systems adopt a trade confirmation or trade matching procedure for member firms to match trade details. This may be via a trade matching system, such as TRAX, into which trade details are entered by member firms, or via an inter-dealer broker (IDB). Trade capture via an IDB may be via a screen-based electronic trading system. Another method is via an Automated Trading System such as Reuters dealing system or SWIFT. For instance, RepoClear uses the TRAX system, while the GSCC uses a real-time proprietary system that matches repo trades.

> ### Government Securities Clearing Corporation (GSCC)
> The GSCC introduced a centralised netting system for repo trading in 1995. It had introduced previously a central system for cash bond trading in 1989. It enables member firms to benefit from automated trade matching, netting and central settlement in US Treasury securities. During 2000 it cleared $216.6 trillion nominal of trading, and repo transactions comprised approximately $132 trillion.[3]
>
> The GSCC clears repo in Treasury securities including Bills and Strips, and in government and federal agency conventional bonds. Trade matching is via the GSCC's own confirmation system, and the depositary used is the Fed Wire. This enables same-day settlement.

---

[3]   Source: GSCC

Clearnet

Clearnet is the centralised clearing and netting system operated by the Paris bourse. It has been recognised as the central clearing system for the French market since June 1999, and with the creation of the Euronext exchange in 2000 it extended its clearing services to the Amsterdam and Brussels exchanges in March 2001. Clearing services are available for exchange-listed equities and bonds, as well as OTC-traded euro-denominated government bonds and repo. Clearnet is a wholly-owned subsidiary of Euronext, although member firms of this Exchange are permitted to become shareholders. The international depositary Euroclear has an option to purchase a 20% shareholding.

Settlement and netting services for government bond repo has been available from November 1998. The development of a centralised clearing service was driven by four factors:

- the increasing costs associated with collateral and custody services, and the increasing need for the reduced counterparty risk associated with a central clearing house;
- the belief that counterparty risks associated with OTC market trading were increasing;
- the adoption of "blind brokerage" trading platforms, with which no "name give-up" is involved, which necessitated the use of a central counterparty;
- new pan-European trading opportunities associated with the introduction of the euro.

The Clearnet service is similar in concept to RepoClear as introduced by the London Clearing House. The membership involved in bonds and repo clearing are mainly primary dealers in euro government debt, and as at 1 February 2002 comprised 30 such banks and securities houses.

Services

Repo trades on Clearnet are settled on the following principles:

- novation; that is, the substitution of Clearnet as counterparty to the contract;
- guarantee of the cleared position, so that Clearnet ensures final settlement;
- multilateral netting of participants' positions;
- settlement on a net basis.

The same principles also apply to bond clearing.

Products

Cash market bonds and repo for French and German government euro-denominated bonds, as well as cash market French mortgage bonds ("obligations foncières"). In 2002 the service will be extended to Belgian, Dutch and Portuguese government bonds.

Trade sources

The transactions settled by Clearnet are provided by a number of trade capture mechanisms and electronic trading platforms, including Euro-MTS, E-Speed, MTS France, BrokerTec and Prominnofi.

Risk management

To manage the risk exposure in the event that a member firm defaults and is unable to honour its contractual obligations, Clearnet as guarantor of trades operates a risk-management system that includes:

- daily margin calls and margin maintenance;
- liquidation of defaulting member's positions, and the use of margin deposits to settle liabilities;
- the availability of a clearing fund to cover residual risk not satisfied by the defaulting firm's margin deposits.

The margin system is a key element of the risk-management mechanism at Clearnet. It includes initial margin, the calculation for which is a function of the class and maturity of each security, and variation margin which is the sum of changes in the value of the individual positions from one business day to the next. This system (which is common across exchange clearing houses) provides an element of safety for Clearnet because it will only be exposed (in terms of market price risk) to changes in market values from the previous day. The netting process means that for bond and repo trades, securities are delivered on a net basis.

Member firms must comply with a set of regulatory and financial criteria. These include the stipulation that members must be a bank or authorised investment institution. Individual clearing members must have a minimum capital adequacy of €30 million and a minimum credit rating of A. General clearing members must have a minimum capital balance of €150 million and a minimum A rating.

Transaction overview

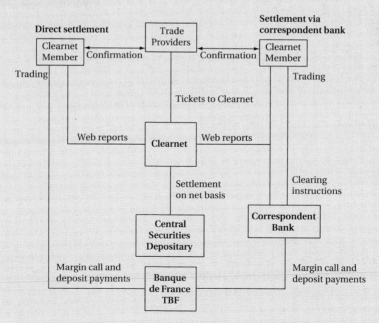

Figure 15.1: Transaction processing in Clearnet. Source: Clearnet.

15.3 Close-out netting under the GMRA

Netting, specifically what is termed *close-out netting*, is a principal means of reducing counterparty risk. In repo it refers to the process of bringing forward all outstanding obligations with a counterparty in the event of default, and offsetting the aggregate set of obligations between the two parties, or *netting out* the outstanding positions. This has two advantages for the counterparty to the defaulting firm. First, by bringing forward all transactions, the risk of adverse movements in the value of collateral is reduced, after there has been confirmation that the counterparty will not be able to fulfil its obligations. The process of bringing forward trades is known as *acceleration*. The netting process (close-out), by combining all individual outstanding claims into one figure, is designed to protect against claims on individual assets of the firm by other creditors. Additional benefits are available if the close-out and netting process is documented, as a net figure can be reported as such for capital adequacy purposes, thus reducing capital allocation charges.

The GMRA treats close-out and netting in paragraph 10. It carries a list of events which, if they occur, constitute an event of default (this includes insolvency of the counterparty). If any of these events take place, the non-defaulting party may serve a notice of default on the counterparty, and upon this, each outstanding repo trade is deemed as maturing that day. The exposures are set-off to produce one net exposure, and the party owing the greater amount is required to pay this.

This is another benefit of treating all repo trades under the GMRA.

Example 15.1:   Electronic trading

Repo is a natural product for incorporation into an automated electronic trading system. It is however, more complex than say, foreign exchange trading in this context, because it has two legs, an accrued interest aspect and collateral consideration. A number of systems have been introduced in North America and Europe, and developments continue, although the majority of trades continue to be conducted on the telephone between participants directly, or via phone brokers – although live prices are frequently quoted on a vendor screen. Two systems in use in Europe are BrokerTec and EuroMTS. BrokerTec is designed to handle a repo trade from inception to settlement; for example, it allows the collateral on a GC trade to be allocated electronically via the system. The majority of trades on both systems is short-term maturity (overnight to one week), with an average of over 50% of all trades being this maturity on BrokerTec (*RISK*, 2001).

15.4 RepoClear

In this section we describe the RepoClear centralised repo netting and clearing system, developed by the London Clearing House (LCH). It is a multilateral centralised clearing and netting system, which began operation in August 1999. It handles both cash bond trading and bond repo trading. Its current and anticipated product range is listed in Appendix 15.1.

RepoClear was developed by the LCH in conjunction with its member firms and the main repo market-making banks in Europe. Following its introduction, it was joined by the European Securities Clearing Corporation (ESCC), which had previously been attempting to introduce a separate netting system. The ESCC system had been a joint enterprise between the GSCC and Euroclear.

15.4.1 *Background*

RepoClear provides for settlement of cash bond and bond repo trades to be settled in their relevant depositaries; for example, for Pfandbriefe securities this is Clearstream AG, Eurobonds are settled via Euroclear and Clearstream International and Belgian government bond repo via Banque Nationale de Belgique. For a repo trade to be eligible for handling via Repo-Clear, both counterparties must be member firms and registered as RepoClear dealers (RD). Before applying for RD status a bank must fulfil the following requirements:

- it must be a member of the LCH, or have a clearing arrangement with a member of lCH, and must have a minimum of £250 million capital base;
- it must be a wholesale market participant, fore example, a registered primary dealer (market maker) in a European government bond market;
- its external foreign currency debt must have an investment grade credit rating.

Repo trading via RepoClear results in the LCH being the counterparty to every trade. This eliminates counterparty default risk for all member firms' repo dealing. To facilitate this, LCH ensures that it holds sufficient margin to cover the maximum potential exposure that would arise should a member firm default and be unable to cover its outstanding positions. This margin is provided by member firms on a daily basis, and the amount required from each firm is dependent on the extent of its trading. This follows the procedure used by derivatives exchange clearing houses. In the event that margin held is insufficient, the LCH itself maintains an extensive capital backing. The principal cover is the Default Fund, which stands at £350 million. This is provided in cash by member firms, again as a variable contribution dependant on the amount of business each firm clears.

Before beginning to use RepoClear, a bank will need to ensure that its internal infrastructure is adequate. This includes:

- a functioning TRAX or EuroMTS system, used to send trade matching data to LCH;
- a settlement system able to accept the change of counterparty and able to reconcile its trades with the LCH netted positions;
- an ability to meet and account for margin calls;
- an adequate communications links so that it can send and receive RepoClear reporting and data.

The RepoClear member firm list (as at August 2001) is given in Appendix 15.2.

15.4.2 *Operation*

Trade data is fed to RepoClear via TRAX, EuroMTS or an automated trading system. On receipt of trade details, the system confirms that both counterparties are RepoClear members and also that the trade is in an acceptable underlying product. It then novates the trade and registers two repos, one with the original seller and one with the original buyer. Dealers may remain anonymous both pre- and post-trade.

All delivery obligations are netted for settlement the following business day. (The netting process takes place daily). LCH calculates the net amount of each bond that each member is due to deliver, and this takes into account the opening and closing legs of all repo trades, together with substitutions and any outstanding failed trades. The netting is run at 1500 hours for Belgian government bonds and 1600 hours for German government bonds (local times). Once netted amounts have been calculated, they are *shaped* to a maximum delivery size, which is currently €150 million. When LCH has determined the net deliveries, it notifies member firms of the details through the RepoClear reporting facility. This enables members to view trade data on screen, which they will need to do to reconcile netted deliveries with their original trades. To help with this all bonds are delivered at the original traded price. Delivery of instructions to the relevant national depositaries is via the member firms, although members can assign a Power of Attorney to LCH so that it can instruct the depositaries direct. Following the settlement netting cycle, if there are no securities delivery obligations, LCH will aggregate all net cash delivery obligations into a single amount for each market, and this is paid through the relevant clearing system. Coupon payments are netted along with the normal cash flows so that there is one cash flow each day. As RepoClear deals currently only with euro-denominated products, there is only one cash flow. A different currency would have its own cash flow. Margin and settlement amounts are also netted.

The ability of LCH and RepoClear to act as the counterparty to all trades is facilitated by the margin system. If a member defaults, LCH will close out the defaulter's positions. The margin facility is described below.

Initial margin
Initial margin is taken to provide cover to LCH for movements in collateral price that may occur before it can close out a defaulting member's position. The position is the aggregate portfolio, calculated from data on all the party's buyers and sellers. Margin may be supplied as cash, bank guarantees such as a letter of credit, or approved government securities. Certain equities are also acceptable. If cash is supplied, LCH pays interest on the amount.

Variation margin
LCH undertakes marking-to-market for all open repo trades, including forward starting repos. Member firms with positive positions, that is, where the value of cash exceeds collateral deposits, must pay this amount to the LCH in cash. LCH then pays this amount to member firms on the opposite side who have negative positions against the LCH. This payment is also cash, and it is returned on termination of the repo.[4] Interest on cash margin amounts is paid or received at the EONIA rate. Cash is required for variation margin because of settlement systems requirements.

The variation margin calculation is based on the net present value (NPV) of members' repo positions at the close of each business day. The NPV is given by the value of the collateral minus the value of cash repoed against it. The change in today's NPV minus the previous day's NPV is the member's variation margin. If the initial margin level has been eaten into by a large amount in one day, LCH will make intra-day margin calls.

Delivery margin
The LCH also collects a delivery margin from member firms to cover the potential risk exposure in the following day's settlements.

---
[4]   In practice there will always be outstanding positions and so the variation margin process is continual, whether this is payment or receipt of cash.

Appendices

Appendix 15.1:   RepoClear product listing[5]

Cash bond and bond repo trading in:

- Austrian, Belgian, Dutch and German government bonds;
- Jumbo Pfandbriefe;
- International bonds (Eurobonds);
- Repo maturity from overnight to one year;
- Fixed rate repo.

Planned products:

- Italian government bonds;
- UK government bonds (Gilts) and DBV repo;
- Buy/sell-back (Italy only);
- Floating-rate repo including variable rate EONIA-linked repo;
- Open repo;
- Tri-party repo.

Appendix 15.2:   RepoClear member firms as at August 2001

ABN Amro Bank N.V.	KBC Bank N.V.
Artesia Banking Corporation N.V.	Lehman Brothers International
Bank of America	Merrill Lynch International
Barclays Capital	Mizuho International plc
Bear Stearns International Limited	Morgan Stanley & Co
BNP Paribas	Nomura International plc
Credit Suisse First Boston	Rabobank
Deutsche Bank AG	Refco Securities
Fortis Bank N.V.	Salomon Brothers International
Goldman Sachs International	Société Genérale
Helaba Bank	UBS Warburg
JPMorgan Chase Bank	Westdeutsche Landesbank Girozentrale

Selected bibliography and references

"Growing pains", *RISK*, August 2001

---

[5]   Source: LCH.

16 Equity Repo

As an investment and financing tool repo is well established in the bond markets, and has a long history in countries such as the US and Italy. Viewed as a secured loan, it is clear that repo can be as easily applied in other capital markets, most notably to that of equities. In this chapter we introduce the basic concepts in equity repo, look briefly at the market terminology in use in the London equity repo market, and also illustrate the types of trades possible using worked examples. The subject has not been widely researched to date, and the author apologies for the lack of a bibliography; hopefully this is an area that will attract more interest amongst writers and academics.

16.1 Introduction

Just as bond traders had long used repo to finance their positions, from the early 1990s equity market-makers began to use equity as collateral in repo trades, and also began to offer equity repo as an investment alternative to cash-rich investors. Prior to this market-makers had obtained stock from the stock borrowing and lending market. The equity repo market is now well established in the USA, UK and other European markets as well as in Japan, although its size is only a fraction of the bond repo market, reflecting the size of the underlying assets. One estimate put it in the region of $30–40 billion.[1] The introduction of equity repo is a logical development in the repo markets. Those market players running large equity positions, such as fund managers and equity market-makers (securities houses), can derive added value from their asset holdings by using them in repo; at the same time, as with bond repo, equity repo is a collateralised loan (investment) for other market players. The invariably lower quality of collateral used means that the repo rate is higher than investment-grade bond repo, which is attractive to certain classes of investors. Essentially then, participants in equity repo are seeking an efficient means by which to place securities or cash in the market, on a secured basis.

As well as the difference in asset class, there are some key institutional differences between equity repo and bond repo. Both the cash bond and bond repo markets are, to a certain extent, mature and well developed, and crucially both the underlying asset and the overlying repo are, in their own way, interest rate positions.[2] Financing in bond markets is carried out primarily using repo. In the equity arena though, the motivation behind repo may differ, and repo itself is one of a number of methods commonly used in equity financing. For the large investment banks though, equity repo is used to cover short positions and also to finance long positions, and this is exactly what occurs in bond repo. Market intermediation between the repo and stock-lending markets is also common, with banks buying securities, financing them through repo and then investing the cash, or borrowing the securities in the lending market and then repoing them out.

---

[1] Source: *RISK*, August 2001, page 89. Given the wide spread this is obviously a very rough estimate!

[2] Obviously this depends on the point of view of the particular market participant and the motivation for entering into the trade. Essentially though, holding bonds is an interest-rate trade, and likewise trading repo.

The market uses the term "equity repo" to describe various mechanisms for equity financing. The classic repo structure is the most common. A primary difference compared to bond repo is the uncertainty of cash flows connected with an equity-asset type. Classic repo requires a legal agreement and with the latest draft of the BMA/ISMA global repo agreement, this is now available. Sell/buy-backs are also used in equity repo. As with bond sell/buy-backs, as this structure does not allow for margin and marking-to-market, it is usually only used for short-term trades.

Equity prices display greater volatility and they are less liquid than government bonds, which immediately suggests that initial margins must be higher for equity repo.

Additionally counterparties must agree how corporate actions will affect trades between them; for instance, when there is a rights issue, how should this affect the seller's portfolio? In all developed market jurisdictions, equity dividends are paid net of withholding tax. The BMA/ISMA agreement now also describes net-paying securities.

In the UK, equity repo is fairly well developed and a liquid market exists for FTSE100 stocks. The market complemented the existing stock lending and borrowing market. Counterparties can deal via brokers, as in the bond repo market, and there are several brokers that provide a screen service to the market, including GarbanICAP and Tullet & Tokyo. The screen service at Tullets was established in 1994, and catered for sell/buy-backs. The two transactions in a sell/buy-back are entered by counterparties into their dealing systems simultaneously, creating a repo trade; repo interest and brokerage are built into the start and end dealing prices. In the US, repo has been adopted as a useful tool to finance equity positions because of the legal, tax and regulatory environment, and the difficulty in pledging equity assets. For this reason, the repo trade is often split into two different transactions, with each side executed with different counterparties.[3] For instance, a bank will enter into a stock loan versus cash trade with one counterparty, and then structure an equity repo against cash with a different counterparty. As equities can be pledged as collateral much more readily in Europe, this structure is rarer in that market. A typical equity repo trade in the London market is described in Example 16.1.

Example 16.1:   Equity repo transaction

An equity market-maker requires equities to act as collateral for a stock loan transaction it is entering into with fund manager client. Another market party is long of equities and wishes to enhance the income stream on this holding. The market maker enters into a repo with the party that is long equities and requires financing, and then uses these securities to post as collateral with the fund manager. If structured properly, the transaction can enhance the revenue stream for the market maker and its client. It is illustrated in Figure 16.1.

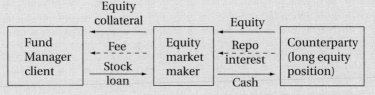

Figure 16.1: Generic equity repo trade.

---

[3]   The Total Return Swap described in Chapter 7 is also common in equity markets for this reason.

312   Part II: Institutional Treatment of Repo

One other key difference between equity repo and bond repo is the notion of a "general collateral" rate. Almost by definition each equity represents the unique features of its issuing corporate entity, and this makes virtually all equity repo deals specific repos. The concept of a general collateral does not therefore exist. The closest that the market comes to a GC rate is the rate bid by banks who are willing to take a blue-chip equity that is part of an index; for example, an S&P 500 or FTSE100 equity.

Financing trades are often carried out for baskets of equities and a repo will be undertaken with a basket of equities as collateral. If this is done for a tracker fund, for instance, and one of the constituents of the index that is being tracked falls out of the index, then the tracker fund will switch its current holding of that equity for its replacement. This necessitates the substitution of that equity in the repo as well.

Index stocks repo

Certain banks making a market in equity repo quote a rate applicable to a certain class of equity; for example, FTSE100 or CAC40 stocks. The uniform rate for all stocks in the index makes this the nearest equivalent to an equity "GC" rate. For example, BNP Paribas quotes a repo bid rate applicable to any FTSE100 security.

Example 16.2:   Equity repo: classic repo structure

Consider a classic repo using equity collateral. The structure will mirror that used in bond repo, but here we assume that none of the issues mentioned above arise during the course of the trade. An equity market-maker, Security House, wishes to finance a holding of 200,000 shares in a FTSE100 company, which are currently trading at a price of £6.00. It enters into a one-month (30 day) repo, at a rate of 5½%. The term of the trade does not run over a dividend date, and no initial margin is called for.

Hence the market value of the equity collateral will equal the value of the loan against it. The repo trade is as shown in Figure 16.2.

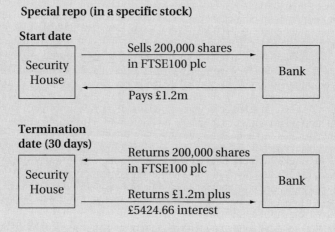

Figure 16.2

At the start of the trade the market-maker has "sold" shares worth £1.2 million, with an agreement to repurchase the shares in 30 days at the original price, plus one month's interest payable at the repo rate.

Let us assume that in 30 days time the share price in FTSE100 plc has risen to £8.25. As this is the termination of the original repo, the market-maker repurchases the shares at the price they sold them at, and pays over the repo interest.

Just as in a bond classic repo, the shares have remained on the market maker's balance sheet. The rise in the share price does not impact on the cash flows in the repo, as we can see in Figure 16.2. The market maker has repurchased shares that are now worth £1.65 million. However if the price of the shares had fallen below the original £6.00, the repo buyer could have called for more collateral (a margin call), as long as this is provided for in the repo agreement between the two counterparties.

16.2 Tri-party equity repo illustration

Precisely because it is not as well documented or as long established as bond repo, equity repo lends itself naturally to tri-party arrangements. A number of banks provide tri-party repo services, including Clearstream International (formerly Cedel Bank), Euroclear and JPMorgan Chase Bank. The service provided is similar to that described for bond tri-party repo in Chapter 5.

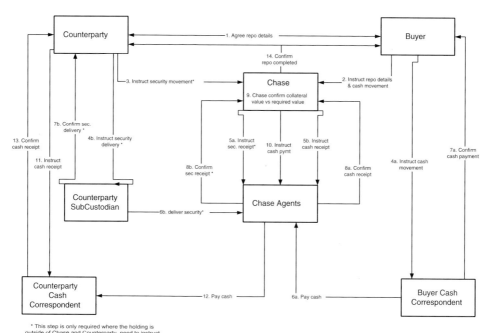

Figure 16.3: Equity tri-party repo structure, JPMorgan Chase Bank.
©JPMorgan Chase Bank. Reproduced with permission.

Figure 16.3 shows the structure for a tri-party equity repo trade with JPMorgan Chase Bank as the tri-party repo agent. During the duration of the repo, the bank ensures on a daily basis that the value of the securities provided as collateral meets the value required by the cash lender, and if there is a shortfall this is notified to both parties. The bank also acts as Custodian for the collateral securities, and if the level of collateral falls short, it would issue a margin call and require "counterparty" to deliver additional securities to JPMorgan Chase, to hold on the repo buyer's behalf.

16.3 The London equity repo market

16.3.1 *Market conventions*

The equity repo market in London has been actively traded since the early 1990s, when many of the trades were brokered via houses such as Tullett & Tokyo. In December 1997 the Stock Lending and Repo Committee of the Bank of England issued its code of best practice, which described the structure of the market in some detail. This document is reproduced in Appendix 16.1.

The conventions in the market follow in essence those introduced by the Bank ahead of the introduction of gilt repo in 1996. In this section we summarise the main points.

16.3.2 *Documentation requirements prior to commencement of trading*

As with bond repo, counterparties require signed legal documentation in place between them. As the latest version of the BMA/ISMA GMRA now contains an annexe that describes equity repo, this is the recommended legal agreement to have in place. The arrangements that should be described in the agreement include:

- margin requirements, procedures to be followed if margin call is made, and acceptable collateral to be supplied in a margin call; additionally, whether calls are made as transfer of additional collateral or as close-out and repricing of trade;
- what type of security is acceptable should there be a stock substitution;
- action to be followed by the buyer in the event of a corporate action;
- the day-count basis for interest calculation. In the London market this is the same as that for sterling money markets: actual/365;
- procedures for marking collateral to market on a daily basis, including acceptable price sources such as Bloomberg or Reuters.

The BoE equity code uses the term *margin ratio* in place of initial margin, although it means exactly the same thing. The margin ratio is given by

$$MR = \frac{P_m}{P_{repo}} \tag{16.1}$$

where P_m is the market price of the securities and P_{repo} is the bid price in the repo. P_{repo} may be adjusted for any margin requirement. If the margin required is 10%, this gives a margin ratio of 1.10 or 110%. If the cash lender provides initial margin of 10% this would be a margin ratio of 0.9091 or 90.91%.

16.3.3 *Entering into the trade*

The convention at the time of trade follows that in the bond repo market, but with more detail on collateral because the trade will be a specific.[4] Otherwise the counterparties will specify the size of the deal, start date and term to maturity, and the repo rate. The repo bid price will be the market value of the shares unless margin ratio has been specified. Unlike GC repo, the pricing basis is not always so clear cut, and the parties will need to agree the pricing basis for the collateral, either beforehand or at the time of trade. In the London market the convention is to use the previous day's closing price on CREST, in effect a CREST reference price for the equity repo market. The content of a repo confirmation as used in the London market is given in Appendix 16.2.

16.3.4 *Margin requirements*

Margin calls are made before noon each day. The convention is that the party being called for margin (whether additional or return of excess) retains the right to deliver margin as either securities or cash. However the security type must be acceptable as collateral to the counter-party. If cash is provided, the receiving party must pay interest on the cash held during the term of the repo. The interest basis needs to be agreed between the two parties, but the convention is that it is paid at the original trade's repo rate. If collateral is held in a pool that covers more than one transaction, the interest rate on cash must be agreed beforehand. Margin calls are settled over CREST.

If a security is repoed out over a dividend date, the CREST system will automatically transfer an amount equal to the net dividend[5] payment from the stock holder to the seller/lender of stock. The Bank's repo code includes a provision for repo sellers to recall securities over a dividend payment record date, if this is required.

16.3.5 *Penalties*

Where a party fails to deliver all or part of the stock in a transaction, in either the opening or closing leg of the trade, a penalty is payable by it as compensation for the failed settlement. This is usually charged at the trade's repo rate, if occurring at the start leg, and ceases if this occurs at the close leg. The party that has suffered a failed settlement may call for margin against any outstanding exposure that results due to the failure.

16.3.6 *Example repo trades*

We now illustrate equity repo mechanics by means of hypothetical trades. These are term trades with specified maturity dates, and are assumed to be cash-driven. The principles will rarely differ where the trade is stock-driven. Although initial margin is invariably taken in equity repo, to provide a comparison with government bond repo we consider the first trade as being with no margin. We then assume a 10% margin level for subsequent trades. Of course, margin levels are a function of the counterparty status and type of collateral involved, exactly as is the case with bond repo. It is frequently determined on a case-specific basis.

The trades all assume the following market factors:

---

4   The exception is the index rate repo mentioned earlier. In such a case the trader may be happy to agree the trade and leave the back office to sort out which collateral is being received.
5   Dividends on equities are paid net of a basic rate withholding tax in the UK.

Security:	ABC plc ordinary shares
Term:	One month (7 June–7 July)
Share price:	£1.00
Cash amount:	£10 million
Repo rate:	6.00%

Trade 1

This is the comparison illustration to GC bond repo, and assumes no initial margin is taken. In equity repo this is virtually unknown. We also assume there is no variation margin call.

Start leg

Cash amount:	£10 million
Number of shares repoed:	£10,000,000/£1.00
	= 10,000,000

The repo buyer pays a total consideration of £10 million, in return for which the seller transfers 10 million shares of ABC plc.

Close leg

On maturity the seller repurchases the shares from the buyer, at the initial sale price together with the repo interest. The repo interest is initial consideration × repo rate × days, which is:

$$10,000,000 \times 6.00\% \times 30/365$$
$$= £49,315.07.$$

The total repurchase price is therefore

$$10,000,000 + 49,315.07$$
$$= £10,049,315.07$$

in return for which the buyer returns the 10 million shares in ABC plc to the original seller.

Trade 2

This is the same trade as Trade 1 but this time with an initial margin of 10% required by the repo buyer. To calculate the number of shares required we multiply the original amount by the margin required:

$$£10,000,000 \times 1.10 = £11,000,000 \text{ market value of shares.}$$

The number of shares transferred by the repo seller is therefore

$$£11,000,000/£1.00 = 11 \text{ million shares.}$$

In the equity repo market the initial margin is expressed as a margin ratio of 0.90909 or 90.91%

The start leg is otherwise identical to Trade 1.

Close leg

The repurchase consideration is the initial purchase price plus interest. The repo interest is payable on £10 million so is identical the interest calculated in Trade 1.

The terms of the trade are:

| Cash amount: | £10 million |
| Share market value: | £11 million |

```
Number of shares:      11 million
Purchase price:        £10 million
Repo rate:             6%
Repo interest:         £49,315.07
Repurchase price:      £10,049,315.07
```

Trade 3

In this example we illustrate a margin call, resulting from a fall in the price of the shares during the trade. As with bond repo, there are two main methods by which margin calls are effected, and we illustrate them here. The end-result of either method is the same, the elimination of collateral shortfall and the restoration of the initial margin level. However, counterparties must therefore agree beforehand which method they will adopt, and this should then be described in the relevant legal agreement.

Assume that the share price has fallen from £1 to £0.90 on 9 June. The market value of the shares is:

$$11,000,000 \times £0.90 \text{ or } £9,900,000.$$

However the repo buyer has lent £10 million cash against the equity and is now undercollateralised. In addition, two days' repo interest has accrued on the trade, and initial margin of 10% had been taken at the start leg. To restore the original margin level of 10%, the repo buyer (cash lender) makes a margin call calculated using the following formula:

Original consideration + repo interest accrued to date $\times (1 + \text{initial margin})$
$-(\text{New share price} \times \text{number of shares})$.

Two days' interest is £3,287.68. The margin call works out as:

$$((10,000,000 + 3,287.68) \times 1.10) - (£0.90 \times 11,000,000)$$
$$= £1,103,616.45.$$

In the London equity repo code, where a margin call has been triggered by a movement in the underlying share price, the repo buyer is entitled to make a call on the repo seller to make up the shortfall. The variation margin trigger (at which a call is made) must be agreed between parties prior to commencement of trading. The repo seller has the right to provide margin either as additional acceptable securities or as cash.

Where a repo is a cash-driven trade, additional shares are delivered to restore the initial margin level. In this case, the terms of the original trade remain unchanged, but the transfer of shares becomes a separate repo of stock against zero cash, and is unwound at the maturity date of the original trade. If the supplier of collateral elects to deliver shares, the additional shares required would be:

$$1,103,616.45/0.90 \text{ or } 1,226,241 \text{ shares (rounded to the nearest whole number).}$$

Where a repo is stock-driven, cash may be supplied as collateral. The market convention is for this cash to earn interest for the collateral supplier at the trade repo rate, or at a rate agreed between the two parties. The interest accrues at act/365 or on a basis agreed between parties.

Trade 4

Here we illustrate the other common method by which margin calls are effected, in which the original repo is closed-out, and then re-opened under new terms. The changed terms of the trade reflect the movement in collateral required to restore margin. This is known as *close-out and repricing* and may be achieved in two ways, depending on whether stock or cash is transferred.

Margin call with securities

In a cash-driven trade it is more appropriate that stock is transferred as collateral. This is carried out as follows.

The original trade priced at £1.00 per share is closed-out for value on 9 June, and a new repo trade effected for 9 June to 7 July, with a share price of £0.90. The number of shares required will be calculated in the usual manner, that is:

>   11,000,000/0.990 or 12,222,222 shares.

This means that a net transfer of 1,222,222 shares is required by the buyer, together with payment of repo interest of £3,287.68 from the original trade. Alternatively the repo interest may be carried forward, this amount may be made up by increasing the number of shares still further, by

$$\frac{3287.68 \times 1.10}{0.90}$$

or 4,018 shares, making the total number of shares required 1,226,240. This is the same number of shares required in example Trade 3.[6]

The terms of the new trade are:

Market value amount:	£11 million
Share price:	£0.90
Number of shares:	12,222,222
Trade date:	9 June
Maturity date:	7 July
Total purchase price	£10,000,000
Repurchase price:	£10,046,027.40

The repurchase price assumes that repo interest from the original trade was settled on its close-out.

Margin call with cash

As before, the original transaction is closed-out for value on 9 June, and re-opened on 9 June. The consideration for the close-out is obtained by adding in two day's accrued interest on the original purchase consideration, as follows:

>   £10,000,000 + £3,287.68
>   = £10,003,287.92.

The purchase price for the new trade is given by the collateral's new (current) market value. This is £0.90 per share, so the purchase consideration is:

$$\frac{0.90 \times 11,000,000}{1.10}$$
>   = £9,000,000.

---

6   There is a small rounding difference.

When the original trade is settled, the closed-out trade is netted against the start leg of the new trade, so that shares do not move between parties, and a cash payment of (£10,003,287.92 – £9,000,000) or £1,003,287.92 is transferred by the provider of cash. The cash transfer includes the two days' repo interest from the first trade.

The terms of the new repo are:

Cash value:	£9,900,000
Share price:	£0.90
Number of shares:	11 million
Trade date:	9 June
Maturity date:	7 June
Purchase price:	£9,000,000
Repo rate:	6%
Repurchase price:	£9,041,424.66

Appendices

Appendix 16.1:   The Bank of England Equity Repo Code of Best Practice[7]

Equity Repo Code of Best Practice

1. The purpose of this Code is to set out standards of best practice for repo transactions in UK equity securities. Its general provisions should also be taken as applying to repos of other UK securities, apart from gilt edged securities which are subject to the Gilt Repo Code of Best Practice.

2. An equity repo is a transaction in which two parties agree that one will sell equity securities to the other and (at the same time and as part of the same transaction) commit to re-purchase equivalent securities on a specified future date, or at call, at a specified price. The terms used in repo markets are clarified in Annex I of this Code. Annex II summarises the market conventions that apply in the equity repo market. Annex III contains a schedule of key times during the equity repo day. Annex IV contains examples of calculations of equity repo transactions.

3. This Code has been drawn up, on the basis of practice in existing repo markets in London, by a working party of market practitioners and regulators under the aegis of the Stock Lending and Repo Committee. A full list of the bodies represented on the working party is attached as Annex V.

Coverage of Code

4. This Code is intended to apply to the full range of activity in repo transactions in UK equity securities by all UK based participants – ie by **market professionals**, **both principals** making markets and trading in equity repo, **and brokers** intermediating in the equity repo

---

7   ©Bank of England. Reproduced with permission. The full text of the BoE Equity Repo Code can be downloaded from the Bank's web site at www.bankofengland.org.uk

market; **end users**, repoing equity from their own portfolios, or undertaking reverse repos in equity collateral; and **agents** (such as fund managers, and custodians), undertaking repo business on behalf of their (principal) clients.

5. This Code relates equally to repos whose principal aim is the borrowing or lending of money secured against equity collateral both in the form of specific securities and in DBVs and to repos whose principal aim is the borrowing or lending of specific equity securities against cash ("specials"). It should be noted that this definition of special is broader than that frequently used in repo markets (where the term special is often restricted to transactions in specific issues where the rate on the repo is particularly low). This Code uses "repo" to mean both repo and reverse repo.

6. Other types of transaction, which are not specifically labelled equity repo, can nevertheless have a similar effect and intent. These include equity stock lending, eg under the Equity and Fixed Interest Stock Lending Agreement; lending of equity securities against other collateral ("stock versus stock" etc); and buy/sellbacks (whether or not under a master agreement). While not all the specific detail of this Code may be appropriate to these alternatives, the same general principles set out below apply.

7. This Code is not intended to apply to transactions in which title to the collateral does not pass, eg cash lending secured against equities under a fixed charge.

8. The words "collateral", "lending", "borrowing" and related expressions used in this Code reflect market terminology. The legal agreements recommended in section F below for use in equity repo, and the standard agreements for the other types of transactions described in paragraph 6 above, ensure under English law that full title to "collateral", and to securities "borrowed" or "lent", passes from one party to another, the party obtaining title being obliged to deliver back equivalent collateral/securities.

Application

9. Equity repos are transactions involving "investments" as defined in the Financial Services Act 1986 ("FS Act"), and "financial instruments" within the Investment Services Directive. Thus many participants in the equity repo market will also be subject to the Principles and to rules made under or by virtue of the FS Act.

10. The market in equity repo is essentially a wholesale, professional, market. Tax regulations require that, in order to avoid being treated as disposals for Stamp Duty purposes, transactions must be conducted on a recognised market and reported to the relevant authorities. Unlike gilt repo, equity repo falls outside the scope of section 43 of the FS Act, and this Code therefore has no direct relation to the London Code of Conduct. However, its object is to set broadly equivalent standards to those of the Gilt Repo Code.

11. The Financial Services Authority supports the approach set out in the Code and encourages authorised firms to have regard to the Code as a statement of best practice. In addition, the Securities & Futures Authority, the Investment Management Regulatory Organisation and the Personal Investment Authority (the Self Regulating Organisations under the FS Act), the London Stock Exchange, and the Bank of England, in relation to the supervision of banks and discount houses under the Banking Act, will have regard to the Code in the execution of their respective supervisory responsibilities.

12. This Code is endorsed as a statement of best practice by those other bodies listed in Annex V.

Queries or Complaints

13. Questions on this Code, or proposals for change or improvement to it or its annexes, should be addressed to the Secretary to the Stock Lending and Repo Committee, c/o the Bank of England. Additional copies of the Code can also be obtained from this source.

14. Complaints relating to possible misconduct in the equity repo market should be reported to the relevant regulatory authority.

A. General Standards

The London wholesale financial markets have a reputation for the professionalism of the firms that participate in them and of their employees. All participants in the equity repo market have a common interest in maintaining this reputation. They also have a common interest in ensuring that the equity repo market operates in a sound and orderly manner. To achieve these aims, it is essential that firms and their staff adopt prudent practices, act at all times with integrity, and observe the highest standards of market conduct. The following paragraphs cover particular aspects of this.

1. Participants in equity repo should at all times treat the names of parties to transactions as confidential to the parties involved.

2. Participants must accept responsibility for the actions of their staff.

3. Participants should act with due skill, care and diligence; to this end, staff should be properly trained in the practices of the equity repo market and be familiar with this Code.

4. Market professionals should pay particular attention to ensuring fair treatment for their clients where conflicts of interest cannot be avoided.

    In order for the benefits from the equity repo market to accrue generally to market participants, it is essential that activity in equity repo does not distort the market either in equity repo or in equity securities themselves. To this end, participants in the equity repo market must not in any circumstances enter into transactions designed to limit the availability of a specific stock with the intention of creating a false or distorted market in the underlying securities.

B. Preliminary Issues

This section deals with issues which participants should address **before** undertaking activity in equity repo. Participants should also review these matters **regularly**.

1. Participants should ensure that there are no legal obstacles to their undertaking equity repo transactions and that, where appropriate, they have obtained any necessary permissions from their regulatory authorities.

2. Where a custodian plans to repo a client's stock, it is fundamental that they should have obtained the necessary authority for this activity from the client in a clear legal agreement. Such an agreement should set down the basis on which repo activity may be entered into

and specify the collateral that may be taken. It may form part of the standard safe custody agreement.

3. Participants should ensure that they have adequate systems and controls for the business they intend to undertake. These should include the following:

   (a) adequate internal controls to ensure that any transactions in equity repo have been properly authorised before cash or stock is released;
   (b) suitable procedures for drawing up and maintaining a list of those authorised to borrow or lend stock;
   (c) suitable credit risk control systems, which cover the risks arising from equity repo transactions;
   (d) clear and timely records, available to management, showing inter alia the value of collateral given/taken (in aggregate and by counterparty to enable accurate monitoring of credit risk);
   (e) adequate systems for ensuring on a timely basis both the valuation of collateral given and received and the appropriate recollateralisation of repo transactions;
   (f) adequate documentation to cover the types of transactions that are to be undertaken;
   (g) adequate systems to account, for tax purposes, for any manufactured dividends in accordance with the relevant regulations; and
   (h) where a participant holds collateral for its counterparties ("hold in custody" repo – see Section H below), adequate systems for segregating and monitoring such collateral – it is particularly important that this area of systems and controls should be subject to independent external audit.

4. Participants should ensure that they have established – and fully understand – their tax position in relation to equity repo transactions.

5. Before undertaking equity repo transactions with a new counterparty, participants should ensure that they have agreed documentation, and have assured themselves of its effectiveness, particularly, for example, in respect of non-UK incorporated counterparties (see also Section F below); and that they have undertaken a rigorous credit assessment of the counterparty.

6. Before undertaking equity repo with a counterparty, participants need to consider whether they would wish to depart from standard practice as set out, inter alia, in this Code and its Annex II on market conventions (eg on deadlines for same day terminations of open repos, margin calls, and substitutions – to note, the daily settlement schedule is also set out in Annex III). Such matters would generally need to be reflected in the legal documentation or otherwise, or would need to be agreed with their counterparty at the time of each trade.

C. Market Professionals

Before dealing in equity repo with a client for the first time, market professionals should either confirm that the client is already aware of this Code and its key contents, or draw them to the client's attention. This section describes what needs to have been covered.

1. Such participants should check whether the new client has a copy of this Code and if not, either send them a copy or advise them to contact the Stock Lending and Repo Committee directly.

2. Such participants should inform the new client, if they are new to equity repo, that the Code recommends that:

    (a) transactions should be under the Equity Repo Legal Agreement (see Section F below), or equivalent;

    (b) transactions should be marked-to-market and recollateralised (see Section G below);

    (c) collateral should be held independently from the repo counterparty (see Section H below);

    and, if appropriate, should remind the client that it is for them to decide if they need to seek independent advice.

3. Such participants should also inform the client that there could be tax consequences from entering into equity repo transactions, in particular with regard to dividends, manufactured dividends and stamp duty on which they might need to seek professional advice.

D. Agents

Annex IV of the PSA/ISMA Global Master Repurchase Agreement sets out how the agreement is varied where one party is acting as agent for a named principal.

This section deals with issues relevant where one of the parties to a equity repo transaction is an agent (such as a fund manager).[1]

1. Participants in an equity repo transaction should ensure that they are clear whether the capacity in which their counterparty is acting is as principal or agent.

2. Where a participant is acting as an agent, the identity of the client who is the principal on whom the risk is taken should be established by the agent before the deal is done and also, at least by means of an agreed identification code, conveyed to the other participant.

3. Where a participant is acting as an agent for more than one principal, the agent needs a clear system for ensuring that each transaction is entered into, and any substitution or mark-to-market adjustment of collateral is made, on behalf of a particular principal whose identity has been determined and recorded.

4. An agent must obtain the necessary prior written authority from the beneficial owners of the cash and securities, or from a party suitably authorised by the beneficial owners, to undertake equity repos; this should cover the basis on which such repos may be carried out, and the collateral that may be taken.

5. An agent should make regular reports to clients, providing them with a full explanation of the equity repo activity carried out on their behalf.

E. Name-Passing Brokers

As well as dealing direct, participants may also wish to trade through broking intermediaries. There are two types of intermediary: a) **matched principals** – participants acting in that capacity are acting as principals; and b) **name-passing brokers**.[2] This section deals with those

---

[1] Those dealing with, or acting as, agents are recommended to study the Financial Law Panel's "Fund Management and Market Transactions, A Practice Recommendation" (September 1995).

[2] To note: subject to any supervisory restrictions, a broker may act both in a name passing and a matched principal capacity in repo, always provided that the nature of the broker's role is apparent at all times to the clients.

matters which are particularly relevant to equity repo business involving name-passing brokers.

1. Name-passing brokers in equity repo should:

    (a) not act as principal to a deal;

    (b) only quote firm prices substantiated by another market participant;

    (c) only receive payment for successfully bringing counterparties together in the form of brokerage, which is freely negotiated; and

    (d) pass the names immediately, when a bid is "hit" or an offer "lifted".

2. While principals and brokers share equal responsibility for maintaining confidentiality, name-passing brokers must exercise particular care. They should ensure that the identity of parties to a transaction is disclosed only after the bid is "hit" or offer "lifted", and then only to the parties involved.

F. Legal Agreement

Equity repo transactions should be subject to a legal agreement between the two participants concerned. A market standard for equity repo has been developed as a variant of the PSA/ISMA Global Master Repurchase Agreement ("the PSA/ISMA agreement"). The PSA/ISMA agreement was drafted with a view to compliance with English law and UK regulatory provisions, and covers the matters which a legal agreement ought to include for principal to principal repo transactions. Part 2 to Annex 1 to the PSA/ISMA agreement has been drawn up to meet the needs of the equity repo market and approved by the Stock Exchange. The PSA/ISMA agreement as extended by this Annex is referred to in this Code as "the Equity Repo Legal Agreement".

The advice of leading Counsel has been sought on the Equity Repo Legal Agreement. Counsel has confirmed that the provisions on close out and netting of outstanding transactions will be effective in a UK insolvency; and that the other provisions of the agreement will take effect in accordance with their terms under English Law.

Participants in the equity repo market are strongly recommended to adopt the Equity Repo Legal Agreement (subject to legal confirmation of its effectiveness, if the specific circumstances in which it is to be used are not straightforward).

Other forms of legal agreement, including variations of the Equity Repo Legal Agreement, may also be effective. It is stressed that whatever form an equity repo transaction takes (eg including buy/sellback), it is highly desirable – and strongly in the interests of both parties – that any transactions are conducted under an appropriate legal agreement.

The matters which a legal agreement needs to cover are the subject of this section.

1. The agreement should provide for the absolute transfer of title to securities (including any securities transferred through substitution or mark-to-market adjustment of collateral).

2. The agreement should provide for daily marking-to-market of transactions.

3. The agreement should provide for appropriate initial margin and for the maintenance of margin whenever the mark-to-market reveals a material change of value.

4. The agreement should specify clearly the events of default and the consequential rights and obligations of the counterparties.

5. The agreement should provide, in the event of default, for full set-off of claims between the counterparties.

6. The agreement should also include provisions clarifying the rights of the parties regarding substitution of securities and the treatment of dividend payments and other rights in respect of securities subject to it, including, for example, the timing of any payments.

7. The agreement should be subject to English law.

G. Margin

Equity repo transactions which are properly structured and under a sound legal agreement inherently involve less credit risk than unsecured loans or undocumented buy/sellbacks. Nevertheless, there is a residual credit risk. This section is concerned with how this risk should be managed.

1. Participants in equity repo should negotiate suitable initial margin reflecting both their assessment of their counterparty's creditworthiness and the market risks involved in the transaction.

2. Repo transactions should be marked-to-market on a daily basis (and participants should consider the need to do so within the day if there has been a large market movement). Such valuations should also take account of any dividend or other benefit which becomes payable to the holder of securities which pass their record date during the life of the repo.

3. It is an essential protection for participants in equity repo transactions that whenever a mark-to-market valuation reveals a material exposure to their counterparty, over and above any agreed initial margin, they should ensure cash or securities are moved in order to eliminate the exposure and restore the initial position. What is "material" is itself a credit judgement. The degree of exposure – called the variation margin – which a counterparty would regard as material, and which would trigger remargining, should be agreed, in advance, with the other counterparty. (To note, this includes the possibility of the two parties agreeing to daily remargining, irrespective of the size of the exposure that had arisen, ie that the agreed variation margin would be zero.)

4. Participants in equity repo transactions should monitor their net exposure to their counterparties on a daily basis.

5. Participants should minimise daylight and settlement exposure by settling equity repo transactions, including substitutions and margin payments, as far as possible through assured payment or DVP settlement systems.

6. Participants should integrate any exposures on equity repo into their credit risk control systems. These should ensure, inter alia, that appropriate exposure limits are established and reviewed on a regular basis, for all counterparties.

7. Participants should set up appropriate custody arrangements for collateral (see the following section).

H. Custody

Custody is an important aspect of equity repo. Taking possession of the collateral or using a third party custodian removes one important potential element of the credit risks involved with equity repo – that, while in possession of the collateral, the other party defaults and that ownership of the collateral subsequently cannot be proven because of administrative error or fraud. This section covers this and other issues relating to custody.

1. Clients need to ensure that stock loan and repo transactions are identified as such to their custodian.

2. Collateral, including where relevant margin and remargin, should be delivered to the account of the counterparty or his agent or a designated third party.

3. Before agreeing to arrangements in which collateral is left with the other party to the transaction ("hold in custody"), participants need to consider why they are content to accept such arrangements and why these are prudent. They need to consider the credit standing of the other party very carefully. They also need to assure themselves that the other party has appropriate, independently audited, systems and controls to ensure segregation and monitoring of collateral.

4. Where a participant is acting through an agent, there should be an agreed arrangement between the agent and that participant for the safeguarding of collateral and the allocation of any earnings on that collateral.

I. Default and Close-Out

This section covers issues which arise when a participant is in a position to exercise the right to declare a counterparty in default under a master agreement and close out its outstanding repo transactions.

1. The decision to declare a default is a major one and senior management of any participant faced with this decision should weigh carefully whether the event which triggers the right requires such action, or is a technical problem which can be resolved in other ways.

2. Once a decision to declare a default has been taken, it is important, in the interests of the participant, the defaulting party and the market, that the process be carried out carefully. In particular:

    (a) the non-defaulting party should do everything within its power to ensure that the default market values used in the close-out calculations are, and can be shown to be, fair; and

    (b) if the non-defaulting party decides to buy or sell securities consequent to the close-out, it should make every effort to do so without unnecessarily disrupting the market.

J. Confirmation and Other Issues

As all those active in financial markets are fully aware, confirmation and settlement are crucial aspects of any trading operation. This section covers aspects of the former, as well as some other, related, issues arising with equity repo transactions.

1. Market professionals should ensure that a written or electronic confirmation covering both legs of an equity repo transaction is issued. This confirmation should cover the items

set out in the section of the conventions annex (Annex II) on confirmations. Confirmations should, whenever possible, be issued on the day of trade.

2. Where material changes, such as margin calls or substitutions of stock, occur during the life of a repo transaction, these should also be confirmed, although in these cases it is sufficient for the change alone to be confirmed. Where appropriate, this may be done via a cross reference to the original repo. Market professionals should also consider whether to confirm rate changes on open repo transactions.

3. Participants should ensure that any confirmations they receive are checked carefully as soon as possible, normally on the day of receipt, and that any queries on their terms are promptly conveyed back to the issuer.

4. Participants undertaking repo in general collateral should, at the time of the trade, confirm whether the trade is against DBVs or specific collateral. In the case of DBVs, the participants should, on a timely basis, agree the DBV class involved; for specific collateral they should, on a timely basis, establish and confirm with their counterparty the precise nature of the collateral. The same applies when collateral is substituted. The market convention for specifying the details of collateral is set out in Section 4 of Annex II to this Code.

5. Participants should consider whether any events relating to any equity which they intend to include in a repo will occur during the life of the repo. Such events include exercise of voting rights, and dividend record dates. If so, they should seek the agreement of the other party to the inclusion of that security in the repo and also agree between them, as necessary, how the event is to be handled. Participants should be aware that where such events occur during the life of a repo, they may give rise to additional credit risks which need to be considered (see G6 above).[3]

Appendix 16.2:   Equity repo trade confirmation content

Contract date/trade date
Purchased securities
Quantity of shares (net of initial margin)
Buyer
Seller
Purchase date
Purchase price
Contractual currency
Total purchase price
Repurchase date (or "Terminable on demand" if open repo)
Repo rate %
Consideration for reverse leg (maturity settlement proceeds)
Buyer's settlement details
Seller's settlement details
Buyer's bank details
Seller's bank details

(Source: Bank of England).

---

[3]   To note: in the case of DBVs, allocation of securities is determined by a CREST selection algorithm which takes no account of dividend record dates.

Part III
Basis Trading and the Implied Repo Rate

The final part of this book might not be considered, by some readers, as logically belonging in a book on repo. However, basis trading and the government bond basis are closely connected with the repo market, because of financing considerations, and nothing illustrates better the close, integrated nature of repo and the wider debt capital markets than basis trading.

There is considerable confusion about basis trading, even amongst market practitioners. Essentially it concerns the financing factor associated with a cash bond position. To set the scene, we discuss forwards and futures pricing, and this enables us to discuss the basis. It is then a short step to basis trading, a form of arbitrage trading. The key part played by the repo rate will be apparent throughout, and is illustrated using worked examples and Bloomberg screens.

We apologise if some readers feel that there is an over-emphasis on the long gilt contract, perhaps to the detriment of more discussion on other contracts. This simply reflects the author's background; however, the principles are very similar for all exchange-traded government bond futures, and there are only very detail differences between say, the Treasury long bond as traded on CBOT and the long gilt traded on LIFFE. Readers should be able to apply the basic principles irrespective of the market that they are working in or researching.

The secret of Tintin's success… is that each story, whatever its significance at the time of writing, transcends the boundaries of its setting today… True, in some respects, the story of Tintin is a sad story; but it also manages to be funny, revealing and dramatic by turns. For lovers of happy endings, it has one of those too.

– Harry Thompson
Tintin: Hergé and his creation
Hodder & Stoughton 1991

"I have to thank you for a good deal," said he. "Perhaps I'll pay my debt some day."
Holmes smiled indulgently.
"I fancy that, for some few years, you will find your time very fully occupied," said he.

Sir Arthur Conan Doyle
"The Adventure of the Norwood Builder"
The Return of Sherlock Holmes

17 The Government Bond Basis, Basis Trading and the Implied Repo Rate I

Basis trading, also known as *cash and carry* trading, refers to the activity of simultaneously trading cash bonds and the related bond futures contract. An open repo market is essential for the smooth operation of basis trading. Most futures exchanges offer at least one bond futures contract. Major exchanges such as CBOT offer contracts along the entire yield curve; others such as LIFFE provide a market in contracts on bonds denominated in a range of major currencies.

The *basis* of a futures contract is the difference between the spot price of an asset and its price for future delivery as implied by the price of a futures contract written on the asset. Futures contracts are exchange-traded standardised instruments, so they are a form of what is termed a *forward* instrument, a contract that describes the forward delivery of an asset at a price agreed today. The pricing of forwards and futures follows similar principles but, as we shall see, contains significant detail differences between the two. The simultaneous trading of futures contracts written on government bonds and the bonds themselves, basis trading, is an important part of the government repo markets; in this, and the two subsequent chapters, we review the essential elements of this type of trading. We begin with basic concepts of forward pricing, before looking at the determinants of the basis, hedging using bond futures, trading the basis and an introduction to trading strategy. We also look at the concept of the *cheapest-to-deliver* bond, and the two ways in which this is measured: the net basis and the *implied repo rate*. As ever, readers are directed to the bibliography, particularly the book by Burghardt *et al* (1994), which is an excellent reference work. It reads very accessibly and contains insights useful for all bond market participants.

We begin with the concepts of forward and futures pricing, and futures contracts. This might look a long way away from the repo market, but please persevere with it as it's essential background enabling us to discuss the implied repo rate and basis trading in a later chapter. The repo desk plays a crucial role in basis trading and, just like forward pricing principles, an appreciation of the repo function is also key to understanding the bond basis. But that comes later. First we discuss some basic concepts in futures pricing and then look at the concept of the bond basis.

17.1 An introduction to forward pricing

17.1.1 *Introduction*

Let's now look at a more qualitative way of considering the forward bond basis, connected with the coupon and running cost on cash bonds. This approach reads more accessibly for those who wish a more specific application to forward pricing on bond assets.

An investor assessing whether an asset is worth purchasing spot or forward must consider two issues: whether there is an income stream associated with the asset, in which case this would be foregone if the asset was purchased forward; and if there is any holding costs associated with the asset if it is purchased spot. The forward price on a bond must reflect these same considerations, so a buyer will consider the effect of income foregone and *carry* costs and assess the relative gain of spot versus forward purchase. In real terms then, we are comparing the income stream of the bond coupon against the interest rate on funds borrowed to purchase the bond.[1]

An investor who is long a cash bond will receive coupon income, and this is accrued on a daily basis. This is a purely accounting convention and has no bearing to the current interest rate or the current price of the bond.[2] An investor who purchases a bond forward is forgoing the income during the time to delivery, and this factor should presumably be incorporated into the forward price. What of the funding (carry) cost involved? This can be calculated from the current money market rate provided the term of the funding is known with certainty. So if we now consider a three-month forward contract on a bond against the current spot price of the same bond, the investor must assess:

■ the coupon income that would be received during the three-month period;

■ the interest charge on funds borrowed during the three-month period.

Let us say that the difference between these two values was exactly 1.00. For the forward contract to be a worthwhile purchase, it would have to be at least 1.00 lower in price than the spot price. This is known as the forward discount. Otherwise the investor is better off buying the bond for spot delivery. However if the price is much lower than 1.00, investors will only buy forward (while cash bond holders would sell their holdings and repurchase forward). This would force the forward price back into line to its *fair value*. The forward price discount is known as the *basis*. The basis exists in all markets where there is a choice available between spot and forward delivery, and not just in financial derivatives. For bonds the basis can be assessed by reference to the current price of the underlying asset, the income stream (coupon), the time to maturity of the forward contract and the current level of interest rates.

17.1.2 *Illustrating the forward bond basis*

Now let us look at an illustration, using the September 2000 long gilt contract. We use the coupon income from the cheapest-to-deliver (CTD) bond, the 5.75% 2009 gilt. We haven't discussed the concept of the CTD yet, however ignore the CTD element for now, and assume a constant money market borrowing rate (the repo rate[3]) during the three months of the futures contract from 29 June 2000 to 27 September 2000.

Intuitively we would expect the basis to move towards zero, as the contract approached maturity. After all, what is the price of something for delivery now if not the spot price? First we consider the yield of the bond against the yield of the futures contract. This is illustrated in Figure 17.1. There is slight convergence towards the end; however, if we plot the basis itself,

---

[1] We assume a leveraged investor: if spot purchase is desired, the investor will borrow the funds used to buy the bond.

[2] Van Deventer (1997) states that the accrued interest concept is "an arbitrary calculation that has no economic meaning". This is because it reflects the coupon and not current interest rates, so in other words it reflects interest rates at the time of issue. The coupon accrued is identical whatever current interest rates may be. It's worth purchasing this reference as it contains accessible accounts of a number of fixed income analytic techniques.

[3] Hurrah! We're back to repo…, patience, we're getting there.

this does converge to zero as expected. This is shown in Figure 17.2. As the contract approaches maturity, the basis becomes more and more sensitive to slight changes in bond price or financing rates, hence the exaggerated spike. For instance if short-term repo rates decrease, while the coupon income on the bond remains unchanged, an investor would be faced with a lower level of foregone return as a result of lower financing costs. This makes it more attractive for an investor to buy the bond spot delivery, and so the basis will rise as demand for the forward (or future, to be precise) declines.

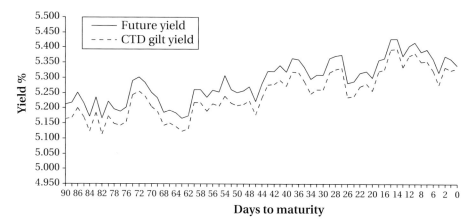

Figure 17.1: Source: LIFFE and Bloomberg.

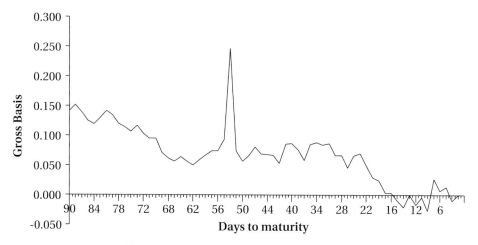

Figure 17.2: Source: LIFFE and Bloomberg.

Essentially, when the repo rate is significantly below the bond yield,[4] the basis will be high. If the repo rate then rises the basis will fall, and this indicates the smaller interest-rate differential between the repo rate and the bond yield. If the repo rate rises to a point where it is above the bond yield, the basis will turn negative. In fact this occurred briefly during the later stages of the life of the September 2000 gilt future as shown above. A negative basis indicates that the price for forward delivery exceeds that for spot delivery.

To reiterate then, the forward basis quantifies the relationship between the income generated by the underlying asset and the costs incurred by owning it.[5] As we are concerned with bond futures, specifically the basis will reflect the relationship between the underlying bond's coupon stream and the repo financing rate if holding the bond. Forward contracts for bonds exhibit the basis. Futures contracts, which are standardised forward contracts traded on an organised exchange, are priced on the same principles as forwards and so therefore also exhibit the basis. The next section considers forward pricing in a more formal way.

17.2 Forwards and futures valuation

Let us now take a more rigorous look at forward valuation. To begin our discussion of derivative instruments, we discuss the valuation and analysis of forward and futures contracts; here, we develop basic valuation concepts. The discussion follows, with permission, the approach described in Rubinstein (1999), as shown in Section 2.2 of that text.[6]

17.2.1 *Introduction*

A forward contract is an agreement between two parties in which the buyer contracts to purchase from the seller a specified asset, for delivery at a future date, at a price agreed today. The terms are set so that the present value of the contract is zero. For the forthcoming analysis we use the following notation:

P is the current price of the underlying asset, also known as the *spot* price;
P_T is the price of the underlying asset at the time of delivery;
X is the delivery price of the forward contract;
T is the term to maturity of the contract in years, also referred to as the time-to-delivery;
r is the risk-free interest rate;
R is the return of the payout or its *yield*;
F is the current price of the forward contract.

The payoff of a forward contract is therefore given by

$$P_T - X \tag{17.1}$$

with X set at the start so that the present value of $(P_T - X)$ is zero. The payout yield is calculated by obtaining the percentage of the spot price that is paid out on expiry.

---

4   The bond's running yield, or flat yield, is usually used.
5   Readers are invited to think of assets for which the forward basis is routinely negative…
6   This is a top book and highly recommended, and for all students and practitioners interested in capital markets, not just those involved with derivative instruments.

17.2.2 *Forwards*

When a forward contract is written, its delivery price is set so that the present value of the payout is zero. This means that the forward price F is then the price on delivery which would make the present value of the payout, on the delivery date, equal to zero. That is, at the start $F = X$. This is the case only on day 1 of the contract however. From then until the contract expiry the value of X is fixed, but the forward price F will fluctuate continuously until delivery. It is the behaviour of this forward price that we wish to examine. For instance, generally as the spot price of the underlying increases, so the price of a forward contract written on the asset also increases; and vice versa. At this stage, it is important to remember that the forward price of a contract is not the same as the value of the contract, and the terms of the agreement are set so that at inception the value is zero. The relationship given above is used to show that an equation can be derived which relates F to P, T, r and R.

Consider first the profit/loss profile for a forward contract. This is shown in Figure 17.3. The price of the forward can be shown to be related to the underlying variables as

$$F = S(r/R)^T,$$
(17.2)

and for the one-year contract highlighted in Figure 17.3 is 52.5, where the parameters are $S = 50$, $r = 1.05$ and $R = 1.00$.

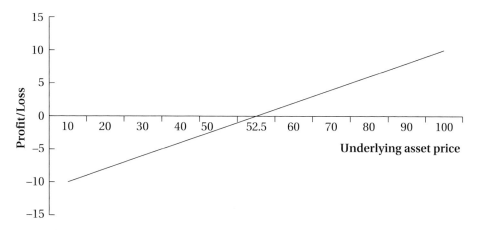

Figure 17.3: Forward contract profit/loss profile.

17.2.3 *Futures*

Forward contracts are tailor-made instruments designed to meet specific individual requirements. *Futures* contracts, on the other hand, are standardized contracts that are traded on recognized futures exchanges. Apart from this, the significant difference between them, and the feature that influences differences between forward and futures prices, is that profits or losses that are gained or suffered in futures trading are paid out at the end of the day. This does not occur with forwards. The majority of trading in futures contracts are always closed-out, that is, the position is netted out to zero before the expiry of the contract. If a position is run into the delivery month, depending on the terms and conditions of the particular exchange, the party that is long future may be delivered into. Settlement is by physical delivery in the case of commodity futures or in cash in the case of certain financial futures. Bond futures are financial futures where any bond that is in the *delivery basket* for that contract will be delivered to the long future. With both physical and financial futures, only a very small percentage of contracts are actually delivered into as the majority of trading is undertaken for hedging and speculative purposes.

With futures contracts, as all previous trading profits and losses have been settled, on the day of expiry only the additional change from the previous day needs to be accounted for. With a forward contract all loss or gain is rolled up until the expiry day and handed over as a total amount on this day.[7]

17.2.4 *Forwards and futures*

Cash flow differences

We can now look at the cash flow treatment of the two contracts in greater detail. This is illustrated in Table 17.1, which uses F to denote the price of the futures contract as well. The table shows the payoff schedule at the end of each trading day for the two instruments; assume that they have identical terms. With the forward there is no cash flow on intermediate dates, whereas with the futures contract there is. As with the forward contract, the price of the future fixes the present value of the futures contract at zero. Each day the change in price, which at the end of the day is *marked-to-market* at the *close* price, will have resulted in either a profit or gain,[8] which is handed over or received each day as appropriate. The process of daily settlement of price movements means that the nominal delivery price can be reset each day so that the present value of the contract is always zero. This means that the future and nominal delivery prices of a futures contract are the same at the end of each trading day.

Time	Forward contract	Futures contract
0	0	0
1	0	$F_1 - F$
2	0	$F_2 - F_1$
3	0	$F_3 - F_2$
4	0	$F_4 - F_3$
5	0	$F_5 - F_4$
...	0	...
...	0	...
...	0	...
$T-1$	0	$F_{T-1} - F_{T-2}$
T	$P_T - F$	$P_T - F_{T-1}$
Total	$P_T - F$	$P_T - F$

Table 17.1: Cash flow process for forwards and futures contracts.

[7] We assume the parties have traded only one forward contract between them. If, as is more accurate to assume, a large number of contracts have been traded across a number of different maturity periods and perhaps instruments, as contracts expire only the net loss or gain is transferred between counterparties.

[8] Or no profit or gain if the closing price is unchanged from the previous day's closing price, a *doji* as technical traders call it.

We see in Table 17.1 that there are no cash flows changing hands between counterparties to a forward contract. The price of a futures contract is reset each day; after day 1 this means it is reset from F to F_1. The amount $(F_1 - F)$ if positive, is handed over by the short future to the long future. If this amount is negative, it is paid by the long future to the short. On the expiry day T of the contract the long future will receive a settlement amount equal to $P_T - F_{T-1}$ which expresses the relationship between the price of the future and the price of the underlying asset. As significant, the daily cash flows transferred when holding a futures contract cancel each other out, so that on expiry the value of the contract is (at this stage) identical to that for a forward, that is $(P_T - F)$.

With exchange-traded contracts all market participants are deemed to conduct their trading with a central counterparty, the exchange's clearing house. This eliminates counterparty risk in all transactions, and the clearing house is able to guarantee each bargain because all participants are required to contribute to its clearing fund. This is by the process of *margin*, by which each participant deposits an *initial margin* and then, as its profits or losses are recorded, deposits further *variation margin* on a daily basis. The marking-to-market of futures contracts is an essential part of this margin process. A good description of the exchange clearing process is contained in Galitz (1995).

This is the key difference between future and forward contracts. If holding a futures position that is recording a daily profit, the receipt of this profit on a daily basis is advantageous because the funds can be reinvested while the position is still maintained. This is not available with a forward. Equally, losses are suffered on a daily basis that are not suffered by the holder of a loss-making forward position.

17.2.5 *Relationship between forward and future price*

Continuing with the analysis contained in Rubinstein (1999), we wish to illustrate that under certain specified assumptions, the price of futures and forwards written with identical terms must be the same.

This can be shown in the following way. Consider two trading strategies of identical term to maturity and written on the same underlying asset; one strategy uses forward contracts while the other uses futures. Both strategies require no initial investment and are *self-financing*. The assumptions are:

■ the absence of risk-free arbitrage opportunities;

■ the existence of an economist's perfect market;

■ certainty of returns.

Under these conditions, it can be shown that the forward and future price must be identical. In this analysis the return r is the daily return (or instantaneous money market rate) and T is the maturity term in days. Let's look further at the strategies.

For the strategy employing forwards, we buy r^T forward contracts. The start forward price is $F = X$ but of course there is no cash outlay at the start, and the payoff on expiry is

$$r^T \left(P_T - F \right).$$

The futures strategy is more involved, due to the daily margin cash flows that are received or paid during the term of the trade. On day 1 we buy r contracts each priced at F. After the close we receive $F_1 - F$. The position is closed-out and the cash received is invested at the daily rate r up to the expiry date. The return on this cash is r^{T-1} which means that on expiry we will receive an amount of

$$r(F_1 - F)r^{T-1}.$$

The next day we purchase r^2 futures contracts at the price of F_1 and at the close the cash flow received of $F_2 - F_1$ is invested at the close of trading at r^{T-2}. Again we will receive on expiry a sum equal to

$$r^2 (F_2 - F_1)r^{T-2}.$$

This process is repeated until the expiry date, which we assume to be the delivery date. What is the net effect of following this strategy? We will receive on the expiry date a set of maturing cash flows that have been invested daily from the end of day 1. The cash sums will be

$$r^T (F_1 - F) + r^T (F_2 - F_1) + r^T (F_3 - F_2) + \cdots + r^T (P_T - F_{T-1}),$$

which nets to

$$r^T (P_T - F),$$

which is also the payoff from the forward contract strategy. Both strategies have a zero cash outlay and are self-financing. The key point is that if indeed we are saying that

$$r^T (P_T - F)_{forward} = r^T (P_T - F)_{future} \qquad (17.3)$$

for the assumption of no arbitrage to hold, then $F_{forward} = F_{future}$.

17.2.6 *The forward-spot parity*

We can use the forward strategy to imply the forward price provided we know the current price of the underlying and the money market interest rate. A numerical example of the forward strategy is given at Figure 17.4, with the same parameters given earlier. We assume no-arbitrage and a perfect frictionless market.

	Cash flows	
	Start date	Expiry
Buy forward contract	0	$P_T - F$
Buy one unit of the underlying asset	−50	P_T
Borrow zero present-value of forward price	$F/1.05$	F
Total	$-50 + F/1.05$	$P_T - F$

Result
Set $-50 + F/1.05$ equal to zero
(no-arbitrage condition)
Therefore $F = 52.5$

Figure 17.4: Forward strategy.

What Figure 17.4 is saying is that it is possible to replicate the payoff profile we observed in Figure 17.3 by a portfolio composed of one unit of the underlying asset, the purchase of which is financed by borrowing a sum that is equal to the present value of the forward price. This borrowing is repaid on maturity and is equal to $(F/1.05) \times 1.05$ which is in fact F. In the absence of arbitrage opportunity the cost of forming the portfolio will be identical to that of the forward itself. However, we have set the current cost of the forward contract at zero, which gives us

$$-50 + F/1.05 = 0$$

We solve this expression to obtain F and this is 52.50.

The price of the forward contract is 52.50, although the present value of the forward contract when it is written is zero. Following Rubinstein, we prove this in Figure 17.5.

	Start date	Expiry
Buy forward contract	0	$P_T - F$
Buy R^{-T} units of the underlying asset	$-PR^{-T}$	P_T
Borrow zero present-value of forward price	Fr^{-T}	$-F$
Total	$-PR^{-T} + Fr^{-T}$	$P_T - F$

$$\text{Set} -PR^{-T} + Fr^{-T} = 0$$
$$\text{Therefore } F = P(r/R)^T$$

Figure 17.5: Algebraic proof of forward price.

What Figure 17.5 states is that the payoff profile for the forward can be replicated precisely by setting up a portfolio that holds R^{-T} units of the underlying asset, which is funded through borrowing a sum equal to the present value of the forward price. This borrowing is repaid at maturity, this amount being equal to

$$(Fr^{-T}) \times r^T = F.$$

The portfolio has an identical payoff profile (by design) to the forward, this being $(P_T - F)$. In a no-arbitrage environment, the cost of setting up the portfolio must be equal to the current price of the forward, as they have identical payoffs and if one was cheaper than the other, there would be a risk-free profit for a trader who bought the cheap instrument and shorted the dear one. However, we set the current cost of the forward (its present value) as zero, which means the cost of constructing the duplicating portfolio must therefore be zero as well. This gives us

$$-PR^{-T} + Fr^{-T} = 0,$$

which allows us to solve for the forward price F.

The significant aspect for the buyer of a forward contract is that the payoff of the forward is identical to that of a portfolio containing an equivalent amount of the underlying asset, which has been constructed using borrowed funds. The portfolio is known as the *replicating portfolio*. The price of the forward contract is a function of the current underlying spot price, the risk-free or money market interest rate, the payoff and the maturity of the contract. To recap then the forward-spot parity states that

$$F = P(r/R)^T. \tag{17.4}$$

It can be shown that neither of the possibilities $F > P(r/R)^T$ or $F < P(r/R)^T$ will hold unless arbitrage possibilities are admitted. The only possibility is (17.4), at which the futures price is *fair value*.

17.2.7 *The basis and implied repo rate*

For later analysis, we introduce now some terms used in the futures markets.

The difference between the price of a futures contract and the current underlying spot price is known as the *basis*. For bond futures contracts, which are written not on a specific bond but a *notional* bond that can in fact be represented by any bond that fits within the contract terms, the size of the basis is given by (17.5):

$$Basis = P_{bond} - \left(P_{fut} \times CF \right),$$ (17.5)

where the basis is the *gross basis* and *CF* is the *conversion factor* for the bond in question. All delivery-eligible bonds are said to be in the *delivery basket*. The conversion factor equalizes each deliverable bond to the futures price.[9] The size of the gross basis represents the cost of carry associated with the bond from today to the delivery date. The bond with the lowest basis associated with it is known as the *cheapest-to-deliver* bond. The magnitude of the basis changes continuously and this uncertainty is termed *basis risk*. Generally the basis declines over time as the maturity of the contract approaches, and converges to zero on the expiry date. The significance of basis risk is greatest for market participants who use futures contracts for hedging positions held in the underlying asset. The basis is positive or negative according to the type of market in question, and is a function of issues such as *cost of carry*. When the basis is positive, that is $F > P$, the situation is described as a *contango*, and is common in precious metals markets. A negative basis $P < F$ is described as *backwardation* and is common in oil contracts and foreign currency markets.

The hedging of futures and the underlying asset requires a keen observation of the basis. To hedge a position in a futures contract, one could run an opposite position in the underlying. However, running such a position incurs the cost of carry referred to above, which depending on the nature of the asset, may include storage costs, opportunity cost of interest foregone, funding costs of holding the asset and so on. The futures price may be analyzed in terms of the forward-spot parity relationship and the risk-free interest rate. If we say that the risk-free rate is

$$r - 1$$

and the forward-spot parity is

$$F = P(r/R)^T ;$$

we can set

$$r - 1 = R(F/P)^{1/T} - 1$$ (17.6)

which must hold because of the no-arbitrage assumption.

---

[9]   For a description and analysis of bond futures contracts, the basis, implied repo and the cheapest-to-deliver bond, see Burghardt *et al.* (1994), an excellent account of the analysis of the Treasury bond basis. Plona (1997) is also a readable treatment of the European government bond basis.

This interest rate is known as the *implied repo rate*, because it is similar to a repurchase agreement carried out with the futures market. Generally, a relatively high implied repo rate is indicative of high futures prices, and the same for low implied repo rates. The rates can be used to compare contracts with each other, when these have different terms to maturity and even underlying assets. The implied repo rate for the contract is more stable than the basis; as maturity approaches the level of the rate becomes very sensitive to changes in the futures price, spot price and (by definition) time to maturity.

17.3 The bond basis: basic concepts

17.3.1 *Introduction*

The previous section introduced the no-arbitrage forward pricing principle and the concept of the basis. We will look at this again later. So we know that the price of an asset, including a bond, that is agreed today for immediate delivery is known as its *spot* price.[10] In essence the forward price of an asset, agreed today for delivery at some specified future date, is based on the spot price and the cost or income of foregoing delivery until the future date. If an asset carries an income stream, withholding delivery until, say, three months in the future would present an opportunity cost to an investor in the asset, so the prospective investor would require a discount on the spot price as the price of dealing in a forward. However, if an asset comes with a holding cost, for example storage costs, then an investor might would expect to pay a premium on the spot price, as it would not be incurring the holding costs that are otherwise associated with the asset.

Commodities such as wheat or petroleum are good examples of assets whose forward delivery is associated with a holding cost. For a commodity whose price is agreed today but for which delivery is taken at a forward date, economic logic dictates that the futures price must exceed the spot price. That is, a commodity basis is usually negative. Financial assets such as bonds have zero storage costs, as they are held in electronic form in a clearing system such as CREST/CGO; moreover they provide an income stream that would offset the cost of financing a bondholding until a future date. Under most circumstances when the yield curve is positively sloping, the holding of a bond position until delivery at a future date will generate a net income to the holder. For these and other reasons it is common for the bond basis to be positive, as the futures price is usually below the spot price.

As we shall see shortly, bond futures contracts do not specify a particular bond, rather a generic or *notional* bond. The actual bond that is delivered against an expired futures contract is the one that makes the cost of delivering it as low as possible. The bond that is selected is known as the cheapest-to-deliver. Considerable research has been undertaken into the concept of the *cheapest-to-deliver* (CTD) bond. In fact, certain commodity contracts also trade with an underlying CTD. Burghardt (*ibid*) points out that wheat is not an homogenous product, as wheat from one part of the country exhibits different characteristics to wheat from another part of the country, and may have to be transported a longer distance (hence at greater cost) to delivery. Therefore a wheat contract is also priced based on the designated cheapest-to-deliver. There is no physical location factor with government bonds, but futures contracts specify that any bond may be delivered that falls into the required maturity period.

---

[10] We use the term "immediate" delivery although for operational, administrative and settlement reasons, actual delivery may be a short period in the future, say anything up to several days or even longer.

In this section we look at the basic concepts, necessary for an understanding of the bond basis, and introduce all the key topics. Basis trading itself is the simultaneous trading of cash bond and the bond futures contract, an arbitrage trade that seeks to exploit any mis-pricing of the future against the cash or vice versa.[11] In liquid and transparent markets such mis-pricing is rare, of small magnitude and very short-lived. The arbitrageur will therefore also try to make a gain from the difference between the costs of holding (or shorting) a bond against that of delivering (or taking delivery of) it at the futures expiry date; essentially, then, the difference between the bond's running yield and its repo financing cost. We'll save the trading principles for the next chapter. First let us introduce basic terminology.

17.3.2 *Futures contract specifications*

When speaking of bond futures contracts people generally think of the US Treasury bond contract, the Bund contract or the long Gilt contract, but then it does depend in which market one is working in or researching. The contract specifications for these contracts are given in Table 17.2, the two US contracts as traded on CBOT and the two European contracts as traded on LIFFE.

Term	Treasury Bond (CBOT)	5-Year Note (CBOT)	Long Gilt (LIFFE)	Bund (LIFFE)
Unit of trading	$100,000 nominal value	$100,000 nominal value	£100,000 nominal value	€100,000 nominal value
Underlying bond	US Treasury bond with a minimum of 15 years remaining to maturity	Original issue US Treasury note with an original maturity of not more than 5.25 years and not less than 4.25 years	UK Gilt with notional 7% coupon and term to maturity of 8.75–13 years	German government bond with 6% coupon and remaining term to maturity of 8.5–10.5 years
Delivery months	March, June, September, December	March, June, September, December	March, June, September, December	March, June, September, December
First notice day			Two business days prior to first day of delivery month	
Last notice day			First business day after last trading day	
Delivery day	Any business day during delivery month		Any business day in delivery month (at seller's choice)	Tenth calendar day of delivery month. If not a business day in Frankfurt, the following Frankfurt business day

Continued overleaf ▶

---

[11]   Another term for basis trading is *cash-and-carry* trading. The terms are used interchangeably.

Term	Treasury Bond (CBOT)	5-Year Note (CBOT)	Long Gilt (LIFFE)	Bund (LIFFE)
Last trading day	12:00 noon on the 8th to the last business day of the delivery month	12:00 noon on the 8th to the last business day of the delivery month	11:00 two business days prior to the last business day in the delivery month	12.30 two Frankfurt business days prior to the delivery day
Last delivery day	Last business day of the delivery month	Last business day of the delivery month		
Price Quotation	Points and 32nds of a point per $100 nominal	Points and 32nds of a point per $100 nominal	Per £100 nominal	Per €100 nominal
Tick size and value	1/32nd of a point ($31.25)	1.2 of 1/32nd of a point ($15.625)	0.01 (£10)	0.01 (€10)
Daily price limit	3 points	3 points		
Trading hours	7:20am – 2:00pm (Pit)	7:20am – 2:00pm (Pit)	08.00 – 18.00	07.00 – 18.00
	5:20pm – 8.05pm (CST)	5:20pm – 8.05pm (CST)	LIFFE CONNECT	LIFFE CONNECT
	10.30pm – 6.00am (Globex)	6.20pm – 9.05pm (CDST)		

Notes
All times are local.
The notional coupon of the Treasury bond, while deprecated as a concept by some writers, is 6%. It was changed from 8% from the March 2000 contract onwards.

Table 17.2: Selected futures contract specifications.

Remember that a futures contract is a standardised forward contract, traded on an organised exchange. So the bond futures contracts described in Table 17.2 represent a forward trade in the underlying cash bond. Only a small minority of the futures contracts traded are actually held through to delivery (unlike the case for say, agricultural commodity contracts), but if one does hold a long position at any time in the delivery month, there is a possibility that one will be delivered into.

The notional coupon in the contract specification has relevance in that it is the basis of the calculation of each bond's *price factor* or *conversion factor*; otherwise it has no bearing on understanding the price behaviour of the futures contract. Remember the contract is based on a *notional* bond, as there will be more than one bond that is eligible for delivery into the contract. The set of deliverable bonds is known as the *delivery basket*. Therefore the futures price is not based on one particular bond, but acts rather like a hybrid of all the bonds in the basket (see Burghardt, page 4). What can we say about Table 17.2? For instance, exchanges specify minimum price movements, which is 0.01 for European contracts and 1/32nd for the US contracts.

Every bond in the delivery basket will have its own *conversion factor*, which is intended to compensate for the coupon and timing differences of deliverable bonds. The exchange publishes tables of conversion factors in advance of a contract starting to trade, and these remain fixed for the life of the contract. These numbers will be smaller than 1.0 for bonds having coupons less than the notional coupon for the bond in the contract, and greater than 1.0 otherwise.

The definition of the gilt contract detailed in Table 17.2 calls for the delivery of a UK gilt with an effective maturity of between 8¾ to 13 years and a 7% notional coupon. We emphasise that the notional coupon should not be an object of a trader's or investor's focus. It exists simply because there would be problems if the definition of deliverable gilts were restricted solely to those with a coupon of exactly 7%. At times there may be no bonds having this precise coupon. Where there was one or more such bonds, the size of the futures market in relation to the size of the bond issue would expose the market to price manipulation. To avoid this, futures exchanges design contracts in such a way as to prevent anyone dominating the market. In the case of the Long Gilt and most similar contracts this is achieved by allowing the delivery of *any* bond with a sufficient maturity, as we have noted. The holder of a long position in futures would prefer to receive a high-coupon bond with significant accrued interest, while those short of the future would favour delivering a cheaper low-coupon bond shortly after the coupon date. This conflict of interest is resolved by adjusting the *invoice amount*, the amount paid in exchange for the bond, to account for coupon rate and timing of the bond actually delivered.

Equation (17.7) gives this invoice amount.

$$Inv_{amt} = \left(P_{fut} \times CF \right) + AI \tag{17.7}$$

where

Inv_{amt}	is the invoice amount;
P_{fut}	is the futures price;
CF	is the conversion factor;
AI	is the accrued interest.

We will consider invoice and settlement amounts again later.

17.3.3 *The conversion factor*

So, we know that a bond futures contract represents any bond whose maturity date falls in the period described in the contract specifications. During the delivery month, and up to the expiry date, the party that is short the future has the option on which bond to deliver and on what day in the month to deliver it. Let us consider the long Gilt contract on LIFFE. If we assume the person that is short the future delivers on the expiry date, for each contract they must deliver to the exchange's clearing house £100,000 nominal of a notional 7% gilt of between 8¾ and 13 years' maturity.[12] Of course no such specific bond exists, so the seller delivers a bond from within the delivery basket. However if the seller delivers a bond of say, 6% coupon and 9 years maturity, intuitively we see that the value of this bond is lower than a 7%

---

[12] In our example, to the London Clearing House. The LCH then on-delivers to the party that is long the contract. The long pays the settlement invoice price.

bond of 13 years maturity. While the short future may well think, "fine by me", the long future will most certainly think not. There would be the same aggrieved feelings, just reversed, if the seller was required to deliver a bond of 8% coupon. To equalise all bonds, irrespective of which actual bond is delivered, the futures exchange assigns a *conversion factor* to each bond in the delivery basket. This serves to make the delivery acceptable to both parties. Conversion factors are used in the invoice process to calculate the value of the delivered bond that is equal to that specified by the contract. In some texts the conversion factor is known as the *price factor*. The concept of the conversion factor was developed by CBOT in the 1970s.

Table 17.3 shows the conversion factors for all gilts that were eligible for delivery as of 30 August 2001 for the September 2001 to September 2002 contracts. Notice how the conversion factors exhibit the "pull to par", decreasing towards 1.00 for those with a coupon above the notional 7% and increasing towards 1.00 for bonds with a coupon below 7%. The passage of time also shows bonds falling out of the delivery basket, and the introduction of a new issue into the basket, the 5% gilt maturing 7 March 2012.

Futures Contract

Gilt	Dec00	Mar01	Jun01	Sep01	Dec01	Mar02
5.75% Treasury 2009	0.9174728	0.9189802				
6.25% Treasury 2010	0.9467478	0.9475611	0.9486415	0.9494956	0.9505874	
9% Conversion 2011	1.1479281	1.1455578	1.1431026	1.1405936	1.1381240	1.1355859
5% Treasury 2012				0.8528791	0.8551727	0.8577270
9% Treasury 2012	1.1576368	1.1555512	1.1531626			
8% Treasury 2013	1.0835676	1.0826206	1.0814990	1.0805114	1.0793560	1.0783363

Table 17.3: Conversion factors for deliverable gilts, Dec00 to Mar02 long gilt contracts. Source: LIFFE.

The yield obtainable on bonds that have different coupons but identical maturities can be equalised by adjusting the price for each bond. This principle is used to calculate the conversion factors for different bonds. The conversion factor for a bond is the price per £1 (or per $1, €1, and so on) at which the bond would give a yield equal to the yield of the notional coupon specified in the futures contract. This is 7% in the case of the long gilt contract, 6% for the Treasury long bond, and so on. In other words the conversion factor for each bond is the price such that every bond would provide an investor with the same yield if purchased; or, the price at which a deliverable bond would trade if its gross redemption yield was 7% (or 6%, and so on). The yield calculation is rounded to whole quarters, given the delivery month cycle of futures. Futures exchanges calculate conversion factors effective either on the exact delivery date, where a single date is defined, or (as at LIFFE) on the first day of the delivery month if delivery can take place at any time during the delivery month.

The conversion factor is assigned by the exchange to each bond in the delivery basket at the start of trading of each contract. It remains constant throughout the life of the contract. A particular bond that remains in the delivery basket over a length of time will have different conversion factors for successive contracts. For example the 9% UK Treasury maturing on 13 October 2008 had conversion factors of 1.1454317, 1.1429955 and 1.1407155 for the LIFFE long gilt contracts that matured in June, September and December 1998 respectively.

Other things being equal, bonds with a higher coupon will have larger conversion factors than those with lower coupons. For bonds with the same coupon, maturity has an influence, though this is slightly less obvious. For bonds with coupons below the notional rate defined in the contract description, the conversion factor is smaller for bonds with a longer maturity. The opposite is true for bonds carrying coupons in excess of the notional coupon rate, for which the conversion factor will be larger the longer the maturity. This effect arises from the mathematics of fixed-interest securities. Bonds with coupon below current market yields will trade at a discount. This discount is larger the longer the maturity, because it is a disadvantage to hold a bond paying a coupon lower than current market rates, and this disadvantage is greater the longer the period to the bond maturing. Conversely, bonds with coupons above current market yields trade at a premium which will be greater the longer the maturity.

To help calculate the *invoice price* of a bond on delivery, we multiply the price of the final settlement price of the futures contract with its conversion factor. This gives us the *converted price*. The price payable by the long future on delivery of the bond is the invoice price, and this is the futures settlement price plus accrued interest. This was shown in simple fashion as (17.1). The actual invoice price, calculated once the actual bond being delivered is known, is given by

$$P_{Inv} = \left(M_{fut} \times P_{futsett} \times CF \right) + AI \tag{17.8}$$

where

P_{Inv} is the invoice price;

M_{fut} is the nominal value of the delivered bonds as specified in the contract;

$P_{futsett}$ is the futures settlement price.

Invoice amount

When the bond is delivered, the long pays the short an invoice amount:

$$Invoiced = \left(EDSP/100 \times CF \times \text{Nominal} \right) + AI \tag{17.9}$$

The settlement price (or *exchange delivery settlement price*, EDSP) is the trading price per £100 nominal for the futures contract on the last day of trading, and is confirmed by the Exchange. The invoice amount includes accrued interest because the futures contract is traded at a *clean* price and does not include accrued interest.

Example 17.1: Calculating the invoice price

A futures contract settles at 102.50. The contract specifies £100,000 nominal of the underlying bond. The delivered bond has a conversion factor of 1.14579 and accrued interest of 0.73973. The settlement price is equal to 1.025% of the nominal value (par value). The invoice price is calculated as

$$P_{Inv} = \left(100,000 \times 1.025 \times 1.14579 \right) + 0.73973$$
$$= £117,443 + 0.73973$$

For the Treasury long bond the conversion factor is calculated using (17.10),

$$CF = \frac{1}{1.03^{t/6}} \left[\frac{C}{2} + \frac{C}{0.06} \left(1 - \frac{1}{1.03^{2N}} \right) + \frac{1}{1.03^{2N}} \right] \tag{17.10}$$

where

N is the complete years to maturity as at the delivery month;

t is the number of months in excess of the whole N (rounded *down* to whole quarters).

The LIFFE conversion factor for the long gilt is reproduced in Appendix 17.1. The formula is actually the same, beginners are invited to explain that this is indeed so. To illustrate (17.10), if a deliverable Treasury bond has a maturity of 19 years and 5 months, t is 3 because the 5 months is rounded down to one quarter or 3 months. Hence if the maturity is 19 years and 9 months, t is 6.

It is worth summarising what we know so far about conversion factors:

- conversion factors remain constant for a bond from the moment they are assigned to the expiry of the contract;

- conversion factors are different for each bond and for each contract;[13] from Table 17.3, which relates to the long gilt contract and its notional coupon of 7%, we see that conversion factors for bonds with coupons higher than 7% diminish in value for each successive contract month, while those for bonds with coupons lower than 7% rise in value for successive contract months. This reflects the "pull to par" effect, which for bonds with the higher coupon is falling from a premium and for bonds with the lower coupon is rising from a discount;

- the conversion factor is used to calculate the invoice price of a bond that is delivered into a futures contract;

- bonds with coupons greater than the notional coupon of the futures contract have a conversion factor higher than 1, while bonds with coupons lower than the notional coupon have a conversion factor lower than 1.

The conversion factor is not a hedge ratio, as has been strongly emphasised by both Burghardt and Galitz,[14] and should not be used as such. Certain textbooks and market practitioners have suggested that using the ratio of two bonds' conversion factors can be an effective hedge ratio, for hedging a bond position, rather than the traditional approach of using the ratio of basis point values. This is fallacious and will lead to serious errors. The conversion factor of a bond is influenced primarily by its coupon, whereas the modified duration of a bond (from which is derived the BPV) is a function mainly of its term to maturity. Hence it is not correct to substitute them. If an investor was hedging a position in a long-dated bond of low coupon, and the current CTD bond was a short-dated bond of high coupon, the volatility ratio calculated using the respective conversion factors would be lower than unity. However, using respective BPVs would result in a volatility ratio higher than one. This example illustrates how using a ratio of conversion factors can result in serious hedging errors, and this approach must not be adopted.

Using conversion factors provides an effective system for making all deliverable bonds perfect substitutes for one another. The system is not perfect of course. Conversion factors are calculated to equalise returns at a single uniform yield, the notional coupon rate specified in the contract specification. In practice though bonds trade at different yields, resulting in the yield curve. Hence despite the use of conversion factors, bonds will not be precisely "equal" at the time of delivery. Some bonds will be relatively more expensive, some cheaper; one particular bond will be the *cheapest-to-deliver* bond. The cheapest-to-deliver (CTD) bond is an important concept in the pricing of bond futures contracts.

---

[13] If two bonds had identical coupons and maturity dates, then they would have the same conversion factor for a specific contract. However, under these terms the two bonds would be identical as well…

[14] Burghardt (*ibid*), page 9 and Chapter 5; Galitz (1995), page 398.

17.3.4 *The bond basis*

Basis trading arises from the difference between the current clean price of a bond and the (implied) forward clean price at which the bond is bought through the purchase of a futures contract. The difference between these two prices is known as the *gross basis*. This is the bond basis to which the market refers, the difference between the bond's spot cash price and the price implied by the current price of the futures contract. The latter is given by multiplying the futures price by the relevant bond's conversion factor.

The formula for calculating the gross basis is therefore:

$$Basis = P_{bond} - \left(P_{fut} \times CF \right). \tag{17.11}$$

From (17.11) we might think that if we sell a futures contract short, in effect this guarantees an ability to deliver the bond at the futures delivery date and receive a known price for the bond. However, the price payable for the bond at delivery is based on the future's final settlement price, and not the trading price of the future at any time beforehand, and so this thinking is erroneous.

In the Treasury market both cash and futures prices are quoted as points and ticks (32nds) per $100 nominal value, and if necessary as half-ticks or 64ths. A 64th price is indicated by a +.

The gross basis can be explained essentially as the difference between the running yield on the bond and the current repo (money market) rate. However, a residual factor exists due to the delivery option implicit in the design of the futures contract and to the daily marking-to-market of the contract, both of which are more difficult to quantify. This residual amount is known as the *net basis*. Net basis is the gross basis adjusted for net carry. Net carry is the actual coupon income and re-investment less borrowing expense, which is at the security's actual repo or money market financing rate.

Figure 17.6 is the Bloomberg page DLV of the deliverable bonds for the June 2000 long gilt contract, and shows the conversion factors and gross basis value for each bond in the basket.

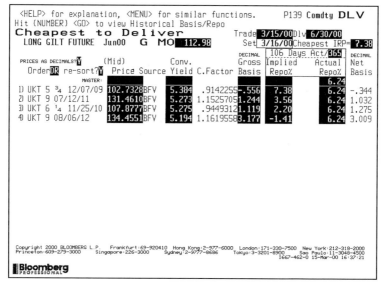

Figure 17.6: Delivery basket for Jun00 long gilt, Bloomberg page DLV, 15 March 2000. ©Bloomberg L.P. Reproduced with permission.

> **Example 17.2: The gross basis**
> Consider the following market details, all relating to one instantaneous point in time:
>
> | | |
> |---|---|
> | Settlement date | 16 March 2000 |
> | Futures delivery date | 30 June 2000 |
> | Days to delivery | 106 |
> | Bond price (UKT 9% 2011) | 131.4610 |
> | Accrued interest | 1.5780822 |
> | Accrued to delivery | 4.1917808 |
> | Futures price (M0 LIFFE long gilt) | 112.98 |
> | Conversion factor | 1.1525705 |
> | Cash market repo rate | 6.24% |
>
> We can calculate the gross basis that would apply in a hypothetical cash-and-carry trade, where there is a simultaneous purchase of the bond and sale of the futures contract as shown below.
>
> bond purchase – outflow of funds: $131.461 + 1.5781 = 133.0390822$
> futures sale – inflow of funds: $(112.98 \times 1.1525705) + 4.192 = 134.409196$.
>
> The gross basis is $131.4610 - (112.98 \times 1.1525705)$ or 1.24358491.

17.3.5 *The net basis*

We've seen from the previous section that gross basis measures the carry on a bond that applies during the life of the futures contract. Because of other factors associated with the delivery into a futures contract, principally that delivery is at the option of the short future, the gross basis is not the actual carry that would be incurred if a trader put on a cash versus futures trade. This is measured by the *net basis*. The net basis causes much confusion amongst market participants, but it is a straightforward concept. Burghardt states that the net basis is the difference between a bond's basis and its total carry to delivery.[15] Plona describes net basis as the difference between the *implied repo rate* and the general collateral repo rate. We consider the implied repo rate (IRR) in the next section.[16]

Both descriptions are good ways in which to consider net basis. Essentially the net basis is the gross basis adjusted for net carry. Net carry is the actual coupon income (and any re-investment income) minus borrowing expense, which is at the security's actual repo (money market) rate. The net basis is therefore the true "economic basis" and measures the net gain from a simultaneous position in the cash bond and the futures contract. A positive value represents a *loss* or net cost to the long cash/short futures position, and the net basis is the expected *profit* for the short cash/long futures position (where the actual repo rate used is the reverse repo rate). The opposite is true for negative net basis values.

The net basis is calculated on the assumption that a basis trade is conducted by the arbitrageur borrowing funds to purchase the cheapest-to-deliver bond, financing it in the repo market, and shorting the futures contract. It measures the maximum *loss* that would be suffered by holding this position until the contract expiry date. The net basis should be nega-

---

[15] *Ibid*, page 33. It is also known as the *basis net of carry*.
[16] Plona (or *Ibid*), page 32.

tive as a loss measure; a positive net basis indicates the potential profit from such a trade.[17] On the other hand, a negative net basis theoretically indicates the potential profit from a short bond/long futures position.

To calculate the net basis, we need to make an assumption about the financing rates that would apply to a basis trade.[18] This centres on the repo rate that is applicable to the cash bond element of the trade. Analysts use one of two methods:

- Using the specific repo rate for the cash bond, fixed to the maturity date. This is a logical approach, as it provides an accurate measure of the financing cost associated with running a long position in the bond, and then delivering it into the futures exchange. Calculating net basis under this method provides a measure of the value of the delivery option;

- Using the overnight GC repo rate, assuming therefore that the bond position is financed on a daily basis. Assuming that the overnight rate will be maintained more or less over the term of the trade is risky.

The box illustrates calculation of the net basis.

Example 17.3:   The net basis

Consider this calculation for the June 1998 long gilt future contract. At this time the "special ex" rule applies to delivery of bonds into the contract, something that no longer applied with the removal of special ex-trading in August 1998.

Trade date	24 April 1998
Settlement date	25 April 1998
M8 long gilt future price	109.65625
CTD bond (8½% Treasury 2007)	106.34375
Accrued interest	2.30548
Accrued to delivery	3.4232882
Dirty price	108.64932
Conversion factor (8½% 2007)	0.9674064
Repo rate	6.36%

The converted price of the bond (that is, through the futures contract) is:

$$109.65625 \times 0.9674064 = 106.08216.$$

The market clean price is 106.34375, therefore the gross basis is:

$$106.34375 - 106.08216 = 0.26159.$$

Due to the special-ex rule in this case, the last day for delivery of 8½% Treasury 2007 into the futures contract is 12 June. This makes the term 48 days. The total price paid including accrued interest will be 108.64923. To finance that using repo for 48 days until 12 June will cost £0.9087243. The holder of the gilt will however earn 48 days' accrued interest of £1.1178082. Therefore, buying the bond direct gives the owner an income advantage of £0.2090839.

---

[17] Note that in some cases and vendor systems, the net basis appears to be positive because the negative sign is left off, under the assumption that users are aware that the net basis represents the loss from a long cash/short futures trade.

[18] As we shall see in the next section, no assumptions need to be made when determining the implied repo rate, which is calculated from actual market-observed prices.

The difference between the gross basis and this income advantage is £0.216159 – £0.2090839, that is £0.0525. It therefore represents the gain by buying the gilt using the futures contract rather than buying directly in the market.

Of course the long gilt contract gives the futures seller the right to deliver any of the gilts in the delivery basket and on any day of the delivery month. If the CTD is bought through a futures contract the buyer may find that because of market movements, a different gilt is delivered. The futures short in effect holds an option which decreases the value of the futures contract to the long.

For this reason the *net* basis is usually positive. The futures contract is also marked-to-market which means that the gain or loss on the contract is spread over the life of the contract, in contrast to a forward contract. This effect is small but will again lead to the net basis differing from zero.

The net basis is given by

$$NetBasis = (108.64923 \times (1 + 6.36 \times (48/36500))) - ((109.65625 \times 0.9674064) + 3.423882)$$
$$= 109.5579543 - 109.50544625$$
$$= 0.05250805.$$

17.3.6 *The implied repo rate*

In a basis trade the rate implied by the strategy is known as a repo rate because it is equivalent to a *repurchase* agreement with the futures market. In effect the short future lends money to the futures market: the short future agrees to buy a bond with a simultaneous provision to sell it back to the market at a predetermined price and to receive a rate of interest on his money, the repo rate. It is the *implied repo rate* because it is an expected repo rate gain if the trade was carried out. In some literature it is suggested as a complex and obscure calculation, in fact the implied repo rate (IRR) is very straightforward to calculate. It is the theoretical return from a basis trade of long cash bond against short future, with the bond delivered into the future on expiry.

The IRR is a measure of return from a basis trade. Consider the cash flows involved when one is long bond/short future. We have:

- a cash outflow from purchasing the bond;
- a cash inflow on delivery into the future, including the accrued interest to the delivery date;
- the cash borrowed to finance the trade.

We simply therefore wish to have the percentage return of the investment over the borrowing cost. That is,

$$\text{IRR} = \frac{((P_{futs} \times CF) + AI_{del}) - (P_{bond} + AI)}{P_{bond} + AI} \times \frac{M}{Days} \tag{17.12}$$

where M is the day-base, either 360 or 365 and *Days* is the term of the trade. There is no need to remember this version though, Burghardt[19] simplifies it to

---

[19] *Ibid*, page 14.

$$\text{IRR} = \left(\frac{P_{invoice} - P_{bond}}{P_{bond}} \right) \times \left(\frac{360}{n} \right) \tag{17.13}$$

which is identical to (17.12), with n for the number of days to delivery, and all prices still include accrued interest, at the time of the trade (bond) or to delivery (future). The formula written as (17.13) is easy to explain. The invoice price is the futures invoice price, the amount from the delivery on expiry. Of course the actual invoice price is a function of the final futures settlement price, but we adjust the current futures price with the conversion factor to allow for this.

Note that Bloomberg quotes the formula in still more simplified fashion, as

$$\text{IRR} = \left(\frac{P_{FutsInvoice}}{P_{bond}} - 1 \right) \times \left(\frac{360}{n} \right) \tag{17.14}$$

with the 360-day base associated with the US Treasury market.

Both (17.12) and (17.13) assume that no coupon is paid during the trade. If a coupon is paid during the trade, it is considered as being reinvested, and the cash flow total must therefore include both the coupon and the reinvestment income generated. The reinvestment rate used in the market is one of the following:

■ the implied repo rate;

■ the bond's yield-to-maturity. This is described as being consistent with the bond yield calculation itself, which assumes reinvestment of coupon at the bond yield;

■ the overnight repo rate, and rolled over. This is justified on the basis that traders in fact do not reinvest the coupon but use the funds to reduce funding costs.

The first two are assumed to apply to maturity, while the second must be calculated at the prevailing rate each day. If the reinvestment rate is assumed to be the IRR, it is the rate that results in

$$P_{bond} \times \left(1 + \text{IRR}\left(\frac{n}{M} \right) \right) = P_{Invoice} + \left(\frac{C}{2} \right) \times \left(1 + \text{IRR}\left(\frac{n_2}{M} \right) \right) \tag{17.15}$$

where n_2 is the number of days between the coupon payment and the futures expiry (delivery) date. Expression (17.15) is then rearranged for the implied repo rate, to give us

$$\text{IRR} = \frac{\left(P_{Invoice} + \frac{C}{2} - P_{bond} \right) \times M}{\left(P_{bond} \times n \right) - \left(\frac{C}{2} \times n_2 \right)}. \tag{17.16}$$

The deliverable bond that has the highest implied repo rate is the *cheapest-to-deliver* bond or CTD. We see from (17.16) that the IRR is a function of the bond price, the value of which is compared to the forward price for the bond implied by futures price. As such the status of CTD bond reflects the bond's price (in other words its yield). If the yield of a bond within the delivery basket moves sufficiently vis-à-vis the other deliverable bonds, it may become the CTD bond. A change in the cheapest bond is an important development and any such change should be anticipated in advance by good traders.

The bond with the highest implied repo rate will, almost invariably, have the lowest net basis. On rare occasions this will not be observed. When two bonds each have implied repo rates that are very similar, it is sometimes the case that the bond with the (slightly) lower implied repo rate has a (slightly) lower net basis.

The CTD bond is just that: it is the cheapest bond to deliver into the futures contract in terms of running costs. The short future has the delivery option, and will elect to deliver the CTD bond unless there is a reason it cannot, in which case it will deliver the next cheapest at greater cost to itself. Assuming that a basis trade is put on with the CTD bond against the future, if the CTD changes then the position becomes useless and will be unwound at great loss. The CTD bond is what the market will treat as the actual underlying bond of the futures contract, and it is closely observed. Pricing theory informs us that the futures price will track the CTD bond price; in fact it is the other way around, with the liquidity and transparency of the futures contract and its price meaning that the CTD bond price tracks that of the future. Under the terms of the long gilt contract, the CTD gilt can be delivered on any business day of the delivery month, but in practice only one of two days are ever used to make delivery: the first (business) day of the delivery month or the last (delivery) day of the month. If the current yield on the CTD gilt exceeds the money market repo rate, the bond will be delivered on the last business day of the month, because the short future earns more by holding on to the bond than by delivering it and investing the proceeds in the money market; otherwise the bond will be delivered on the first business day of the delivery month. Until very recently a gilt that was eligible for trading *special ex-dividend* on any day of the delivery month was not eligible for delivery into that gilt contract. However, from August 1998 the provision for special ex-dividend trading was removed from gilts, so this consideration no longer applies. Other gilts that are not eligible for delivery are index-linked, partly paid or convertible gilts.[20] For gilts the IRR for all deliverable bonds can be calculated using (17.12) in the normal way. However if a bond goes ex-dividend between trade date and delivery date, a modification is required in which the interest accrued is negative during the ex-dividend period.

Example 17.4:   The implied repo rate

Another way of looking at the concept of the cheapest-to-deliver bond is in terms of the implied repo rate. The CTD bond is the bond that gives the highest implied repo rate (IRR) to the short from a cash-and-carry trade, that is a strategy of buying the bond (with borrowed funds) in the cash market and selling it forward into the futures market. The bond is funded in the repo market, and by selling it forward the trade is in effect a repo with the futures market, hence *implied* repo rate.

To illustrate we calculate the IRR for the 9% Treasury 2008, a UK gilt, at the time that

---

[20] Gilts go ex-dividend seven business days before the coupon date, this being the record date to determine the investors that will receive the coupon. Prior to its withdrawal, counterparties could agree between themselves to trade ex-dividend up to two weeks before the ex-dividend date, this being known as *special ex-dividend*. During trading for the September 1997 long gilt contract, some market participants forgot (or were unaware) that gilts that were special ex-dividend at any time during the delivery month became ineligible for delivery, and had traded in the current CTD bond, the 9% 2008 under the assumption that they could deliver, or would be delivered into, of this bond. When the CTD bond changed it resulted in losses for parties that had not been aware of this. This despite the fact that LIFFE sent out a notice informing the market that the CTD for September 1997 would not be the 9% 2008 for this reason…

the "front month" contract was the December 1998 contract. The price of the gilt is 129.0834. The December 1998 long gilt futures contract is trading at 114.50. The date is 1 October. The money market rate on this date is 7.25%. As the current (or *running*) yield on the 9% 2008, at 6.972% is lower than the money market rate, it will be delivered at the beginning of December (that is, in 61 days from now). To identify the CTD bond we would need to calculate the IRR for all eligible bonds. We use the conversion factor for the bond which is 1.140715, calculated and given out by LIFFE before the futures contract began trading.

The cash outflow in a cash-and-carry trade is:

bond dirty price	129.0834
interest cost	
(1 October – 1 December)	$129.0834 \times (0.0725 \times (61/365))$
Total outflow	130.6474.

The bond (whose price includes 171 days' accrued interest on 1 October) has to be financed at the money market rate of 7.25% for the 61 days between 1 October and 1 December, when the bond (if it is still the CTD) is delivered into the futures market. The cash inflow per £100 nominal as a result of this trade is:

Implied clean price of bond on 1 December	
(futures price on 1 October multiplied	
by conversion factor)	114.50×1.1407155
Accrued interest (1 October – 1 December)	$£9 \times (61/365)$
Total inflow	132.11603

The implied price of the bond on 1 December equals the futures price on 1 October multiplied by the conversion factor for the bond. Because the futures price is quoted clean, accrued interest has to be added to obtain the implied dirty price on 1 December.

This cash-and-carry trade which operates for 61 days from 1 October to 1 December generates a rate of return or *implied repo rate* of:

$$\text{IRR} = \left(\frac{132.11603 - 130.6474}{130.6474} \right) \times \frac{365}{61} \times 100$$
$$= 6.726\%.$$

Example 17.5: Calculating gross basis, net basis and implied repo rate

The gross basis is the difference between the actual price of the bond and the forward price of the bond as implied by the price of the futures contract, and represents the carrying cost of the bond. This is the actual difference between the coupon gain and re-investment minus the carry costs (which is at the actual money market repo rate). A positive net basis represents the loss that would result from a long cash/short futures position, and therefore the theoretical gain from a short cash/long futures trade, where the actual repo rate is the reverse repo rate transacted when covering the short cash position. The implied repo rate is the theoretical return from a long cash/short futures trade, assuming that the trader is short the number of futures equal to the bond's conversion factor for each £100,000 nominal of bonds held. Any coupon payments are assumed to be reinvested at the implied repo rate.

Earlier in this book we presented the formulae for gross basis and implied repo rate. The net basis is given by:

$$\text{Net basis} = \left(P_{bond} \times \left(1 + r \times Del/36500\right)\right) - \left(\left(P_{fut} \times CF\right) + AI_{del}\right)$$

where

P_{bond} is the bond dirty price;
r is the actual repo rate (expressed as per cent × 100);
Del is the days to delivery;
P_{fut} is the futures price;
CF is the bond's conversion factor;
AI_{del} is the bond's accrued interest to delivery.

For net basis calculations in Treasury or euro markets the appropriate 360-day basis is used.

The calculations are for the CTD bond for the long gilt contract, which was the 6¼% 2010 gilt. We use mid prices for the bond. The trade is buying the cash and simultaneously selling the future. Note that gilts accrue on actual/actual basis and there were 184 days in the interest period 25 May–25 November 2001. The accrued interest calculation is therefore $(80/184 \times (6.25 \times 0.5))$ for the first date and $(126/184 \times (6.25 \times 0.5))$ for the delivery date.

Settlement date	13 August 2001
Futures price	115.94
6¼% Treasury 25/11/10 price	110.20
Conversion factor	0.9494956
Repo rate	4.90%

Calculations

Cash out on 13/8/2001	110.20 plus accrued (80 days)	=	111.558696
Cash in on 28/9/021	(115.94 × 0.9494956) plus accrued	=	110.08452 + 2.139946
			(46 days later)
		=	112.2244659

Gross basis

110.20 – 110.0845199	=	**0.1154801**

Net basis

(111.558696 × (1 + 4.90 × 46/36500)) – 112.2244659	=	**0.0231432**

Implied repo rate

(112.2244659/111.558696 – 1) × (365/46) × 100	=	**4.735390%**

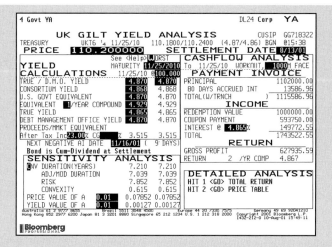

Figure 17.7: Bloomberg YA page for 6¼% 2010 gilt, showing accrued interest for value 13 August 2001. ©Bloomberg L.P. Reproduced with permission.

These calculations are confirmed by looking at the Bloomberg screens YA and DLV for value on 13 August 2001, as shown in Figures 17.7 and 17.8 respectively. Figure 17.7 is selected for the 6¼% 2010 gilt and Figure 17.8 is selected for the front month contract at the time, the Sep01 gilt future. Figure 17.9 shows the change in CTD bond status between the 6¼% 2010 gilt and the 9% 2011 gilt, the second cheapest bond at the time of the analysis, with changes in the futures price. The change of CTD status with changes in the implied repo rate is shown in Figure 17.10. Both are Bloomberg page HCG.

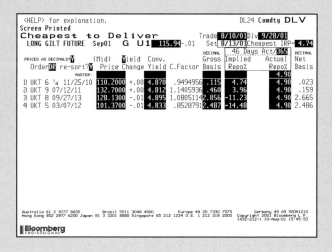

Figure 17.8: Bloomberg DLV page for Sep01 (U1) gilt contract, showing gross basis, net basis and IRR for trade date 12 August 2001. ©Bloomberg L.P. Reproduced with permission.

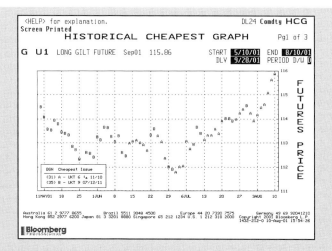

Figure 17.9: Bloomberg HCG page for Sep01 (U1) gilt contract, showing CTD bond history up to 12 August 2001 with changes in futures price. ©Bloomberg L.P. Reproduced with permission.

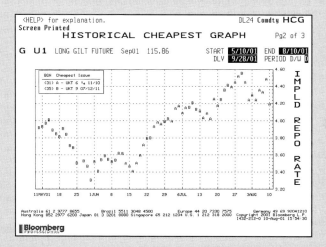

Figure 17.10: Bloomberg HCG page for Sep01 (U1) gilt contract, showing CTD bond history up to 12 August 2001, with changes in implied repo rate. ©Bloomberg L.P. Reproduced with permission.

Page DLV on Bloomberg lists deliverable bonds for any selected futures contract. Bonds are listed in order of declining *implied repo rate*; the user can select in increasing or decreasing order of implied repo rate, basis, yield, maturity, coupon or duration. The user can also select the price source for the bonds (in our example set at "Bloomberg Generic" rather than any specific bank or market maker) and the current cash repo rate.

17.4 Selecting the cheapest-to-deliver bond

As we've discussed just now there are two competing definitions for identifying the bond that is the cheapest-to-deliver issue, and they almost always, but not always, identify the same issue as "cheapest". The general rule is that the issue with the highest implied repo rate, and/or the issue with the lowest net basis is the CTD bond. Most academic literature uses the first definition, whereas market practitioners often argue that the net basis method should be used since it measures the actual profit & loss for an actual cash-and-carry trade.

It is up to the individual trader to decide which method to use as the basis for analysis. For example, Bloomberg terminals use the IRR method. The justification for this is that many market participants accept that the IRR method is appropriate to the cash-and-carry investor seeking maximum return per dollar invested. The main area of disagreement regards those cases where an arbitrageur finances (repos) the cash side of the trade and the net basis measures their resulting profit or loss. In a Bloomberg analysis this net basis is presented as percentage points of par (the same units as price), although some practitioners express it as p&l per million bonds. It is primarily because the net basis is per par amount rather than per pound invested that the two methods occasionally identify different "cheapest" issues. Note that in practice net basis will always be a loss, otherwise traders would arbitrage an infinite amount of any issue with a profitable net basis. Therefore the basis method identifies the issue which has the *smallest loss* per million pounds nominal as the cheapest issue.

The only reason a trader is willing to accept this guaranteed loss is that they don't intend to follow through exactly with this trade to maturity. Being long of the basis, that is short futures, essentially gives the trader numerous delivery and trading options; the cost of these is the net basis that the trader pays. In effect the trader is buying options for the cost of the net basis. The number of options they buy is indicated by the *conversion factor* since that is the hedge factor for the cheapest issue. Therefore the cost per option is the net basis divided by the conversion factor. When ranked by net basis per contract (that is, divided by the conversion factor), the cheapest by this method invariably agrees with the IRR method.

17.5 Trading the basis

17.5.1 *The basis position*

Basis trading or cash-and-carry trading is an arbitrage-driven activity that involves the simultaneous trading of cash bonds and exchange-traded bond futures contracts. Traders speak of going "long the basis" or of "buying the basis" when they buy the bond and sell the future. The equivalent number of futures contracts to trade per 100,000 nominal value of cash bond is given by the conversion factor. The opposite position, buying the future and selling the cash bond, is known as "selling the basis" or "going short the basis". Someone who is long the basis has bought the basis itself (hence the expression!) and will therefore profit if the basis increases, that is, the price of the bond increases relative to the price of the futures contract.[21] A trader who has sold the basis will gain if the basis decreases, that is the price of the bond falls relative to the futures contract price.

Ideally each side of the position will be executed simultaneously, and most derivatives exchanges have a basis trading facility that enables a party to undertake this. Certain govern-

---

[21] Remember, when we say the price of the future, we mean the price as adjusted by the relevant conversion factor.

ment bond primary dealers will quote a price in the basis as well. If this is not possible, the trade can be put on separately, known as "legging into the trade" as each leg is carried out at different times. To do this, generally the cash bond position is put on first and then the futures position, as the latter is more liquid and transparent. Whichever way round the trade is effected though, this method carries with it some risk, as the price of the leg yet to be traded can move against you, complicating the completion of the trade.[22] If this happens there is a danger that the second leg is put on one or two ticks offside, and straight away the trade starts off at a loss. This should be avoided if at all possible. There is also a bid-offer spread to take into account, for both cash and future positions.

The arbitrageur hopes to generate profit from a basis trade, and this will be achieved from changes in the basis itself and/or gains from the funding or carry. If the net funding cost is positive, then this will add to any profit or reduce losses arising from changes in the basis. This is where the repo rate comes in. The trader may elect to fund the bond position, whether long or short, in overnight repo but generally the best approach is to fix a term repo, with expiry date matching the date at which the trader hopes to unwind the trade. This may be to the contract expiry date or before. If short the basis, it is vital that the repo desk is aware if there is any chance that the bond goes special, as this could prove costly unless the repo is fixed to the trade maturity. There is also a bid-offer spread to consider with the repo rate, and while this is usually quite small for GC repo, say as little as 3 basis points, it may be wider for specifics, from 10 to 20 basis points.

In the next chapter we consider further issues in trading the basis.

A summary of the basic position

Cash-and-carry trading
In this trade, we undertake simultaneous transactions in:

- buying the cash bond;
- selling the bond futures contract.

The trader buys the cheapest-to-deliver bond, the financing of which is fixed in the repo market (trader pays the repo rate). The trader believes that the bond is cheaper in the cash market than its forward price implied by the price of the futures contract. On the expiry date of the futures contract, any bond in the deliverable basket is eligible for delivery, but (assuming no change in CTD status) the trader will deliver the bond they are long of. The trader's potential gain arises from the mis-pricing of the bond in the cash market.

Reverse cash-and-carry trading
In this trade we undertake simultaneous transactions by:

- selling the CTD bond in the cash market, and covering the position by entering into reverse repo (the trader receives the repo rate);
- buying the equivalent number of futures contracts.

For the reverse basis trade to generate profit there can be no change in the CTD status

---

[22] From personal experience the author will testify that this is an extremely stressful position to be in! Don't leg into the trade unless there's no alternative.

of the bond; if another bond becomes the CTD at contract expiry, a loss will result. On futures expiry, the trader is delivered into the bond in which they have a short position, and this also enables them to close-out the repo trade. Theoretical profit is generated because the invoice price paid for the bond is lower than the price received at the start of the trade in the cash market, once funding costs have been taken into account.

Appendices

Appendix 17.1:   The LIFFE long gilt conversion factor

Here we describe the process used for the calculation of the *conversion factor* or *price factor* for deliverable bonds of the long gilt contract. The contract specifies a bond of maturity 8¾-13 years and a notional coupon of 7%. For each bond that is eligible to be in the delivery basket, the conversion factor is given by the following expression: $P(7)/100$ where the numerator $P(7)$ is equal to the price per £100 nominal of the deliverable gilt at which it has a gross redemption yield of 7%, calculated as at the first day of the delivery month, less the accrued interest on the bond on that day. This calculation uses the formula given at (17.17) and the expression used to calculate accrued interest. The analysis is adapted, with permission, from LIFFE's technical document.

The numerator $P(7)$ is given by (17.17):

$$P(7) = \frac{1}{1.035^{t/s}}\left(c_1 + \frac{c_2}{1.035} + \frac{C}{0.07}\left(\frac{1}{1.035} - \frac{1}{1.035^n}\right) + \frac{100}{1.035^n}\right) - AI \tag{17.17}$$

where

c_1 is the cash flow due on the following quasi-coupon date, per £100 nominal of the gilt. c_1 will be zero if the first day of the delivery month occurs in the ex-dividend period or if the gilt has a long first coupon period and the first day of the delivery month occurs in the first full coupon period. c_1 will be less than $C/2$ if the first day of the delivery month falls in a short first coupon period. c_1 will be greater than $C/2$ if the first day of the delivery month falls in a long first coupon period and the first day of the delivery month occurs in the second full coupon period;

c_2 is the cash flow due on the next but one quasi-coupon date, per £100 nominal of the gilt. c_2 will be greater than $C/2$ if the first day of the delivery month falls in a long first coupon period and in the first full coupon period. In all other cases, $c_2 = C/2$;

C is the annual coupon of the gilt, per £100 nominal;

t is the number of calendar days from and including the first day of the delivery month up to but excluding the next quasi-coupon date;

s is the number of calendar days in the full coupon period in which the first day of the delivery month occurs;

n is the number of full coupon periods between the following quasi-coupon date and the redemption date;

AI is the accrued interest per £100 nominal of the gilt.

The accrued interest used in the formula above is given according to the following procedures.

- If the first day of the delivery month occurs in a standard coupon period, and the first day of the delivery month occurs on or before the ex-dividend date, then

$$AI = \frac{t}{s} \times \frac{C}{2}. \qquad (17.18)$$

- If the first day of the delivery month occurs in a standard coupon period, and the first day of the delivery month occurs after the ex-dividend date, then:

$$AI = \left(\frac{t}{s} - 1\right) \times \frac{C}{2}, \qquad (17.19)$$

where

t is the number of calendar days from and including the last coupon date up to but excluding the first day of the delivery month;

s is the number of calendar days in the full coupon period in which the first day of the delivery month occurs.

- If the first day of the delivery month occurs in a short first coupon period, and the first day of the delivery month occurs on or before the ex-dividend date, then

$$AI = \frac{t^*}{s} \times \frac{C}{2}. \qquad (17.20)$$

- If the first day of the delivery month occurs in a short first coupon period, and the first day of the delivery month occurs after the ex-dividend date, then

$$AI = \left(\frac{t^* - n}{s}\right) \times \frac{C}{2}, \qquad (17.21)$$

where

t^* is the number of calendar days from and including the issue date up to but excluding the first day of the delivery month;

n is the number of calendar days from and including the issue date up to but excluding the next quasi-coupon date.

- If the first day of the delivery month occurs in a long first coupon period, and during the first full coupon period, then

$$AI = \frac{u}{s_1} \times \frac{C}{2}. \qquad (17.22)$$

- If the first day of the delivery month occurs in a long first coupon period, and during the second full coupon period and on or before the ex-dividend date, then

$$AI = \left(\frac{p_1}{s_1} + \frac{p_2}{s_2}\right) \times \frac{C}{2}. \qquad (17.23)$$

- If the first day of the delivery month occurs in a long first coupon period, and during the second full coupon period and after the ex-dividend date, then

$$AI = \left(\frac{p_2}{s_2} - 1\right) \times \frac{C}{2},$$ (17.24)

where

u is the number of calendar days from and including the issue date up to but excluding the first day of the delivery month;

s_1 is the number of calendar days in the full coupon period in which the issue date occurs;

s_2 is the number of days in the next full coupon period after the full coupon period in which the issue date occurs;

p_1 is the number of calendar days from and including the issue date up to but excluding the next quasi-coupon date;

p_2 is the number of calendar days from and including the quasi-coupon date after the issue date up to but excluding the first day of the delivery month, which falls in the next full coupon period after the full coupon period in which the issue date occurs.

Selected bibliography and references

Benninga, S., Weiner, Z., "An Investigation of Cheapest-to-Deliver on Treasury Bond Futures Contracts", *Journal of Computational Finance 2*, 1999, pp. 39–56

Boyle, P., "The Quality Option and the Timing Option in Futures Contracts", *Journal of Finance 44*, 1989, pp. 101–113

Burghardt, G., *et al*, *The Treasury Bond Basis*, revised edition, Irwin 1994

Galitz, L., *Financial Engineering*, revised edition, FT Pitman, 1995, Chapter 8

Fabozzi, F., *Treasury Securities and Derivatives*, FJF Associates, 1998

Fabozzi, F., *Bond Portfolio Management*, 2nd edition, FJF Associates, 2001, Chapters 6, 17

Plona, C., *The European Bond Basis*, McGraw-Hill 1997

Rubinstein, M., *Rubinstein on Derivatives*, RISK Books, 1999

Jonas, S., "The change in the cheapest-to-deliver in Bond and Note Futures", in Dattatreya, R., (ed.), *Fixed Income Analytics*, McGraw-Hill 1991

Van Deventer, D., Imai, K., *Financial Risk Analytics: A Term Structure Model Approach for Banking, Insurance and Investment Management*, Irwin 1997, page 11

Questions and exercises

The author still quite likes the questions and exercises from Chapter 34 of his book *The Bond and Money Markets*, so these are reproduced here for readers' amusement and market practitioners incredulity. But have a read through Chapter 18 first.

1.   The gilt future is trading at 114.55. Which of the following gilts is the cheapest-to-deliver?

Bond	Price	Conversion factor
9% 2008	130.7188	1.1407155
7% 2007	116.375	1.0165266
8% 2009	125.4375	1.0750106
9% 2011	136.1536	1.1655465

2.   A bond desk puts on an arbitrage trade consisting of a long cash and short futures position. What risks does this trade expose the desk to?

3.   Assume that the cheapest-to-deliver bond for a futures contract has a coupon of 6% and has precisely nine years to maturity. Its price is 103.5625. If its conversion factor is 0.90123564, what is the current price of the futures contract?

4.   Assess the following market information and determine if there is an arbitrage opportunity available from undertaking a basis trade:

Bond coupon	8.875%
Maturity	December 2003
Price	102.71
Accrued interest	3.599
Futures price	85.31
Conversion factor	1.20305768
Repo rate	6.803%
Days to delivery	23
Contract size	100,000
Accrued interest on delivery	4.182

5.   The terms of the LIFFE long gilt contract state that delivery may take place on any day during the delivery month. On 30 May 1999 the yield on the cheapest-to-deliver gilt is 5.716% while the repo rate is 6.24%. On what day will a short future deliver the bond if:

     (a)   he already owns the cash bond;
     (b)   if he does not yet own the bond? Explain your answer.

     Will there be any change in the current cheapest-to-deliver bond if there is a parallel shift in the yield curve of 50 basis point?

6.   The first day of trading of a new futures contract is about to commence. What is the fair price of the contract?

7.   Consider the following market data, with prices for UK gilts and the LIFFE long gilt contract. Gilts pay semi-annual coupon on an act/act basis.

UKT 5.75% 7 Dec 2009	£102.7328	Conversion factor 0.9142255
UKT 6.25% 25 Nov 2010	107.8777	Conversion factor 0.9449312
UKT 9% 6 Aug 2012	134.4551	Conversion factor 1.1619558
Futures price	112.98	
Settlement date	16 March 2000	
Futures expiry	30 June 2000	
Actual repo rate	6.24%	

     Calculate the gross basis, the net basis and the implied repo rate for each bond. Which bond is the cheapest-to-deliver? Relative to the futures contract, what is the difference in price between the cheapest-to-deliver bond and the most expensive-to-deliver bond? What does a negative net basis indicate?

8.   We wish to determine by how much the yield of a deliverable bond would have to change in order for it to become the cheapest-to-deliver bond. How could we do this?

9.   A junior trader feels that there are some arbitrage opportunities available in the basis, which is net positive for the cheapest-to-deliver bond, if they put on a strategy of long futures versus short in the cheapest-to-deliver. What factors may contribute to preventing them from realising a profit equal to the current value of the net basis?

10. A long bond futures contract matures in 56 days, and its current price is 107.55. The price of the cheapest-to-deliver is 129.875, and it has a coupon of 9% and accrued interest of 79 days (act/act). What is the implied repo rate?

18 The Government Bond Basis, Basis Trading and the Implied Repo Rate II

In this chapter we look in more detail at some fundamentals behind the basis, including the factors that drive its behaviour, and we also consider implications of the short future's delivery option. There is also recent delivery history for the long gilt future, for illustrative purposes.

18.1 Analysing the basis

Having discussed, in the previous chapter, the theoretical foundation behind futures prices, it is nevertheless the case that they move out of sync with the no-arbitrage price and present arbitrage trading opportunities. A review of the US Treasury or the gilt bond basis relative to the bond carry would show that the basis has frequently been greater than the carry, and this would indicate mis-pricing in the futures contracts.[1] The anomalies in pricing are due to a number of factors, the principal one of which is that the short future has the option of delivery. That is, the short picks which bond to deliver from the basket, and the time at which it is delivered. The long future simply accepts the bond that is delivered. It is this inequality that is the option element of the contract.

We will take a look at this, but first let's consider the principle behind no-arbitrage delivery.

18.1.1 *No-arbitrage futures price*[2]

At the expiration of a futures contract, after the exchange delivery settlement price is being determined, there should be no opportunity for a market participant to generate an arbitrage profit by buying bonds and selling futures; by definition, because on the last day of trading there is no uncertainty with regard to the carry costs of the bond to delivery. In fact certain exchanges arrange it so that the time between the last trading day and date for delivery is identical to the settlement process in the cash market.[3] On the last day, someone buying cash bonds will receive value on the same day, and with the same accrued interest, as a long future being delivered into. Thus carry cost is no longer an uncertainty and the price of the futures contract in theory must equate that of the cash bond. In other words, the basis is zero at this point.

Consider Figure 18.2, the delivery basket for the December 2001 long gilt contract. The bonds have been priced so that they all yield 7%, the notional coupon. Under these condi-

---

[1] Burghardt (*ibid.*), page 27. Apologies, but I must surrender to an urge to quote again from the same page, to wit: "The players in the bond market are some of the brightest people in the financial world…" (!). I am sure he is right, although I suppose there are exceptions to every rule…

[2] We follow the approach also used in Plona (*ibid*, Chapter 3).

[3] For instance, the Bund contract on Eurex.

tions, only one futures price will satisfy the no-arbitrage principle. As carry is not an issue on expiry, the no-arbitrage condition is met provided there is a zero basis for one of the deliverable bonds and no negative basis for any of the other bonds. For instance, at a futures price of 100.09, following the price factor conversion the equivalent bond price would be below the market price of the 8% Treasury 2013 (the cheapest-to-deliver bond at this level) and thus maintain a positive basis. However, for the 6.25% Treasury 2010 bond, this futures price would be equivalent to a converted bond price of 95.1443. The market price of this bond is lower than this, at 94.9685. In theory a trader can buy the bond at this price, sell the futures contract at 100.09 and realise a trading gain of 0.1758 (the difference between the two prices). This is the arbitrage profit. So the initial suggested price for the futures contract is too high. At a price of 100.06 the future no longer presents an opportunity for profit if buying the basis; however, in theory, selling the basis against the 9% 2011 bond still generates profit. The long future must accept delivery of any of the bonds in the basket however, and will not be delivered this bond. So the adjusted futures price is too low.

Hence we know that the arbitrage-free futures price lies between these two levels. In fact we obtain the no-arbitrage price by dividing the bonds' market prices by their respective conversion factor. These are shown in Table 18.1. The prices in Table 18.1 are the futures prices at which there exists a zero basis for that particular underlying bond. We can determine this relationship easily from the definition of the basis, as shown below:

$$Basis = P_{bond} - \left(P_{fut} \times CF \right), \tag{18.1}$$

$$P_{bond} = Basis + \left(P_{fut} \times CF \right). \tag{18.2}$$

If we set the basis at zero, we obtain

$$P_{fut} = \frac{P_{bond}}{CF}, \tag{18.3}$$

which illustrates how the deliverable bond price divided by its conversion factor is equal to the zero-basis futures price.

Taking this further, the futures price that would ensure that all the deliverable bonds have a basis that is either zero, or greater than zero, is the lowest possible zero-basis futures price. The price cannot exceed this otherwise there would be an arbitrage opportunity. If we calculate the zero-basis futures price at different yield levels, we will observe that when yields lie above the contract notional coupon, generally the shortest-dated bond carries the lowest zero-basis futures price. If yields lie below the notional coupon, frequently the longest-dated bond carries the lowest zero-basis futures price, and so is the CTD bond. This has been observed empirically by a number of authors, and formalised by Benninga (2001), for instance.[4] The observation reflects a bias in the conversion factor. We illustrate this bias in Figure 18.3, for the shortest-dated and longest-dated deliverable bonds for the June 2000 long gilt future. It shows where the futures price meets for both bonds is at the contract notional coupon of 7%, this being known as the *inflection point*. The conversion factor bias determines which bond is the cheapest-to-deliver bond, based on yield levels of bonds in the basket and their position relative to the contract notional coupon.

---

4   See also Appendix 18.2 for a short chat on a general model of the CTD bond.

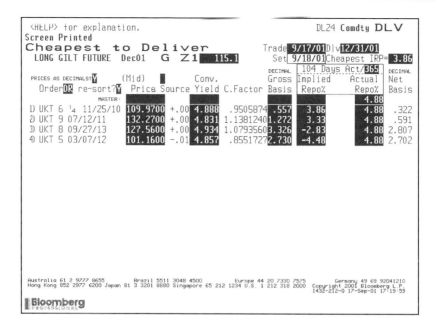

Figure 18.1: Dec01 long gilt delivery basket as at 17 September 2001.
©Bloomberg L.P. Reproduced with permission.

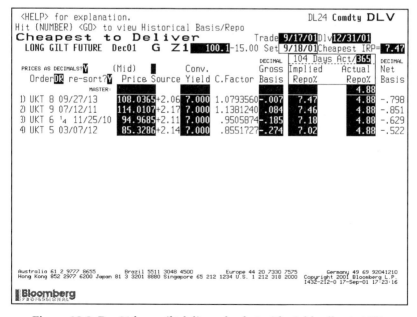

Figure 18.2: Dec01 long gilt delivery basket with yields all set at 7%.
©Bloomberg L.P. Reproduced with permission.

Bond	Conversion factor	Price at 7% yield	Price divided by factor
6.25% Treasury 2010	0.9505874	94.9685	99.90506922
9% Converison 2011	1.1381240	114.0107	100.1742341
8% Treasury 2013	1.0793560	108.0365	100.0894817
5% Treasury 2012	0.8551727	85.3286	99.7793779

Table 18.1: December 2001 long gilt delivery basket, price at 7% notional yield level, and zero-basis futures price.

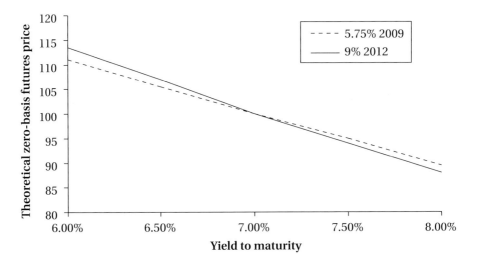

Figure 18.3: Illustrating bias in the conversion factor, June 2000 long gilt future.

The relative bias of the conversion factor is a function of the duration property of the bonds. For further information on this see Meisner and Labuszewski (1984) and Arak *et al* (1986).

18.1.2 *Options embedded in bond futures contracts*
In the US Treasury bond contract, the short future has the following options with regard to delivery:

- the *wild card* or *time to deliver* option;
- the *quality* option.

The short future may deliver during any business day of the delivery month, although the administrative process involved takes place over three days. The first day is the *position day*, the first day on which the short declares an intent to deliver. The first possible day that this can occur is the second-to-last business day before the first day of the delivery month. There is an important advantage to the short future on this day: at 14:00 hours that day the exchange settlement price and hence the invoice amount to be received by the short are fixed. However, the short does not have to announce an intent to deliver until 20:00 hours on that day. During the six hours after the settlement price, if interest rates rise and the bond price falls, the short will earn the difference between the actual price received for the bond, which is the EDSP set at 14:00, and the price that they will have to pay to acquire the bond. Equally if the bond is in the short's possession, the price received for the short future delivery will be higher than the market price of the bond. The second day is the *notice of intention day*, and during this day the exchange clearing house identifies the short and long parties to each other. The third day is the *delivery day*; during this day the short future must deliver the bond to the clearing house. The long future pays the invoice amount based on the settlement price fixed on the position day.

The short future has an option of when to exercise the *time to deliver* option from the penultimate business day prior to the start of the delivery month up to the last business day of the delivery month, known as the *last trading day*. At 14:00 hours on that day the final settlement price is determined, which stays constant to the end of the month. The short future is left with one more wild card at this point, known as the *end-of-the-month* option. Assuming that the short has not declared an intent to deliver until now, the settlement price for the contract is now irrevocably fixed. At this point the short still has five more days before having to declare an intention. In this case the possibility still exists for profit generation if, for example, the trader purchases the bond at the settlement price and holds it to delivery, earning the accrued interest. This will generate a carry profit if the bond's running yield is higher than its specific repo offer rate.

The last option advantage of the short future is the quality option. This is the option to deliver any of the bonds within the delivery basket. As we have seen the bonds can vary widely in coupon and maturity, and hence yield, and despite the conversion factor equalisation there is a bias in this factor that means at yield levels above the notional coupon, long-dated bonds are the cheapest, and vice versa if yields are below the notional level. The quality option also presents the long future with potential problems if there is a change in yields sufficient to change the CTD from one bond to another. If this comes as a surprise to the basis trader, it can be potentially very serious.

The delivery options available to the short future carry value, and this is reflected in the difference between the gross basis and the net basis. In theory the value of the delivery options, when added to the price of the futures contract, should equal the value of the bond together with the carry.

18.2 Bond delivery factors

18.2.1 *The cheapest-to-deliver*

The deliverable bond is of course the cheapest-to-deliver bond. This is not, as a junior trader once suggested to the author, the bond with the lowest market price (although it might well be). The CTD bond is the one that maximises the return to the arbitrageur engaging in buying the basis, that is, buying the bond and simultaneously selling the future, holding the bond to expiry and then delivering it into the futures contract. Some market practitioners use the implied repo rate to identify the CTD, while others prefer the net basis method. We assess both now.

Essentially a good approximation for the CTD is to compare the basis for a bond with its total carry costs to delivery. The difference between the two is the net basis. However, this method may produce incorrect CTD rankings when the net basis values for two bonds are very close. When this happens the net basis for the bond that is actually the cheapest is higher than another bond in the basket, despite the fact that it is the cheapest. This happens because since the net basis method measures cheapness by comparing net basis to the dirty price of the bond, and this price is related to coupon size, maturity and given yield levels, the actual running cost is sometimes not captured. This can produce a lower net basis for a bond that is not actually the cheapest. For this reason the most accurate method by which to identify the CTD is to pick the bond with the highest implied repo rate. From the previous chapter we saw that the IRR is the hypothetical return achieved by going long the basis and running this position to expiry. It is in effect a repo agreement with the futures market, and the calculation fully accounts for the bond's purchase price. The IRR method is recommended by academic writers because of the way that it is calculated; to reiterate from Chapter 17:

$$\text{IRR} = \left(\frac{P_{invoice}}{P_{bond}} - 1 \right) \times \left(\frac{M}{n} \right),$$

(18.4)

where

$P_{invoice}$ is the invoice price;
P_{bond} is the cash bond purchase price;
M is the day base (365 or 360);
n is the days to delivery.

From (18.4) we see that the bond currently trading at a price that results in the highest ratio of futures invoice price to the purchase price will have the highest implied repo rate. In other words, the bond with the lowest purchase price *relative to its invoice price* is the CTD bond.

Nevertheless net basis is still popular amongst traders because it identifies the actual loss (when negative) from the basis trade, and as such is a more quantitative measure.

18.2.2 Selecting delivery time

Another advantage of the IRR measure is that it clearly indicates the time that the short future should deliver the bond. Consider Table 18.2 for the December 2000 long gilt contract.

Bond	Closing day cash price	Conversion factor	Gross basis	Net basis	IRR to first delivery day %	IRR to last delivery day %	Actual repo rate %
5.75% 7 Dec 2009	106.0590	0.9174728	−0.166	−0.300	1.04	6.26	4.52
9% 12 Jul 2011	133.8585	1.1479281	0.951	0.509	−3.32	2.16	4.52
6.25% 25 Nov 2010	110.8310	0.9467478	1.217	1.040	−5.79	−1.28	4.52
9% 6 Aug 2012	136.2685	1.1576368	2.237	1.808	−6.78	−3.74	4.52
8% 27 Sep 2013	129.9925	1.0835676	4.537	4.190	−22.70	−15.74	4.52

Table 18.2: Identifying the cheapest-to-deliver and the optimum delivery time, December 2000 long gilt basket. Source: LIFFE, JPMorgan Chase Bank.

This shows the implied repo rates for delivery on the first day of the delivery month and the last day of the month. For all of the bonds the IRR for delivery on the last day is higher than that for delivery on the first day. It is apparent that the (theoretical) return from a long basis trade would be higher if the delivery date was delayed to the last possible moment, and so in this case the short future would elect to deliver on the last business day.

In fact our illustration is a peculiar one, because the gilt yield curve was inverted at this time. In a positively-sloped yield curve environment, higher IRRs will result for longer-term trades and the decision of the short over when to deliver is an obvious one. The other reason why the short future would prefer to delay delivery is because early delivery eliminates the value of the option element that the short future possesses. It is a bit like early exercise of an American option eliminating the option's time value. In a negative yield curve environment the decision is not so clear cut, although early delivery still removes the short's option advantage. However the market repo rate would need to be considerably higher than the IRRs to justify early delivery, and this was not the case here. Where the market repo rate is higher, the short future will be running a carry cost each day the basis position is maintained, so this will suggest early delivery.

September 1996			December 1998	
Date	9% 2011	7.75% 2006	Date	9% 2008
2			1	1238
3			2	1787
4			3	26
5			4	4116
6			7	
9			8	200
10			9	
11			10	
12			11	8
13			14	
16			15	
17			16	
18			17	
19			18	3
20			21	
23			22	
24			23	
25	16		24	
26			29	
27	3500	4515	30	
Total	3516	4515		7378

Table 18.3: Bond delivery patterns for two gilt futures contracts, reflecting the shape of the yield curve at time of delivery.

In theory there should only be two days when the short future delivers: the start or end of the delivery month; but changes in the yield curve, a particular bond yield level, and market repo rates may make it necessary to deliver on dates in between. Consider Table 18.3, which shows the delivery pattern for the September 1996 and December 1998 long gilt contract on LIFFE. In September 1996 the gilt yield curve was conventional and positively sloping, and apart from a small handful of deliveries just prior, all deliveries were made on the last eligible day of the month. In December 1998 however, the yield curve was negatively sloping, and this is reflected in the pattern of deliveries. It would appear that some market participants had confused ideas, and although in general bonds were delivered early in the month, some deliveries were still being made right in to the middle of the month. This despite the fact the delivery parties would be experiencing negative carry each day they did not deliver. Essentially, this would have been a cost to all those that did not deliver on the first day.

For readers' interest we list the delivery histories from March 1996 long gilt contract through to the June 2001 contract, in Appendix 18.1.

18.2.3 *Changes in CTD status*

A bond may be replaced as CTD if there are changes in relative yield levels of deliverable bonds, if the shape of the yield curve changes or if specific repo rates turn special for certain bonds and not others. Benninga (2001) amongst others has identified the following general rules:

■ where the yield level is below the notional coupon level, the bond with the lowest duration will be the CTD. If the yield level is higher than the notional, the bond with the highest duration will be the CTD;

■ where bonds have roughly identical durations, the bond with the highest yield will be the CTD.

Bond yields are relative however, and the bonds in the basket will trade at different yield levels. A large *relative* shift can bring about a change in CTD status, while overall yields remain roughly at the same level. A more significant yield shift or change in the shape of the curve can also have this effect. The yield on any particular bond is market-determined, and is a function of a number of factors, such as its liquidity, benchmark status, and so on. If there are two or more bonds in the delivery basket with approximately identical duration values, the bond with the higher yield would have the lower converted price, and therefore would be the CTD bond.

Remember that duration[5] is an approximate measure of the percentage change in the price of a bond for a 1% change in the bond's yield. For a given change in yield then, the prices of bonds of higher-duration will change by a greater amount than lower-duration bonds. This is worth bearing in mind because it is behind the bias in the conversion factor introduced in the previous section. Let's reiterate this here. A contract's conversion factors are the approximate prices at which deliverable bonds yield the notional yield level. For the Treasury long bond then, all conversion factors are approximately neutral at a yield level of 6%. If every bond in the delivery basket was trading at 6% yield, their converted prices (the price at this yield, divided by the relevant conversion factor) should be equal to 100, or close to 100. At this yield level then, the short future is in theory indifferent as to which bond to deliver. However, at yield levels above or below the notional level of 6%, duration of the deliverable bonds becomes relevant.

At yields below 6%, as yields fall the rise in price of a lower-duration bond is relatively lower than the price rise of a higher-duration bond. Thus, the low-duration bond becomes the CTD bond. As yields rise above 6%, the higher-duration bond experiences a smaller fall in price than the lower-duration bond, and it becomes the CTD bond.

---

[5]   We refer here of course to modified duration, which is usually simply termed "duration" in the US Treasury market.

Appendices

Appendix 18.1:   LIFFE Long Gilt delivery history, March 1996–June 2001

LONG GILT CONTRACT
DELIVERY NOTICES
DELIVERY MONTH – MARCH 1996

	NOTICE DAY	EDSP	Number of Lots to be Delivered	Cumulative Total
February	28	107-07	0	0
	29	106-28	0	0
March	1	107-17	0	0
	4	108-03	0	0
	5	108-08	0	0
	6	107-30	0	0
	7	107-22	0	0
	8	107-11	0	0
	11	104-20	0	0
	12	105-12	0	0
	13	105-21	0	0
	14	105-23	0	0
	15	105-27	0	0
	18	105-19	0	0
	19	105-22	0	0
	20	105-15	0	0
	21	106-09	0	0
	22	106-05	0	0
	25	105-22	0	0
	26	105-25	0	0
	27 final	**105-29**	0	0
	28		2,359	2,359
	Total Mar 96 Deliveries		2,359	2,359

Source: LIFFE.

(Delivery Day is two business days after Notice Day except on Last Notice Day when delivery is next day; final delivery day being 28 March 1996)

Stock delivered 28 March 1996:   **Treasury 8.5% 16 Jul 2007**   **2,359 lots**

LONG GILT CONTRACT
DELIVERY NOTICES
DELIVERY MONTH – JUNE 1996

	NOTICE DAY	EDSP	Number of Lots to be Delivered	Cumulative Total
May	30	105-21	0	0
	31	105-25	0	0
June	3	105-23	0	0
	4	106-03	0	0
	5	106-13	0	0
	6	106-13	0	0
	7	106-29	0	0
	10	106-10	0	0
	11	105-30	0	0
	12	106-07	0	0
	13	106-08	0	0
	14	106-00	0	0
	17	105-20	0	0
	18	105-24	0	0
	19	106-02	0	0
	20	105-28	0	0
	21	106-06	0	0
	24	106-23	0	0
	25	106-21	0	0
FINAL EDSP	26	**106-27**	0	0
	28		6,650	6,650
	Total Jun 96 Deliveries		6,650	6,650

Source: LIFFE.

(Delivery Day is two business days after Notice Day except on Last Notice Day when delivery is next day; final delivery day being 28 June 1996)

Stock delivered 28 June 1996:   **Treasury 9.0% 13 Oct 2008**   **6,650 lots**

LONG GILT CONTRACT
DELIVERY NOTICES
DELIVERY MONTH – SEPTEMBER 1996

	NOTICE DAY	EDSP	Number of Lots to be Delivered	Cumulative Total
August	29	107-10	0	0
	30	107-06	0	0
September	2	106-31	0	0
	3	106-31	0	0
	4	107-05	0	0
	5	107-05	0	0
	6	106-28	0	0
	9	107-09	0	0
	10	107-15	0	0
	11	107-11	0	0
	12	107-11	0	0
	13	107-21	0	0
	16	108-21	0	0
	17	108-13	0	0
	18	108-09	0	0
	19	108-01	0	0
	20	108-12	0	0
	23	108-00	0	0
	24	108-04	0	0
	25	108-04	16	16
FINAL EDSP	26	**109-00**	0	0
	27		8,015	8,031
	Total Sep 96 Deliveries		8,031	8,031

Source: LIFFE.

(Delivery Day is two business days after Notice Day except on Last Notice Day when delivery is next day; final delivery day being 27 September 1996)

Stock delivered 28 September 1996:   **Conversion 9.0% 12 Jul 2011   3,500 lots**
Treasury   7.75% 8 Sep 2006   4,531 lots

LONG GILT CONTRACT
DELIVERY NOTICES
DELIVERY MONTH – DECEMBER 1996

	NOTICE DAY	EDSP	Number of Lots to be Delivered	Cumulative Total
November	28	110-26	0	0
	29	111-10	0	0
December	2	112-00	0	0
	3	112-09	0	0
	4	111-11	0	0
	5	111-19	0	0
	6	109-18	0	0
	9	110-02	0	0
	10	110-06	0	0
	11	110-03	1,167	1,167
	12	109-31	0	1,167
	13	109-07	0	1,167
	16	110-04	0	1,167
	17	109-29	0	1,167
	18	109-08	0	1,167
	19	109-16	0	1,167
	20	110-00	0	1,167
	23	110-00	0	1,167
	24	110-18	0	1,167
FINAL EDSP	27	**110-26**	3,063	4,230
	30		3,063	4,230
	Total Dec 96 Deliveries		4,230	4,230

Source: LIFFE.

(Delivery Day is two business days after Notice Day except on Last Notice Day when delivery is next day; final delivery day being 30 December 1996)

Stock delivered 13 December 1996:	Treasury 8.5% 16 Jul 2007	1,167 lots
Stock delivered 30 December 1996:	Treasury 7.5% 7 Dec 2006	3,062 lots
	Treasury 6.25% 25 Nov 2010	1 lot

LONG GILT CONTRACT
DELIVERY NOTICES
DELIVERY MONTH – MARCH 1997

	NOTICE DAY	EDSP	Number of Lots to be Delivered	Cumulative Total
February	27	112-16	0	0
	28	113-05	0	0
March	3	112-14	0	0
	4	112-24		
	5	112-10	0	0
	6	111-31	0	0
	7	111-20	0	0
	10	112-14	0	0
	11	112-20	0	0
	12	112-00	0	0
	13	111-22	0	0
	14	111-16	0	0
	17	111-11	0	0
	18	110-24	0	0
	19	110-03	0	0
	20	109-24	0	0
	21	109-28	0	0
	24	109-20	0	0
	25 final	109-27	0	0
	26		15,424	15,424
	Total Mar 97 Deliveries	15,424	15,424	

Source: LIFFE.

(Delivery Day is two business days after Notice Day except on Last Notice Day when delivery is next day; final delivery day being 26 March 1997)

Stock delivered 26 March 1997:   **Treasury 8.5% 16 Jul 2007**   **15,424 lots**

LONG GILT CONTRACT
DELIVERY NOTICES
DELIVERY MONTH – JUNE 1997

	NOTICE DAY	EDSP	Number of Lots to be Delivered	Cumulative Total
June	2	112-16	0	0
	3	113-05	0	0
	4	112-31	0	0
	5	113-07	0	0
	6	113-05	0	0
	9	113-06	26,407	26,407
	10	113-25	21,637	48,044
	11	114-03	0	48,044
	12	114-06	0	48,044
	13	114-07	0	48,044
	16	114-32	0	48,044
	17	114-22	0	48,044
	18	114-01	0	48,044
	19	114-01	0	48,044
	20	113-18	0	48,044
	23	113-14	0	48,044
	24	113-16	0	48,044
	25	113-31	0	48,044
	26	114-07	206	48,250
Last Trading Day	27	114-07	792	49,042
	28	114-07	0	49,042
	Total Jun 97 Deliveries		49,042	49,042

Source: LIFFE.

(Delivery Day is two business days after Notice Day except on Last Notice Day when delivery is next day; final delivery day being 30 June 1997)

Stock delivered
Stock delivered June 1997:   **Treasury 9.0% 13 Oct 2008**   **49,042 lots**

LONG GILT CONTRACT
DELIVERY NOTICES
DELIVERY MONTH – SEPTEMBER 1997

	NOTICE DAY	EDSP	Number of Lots to bc Delivered	Cumulative Total
August	28	114-13	0	0
	29	114-19	0	0
September	1	114-21	0	0
	2	114-28		
	3	115-03	0	0
	4	115-00	0	0
	5	115-10	25,853	25,853
	8	115-18	0	25,853
	9	115-15	0	25,853
	10	115-13	0	25,853
	11	115-15	0	25,853
	12	115-23	0	25,853
			0	25,853
	15	116-04	0	25,853
	16	116-26	0	25,853
	17	117-24	0	25,853
	18	117.27	0	25,853
	19	118-00	200	26,053
	22	118-16	13	26,066
	23	118-07	0	26,066
	24	118-12	0	26,066
	25	118-14	74	26,140
	26 final	120-06	58	26,198
	27		1137	27335
	Total Sep 97 Deliveries		27,335	27,335

Source: LIFFE.

(Delivery Day is two business days after Notice Day except on Last Notice Day when delivery is next day; final delivery day being 29 September 1997)

Stock delivered September 1997:   **Treasury 7.25% 7 Dec 2007**   **27,335 lots**

LONG GILT CONTRACT
DELIVERY NOTICES
DELIVERY MONTH – DECEMBER 1997

	NOTICE DAY	EDSP	Number of Lots to be Delivered	Cumulative Total
November	27	118-21	1846	0
	28	118-19	193	2039
December	1	119-07	312	2351
	2	119-04	24	2375
	3	119-08	0	2375
	4	119-10	406	2781
	5	118-24	0	0
	8	119-04	0	0
	9	119-13	3480	6261
	10	119-22	3	6264
	11	120-11	0	6264
	12	121-02	0	6264
	15	121-02	700	6964
	16	120-29	6	6970
	17	120-08	3887	10857
	18	120-20	0	10857
	19	121-01	780	11637
	22	121-06	3204	14841
	23	121-14	0	14841
	24	121-18	1210	16051
	29 final	**121-22**	4508	20559
	Total Dec 97 Deliveries			20559

Source: LIFFE.

(Delivery Day is two business days after Notice Day except on Last Notice Day when delivery is next day; final delivery day being 30 December 1997)

Stock delivered 1–31 December 1997:   **Treasury 7.25% 7 Dec 2007**   **20,559 lots**

**LONG GILT CONTRACT
DELIVERY NOTICES
DELIVERY MONTH – MARCH 1998**

	NOTICE DAY	EDSP	Number of Lots to be Delivered	Cumulative Total
February	26	123-09	32898	32898
	27	122-31	9753	42651
March	2	122-26	9423	52074
	3	122-24	9514	61588
	4	122-09	6155	67743
	5	124-12	24648	92391
	6	124-06	0	92391
	9	125-04	0	92391
	10	125-10	0	92391
	11	125-15	0	92391
	12	125-18	0	92391
	13	125-22	101	92492
	16	125-30	0	92492
	17	126-10	0	92492
	18	126-11	0	92492
	19	126-04	0	92492
	20	125-25	0	92492
	23	126-03	75	92567
	24	125-29	0	92567
	25	126-08	0	92567
	26	126-21	0	92567
	27	125-24	100	92667
	28	125-24	192	92859
Total March 98 Deliveries			**92,859**	

Source: LIFFE.

(Delivery Day is two business days after Notice Day except on Last Notice Day when delivery is next day; final delivery day being 31 March 1998)

Stock delivered 1–31 March 1998:   **Treasury 9% 13 Oct 2008   92391 Lots**
Conversion factor 0.9999442
Treasury 8% 25 Sep 2009   468 Lots
Conversion factor 0.9292558

LONG GILT CONTRACT
DELIVERY NOTICES
DELIVERY MONTH – JUNE 1998

	NOTICE DAY	EDSP	Number of Lots to be Delivered	Cumulative Total
May	28	108.96	1818	1818
	29	109.15	111	1929
June	1	109.28	29002	30931
	2	109.73	2254	33185
	3	109.79	106	33291
	4	109.64	1270	34561
	5	109.08	1667	36228
	8	109.19	9	36237
	9	108.93	125	36362
	10	109.39	1	36363
	11	109.94	0	36363
	12	110.06	3132	39495
	15	110.42	99	39594
	16	109.61	2201	41795
	17	108.86	557	42352
	18	108.25	463	42815
	19	108.21	0	42815
	22	108.31	0	42815
	23	108.30	0	42815
	24	108.59	550	43365
	25	108.73	631	43996
	26	108.08	2200	46196
	30	108.08	4342	50538
Total June 98 Deliveries				50538

Source: LIFFE.

(Delivery Day is two business days after Notice Day except on Last Notice Day when delivery is next day; final delivery day being 30 June 1998)

Stock delivered June 1998:   **9% 13 OCT 08**   **50,538 lots**
                                         Conversion factor 1.1454317

**LONG GILT CONTRACT
DELIVERY NOTICES
DELIVERY MONTH – SEPTEMBER 1998**

	NOTICE DAY	EDSP	Number of Lots to be Delivered	Cumulative Total
August	27	111.62	12478	12478
	28	112.33	2947	15425
September	1	112.21	457	15882
	2	111.41	813	16695
	3	111.90	292	16987
	4	111.99	0	16987
	7	112.29	1402	18389
	8	112.10	0	18389
	9	112.49	0	18389
	10	112.91	0	18389
	11	113.96	0	18389
	14	113.41	0	18389
	15	113.94	0	18389
	16	113.87	0	18389
	17	114.47	0	18389
	18	114.85	0	18389
	21	115.57	0	18389
	22	114.85	0	18389
	23	114.64	0	18389
	24	114.26	0	18389
	25	114.97	0	18389
	28	115.16	0	18389
	29	115.16	3421	21810
Total September 98 Deliveries				**21810**

Source: LIFFE.

(Delivery Day is two business days after Notice Day except on Last Notice Day when delivery is next day; final delivery day being 30 September 1998)

Stock delivered September 1998:   **9% Treasury 13-Oct-08   21810 Lots
Conversion factor 1.1429955**

LONG GILT CONTRACT
DELIVERY NOTICES
DELIVERY MONTH – DECEMBER 1998

	NOTICE DAY	EDSP	Number of Lots to be Delivered	Cumulative Total
November	27	116.76	600	600
	30	116.81	23	23
December	1	117.30	1238	1861
	2	117.17	1787	3648
	3	117.71	26	3674
	4	117.55	4116	7790
	7	117.84	0	7790
	8	117.73	200	7990
	9			
	10			
	11	117.49	8	7998
	14			
	15			
	16			
	17			
	18	118.35	3	8001
	21			
	22			
	23			
	24			
	29			
	30			
	Total December 98 Deliveries			

Source: LIFFE.

(Delivery Day is two business days after Notice Day except on Last Notice Day when delivery is next day; final delivery day being 30 December 1998)

Stock delivered December 1998:   **9% 13-Oct-08**   **8,001 Lots**
                                            Conversion factor 1.1406361

LONG GILT CONTRACT
DELIVERY NOTICES
DELIVERY MONTH – MARCH 1999

	NOTICE DAY	EDSP	Number of Lots to be Delivered	Cumulative Total
February	25	117.17	0	0
	26	115.98	0	0
March	1	115.87	0	0
	2	115.67	0	0
	3	115.96	0	0
	4	114.97	0	0
	5	115.57	0	0
	8	115.8	0	0
	9	115.33	229	229
	10	115.32	0	229
	11	115.82	0	229
	12	115.95	0	229
	15	116.09	0	229
	16	116.32	0	229
	17	117.02	0	229
	18	117.1	0	229
	19	117.22	0	229
	22	116.59	0	229
	23	116.45	0	229
	24	116.74	1	230
	25	116.72	0	230
	26	116.5	231	461
LTD	29	116.04	1110	1571
LND	30	–	3482	5053

Source: LIFFE.

(Delivery Day is two business days after Notice Day except on Last Notice Day when delivery is next day; final delivery day being 31 March 1999)

Stock delivered March 1999:	**7.25% 07 December 2007**	**5053**
	Total	**5053**

LONG GILT CONTRACT
DELIVERY NOTICES
DELIVERY MONTH – JUNE 1999

	NOTICE DAY	EDSP	Number of Lots to be Delivered	Cumulative Total
May	28	113.98	0	0
June	1	113.63	0	0
	2	112.84	0	0
	3	113.35	0	0
	4	112.92	0	0
	7	112.90	0	0
	8	113.36	0	0
	9	112.87	0	0
	10	112.38	0	0
	11	112.19	0	0
	14	111.92	0	0
	15	112.68	0	0
	16	112.75	0	0
	17	112.95	0	0
	18	113.56	0	0
	21	113.22	0	0
	22	112.08	0	0
	23	111.71	0	0
	24	111.46	0	0
	25	110.36	638	638
LTD	28	110.74	3166	3804
LND	29	–	3602	7406

Source: LIFFE.

(Delivery Day is two business days after Notice Day except on Last Notice Day when delivery is next day; final delivery day being 30 June 1999)

Stock delivered June 1999:   **9.00% 13 October 2008**   **7406**
                                       Total   **7406**

LONG GILT CONTRACT
DELIVERY NOTICES
DELIVERY MONTH – SEPTEMBER 1999

	NOTICE DAY	EDSP	Number of Lots to be Delivered	Cumulative Total
August	27	111.15	0	0
	31	110.08	0	
September	1	110.14	0	0
	2	109.72	0	0
	3	109.16	0	0
	6	109.35	0	0
	7	109.31	0	0
	8	108.50	0	0
	9	107.44	0	0
	10	107.43	0	0
	13	107.04	0	0
	14	107.31	0	0
	15	106.91	0	0
	16	106.88	0	0
	17	107.86	0	0
	20	108.08	0	0
	21	107.29	0	0
	22	107.11	0	0
	23	106.76	0	0
	24	107.71	0	0
	27	107.53	0	0
LTD	28	106.8	1091	1091
LND	29	106.8	1914	3005

(Source: LIFFE.)

(Delivery Day is two business days after Notice Day except on Last Notice Day when delivery is next day; final delivery day being 30 September 1999)

Stock delivered June 1999:   **9.00% 13 October 2008**   **3005 lots**

LONG GILT CONTRACT
DELIVERY NOTICES
DELIVERY MONTH – DECEMBER 1999

	NOTICE DAY	EDSP	Number of Lots to be Delivered	Cumulative Total
November	29	108.39	0	0
	30	108.73	0	
December	1	108.89	0	0
	2	108.98	0	0
	3	108.42	0	0
	6	108.47	0	0
	7	108.77	73	73
	8	109.73	3	76
	9	109.34	0	76
	10	109.86	0	76
	13	109.94	0	76
	14	110.04	0	76
	15	109.79	0	76
	16	109.58	0	76
	17	108.72	0	76
	20	108.88	519	595
	21	108.81	0	595
	22	108.13	0	595
	23	108.07	0	595
LTD	24	108.23	1399	1994
LND	29	108.23	3349	5343
	30	–		5343

(Source: LIFFE.)

(Delivery Day is two business days after Notice Day except on Last Notice Day when delivery is next day; final delivery day being 30 December 1999)

Stock delivered December 1999:   **9.00% 13 October 2008**   **5343 Lots**
                                             Conversion factor   **1.1303221**

LONG GILT CONTRACT
DELIVERY NOTICES
DELIVERY MONTH – MARCH 2000

	NOTICE DAY	EDSP	Number of Lots to be Delivered	Cumulative Total
February	28	112.69	0	0
	29	112.65	0	
March	1	112.31	0	0
	2	112.01	0	0
	3	112.02	0	0
	6	113.16	200	200
	7	113.76	252	452
	8	113.18	1	453
	9	113.81	0	453
	10	114.12	0	453
	13	113.51	0	453
	14	113.39	0	453
	15	113.22	0	453
	16	113.88	0	453
	17	114.74	670	1123
	20	114.49	0	1123
	21	114.18	0	1123
	22	113.99	1264	2387
	23	113.93	0	2387
	24	113.90	0	2387
	27	113.15	0	2387
	28	112.79	296	2683
LTD	29	112.95	1095	3778
LND	30	–	2865	6643

(Source: LIFFE.)

(Delivery Day is two business days after Notice Day except on Last Notice Day when delivery is next day; final delivery day being 31 March 2000)

			Conversion factor
Stock delivered March 2000:	**5.75% Dec 2009**	**5379 lots**	0.9124950
	9% Jul 2011	**1264 lots**	1.1548471
	Total	**6643 lots**	

LONG GILT CONTRACT
DELIVERY NOTICES
DELIVERY MONTH – JUNE 2000

	NOTICE DAY	EDSP	Number of Lots to be Delivered	Cumulative Total
May	30	113.41	0	0
	31	113.30	0	
June	1	113.92	0	0
	2	114.68	0	0
	5	115.20	0	0
	6	114.96	0	0
	7	114.48	0	0
	8	114.60	0	0
	9	114.26	0	0
	12	114.64	0	0
	13	114.50	0	0
	14	114.53	0	0
	15	114.37	0	0
	16	114.49	0	0
	19	114.89	0	0
	20	114.59	0	0
	21	113.82	0	0
	22	113.50	0	0
	23	113.48	0	0
	26	113.05	0	0
	27	113.57	2291	2291
LTD	28	113.40	0	2291
LND	29	–	5068	7359

(Source: LIFFE.)

(Delivery Day is two business days after Notice Day except on Last Notice Day when delivery is next day; final delivery day being 30 June 2000)

Stock delivered June 2000:   5.75% Dec 2009   **7359 lots**
                                        Conversion factor   **0.9142255**

LONG GILT CONTRACT
DELIVERY NOTICES
DELIVERY MONTH – SEPTEMBER 2000

	NOTICE DAY	EDSP	Number of Lots to be Delivered	Cumulative Total
August	30	112.45	0	0
	31	112.37	0	0
September	1	112.43	0	0
	4	113.38	0	0
	5	113.12	0	0
	6	112.92	0	0
	7	112.79	0	0
	8	112.80	0	0
	11	112.54	0	0
	12	112.60	0	0
	13	112.01	0	0
	14	112.96	0	0
	15	112.34	0	0
	18	111.75	0	0
	19	112.20	0	0
	20	112.26	0	0
	21	112.44	0	0
	22	112.78	0	0
	25	112.74	0	0
	26	112.45	0	0
LTD	27	112.37	0	0
LND	28	–	656	656

(Source: LIFFE.)

(Delivery Day is two business days after Notice Day except on Last Notice Day when delivery is next day; final delivery day being 29 September 2000)

Stock delivered September 2000:   **5.75% Dec 2009**   **656 lots**
                                                                          Conversion factor   **0.9157042**

LONG GILT CONTRACT
DELIVERY NOTICES
DELIVERY MONTH – DECEMBER 2000

	NOTICE DAY	EDSP	Number of Lots to be Delivered	Cumulative Total
November	29	115.85	0	0
	30	115.69	0	0
December	1	116.12	0	0
	4	116.27	0	0
	5	115.94	0	0
	6	116.08	0	0
	7	116.10	0	0
	8	115.93	0	0
	11	115.48	0	0
	12	115.48	0	0
	13	115.34	0	0
	14	115.52	0	0
	15	115.57	0	0
	18	115.78	0	0
	19	115.53	0	0
	20	115.87	46	46
	21	114.98	0	46
	22	115.30	0	46
LTD	27	115.78	36	82
LND	28	–	817	899

(Source: LIFFE.)

(Delivery Day is two business days after Notice Day except on Last Notice Day when delivery is next day; final delivery day being 29 December 2000)

Stock delivered December 2000:   **5.75% Dec 2009**   **899 lots**
                                             Conversion factor   **0.9174728**

LONG GILT CONTRACT
DELIVERY NOTICES
DELIVERY MONTH – MARCH 2001

	NOTICE DAY	EDSP	Number of Lots to be Delivered	Cumulative Total
February	27	114.91	0	0
	28	115.42	0	0
March	1	115.73	0	0
	2	115.54	0	0
	5	115.55	0	0
	6	115.38	0	0
	7	115.70	0	0
	8	115.57	0	0
	9	115.79	0	0
	12	115.74	0	0
	13	115.65	0	0
	14	116.12	0	0
	15	116.66	0	0
	16	117.11	0	0
	19	117.40	0	0
	20	117.27	0	0
	21	117.43	0	0
	22	117.23	150	150
	23	117.13	4	154
	26	116.97	0	154
	27	116.75	0	154
LTD	28	116.25	950	1104
LND	29	–	2768	3872

(Source: LIFFE.)

(Delivery Day is two business days after Notice Day except on Last Notice Day when delivery is next day; final delivery day being 30 March 2001)

Stock delivered March 2001:	**5.75% Dec 2009**	**3872 lots**
	Conversion factor	**0.9189802**

LONG GILT CONTRACT
DELIVERY NOTICES
DELIVERY MONTH – JUNE 2001

	NOTICE DAY	EDSP	Number of Lots to be Delivered	Cumulative Total
May	30	113.23	0	0
	31	113.06	0	0
June	1	113.56	0	0
	4	113.95	0	0
	5	113.70	0	0
	6	114.17	0	0
	7	114.16	0	0
	8	113.73	0	0
	11	114.03	0	0
	12	113.47	0	0
	13	113.19	0	0
	14	113.38	0	0
	15	113.80	0	0
	18	113.95	0	0
	19	113.90	0	0
	20	113.80	0	0
	21	113.48	0	0
	22	113.76	0	0
	25	114.19	0	0
	26	113.86	0	0
LTD	27	113.88	0	0
LND	28	–	6362	6362

(Source: LIFFE.)

(Delivery Day is two business days after Notice Day except on Last Notice Day when delivery is next day; final delivery day being 30 June 2000)

Stock delivered June 2000:   **6.25% Treasury Nov 2010**   **6362 lots**
                                        Conversion factor   **0.9486415**

Appendix 18.2:   General rules of the CTD bond

Beninnga (1997) has suggested some general rules in a non-flat yield curve environment that may be taken to be a general model for basis trading. His study analysed the character of the CTD bond under four different scenarios, as part of a test of the following circumstances. When the term structure is flat, the CTD bond is the one with:

- the highest duration if the market interest rate is higher than the notional coupon;
- the lowest duration if the market interest rate is lower than the notional coupon.

Benninga suggests that under certain scenarios, notably when:

- the market yield is higher than the notional coupon and there are no deliverable bonds with a coupon lower than the notional coupon, and when the market yield is higher than the notional coupon, and
- there are no deliverable bonds with a coupon higher than the notional,

the duration rule does not always apply.

The conclusions of his analysis are that:

- the CTD bond invariably has the highest coupon of the deliverable bonds, where the market yield is lower than the notional coupon, otherwise it has the lowest coupon of the deliverable bonds. The analysis assumes that the bonds possess positive convexity, but the results are not dependent on the shape of the yield curve;
- when market rates are lower than the notional coupon, the maturity of the CTD is the shortest of all deliverable bonds; again, if the market rate lies above the notional coupon, the CTD bond will have the longest maturity if it also has a coupon greater than the notional coupon. If the coupon of the CTD bond is lower than the notional coupon, Benningna concludes that the CTD will have neither the longest or the shortest maturity in the delivery basket.

Certain anecdotal observation appears to confirm these generalities.

Appendix 18.3:   A general model of the CTD bond

The price today (or at time 0) of a bond is generally given by (18.5):

$$P = \int_0^T C e^{-rt}\, dt + 100 e^{-rT}, \qquad (18.5)$$

where C is the bond cash flow and T is the bond maturity date.

The discount factor at time t for one unit of cash at time $s \geq t$ when the time t spot interest-rate is r is given by e^{-rt}. The value of the conversion factor for a bond with maturity T and coupon C delivered at time F, the expiry date of the futures contract, is given by (18.6):

$$
\begin{aligned}
CF &= \int_0^{T-F} C e^{-cs}\, ds + e^{-c(T-F)} \\
&= \frac{C e^{-cs}}{-c}\Big|_0^{T-F} + e^{-c(T-F)} = \frac{C\left(1 - e^{-c(T-F)}\right)}{-c} + e^{-c(T-F)},
\end{aligned}
\qquad (18.6)
$$

where c is the notional coupon of the futures contract.

Selected bibliography and references

Arak, M., Goodman, L., Ross, S., "The Cheapest to Deliver Bond on the Treasury Bond Futures Contract", *Advances in Futures and Options Research 1*,1986, pp. 49–74

Benninga, S., *Financial Modeling*, MIT, 1997, Chapter 18

Kolb, R., *Understanding Futures Markets*, Kolb Publishing 1994, Chapter 9

Meisner, J., Labuszewski, J., "Treasury Bond Futures Delivery Bias", *Journal of Futures Markets*, Winter 1984, pp. 569–572

19 An Introduction to Fundamentals of Basis Trading

In this chapter we consider some further issues of basis trading and look at the impact of repo rates on an individual's trading approach.

19.1 Rates and spread history

19.1.1 *Net basis history*

One of the first considerations for basis traders is the recent (and not so recent) history of the basis. For instance if the basis is historically high, a strategy might involve selling the basis, in anticipation that the levels will fall back to more "normal" levels. The trader can sell the basis of the CTD bond or another bond in the delivery basket. Let us consider one approach here, tracking the basis of the CTD in an attempt to identify trade opportunities.

By tracking the net basis for the CTD, we are able to see the impact of the delivery option possessed by the short on the level of the basis. Figures 19.1 to 19.3 illustrate the behaviour of the net basis for the 6.25% 2010 gilt during the period September 2000 to September 2001. This bond was the CTD bond during this period.

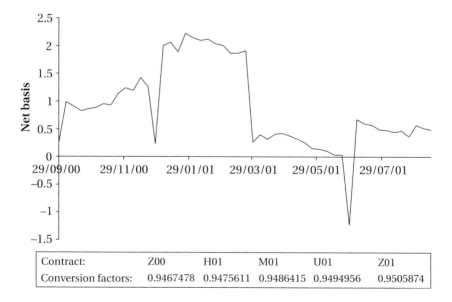

Contract:	Z00	H01	M01	U01	Z01
Conversion factors:	0.9467478	0.9475611	0.9486415	0.9494956	0.9505874

Figure 19.1: Long gilt cheapest-to-deliver bond net basis history, front month contract (CTD bond is 6.25% Treasury 2010).

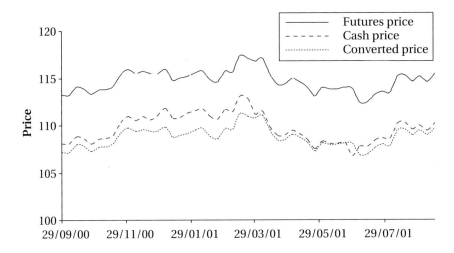

Figure 19.2: CTD bond price histories.

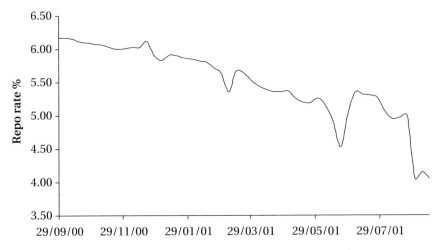

Figure 19.3: Repo rates during September 2000 to September 2001.

Tracking the net basis allows us to observe the value placed by the market on the short future's delivery options. For purposes of illustration we also show the futures price, cash bond price and converted bond price in Figure 19.2 and the actual market repo rate in Figure 19.3 during the same period. The net basis is measured in price decimals, just like the futures and cash price. We observe that, as expected, there is a pattern of convergence towards a zero basis as each contract approaches final delivery date. We also observe that profit can be obtained by selling the basis at times of approaching the delivery month, assuming that this bond remains the CTD throughout the period. If there is any change in the CTD status this will reduce or eliminate profits, because then instead of the trader gaining the entire net carry basis, some or all of it will have been given up. A good way of assessing a position of being short the basis is to assume one is short of an out-of-the-money option. The maximum profit is the option premium, and this is earned gradually over the term of the trade as the time value of the option decays. In this case the equivalent to the option premium is the net basis itself. As the basis converges to zero, and the futures contract approaches expiry, the net basis is gained. However, the risk is potentially high: identical to the trader who has written an option, and potentially unlimited.

The same approach may be adopted when buying the basis, observing when it is historically cheap. A long position in the basis is similar to being long a call option on a bond or a bond future.

An analysis of the net basis history in isolation is not necessarily sufficient to formulate trade decisions however, because it would not indicate changes in the status of the CTD bond. In itself, it merely tracks the net basis of the bond that is the CTD at that precise moment. A change in the CTD bond can have serious repercussions for the basis trader. A trade idea based on selling the basis of the CTD bond will be successful only if the bond remains the CTD during the term of the trade. So if a trader sells the basis, with the intention of running the trade to contract delivery, then as long as that bond remains the CTD then the entire basis is the theoretical profit. If there is a change in status amongst the deliverable bonds, then this profit may be reduced, wiped out or turned into a loss.

Another approach when looking at the net basis is to buy it when it is historically cheap. This anticipates a rise in the basis value, so it should not be undertaken when the futures contract has a relatively short time to expiry. Remember that a contract ceases to be the *front month* contract[1] fairly immediately once we move into the delivery month, buying the basis when it is cheap is a tactic that is often carried out before a future becomes the front month contract. A long basis position essentially is similar to a long position in an option.[2] So the downside exposure is limited to the net basis at the time the trade is put on, while the potential upside gain is, in theory, unlimited. As with a long option position, a long basis position may be put on to reflect a number of views, and can be bullish or bearish, or may not be directional at all. A long basis trade then is an alternative to buying a call option, put option or what are known as *straddles* or *strangles*.[3]

19.1.2 *The implied repo rate*

In Chapter 18 we discussed how the implied repo rate measure was the best indicator of the CTD bond, with this bond having the highest IRR. It is worth bearing in mind that at the start of the delivery cycle the differences in IRRs are fairly small. Identifying one bond at this stage is only a forecast of the eventual outcome, and indeed it possible for the CTD at the start of

---

[1]   Called the *lead contract* in the US market. This is the liquid contract traded under normal circumstances for hedging and simple speculation trading.

[2]   As confirmed by Burghardt (*Ibid*, page 127), the basis of a bond of high-duration value acts roughly the same as a bond future or a call option on a bond, while the basis of a low-duration bond is similar in behaviour to a put option on a bond. The basis of bonds of neither high nor low duration moves like a straddle or strangle.

[3]   A straddle is a combination option position made up of a put option and a call option that have the same characteristics (that is, both options have identical strike prices, time to maturity and the same underlying asset). A long straddle is buying the put and the call option, while a short straddle is selling the put and call options. Straddles require a large shift in price of the underlying to be profitable, but gain in the meantime from a change in the implied volatility (a rise in implied volatility for a long straddle). A strangle is similar to a straddle but is constructed using options with different strike prices. There is a whole library of books one could buy on options, the author recommends Galitz's *Financial Engineering* (FT Pitman, 1995), David Blake's *Financial Market Analysis* (Wiley, 2000), and Jarrow and Turnbull's *Derivative Securities* (South-Western, 1999).

the contract's trading to drop down to third or even fourth cheapest. We noted earlier that traders often prefer the net basis method over the IRR approach; this is because the IRR can also mislead. Remember that the IRR measures the return based on the dirty purchase price and the invoice price. In other words, it is a function of coupon income during the trade term and the cost of making delivery. As the time span to delivery decreases, small changes in the basis have a larger and larger impact on the IRR calculation. The danger of this is that a very small change in a bond's basis, while not altering its cheapest delivery status, can affect quite significantly the bond's IRR.

Figure 19.4 shows the IRR of the cheapest-to-deliver bond for the Dec01 long gilt contract. Notice how at the start of trading two bonds were vying for CTD status, and switched positions almost daily, before it settled down as the 6.25% 2010 gilt. This is perhaps good news for the basis trader, as IRR volatility is conducive to a profitable trading environment. More valuable though is the later stability of the contract's CTD status, which lowers the risk for the basis trader.

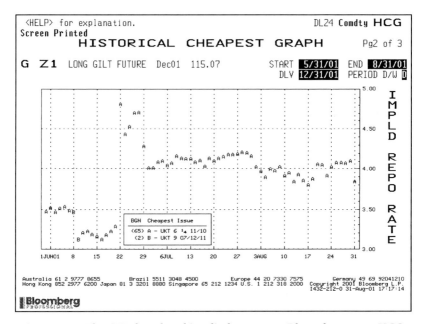

Figure 19.4: The CTD bond and implied repo rate, Bloomberg page HCG.
© Bloomberg L.P. Used with permission.

Figure 19.5 shows the historical pattern for the Sep01 contract, part of page DLV on Bloomberg.

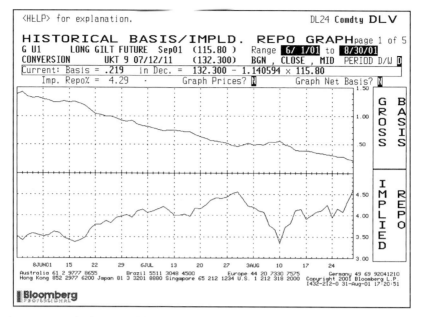

Figure 19.5: The historical basis and implied repo rate, Sep01 long gilt contract.
© Bloomberg L.P. Used with permission.

19.2 Impact of the repo rate

Basis trading sounds excellent in theory but market participants also must take into account some practical issues that can complicate matters. Possibly the most important consideration is that of financing the trade, and the specific repo rates for the bond concerned. We consider this here.

19.2.1 *The repo rate*

A key issue, possibly *the* key issue in a basis trade involves its financing. From our look at the size of the net basis, we know that the potential profit in a basis trade is usually quite small (this being the main reason that arbitrageurs undertake basis trades in very large size, $750 million being a not uncommon nominal value). Financing a trade, whether this is a long bond position or investing the proceeds of a short sale, can have a significant impact on its profitability. The trader must decide whether to fix the repo financing for the proposed term of the trade, for part of the term, or on an overnight roll basis. The financing rate is the specific repo rate for the bond traded. For virtually all applications, the closer this specific rate is to the GC rate the better. In a long bond position the repo rate is paid, so a specific rate that is special will probably render the trade uneconomic. For a short bond position, the repo rate is being received; however if this is special it would indicate that the bond itself is probably overpriced in the cash market or in danger of being squeezed or made undeliverable, which would introduce complications.

Generally traders prefer to fix the funding on the trade for a term, either part or the whole term. Financing a basis trade in the overnight does have some advantages however; for instance, if the short-term yield curve is positively sloping, overnight financing should prove cheaper than a term repo, as long as overnight rates are not volatile. The key advantage though is that if financing overnight, the trade may be unwound with much more ease. In a term repo, the trader is more or less fixed through to his original anticipated maturity date, and under changing circumstances this might be uneconomic. The risk in overnight funding is that a shift in the short-term yield curve can raise overnight rates to painful levels. If long the basis, a rise in the overnight rate will increase the funding cost of the trade and reduce its profitability. If short the basis, a fall in the overnight rate will reduce the (reverse) repo interest on the trade and so reduce profit. In addition there is the bid-offer spread to consider: someone entering into reverse repo to cover a short bond position receives the repo market-maker's offered rate, which is around 6 basis points lower than the bid rate for GC, but which may be 10–20 basis points lower for a specific repo.

Where one or more of the bonds in the delivery basket is special, it can cloud the identification of the CTD bond. Remember that one method of assessing the CTD is to pick that which has the highest implied repo rate (IRR), and if all deliverable bonds are trading close to GC this would be reasonable. However, this may not be the case if a bond is special. To remove confusion, it is better to compare each bond's IRR with its specific term repo rate, and identify the bond that has the biggest difference between its IRR and its specific repo. This bond is the CTD bond.

Uncertainty about specific repo rates can become a motivation behind a basis trade, as it also presents profit opportunities. For example, if an arbitrageur has decided that a short future/long bond basis trade is worthwhile, and their repo desk suggests that this bond may *shortly* become special, overall profitability can be significantly enhanced when the bond is then used as collateral in a repo. Of course, the financing of the long position must be secured first, in a term repo, before it subsequently goes special.

Nonetheless the issue of financing remains a source of uncertainty in a basis trade and therefore a source of risk. The specific issues are:

- **if long the basis:** for a bond that is currently special, as the bond ceases being special and starts to trade close to GC again, as its specific repo rate rises its net basis will decline;
- **if short the basis:** for a bond that is currently trading close to GC in repo, the risk is that if it starts to trade special, the specific repo rate (reverse repo rate) will fall and therefore the bond's basis will rise.

In either case, this results in a mark-to-market loss. Good market intelligence for the bond forming part of a basis trade, obtained from the repo desk, is essential in the trade.

Trade opportunities can arise based on a bond's status in the repo market. As an example consider where a bond is trading special in the repo market for term trades but is still available close to GC in the *short dates*, say overnight to three days. In this case the bond's net basis will be a function of the term repo rate, which is special. An arbitrageur can sell the basis, but realise a funding gain by financing the trade in the overnight repo market.[4]

---

[4] It is rare that a bond that is special to any significant degree would still be available at GC on an overnight basis. The trade sounds good in theory though, although the risk remains that, in financing the trade on an overnight basis, if it then turns special in overnight the trade will suffer. (And so will the trader…)

19.2.2 *Short bond position squeeze*

A market participant running a short position in a bond is always at risk if that bond becomes illiquid and thus unavailable for borrowing either in stock loan or in repo. A basis trader selling the basis is exposed to the same risk. We discussed the issues when a bond goes special in the previous section. The extent of funding loss when the (reverse) repo rate for a bond in which a trader is running a short goes special can be very large indeed; there is no limit to the extent of "specialness" and the repo rate can even go negative. If the bond becomes unavailable for borrowing and so cannot be delivered, it may be difficult to cover and also to buy the bond back and flatten out the position.

In some cases the overall market short in a particular bond issue may exceed the amount of the issue available to trade. This is known as a *short squeeze*. If the CTD bond has a small issue size, it can suffer from a squeeze precisely because arbitrageurs are putting on basis trades in the bond.

To reduce risk of loss from short squeezes, before entering into the trade the arbitrage desk must ensure that:

- the issue size is sufficiently large;

- the stock is available for borrowing in repo and/or the securities-lending market, and is sufficiently liquid such that it should not be a problem to buy back the bond (if a short basis trade);

- both the overnight and the term repo rates are not special, that is, no more than 30–35 basis points below the GC rate. If there are special considerations involved, a specific repo rate that is, say, 50 basis points below the GC does not preclude the trade being undertaken; however, the danger with this is that it is an indication that the stock may trade much more special later.

Once the trade is put on, part of its ongoing monitoring will involve checking that the bond is not about to be squeezed. Indications of this might include:

- a falling specific repo rate, entering into special territory;

- large-size short sales of the bond elsewhere in the market. It is difficult to be aware of this until too late afterwards – a good relationship with one's inter-dealer broker might help here;

- a tightening of the bond's yield against the yield curve, that is, the bond beginning to trade expensive to the curve in the cash market. This is one indication that the bond may be going special in repo.

As part of normal discipline in a relative value trade, there should also be a stop-loss limit, beyond which the trade is unwound.[5] A common approach is to place this limit at half the expected profit on the trade.

---

[5] For an introduction to relative value and yield curve bond trading, see Chapter 13 in the author's book *Bond Market Securities* (FT Prentice Hall, 2001).

19.3 Basis trading mechanics

Basis trading or cash-and-carry trading is putting on a combined simultaneous position in a deliverable bond and the bond futures contract. Buying the basis or going long the basis is buying the cash bond and selling the future, while selling the basis is selling the cash bond and buying the future. The trade need not be in the CTD bond, but in any bond that is in the futures delivery basket.

In this section, which is the furthest away from the general area of "repo markets", we consider some issues in actually trading the basis. It is still of concern to repo market participants though, because the repo desk is always closely involved with basis trading, not least as a source of market intelligence on particular bonds.

19.3.1 *Using the conversion factor*

A basis trade is the only type of trade that uses the specific bond's conversion factor to calculate the amount of futures contracts to put on against the cash position. This is sometimes known as the "hedge ratio", but this term is not recommended as a hedge ratio in any other type of trade is not carried out using conversion factors.

To calculate how many contracts to use in a basis trade, we use (19.1),

$$Number = \frac{M_{bond}}{M_{fut}} \times CF_{bond},$$ (19.1)

where

M_{bond} is the nominal amount of the cash bond;
M_{fut} is the notional size of one futures contract;
CF_{bond} is the bond's conversion factor.

So for the December 2001 long gilt a basis trade in £100 million of the 6¼% 2010 gilt, which has a conversion factor of 0.950587, would require

  $(100,000,000/100,000) \times 0.950587$

or 951 contracts. The number of contracts is rounded to the nearest integer although traders round up or down depending on their views on market direction.

Conversion factor ratios are used because they determine the bond's basis itself. This means that a trade calculated using a conversion factor ratio should track the basis. In some cases a trade will be constructed using a duration-based hedge ratio, particularly when trading in a bond that is not the current CTD.[6]

---

[6] It is important to remember that the *only* time when the conversion factor is used to structure a trade is in a basis trade. Hedge ratios for a position of two bonds or bonds and futures should be constructed using modified duration values. The author has come across suggestions that if a hedge is put on using one cash bond against another, and both bonds are deliverable bonds, then the ratio of both bonds' conversion factors can be used to calculate the relative volatility and the amount of the hedging bond required. This is not correct practice. A conversion factor is a function primarily of the bond's coupon, whereas price volatility is influenced more by a bond's term to maturity. They are not therefore substitutes for one another, and hedge ratios should always be calculated using modified duration. To illustrate, consider a bond position that is being hedged using the CTD bond, and assume that the bond to be hedged is a shorter-dated high-coupon bond, while the CTD bond is a long-dated low-coupon bond. A ratio of their modified durations would be less than one, but the

19.3.2 *Trading profit and loss*

The size of the net basis for a bond gives an indication of the expected profit from a basis trade in that bond. Constructing the trade using the conversion factor ratio should ensure that the trade produces a profit (or loss) related to a change in the basis during the trade's term. Such a profit (loss) will occur as a result of changes in the cash bond price that are not matched by movement in the futures price; so for example a long basis trade will generate profit if the bond price increases by an amount greater than the converted bond price (futures price multiplied by conversion factor). It also gains if there is a fall in the cash price that is less than the fall in the converted bond price. A short basis trade gains in the opposite case: a rise in cash price less than the converted price or a fall in cash price that is greater than the fall in the converted price.

The other key source of profit or loss is the funding, and this sometimes outweighs the consideration arsing from movement in market prices. The long basis trade has a net carry cost, comprised of coupon income minus repo interest, and this is usually positive. The short basis trade has a net carry cost comprised of repo interest minus coupon payments, and this is usually negative. This is sometimes reversed in an inverted yield curve environment. What this means is that the passage of time impacts long and short basis trades in different ways. The long basis will, in most cases, be earning net carry. This will result in profit even if there is no movement in the basis itself, or it may offset losses arising from the latter. The short basis trade will usually be incurring a financing loss, and the movement in the basis must not only be in the right direction but sufficient to offset the ongoing funding loss.

19.4 Timing the basis trade using the implied repo rate

19.4.1 *The implied repo rate (again)*

From the previous section we are aware how trades can be put on that generate profit from movements in the bond basis and possibly also from funding the trade in repo. The key to successful treading is often correct timing, and in this case the correct time to buy or sell the basis. The decision to enter into the trade is based on an analysis of current conditions and historical spreads, together with a combination of past experience, current market view and risk/reward taste of the individual trader. In this section we consider how observing the implied repo rate pattern can assist with market entry timing.

We know that three different values measure the relationship between the current (spot) price of the cash bond and its (implied) price for forward delivery given by the current futures price. These are the gross basis, the gross basis adjusted for net carry or net basis, and the implied repo rate. We also suggested that the net basis was perhaps the preferred measure used in the market to identify the value of the short future's delivery option, and hence also the CTD bond. Figure 19.6 illustrates the three measures for the 9% Treasury 2008, the CTD bond for the long gilt contract from March 1998 through to December 1999. The gross basis and the net basis follow a rough convergence towards zero, while the IRR does not follow such a convergence. The pattern of the IRR also exhibits a certain degree of volatility, apparently uncorrelated to the time to delivery of each contract. The volatility of the IRR has been com-

---

ratio of their conversion factors would be higher than one. This produces two different hedge values for the CTD bond, and the one using conversion factors would not be an accurate reflection of the two bonds' relative price volatility. It is important to remember that conversion factors should not be used to measure bond price volatilities when constructing hedge positions.

pared to the implied volatility of an option contract.[7] Plotting the basis against the IRR of the CTD will also show a relationship between the two; generally, a fall in the IRR occurs simultaneously with a rise in the basis, with peaks and troughs for the one being balanced by the opposite for the other. Further, a peak in the IRR indicates a basis value that is relatively low, while a trough in the IRR suggests a relatively high basis. We say "relative" because the basis is usually measured across several contracts, and a "low" basis in March can be "high" by June. However, the general relationship holds true.

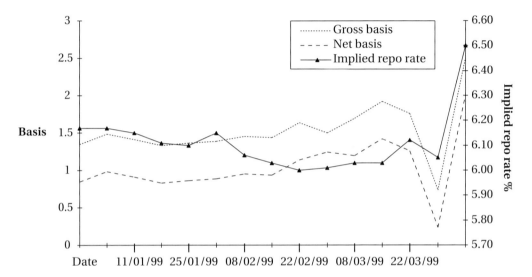

Figure 19.6: Gross basis, net basis and implied repo rate for cheapest-to-deliver bond (9% Treasury 2008), towards contract delivery. Source: Bloomberg.

Therefore the IRR is a most useful measure for the basis trader because it provides an indication of a bond's basis but unrelated to the convergence over time. It also provides "real" values, not relative ones, as a high IRR is high at any stage of the cycle. Similarly, a "low" IRR can be viewed as a true low value, irrespective of the time of the year that it is observed, or whether we are approaching a delivery period or not. When we speak of high or low values for the IRR, we mean high or low against the actual market repo rate. Figure 19.7 shows the IRR for the 9% 2008 bond shown in Figure 19.6, this time plotted against the specific overnight repo rate (mid-rate) for that bond.

Using the actual repo rate as a benchmark for comparison, we can check when the IRR is indeed at high levels and use this to plan a trade. From visual observation of Figure 19.7 we note that the IRR is almost, but not quite, always within a range that is 80–90% of the overnight repo rate. It only rarely outside this range, whether approaching the overnight rate or below the bottom part of the range. (Of course, we would be more scientific if undertaking actual analysis preparatory to a trade, and calculate the actual range of the IRR from recorded values rather than just look at the graph!). Bearing in mind that a high implied repo rate indicates a low gross basis, identifying a high IRR would suggest that the basis has fallen to a

---

7   See for instance Plona (*Ibid*), page 290ff.

lower level than would be "normal" at this stage of the convergence cycle. In other words, this is a possible point to buy the basis. If the analysis is proved correct, the basis will rise over the following days and the trade will produce profit.

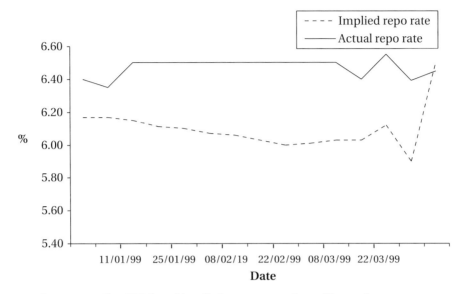

Figure 19.7: The CTD bond implied repo rate and specific market repo rate.
Source: Bloomberg.

19.4.2 *The implied repo rate across futures contracts: Bloomberg illustration*

The implied repo rate for the CTD can be used in association with the actual repo rates across three contracts on Bloomberg page CBSD. This is illustrated at Figure 19.8, which calculates the swap yield spread at which the long future delivered bond is swapped into a bond that is the *new* CTD and delivered into a short future. Thus this analysis can be carried out whenever the CTD for one contract is not the same as that for the next contract. The swap spread is user-defined but starts off as the current yield spread between the two bonds. We see from Figure 19.8 that the "Deliver" bond is the CTD for each contract; the converted price is given as "Dlvy price".

The contracts listed under "LONG" are the long positions in the implied repo analysis, while the actual market repo rates are indicated alongside as user-specified rates. These represent the basis trade return (or cash-and-carry return) for the number of days to contract expiry. In other words, the return generated from buying the basis, that is shorting the future, buying the CTD bond, holding this bond for the number of days shown and then delivering this bond into the short futures contract on the delivery date.

The implied repo rate indicates the relative richness of cheapness of the bond to the future, but using page CBSD we identify whether the near-dated futures contract is cheap relative to the far-dated contract. This is indicated when the IRR is relatively low or high, with the former suggesting that the near contract is expensive compared to the far contract. Here then we are using the IRR as part of a futures spread strategy. In such a trade, we sell the far-dated contract and simultaneously purchase the near-dated contract. On expiration of the front month contract, the long will be delivered into, with this bond being held and funded in repo until the second contract expiry. We calculate the funding rate that would allow us to run the position at positive carry using the page as shown in Figure 19.8, from market repo rates.

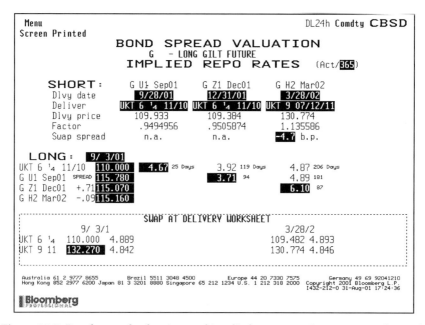

Figure 19.8: Bond spread valuation and implied repo rate, Sep01–Mar02 long gilt future, 24 August 2001. ©Bloomberg L.P. Reproduced with permission.

Appendix A

The BMA/ISMA Global Master Repurchase Agreement[1]

The Bond Market Association New York • Washington • London www.bondmarkets.com	International Securities Market Association Rigistrasse 60, P.O. Box, CH-8033, Zürich www.isma.org

2000 VERSION

TBMA/ISMA

GLOBAL MASTER REPURCHASE AGREEMENT

Dated as of_____

Between:

_____("Party A")

and

_____("Party B")

1.   **Applicability**

(a)   From time to time the parties hereto may enter into transactions in which one party,
        acting through a Designated Office, ("Seller") agrees to sell to the other, acting through
        a Designated Office, ("Buyer") securities and financial instruments ("Securities")

(subject to paragraph 1(c), other than equities and Net Paying Securities) against the payment of the purchase price by Buyer to Seller, with a simultaneous agreement by Buyer to sell to Seller Securities equivalent to such Securities at a date certain or on demand against the payment of the repurchase price by Seller to Buyer.

(b)   Each such transaction (which may be a repurchase transaction ("Repurchase Transaction") or a buy and sell back transaction ("Buy/Sell Back Transaction")) shall be referred to herein as a "Transaction" and shall be governed by this Agreement, including any supplemental terms or conditions contained in Annex I hereto, unless otherwise agreed in writing.

(c)   If this Agreement may be applied to –

     (i)   Buy/Sell Back Transactions, this shall be specified in Annex I hereto, and the provisions of the Buy/Sell Back Annex shall apply to such Buy/Sell Back Transactions;

     (ii)   Net Paying Securities, this shall be specified in Annex I hereto and the provisions of Annex I, paragraph 1(b) shall apply to Transactions involving Net Paying Securities.

(d)   If Transactions are to be effected under this Agreement by either party as an agent, this shall be specified in Annex I hereto, and the provisions of the Agency Annex shall apply to such Agency Transactions.

2. Definitions

(a)   "Act of Insolvency" shall occur with respect to any party hereto upon –

     (i)   its making a general assignment for the benefit of, entering into a reorganisation, arrangement, or composition with creditors; or

     (ii)   its admitting in writing that it is unable to pay its debts as they become due; or

     (iii)   its seeking, consenting to or acquiescing in the appointment of any trustee, administrator, receiver or liquidator or analogous officer of it or any material part of its property; or

     (iv)   the presentation or filing of a petition in respect of it (other than by the counterparty to this Agreement in respect of any obligation under this Agreement) in any court or before any agency alleging or for the bankruptcy, winding-up or insolvency of such party (or any analogous proceeding) or seeking any reorganisation, arrangement, composition, re-adjustment, administration, liquidation, dissolution or similar relief under any present or future statute, law or regulation, such petition (except in the case of a petition for winding-up or any analogous proceeding, in respect of which no such 30 day period shall apply) not having been stayed or dismissed within 30 days of its filing; or

(v)   the appointment of a receiver, administrator, liquidator or trustee or analogous officer of such party or over all or any material part of such party's property; or

(vi)   the convening of any meeting of its creditors for the purposes of considering a voluntary arrangement as referred to in section 3 of the Insolvency Act 1986 (or any analogous proceeding);

(b)   "Agency Transaction", the meaning specified in paragraph 1 of the Agency Annex;

(c)   "Appropriate Market", the meaning specified in paragraph 10;

(d)   "Base Currency", the currency indicated in Annex I hereto;

(e)   "Business Day" –

(i)   in relation to the settlement of any Transaction which is to be settled through Clearstream or Euroclear, a day on which Clearstream or, as the case may be, Euroclear is open to settle business in the currency in which the Purchase Price and the Repurchase Price are denominated;

(ii)   in relation to the settlement of any Transaction which is to be settled through a settlement system other than Clearstream or Euroclear, a day on which that settlement system is open to settle such Transaction;

(iii)   in relation to any delivery of Securities not falling within (i) or (ii) above, a day on which banks are open for business in the place where delivery of the relevant Securities is to be effected; and

(iv)   in relation to any obligation to make a payment not falling within (i) or (ii) above, a day other than a Saturday or a Sunday on which banks are open for business in the principal financial centre of the country of which the currency in which the payment is denominated is the official currency and, if different, in the place where any account designated by the parties for the making or receipt of the payment is situated (or, in the case of a payment in euro, a day on which TARGET operates);

(f)   "Cash Margin", a cash sum paid to Buyer or Seller in accordance with paragraph 4;

(g)   "Clearstream", Clearstream Banking, société anonyme, (previously Cedelbank) or any successor thereto;

(h)   "Confirmation", the meaning specified in paragraph 3(b);

(i)   "Contractual Currency", the meaning specified in paragraph 7(a);

(j)   "Defaulting Party", the meaning specified in paragraph 10;

(k)   "Default Market Value", the meaning specified in paragraph 10;

(l)   "Default Notice", a written notice served by the non-Defaulting Party on the Default-
        ing Party under paragraph 10 stating that an event shall be treated as an Event of De-
        fault for the purposes of this Agreement;

(m)   "Default Valuation Notice", the meaning specified in paragraph 10;

(n)   "Default Valuation Time", the meaning specified in paragraph 10;

(o)   "Deliverable Securities", the meaning specified in paragraph 10;

(p)   "Designated Office", with respect to a party, a branch or office of that party which is
        specified as such in Annex I hereto or such other branch or office as may be agreed to
        by the parties;

(q)   "Distributions", the meaning specified in sub-paragraph (w) below;

(r)   "Equivalent Margin Securities", Securities equivalent to Securities previously
        transferred as Margin Securities;

(s)   "Equivalent Securities", with respect to a Transaction, Securities equivalent to Pur-
        chased Securities under that Transaction. If and to the extent that such Purchased Se-
        curities have been redeemed, the expression shall mean a sum of money equivalent to
        the proceeds of the redemption;

(t)   Securities are "equivalent to" other Securities for the purposes of this Agreement if
        they are: (i) of the same issuer; (ii) part of the same issue; and (iii) of an identical type,
        nominal value, description and (except where otherwise stated) amount as those other
        Securities, provided that –

        (A)   Securities will be equivalent to other Securities notwithstanding that those Secu-
               rities have been redenominated into euro or that the nominal value of those Se-
               curities has changed in connection with such redenomination; and

        (B)   where Securities have been converted, subdivided or consolidated or have be-
               come the subject of a takeover or the holders of Securities have become entitled
               to receive or acquire other Securities or other property or the Securities have be-
               come subject to any similar event, the expression "equivalent to" shall mean Se-
               curities equivalent to (as defined in the provisions of this definition preceding
               the proviso) the original Securities together with or replaced by a sum of money
               or Securities or other property equivalent to (as so defined) that receivable by
               holders of such original Securities resulting from such event;

(u)   "Euroclear", Morgan Guaranty Trust Company of New York, Brussels office, as opera-
        tor of the Euroclear System or any successor thereto;

(v)   "Event of Default", the meaning specified in paragraph 10;

(w)   "Income", with respect to any Security at any time, all interest, dividends or other
        distributions thereon, but excluding distributions which are a payment or repayment
        of principal in respect of the relevant securities ("Distributions");

(x)   "1ncome Payment Date", with respect to any Securities, the date on which Income is paid in respect of such Securities or, in the case of registered Securities, the date by reference to which particular registered holders are identified as being entitled to payment of Income;

(y)   "LIBOR", in relation to any sum in any currency, the one month London Inter Bank Offered Rate in respect of that currency as quoted on page 3750 on the Bridge Telerate Service (or such other page as may replace page 3750 on that service) as of 11:00 a.m., London time, on the date on which it is to be determined;

(z)   "Margin Ratio", with respect to a Transaction, the Market Value of the Purchased Securities at the time when the Transaction was entered into divided by the Purchase Price (and so that, where a Transaction relates to Securities of different descriptions and the Purchase Price is apportioned by the parties among Purchased Securities of each such description, a separate Margin Ratio shall apply in respect of Securities of each such description), or such other proportion as the parties may agree with respect to that Transaction;

(aa)   "Margin Securities", in relation to a Margin Transfer, Securities reasonably acceptable to the party calling for such Margin Transfer;

(bb)   "Margin Transfer", any, or any combination of, the payment or repayment of Cash Margin and the transfer of Margin Securities or Equivalent Margin Securities;

(cc)   "Market Value", with respect to any Securities as of any time on any date, the price for such Securities at such time on such date obtained from a generally recognised source agreed to by the parties (and where different prices are obtained for different delivery dates, the price so obtainable for the earliest available such delivery date) (provided that the price of Securities that are suspended shall (for the purposes of paragraph 4) be nil unless the parties otherwise agree and (for all other purposes) shall be the price of those Securities as of close of business on the dealing day in the relevant market last preceding the date of suspension) plus the aggregate amount of Income which, as of such date, has accrued but not yet been paid in respect of the Securities to the extent not included in such price as of such date, and for these purposes any sum in a currency other than the Contractual Currency for the Transaction in question shall be converted into such Contractual Currency at the Spot Rate prevailing at the relevant time;

(dd)   "Net Exposure", the meaning specified in paragraph 4(c);

(ee)   the "Net Margin" provided to a party at any time, the excess (if any) at that time of (i) the sum of the amount of Cash Margin paid to that party (including accrued interest on such Cash Margin which has not been paid to the other party) and the Market Value of Margin Securities transferred to that party under paragraph 4(a) (excluding any Cash Margin which has been repaid to the other party and any Margin Securities in respect of which Equivalent Margin Securities have been transferred to the other party) over (ii) the sum of the amount of Cash Margin paid to the other party (including accrued interest on such Cash Margin which has not been paid by the other party) and the Market Value of Margin Securities transferred to the other party under paragraph 4(a) (excluding any Cash Margin which has been repaid by the other party and any Margin Securities in respect of which Equivalent Margin Securities have been transferred by the other party) and for this purpose any amounts not denominated in the Base Currency shall be converted into the Base Currency at the Spot Rate prevailing at the relevant time;

(ff)   "Net Paying Securities", Securities which are of a kind such that, were they to be the subject of a Transaction to which paragraph 5 applies, any payment made by Buyer under paragraph 5 would be one in respect of which either Buyer would or might be required to make a withholding or deduction for or on account of taxes or duties or Seller might be required to make or account for a payment for or on account of taxes or duties (in each case other than tax on overall net income) by reference to such payment;

(gg)   "Net Value", the meaning specified in paragraph 10;

(hh)   "New Purchased Securities", the meaning specified in paragraph 8(a);

(ii)   "Price Differential", with respect to any Transaction as of any date, the aggregate amount obtained by daily application of the Pricing Rate for such Transaction to the Purchase Price for such Transaction (on a 360 day basis or 365 day basis in accordance with the applicable ISMA convention, unless otherwise agreed between the parties for the Transaction), for the actual number of days during the period commencing on (and including) the Purchase Date for such Transaction and ending on (but excluding) the date of calculation or, if earlier, the Repurchase Date;

(jj)   "Pricing Rate", with respect to any Transaction, the per annum percentage rate for calculation of the Price Differential agreed to by Buyer and Seller in relation to that Transaction;

(kk)   "Purchase Date", with respect to any Transaction, the date on which Purchased Securities are to be sold by Seller to Buyer in relation to that Transaction;

(11)   "Purchase Price", on the Purchase Date, the price at which Purchased Securities are sold or are to be sold by Seller to Buyer;

(mm) "Purchased Securities", with respect to any Transaction, the Securities sold or to be sold by Seller to Buyer under that Transaction, and any New Purchased Securities transferred by Seller to Buyer under paragraph 8 in respect of that Transaction;

(nn)   "Receivable Securities", the meaning specified in paragraph 10;

(oo)   "Repurchase Date", with respect to any Transaction, the date on which Buyer is to sell Equivalent Securities to Seller in relation to that Transaction;

(pp)   "Repurchase Price", with respect to any Transaction and as of any date, the sum of the Purchase Price and the Price Differential as of such date;

(qq)   "Special Default Notice", the meaning specified in paragraph 14;

(rr)   "Spot Rate", where an amount in one currency is to be converted into a second currency on any date, unless the parties otherwise agree, the spot rate of exchange quoted by Barclays Bank PLC in the London inter-bank market for the sale by it of such second currency against a purchase by it of such first currency;

(ss)   "TARGET", the Trans-European Automated Real-time Gross Settlement Express Transfer System;

(tt)   "Term", with respect to any Transaction, the interval of time commencing with the Purchase Date and ending with the Repurchase Date;

(uu)   "Termination", with respect to any Transaction, refers to the requirement with respect to such Transaction for Buyer to sell Equivalent Securities against payment by Seller of the Repurchase Price in accordance with paragraph 3(f), and reference to a Transaction having a "fixed term" or being "terminable upon demand" shall be construed accordingly;

(vv)   "Transaction Costs", the meaning specified in paragraph 10;

(ww)   "Transaction Exposure", with respect to any Transaction at any time during the period from the Purchase Date to the Repurchase Date (or, if later, the date on which Equivalent Securities are delivered to Seller or the Transaction is terminated under paragraph 10(g) or 10(h)), the difference between (i) the Repurchase Price at such time multiplied by the applicable Margin Ratio (or, where the Transaction relates to Securities of more than one description to which different Margin Ratios apply, the amount produced by multiplying the Repurchase Price attributable to Equivalent Securities of each such description by the applicable Margin Ratio and aggregating the resulting amounts, the Repurchase Price being for this purpose attributed to Equivalent Securities of each such description in the same proportions as those in which the Purchase Price was apportioned among the Purchased Securities) and (ii) the Market Value of Equivalent Securities at such time. If (i) is greater than (ii), Buyer has a Transaction Exposure for that Transaction equal to that excess. If (ii) is greater than (i), Seller has a Transaction Exposure for that Transaction equal to that excess; and

(xx)   except in paragraphs 14(b)(i) and 18, references in this Agreement to "written" communications and communications "in writing" include communications made through any electronic system agreed between the parties which is capable of reproducing such communication in hard copy form.

3.   Initiation; Confirmation; Termination

(a)   A Transaction may be entered into orally or in writing at the initiation of either Buyer or Seller.

(b)   Upon agreeing to enter into a Transaction hereunder Buyer or Seller (or both), as shall have been agreed, shall promptly deliver to the other party written confirmation of such Transaction (a "Confirmation").

The Confirmation shall describe the Purchased Securities (including CUSIP or ISIN or other identifying number or numbers, if any), identify Buyer and Seller and set forth –

(i)   the Purchase Date;

(ii)   the Purchase Price;

(iii)   the Repurchase Date, unless the Transaction is to be terminable on demand (in which case the Confirmation shall state that it is terminable on demand);

(iv)   the Pricing Rate applicable to the Transaction;

(v)   in respect of each party the details of the bank account[s] to which payments to be made hereunder are to be credited;

(vi)   where the Buy/Sell Back Annex applies, whether the Transaction is a Repurchase Transaction or a Buy/Sell Back Transaction;

(vii)   where the Agency Annex applies, whether the Transaction is an Agency Transaction and, if so, the identity of the party which is acting as agent and the name, code or identifier of the Principal; and

(viii)   any additional terms or conditions of the Transaction;

and may be in the form of Annex II hereto or may be in any other form to which the parties agree.

The Confirmation relating to a Transaction shall, together with this Agreement, constitute prima facie evidence of the terms agreed between Buyer and Seller for that Transaction, unless objection is made with respect to the Confirmation promptly after receipt thereof. In the event of any conflict between the terms of such Confirmation and this Agreement, the Confirmation shall prevail in respect of that Transaction and those terms only.

(c)   On the Purchase Date for a Transaction, Seller shall transfer the Purchased Securities to Buyer or its agent against the payment of the Purchase Price by Buyer.

(d)   Termination of a Transaction will be effected, in the case of on demand Transactions, on the date specified for Termination in such demand, and, in the case of fixed term Transactions, on the date fixed for Termination.

(e)   In the case of on demand Transactions, demand for Termination shall be made by Buyer or Seller, by telephone or otherwise, and shall provide for Termination to occur after not less than the minimum period as is customarily required for the settlement or delivery of money or Equivalent Securities of the relevant kind.

(f)   On the Repurchase Date, Buyer shall transfer to Seller or its agent Equivalent Securities against the payment of the Repurchase Price by Seller (less any amount then payable and unpaid by Buyer to Seller pursuant to paragraph 5).

4.   Margin Maintenance

(a)   If at any time either party has a Net Exposure in respect of the other party it may by notice to the other party require the other party to make a Margin Transfer to it of an aggregate amount or value at least equal to that Net Exposure.

(b)   A notice under sub-paragraph (a) above may be given orally or in writing.

(c)   For the purposes of this Agreement a party has a Net Exposure in respect of the other party if the aggregate of all the first party's Transaction Exposures plus any amount payable to the first party under paragraph 5 but unpaid less the amount of any Net Margin provided to the first party exceeds the aggregate of all the other party's Transaction Exposures plus any amount payable to the other party under paragraph 5 but unpaid less the amount of any Net Margin provided to the other party; and the amount of the Net Exposure is the amount of the excess. For this purpose any amounts not denominated in the Base Currency shall be converted into the Base Currency at the Spot Rate prevailing at the relevant time.

(d)   To the extent that a party calling for a Margin Transfer has previously paid Cash Margin which has not been repaid or delivered Margin Securities in respect of which Equivalent Margin Securities have not been delivered to it, that party shall be entitled to require that such Margin Transfer be satisfied first by the repayment of such Cash Margin or the delivery of Equivalent Margin Securities but, subject to this, the composition of a Margin Transfer shall be at the option of the party making such Margin Transfer.

(e)   Any Cash Margin transferred shall be in the Base Currency or such other currency as the parties may agree.

(f)   A payment of Cash Margin shall give rise to a debt owing from the party receiving such payment to the party making such payment. Such debt shall bear interest at such rate, payable at such times, as may be specified in Annex I hereto in respect of the relevant currency or otherwise agreed between the parties, and shall be repayable subject to the terms of this Agreement.

(g)   Where Seller or Buyer becomes obliged under sub-paragraph (a) above to make a Margin Transfer, it shall transfer Cash Margin or Margin Securities or Equivalent Margin Securities within the minimum period specified in Annex I hereto or, if no period is there specified, such minimum period as is customarily required for the settlement or delivery of money, Margin Securities or Equivalent Margin Securities of the relevant kind.

(h)   The parties may agree that, with respect to any Transaction, the provisions of sub-paragraphs (a) to (g) above shall not apply but instead that margin may be provided separately in respect of that Transaction in which case –

       (i)   that Transaction shall not be taken into account when calculating whether either party has a Net Exposure;

       (ii)   margin shall be provided in respect of that Transaction in such manner as the parties may agree; and

       (iii)   margin provided in respect of that Transaction shall not be taken into account for the purposes of sub-paragraphs (a) to (g) above.

(i)   The parties may agree that any Net Exposure which may arise shall be eliminated not by Margin Transfers under the preceding provisions of this paragraph but by the repricing of Transactions under sub-paragraph (j) below, the adjustment of Transactions under sub-paragraph (k) below or a combination of both these methods.

(j)   Where the parties agree that a Transaction is to be repriced under this sub-paragraph, such repricing shall be effected as follows –

(i)   the Repurchase Date under the relevant Transaction (the "Original Trans-action") shall be deemed to occur on the date on which the repricing is to be effected (the "Repricing Date");

(ii)   the parties shall be deemed to have entered into a new Transaction (the "Re-priced Transaction") on the terms set out in (iii) to (vi) below;

(iii)   the Purchased Securities under the Repriced Transaction shall be Securities equivalent to the Purchased Securities under the Original Transaction;

(iv)   the Purchase Date under the Repriced Transaction shall be the Repricing Date;

(v)   the Purchase Price under the Repriced Transaction shall be such amount as shall, when multiplied by the Margin Ratio applicable to the Original Transac-tion, be equal to the Market Value of such Securities on the Repricing Date;

(vi)   the Repurchase Date, the Pricing Rate, the Margin Ratio and, subject as afore-said, the other terms of the Repriced Transaction shall be identical to those of the Original Transaction;

(vii)   the obligations of the parties with respect to the delivery of the Purchased Securities and the payment of the Purchase Price under the Repriced Trans-action shall be set off against their obligations with respect to the delivery of Equivalent Securities and payment of the Repurchase Price under the Origi-nal Transaction and accordingly only a net cash sum shall be paid by one party to the other. Such net cash sum shall be paid within the period specified in sub-paragraph (g) above.

(k)   The adjustment of a Transaction (the "Original Transaction") under this sub-para-graph shall be effected by the parties agreeing that on the date on which the adjust-ment is to be made (the "Adjustment Date") the Original Transaction shall be termi-nated and they shall enter into a new Transaction (the "Replacement Transaction") in accordance with the following provisions –

(i)   the Original Transaction shall be terminated on the Adjustment Date on such terms as the parties shall agree on or before the Adjustment Date;

(ii)   the Purchased Securities under the Replacement Transaction shall be such Securities as the parties shall agree on or before the Adjustment Date (being Securities the aggregate Market Value of which at the Adjustment Date is sub-stantially equal to the Repurchase Price under the Original Transaction at the Adjustment Date multiplied by the Margin Ratio applicable to the Original Transaction);

(iii)   the Purchase Date under the Replacement Transaction shall be the Adjustment Date;

(iv)   the other terms of the Replacement Transaction shall be such as the parties
shall agree on or before the Adjustment Date; and

(v)   the obligations of the parties with respect to payment and delivery of Securities on the Adjustment Date under the Original Transaction and the Replacement Transaction shall be settled in accordance with paragraph 6
within the minimum period specified in sub-paragraph (g) above.

5.   Income Payments

Unless otherwise agreed –

(i)   where the Term of a particular Transaction extends over an Income Payment
Date in respect of any Securities subject to that Transaction, Buyer shall on
the date such Income is paid by the issuer transfer to or credit to the account
of Seller an amount equal to (and in the same currency as) the amount paid
by the issuer;

(ii)   where Margin Securities are transferred from one party ("the first party") to
the other party ("the second party") and an Income Payment Date in respect
of such Securities occurs before Equivalent Margin Securities are transferred
by the second party to the first party, the second party shall on the date such
Income is paid by the issuer transfer to or credit to the account of the first
party an amount equal to (and in the same currency as) the amount paid by
the issuer;

and for the avoidance of doubt references in this paragraph to the amount of any Income paid by the issuer of any Securities shall be to an amount paid without any withholding or deduction for or on account of taxes or duties notwithstanding that a
payment of such Income made in certain circumstances may be subject to such a
withholding or deduction.

6.   Payment and Transfer

(a)   Unless otherwise agreed, all money paid hereunder shall be in immediately available
freely convertible funds of the relevant currency. All Securities to be transferred hereunder (i) shall be in suitable form for transfer and shall be accompanied by duly executed instruments of transfer or assignment in blank (where required for transfer) and
such other documentation as the transferee may reasonably request, or (ii) shall be
transferred through the book entry system of Euroclear or Clearstream, or (iii) shall be
transferred through any other agreed securities clearance system or (iv) shall be transferred by any other method mutually acceptable to Seller and Buyer.

(b)   Unless otherwise agreed, all money payable by one party to the other in respect of any
Transaction shall be paid free and clear of, and without withholding or deduction for,
any taxes or duties of whatsoever nature imposed, levied, collected, withheld or assessed by any authority having power to tax, unless the withholding or deduction of
such taxes or duties is required by law. In that event, unless otherwise agreed, the pay-

ing party shall pay such additional amounts as will result in the net amounts receivable by the other party (after taking account of such withholding or deduction) being equal to such amounts as would have been received by it had no such taxes or duties been required to be withheld or deducted.

(c)   Unless otherwise agreed in writing between the parties, under each Transaction transfer of Purchased Securities by Seller and payment of Purchase Price by Buyer against the transfer of such Purchased Securities shall be made simultaneously and transfer of Equivalent Securities by Buyer and payment of Repurchase Price payable by Seller against the transfer of such Equivalent Securities shall be made simultaneously.

(d)   Subject to and without prejudice to the provisions of sub-paragraph 6(c), either party may from time to time in accordance with market practice and in recognition of the practical difficulties in arranging simultaneous delivery of Securities and money waive in relation to any Transaction its rights under this Agreement to receive simultaneous transfer and/or payment provided that transfer and/or payment shall, notwithstanding such waiver, be made on the same day and provided also that no such waiver in respect of one Transaction shall affect or bind it in respect of any other Transaction.

(e)   The parties shall execute and deliver all necessary documents and take all necessary steps to procure that all right, title and interest in any Purchased Securities, any Equivalent Securities, any Margin Securities and any Equivalent Margin Securities shall pass to the party to which transfer is being made upon transfer of the same in accordance with this Agreement, free from all liens, claims, charges and encumbrances.

(f)   Notwithstanding the use of expressions such as "*Repurchase Date*", "*Repurchase Price*", "*margin*", "*Net Margin*", "*Margin Ratio*" and "*substitution*", which are used to reflect terminology used in the market for transactions of the kind provided for in this Agreement, all right, title and interest in and to Securities and money transferred or paid under this Agreement shall pass to the transferee upon transfer or payment, the obligation of the party receiving Purchased Securities or Margin Securities being an obligation to transfer Equivalent Securities or Equivalent Margin Securities.

(g)   Time shall be of the essence in this Agreement.

(h)   Subject to paragraph 10, all amounts in the same currency payable by each party to the other under any Transaction or otherwise under this Agreement on the same date shall be combined in a single calculation of a net sum payable by one party to the other and the obligation to pay that sum shall be the only obligation of either party in respect of those amounts.

(i)   Subject to paragraph 10, all Securities of the same issue, denomination, currency and series, transferable by each party to the other under any Transaction or hereunder on the same date shall be combined in a single calculation of a net quantity of Securities transferable by one party to the other and the obligation to transfer the net quantity of Securities shall be the only obligation of either party in respect of the Securities so transferable and receivable.

(j)   If the parties have specified in Annex I hereto that this paragraph 6(j) shall apply, each obligation of a party under this Agreement (other than an obligation arising under paragraph 10) is subject to the condition precedent that none of those events specified in paragraph 10(a) which are identified in Annex I hereto for the purposes of this paragraph 6(j) (being events which, upon the serving of a Default Notice, would be an Event of Default with respect to the other party) shall have occurred and be continuing with respect to the other party.

7.   Contractual Currency

(a)   All the payments made in respect of the Purchase Price or the Repurchase Price of any Transaction shall be made in the currency of the Purchase Price (the "Contractual Currency") save as provided in paragraph 10(c)(ii). Notwithstanding the foregoing, the payee of any money may, at its option, accept tender thereof in any other currency, provided, however, that, to the extent permitted by applicable law, the obligation of the payer to pay such money will be discharged only to the extent of the amount of the Contractual Currency that such payee may, consistent with normal banking procedures, purchase with such other currency (after deduction of any premium and costs of exchange) for delivery within the customary delivery period for spot transactions in respect of the relevant currency.

(b)   If for any reason the amount in the Contractual Currency received by a party, including amounts received after conversion of any recovery under any judgment or order expressed in a currency other than the Contractual Currency, falls short of the amount in the Contractual Currency due and payable, the party required to make the payment will, as a separate and independent obligation, to the extent permitted by applicable law, immediately transfer such additional amount in the Contractual Currency as may be necessary to compensate for the shortfall.

(c)   If for any reason the amount in the Contractual Currency received by a party exceeds the amount of the Contractual Currency due and payable, the party receiving the transfer will refund promptly the amount of such excess.

8.   Substitution

(a)   A Transaction may at any time between the Purchase Date and Repurchase Date, if Seller so requests and Buyer so agrees, be varied by the transfer by Buyer to Seller of Securities equivalent to the Purchased Securities, or to such of the Purchased Securities as shall be agreed, in exchange for the transfer by Seller to Buyer of other Securities of such amount and description as shall be agreed ("New Purchased Securities") (being Securities having a Market Value at the date of the variation at least equal to the Market Value of the Equivalent Securities transferred to Seller).

(b)   Any variation under sub-paragraph (a) above shall be effected, subject to paragraph 6(d), by the simultaneous transfer of the Equivalent Securities and New Purchased Securities concerned.

(c)   A Transaction which is varied under sub-paragraph (a) above shall thereafter continue in effect as though the Purchased Securities under that Transaction consisted of or included the New Purchased Securities instead of the Securities in respect of which Equivalent Securities have been transferred to Seller.

(d)   Where either party has transferred Margin Securities to the other party it may at any time before Equivalent Margin Securities are transferred to it under paragraph 4 request the other party to transfer Equivalent Margin Securities to it in exchange for the transfer to the other party of new Margin Securities having a Market Value at the time of transfer at least equal to that of such Equivalent Margin Securities. If the other party agrees to the request, the exchange shall be effected, subject to paragraph 6(d), by the simultaneous transfer of the Equivalent Margin Securities and new Margin Securities concerned. Where either or both of such transfers is or are effected through a settlement system in circumstances which under the rules and procedures of that settlement system give rise to a payment by or for the account of one party to or for the account of the other party, the parties shall cause such payment or payments to be made outside that settlement system, for value the same day as the payments made through that settlement system, as shall ensure that the exchange of Equivalent Margin Securities and new Margin Securities effected under this sub-paragraph does not give rise to any net payment of cash by either party to the other.

9.   **Representations**

        Each party represents and warrants to the other that –

(a)   it is duly authorised to execute and deliver this Agreement, to enter into the Transactions contemplated hereunder and to perform its obligations hereunder and thereunder and has taken all necessary action to authorise such execution, delivery and performance;

(b)   it will engage in this Agreement and the Transactions contemplated hereunder (other than Agency Transactions) as principal;

(c)   the person signing this Agreement on its behalf is, and any person representing it in entering into a Transaction will be, duly authorised to do so on its behalf;

(d)   it has obtained all authorisations of any governmental or regulatory body required in connection with this Agreement and the Transactions contemplated hereunder and such authorisations are in full force and effect;

(e)   the execution, delivery and performance of this Agreement and the Transactions contemplated hereunder will not violate any law, ordinance, charter, by-law or rule applicable to it or any agreement by which it is bound or by which any of its assets are affected;

(f)   it has satisfied itself and will continue to satisfy itself as to the tax implications of the Transactions contemplated hereunder;

(g)   in connection with this Agreement and each Transaction –

        (i)   unless there is a written agreement with the other party to the contrary, it is not relying on any advice (whether written or oral) of the other party, other than the representations expressly set out in this Agreement;

        (ii)   it has made and will make its own decisions regarding the entering into of any Transaction based upon its own judgment and upon advice from such professional advisers as it has deemed it necessary to consult;

(iii)   it understands the terms, conditions and risks of each Transaction and is willing to assume (financially and otherwise) those risks; and

(h)   at the time of transfer to the other party of any Securities it will have the full and unqualified right to make such transfer and that upon such transfer of Securities the other party will receive all right, title and interest in and to those Securities free of any lien, claim, charge or encumbrance.

On the date on which any Transaction is entered into pursuant hereto, and on each day on which Securities, Equivalent Securities, Margin Securities or Equivalent Margin Securities are to be transferred under any Transaction, Buyer and Seller shall each be deemed to repeat all the foregoing representations. For the avoidance of doubt and notwithstanding any arrangements which Seller or Buyer may have with any third party, each party will be liable as a principal for its obligations under this Agreement and each Transaction.

10.   Events of Default

(a)   If any of the following events (each an "Event of Default") occurs in relation to either party (the "Defaulting Party", the other party being the "non-Defaulting Party") whether acting as Seller or Buyer –

(i)   Buyer fails to pay the Purchase Price upon the applicable Purchase Date or Seller fails to pay the Repurchase Price upon the applicable Repurchase Date, and the non-Defaulting Party serves a Default Notice on the Defaulting Party; or

(ii)   if the parties have specified in Annex I hereto that this sub-paragraph shall apply, Seller fails to deliver Purchased Securities on the Purchase Date or Buyer fails to deliver Equivalent Securities on the Repurchase Date, and the non-Defaulting Party serves a Default Notice on the Defaulting Party; or

(iii)   Seller or Buyer fails to pay when due any sum payable under sub-paragraph (g) or (h) below, and the non-Defaulting Party serves a Default Notice on the Defaulting Party; or

(iv)   Seller or Buyer fails to comply with paragraph 4 and the non-Defaulting Party serves a Default Notice on the Defaulting Party; or

(v)   Seller or Buyer fails to comply with paragraph 5 and the non-Defaulting Party serves a Default Notice on the Defaulting Party; or

(vi)   an Act of Insolvency occurs with respect to Seller or Buyer and (except in the case of an Act of Insolvency which is the presentation of a petition for winding-up or any analogous proceeding or the appointment of a liquidator or analogous officer of the Defaulting Party in which case no such notice shall be required) the non-Defaulting Party serves a Default Notice on the Defaulting Party; or

(vii)   any representations made by Seller or Buyer are incorrect or untrue in any material respect when made or repeated or deemed to have been made or

repeated, and the non-Defaulting Party serves a Default Notice on the Defaulting Party; or

(viii)   Seller or Buyer admits to the other that it is unable to, or intends not to, per-
          form any of its obligations hereunder and/or in respect of any Transaction
          and the non-Defaulting Party serves a Default Notice on the Defaulting Party;
          or

(ix)   Seller or Buyer is suspended or expelled from membership of or participation
          in any securities exchange or association or other self regulating organisation,
          or suspended from dealing in securities by any government agency, or any of
          the assets of either Seller or Buyer or the assets of investors held by, or to the
          order of, Seller or Buyer are transferred or ordered to be transferred to a trus-
          tee by a regulatory authority pursuant to any securities regulating legislation
          and the non-Defaulting Party serves a Default Notice on the Defaulting Party;
          or

(x)   Seller or Buyer fails to perform any other of its obligations hereunder and
          does not remedy such failure within 30 days after notice is given by the non-
          Defaulting Party requiring it to do so, and the non-Defaulting Party serves a
          Default Notice on the Defaulting Party;

then sub-paragraphs (b) to (f) below shall apply.

(b)   The Repurchase Date for each Transaction hereunder shall be deemed immediately
          to occur and, subject to the following provisions, all Cash Margin (including interest
          accrued) shall be immediately repayable and Equivalent Margin Securities shall be
          immediately deliverable (and so that, where this sub-paragraph applies, performance
          of the respective obligations of the parties with respect to the delivery of Securities, the
          payment of the Repurchase Prices for any Equivalent Securities and the repayment of
          any Cash Margin shall be effected only in accordance with the provisions of sub-
          paragraph (c) below).

(c)   (i)   The Default Market Values of the Equivalent Securities and any Equivalent
                   Margin Securities to be transferred, the amount of any Cash Margin (includ-
                   ing the amount of interest accrued) to be transferred and the Repurchase
                   Prices to be paid by each party shall be established by the non-Defaulting
                   Party for all Transactions as at the Repurchase Date; and

          (ii)   on the basis of the sums so established, an account shall be taken (as at the
                   Repurchase Date) of what is due from each party to the other under this
                   Agreement (on the basis that each party's claim against the other in respect of
                   the transfer to it of Equivalent Securities or Equivalent Margin Securities un-
                   der this Agreement equals the Default Market Value therefor) and the sums
                   due from one party shall be set off against the sums due from the other and
                   only the balance of the account shall be payable (by the party having the
                   claim valued at the lower amount pursuant to the foregoing) and such bal-
                   ance shall be due and payable on the next following Business Day. For the
                   purposes of this calculation, all sums not denominated in the Base Currency
                   shall be converted into the Base Currency on the relevant date at the Spot
                   Rate prevailing at the relevant time.

(d)　For the purposes of this Agreement, the "Default Market Value" of any Equivalent Securities or Equivalent Margin Securities shall be determined in accordance with sub-paragraph (e) below, and for this purpose –

(i)　the "Appropriate Market" means, in relation to Securities of any description, the market which is the most appropriate market for Securities of that description, as determined by the non-Defaulting Party;

(ii)　the "Default Valuation Time" means, in relation to an Event of Default, the close of business in the Appropriate Market on the fifth dealing day after the day on which that Event of Default occurs or, where that Event of Default is the occurrence of an Act of Insolvency in respect of which under paragraph 10(a) no notice is required from the non-Defaulting Party in order for such event to constitute an Event of Default, the close of business on the fifth dealing day after the day on which the non-Defaulting Party first became aware of the occurrence of such Event of Default;

(iii)　"Deliverable Securities" means Equivalent Securities or Equivalent Margin Securities to be delivered by the Defaulting Party,

(iv)　"Net Value" means at any time, in relation to any Deliverable Securities or Receivable Securities, the amount which, in the reasonable opinion of the non-Defaulting Party, represents their fair market value, having regard to such pricing sources and methods (which may include, without limitation, available prices for Securities with similar maturities, terms and credit characteristics as the relevant Equivalent Securities or Equivalent Margin Securities) as the non-Defaulting Party considers appropriate, less, in the case of Receivable Securities, or plus, in the case of Deliverable Securities, all Transaction Costs which would be incurred in connection with the purchase or sale of such Securities;

(v)　"Receivable Securities" means Equivalent Securities or Equivalent Margin Securities to be delivered to the Defaulting Party; and

(vi)　"Transaction Costs" in relation to any transaction contemplated in paragraph 10(d) or (e) means the reasonable costs, commission, fees and expenses (including any mark-up or mark-down) that would be incurred in connection with the purchase of Deliverable Securities or sale of Receivable Securities, calculated on the assumption that the aggregate thereof is the least that could reasonably be expected to be paid in order to carry out the transaction;

(e)　(i)　If between the occurrence of the relevant Event of Default and the Default Valuation Time the non-Defaulting Party gives to the Defaulting Party a written notice (a "Default Valuation Notice") which –

(A)　states that, since the occurrence of the relevant Event of Default, the non-Defaulting Party has sold, in the case of Receivable Securities, or purchased, in the case of Deliverable Securities, Securities which form part of the same issue and are of an identical type and description as those Equivalent Securities or Equivalent Margin Securities, and that the non-Defaulting Party elects to treat as the Default Market Value –

(aa)   in the case of Receivable Securities, the net proceeds of such sale after deducting all reasonable costs, fees and expenses incurred in connection therewith (provided that, where the Securities sold are not identical in amount to the Equivalent Securities or Equivalent Margin Securities, the non-Defaulting Party may either (x) elect to treat such net proceeds of sale divided by the amount of Securities sold and multiplied by the amount of the Equivalent Securities or Equivalent Margin Securities as the Default Market Value or (y) elect to treat such net proceeds of sale of the Equivalent Securities or Equivalent Margin Securities actually sold as the Default Market Value of that proportion of the Equivalent Securities or Equivalent Margin Securities, and, in the case of (y), the Default Market Value of the balance of the Equivalent Securities or Equivalent Margin Securities shall be determined separately in accordance with the provisions of this paragraph 10(e) and accordingly may be the subject of a separate notice (or notices) under this paragraph 10(e)(i)); or

(bb)   in the case of Deliverable Securities, the aggregate cost of such purchase, including all reasonable costs, fees and expenses incurred in connection therewith (provided that, where the Securities purchased are not identical in amount to the Equivalent Securities or Equivalent Margin Securities, the non-Defaulting Party may either (x) elect to treat such aggregate cost divided by the amount of Securities sold and multiplied by the amount of the Equivalent Securities or Equivalent Margin Securities as the Default Market Value or (y) elect to treat the aggregate cost of purchasing the Equivalent Securities or Equivalent Margin Securities actually purchased as the Default Market Value of that proportion of the Equivalent Securities or Equivalent Margin Securities, and, in the case of (y), the Default Market Value of the balance of the Equivalent Securities or Equivalent Margin Securities shall be determined separately in accordance with the provisions of this paragraph 10(e) and accordingly may be the subject of a separate notice (or notices) under this paragraph 10(e)(i));

(B)   states that the non-Defaulting Party has received, in the case of Deliverable Securities, offer quotations or, in the case of Receivable Securities, bid quotations in respect of Securities of the relevant description from two or more market makers or regular dealers in the Appropriate Market in a commercially reasonable size (as determined by the non-Defaulting Party) and specifies –

(aa)   the price or prices quoted by each of them for, in the case of Deliverable Securities, the sale by the relevant market marker or dealer of such Securities or, in the case of Receivable Securities, the purchase by the relevant market maker or dealer of such Securities;

(bb)   the Transaction Costs which would be incurred in connection with such a transaction; and

(cc)   that the non-Defaulting Party elects to treat the price so quoted (or, where more than one price is so quoted, the arithmetic mean of the prices so quoted), after deducting, in the case of Receivable Securities, or adding, in the case of Deliverable Securities, such Transaction Costs, as the Default Market Value of the relevant Equivalent Securities or Equivalent Margin Securities; or

(C)   states –

(aa)   that either (x) acting in good faith, the non-Defaulting Party has endeavoured but been unable to sell or purchase Securities in accordance with sub-paragraph (i)(A) above or to obtain quotations in accordance with sub-paragraph (i)(B) above (or both) or (y) the non-Defaulting Party has determined that it would not be commercially reasonable to obtain such quotations, or that it would not be commercially reasonable to use any quotations which it has obtained under sub-paragraph (i)(B) above; and

(bb)   that the non-Defaulting Party has determined the Net Value of the relevant Equivalent Securities or Equivalent Margin Securities (which shall be specified) and that the non-Defaulting Party elects to treat such Net Value as the Default Market Value of the relevant Equivalent Securities or Equivalent Margin Securities,

then the Default Market Value of the relevant Equivalent Securities or Equivalent Margin Securities shall be an amount equal to the Default Market Value specified in accordance with (A), (B)(cc) or, as the case may be, (C)(bb) above.

(ii)   If by the Default Valuation Time the non-Defaulting Party has not given a Default Valuation Notice, the Default Market Value of the relevant Equivalent Securities or Equivalent Margin Securities shall be an amount equal to their Net Value at the Default Valuation Time; provided that, if at the Default Valuation Time the non-Defaulting Party reasonably determines that, owing to circumstances affecting the market in the Equivalent Securities or Equivalent Margin Securities in question, it is not possible for the non-Defaulting Party to determine a Net Value of such Equivalent Securities or Equivalent Margin Securities which is commercially reasonable, the Default Market Value of such Equivalent Securities or Equivalent Margin Securities shall be an amount equal to their Net Value as determined by the non-Defaulting Party as soon as reasonably practicable after the Default Valuation Time.

(f)   The Defaulting Party shall be liable to the non-Defaulting Party for the amount of all reasonable legal and other professional expenses incurred by the non-Defaulting Party in connection with or as a consequence of an Event of Default, together with interest thereon at LIBOR or, in the case of an expense attributable to a particular Transaction, the Pricing Rate for the relevant Transaction if that Pricing Rate is greater than LIBOR.

(g)   If Seller fails to deliver Purchased Securities to Buyer on the applicable Purchase Date Buyer may –

    (i)   if it has paid the Purchase Price to Seller, require Seller immediately to repay the sum so paid;

    (ii)   if Buyer has a Transaction Exposure to Seller in respect of the relevant Transaction, require Seller from time to time to pay Cash Margin at least equal to such Transaction Exposure;

    (iii)   at any time while such failure continues, terminate the Transaction by giving written notice to Seller. On such termination the obligations of Seller and Buyer with respect to delivery of Purchased Securities and Equivalent Securities shall terminate and Seller shall pay to Buyer an amount equal to the excess of the Repurchase Price at the date of Termination over the Purchase Price.

(h)   If Buyer fails to deliver Equivalent Securities to Seller on the applicable Repurchase Date Seller may –

    (i)   if it has paid the Repurchase Price to Buyer, require Buyer immediately to repay the sum so paid;

    (ii)   if Seller has a Transaction Exposure to Buyer in respect of the relevant Transaction, require Buyer from time to time to pay Cash Margin at least equal to such Transaction Exposure;

    (iii)   at any time while such failure continues, by written notice to Buyer declare that that Transaction (but only that Transaction) shall be terminated immediately in accordance with sub-paragraph (c) above (disregarding for this purpose references in that sub-paragraph to transfer of Cash Margin and delivery of Equivalent Margin Securities and as if references to the Repurchase Date were to the date on which notice was given under this sub-paragraph).

(i)   The provisions of this Agreement constitute a complete statement of the remedies available to each party in respect of any Event of Default.

(j)   Subject to paragraph 10(k), neither party may claim any sum by way of consequential loss or damage in the event of a failure by the other party to perform any of its obligations under this Agreement.

(k)   (i)   Subject to sub-paragraph (ii) below, if as a result of a Transaction terminating before its agreed Repurchase Date under paragraphs 10(b), 10(g)(iii) or 10(h)(iii), the non-Defaulting Party, in the case of paragraph 10(b), Buyer, in the case of paragraph 10(g)(iii), or Seller, in the case of paragraph 10(h)(iii), (in each case the "first party") incurs any loss or expense in entering into replacement transactions, the other party shall be required to pay to the first party the amount determined by the first party in good faith to be equal to the loss or expense incurred in connection with such replacement transactions (including all fees, costs and other expenses) less the amount of any profit or gain made by that party in connection with such replacement transactions; provided that if that calculation results in a negative number, an amount equal to that number shall be payable by the first party to the other party.

(ii)   If the first party reasonably decides, instead of entering into such replacement transactions, to replace or unwind any hedging transactions which the first party entered into in connection with the Transaction so terminating, or to enter into any replacement hedging transactions, the other party shall be required to pay to the first party the amount determined by the first party in good faith to be equal to the loss or expense incurred in connection with entering into such replacement or unwinding (including all fees, costs and other expenses) less the amount of any profit or gain made by that party in connection with such replacement or unwinding; provided that if that calculation results in a negative number, an amount equal to that number shall be payable by the first party to the other party.

(1)   Each party shall immediately notify the other if an Event of Default, or an event which, upon the serving of a Default Notice, would be an Event of Default, occurs in relation to it.

11.   Tax Event

(a)   This paragraph shall apply if either party notifies the other that –

(i)   any action taken by a taxing authority or brought in a court of competent jurisdiction (regardless of whether such action is taken or brought with respect to a party to this Agreement); or

(ii)   a change in the fiscal or regulatory regime (including, but not limited to, a change in law or in the general interpretation of law but excluding any change in any rate of tax),

has or will, in the notifying party's reasonable opinion, have a material adverse effect on that party in the context of a Transaction.

(b)   If so requested by the other party, the notifying party will furnish the other with an opinion of a suitably qualified adviser that an event referred to in sub-paragraph (a)(i) or (ii) above has occurred and affects the notifying party.

(c)   Where this paragraph applies, the party giving the notice referred to in sub-paragraph (a) may, subject to sub-paragraph (d) below, terminate the Transaction with effect from a date specified in the notice, not being earlier (unless so agreed by the other party) than 30 days after the date of the notice, by nominating that date as the Repurchase Date.

(d)   If the party receiving the notice referred to in sub-paragraph (a) so elects, it may override that notice by giving a counter-notice to the other party. If a counter-notice is given, the party which gives the counter-notice will be deemed to have agreed to indemnify the other party against the adverse effect referred to in sub-paragraph (a) so far as relates to the relevant Transaction and the original Repurchase Date will continue to apply.

(e)   Where a Transaction is terminated as described in this paragraph, the party which has given the notice to terminate shall indemnify the other party against any reasonable legal and other professional expenses incurred by the other party by reason of the termination, but the other party may not claim any sum by way of consequential loss or damage in respect of a termination in accordance with this paragraph.

(f)   This paragraph is without prejudice to paragraph 6(b) (obligation to pay additional amounts if withholding or deduction required); but an obligation to pay such additional amounts may, where appropriate, be a circumstance which causes this paragraph to apply.

12.   Interest

To the extent permitted by applicable law, if any sum of money payable hereunder or under any Transaction is not paid when due, interest shall accrue on the unpaid sum as a separate debt at the greater of the Pricing Rate for the Transaction to which such sum relates (where such sum is referable to a Transaction) and LIBOR on a 360 day basis or 365 day basis in accordance with the applicable ISMA convention, for the actual number of days during the period from and including the date on which payment was due to, but excluding, the date of payment.

13.   Single Agreement

Each party acknowledges that, and has entered into this Agreement and will enter into each Transaction hereunder in consideration of and in reliance upon the fact that all Transactions hereunder constitute a single business and contractual relationship and are made in consideration of each other. Accordingly, each party agrees (i) to perform all of its obligations in respect of each Transaction hereunder, and that a default in the performance of any such obligations shall constitute a default by it in respect of all Transactions hereunder, and (ii) that payments, deliveries and other transfers made by either of them in respect of any Transaction shall be deemed to have been made in consideration of payments, deliveries and other transfers in respect of any other Transactions hereunder.

14.   Notices and Other Communications

(a)   Any notice or other communication to be given under this Agreement –

        (i)   shall be in the English language, and except where expressly otherwise provided in this Agreement, shall be in writing;

        (ii)   may be given in any manner described in sub-paragraphs (b) and (c) below;

(iii)   shall be sent to the party to whom it is to be given at the address or number, or in accordance with the electronic messaging details, set out in Annex I hereto.

(b)   Subject to sub-paragraph (c) below, any such notice or other communication shall be effective –

(i)   if in writing and delivered in person or by courier, at the time when it is delivered;

(ii)   if sent by telex, at the time when the recipient's answerback is received;

(iii)   if sent by facsimile transmission, at the time when the transmission is received by a responsible employee of the recipient in legible form (it being agreed that the burden of proving receipt will be on the sender and will not be met by a transmission report generated by the sender's facsimile machine);

(iv)   if sent by certified or registered mail (airmail, if overseas) or the equivalent (return receipt requested), at the time when that mail is delivered or its delivery is attempted;

(v)   if sent by electronic messaging system, at the time that electronic message is received;

except that any notice or communication which is received, or delivery of which is attempted, after close of business on the date of receipt or attempted delivery or on a day which is not a day on which commercial banks are open for business in the place where that notice or other communication is to be given shall be treated as given at the opening of business on the next following day which is such a day.

(c)   If –

(i)   there occurs in relation to either party an event which, upon the service of a Default Notice, would be an Event of Default; and

(ii)   the non-Defaulting Party, having made all practicable efforts to do so, including having attempted to use at least two of the methods specified in sub-paragraph (b)(ii), (iii) or (v), has been unable to serve a Default Notice by one of the methods specified in those sub-paragraphs (or such of those methods as are normally used by the non-Defaulting Party when communicating with the Defaulting Party),

the non-Defaulting Party may sign a written notice (a "Special Default Notice") which –

(aa)   specifies the relevant event referred to in paragraph 10(a) which has occurred in relation to the Defaulting Party;

(bb)   states that the non-Defaulting Party, having made all practicable efforts to do so, including having attempted to use at least two of the methods specified in sub-paragraph (b)(ii), (iii) or (v), has been unable to serve a Default Notice by one of the methods specified in those sub-paragraphs (or such of those methods as are normally used by the non-Defaulting Party when communicating with the Defaulting Party);

(cc)   specifies the date on which, and the time at which, the Special Default Notice is signed by the non-Defaulting Party; and

(dd)   states that the event specified in accordance with sub-paragraph (aa) above shall be treated as an Event of Default with effect from the date and time so specified.

On the signature of a Special Default Notice the relevant event shall be treated with effect from the date and time so specified as an Event of Default in relation to the Defaulting Party, and accordingly references in paragraph 10 to a Default Notice shall be treated as including a Special Default Notice. A Special Default Notice shall be given to the Defaulting Party as soon as practicable after it is signed.

(d)   Either party may by notice to the other change the address, telex or facsimile number or electronic messaging system details at which notices or other communications are to be given to it.

15.   **Entire Agreement; Severability**

This Agreement shall supersede any existing agreements between the parties containing general terms and conditions for Transactions. Each provision and agreement herein shall be treated as separate from any other provision or agreement herein and shall be enforceable notwithstanding the unenforceability of any such other provision or agreement.

16.   **Non-assignability; Termination**

(a)   Subject to sub-paragraph (b) below, neither party may assign, charge or otherwise deal with (including without limitation any dealing with any interest in or the creation of any interest in) its rights or obligations under this Agreement or under any Transaction without the prior written consent of the other party. Subject to the foregoing, this Agreement and any Transactions shall be binding upon and shall inure to the benefit of the parties and their respective successors and assigns.

(b)   Sub-paragraph (a) above shall not preclude a party from assigning, charging or otherwise dealing with all or any part of its interest in any sum payable to it under paragraph 10(c) or (f) above.

(c)   Either party may terminate this Agreement by giving written notice to the other, except that this Agreement shall, notwithstanding such notice, remain applicable to any Transactions then outstanding.

(d)   All remedies hereunder shall survive Termination in respect of the relevant Transaction and termination of this Agreement.

(e)   The participation of any additional member State of the European Union in economic and monetary union after 1 January 1999 shall not have the effect of altering any term of the Agreement or any Transaction, nor give a party the right unilaterally to alter or terminate the Agreement or any Transaction.

17.   **Governing Law**

This Agreement shall be governed by and construed in accordance with the laws of England. Buyer and Seller hereby irrevocably submit for all purposes of or in connection with this Agreement and each Transaction to the jurisdiction of the Courts of England.

Party A hereby appoints the person identified in Annex I hereto as its agent to receive on its behalf service of process in such courts. If such agent ceases to be its agent, Party A shall promptly appoint, and notify Party B of the identity of, a new agent in England.

Party B hereby appoints the person identified in Annex I hereto as its agent to receive on its behalf service of process in such courts. If such agent ceases to be its agent, Party B shall promptly appoint, and notify Party A of the identity of, a new agent in England.

Each party shall deliver to the other, within 30 days of the date of this Agreement in the case of the appointment of a person identified in Annex I or of the date of the appointment of the relevant agent in any other case, evidence of the acceptance by the agent appointed by it pursuant to this paragraph of such appointment.

Nothing in this paragraph shall limit the right of any party to take proceedings in the courts of any other country of competent jurisdiction.

18.   **No Waivers, etc.**

No express or implied waiver of any Event of Default by either party shall constitute a waiver of any other Event of Default and no exercise of any remedy hereunder by any party shall constitute a waiver of its right to exercise any other remedy hereunder. No modification or waiver of any provision of this Agreement and no consent by any party to a departure herefrom shall be effective unless and until such modification, waiver or consent shall be in writing and duly executed by both of the parties hereto. Without limitation on any of the foregoing, the failure to give a notice pursuant to paragraph 4(a) hereof will not constitute a waiver of any right to do so at a later date.

19.   **Waiver of Immunity**

Each party hereto hereby waives, to the fullest extent permitted by applicable law, all immunity (whether on the basis of sovereignty or otherwise) from jurisdiction, attachment (both before and after judgment) and execution to which it might otherwise be entitled in any action or proceeding in the Courts of England or of any other country or jurisdiction, relating in any way to this Agreement or any Transaction, and agrees that it will not raise, claim or cause to be pleaded any such immunity at or in respect of any such action or proceeding.

20.   **Recording**

The parties agree that each may electronically record all telephone conversations between them.

21.   **Third Party Rights**

No person shall have any right to enforce any provision of this Agreement under the Contracts (Rights of Third Parties) Act 1999.

[Name of Party]   [Name of Party]

By   _____   By   _____
Title _____   Title _____
Date   _____   Date   _____

ANNEX I

Supplemental Terms or Conditions

Paragraph references are to paragraphs in the Agreement.

1 .   The following elections shall apply –

[(a)   paragraph 1(c)(i). Buy/Sell Back Transactions [may/may not] be effected under this Agreement, and accordingly the Buy/Sell Back Annex [shall/shall not] apply.]*

[(b)   paragraph 1(c)(ii). Transactions in Net Paying Securities [may/may not] be effected under this Agreement, and accordingly the provisions of sub-paragraphs (i) and (ii) below [shall/shall not] apply.

   (i)   The phrase "other than equities and Net Paying Securities" shall be replaced by the phrase "other than equities".

   (ii)   In the Buy/Sell Back Annex the following words shall be added to the end of the definition of the expression "IR": "and for the avoidance of doubt the reference to the amount of Income for these purposes shall be to an amount paid without withholding or deduction for or on account of taxes or duties notwithstanding that a payment of such Income made in certain circumstances may be subject to such a withholding or deduction".]*

[(c)   paragraph 1(d). Agency Transactions [may/may not] be effected under this Agreement, and accordingly the Agency Annex [shall/shall not] apply.]*

(d)   paragraph 2(d). The Base Currency shall be:_____.

(e)   paragraph 2(p). [list Buyer's and Seller's Designated Offices]

(f)   paragraph 2(cc). The pricing source for calculation of Market Value shall be: _____.

(g)   paragraph 2(rr). Spot rate to be: _____.

(h)   paragraph 3(b). [Seller/Buyer/both Seller and Buyer]* to deliver Confirmation.

(i)   paragraph 4(f). Interest rate on Cash Margin to be   [ ]% for _____currency.

                                                                [ ]% for_____currency.

        Interest to be payable [payment intervals and dates].

(j)   paragraph 4(g). Delivery period for margin calls to be: _____.

[(k)   paragraph 6(j). Paragraph 6(j) shall apply and the events specified in paragraph 10(a) identified for the purposes of paragraph 6(j) shall be those set out in sub paragraphs [   ] of paragraph 10(a) of the Agreement.]*

[(1)   paragraph 10(a)(ii). Paragraph 10(a)(ii) shall apply.]*

---

* Delete as appropriate.

(m)   paragraph 14. For the purposes of paragraph 14 of this Agreement –

        (i)   Address for notices and other communications for Party A –

                 Address:
                 Attention:
                 Telephone:
                 Facsimile:
                 Telex:
                 Answerback:
                 Other:

        (ii)   Address for notices and other communications for Party B –

                 Address:
                 Attention:
                 Telephone:
                 Facsimile:
                 Telex:
                 Answerback:
                 Other:

[(n)   paragraph 17. For the purposes of paragraph 17 of this Agreement–

        (i)   Party A appoints [   ] as its agent for service of process;

        (ii)   Party B appoints [   ] as its agent for service of process.] *

2.   The following supplemental terms and conditions shall apply–

[Existing Transactions

(a)   The parties agree that this Agreement shall apply to all transactions which are subject
        to the PSA/ISMA Global Master Repurchase Agreement between them dated _____ and
        which are outstanding as at the date of this Agreement so that such transactions shall
        be treated as if they had been entered into under this Agreement, and the terms of
        such transactions are amended accordingly with effect from the date of this Agree-
        ment.] *

[Forward Transactions

(b)   The parties agree that Forward Transactions (as defined in sub-paragraph (i)(A)
        below) may be effected under this Agreement and accordingly the provisions of sub-
        paragraphs (i) to (iv) below shall apply.

        (i)   The following definitions shall apply–

_____

* Delete as appropriate.

(A)   "Forward Transaction", a Transaction in respect of which the Purchase Date is at least [three] Business Days after the date on which the Transaction was entered into and has not yet occurred;

(B)   "Forward Repricing Date", with respect to any Forward Transaction the date which is such number of Business Days before the Purchase Date as is equal to the minimum period for the delivery of margin applicable under paragraph 4(g).

(ii)   The Confirmation relating to any Forward Transaction may describe the Purchased Securities by reference to a type or class of Securities, which, without limitation, may be identified by issuer or class of issuers and a maturity or range of maturities. Where this paragraph applies, the parties shall agree the actual Purchased Securities not less than two Business Days before the Purchase Date and Buyer or Seller (or both), as shall have been agreed, shall promptly deliver to the other party a Confirmation which shall describe such Purchased Securities.

(iii)   At any time between the Forward Repricing Date and the Purchase Date for any Forward Transaction the parties may agree either–

(A)   to adjust the Purchase Price under that Forward Transaction; or

(B)   to adjust the number of Purchased Securities to be sold by Seller to Buyer under that Forward Transaction.

(iv)   Where the parties agree to an adjustment under paragraph (iii) above, Buyer or Seller (or both), as shall have been agreed, shall promptly deliver to the other party a Confirmation of the Forward Transaction, as adjusted under paragraph (iii) above.

(c)   Where the parties agree that this paragraph shall apply, paragraphs 2 and 4 of the Agreement are amended as follows.

(i)   Paragraph 2(ww) is deleted and replaced by the following–

"(ww) "Transaction Exposure" means–

(i)   with respect to any Forward Transaction at any time between the Forward Repricing Date and the Purchase Date, the difference between (A) the Market Value of the Purchased Securities at the relevant time and (B) the Purchase Price;

(ii)   with respect to any Transaction at any time during the period (if any) from the Purchase Date to the date on which the Purchased Securities are delivered to Buyer or, if earlier, the date on which the Transaction is terminated under paragraph 10(g), the difference between (A) the Market Value of the Purchased Securities at the relevant time and (B) the Repurchase Price at the relevant time;

(iii)   with respect to any Transaction at any time during the period from the Purchase Date (or, if later, the date on which the Purchased Securities are delivered to Buyer or the Transaction is terminated under paragraph 10(g)) to the Repurchase Date (or, if later, the date on which Equivalent Securities are delivered to Seller or the Transaction is terminated under paragraph 10(h)), the difference between (A) the Repurchase Price at the relevant time multiplied by the applicable Margin Ratio (or, where the Transaction relates to Securities of more than one description to which different Margin Ratios apply, the amount produced by multiplying the Repurchase Price attributable to Equivalent Securities of each such description by the applicable Margin Ratio and aggregating the resulting amounts, the Repurchase Price being for this purpose attributed to Equivalent Securities of each such description in the same proportions as those in which the Purchase Price was apportioned among the Purchased Securities) and (B) the Market Value of Equivalent Securities at the relevant time.

In each case, if (A) is greater than (B), Buyer has a Transaction Exposure for that Transaction equal to the excess, and if (B) is greater than (A), Seller has a Transaction Exposure to Buyer equal to the excess."

(ii)   In paragraph 4(c)–

(aa)   the words "any amount payable to the first party under paragraph 5 but unpaid" are deleted and replaced by "any amount which will become payable to the first party under paragraph 5 during the period after the time at which the calculation is made which is equal to the minimum period for the delivery of margin applicable under paragraph 4(g) or which is payable to the first party under paragraph 5 but unpaid"; and

(bb)   the words "any amount payable to the other party under paragraph 5 but unpaid" are deleted and replaced by "any amount which will become payable to the other party under paragraph 5 during the period after the time at which the calculation is made which is equal to the minimum period for the delivery of margin applicable under paragraph 4(g) or which is payable to the other party under paragraph 5 but unpaid".]*

---

* Delete as appropriate.

ANNEX II

Form of Confirmation

To: _____

From: _____

Date: _____

Subject: [Repurchase] [Buy/Sell Back]* Transaction
               (Reference Number:)

Dear Sirs,

The purpose of this [letter]/[facsimile]//[telex], a "Confirmation" for the purposes of the Agreement, is to set forth the terms and conditions of the above repurchase transaction entered into between us on the Contract Date referred to below.

This Confirmation supplements and forms part of, and is subject to, the Global Master Repurchase Agreement as entered into between us as of [   ] as the same may be amended from time to time (the "Agreement"). All provisions contained in the Agreement govern this Confirmation except as expressly modified below. Words and phrases defined in the Agreement and used in this Confirmation shall have the same meaning herein as in the Agreement.

1.   Contract Date:

2.   Purchased Securities [state type[s] and nominal value[s]]:

3.   CUSIP, ISIN or other identifying number[s]:

4.   Buyer:

5.   Seller:

6.   Purchase Date:

7.   Purchase Price:

8.   Contractual Currency:

[9.   Repurchase Date]:*

[10.   Terminable on demand]:*

11.   Pricing Rate:

[12.   Sell Back Price:]*

13.   Buyer's Bank Account[s] Details:

14.   Seller's Bank Account[s] Details:

[15.   The Transaction is an Agency Transaction. [Name of Agent] is acting as agent for [name or identifier of Principal]]: *

[16.   Additional Terms]: *

Yours faithfully,

_____

* Delete as appropriate.

Appendix B

List of Annexes to the GMRA 2000[1]

Published by ISMA and TBMA:

– Agency Annex	Supplemental terms and conditions for agency transactions. There is also an addendum to the Agency Annex incorporating amendments for transactions with multiple principals
– Bills of Exchange Annex	Supplemental terms and conditions where the securities are Treasury bills, local authority bills, bills of exchange
– Buy/Sell Back Annex	Supplemental terms and conditions for buy/sell back transactions
– Equities Annex	Supplemental terms and conditions where the securities are equity securities
– Italian Annex	Supplemental terms and conditions where the securities are Italian domestic securities
– Netherlands Annex	Supplemental terms and conditions for transactions with counterparties in the Netherlands

Published by other bodies:

– AFMA annex	Supplemental terms and conditions for use with Australian counterparties published by the Australian Financial Markets Association (AFMA), Sydney
– RITS Annex	Supplemental terms and conditions for use with the Australian Reserve Bank Information and Transfer System published by the Reserve Bank of Australia, Sydney

---

[1]   ©TBMA/ISMA. Reproduced with permission.

| – | Swiss Annex | Supplemental terms and conditions for transactions with counterparties in Switzerland published by the Swiss National Bank, Zurich |
| – | Gilts Annex | Supplemental terms and conditions where the securities are UK gilt-edged securities published by the Bank of England, London |

Status: October 20, 2000/TH/ys

Appendix C

Buy/Sell Back Annex[1]

TBMA/ISMA GLOBAL MASTER REPURCHASE AGREEMENT (2000 VERSION)

BUY/SELL BACK ANNEX

Supplemental terms and conditions for Buy/Sell Back Transactions

This Annex constitutes an Annex to the TBMA/ISMA, Global Master Repurchase Agreement dated _____ between .... and ....
(the "Agreement").

1.   Scope

(a)   The parties have agreed that the Transactions to which this Agreement applies may include Buy/Sell Transactions.

(b)   In relation to Buy/Sell Back Transactions, the Agreement shall be construed as if it had been amended and supplemented as set out in paragraphs 3 to 5 of this Annex.

2.   Interpretation

(a)   In this Annex–

(i)   "Accrued Interest", with respect to any Purchased Securities subject to a Buy/Sell Back Transaction, unpaid Income that has accrued during the period from (and including) the issue date or the last Income Payment Date (whichever is the later) in respect of such Purchased Securities to (but excluding) the date of calculation. For these purposes unpaid Income shall be deemed to accrue on a daily basis from (and including) the issue date or the last Income Payment Date (as the case may be) to (but excluding) the next Income Payment Date or the maturity date (whichever is the earlier);

(ii)   "Sell Back Differential", with respect to any Buy/Sell Back Transaction as of any date, the aggregate amount obtained by daily application of the Pricing Rate for such Buy/Sell Back Transaction (on a 360 day basis or 365 day basis in accordance with the applicable ISMA convention, unless otherwise agreed between the parties for the Transaction) to the sum of (a) the Purchase Price and (b) Accrued Interest paid on the Purchase Date for such Transaction for the actual number of days during the period commencing on (and including) the Purchase Date for such Buy/Sell Back Transaction and ending on (but excluding) the date of calculation;

---
[1]   ©TBMA/ISMA. Reproduced with permission.

    (iii)   "Sell Back Price", with respect to any Buy/Sell Back Transaction, means–

        (x)   in relation to the date originally specified by the parties as the Repurchase Date pursuant to paragraph 3(b)(iii) of the Agreement, the price agreed by the Parties in relation to that Buy/Sell Back Transaction, and

        (y)   in any other case (including for the purposes of the application of paragraph 4 (margin maintenance) or paragraph 10 (Events of Default) of the Agreement), the product of the formula $(P +AI +D) (IR +C)$, where–

P = the Purchase Price

AI = the amount, equal to Accrued Interest at the Purchase Date, paid under paragraph 3(f) of this Annex

D = the Sell Back Differential

IR = the amount of any income in respect of the Purchased Securities payable by the issuer on or, in the case of registered Securities, by reference to, any date failing between the Purchase Date and the Repurchase Date

C = the aggregate amount obtained by daily application of the Pricing Rate for such Buy/Sell Back Transaction to any such Income from (and including) the date of payment by the issuer to (but excluding) the date of calculation

(b)   References to "Repurchase Price" throughout the Agreement shall be construed as references to "Repurchase Price or the Sell Back Price, as the case may be".

(c)   In Paragraph 10(c)(i) of the Agreement (relating to Events of Default), the reference to the "Repurchase Prices" shall be construed as a reference to "Repurchase Prices and Sell Back Prices".

(d)   In the event of any conflict between the terms of this Annex III and any other term of the Agreement, the terms in this Annex shall prevail.

3.   Initiation; Confirmation; Termination

(a)   Each Transaction shall be identified at the time it is entered into and in the Confirmation relating to it as either a Repurchase Transaction or a Buy/Sell Back Transaction.

(b)   In the case of a Buy/Sell Back Transaction the Confirmation delivered in accordance with paragraph 3 of the Agreement may consist of a single document in respect of both of the transactions which together form the Buy/Sell Back Transaction or separate Confirmations may be delivered in respect of each such transaction. Such Confirmations may be in the form of Annex II to the Agreement except that, subject to sub-paragraph (c) below, such Confirmations shall not include the item specified in paragraph 10 of Annex II.

(c)   When entering into a Buy/Sell Back Transaction the parties shall also agree the Sell Back Price and the Pricing Rate to apply in relation to that Transaction on the scheduled Repurchase Date. The parties shall record the Pricing Rate in at least one Confirmation applicable to that Buy/Sell Back Transaction.

(d)   Buy/Sell Back Transactions shall not be terminable on demand.

(e)   In the case of a Buy/Sell Back Transaction, the Purchase Price shall be quoted exclusive of Accrued Interest to the Purchase Date on the Purchased Securities and the Sell Back Price shall be quoted exclusive of Accrued Interest.

(f)   For the purposes of paragraph 3(c) of the Agreement, in the case of a Buy/Sell Back Transaction, the Purchased Securities shall be transferred to Buyer or its agent against the payment of the Purchase Price plus an amount equal to Accrued Interest to the Purchase Price on such Purchased Securities.

(g)   In the case of a Buy/Sell Back Transaction, paragraph 3(f) of the Agreement shall not apply. Termination of such a Transaction will be effected on the Repurchase Date by transfer to Seller or its agent of Equivalent Securities against the payment by Seller of (i) in a case where the Repurchase Date is the date originally scheduled by the parties pursuant to paragraph 3(b)(iii) of the Agreement, the Sell Back Price referred to in paragraph 2(iii)(x) of this Annex plus an amount equal to Accrued Interest to the Repurchase Date; and (ii) in any other case, the Sell Back Price referred to in paragraph 2(iii)(y) of this Annex.

4.   Margin maintenance: "repricing"

If the parties agree that a Buy/Sell Back Transaction is to be repriced in accordance with paragraph 4(i) of the Agreement, they shall at the time of such repricing agree the Purchase Price, the Sell Back Price and the Pricing Rate applicable to the Repriced Transaction.

5.   Income Payments

Paragraph 5 of the Agreement (relating to Income payments) shall not apply to Buy/Sell Back Transactions.

Glossary

Agent: A market participant in the market such as fund managers and custodians who undertake repo transactions on behalf of (principal) clients.

Airbus A340: The four-engined long-range civil airliner developed by Airbus Industrie.

All-in price: See *Dirty price*.

Arbitrage: A guaranteed or risk-free profit from simultaneously buying and selling instruments that are perfect equivalents, one being cheaper than the other.

Asset-backed security: A debt market instrument that is collateralised by bundled assets such as mortgages, car loans, credit card debt or other cash receivables. This class of securities includes mortgage-backed securities, and are related to repackaged securities and collateralised debt obligations.

Asset & liability management: The practice of matching the term structure and cash flows of an institution's asset and liability portfolios, in order to maximise returns and minimise interest rate risk. A simple example is a bank using an interest rate swap to convert a fixed-rate loan (asset) to match the interest basis of its floating-rate deposits (liability).

Ask: The offered price, in repo the rate at which the market "sells" stock, in other words the rate at which it pays money on borrowed funds

Assured payment: A payment generated by an irrevocable instruction simultaneously with the movement of securities between counterparty accounts, which occurs for example in CREST/CGO.

Backwardation: The case when the cash or spot price of a commodity is greater than its forward price. A backwardation occurs when there exists insufficient supply to satisfy nearby demand in a commodity market. The size of the backwardation is determined by differences between supply and demand factors in the nearby positions compared with the same factors on the forward position. It is also known as a *back*.

Bank for International Settlements (BIS): The Basel-based body that serves as a bank for central banks. Responsible for drafting the "Basel rules" in 1988.

Basel II: *See Basel Capital Accord.*

Basel Capital Accord: The capital rules issued by the Basel Committee on Banking Supervision in 1988, and which set minimum rules for capital allocation, to be enforced by national regulatory authorities. The Basel Committee issued updated proposals in 1999, now known as Basel II, which are intended for implementation in 2002.

Basis: The difference between the price of a futures contract and the cash market underlying asset.

Basis risk: A form of market risk that arises whenever one kind of risk exposure is hedged with an instrument that behaves in a similar, but not necessarily identical way. For instance, a bank trading desk may use three–month interest rate futures to hedge its commercial paper or euronote programme. Although eurocurrency rates, to which futures prices respond, are well correlated with commercial paper rates they do not always move in lock step. If therefore commercial paper rates move by 10 basis points but futures prices dropped by only 7 basis points, the 3 bp gap would be the basis risk.

Basis trading: Simultaneous trading in a derivative contract (normally a futures contract) and the underlying asset. The purpose of basis trading is to exploit an arbitrage-type profit potential, or to cover a short derivative position. Arbitrage basis trading is designed to take advantage of mispricing of cash and/or futures or is based on speculation that the basis risk will change.

Bid: The repo rate that the cash investor demands from the seller; to "bid" for stock, that is, lend the cash. This is the same terminology and price quote as for CDs. The repo buyer is the cash lender, and has actually traded a *reverse repo.*

Bilateral netting: An agreement between two counterparties whereby the value of all transactions on which funds are owed is offset against the value of transactions where funds are due, resulting in a single net exposure amount owed by one counterparty to the other. Bilateral netting can cover the entire range of products, including repo, swaps, and options, to produce one net exposure.

Bond Market Association: Formerly known as the Public Securities Association (PSA), this is the trade association of the US domestic bond market. As the PSA it produced the original master repo agreement for use in the US dollar market, subsequently used at the basis for the PSA/ISMA master repo agreement used in international repo markets.

Bonds borrowed: Stock borrowed in a securities lending transaction.

Borrower: In a classic repo, the counterparty that is taking stock, in other words *lending* cash. In stock lending, the counterparty borrowing a specified security and supplying cash or stock as collateral.

Broker: An intermediary who brokes repo, either on a matched principal or name-passing basis.

Bulldog: Sterling domestic bonds issued by non-UK domiciled borrowers. These bonds under a similar arrangement to gilts and are settled via the CREST/CGO clearing system.

Buy/sell-back or **sell/buy-back:** A sale and spot purchase (for froward settlement) of securities transacted simultaneously. It is not specifically repo but has the same effect and intent and consists of a simultaneous matching purchase and sale of the same quantity of securities for different value dates. The UK's Gilt Repo Code recommends that buy/sell-backs should only be carried out under a master agreement with the same protections as those in the Gilt Repo Legal Agreement. A buy/sell-back is equivalent to a reverse repo, while a sell/buy-back is equivalent to a repo.

Calling the mark: The process of calling for margin to be reinstated following a mark-to-market revaluation of a repo transaction.

Capital Adequacy Directive: The European Union's set of rules issued in 1993 and implemented in 1996 designed to apply a building-block approach to market risk in a bank's trading book, and foreign exchange risk across banking and trading books.

Cash: Also called the *cash market* or the *underlying*, a reference to the actual asset such as a bushel of wheat or a bond.

Cash-and-carry arbitrage: A strategy used in the bond futures market in which a trader sells a futures contract and simultaneously buys the underlying bond to deliver into it, to generate a riskless profit. For the strategy to be successful the futures contract must be theoretically expensive compared to the cash. The value of the futures contract is determined by reference to the *implied repo rate*; if the implied repo rate is higher than the actual market repo rate, then the futures contract is said to be cheap.

Cash-driven repo: A repo transaction iniated by a party that wishes to invest cash against security collateral.

CBOT: The Chicago Board of Trade, one of the two futures exchanges in Chicago, USA and one of the largest in the world. It lists the US Treasury Bond futures contract, and the 10-year, 5-year and 2-year note contracts, amongst others.

Central Gilts Office: The office of the Bank of England which runs the computer-based settlement system for gilt-edged securities and certain other securities (mostly Bulldogs) for which the Bank acts as Registrar. It merged with CRESTCo, the London market equity settlement system, in July 2000 and is now known as CREST/CGO or simply CREST.

CGO reference prices: Daily prices of gilt-edged and other securities held in CREST/CGO which are used by CREST/CGO and market makers in various processes, including revaluing stock loan transactions, calculating total consideration in a repo transaction, and DBV assembly. Now referred to a CREST reference prices or DMO prices (because the prices are published by the UK Debt Management Office).

Classic repo: The term used to refer to a generic sale and repurchase transaction. Originally introduced by ISMA as a term for repo as practised in the US market.

Clean-up of interest: The practice of transferring repo interest prior to the repo termination date. The most common reason for this is when *close-out and repricing* of a repo transaction takes place.

Clearstream: Formerly CEDEL or its banking arm known as Cedel Bank, the international clearing system owned by a consortium of banks, and which also offers Tri-party repo facilities. It was formed following the merger of Cedel with Deutsche Bourse. The German domestic clearing system is known as Clearstream AG, while Eurobonds clear through Clearstream International.

Close-out and repricing: A method of removing mark-to-market credit exposure in a repo and restoring margin balance. It involves terminating the current repo and re-startng it to the original termination date with margin balance restored.

Closing leg: The second (terminating) stage of a repo transaction. A repo involves two trades in the same security, one for a near value date and the other for a value date in the future. The closing leg refers to the second trade. Also known as *second* leg, *far* leg, *end* leg, *reverse* leg, *termination* leg or *offside* leg.

Collateral: A general term used in the market to cover any securities exchanged in a repo trans-action, both initially and subsequently during the period before the repo matures. Used as security against the transfer of cash. Or, in stock lending, of securities. Under the BMA/ISMA and Gilt Repo Legal agreements, full title to collateral passes from one party to another, the party obtaining title being obliged to deliver back *equivalent* securities.

Collateralised debt obligation (CDO): A multi-asset and multi-tranche debt structure, with the underlying assets comprised of bonds (collate-ralised bond obligation), loans (collateralised loan obligation) or a mixture of both.

Conversion factor: A value assigned by the futures exchange to all bonds deliverable into a futures contract, being the price at which the bond would have a yield-to-maturity equal to the notional coupon of the futures contract specification. Also known as the *price factor*.

Convexity: A measure of a bond's price sensi-tivity in practice compared to the level implied by its modified duration.

Counterparty credit risk: The risk of financial loss arising out of holding a particular contract or portfolio of contracts as a result of one party to the contract(s) failing to fulfil its contractual obligations. Counterparty credit risk is assessed as a function of three variables: (i) the value of the position exposed to default (the credit or credit risk exposure); (ii) the proportion of the value that would be recovered in the event of a default; and (iii) the likelihood of a default occurring.

Credit default swap: A bilateral financial contract in which one counterparty, known as the protection buyer, pays a premium in the form of a periodic fee, to the other counterparty

known as the protection seller. The fee is expressed in basis points of the nominal value of the contract. The contract is written on a reference asset, and in the event of a predefined credit event the protection buyer will deliver the asset to the protection seller, in return for a payment of the nominal value of the contract from the protection seller.

Credit derivative: A bilateral contract that isolates credit risk from an underlying specified reference asset and transfers this risk from one party of the contract (the buyer) to the other party (the seller). The seller receives a one-off or periodic premium payment in return for taking on the credit risk. The most common credit derivatives are *credit default swaps* and *total return swaps*.

Credit risk: The risk of loss that will be incurred if a counterparty to a transaction does not fulfil its financial obligations under the transaction contract. It also refers to financial loss suffered by a bondholder as a result of default of the issuer of the bond held. Also known as *default risk*.

CREST: The London equity market electronic book-entry clearing and settlement system, with which the CGO merged in July 2000.

Cross-currency repo: A repo transaction in which the collateral transferred is denominated in a different currency to that of the cash lent out.

Customer repo: A term used in the US Treasury market, where the Federal Reserve Bank of New York places cash in the market on behalf of its customers.

Day count: The convention used to calculate accrued interest on bonds and interest on cash. For UK gilts the accrued interest convention changed to actual/actual from actual/365 on 1 November 1998. For cash the interest basis in money markets is actual/365 for sterling and actual/360 for US dollar and euro.

DBV (delivery by value): A mechanism whereby a CREST/CGO member may borrow from or lend money to another CREST/CGO member against overnight gilt collateral. The CGO system automatically selects and delivers securities to a specified aggregate value on the basis of the previous night's CGO reference prices; equi-valent securities are returned the following day. The DBV functionality allows the giver and taker of collateral to specify the classes of security to be included within the DBV. The options are: all classes of security held within CGO, including strips and bulldogs; coupon-bearing gilts and bulldogs; coupon-bearing gilts and strips; only coupon-bearing gilts.

DBV repo: A repo transaction in which the delivery of securities is by means of the DBV facility in CREST/CGO.

Deliver-out repo: A term for a conventional classic repo where the buyer takes delivery of the collateral.

Delivery repo: A term used in the US market to refer to a repo in which the lender of cash takes actual delivery of the collateral, as opposed to a *hold-in-custody* repo.

Delivery versus payment (DVP): The simultaneous exchange of securities and cash. The assured payment mechanism of CREST/CGO achieves the same protection.

Demand repo: Another term for open repo, a repo trade that has no fixed maturity term, and is renewed at one or both counterparties' agreement each morning.

Dirty price: The price of a bond including accrued interest. Also known as the *all-in* price.

Dollar repo: A repo transaction in which collateral returned at the maturity of the trade need not be exactly the same as that originally transferred over. This is actually incorporated in the BMA/ISMA GMRA, which states the the obligation is only to return "equivalent" securities. In the US mortgage market also known as a *dollar roll*, but there are some detail differences between this and repo.

Dollar roll: A transaction with a number of similarities to repo, used exclusively for mortgage-backed securities, in the US market.

Duration: The weighted average maturity of a bond, given by the present values of the bond's cash flows. In the US market the *modified duration* of a bond, a measure of the change in price of a bond for a given change in its yield.

Duration weighting: The process of using the modified duration value for bonds to calculate the exact nominal holdings in a spread position. This is necessary because £1 million nominal of a two-year bond is not equivalent to £1 million of, say, a five-year bond. The modified duration

value of the five-year bond will be higher, indicating that its "basis point value" (bpv) will be greater, and that therefore £1 million worth of this bond represents greater sensitivity to a move in interest rates (risk). As another example consider a fund manager holding £10 million of five-year bonds. The fund manager wishes to switch into a holding of two-year bonds with the same overall risk position. The basis point values of the bonds are 0.041583 and 0.022898 respectively. The ratio of the bpvs are:

0.041583/0.022898 = 1.816.

The fund manager therefore needs to switch into £10m × 1.816 = £18.160 million of the two-year bond.

EONIA: The euro overnight interest rate reference index. It is calculated as the average of the range of overnight interest rates during the day.

Equity repo legal agreement: The 1995 PSA/ISMA GMRA when extended to cover equity repo, now stated in Annex IV of the October 2000 agreement.

Equivalent securities: A term used in repo to denote that the securities returned must be of identical issue (and *tranche*, where relevant) and nominal value to those repoed in.

Euroclear: The international bond and equity clearing system, based in Brussels and owned by a consortium of banks.

Ex-dividend (xd) date: A bond's record date for the payment of coupons. The coupon payment will be made to the person who is the registered holder of the stock on the xd date. For gilts this is seven business days before the coupon date.

F-86 Sabre: The single-seat jet fighter developed by North American Aviation, introduced by the US Air Force in 1950 and used operationally by air forces around the world.

Failure *or* **failed trade**: A trade that does not complete because the seller is unable to deliver the stock on time.

Fed repo: A repo trade entered into between the US Federal Reserve ("Fed") and US Treasury primary dealers, similar to the Bank of England open market operations. The Fed undertakes this in order to supply liquidity to the market. The typical term of a Fed repo is 15 days and is at the Fed funds rate. The collateral accepted is Treasury or Agency securities.

Fixed-coupon repo: Similar to a *dollar repo*, except that the collateral returned must have the same coupon as that originally transferred.

Flat repo: Repo undertaken with no margin. Also known as *flat basis*.

Flex repo: Classic repo trade in which the lender of cash may draw down the cash supplied in accordance with a schedule agreed at trade inception.

Forward rate agreement (FRA): An off-balance-sheet instrument that allows parties to fix the interest rate for a specified period in the future. One party pays fixed, the other an agreed variable rate. The trade is written on a notional amount and only the difference between contracted and actual interest rates is paid on the expiry of the contract. If rates have risen at the time of expiry, the buyer receives the difference in rates from the seller, and vice versa.

Gap: The maturity mismatch between differing maturities of deposits and loans. Gives rise to gap risk.

General collateral (GC): Securities, which are not "special", used as collateral against cash borrowing. A repo buyer will accept GC at any time that a specific stock is not quoted as required in the transaction. In the gilts market GC includes DBVs. There is no strandard accepted GC in equity repo, although some participants make markets in blue-chip index stocks, a quasi equity GC.

GMRA: The Global Master Repurchase Agreement, the standard legal agreement used to cover classic repo (and subsequently) sell/buy-backs and equity repo. It was originally introduced by the PSA (now BMA) and ISMA in 1992. Although based on the original PSA document, it is governed by English law, and is generally referred to as the PSA/ISMA agreement.

Gross basis: The difference between the price of an asset and its implied price given by the price of a futures contract. The gross basis for a government bond futures contract is given by:

$$Basis = P_{bond} - \left(P_{fut} \times CF \right)$$

where *CF* is the bond's conversion factor.

Haircut: The term used in the US market for *initial margin*.

Hard stock: Another term for a *special* stock. In the US market the term *hot stock* is also used.

Hold in custody (HIC) repo: A repo in which the party who receives cash does not deliver the securities to the counterparty but segregates them in an internal account for the benefit of the cash provider. In the US market also known as a *trust me* repo.

Hot stock or **hard stock:** A security in high demand, and therefore special in the repo market.

Icing: The term used to reserve stock, ahead of possibly borrowing it, in the stock-lending market. Stock that has been iced is *open to challenge*.

Implied repo rate: The rate used to measure which stock is the cheapest-to-deliver (CTD) into the government bond futures contract. The bond with the highest implied repo rate is the CTD bond. It is given by

$$\frac{P_{fut} - P_{bond}}{P_{bond}} \times \frac{365}{N} \times 100$$

where P_{fut} is the dirty futures price, P_{bond} is the dirty cash price and N is the number of days to expiry of the futures contract. The dirty futures price is the cash inflow from selling the futures contract and the dirty cash price is the cash outflow from simultaneously buying the CTD bond. The term *implied repo rate* is also used, erroneously, to refer to the repo rate "implied" in a sell/buy-back transaction but incorporated in the forward buy-back price.

Indexed repo: A repo transaction where the repo rate is linked to an external, specified index such as Libor.

Initial margin: The excess either of cash over the value of securities, or of the value of securities over cash in a repo transaction at the time it is executed and subsequently, after margin calls.

Interest rate swap: An agreement between two parties in which one party pays interest on the agreed notional amount at a specified fixed rate, and the other party pays at a floating rate linked to Libor. Only net cash flows are actually transferred, based on the difference between the fixed rate and the prevailing floating-rate fix. Interest rate swaps are used to transform the interest rate basis of an asset or liability. Swaps in liquid currencies such as dollar, sterling and euro can be transacted out to 30 years maturity, and the swap rate is calculated from the government bond zero-coupon yield curve.

Investor: A corporate counterparty that is long cash in a repo transaction, and therefore a taker of collateral.

ISMA: The International Securities Market Association. This association compiled, with the PSA (now renamed the Bond Market Association), the PSA/ISMA Global Master Repurchase Agreement.

Lender: The provider of collateral in a repo or sell/buy-back, and therefore a *borrower* of cash; or the lender of stock (and taker of collateral) in a stock loan transaction.

Libor: The London Interbank Offered Rate, the rate for all major currencies up to a one-year term, set at 11:00 hours each day by the British Bankers Association. This is the rate at which banks lend to each other.

LIFFE: The London International Financial Futures Exchange, a premier futures and options exchange in Europe. It trades government bond contracts such as the Long Gilt, short-term interest-rate contracts such as short sterling as well as the interest-rate swap contract SwapNote.

Liquidity risk: The risk associated with undertaking transactions in illiquid markets, which are characterised by wide bid-offer spreads, lack of transparency, small number of market makers and large movements in price after a deal of large size. In the context of banking asset & liability management, the risk of having insufficient funds available to meet a sudden large-scale demand for funds from depositors.

Manufactured dividend: The payment (of an amount equal to the gross coupon on the security concerned) which the acquirer of the security in a repo is generally contractually obliged to make to the other party when the acquirer receives a coupon on a security which passes the ex-dividend date during the course of the repo.

Margin: In the context of repo markets, the level of overcollateralisation required by the buyer (lender). Made up of *initial margin* at the time of trade and subsequent *variation margin* if required by a fall in value of collateral.

Margin call: A request following marking-to-market of a repo transaction for the initial margin to be reinstated or, where no initial margin has been taken to restore the cash/securities ratio to parity.

Margin ratio: A term used in the GMRA and the Equity Legal Agreement, and a term for the initial margin. It is defined as the ratio of the market price of the securities to their purchase price.

Mark-to-market: In repo transactions the act of revaluing securities to current market values. Such revaluations should include both coupon accrued on the securities outstanding and interest accrued on the cash; it should also take into account any coupon which passes its ex-dividend date during the life of the repo.

Matched book: Running a market-making operation in repo. Alternatively, only trading repo to cover your own financing requirements. Also refers to the matching by a repo trader of securities repoed in and out. It carries no implications that the trader's position is "matched" in terms of exposure or term to maturity; for example, to short-term interest rates, and in fact books are "mismatched" to reflect views on interest rates.

Monte Titole: The Italian domestic market clearing system.

Net basis: The gross basis of a futures-deliverable bond, adjusted for net carry.

Netting: The practice of counterparties taking the net exposure of all the trades they have outstanding between them and only settling the net difference. When used in conjunction with a centralised clearing counterparty (similar to a derivatives exchange clearing house), a process that eliminates counterparty credit risk and simplifies stock and cash movements.

Offer: The repo rate that the seller is willing to pay on cash received; to "offer" the stock, that is, take the cash.

Open book: A term for a "mismatched" book. However the term "mismatched" book is not itself generally used by traders.

Open to challenge: A request to *ice* a stock is open to challenge if the party making the icing request has not confirmed the order, and a second party subsequently approaches the stock lender with a firm request to borrow. The first party retains first option on the stock it has iced.

Opening leg: The first half of a repo transaction. Also known as *start* leg, *first* leg, *near* leg or *onside* leg. See also *Closing leg*.

Open repo: A repo trade with no fixed maturity date, with the daily possibility of terminating the repo or re-fixing its terms or substituting collateral.

OTC: Over-the-counter. Strictly speaking any transaction not conducted on a registered stock exchange. Trades conducted via the telephone between banks are said to be OTC as are contracts such as FRAs and (non-exchange traded) options. Repo is also traded as an OTC instrument.

Overcollateralised: Where the value of collateral exceeds that of the cash lent against it. Used to protect against counterparty and market risk.

Pair-off: The netting of consideration and stock in the settlement of two trades (one buy, one sell) in the same security, possible where value dates are identical, to allow settlement of the net differences only.

Pension: The French domestic market classic repo. Formally documented in law in December 1993, previously known as *pension livrée*.

Price differential: A term used in the Equity Repo Agreement to describe the accrued return on the cash involved in a repo.

Price factor: Another term for the *conversion factor*.

Pricing rate: Another term for repo rate.

Principal: A party to a repo transaction who acts on their own behalf. Also, a term used to refer to the nominal value of a bond.

PSA: The Public Securities Association. A US-based organisation which developed the market standard documentation for repo in the US domestic market and which developed, with the ISMA, the Global Master Repurchase Agreement. It recently changed its name to the Bond Market Association.

PSA/ISMA Global Master Repurchase Agreement: Developed jointly by PSA and ISMA, this is the market standard documentation for non-dollar repo markets. A revised edition was issued in November 1995. The Gilt Repo Legal Agreement is an amended version of the revised edition (through the inclusion of a Part 2 to its Annex I and modified by a side letter in connection with the upgrade of the CGO service in 1997) designed to meet the needs of the gilt repo market. Now designated TBMA/BMA GMRA.

Rebate: The fee payable by a borrower of stock in the stock loan market.

Recall: Where the repo is an open transaction, a request to return repoed securities.

Refer: The practice whereby a trader instructs a broker to put "under reference" any prices or rates they have quoted to them, meaning that they are no longer "firm" and the broker must refer to the trader before they can trade on the price initially quoted.

Regulatory capital: The amount of capital that a financial institution is required to set aside against its assets (loans), as required by the national regulatory authority.

Repo rate: The return earned on a repo transaction expressed as an interest rate on the cash side of the transaction.

Repo (reverse repo) to maturity: A repo or reverse repo where the security repoed matures on the same day as the closing leg.

Repricing: At a variation margin call, when a repo is closed-out and re-started to reflect margin delivery. Also used as another term for *marking-to-market*.

Reverse repo: A repo, but from the point of view of the counterparty taking in stock. The US AIMR, in its CFA exam syllabus, defines a reverse repo as one undertaken by a corporate customer with a banking counterparty (who engages in repo).

Reversing: Entering into reverse repo, as in "reverse in" securities.

Right of substitution: The right of the party to a repo, which has delivered securities, to substitute equivalent collateral during the life of the repo.

Roll: To renew a repo trade at its maturity.

Rollover: See *Roll*.

Safe custody repo: Also known as *safekeeping* repo, where the borrower of cash keeps hold of collateral pledged, placing it in a segregated client account.

Sale and repurchase agreement: A repo trade.

Securities lending: The market in borrowing and lending stock, for a fee, against collateral.

Sell/buy-back: A trade economically identical to a classic repo, but conducted as a spot sale and simultaneous repurchase of stock, with the forward repurchase price adjusted to account for interest payable on borrowed funds. The repurchase price is in no way connected to the actual market price of the stock on repurchase date.

Seller: The counterparty that "sells" collateral in a repo or sell/buy-back, in other words the party borrowing funds.

Set off: The practice of netting obligations between two counterparties, in the event of default.

Short dates: The term for short maturity deposits, typically overnight, tom-next, and 2–3 day maturity trades. Sometimes the one-week term will be considered amongst the short dates.

Special: A security which for any reason is sought after in the repo market, thereby enabling any holder of the security to earn incremental income (in excess of GC) through lending them via a repo transaction. The repo rate for a special will be below the GC rate, as this is the rate the borrower of the cash is paying in return for supplying the special bond as collateral.

Specific: A repo in which the collateral is specified, that is, it is not GC. A specific security is not necessarily special.

Stock-driven repo: A repo initiated by a party who is motivated by the need to borrow a specific security or repo out a specific security for funding purposes. A stock-driven trade usually involves a round nominal amount of stock.

Stock lending: The UK market term for securities lending.

Strip: A zero-coupon bond which is produced by separating a standard coupon-bearing bond into its constituent principal and interest components.

Substitution: The practice of replacing collateral with another of equivalent credit quality during the term of a repo trade. This is initiated by the supplier of collateral, but must be agreed beforehand by the lender of cash.

Synthetic CDO: A synthetic CDO uses credit derivatives such as credit default swaps or total return swaps to transfer credit risk in a portfolio of assets. This contrasts with a cash flow CDO which uses the cash flows from the assets as asset backing for the issues of notes to investors. A synthetic CDO transfers the total return in a portfolio via the credit derivative. Synthetic CDOs may be balance sheet CDOs, which are typically executed by banks to obtain regulatory capital relief, or arbitrage CDOs, which are used by insurance companies and asset managers to exploit the yield spread between the underlying assets and the expense of servicing the CDO structure.

Tail: The interest rate *gap* between a deposit and loan (or reverse repo and repo) of differing maturities, representing interest rate risk.

Terminable on demand: A repo trade that may terminated on a daily basis, in other words an *open repo.*

Termination: The maturity date.

Term repo: Repo trades (of a maturity over one day) with a fixed maturity date.

Total return swap: A bilateral financial contract in which one party (the total return payer) makes floating-rate payments to the other party (the total return receiver) equal to the total return on a specified asset or index, in return for amounts which generally equal the total return payer's cost of holding the specified asset on its balance sheet. Price appreciation or depreciation may be calculated and exchanged at maturity or on an interim basis. Total return swaps are economically similar to a repo trade, and may be considered as synthetic repos or as a form of credit derivative. However, a total return swap is distinct from a credit default swap in that the floating payments are based on the total economic performance of the specified asset, and are not contingent upon the occurrence of a credit event.

Translation risk: An accounting or financial reporting risk where the earnings of a company can be adversely affected due to its method of accounting for foreign earnings.

Tri-party repo: A repo in which an independent agent bank or clearing house oversees a standard two-party repo transaction. The responsibilities of the tri-party agent include maintaining acceptable and adequate collateral and overall maintenance of the outstanding repo trades.

Trust account repo: Another term for *safe custody repo.*

Underlying: The cash market asset on which a futures or option contract is written. Also, the reference asset in a credit derivative.

Value: The date that the cash is received for stock sold (and vice versa), the value date. Alternatively the date from which interest begins to commence.

Variation margin: The band agreed between the parties to a repo transaction at the outset within which the value of the collateral may fluctuate before triggering a right to call for cash or securities to reinstate the initial margin on the repo transaction.

Volatility: A measure of the variability of the price of a financial asset. It is defined as the annualised standard deviation of the natural logarithm of the ratio of two successive prices. *Historical volatility* is a measure of the standard deviation of an asset over a specified period in the past. *Implied volatility* is the volatility of the underlying asset implied by the price of an option contract that has been written on it. Volatility is not the measure of the direction of an asset's price. The distribution of asset prices is assumed to follow a lognormal distribution, because the logarithm of the prices is normally distributed (we assume lognormal rather than normal distribution to allow for the fact that prices cannot – as could be the case in a normal distribution – have negative values). Returns are defined as the logarithm of the price relatives and are assumed to follow the normal distribution such that:

$$\ln\left(\frac{S_t}{S_0}\right) \sim N(\mu t, \sigma\sqrt{t})$$

where

S_0	is the price at time 0;
S_t	is the price at time t;
$N(m, s)$	is a random variable with mean m and standard deviation s;
μ	is the annual rate of return;
σ	is the annualised standard deviation of returns;

and the symbol ~ means "is distributed according to".

Volatility is defined in the equation above as the annualised standard deviation of returns. This definition does not refer to the variability of the prices directly but to the variability of the returns that generate these prices. Price relatives are calculated from the ratio of successive closing prices. Returns are then calculated according to the following equation as the logarithm of the price relatives:

$$\text{return} = \ln\left(\frac{S_{t+1}}{S_t}\right)$$

where

S_t	is the market price at time t;
S_{t+1}	is the price one period later.

The mean and standard deviation of returns follow standard statistical techniques using the following formula:

$$\mu = \sum_{i=1}^{N}\frac{x_i}{N} \quad \text{and} \quad \sigma = \sqrt{\sum_{i=1}^{N}\frac{(x_i - \mu)^2}{N-1}}$$

where

x_i	is the i'th price relative;
N	is the total number of observations.

This gives a standard deviation or volatility of daily price returns. To convert this to an annual figure, it is necessary to multiply it by the square root of the number of working days in a year, normally taken to be 250.

Yield curve: A graphical representation of interest rates plotted against terms to maturity. Most commonly government bond yields are plotted against their respective maturities. The plot of zero-coupon rates against maturity is known as the *term structure of interest rates.* Only assets of homogenous quality can be used when plotting yields. A *positive* yield curve exhibits an increasing level of interest rates over longer maturity periods, while a *negative* or *inverted* yield curve exhibits diminishing yields over time.

Zero-coupon bond: A bond issued at a discount and redeemed at par, on account that is pays no coupons during its life.

Zero-coupon rate: The yield on a zero-coupon bond.

Zone A: The categorisation of certain countries into a category under Basel rules; these sovereign borrowers attract the lowest risk weighting.

When I get to a fight against a kid who can really fight, at the end of the day it's who's got the heart and who's got the skill. When that happens, I've got to pull through. I have to have the heart and the courage to make my opponent back up, to pull me through the fight.

– Prince Naseem Hamed, quoted in Pitt, N.,
The Paddy and the Prince, Yellow Jersey Press, 1998, p. 5

Don't drink, don't smoke, don't gamble, don't do drugs and don't chase women.

– Brendan Ingle, *Ibid*, p.29

Author index

Amihud and Mendelson 180
Avellaneda 54
Baxter and Rennie 54
Benninga 366, 395
Blake 9, 399
Butler 42, 265
Burghardt 35, 331, 341, 347, 349, 351, 365, 399
Campbell 51, 53–4, 60
Choudhry 42, 54, 81
Cornell and Shapiro 180
Corrigan 109
Cox, Ingersoll and Ross 67
Culbertson 67
Das 186
Deacon and Derry 63
Decovny 186
Duffie 180–183
Fabozzi 47, 104, 116, 163
Fabozzi, Mann and Choudhry 186
Fabozzi and Yuen 118
Fisher 65
Francis 146
Galitz 186, 337, 347, 399
Georgiou 8
Grandville 53
Gollow 8
Gujarati 64

Gup and Brooks 190
Hicks 65–66
Hu 116, 119
Hull 51
Ingersoll 9, 61, 65
Jarrow 9, 51–52, 54, 61, 65
Jarrow and Turnbull 186, 399
Kasapi 161
McCulloch 63
Marshall and Bansal 188–9
Modigliani and Sutch 67
Neftci 9, 54–6
Nelson and Siegel 63
Plona 349, 365
Ramamurthy 186
Ross 54, 56, 67
Roth 8
Rubinstein 334, 337, 339
Schaefer 63
Shiller 9, 54, 61, 65
Steiner, B 8
Sundaresan 9, 48–9, 54
Van Deventer 9, 30, 63, 332
Van Horne 9
Waggoner 63
Windas 57
Wong 249

Main index

Note to reader: Top-level index entries are in **bold type**, second-level entries are in "normal" type and third-level entries are in *italic type*.

A

AAA-rated collateral 123
ABN Amro 131
Acceptance financing 76 – see also *Bankers acceptances*
Accounting and repo 275
  and legal definition of repo 275
  repo as actual sale vs. loan of cash 275
  rules
    overview of 275
    balance sheet 275
    de-recognition 276
    and repo buyer 276
    and repo seller 276
    variation margin 276

United Kingdom 277
  balance sheet netting 277
  British Bankers Association 277
  Financial Reporting Standards (FRS) 277
  FRS-5 and application to repo 277, 283
  and repo to maturity 277
United States 277
  FASB-39 278
  netting provisions 278
  Securities and Exchange Commission regulations 277
  SFAS-125 277, 278
  Statements of Financial Accounting Standards (SFAS) 277

D

E

S

Sunrise doesn't last all day
A cloudburst doesn't last all day
Seems my love is up,
And has left you with no warning
But it's not always going to be this grey

All things must pass, all things must pass away

Sunset doesn't last all evening
A mind can blow those clouds away
After all this my love is up and must be leaving
But it's not always going to be this grey

None of life's strings can last
So, I must be on my way
And face another day

Now the darkness only stays at night time
In the morning it will fade away
Daylight is good at arriving at the right time
No it's not always going to be this grey

All Things Must Pass
(Apple Records 1970)

George Harrison
25 February 1943 – 29 November 2001
RIP